THE NATIONAL TEMPER

under the general editorship of **John M. Blum**
Yale University

THE NATIONAL TEMPER

Readings in American History

edited by

LAWRENCE W. LEVINE

and

ROBERT MIDDLEKAUFF

University of California, Berkeley

HARCOURT, BRACE & WORLD, INC.

New York   Chicago   San Francisco   Atlanta

LIBRARY OF CONGRESS CATALOG CARD NUMBER: 68-24779

PRINTED IN THE UNITED STATES OF AMERICA

CONTENTS

PART THREE

THE TWENTIETH CENTURY   285

PREFACE

In an essay in this book Professor Sigmund Diamond declares that "in scholarship, if not in manufacturing, novelty is a virtue that has limits." We do not pretend to know much about manufacturing, but we do subscribe to the statement as it applies to historical scholarship. Since we realize that a glance at our table of contents may persuade some readers that we have lusted after the novel, we wish to explain the intentions that guided our selection of articles.

While we believe that most of the subjects treated in textbooks and general histories are important, and while we have chosen articles that relate to the important problems in American history, we have not turned to the conventional formulations of those problems. Rather we have sought to include articles that bear on important issues in unusual, even offbeat, ways. Thus some of the subjects of these pieces are novel—as far as a traditional approach to history is concerned. For example, such topics as sexual practices, cowboy heroes, popular novels, and gangster films rarely draw historians' interest as fields of study. But as the articles in this collection demonstrate, they can be dealt with in ways that illuminate cultural development. We have also included the kind of article that takes its distinction largely from its method, though it may deal with an unconventional subject as well. Several of the literary analyses and the sociological studies in our collection fall into this category.

All the selections bear on concerns important to American historians. They are serious attempts to extract meaning from the American past. Considered alone or in this collection, the articles do not exhaust the possibilities for investigation into American history. But used seriously, say as supplements to a textbook, a general history, or more ambitious specialized studies, they can inform as well as stimulate. All repay close reading; and though we believe that they may be most profitable to students in a general American history course, we also hope that any student of the American past will find them rewarding.

We are grateful to the authors and publishers of these essays for permission to reprint them. We particularly wish to thank Professor Stanley N. Katz of the University of Wisconsin for his perceptive and constructive critique of our manuscript.

Lawrence W. Levine
Robert Middlekauff

PART ONE

THE COLONIAL PERIOD

DAVID M. POTTER

THE QUEST FOR
THE NATIONAL CHARACTER

This essay by David Potter considers explicitly what every piece in this volume touches implicitly—the question of the American national character. Potter maintains that almost all theories of the American character fall into two primary types. One, first offered by Jefferson, describes the American as an individualist with profound, idealistic impulses; the other, formulated by Alexis de Tocqueville, sees him as a conformist with immense materialistic drives. Although Potter does not contend that the dedication to equality implied in both conceptions effectively reconciles these contrasting images, he does find in its various manifestations a new focus for understanding much that has been persistent in the American character.

David Potter, People of Plenty * *(1954), and the symposium edited by Elting E. Morison,* The American Style *(1958), are rewarding reading for students interested in pursuing this subject.*

---

* *All books marked with an asterisk are available in paperback.*

Unlike most nationality groups in the world today, the people of the United States are not ethnically rooted in the land where they live. The French have remote Gallic antecedents; the Germans, Teutonic; the English, Anglo-Saxon; the Italians, Roman; the Irish, Celtic; but the only people in America who can claim ancient American origins are a remnant of Red Indians. In any deep dimension of time, all other Americans are immigrants. They began as Europeans (or in the case of 10 per cent of the population, as Africans), and if they became Americans it was only, somehow, after a relatively recent passage westbound across the Atlantic.

It is, perhaps, this recency of arrival which has given to Americans a somewhat compulsive preoccupation with the question of their Americanism. No people can really qualify as a nation in the true sense unless they are united by important qualities or values in common. If they share the same ethnic, or linguistic, or religious, or political heritage, the foundations of nationality can hardly be questioned. But when their ethnic, religious, linguistic, and political heritage is mixed, as in the case of the American people, nationality can hardly exist at all unless it takes the form of a common adjustment to conditions of a new land, a common commitment to shared values, a common esteem for certain qualities of character, or a common set of adaptive traits and attitudes. It is partly for this reason that Americans, although committed to the principle of freedom of thought, have nevertheless placed such heavy emphasis upon the obligation to accept certain undefined tenets of "Americanism." It is for this same reason, also, that Americans have insisted upon their distinctiveness from the Old World from which they are derived. More than two centuries ago Hector St. John de Crèvecoeur asked a famous question, "What then is the American, this new man?" He simply assumed, without arguing the point, that the American is a new man, and he only inquired wherein the American is different. A countless array of writers, including not only careful historians and social scientists but also professional patriots, hit-and-run travellers, itinerant lecturers, intuitive-minded amateurs of all sorts, have been repeating Crèvecoeur's question and seeking to answer it ever since.

A thick volume would hardly suffice even to summarize the diverse interpretations which these various writers have advanced in describing or explaining the American character. Almost every trait, good or bad, has been attributed to the American people by someone,[1] and almost every explana-

---

[1] Lee Coleman, "What Is American: A Study of Alleged American Traits," in *Social Forces*, XIX (1941), surveyed a large body of the literature on the American character and concluded that "almost every conceivable value or trait has at one time or another been imputed to American culture by authoritative observers."

FROM David M. Potter, "The Quest for the National Character," in John Higham, ed., *The Reconstruction of American History*, New York: Harper & Row Torchbooks, 1962, pp. 197–220. Reprinted by permission.

tion, from Darwinian selection to toilet-training, has been advanced to account for the attributed qualities. But it is probably safe to say that at bottom there have been only two primary ways of explaining the American, and that almost all of the innumerable interpretations which have been formulated can be grouped around or at least oriented to these two basic explanations, which serve as polar points for all the literature.

The most disconcerting fact about these two composite images of the American is that they are strikingly dissimilar and seemingly about as inconsistent with one another as two interpretations of the same phenomenon could possibly be. One depicts the American primarily as an individualist and an idealist, while the other makes him out as a conformist and a materialist. Both images have been developed with great detail and elaborate explanation in extensive bodies of literature, and both are worth a close scrutiny.

For those who have seen the American primarily as an individualist, the story of his evolution as a distinctive type dates back possibly to the actual moment of his decision to migrate from Europe to the New World, for this was a process in which the daring and venturesome were more prone to risk life in a new country while the timid and the conventional were more disposed to remain at home. If the selective factors in the migration had the effect of screening out men of low initiative, the conditions of life in the North American wilderness, it is argued, must have further heightened the exercise of individual resourcefulness, for they constantly confronted the settler with circumstances in which he could rely upon no one but himself, and where the capacity to improvise a solution for a problem was not infrequently necessary to survival.

In many ways the colonial American exemplified attitudes that were individualistic. Although he made his first settlements by the removal of whole communities which were transplanted bodily—complete with all their ecclesiastical and legal institutions—he turned increasingly, in the later process of settlement, to a more and more individualistic mode of pioneering, in which one separate family would take up title to a separate, perhaps an isolated, tract of land, and would move to this land long in advance of any general settlement, leaving churches and courts and schools far behind. His religion, whether Calvinistic Puritanism or emotional revivalism, made him individually responsible for his own salvation, without the intervention of ecclesiastical intermediaries between himself and his God. His economy, which was based very heavily upon subsistence farming, with very little division of labor, also impelled him to cope with a diversity of problems and to depend upon no one but himself.

With all of these conditions at work, the tendency to place a premium upon individual self-reliance was no doubt well developed long before the cult of the American as an individualist crystallized in a conceptual form. But it did crystallize, and it took on almost its classic formulation in the thought of Thomas Jefferson.

It may seem paradoxical to regard Jefferson as a delineator of American national character, for in direct terms he did not attempt to describe the American character at all. But he did conceive that one particular kind of society was necessary to the fulfillment of American ideals, and further that one particular kind of person, namely the independent farmer, was a necessary component in the optimum society. He believed that the principles of liberty and equality, which he cherished so deeply, could not exist in a hierarchical society, such as that of Europe, nor, indeed, in any society where economic and social circumstances enabled one set of men to dominate and exploit the rest. An urban society or a commercial society, with its concentration of financial power into a few hands and its imposition of dependence through a wage system, scarcely lent itself better than an aristocracy to his basic values. In fact, only a society of small husbandmen who tilled their own soil and found sustenance in their own produce could achieve the combination of independence and equalitarianism which he envisioned for the ideal society. Thus, although Jefferson did not write a description of the national character, he erected a model for it, and the model ultimately had more influence than a description could ever have exercised. The model American was a plain, straightforward agrarian democrat, an individualist in his desire for freedom for himself, and an idealist in his desire for equality for all men.

Jefferson's image of the American as a man of independence, both in his values and in his mode of life, has had immense appeal to Americans ever since. They found this image best exemplified in the man of the frontier, for he, as a pioneer, seemed to illustrate the qualities of independence and self-reliance in their most pronounced and most dramatic form. Thus, in a tradition of something like folklore, half-legendary figures like Davy Crockett have symbolized America as well as symbolizing the frontier. In literature, ever since J. Fenimore Cooper's Leatherstocking tales, the frontier scout, at home under the open sky, free from the trammels of an organized and stratified society, has been cherished as an incarnation of American qualities.[2] In American politics the voters showed such a marked preference for men who had been born in log cabins that many an ambitious candidate pretended to pioneer origins which were in fact fictitious.

The pioneer is, of course, not necessarily an agrarian (he may be a hunter, a trapper, a cowboy, a prospector for gold), and the agrarian is not necessarily a pioneer (he may be a European peasant tilling his ancestral acres), but the American frontier was basically an agricultural frontier, and the pioneer was usually a farmer. Thus it was possible to make an equation between the pioneer and the agrarian, and since the pioneer evinced the

---

[2] Henry Nash Smith, *Virgin Land: The American West as Symbol and Myth* (1950), brilliantly analyzes the power which the image of the Western pioneer has had upon the American imagination.

agrarian traits in their most picturesque and most appealing form there was a strong psychological impulse to concentrate the diffused agrarian ideal into a sharp frontier focus. This is, in part, what Frederick Jackson Turner did in 1893 when he wrote *The Significance of the Frontier in American History.* In this famous essay Turner offered an explanation of what has been distinctive in American history, but it is not as widely realized as it might be that he also penned a major contribution to the literature of national character. Thus Turner affirmed categorically that "The American intellect owes its striking characteristics to the frontier. That coarseness and strength, combined with acuteness and acquisitiveness; that practical inventive turn of mind, quick to find expedients; that masterful grasp of material things, lacking in the artistic but powerful to effect great ends; that restless, nervous energy; that dominant individualism, working for good and for evil; and withal, that buoyancy and exuberance which comes with freedom—these are traits of the frontier, or traits called out elsewhere because of the existence of the frontier." [3]

A significant but somewhat unnoticed aspect of Turner's treatment is the fact that, in his quest to discover the traits of the American character, he relied for proof not upon descriptive evidence that given traits actually prevailed, but upon the argument that given conditions in the environment would necessarily cause the development of certain traits. Thus the cheapness of land on the frontier would make for universal land-holding which in turn would make for equalitarianism in the society. The absence of division of labor on the frontier would force each man to do most things for himself, and this would breed self-reliance. The pitting of the individual man against the elemental forces of the wilderness and of nature would further reinforce this self-reliance. Similarly, the fact that a man had moved out in advance of society's institutions and its stratified structure would mean that he could find independence, without being overshadowed by the institutions, and could enjoy an equality unknown to stratified society. All of this argument was made without any sustained effort to measure exactly how much recognizable equalitarianism and individualism and self-reliance actually were in evidence either on the American frontier or in American society. There is little reason to doubt that most of his arguments were valid or that most of the traits which he emphasized did actually prevail, but it is nevertheless ironical that Turner's interpretation, which exercised such vast influence upon historians, was not based upon the historian's kind of proof, which is from evidence, but upon an argument from logic which so often fails to work out in historical experience.

But no matter how he arrived at it, Turner's picture reaffirmed some by-now-familiar beliefs about the American character. The American was equal-

---

[3] Frederick J. Turner, *The Frontier in American History* (Henry Holt and Co., 1920), p. 37.

itarian, stoutly maintaining the practices of both social and political democracy; he had a spirit of freedom reflected in his buoyance and exuberance; he was individualistic—hence "practical and inventive," "quick to find expedients," "restless, nervous, acquisitive." Turner was too much a scholar to let his evident fondness for the frontiersman run away with him entirely, and he took pains to point out that this development was not without its sordid aspects. There was a marked primitivism about the frontier, and with it, to some extent, a regression from civilized standards. The buoyant and exuberant frontiersman sometimes emulated his Indian neighbors in taking the scalps of his adversaries. Coarse qualities sometimes proved to have more survival value than gentle ones. But on the whole this regression was brief, and certainly a rough-and-ready society had its compensating advantages. Turner admired his frontiersman, and thus Turner's American, like Jefferson's American, was partly a realistic portrait from life and partly an idealized model from social philosophy. Also, though one of these figures was an agrarian and the other was a frontiersman, both were very much the same man—democratic, freedom-loving, self-reliant, and individualistic.

An essay like this is hardly the place to prove either the validity or the invalidity of the Jeffersonian and Turnerian conception of the American character. The attempt to do so would involve a review of the entire range of American historical experience, and in the course of such a review the proponents of this conception could point to a vast body of evidence in support of their interpretation. They could argue, with much force, that Americans have consistently been zealous to defend individualism by defending the rights and the welfare of the individual, and that our whole history is a protracted record of our government's recognizing its responsibility to an ever broader range of people—to men without property, to men held in slavery, to women, to small enterprises threatened by monopoly, to children laboring in factories, to industrial workers, to the ill, to the elderly, and to the unemployed. This record, it can further be argued, is also a record of the practical idealism of the American people, unceasingly at work.

But without attempting a verdict on the historical validity of this image of the American as individualist and idealist, it is important to bear in mind that this image has been partly a portrait, but also partly a model. In so far as it is a portrait—a likeness by an observer reporting on Americans whom he knew—it can be regarded as authentic testimony on the American character. But in so far as it is a model—an idealization of what is best in Americanism, and of what Americans should strive to be, it will only be misleading if used as evidence of what ordinary Americans are like in their everyday lives. It is also important to recognize that the Jefferson-Turner image posited several traits as distinctively American, and that they are not all necessarily of equal validity. Particularly, Jefferson and Turner both believed that love of equality and love of liberty go together. For Jefferson the very fact, stated in the Declaration of Independence, that "all men are created equal," carried with it the corollary that they are all therefore "entitled to [and would be eager for] life, liberty, and the pursuit of happiness." From this premise it is easy to slide imperceptibly into the position of holding that equalitarianism and individualism are inseparably linked, or even that they are somehow the same thing. This is, indeed, almost an officially sanctioned ambiguity in the American creed. But it requires only a little thoughtful reflection to recognize that equalitarianism and individualism do not necessarily go together. Alexis de Tocqueville understood this fact more than a century ago, and out of his recognition he framed an analysis which is not only the most brilliant single account of the American character, but is also the only major alternative to the Jefferson-Turner image.

After travelling the length and breadth of the United States for ten months at the height of Andrew Jackson's ascendancy, Tocqueville felt no doubt of the depth of the commitment of Americans to democracy. Throughout two volumes which ranged over every aspect of American life, he consistently emphasized democracy as a pervasive factor. But the democracy which he wrote about was far removed from Thomas Jefferson's dream.

"Liberty," he observed of the Americans, "is not the chief object of their desires; equality is their idol. They make rapid and sudden efforts to obtain liberty, and if they miss their aim resign themselves to their disappointment; but nothing can satisfy them without equality, and they would rather perish than lose it." [4]

This emphasis upon equality was not, in itself, inconsistent with the most orthodox Jeffersonian ideas, and indeed Tocqueville took care to recognize that under certain circumstances equality and freedom might "meet and blend." But such circumstances would be rare, and the usual effects of equality would be to encourage conformity and discourage individualism, to regiment opinion and to inhibit dissent. Tocqueville justified this seemingly paradoxical conclusion by arguing that:

> When the inhabitant of a democratic country compares himself individually with all those about him, he feels with pride that he is the equal of any one of them; but when he comes to survey the totality of his fellows, and to place himself in contrast with so huge a body, he is instantly overwhelmed by the sense of his own insignificance and weakness. The same equality that renders him independent of each of his fellow citizens, taken severally, exposes him alone and unprotected to the influence of the greater number. The public, therefore, among a democratic people, has a singular power, which aristocratic nations cannot conceive; for it does not persuade others to its beliefs, but it imposes them and makes them permeate the thinking of everyone by a sort of enormous pressure of the mind of all upon the individual intelligence. [5]

---

[4] Alexis de Tocqueville, *Democracy in America,* edited by Phillips Bradley (Alfred A. Knopf, 1946), I, pp. 53–4.

[5] *Ibid.,* II, p. 94; II, p. 10.

At the time when Tocqueville wrote, he expressed admiration for the American people in many ways, and when he criticized adversely his tone was abstract, bland, and free of the petulance and the personalities that characterized some critics, like Mrs. Trollope and Charles Dickens. Consequently, Tocqueville was relatively well received in the United States, and we have largely forgotten what a severe verdict his observations implied. But, in fact, he pictured the American character as the very embodiment of conformity, of conformity so extreme that not only individualism but even freedom was endangered. Because of the enormous weight with which the opinion of the majority pressed upon the individual, Tocqueville said, the person in the minority "not only mistrusts his strength, but even doubts of his right; and he is very near acknowledging that he is in the wrong when the greater number of his countrymen assert that he is so. The majority do not need to force him; they convince him." "The principle of equality," as a consequence, had the effect of "prohibiting him from thinking at all," and "freedom of opinion does not exist in America." Instead of reinforcing liberty, therefore, equality constituted a danger to liberty. It caused the majority "to despise and undervalue the rights of private persons," and led on to the pessimistic conclusion that "Despotism appears . . . peculiarly to be dreaded in democratic times." [6]

Tocqueville was perhaps the originator of the criticism of the American as conformist, but he also voiced another criticism which has had many echoes, but which did not originate with him. This was the condemnation of the American as a materialist. As early as 1805 Richard Parkinson had observed that "all men there [in America] make it [money] their pursuit," and in 1823 William Faux had asserted that "two selfish gods, pleasure and gain, enslave the Americans." In the interval between the publication of the first and second parts of Tocqueville's study, Washington Irving coined his classic phrase concerning "the almighty dollar, that great object of universal devotion throughout the land." [7] But it remained for Tocqueville, himself, to link materialism with equality, as he had already linked conformity.

"Of all passions," he said, "which originate in or are fostered by equality, there is one which it renders peculiarly intense, and which it also infuses into the heart of every man: I mean the love of well-being. The taste for well-being is the prominent and indelible feature of democratic times. . . . The effort to satisfy even the least wants of the body and to provide the little conveniences of life is uppermost in every mind."

---

[6] *Ibid.*, II, p. 261; II, p. 11; I, p. 265; II, p. 326; II, p. 322.

[7] Richard Parkinson, *A Tour in America in 1798–1800* (2 vols., 1805), vol. II, p. 652; William Faux, *Memorable Days in America* (1823), p. 417; Washington Irving, "The Creole Village," in *The Knickerbocker Magazine,* November 1836.

He described this craving for physical comforts as a "passion," and affirmed that "I know of no country, indeed, where the love of money has taken stronger hold on the affections of men." [8]

For more than a century we have lived with the contrasting images of the American character which Thomas Jefferson and Alexis de Tocqueville visualized. Both of these images presented the American as an equalitarian and therefore as a democrat, but one was an agrarian democrat while the other was a majoritarian democrat; one an independent individualist, the other a mass-dominated conformist; one an idealist, the other a materialist. Through many decades of self-scrutiny Americans have been seeing one or the other of these images whenever they looked into the mirror of self-analysis.

The discrepancy between the two images is so great that it must bring the searcher for the American character up with a jerk, and must force him to grapple with the question whether these seemingly antithetical versions of the American can be reconciled in any way. Can the old familiar formula for embracing opposite reports—that the situation presents a paradox—be stretched to encompass both Tocqueville and Jefferson? Or is there so grave a flaw somewhere that one must question the whole idea of national character and call to mind all the warnings that thoughtful men have uttered against the very concept that national groups can be distinguished from one another in terms of collective group traits.

Certainly there is a sound enough basis for doubting the validity of generalizations about national character. To begin with, many of these generalizations have been derived not from any dispassionate observation or any quest for truth, but from superheated patriotism which sought only to glorify one national group by invidious comparison with other national groups, or from a pseudoscientific racism which claimed innately superior qualities for favored ethnic groups. Further, the explanations which were offered to account for the ascribed traits were as suspect as the ascriptions themselves. No one today will accept the notions which once prevailed that such qualities as the capacity for self-government are inherited in the genes, nor will anyone credit the notion that national character is a unique quality which manifests itself mystically in all the inhabitants of a given country. Between the chauvinistic purposes for which the concept of national character was used, and the irrationality with which it was supported, it fell during the 1930's into a disrepute from which it has by no means fully recovered.

Some thinkers of a skeptical turn of mind had rejected the idea of national character even at a time when most historians accepted it without question. Thus, for instance, John Stuart Mill as early as 1849 observed that "of all vulgar modes of escaping from the consideration of the effect of social and moral influences on the human mind, the most vulgar is that of at-

---

[8] Tocqueville, *Democracy in America,* II, p. 26; II, p. 128; II, p. 129; I, p. 51.

tributing diversities of character to inherent natural differences." Sir John Seely said, "no explanation is so vague, so cheap, and so difficult to verify." [9]

But it was particularly at the time of the rise of Fascism and Naziism, when the vicious aspects of extreme nationalism and of racism became glaringly conspicuous, that historians in general began to repudiate the idea of national character and to disavow it as an intellectual concept, even though they sometimes continued to employ it as a working device in their treatment of the peoples with whose history they were concerned. To historians whose skepticism had been aroused, the conflicting nature of the images of the American as an individualistic democrat or as a conformist democrat would have seemed simply to illustrate further the already demonstrated flimsiness and fallacious quality of all generalizations about national character.

But to deny that the inhabitants of one country may, as a group, evince a given trait in higher degree than the inhabitants of some other country amounts almost to a denial that the culture of one people can be different from the culture of another people. To escape the pitfalls of racism in this way is to fly from one error into the embrace of another, and students of culture—primarily anthropologists, rather than historians—perceived that rejection of the idea that a group could be distinctive, along with the idea that the distinction was eternal and immutable in the genes, involved the ancient logical fallacy of throwing out the baby along with the bath. Accordingly, the study of national character came under the special sponsorship of cultural anthropology, and in the forties a number of outstanding workers in this field tackled the problem of national character, including the American character, with a methodological precision and objectivity that had never been applied to the subject before. After their investigations, they felt no doubt that national character was a reality—an observable and demonstrable reality. One of them, Margaret Mead, declared that "In every culture, in Samoa, in Germany, in Iceland, in Bali, and in the United States of America, we will find consistencies and regularities in the way in which newborn babies grow up and assume the attitudes and behavior patterns of their elders—and this we may call 'character formation.' We will find that Samoans may be said to have a Samoan character structure and Americans an American character structure." [10] Another, the late Clyde Kluckhohn, wrote: "The statistical prediction can safely be made that a hundred Americans, for example, will display certain defined characteristics more frequently than will a hundred

---

[9] Mill, *The Principles of Political Economy* (1849), I, p. 390; Seely, quoted by Boyd C. Shafer, "Men Are More Alike," in *American Historical Review*, LVII (1952), p. 606.

[10] Margaret Mead, *And Keep Your Powder Dry* (William Morrow and Co., 1942), p. 21. Miss Mead also says, "The way in which people behave is all of a piece, their virtues and their sins, the way they slap the baby, handle their court cases, and bury their dead."

Englishmen comparably distributed as to age, sex, social class, and vocation." [11]

If these new students were correct, it meant that there was some kind of identifiable American character. It might conform to the Jeffersonian image; it might conform to the Tocquevillian image; it might conform in part to both; or it might conform to neither. But in any event discouraged investigators were enjoined against giving up the quest with the conclusion that there is no American character. It has been said that a philosopher is a blind man in a dark room looking for a black cat that isn't there; the student of national character might also, at times, resemble a blind man in a dark room, looking for a black cat, but the cultural anthropologists exhorted him to persevere in spite of the problems of visibility, for the cat was indubitably there.

Still confronted with the conflicting images of the agrarian democrat and the majoritarian democrat, the investigator might avoid an outright rejection of either by taking the position that the American character has changed, and that each of these images was at one time valid and realistic, but that in the twentieth century the qualities of conformity and materialism have grown increasingly prominent, while the qualities of individualism and idealism have diminished. This interpretation of a changing American character has had a number of adherents in the last two decades, for it accords well with the observation that the conditions of the American culture have changed. As they do so, of course the qualities of a character that is derived from the culture might be expected to change correspondingly. Thus, Henry S. Commager, in his *The American Mind* (1950), portrayed in two contrasting chapters "the nineteenth-century American" and "the twentieth-century American." Similarly, David Riesman, in *The Lonely Crowd* (1950), significantly sub-titled *A Study of the Changing American Character,* pictured two types of Americans, first an "inner-directed man," whose values were deeply internalized and who adhered to these values tenaciously, regardless of the opinions of his peers (clearly an individualist), and second an "other-directed man," who subordinated his own internal values to the changing expectations directed toward him by changing peer groups (in short, a conformist).

Although he viewed his inner-directed man as having been superseded historically by his other-directed man, Riesman did not attempt to explain in historical terms the reason for the change. He made a rather limited effort to relate his stages of character formation to stages of population growth, but he has since then not used population phase as a key. Meanwhile, it is fairly clear, from Riesman's own context, as well as from history in general, that

---

[11] Clyde Kluckhohn and Henry A. Murray, *Personality in Nature, Society, and Culture* (Alfred A. Knopf, 1949), p. 36.

there were changes in the culture which would have accounted for the transition in character. Most nineteenth-century Americans were self-employed; most were engaged in agriculture; most produced a part of their own food and clothing. These facts meant that their well-being did not depend on the goodwill or the services of their associates, but upon their resourcefulness in wrestling with the elemental forces of Nature. Even their physical isolation from their fellows added something to the independence of their natures. But most twentieth-century Americans work for wages or salaries, many of them in very large employee groups; most are engaged in office or factory work; most are highly specialized, and are reliant upon many others to supply their needs in an economy with an advanced division of labor. Men now do depend upon the goodwill and the services of their fellows. This means that what they achieve depends less upon stamina and hardihood than upon their capacity to get along with other people and to fit smoothly into a co-operative relationship. In short the culture now places a premium upon the qualities which will enable the individual to function effectively as a member of a large organizational group. The strategic importance of this institutional factor has been well recognized by William H. Whyte, Jr., in his significantly titled book *The Organization Man* (1956)—for the conformity of Whyte's bureaucratized individual results from the fact that he lives under an imperative to succeed in a situation where promotion and even survival depend upon effective inter-action with others in an hierarchical structure.

Thus, by an argument from logic (always a treacherous substitute for direct observation in historical study), one can make a strong case that the nineteenth-century American should have been (and therefore must have been) an individualist, while the twentieth-century American should be (and therefore is) a conformist. But this formula crashes headlong into the obdurate fact that no Americans have ever been more classically conformist than Tocqueville's Jacksonian democrats—hardy specimens of the frontier breed, far back in the nineteenth century, long before the age of corporate images, peer groups, marginal differentiation, and status frustration. In short, Tocqueville's nineteenth-century American, whether frontiersman or no, was to some extent an other-directed man. Carl N. Degler has pointed out this identity in a very cogent paper not yet published, in which he demonstrates very forcibly that most of our easy assumptions about the immense contrast between the nineteenth-century American and the twentieth-century American are vulnerable indeed.[12]

This conclusion should, perhaps, have been evident from the outset, in view of the fact that it was Tocqueville who, in the nineteenth century, gave us the image which we now frequently identify as the twentieth-century American. But in any case, the fact that he did so means that we can hardly

---

[12] Delivered on 30 December 1960, at the annual meeting of the American Historical Association in New York.

resolve the dilemma of our individualist democrat and our majoritarian democrat by assuming that both are historically valid but that one replaced the other. The problem of determining what use we can make of either of these images, in view of the fact that each casts doubt upon the other, still remains. Is it possible to uncover common factors in these apparently contradictory images, and thus to make use of them both in our quest for a definition of the national character? For no matter whether either of these versions of the American is realistic as a type or image, there is no doubt that both of them reflect fundamental aspects of the American experience.

There is no purpose, at this point in this essay, to execute a neat, prearranged sleight-of-hand by which the individualist democrat and the conformist democrat will cast off their disguises and will reveal themselves as identical twin Yankee Doodle Dandies, both born on the fourth of July. On the contrary, intractable, irresolvable discrepancies exist between the two figures, and it will probably never be possible to go very far in the direction of accepting the one without treating the other as a fictitious image, to be rejected as reflecting an anti-democratic bias and as at odds with the evidence from actual observation of the behavior of *Homo Americanus* in his native haunts. At the same time, however, it is both necessary to probe for the common factors, and legitimate to observe that there is one common factor conspicuous in the extreme—namely the emphasis on equality, so dear both to Jefferson's American and to Tocqueville's. One of these figures, it will be recalled, has held no truth to be more self-evident than that all men are created equal, while the other has made equality his "idol," far more jealously guarded than his liberty.

If the commitment to equality is so dominant a feature in both of these representations of the American, it will perhaps serve as a key to various facets of the national character, even to contradictory aspects of this character. In a society as complex as that of the United States, in fact, it may be that the common factors underlying the various manifestations are all that our quest should seek. For it is evident that American life and American energy have expressed themselves in a great diversity of ways, and any effort to define the American as if nearly two hundred million persons all corresponded to a single type would certainly reduce complex data to a blunt, crude, and oversimplified form. To detect what qualities Americans share in their diversity may be far more revealing than to superimpose the stereotype of a fictitious uniformity. If this is true, it means that our quest must be to discover the varied and dissimilar ways in which the commitment to equality expresses itself—the different forms which it takes in different individuals—rather than to regard it as an undifferentiated component which shows in all individuals in the same way. Figuratively, one might say that in seeking for what is common, one should think of the metal from which Americans are forged, no matter into how many shapes this metal may be cast, rather than thinking of a die with which they all are stamped into an identical shape. If the problem is viewed in this way, it will be readily apparent that Tocqueville made a pregnant statement when he observed that the idea of equality was "the fundamental fact from which all others seem to be derived."

The term "equality" is a loose-fitting garment and it has meant very different things at very different times. It is very frequently used to imply parity or uniformity. The grenadiers in the King of Prussia's guard were equal in that they were all, uniformly, over six feet six inches tall. Particularly, it can mean, and often does mean in some social philosophies, uniformity of material welfare—of income, of medical care, etc. But people are clearly not uniform in strength or intelligence or beauty, and one must ask, therefore, what kind of uniformity Americans believed in. Did they believe in an equal sharing of goods? Tocqueville himself answered this question when he said, "I know of no country . . . where a profounder contempt is expressed for the theory of the permanent equality of property." [13]

At this point in the discussion of equality, someone, and very likely a business man, is always likely to break in with the proposition that Americans believe in equality of opportunity—in giving everyone what is called an equal start, and in removing all handicaps such as illiteracy and all privileges such as monopoly or special priority, which will tend to give one person an advantage over another. But if a person gains the advantage without having society give it to him, by being more clever or more enterprising or even just by being stronger than someone else, he is entitled to enjoy the benefits that accrue from these qualities, particularly in terms of possessing more property or wealth than others.

Historically, equality of opportunity was a particularly apt form of equalitarianism for a new, undeveloped frontier country. In the early stages of American history, the developed resources of the country were so few that an equality in the division of these assets would only have meant an insufficiency for everyone. The best economic benefit which the government could give was to offer a person free access in developing undeveloped resources for his own profit, and this is what America did offer. It was an ideal formula for everyone: for the individual it meant a very real chance to gain more wealth than he would have secured by receiving an equal share of the existing wealth. For the community, it meant that no one could prosper appreciably without activities which would develop undeveloped resources, at a time when society desperately needed rapid economic development. For these reasons, equality of opportunity did become the most highly sanctioned form of equalitarianism in the United States.

Because of this sanction, Americans have indeed been tolerant of great discrepancies in wealth. They have approved of wealth much more readily when they believed that it had been earned—as in the case, for instance, of Henry Ford—than when they thought it had been acquired by some special

---

[13] Tocqueville, *Democracy in America,* I, pp. 57–8.

privilege or monopoly. In general, however, they have not merely condoned great wealth; they have admired it. But to say that the ideal of equality means only equality of opportunity is hardly to tell the whole story. The American faith has also held, with intense conviction, the belief that all men are equal in the sense that they share a common humanity—that all are alike in the eyes of God—and that every person has a certain dignity, no matter how low his circumstances, which no one else, no matter how high *his* circumstances, is entitled to disregard. When this concept of the nature of man was translated into a system of social arrangements, the crucial point on which it came to focus was the question of rank. For the concept of rank essentially denies that all men are equally worthy and argues that some are better than others—that some are born to serve and others born to command. The American creed not only denied this view, but even condemned it and placed a taboo upon it. Some people, according to the American creed, might be more fortunate than others, but they must never regard themselves as better than others. Pulling one's rank has therefore been the unforgivable sin against American democracy, and the American people have, accordingly, reserved their heartiest dislike for the officer class in the military, for people with upstage or condescending manners, and for anyone who tries to convert power or wealth (which are not resented) into overt rank or privilege (which are). Thus it is permissible for an American to have servants (which is a matter of function), but he must not put them in livery (which is a matter of rank); permissible to attend expensive schools, but not to speak with a cultivated accent; permissible to rise in the world, but never to repudiate the origins from which he rose. The most palpable and overt possible claim of rank is, of course, the effort of one individual to assert authority, in a personal sense, over others, and accordingly the rejection of authority is the most pronounced of all the concrete expressions of American beliefs in equality.

In almost any enterprise which involves numbers of people working in conjunction, it is necessary for some people to tell other people what to do. This function cannot be wholly abdicated without causing a breakdown, and in America it cannot be exercised overtly without violating the taboos against authority. The result is that the American people have developed an arrangement which skillfully combines truth and fiction, and maintains that the top man does not rule, but leads; and does not give orders, but calls signals; while the men in the lower echelons are not underlings, but members of the team. This view of the relationship is truthful in the sense that the man in charge does depend upon his capacity to elicit the voluntary or spontaneous co-operation of the members of his organization, and he regards the naked use of authority to secure compliance as an evidence of failure; also, in many organizations, the members lend their support willingly, and contribute much more on a voluntary basis than authority could ever exact from them. But the element of fiction sometimes enters, in terms of the fact that both sides understand that in many situations authority would have to be invoked if voluntary compliance were not forthcoming. This would be humiliating to all parties—to the top man because it would expose his failure as a leader and to the others because it would force them to recognize the carefully concealed fact that in an ultimate sense they are subject to coercion. To avoid this mutually undesirable exploration of the ultimate implications, both sides recognize that even when an order has to be given, it is better for it to be expressed in the form of a request or a proposal, and when compliance is mandatory, it should be rendered with an appearance of consent.

It is in this way that the anti-authoritarian aspect of the creed of equality leads to the extraordinarily strong emphasis upon permissiveness, either as a reality or as a mere convention in American life. So strong is the taboo against authority that the father, once a paternal authority, is now expected to be a pal to his children, and to persuade rather than to command. The husband, once a lord and master, to be obeyed under the vows of matrimony, is now a partner. And if, perchance, an adult male in command of the family income uses his control to bully his wife and children, he does not avow his desire to make them obey, but insists that he only wants them to be co-operative. The unlimited American faith in the efficacy of discussion as a means of finding solutions for controversies reflects less a faith in the powers of rational persuasion than a supreme reluctance to let anything reach a point where authority will have to be invoked. If hypocrisy is the tribute that vice pays to virtue, permissiveness is, to some extent, the tribute that authority pays to the principle of equality.

When one recognizes some of these varied strands in the fabric of equalitarianism it becomes easier to see how the concept has contributed to the making both of the Jeffersonian American and the Tocquevillian American. For as one picks at the strands they ravel out in quite dissimilar directions. The strand of equality of opportunity, for instance, if followed out, leads to the theme of individualism. It challenged each individual to pit his skill and talents in a competition against the skill and talents of others and to earn the individual rewards which talent and effort might bring. Even more, the imperatives of the competitive race were so compelling that the belief grew up that everyone had a kind of obligation to enter his talents in this competition and to "succeed." It was but a step from the belief that ability and virtue would produce success to the belief that success was produced by—and was therefore an evidence of—ability and virtue. In short, money not only represented power, it also was a sign of the presence of admirable qualities in the man who attained it. Here, certainly, an equalitarian doctrine fostered materialism, and if aggressiveness and competitiveness are individualistic qualities, then it fostered individualism also.

Of course, neither American individualism nor American materialism can be explained entirely in these terms. Individualism must have derived great strength, for instance, from the reflection that if all men are equal, a man might as well form his own convictions as accept the convictions of someone else no better than himself. It must also have been reinforced by the frontier experience, which certainly compelled every man to rely upon himself. But this kind of individualism is not the quality of independent-mindedness, and it is not the quality which Tocqueville was denying when he said that Americans were conformists. A great deal of confusion has resulted, in the discussion of the American character, from the fact that the term individualism is sometimes used (as by Tocqueville) to mean willingness to think and act separately from the majority, and sometimes (as by Turner) to mean capacity to get along without help. It might be supposed that the two would converge, on the theory that a man who can get along by himself without help will soon recognize that he may as well also think for himself without help. But in actuality, this did not necessarily happen. Self-reliance on the frontier was more a matter of courage and of staying power than of intellectual resourcefulness, for the struggle with the wilderness challenged the body rather than the mind, and a man might be supremely effective in fending for himself, and at the same time supremely conventional in his ideas. In this sense, Turner's individualist is not really an antithesis of Tocqueville's conformist at all.

Still, it remains true that Jefferson's idealist and Tocqueville's conformist both require explanation, and that neither can be accounted for in the terms which make Jefferson's individualist and Tocqueville's materialist understandable. As an explanation of these facets of the American character, it would seem that the strand of equalitarianism which stresses the universal dignity of all men, and which hates rank as a violation of dignity, might be found quite pertinent. For it is the concept of the worth of every man which has stimulated a century and a half of reform, designed at every step to realize in practice the ideal that every human possesses potentialities which he should have a chance to fulfill. Whatever has impeded this fulfillment, whether it be lack of education, chattel slavery, the exploitation of the labor of unorganized workers, the hazards of unemployment, or the handicaps of age and infirmity, has been the object, at one time or another, of a major reforming crusade. The whole American commitment to progress would be impossible without a prior belief in the perfectibility of man and in the practicability of steps to bring perfection nearer. In this sense, the American character has been idealistic. And yet its idealism is not entirely irreconcilable with its materialism, for American idealism has often framed its most altruistic goals in materialistic terms—for instance, of raising the standard of living as a means to a better life. Moreover, Americans are committed to the view that materialistic means are necessary to idealistic ends. Franklin defined what is necessary to a virtuous life by saying "an empty sack cannot stand upright," and Americans have believed that spiritual and humanitarian goals are best achieved by instrumentalities such as universities and hospitals which carry expensive price tags.

If the belief that all men are of equal worth has contributed to a feature of American life so much cherished as our tradition of humanitarian reform, how could it at the same time have contributed to a feature so much deplored as American conformity? Yet it has done both, for the same respect of the American for his fellow men, which has made many a reformer think that his fellow citizens are worth helping, has also made many another American think that he has no business to question the opinions that his neighbors have sanctioned. True, he says, if all men are equal, each ought to think for himself, but on the other hand, no man should consider himself better than his neighbors, and if the majority have adopted an opinion on a matter, how can one man question their opinion, without setting himself up as being better than they. Moreover, it is understood that the majority are pledged not to force him to adopt their opinion. But it is also understood that in return for this immunity he will voluntarily accept the will of the majority in most things. The absence of a formal compulsion to conform seemingly increases the obligation to conform voluntarily. Thus, the other-directed man is seen to be derived as much from the American tradition of equalitarianism as the rugged individualist, and the compulsive seeker of an unequally large share of wealth as much as the humanitarian reformer striving for the fulfillment of democratic ideals.

To say that they are all derived from the same tradition is by no means to say that they are, in some larger, mystic sense, all the same. They are not, even though the idealism of the reformer may seek materialistic goals, and though men who are individualists in their physical lives may be conformists in their ideas. But all of them, it may be argued, do reflect circumstances which are distinctively American, and all present manifestations of a character which is more convincingly American because of its diversity than any wholly uniform character could possibly be. If Americans have never reached the end of their quest for an image that would represent the American character, it may be not because they failed to find one image but because they failed to recognize the futility of attempting to settle upon one, and the necessity of accepting several.

PERRY MILLER

ERRAND INTO THE WILDERNESS

Perry Miller raises a question that perplexes Americans today as it per-plexed Puritans three centuries ago: what is the meaning of America? Just as the Puritans first formulated the question, so also they first offered an answer, one that retains much of its original relevance in the present age. Puritans conceived of an American mission as the fulfillment of divine intentions through the actions of human beings; and though, as Miller explains, they felt oppressed by their inability to carry out God's will as well as they might, they never doubted the worth of their conviction. Since the seventeenth century other Americans have redefined their country's purposes and have pointed out its failures of mind and performance. Whatever these departures from the Puritans' sense of destiny, the American character, even a part of its critical cast of mind, owes something to the original formulation of mission as it was defined by the Puritans. Miller's evocative essay deserves our attention for what it tells us both about the Puritans and about ourselves.

For a fuller explication of the ideas expressed in this essay, students should see Perry Miller, The New England Mind: From Colony to Province * (1953), and Orthodoxy in Massachusetts * (1933).

It was a happy inspiration that led the staff of the John Carter Brown Library to choose as the title of its New England exhibition of 1952 a phrase from Samuel Danforth's election sermon, delivered on May 11, 1670: *A Brief Recognition of New England's Errand into the Wilderness.* It was of course an inspiration, if not of genius at least of talent, for Danforth to invent his title in the first place. But all the election sermons of this period—that is to say, the major expressions of the second generation, which, delivered on these forensic occasions, were in the fullest sense community expression—have interesting titles; a mere listing tells the story of what was happening to the minds and emotions of the New England people: John Higginson's *The Cause of God and His People In New England* in 1663, William Stoughton's *New England's True Interest, Not to Lie* in 1668, Thomas Shepard's *Eye-Salve* in 1672, Urian Oakes's *New England Pleaded With* in 1673, and, climactically and most explicitly, Increase Mather's *A Discourse Concerning the Danger of Apostasy* in 1677.

All of these show by their title pages alone—and, as those who have looked into them know, infinitely more by their contents—a deep disquietude. They are troubled utterances, worried, fearful. Something has gone wrong. As in 1662 Wigglesworth already was saying in verse, God has a controversy with New England; He has cause to be angry and to punish it because of its innumerable defections. They say, unanimously, that New England was sent on an errand, and that it has failed.

To our ears these lamentations of the second generation sound strange indeed. We think of the founders as heroic men—of the towering stature of Bradford, Winthrop, and Thomas Hooker—who braved the ocean and the wilderness, who conquered both, and left to their children a goodly heritage. Why then this whimpering?

Some historians suggest that the second and third generations suffered a failure of nerve; they weren't the men their fathers had been, and they knew it. Where the founders could range over the vast body of theology and ecclesiastical polity and produce profound works like the treatises of John Cotton or the subtle psychological analyses of Hooker, or even such a gusty though wrongheaded book as Nathaniel Ward's *Simple Cobler,* let alone such lofty and rightheaded pleas as Roger Williams' *Bloudy Tenent,* all these children could do was tell each other that they were on probation and that their chances of making good did not seem very promising.

Since Puritan intellectuals were thoroughly grounded in grammar and rhetoric, we may be certain that Danforth was fully aware of the ambiguity concealed in his word "errand." It already had taken on the double meaning which it still carries with us. Originally, as the word first took form in Eng-

FROM Perry Miller, *Errand into the Wilderness,* Cambridge: Belknap Press of Harvard University Press, 1956. Reprinted by permission of Mrs. Elizabeth Miller.

lish, it meant exclusively a short journey on which an inferior is sent to convey a message or to perform a service for his superior. In that sense we today speak of an "errand boy"; or the husband says that while in town on his lunch hour, he must run an errand for his wife. But by the end of the Middle Ages, errand developed another connotation: it came to mean the actual business on which the actor goes, the purpose itself, the conscious intention in his mind. In this signification, the runner of the errand is working for himself, is his own boss; the wife, while the husband is away at the office, runs her own errands. Now in the 1660's the problem was this: which had New England originally been—an errand boy or a doer of errands? In which sense had it failed? Had it been despatched for a further purpose, or was it an end in itself? Or had it fallen short not only in one or the other, but in both of the meanings? If so, it was indeed a tragedy, in the primitive sense of a fall from a mighty designation.

If the children were in grave doubt about which had been the original errand—if, in fact, those of the founders who lived into the later period and who might have set their progeny to rights found themselves wondering and confused—there is little chance of our answering clearly. Of course, there is no problem about Plymouth Colony. That is the charm about Plymouth: its clarity. The Pilgrims, as we have learned to call them, were reluctant voyagers; they had never wanted to leave England, but had been obliged to depart because the authorities made life impossible for Separatists. They could, naturally, have stayed at home had they given up being Separatists, but that idea simply did not occur to them. Yet they did not go to Holland as though on an errand; neither can we extract the notion of a mission out of the reasons which, as Bradford tells us, persuaded them to leave Leyden for "Virginia." The war with Spain was about to be resumed, and the economic threat was ominous; their migration was not so much an errand as a shrewd forecast, a plan to get out while the getting was good, lest, should they stay, they would be "intrapped or surrounded by their enemies, so as they should neither be able to fight nor flie." True, once the decision was taken, they congratulated themselves that they might become a means for propagating the gospel in remote parts of the world, and thus of serving as steppingstones to others in the performance of this great work; nevertheless, the substance of their decision was that they "thought it better to dislodge betimes to some place of better advantage and less danger, if any such could be found." The great hymn that Bradford, looking back in his old age, chanted about the landfall is one of the greatest passages, if not the very greatest, in all New England's literature; yet it does not resound with the sense of a mission accomplished—instead, it vibrates with the sorrow and exultation of suffering, the sheer endurance, the pain and the anguish, with the somberness of death faced unflinchingly:

May not and ought not the children of these fathers rightly say: Our fathers were Englishmen which came over this great ocean, and were ready to perish in this wilderness; but they cried unto the Lord, and he heard their voyce, and looked on their adversitie. . . .

We are bound, I think, to see in Bradford's account the prototype of the vast majority of subsequent immigrants—of those Oscar Handlin calls "The Uprooted": they came for better advantage and for less danger, and to give their posterity the opportunity of success.

The Great Migration of 1630 is an entirely other story. True, among the reasons John Winthrop drew up in 1629 to persuade himself and his colleagues that they should commit themselves to the enterprise, the economic motive frankly figures. Wise men thought that England was overpopulated and that the poor would have a better chance in the new land. But Massachusetts Bay was not just an organization of immigrants seeking advantage and opportunity. It had a positive sense of mission—either it was sent on an errand or it had its own intention, but in either case the deed was deliberate. It was an act of will, perhaps of willfulness. These Puritans were not driven out of England (thousands of their fellows stayed and fought the Cavaliers) —they went of their own accord.

So, concerning them, we ask the question, why? If we are not altogether clear about precisely how we should phrase the answer, this is not because they themselves were reticent. They spoke as fully as they knew how, and none more magnificently or cogently than John Winthrop in the midst of the passage itself, when he delivered a lay sermon aboard the flagship *Arbella* and called it "A Modell of Christian Charity." It distinguishes the motives of this great enterprise from those of Bradford's forlorn retreat, and especially from those of the masses who later have come in quest of advancement. Hence, for the student of New England and of America, it is a fact demanding incessant brooding that John Winthrop selected as the "doctrine" of his discourse, and so as the basic proposition to which, it then seemed to him, the errand was committed, the thesis that God had disposed mankind in a hierarchy of social classes, so that "in all times some must be rich, some poor, some highe and eminent in power and dignitie; others mean and in subjeccion." It is as though, preternaturally sensing what the promise of America might come to signify for the rank and file, Winthrop took the precaution to drive out of their heads any notion that in the wilderness the poor and the mean were ever so to improve themselves as to mount above the rich or the eminent in dignity. Were there any who had signed up under the mistaken impression that such was the purpose of their errand, Winthrop told them that, although other peoples, lesser breeds, might come for wealth or pelf, this migration was specifically dedicated to an avowed end that had nothing to do with incomes. We have entered into an explicit covenant with God, "we haue professed to enterprise these accions vpon these and these ends"; we have drawn up indentures with the Almighty, wherefore if we succeed and do not let ourselves get diverted into making money, He will reward us.

Whereas if we fail, if we "fall to embrace this present world and prosecute our carnall intencions, seekeing great things for our selves and our posterity, the Lord will surely breake out in wrathe against us be revenged of such a periured people and make us knowe the price of the breache of such a Covenant."

Well, what terms were agreed upon in this covenant? Winthrop could say precisely—"It is by a mutuall consent through a specially overruleing providence, and a more than ordinary approbation of the Churches of Christ to seeke out a place of Cohabitation and Consorteshipp under a due forme of Government both civill and ecclesiasticall." If it could be said thus concretely, why should there be any ambiguity? There was no doubt whatsoever about what Winthrop meant by a due form of ecclesiastical government: he meant the pure Biblical polity set forth in full detail by the New Testament, that method which later generations, in the days of increasing confusion, would settle down to calling Congregational, but which for Winthrop was no denominational peculiarity but the very essence of organized Christianity. What a due form of civil government meant, therefore, became crystal clear: a political regime, possessing power, which would consider its main function to be the erecting, protecting, and preserving of this form of polity. This due form would have, at the very beginning of its list of responsibilities, the duty of suppressing heresy, of subduing or somehow getting rid of dissenters—of being, in short, deliberately, vigorously, and consistently intolerant.

Regarded in this light, the Massachusetts Bay Company came on an errand in the second and later sense of the word: it was, so to speak, on its own business. What it set out to do was the sufficient reason for its setting out. About this Winthrop seems to be perfectly certain, as he declares specifically what the due forms will be attempting: the end is to improve our lives to do more service to the Lord, to increase the body of Christ, and to preserve our posterity from the corruptions of this evil world, so that they in turn shall work out their salvation under the purity and power of Biblical ordinances. Because the errand was so definable in advance, certain conclusions about the method of conducting it were equally evident: one, obviously, was that those sworn to the covenant should not be allowed to turn aside in a lust for mere physical rewards; but another was, in Winthrop's simple but splendid words, "we must be knit togeher in this worke as one man, wee must entertaine each other in brotherly affection." we must actually delight in each other, "always having before our eyes our Commission and community in the worke, our community as members of the same body." This was to say, were the great purpose kept steadily in mind, if all gazed only at it and strove only for it, then social solidarity (within a scheme of fixed and unalterable class distinctions) would be an automatic consequence. A society despatched upon an errand that is its own reward would want no other rewards: it could go forth to possess a land without ever becoming possessed by it; social gradations would remain eternally what God had originally appointed; there would be no internal contention among groups or interests, and though there would be hard work for everybody, prosperity would be bestowed not as a consequence of labor but as a sign of approval upon the mission itself. For once in the history of humanity (with all its sins), there would be a society so dedicated to a holy cause that success would prove innocent and triumph not raise up sinful pride or arrogant dissension.

Or, at least, this would come about if the people did not deal falsely with God, if they would live up to the articles of their bond. If we do not perform these terms, Winthrop warned, we may expect immediate manifestations of divine wrath; we shall perish out of the land we are crossing the sea to possess. And here in the 1600's and 1670's, all the jeremiads (of which Danforth's is one of the most poignant) are castigations of the people for having defaulted on precisely these articles. They recite the long list of afflictions an angry God had rained upon them, surely enough to prove how abysmally they had deserted the covenant: crop failures, epidemics, grasshoppers, caterpillars, torrid summers, arctic winters, Indian wars, hurricanes, shipwrecks, accidents, and (most grievous of all) unsatisfactory children. The solemn work of the election day, said Stoughton in 1668, is "Foundation-work"—not, that is, to lay a new one, "but to continue, and strengthen, and beautifie, and build upon that which has been laid." It had been laid in the covenant before even a foot was set ashore, and thereon New England should rest. Hence the terms of survival, let alone of prosperity, remained what had first been propounded:

If we should so frustrate and deceive the Lords Expectations, that his Covenant-interest in us, and the Workings of his Salvation be made to cease, then All were lost indeed; Ruine upon Ruine, Destruction upon Destruction would come, until one stone were not left upon another.

Since so much of the literature after 1660—in fact, just about all of it—dwells on this theme of declension and apostasy, would not the story of New England seem to be simply that of the failure of a mission? Winthrop's dread was realized: posterity had not found their salvation amid pure ordinances but had, despite the ordinances, yielded to the seductions of the good land. Hence distresses were being piled upon them, the slaughter of King Philip's War and now the attack of a profligate king upon the sacred charter. By about 1680, it did in truth seem that shortly no stone would be left upon another, that history would record of New England that the founders had been great men, but that their children and grandchildren progressively deteriorated.

This would certainly seem to be the impression conveyed by the assembled clergy and lay elders who, in 1679, met at Boston in a formal synod, under the leadership of Increase Mather, and there prepared a report on why the land suffered. The result of their deliberation, published under the title *The Necessity of Reformation,* was the first in what has proved to be a distressingly long succession of investigations into the civic health of Americans, and it is probably the most pessimistic. The land was afflicted, it said, because corruption had proceeded apace; assuredly, if the people did not quickly reform, the last blow would fall and nothing but desolation be left. Into what a moral quagmire this dedicated community had sunk, the synod did not leave to imagination; it published a long and detailed inventory of sins, crimes, misdemeanors, and nasty habits, which makes, to say the least, interesting reading.

We hear much talk nowadays about corruption, most of it couched in generalized terms. If we ask our current Jeremiahs to descend to particulars, they tell us that the republic is going on the rocks, or to the dogs, because the wives of politicians aspire to wear mink coats and their husbands take a moderate five per cent cut on certain deals to pay for the garments. The Puritans were devotees of logic, and the verb "methodize" ruled their thinking. When the synod went to work, it had before it a succession of sermons, such as that of Danforth and the other election-day or fast-day orators, as well as such works as Increase Mather's *A Brief History of the Warr With the Indians,* wherein the decimating conflict with Philip was presented as a revenge upon the people for their transgressions. When the synod felt obliged to enumerate the enormities of the land so that the people could recognize just how far short of their errand they had fallen, it did not, in the modern manner, assume that regeneration would be accomplished at the next election by turning the rascals out, but it digested this body of literature; it reduced the contents to method. The result is a staggering compendium of iniquity, organized into twelve headings.

First, there was a great and visible decay of godliness. Second, there were several manifestations of pride—contention in the churches, insubordination of inferiors toward superiors, particularly of those inferiors who had, unaccountably, acquired more wealth than their betters, and, astonishingly, a shocking extravagance in attire, especially on the part of these of the meaner sort, who persisted in dressing beyond their means. Third, there were heretics, especially Quakers and Anabaptists. Fourth, a notable increase in swearing and a spreading disposition to sleep at sermons (these two phenomena seemed basically connected). Fifth, the Sabbath was wantonly violated. Sixth, family government had decayed, and fathers no longer kept their sons and daughters from prowling at night. Seventh, instead of people being knit together as one man in mutual love, they were full of contention, so that lawsuits were on the increase and lawyers were thriving. Under the eighth head, the synod described the sins of sex and alcohol, thus producing some of the juiciest prose of the period: militia days had become orgies, taverns were crowded; women threw temptation in the way of befuddled men by wearing false locks and displaying naked necks and arms "or, which is more abominable, naked Breasts"; there were "mixed Dancings," along with light behavior and "Company-keeping" with vain persons, wherefore the bastardy rate was rising. In 1672, there was actually an attempt to supply Boston with a brothel (it was suppressed, but the synod was bearish about the future). Ninth, New Englanders were betraying a marked disposition to tell lies, especially when selling anything. In the tenth place, the business morality of even the most righteous left everything to be desired: the wealthy speculated in land and raised prices excessively; "Day-Labourers and Mechanicks are unreasonable in their demands." In the eleventh place, the people showed no disposition to reform, and in the twelfth, they seemed utterly destitute of civic spirit.

"The things here insisted on," said the synod, "have been oftentimes mentioned and inculcated by those whom the Lord hath set as Watchmen to the house of Israel." Indeed they had been, and thereafter they continued to be even more inculcated. At the end of the century, the synod's report was serving as a kind of handbook for preachers: they would take some verse of Isaiah or Jeremiah, set up the doctrine that God avenges the iniquities of a chosen people, and then run down the twelve heads, merely bringing the list up to date by inserting the new and still more depraved practices an ingenious people kept on devising. I suppose that in the whole literature of the world, including the satirists of imperial Rome, there is hardly such another uninhibited and unrelenting documentation of a people's descent into corruption.

I have elsewhere endeavored to argue [1] that, while the social or economic historian may read this literature for its contents—and so construct from the expanding catalogue of denunciations a record of social progress—the cultural anthropologist will look slightly askance at these jeremiads; he will exercise a methodological caution about taking them at face value. If you read them all through, the total effect, curiously enough, is not at all depressing: you come to the paradoxical realization that they do not bespeak a despairing frame of mind. There is something of a ritualistic incantation about them; whatever they may signify in the realm of theology, in that of psychology they are purgations of soul; they do not discourage but actually encourage the community to persist in its heinous conduct. The exhortation to a reformation which never materializes serves as a token payment upon the obligation, and so liberates the debtors. Changes there had to be: adaptations to environment, expansion of the frontier, mansions constructed, commercial adventures undertaken. These activities were not specifically nominated in the bond Winthrop had framed. They were thrust upon the society by American experience; because they were not only works of necessity but of excitement, they proved irresistible—whether making money, haunting

---

[1] See *The New England Mind: From Colony to Province* (1952), Chapter II.

taverns, or committing fornication. Land speculation meant not only wealth but dispersion of the people, and what was to stop the march of settlement? The covenant doctrine preached on the *Arbella* had been formulated in England, where land was not to be had for the taking; its adherents had been utterly oblivious of what the fact of a frontier would do for an imported order, let alone for a European mentality. Hence I suggest that under the guise of this mounting wail of sinfulness, this incessant and never successful cry for repentance, the Puritans launched themselves upon the process of Americanization.

However, there are still more pertinent or more analytical things to be said of this body of expression. If you compare it with the great productions of the founders, you will be struck by the fact that the second and third generations had become oriented toward the social, and only the social, problem; herein they were deeply and profoundly different from their fathers. The finest creations of the founders—the disquisitions of Hooker, Shepard, and Cotton—were written in Europe, or else, if actually penned in the colonies, proceeded from a thoroughly European mentality, upon which the American scene made no impression whatsoever. The most striking example of this imperviousness is the poetry of Anne Bradstreet: she came to Massachusetts at the age of eighteen, already two years married to Simon Bradstreet; there, she says, "I found a new world and new manners, at which my heart rose" in rebellion, but soon convincing herself that it was the way of God, she submitted and joined the church. She bore Simon eight children, and loved him sincerely, as her most charming poem, addressed to him, reveals:

> If ever two were one, then surely we;
> If ever man were loved by wife, then thee.

After the house burned, she wrote a lament about how her pleasant things in ashes lay and how no more the merriment of guests would sound in the hall; but there is nothing in the poem to suggest that the house stood in North Andover or that the things so tragically consumed were doubly precious because they had been transported across the ocean and were utterly irreplaceable in the wilderness. In between rearing children and keeping house she wrote her poetry; her brother-in-law carried the manuscript to London, and there published it in 1650 under the ambitious title, *The Tenth Muse Lately Sprung Up in America.* But the title is the only thing about the volume which shows any sense of America, and that little merely in order to prove that the plantations had something in the way of European wit and learning, that they had not receded into barbarism. Anne's flowers are English flowers, the birds, English birds, and the landscape is Lincolnshire. So also with the productions of immigrant scholarship: such a learned and acute work as Hooker's *Survey of the Summe of Church Discipline,* which is specifically about the regime set up in America, is written entirely within the logical patterns, and out of the religious experience, of Europe; it makes no concession to new and peculiar circumstances.

The titles alone of productions in the next generation show how concentrated have become emotion and attention upon the interest of New England, and none is more revealing than Samuel Danforth's conception of an errand into the wilderness. Instead of being able to compose abstract treatises like those of Hooker upon the soul's preparation, humiliation, or exultation, or such a collection of wisdom and theology as John Cotton's *The Way of Life* or Shepard's *The Sound Believer,* these later saints must, over and over again, dwell upon the specific sins of New England, and the more they denounce, the more they must narrow their focus to the provincial problem. If they write upon anything else, it must be about the halfway covenant and its manifold consequences—a development enacted wholly in this country—or else upon their wars with the Indians. Their range is sadly constricted, but every effort, no matter how brief, is addressed to the persistent question: what is the meaning of this society in the wilderness? If it does not mean what Winthrop said it must mean, what under Heaven is it? Who, they are forever asking themselves, who are we?—and sometimes they are on the verge of saying, who the Devil are we, anyway?

This brings us back to the fundamental ambiguity concealed in the word "errand," that *double entente* of which I am certain Danforth was aware when he published the words that give point to the exhibition. While it was true that in 1630, the covenant philosophy of a special and peculiar bond lifted the migration out of the ordinary realm of nature, provided it with a definite mission which might in the secondary sense be called its errand, there was always present in Puritan thinking the suspicion that God's saints are at best inferiors, despatched by their Superior upon particular assignments. Anyone who has run errands for other people, particularly for people of great importance with many things on their minds, such as army commanders, knows how real is the peril that, by the time he returns with the report of a message delivered or a bridge blown up, the Superior may be interested in something else; the situation at headquarters may be entirely changed, and the gallant errand boy, or the husband who desperately remembered to buy the ribbon, may be told that he is too late. This tragic pattern appears again and again in modern warfare: an agent is dropped by parachute and, after immense hardships, comes back to find that, in the shifting tactical or strategic situations, his contribution is no longer of value. If he gets home in time and his service proves useful, he receives a medal; otherwise, no matter what prodigies he has performed, he may not even be thanked. He has been sent, as the devastating phrase has it, upon a fool's errand, than which there can be a no more shattering blow to self-esteem.

The Great Migration of 1630 felt insured against such treatment from on high by the covenant; nevertheless, the God of the covenant always remained an unpredictable Jehovah, a *Deus Absconditus.* When God promises to abide by stated terms, His word, of course, is to be trusted; but then, what is man that he dare accuse Omnipotence of tergiversation? But if any such apprehension was in Winthrop's mind as he spoke on the *Arbella,* or in the minds of other apologists for the enterprise, they kept it far back and allowed it no utterance. They could stifle the thought, not only because Winthrop and his colleagues believed fully in the covenant, but because they could see in the pattern of history that their errand was not a mere scouting expedition: it was an essential maneuver in the drama of Christendom. The Bay Company was not a battered remnant of suffering Separatists thrown up on a rocky shore; it was an organized task force of Christians, executing a flank attack on the corruptions of Christendom. These Puritans did not flee to America; they went in order to work out that complete reformation which was not yet accomplished in England and Europe, but which would quickly be accomplished if only the saints back there had a working model to guide them. It is impossible to say that any who sailed from Southampton really expected to lay his bones in the new world; were it to come about—as all in their heart of hearts anticipated—that the forces of righteousness should prevail against Laud and Wentworth, that England after all should turn toward reformation, where else would the distracted country look for leadership except to those who in New England had perfected the ideal polity and who would know how to administer it? This was the large unspoken assumption in the errand of 1630: if the conscious intention were realized, not only would a federated Jehovah bless the new land, but He would bring back these temporary colonials to govern England.

In this respect, therefore, we may say that the migration was running an errand in the earlier and more primitive sense of the word—performing a job not so much for Jehovah as for history, which was the wisdom of Jehovah expressed through time. Winthrop was aware of this aspect of the mission—fully conscious of it. "For wee must Consider that wee shall be as a Citty upon a Hill, the eies of all people are uppon us." More was at stake than just one little colony. If we deal falsely with God, not only will He descend upon us in wrath, but even more terribly, He will make us "a story and a by-word through the world, wee shall open the mouthes of enemies to speake evill of the wayes of god and all professours for Gods sake." No less than John Milton was New England to justify God's ways to man, though not, like him, in the agony and confusion of defeat but in the confidence of approaching triumph. This errand was being run for the sake of Reformed Christianity; and while the first aim was indeed to realize in America the due form of government, both civil and ecclesiastical, the aim behind that aim was to vindicate the most rigorous ideal of the Reformation, so that ultimately all Europe would imitate New England. If we succeed, Winthrop told his audience, men will say of later plantations, "the lord make it like that of New England." There was an elementary prudence to be observed: Winthrop said that the prayer would arise from subsequent plantations, yet what was England itself but one of God's plantations? In America, he promised, we shall see, or may see, more of God's wisdom, power, and truth "then formerly wee have beene acquainted with." The situation was such that, for the moment, the model had no chance to be exhibited in England; Puritans could talk about it, theorize upon it, but they could not display it, could not prove that it would actually work. But if they had it set up in America—in a bare land, devoid of already established (and corrupt) institutions, empty of bishops and courtiers, where they could start *de novo,* and the eyes of the world were upon it —and if then it performed just as the saints had predicted of it, the Calvinist internationale would know exactly how to go about completing the already begun but temporarily stalled revolution in Europe.[2]

When we look upon the enterprise from this point of view, the psychology of the second and third generations becomes more comprehensible. We realize that the migration was not sent upon its errand in order to found the United States of America, nor even the New England conscience. Actually, it would not perform its errand even when the colonists did erect a due form of government in church and state: what was further required in order for this mission to be a success was that the eyes of the world be kept fixed upon it in rapt attention. If the rest of the world, or at least of Protestantism, looked elsewhere, or turned to another model, or simply got distracted and forgot about New England, if the new land was left with a polity nobody in the great world of Europe wanted—then every success in fulfilling the terms of the covenant would become a diabolical measure of failure. If the due form of government were not everywhere to be saluted, what would New England have upon its hands? How give it a name, this victory nobody could utilize? How provide an identity for something conceived under misapprehensions? How could a universal which turned out to be nothing but a provincial particular be called anything but a blunder or an abortion?

If an actor, playing the leading role in the greatest dramatic spectacle of the century, were to attire himself and put on his make-up, rehearse his lines, take a deep breath, and stride onto the stage, only to find the theater dark and empty, no spotlight working, and himself entirely alone, he would feel as did New England around 1650 or 1660. For in the 1640's, during the Civil Wars, the colonies, so to speak, lost their audience. First of all, there proved to be, deep in the Puritan movement, an irreconcilable split between the Presbyterian and Independent wings, wherefore no one system could be imposed upon England, and so the New England model was unserviceable. Secondly—most horrible to relate—the Independents, who in polity were carrying New England's banner and were supposed, in the schedule of his-

---

[2] See the perceptive analysis of Alan Heimert (*The New England Quarterly,* XXVI, September 1953) of the ingredients that ultimately went into the Puritans' metaphor of the "wilderness," all the more striking a concoction because they attached no significance a priori to their wilderness destination. To begin with, it was simply a void.

tory, to lead England into imitation of the colonial order, betrayed the sacred cause by yielding to the heresy of toleration. They actually welcomed Roger Williams, whom the leaders of the model had kicked out of Massachusetts so that his nonsense about liberty of conscience would not spoil the administrations of charity.

In other words, New England did not lie, did not falter; it made good everything Winthrop demanded—wonderfully good—and then found that its lesson was rejected by those choice spirits for whom the exertion had been made. By casting out Williams, Anne Hutchinson, and the Antinomians, along with an assortment of Gortonists and Anabaptists, into that cesspool then becoming known as Rhode Island, Winthrop, Dudley, and the clerical leaders showed Oliver Cromwell how he should go about governing England. Instead, he developed the utterly absurd theory that so long as a man made a good soldier in the New Model Army, it did not matter whether he was a Calvinist, an Antinomian, an Arminian, an Anabaptist or even—horror of horrors—a Socinian! Year after year, as the circus tours this country, crowds howl with laughter, no matter how many times they have seen the stunt, at the bustle that walks by itself: the clown comes out dressed in a large skirt with a bustle behind; he turns sharply to the left, and the bustle continues blindly and obstinately straight ahead, on the original course. It is funny in a circus, but not in history. There is nothing but tragedy in the realization that one was in the main path of events, and now is sidetracked and disregarded. One is always able, of course, to stand firm on his first resolution, and to condemn the clown of history for taking the wrong turning: yet this is a desolating sort of stoicism, because it always carries with it the recognition that history will never come back to the predicted path, and that with one's own demise, righteousness must die out of the world.

The most humiliating element in the experience was the way the English brethren turned upon the colonials for precisely their greatest achievement. It must have seemed, for those who came with Winthrop in 1630 and who remembered the clarity and brilliance with which he set forth the conditions of their errand, that the world was turned upside down and inside out when, in June 1645, thirteen leading Independent divines—such men as Goodwin, Owen, Nye, Burroughs, formerly friends and allies of Hooker and Davenport, men who might easily have come to New England and helped extirpate heretics—wrote the General Court that the colony's law banishing Anabaptists was an embarrassment to the Independent cause in England. Opponents were declaring, said these worthies, "that persons of our way, principall and spirit cannot beare with Dissentors from them, but Doe correct, fine, imprison and banish them wherever they have power soe to Doe." There were indeed people in England who admired the severities of Massachusetts, but we assure you, said the Independents, these "are utterly your enemyes and Doe seeke your extirpation from the face of the earth: those who now in power are your friends are quite otherwise minded, and doe professe they are much offended with your proceedings." Thus early commenced that chronic weakness in the foreign policy of Americans, an inability to recognize who in truth constitute their best friends abroad.

We have lately accustomed ourselves to the fact that there does exist a mentality which will take advantage of the liberties allowed by society in order to conspire for the ultimate suppression of those same privileges. The government of Charles I and Archbishop Laud had not, where that danger was concerned, been liberal, but it had been conspicuously inefficient; hence, it did not liquidate the Puritans (although it made halfhearted efforts), nor did it herd them into prison camps. Instead, it generously, even lavishly, gave a group of them a charter to Massachusetts Bay, and obligingly left out the standard clause requiring that the document remain in London, that the grantees keep their office within reach of Whitehall. Winthrop's revolutionaries availed themselves of this liberty to get the charter overseas, and thus to set up a regime dedicated to the worship of God in the manner they desired—which meant allowing nobody else to worship any other way, especially adherents of Laud and King Charles. All this was perfectly logical and consistent. But what happened to the thought processes of their fellows in England made no sense whatsoever. Out of the New Model Army came the fantastic notion that a party struggling for power should proclaim that, once it captured the state, it would recognize the right of dissenters to disagree and to have their own worship, to hold their own opinions. Oliver Cromwell was so far gone in this idiocy as to become a dictator, in order to impose toleration by force! Amid this shambles, the errand of New England collapsed. There was nobody left at headquarters to whom reports could be sent.

Many a man has done a brave deed, been hailed as a public hero, had honors and ticker tape heaped upon him—and then had to live, day after day, in the ordinary routine, eating breakfast and brushing his teeth, in what seems protracted anticlimax. A couple may win their way to each other across insuperable obstacles, elope in a blaze of passion and glory—and then have to learn that life is a matter of buying the groceries and getting the laundry done. This sense of the meaning having gone out of life, that all adventures are over, that no great days and no heroism lie ahead, is particularly galling when it falls upon a son whose father once was the public hero or the great lover. He has to put up with the daily routine without ever having known at first hand the thrill of danger or the ecstasy of passion. True, he has his own hardships—clearing rocky pastures, hauling in the cod during a storm, fighting Indians in a swamp—but what are these compared with the magnificence of leading an exodus of saints to found a city on a hill, for the eyes of all the world to behold? He might wage a stout fight against the Indians and one out of ten of his fellows might perish in the struggle, but the world was no longer interested. He would be reduced to writing accounts of himself and scheming to get a publisher in London, in a desperate effort to tell a heedless world, "Look, I exist!"

His greatest difficulty would be not the stones, storms, and Indians, but the problem of his identity. In something of this sort, I should like to suggest, consists the anxiety and torment that inform productions of the late seventeenth and early eighteenth centuries—and should I say, some thereafter? It appears most clearly in *Magnalia Christi Americana,* the work of that soul most tortured by the problem, Cotton Mather: "I write the Wonders of the Christian Religion, flying from the Depravations of Europe, to the American Strand." Thus he proudly begins, and at once trips over the acknowledgment that the founders had not simply fled from depraved Europe but had intended to redeem it. And so the book is full of lamentations over the declension of the children, who appear, page after page, in contrast to their mighty progenitors, about as profligate a lot as ever squandered a great inheritance.

And yet, the *Magnalia* is not an abject book; neither are the election sermons abject, nor is the inventory of sins offered by the synod of 1679. There is bewilderment, confusion, chagrin, but there is no surrender. A task has been assigned upon which the populace are in fact intensely engaged. But they are not sure any more for just whom they are working; they know they are moving, but they do not know where they are going. They seem still to be on an errand, but if they are no longer inferiors sent by the superior forces of the reformation, to whom they should report, then their errand must be wholly of the second sort, something with a purpose and an intention sufficient unto itself. If so, what is it? If it be not the due form of government, civil and ecclesiastical, that they brought into being, how otherwise can it be described?

The literature of self-condemnation must be read for meanings far below the surface, for meanings of which, we may be so rash as to surmise, the authors were not fully conscious, but by which they were troubled and goaded. They looked in vain to history for an explanation of themselves; more and more it appeared that the meaning was not to be found in theology, even with the help of the covenantal dialectic. Thereupon, these citizens found that they had no other place to search but within themselves—even though, at first sight, that repository appeared to be nothing but a sink of iniquity. Their errand having failed in the first sense of the term, they were left with the second, and required to fill it with meaning by themselves and out of themselves. Having failed to rivet the eyes of the world upon their city on the hill, they were left alone with America.

SIGMUND DIAMOND

FROM ORGANIZATION TO SOCIETY
Virginia in the Seventeenth Century

Sociologist Sigmund Diamond describes his article as an effort to rehabilitate the methods of historical sociology. As interesting as those methods are, students will probably find that the results are even more striking. The article reconstructs the transformation of the overseas settlement established by the Virginia Company from a conventional business organization to a colonial society. The major impetus in this process of development was the recruitment of a voluntary labor force by the offer of economic rewards and social status to potential settlers. Virginia demands comparison with the Massachusetts Bay Colony; one difference worth reflection is the contrast between the latter colony, which set its own objectives, and the former, which followed the directives of a parent company in England. Some of the problems raised by Diamond are more fully explored in Charles M. Andrews, The Colonial Period of American History *(1934), and in Wesley F. Craven,* The Dissolution of the Virginia Company *(1932), and* The Southern Colonies in the Seventeenth Century *(1949).*

$\mathbf{F}$ad and fashion play their roles in the world of scholarship as elsewhere, and often products of the intellect may assume the quaint air of artifacts for no better reason than that, with the passage of time, they are made obsolete by the appearance of new, if not necessarily better, models. But in scholarship, if not in manufacturing, novelty is a virtue that has limits; and even old ideas and interests may be resurrected if they demonstrate the existence of problems or give promise of solving problems for which more recent ideas have proved inadequate. So it is that historical sociology, though conceded to be one of the roots from which the discipline itself emerged, has, in this country at least, suffered from the competition of more stylish fashions. And so it is, too, that there is increasing evidence today that historical sociology, so long an outmoded form of inquiry, is once again commending itself as an important subject of research. What follows is, frankly, an attempt to aid in the rehabilitation of historical sociology, not by exhortation, but, it is hoped, by a persuasive demonstration that questions of considerable importance for sociological theory may be raised when problems are examined in historical perspective. Our interest in this essay is in the utilization of certain aspects of the history of Virginia in the early seventeenth century to suggest significant questions concerning the creation of new statuses and the circumstances under which the character of an organization may be so altered as to be transmuted into something which is not, properly speaking, an organization at all but a society.

I

It must be conceded at the outset that the group we have selected for study was pathetically small. In 1607, when the Virginia Company established a settlement at Jamestown, its population numbered 105; and in 1624, when the crown revoked the charter of the Company, the population of Virginia amounted to just over 1,200, despite the fact that the Company had sent more than 5,000 emigrants during that seventeen-year period.[1] But, just as a limited duration of time is no necessary detriment to a study of this kind, because there are periods of history when the rate of change is accelerated, so, too, the limited size of the group affords no accurate measure of the importance of the enterprise. Judged in terms of its outcome, its importance is self-evident. But, judged even in terms of the criteria of importance imposed by contemporaries, the verdict must be the same. The articles on the Virginia

---

[1] Philip Alexander Bruce, *Social Life of Virginia in the Seventeenth Century* (Richmond, 1907), pp. 15, 17–18; "The Virginia Census, 1624–25," *Virginia Magazine of History and Biography*, VII (1899–1900), 364–67; Edward Channing, *A History of the United States* (New York and London, 1905–25), I, 204–5.

FROM Sigmund Diamond, "From Organization to Society: Virginia in the Seventeenth Century," *American Journal of Sociology*, Vol. LXIII (March 1958), pp. 457–75. Reprinted by permission.

settlement in the *Kölnische Zeitung* and the *Mercure françoise;* the running series of reports from the Venetian ambassadors in London to the Doge and Senate; the letters from Jesuit priests in England to the Propaganda Fide in Rome and the newsletters from Venice and Antwerp in the Vatican archives; the continuing stream of dispatches from the Spanish ambassadors to King Philip III, pressing him to attack Jamestown, advising him of the latest decisions of the Virginia Company, and relating their efforts to recruit English spies; and the existence in the royal archives at Simancas of a description of the layout of Jamestown and the earliest known map of the town, the work of an Irish spy in the service of Spain [2]—all this is eloquent testimony of the position of Virginia in the international relations of the seventeenth century and of the concern felt in the capitals of Europe in the Virginia Company's undertaking. Nor was the expression of this concern merely verbal. In August, 1613, when the population of Virginia barely exceeded 200, the settlement at Jamestown had a decidedly cosmopolitan cast, for it contained eighteen prisoners—fifteen Frenchmen, including two Jesuits and several members of the nobility; a Spanish spy, Don Diego de Molina; a renegade Englishman in the pay of Spain; and an Indian princess, Pocahontas.[3]

At the May Day, 1699, exercises at the College of William and Mary, one of the student orators—who must have been a sophomore—exclaimed:

> Methinks we see already that happy time when we shall surpass the Asiaticians in civility, the Jews in religion, the Greeks in philosophy, the Egyptians in geometry, the Phoenicians in arithmetic, and the Chaldeans in astrology. O happy Virginia.[4]

We may be intrigued by the ingenuousness of the student, but we are interested in the statement as evidence of the fact that in 1699—and for some time earlier—Virginia was a society and Virginians were nothing if not ebullient about its prospects. For it had not always been so.

At its inception—and for a number of years thereafter—it had been a formal organization, and, if the joyous outburst of the student reflects its character at a later date, its earlier character is better revealed by the instruc-

---

[2] See, e.g., Alexander Brown, *The Genesis of the United States* (Boston and New York, 1897), I, 142, 180, n. 1, 244–45, 393–99; II, 595–96, 738, 741; *Calendar of State Papers and Manuscripts Relating to English Affairs . . . in the Archives and Collections of Venice . . . ,* Vol. XI, Nos. 52, 466, 794, 821; Carl Russell Fish (ed.), *Guide to the Materials for American History in Roman and Other Italian Archives* (Washington, 1911), pp. 150 ff.; Henry Chandlee Forman, *Jamestown and St. Mary's* (Baltimore, 1938), pp. 37, 38; Alexander Brown, *The First Republic in America* (New York and Boston, 1898), pp. 48, 50, 51–52, 62, 79–80, 121, 123, 125, 152, 160, 184–85, 218–19.

[3] Brown, *Genesis,* II, 700–706.

[4] Quoted in Louis B. Wright, *The First Gentlemen of Virginia* (San Marino, 1940), p. 109.

tions given by the Virginia Company to Sir Thomas Gates on the eve of his departure for Jamestown in May, 1609:

> You must divide yor people into tennes, twenties & so upwards, to every necessary worke a competent nomber, over every one of wch you must appointe some man of Care & still in that worke to oversee them and to take dayly accounte of their laboures, and you must ordayne y^t every overseer of such a nomber of workemen Deliver once a weeke an accounte of the wholle comitted to his Charge . . . you shall doe best to lett them eate together at reasonable howers in some publique place beinge messed by six or five to a messe, in wch you must see there bee equality and sufficient that so they may come and retourne to their worke without any delay and have no cause to complain of measure or to excuse their idleness uppon ye dressinge or want of diet. You may well allowe them three howers in a somers day and two in the winter, and shall call them together by Ringinge of a Bell and by the same warne them againe to worke.[5]

And, if in later years "O happy Virginia" could be a spontaneous outcry of its citizens, it could not have been earlier. Testifying in 1625 about conditions under the administration of Sir Thomas Dale in 1614–16, Mrs. Perry, one of the fortunates who survived more than a few years in the first quarter-century of Virginia's history, revealed that

> in the time of S^r: Thomas Dales Government An leyden and June Wright and other women were appoynted to make shirts for the Colony servants and had six nelds full of silke threed allowed for making of a shirte, wch yf they did not p'forme, They had noe allowance of Dyott, and because theire threed naught and would not sewe, they tooke owt a ravell of ye lower p^{te} of ye shirte to make an end of ye worke, and others y^t had threed of thiere owne made it up wth that, Soe the shirts of those wch had raveled owt proved shorter then the next, for wch fact the said An leyden and June Wright were whipt, And An leyden beinge then wth childe (the same night thereof miscarried).[6]

Our first inquiry, then, must be into the characteristics of the original settlement at Jamestown—characteristics which changed so markedly during the course of the next quarter-century.

Virginia was not established as a colony to take its place among the territories governed by the British crown; it was not a state, and, properly speaking, it was not a political unit at all. It was property, the property of the Virginia Company of London, and it was established to return a profit to the stockholders of that company. Under the political and economic conditions

---

[5] Susan Myra Kingsbury (ed.), *Records of the Virginia Company* (Washington, 1906–35), III, 21.

[6] "Minutes of the Council and General Court," *Virginia Magazine of History and Biography*, XXIII (1915), 138.

of seventeenth-century England, speculators in overseas expansion could count on no support from the government except verbal encouragement and some legal protection—and sometimes precious little of these. Under the circumstances, therefore, colonization had to be undertaken as a private business venture, and the first charge imposed on the property was the return on the shareholder's investment. Traditionally, this episode has been dealt with primarily in terms of the motivation of participants—did they come to establish religious freedom, to seek a haven for the politically persecuted, or to found a "First Republic"?—and it is true that those who joined the Virginia enterprise did so for many reasons. Some, like Richard Norwood, were footloose and fancy-free after having completed their apprenticeships. Robert Evelin wrote his mother that he was "going to the sea, a long and dangerous voyage with other men, to make me to be able to pay my debts, and to restore my decayed estate again . . . and I beseech you, if I do die, that you would be good unto my poor wife and children, which God knows, I shall leave very poor and very mean, if my friends be not good unto them." In its promotional literature the Virginia Company took advantage of this broad spectrum of motives and cast its net wide to snare the purses and bodies of all sorts and conditions of persons in support of a venture in which

> . . . profite doth with pleasure joyne,
> and bids each chearefull heart,
> To this high praysed enterprise,
> performe a Christian part.[7]

But, from the point of view of the managers of the enterprise, recruitment was perceived less as a problem of motivation than of achieving an organizational form through which the resources and energies of the participants could be mobilized. The basic objectives of the promoters in establishing a plantation in Virginia are quite clear: to exploit the mineral resources which they were certain were there; to search for that elusive will-o'-the-wisp—a water route to the Pacific through North America—and to monopolize whatever local trade existed and whatever oriental trade would be developed with the opening-up of the northwest passage.

The organizational form adopted for the venture was not created by the promoters; the roots of the joint-stock company, though it was still subject to considerable experimentation, lay deeply imbedded in English history. Nor were the proprietors themselves totally without experience in the establishment of plantations or unaware of the experience of others. Sir Thomas Smythe, a leader of the Virginia enterprise, was one of the merchant princes of London, a governor of the East India Company, the Muscovy Company,

---

[7] Wesley Frank Craven and Walter B. Hayward, *The Journal of Richard Norwood, Surveyor of Bermuda* (New York, 1945); Brown, *Genesis*, I, 442; "London's Lotterie," *William and Mary Quarterly*, V (3d ser., 1948), 259–64.

and many others. And they had before them the experience—which was, as we shall see, not entirely an unmixed blessing—of the colonizing efforts of Sir Walter Raleigh and Sir Humphrey Gilbert, of the trading posts established by the great commercial companies, of Spain and Portugal, and of the founding of plantations in Ireland.[8]

What they established was a business organization; and, though the form of that organization was changed at various times during the Company's history, those changes were at all times dictated by the need to make the business pay, which, in the words of Sir Edwin Sandys, one of the two great leaders of the Company, was "that whereon all men's eyes were fixed." [9] Its problems were those of any business organization. It sold shares, begged contributions, and organized lotteries to raise the necessary funds; it was concerned to recruit a proper labor force; it had to cope with the problem of adequate supervision and administration so as to maintain its authority; and it engaged in a full-scale advertising campaign to sell to potential adventurers and planters the glories of a land where the "horses are also more beautiful, and fuller of courage. And such is the extraordinarie fertility of that Soyle, that the Does of their Deere yeelde Two Fawnes at a birth, and sometimes three." And it was confronted with the petty harassments of cajoling those whose good will was needed for the success of the organization. "Talking with the King," wrote the Earl of Southampton to Sir Robert Cecil, "by chance I told him of the Virginia Squirrills which they say will fly, whereof there are now divers brought into England, and hee presently and very earnestly asked me if none of them was provided for him. . . . I would not have troubled you with this but that you know so well how he is affected by these toyes." [10]

But though the Company's plans were eminently rational, its grand design suffered from a fatal flaw: reality was far different from what the Company expected. Its model had been the East India Company, and its dream had been to reproduce the Spanish looting of a continent; but conditions in Virginia were not those of India or Mexico and Peru. "It was the Spaniards good hap," wrote Captain John Smith later in the history of the Virginia Company,

---

[8] Herbert Levi Osgood, *The American Colonies in the Seventeenth Century* (New York and London, 1904, 1907), I, 32–34; II, 30–32; Philip Alexander Bruce, *Economic History of Virginia in the Seventeenth Century* (New York and London, 1896), I, 3–4.

[9] Wesley Frank Craven, *Dissolution of the Virginia Company* (New York, 1932), p. 24. For an account of the structure of the Company see William Robert Scott, *The Constitution and Finance of English, Scottish and Irish Joint-Stock Companies to 1720* (Cambridge, 1910), II, 247–59, 266–88.

[10] *A Declaration of the State of the Colonie and Affairs in Virginia* (London, 1620), in Peter Force (ed.), *Tracts and Other Papers, Relating . . . to the . . . Colonies in North America* (Washington, 1836–46), III, 5; Brown, *Genesis,* I, 357.

to happen in those parts where were infinite numbers of people, whoe had manured the ground with that providence that it afforded victuall at all times; and time had brought them to that perfection they had the use of gold and silver, and the most of such commodities as their countries affoorded; so that what the Spaniard got was only the spoile and pillage of those countries people, and not the labours of their owne hands. But had those fruitfull Countries been as Salvage, as barbarous, as ill-peopled, as little planted laboured and manured, as Virginia; their proper labours, it is likely would have produced as small profit as ours. . . .

But we chanced in a land, even as God made it. . . . Which ere wee could bring to recompence our paines, defray our charges, and satisfie our adventurers; wee were to discover the country, subdue the people, bring them to be tractable civil and industrious, and teach them trades that the fruits of their labours might make us recompence, or plant such colonies of our owne that must first make provision how to live of themselves ere they can bring to perfection the commodities of the countrie.[11]

But though the error in conception made by the leaders of the Virginia Company was, from their viewpoint, a grievous one, it is also thoroughly understandable. It is true that the late sixteenth and early seventeenth century was a period of rapid expansion in the organization of trading companies; no less than thirty-four were chartered during that time. But the significant point is that the Virginia Company was the eighteenth to be founded, and, of the previous seventeen, whose experience could be taken as models, all dealt with countries within the European seas, with settled communities along the African coast, or with the advanced societies of Asia. For them, the problem was to exploit the already existing labor force of a settled society.[12] For the Virginia Company, the problem—and it is in this that the crucial difference lies—was to recruit a labor force.

It must be understood, therefore, that, in conformity with its objectives and organizational form, the establishment planted by the Virginia Company at Jamestown was a private estate, which, in the absence of an amenable local labor force, was worked on the basis of imported labor. Basic policies were laid down in London by the General Court of the Company, the body of those who had purchased the £12 10s. shares or who had been admitted for favors in the Company's behalf; the management and direction of affairs were intrusted to agents of the shareholders; and the supervision of those whose labor in Virginia was necessary for the attainment of the Company's objectives was placed in the hands of officials appointed in London.

---

[11] John Smith, *Description of Virginia and Proceedings of the Colonie* (Oxford, 1612), in Lyon Gardiner Tyler (ed.), *Narratives of Early Virginia* (New York, 1907), p. 178.

[12] Susan Myra Kingsbury, "A Comparison of the Virginia Company with the Other English Trading Companies of the Sixteenth and Seventeenth Centuries," *Annual Report of the American Historical Association for the Year 1906* (Washington, 1907), pp. 162–66.

Under the circumstances there were many potent inducements to English investors to purchase the Company's £12 10s. shares, a price, incidentally, which was the Company's estimate of the cost of transporting a settler to Virginia. Under the charter of 1606 they were guaranteed that after a five-year period, during which the settlers in Virginia would be supported by a stream of supplies sent at Company expense, the profits gained through trade and the discovery of minerals would be divided among the investors in proportion to the number of shares they held, and grants of land would be made to them on the same basis. But what were to be the inducements to become the labor force of a company trading post?

It should be noted at once that the English imitated the Spaniards in attempting to mobilize native labor. For the Company the key to the integration of the Indians into the labor force was in the ease with which, it was anticipated, they could be converted to Christianity and thereby won over as well to the secular values of Europeans. To them would accrue spiritual benefits; the Company, already blessed with those, would receive something more substantial. As a certain "Maister Captaine Chester" put it:

> The land full rich, the people easilie wonne,
> Whose gaines shalbe the knowledge of our faith
> And ours such ritches as the country hath.[13]

But though the Company succeeded for a time in exacting some tribute from the local tribal chiefs in the form of goods and weekly labor services, the Indians proved unwilling to accept the Company's spiritual and secular offerings. Long before the Indian uprising of 1622 gave an excuse to the settlers to engage in a campaign of extermination, it was clear that the Virginia Company would be forced to import its own labor force.[14]

Between 1607 and 1609, when its charter was changed, the Virginia Company sent over 300 persons to Jamestown. They were a disparate crew of adventurers and roughnecks, imbued with the hope that after a short period in Virginia they would return home with their fortunes in their purses. The social composition of the original labor force, the tasks they were expected to perform, and the nature of the settlement they were expected to establish can all be inferred from the passenger lists of the first expedition and the three subsequent supplies that were sent out by the Company before its charter was modified in 1609. The original expedition numbered 105 persons, of whom we have the names of 67. Of these 67, 29 were listed as gentlemen and 6 were named to the local council; the rest were listed by occupation—1 preacher, 4 carpenters, 12 laborers, 1 surgeon, 1 blacksmith, 1

---

[13] Quoted in Keith Glenn, "Captain John Smith and the Indians," *Virginia Magazine of History and Biography,* LII (1944), 231, n. 12.

[14] Wesley Frank Craven, "Indian Policy in Early Virginia," *William and Mary Quarterly,* I (3d ser., 1944), 65–82.

sailor, 1 barber, 2 bricklayers, 1 mason, 1 tailor, 1 drummer, and 4 boys—and 2 were unidentified. In the three succeeding supplies, the rather high proportion of gentlemen was not substantially reduced, nor did the range of occupations alter significantly. Seventy-three of the 120 persons in the first supply of 1608 can be identified. In this group, gentlemen exceeded laborers 28 to 21. The remainder was made up of an odd assortment of craftsmen, including jewelers, refiners, and goldsmiths—bespeaking the expectations of the Company—apothecaries, tailors, blacksmiths, and—mute testimony to the fact that gentlemen must be gentlemen whether in the wilds of Virginia or a London drawing room—a perfumer. In brief, the two most striking characteristics of this original labor force are the presence of so high a proportion of gentlemen and the absence of any occupations indicative of an intention to establish a settled agricultural community.[15]

From the point of view of the promoters of the Virginia enterprise, these men were not citizens of a colony; they were the occupants of a status in—to use an anachronistic term—the Company's table of organization, and the status was that of workman. Such other qualities or attributes that they possessed might have been of importance when they were in London, Norwich, or Bristol, but what counted in Virginia was that they should accept the directions of their superiors and that they should be willing to work.

Even under the best of circumstances, the problem of maintaining discipline and authority would have been crucial to the success of the Company. But these were hardly the best of circumstances, for the very social composition of the original labor force intensified what in any case would have been a grievously difficult problem. In the long intervals between the arrival of supplies under the direction of the Company's admiral, Christopher Newport, conditions in Jamestown bordered on anarchy; men were beaten by their officers, plots were hatched to escape the country, and insubordination was rampant. The Company's administrative methods, characterized by the utmost laxness, could not cope with the situation. "I likewise as occasion moved me," wrote President Wingfield, discussing the supplies in Virginia, "spent them in trade or by guift amongst the Indians. So likewise did Captain Newport take of them . . . what he thought good, without any noate of his hand mentioning the certainty; and disposed of them as was fitt for him. Of these likewise I could make no accompt." Nor did the high percentage of aristocrats help matters. Unused to the heavy work of axing timber, they cursed so much at their blisters that the president of the council ordered that at the end of the day's work a can of cold water be poured down the sleeve of each offender for every curse he had uttered. To Captain John Smith, the problem was the presence of too many gentlemen: "For some small number of adventrous Gentlemen . . . nothing were more requisite; but to have

---

[15] John Smith, *Description of Virginia,* in Tyler (ed.), *op. cit.,* pp. 125–26, 140–41, 159–60; Thomas Jefferson Wertenbaker, *Patrician and Plebeian in Virginia* (Charlottesville, 1910), pp. 5–9; Bruce, *Social Life,* pp. 39–43.

more to wait and play than worke, or more commanders and officers than industrious labourers was not so necessarie. For in Virginia, a plaine Souldier that can use a Pickaxe and spade, is better than five Knights." [16]

Clearly, even if the mortality figures had been less gruesome than they were—in July, 1609, between 80 and 100 were alive of the 320 who had been sent since 1607 [17]—qualitative considerations alone would have dictated a change in the composition of the labor force. For the Company the situation was brought to a head with the realization that there were to be no quick returns from metals and trade and that profits would have to be made through the exploitation of agricultural resources.

Never did the Company rely fundamentally on the recruitment of involuntary labor, but so desperate were its labor requirements and so necessary was it to keep the good will of those authorities who favored the transportation of undesirables that it felt compelled to resort to forced labor.

As early as 1609, a letter from Lisbon revealed that the Portuguese were transporting fifteen hundred children over the age of ten to the East Indies and suggested that the same be done in the case of Virginia. Shortly thereafter the Privy Council notified the mayor of London that the plagues of the city were due mainly to the presence of so many poor persons and recommended that a fund be raised, with the help of the commercial companies, to send as many of these as possible to Virginia. The Virginia Company promptly gave an estimate of the expenses involved and of the terms that would be offered to the emigrants; but, though a large sum of money was raised, no persons were actually transported at that time. In 1617, however, the City of London raised £500 to pay the cost of shipping one hundred children to Virginia, where they were to be apprenticed until the age of twenty-one, thereafter to be the fee-simple owners of fifty acres of land each. So delighted were the Company and the Virginia planters that they continued the practice, but it is evident that not all the children were equally pleased by the future arranged for them. In January, 1620, Sandys wrote to Sir Robert Naunton, the king's principal secretary, that "it falleth out that among those children, sundry being ill-disposed, and fitter for any remote place than for this Citie, declare their unwillingness to goe to Virginia: of whom the Citie is especially desirous to be disburdened; and in Virginia under severe Masters they may be brought to goodness." Since the City could not deliver and the Company could not transport "theis persons against their wills," Sandys appealed to the Privy Council for the necessary authority. It was quickly given. Exact figures cannot be determined, but, before the demise of the Company

---

[16] The quotations are in Osgood, op. cit., I, 46–47; Smith, Generall Historie, in Tyler (ed.), op. cit., pp. 331–32; John Smith, The Proceedings of the English Colonie in Virginia (Oxford, 1612), in the A. G. Bradley edition of Edward Arber (ed.), Travels and Works of Captain John Smith (Edinburgh, 1919), I, 149. See also Osgood, op. cit., I, 50, 54–55; Bruce, Economic History, I, 197.

[17] Channing, op. cit., I, 204.

in 1624, additional shipments of children had been delivered to Virginia, and it is evident that several hundred must have been involved.[18]

Concerning the shipment of convicts and rogues and vagabonds the information is scanty. Some convicts were certainly in Virginia before 1624, though we do not know how many; but the Virginia Company was antagonistic to the importation of such persons, and, in any case, convict-dumping on a large scale did not become a characteristic of the colonial scene until the second half of the seventeenth century.[19] So, too, was the Company antagonistic to the importation of rogues, possibly because, unlike the case of the London children, it was forced to assume the cost of transportation. It engaged in the practice under pressure from King James I. For one group of fifty boys sent out in 1619, the Company expected to receive £500 in tobacco from the planters to whom they were indentured; but as late as October, 1622, it had received only £275.15.6, and Governor Yeardley was told that the planters "should be caused to make satisfaccon for the 224^{li}4:6: wch is remayninge due unto the Companie this yeare in good leafe Tobacco." That still others were sent is certain; the Court Book of Bridewell Hospital records that in 1620 Ellen Boulter was "brought in by the Marshall for a Vagrant, that will not be ruled by her father or her friends," to be kept at her father's charges to go to Virginia.[20]

But throughout its history the Company was dependent upon the recruitment of voluntary labor, and especially was this true when it realized that profits would have to be made from agricultural staples and not minerals. The change in objective not only emphasized the necessity of recruiting a larger labor supply but required that it be qualitatively different from the earlier one, for now that the glitter of gold was vanishing the Company needed not soldiers of fortune but sober workmen who would be able to extract from the land the food supplies necessary for their own support and the staples whose export would produce profit for the shareholders.[21] But what could the Company offer as sufficient inducement to motivate large numbers of persons to come to Virginia, especially when—as the evidence indicates —enthusiasm for emigration from England was confined to the wealthy, who themselves were hardly likely to exchange the comforts of life in England for

---

[18] *Calendar of State Papers, East Indies, 1571–1616,* No. 432; Brown, *Genesis,* I, 252–54; E. Ribton-Turner, *A History of Vagrants and Vagrancy* (London, 1887), 141; Kingsbury (ed.), *Records,* I, 304–6, 270, 359; III, 259; *Acts of the Privy Council of England, Colonial Series,* Vol. I, No. 42; Abbot Emerson Smith, *Colonists in Bondage* (Chapel Hill, 1947), pp. 147–49; Richard B. Morris, *Government and Labor in Early America* (New York, 1946), p. 385.

[19] A. E. Smith, *op. cit.,* pp. 94–95; Morris, *op. cit.,* p. 323.

[20] Kingsbury (ed.), *Records,* I, 520, II, 108; A. E. Smith, *op. cit.,* pp. 139–40.

[21] Craven, *Virginia Company,* pp. 29–33; Scott, *op. cit.,* II, 250–52; Philip Alexander Bruce, *Institutional History of Virginia in the Seventeenth Century* (New York and London, 1910), II, 237–41.

the dangers of life in Virginia? [22] The difficulties the Company faced in this respect were exacerbated by the whispering campaign started by settlers who had already returned from Virginia. "Some few of those unruly youths sent thither," said a Virginia Company broadside in 1609,

> (being of most leaued and bad condition) and such as no ground can hold for what of good direction there, were suffered by stealth to get aboard the ships returning thence, and are come for England againe, giving out in all places where they come (to colour their owne misbehaviours, and the cause of their returne with some pretence) most vile and scandalous reports, both of the Country itselfe, and of the Cariage of the business there.[23]

The Company now determined to be discriminating in the selection of settlers:

> And for that former experience hath too clearly taught, how muche and manie waies it hurtheth to suffer Parents to disburden themselves of lascivious sonnes, masters of bad servants and wives of ill husbands, and so to dogge the business with such an idle crue, as did thrust themselves in the last voiage, that will rather starve for hunger, than lay their hands to labor.[24]

It was conceded that some "base and disordered men" might inveigle themselves into the body of settlers, but they could not do too much harm, for, as the Reverend William Crashaw said on the departure of Governor de la Warr to Virginia, "the basest and worst men trained up in a severe discipline, sharp lawes, a hard life, and much labour, do prove good members of a Commonwealth. . . . The very excrements, of a full and swelling state . . . wanting pleasures, and subject to some pinching miseries," will become "good and worthie instruments." [25]

Clearly, if prospective settlers in Virginia faced "severe discipline, sharp lawes, a hard life, and much labour," substantial concessions would have to be offered to induce them to emigrate. The status the Company was asking them to accept was that of servant, employee of the Company, but it was one thing to create a position and quite another to get men to fill it. Since perpetual servitude was obviously no inducement, the Company was required to limit the period of service and to make other concessions. Every settler over the age of ten, whether he paid his own way or was shipped at Com-

---

[22] A. E. Smith, *op. cit.*, pp. 44–46.

[23] Brown, *Genesis*, I, 355.

[24] *Ibid.*, I, 356.

[25] *A Sermon Preached in London before the Right Honourable Lord la warre, Lord governor and Captaine Generall of Virginia* (London, 1610), quoted in Perry Miller, "Religion and Society in the Early Literature: The Religious Impulse in the Founding of Virginia," *William and Mary Quarterly,* VI (3d ed., 1949), 31; Brown, *Genesis,* I, 364.

pany expense, was promised one share of stock in the Company, with potential dividends from the profits of trade and a land grant to be made at the time of the first division after seven years. Every "extraordinarie" man—such as "Divines, Governors, Ministers of State and Justice, Knights, Gentlemen, Physitions" or such as were "of worth for special services"—was given additional shares according to the value of his person. The Company expected, in return for assuming all the costs of maintaining that plantation and providing supplies to the emigrants, that each settler would work at tasks assigned him under the direction of Company-appointed officers. For a period of seven years, all supplies were to be distributed through the Company store, all exports were to be shipped through the Company magazine, and all land was to be held by the Company.[26] In effect, the Company created the status of landowner in order to induce persons to accept the status of non-landowner; it was asking emigrants to accept the present burdens of membership in a lower status in anticipation of the future benefits they would receive upon promotion to a higher status. From the point of view of the structure of an organization, this was simply automatic progression—promotion to a higher position in the table of organization after a limited tenure in a lower position. From the point of view of a society, however, this was a guaranty of social mobility, and, as we shall see, it seriously compromised the Company's ability to secure its organizational objectives.

That the Company expected the combination of limited servitude and potential landownership to solve its labor problem is quite clear; sufficient numbers of workmen would be induced to emigrate to Virginia and, having arrived, would be motivated to do the work that was essential to the Company's success. Virginia planter and London adventurer were to be united in a single relationship. Do not discourage the planters, the London stockholders were admonished, "in growing religious, nor in gathering riches, two especiall bonds (whether severed or cojoined) to keepe them in obedience, the one for conscience sake, the other for fear of losing what they have gotten." How the planter's concern for his own interests was to benefit the Company was quite clear. "The Planters," wrote Alderman Johnson, "will be in such hope to have their owne shares and habitations in those lands, which they have so husbanded, that it will cause contending and emulation among them, which shall bring foorth the most profitable and beneficiall fruites for their ioynt stock." [27]

---

[26] James Curtis Ballagh, *White Servitude in the Colony of Virginia* ("Johns Hopkins University Studies in Historical and Political Science, 13th Series," Vols. VII–VIII [Baltimore, 1895]), pp. 15–17; Craven, *Virginia Company,* pp. 29–33; Craven, *Southern Colonies,* pp. 85–90; A. E. Smith, *op. cit.,* pp. 8–10; Kingsbury, "Comparison," *op. cit.,* pp. 163–69.

[27] *The New Life of Virginea . . . Being the Second Part of Nova Britannia* (London, 1612), in Force (ed.), *op. cit.,* I, 17–18; *Nova Britannia,* in Force (ed.), *op. cit.,* I, 26.

But land for the settlers and profits for the stockholders were affairs of the future, and both were dependent upon the skill and speed with which the planters could be molded into an efficient labor force. It was of the utmost importance, therefore, that the Company establish its authority in Virginia and maintain discipline, and for the achievement of these purposes the Company was not content to rely simply on the self-discipline it hoped would be the by-product of the effort to obtain profits. The first step was taken with the issuance of the new charter of 1609. During its first three years in Virginia, the Company felt, "experience of error in the equality of Governors, and some out-rages, and follies committed by them, had a little shaken so tender a body." To avoid the evils of divided authority, "we did resolve and obtain, to renew our Letters Pattents, and to procure to ourselves, such ample and large priviledges and powers by which we were at liberty to reforme and correct those already discovered, and to prevent such as in the future might threaten us . . . under the conduct of one able and absolute Governor." [28] But changes in the formal structure of authority were not sufficient.

Religion, too, was counted upon to do its part in maintaining order. Doctrinal conflict was minimized from the start by the ban on Catholics, but what really distinguishes the role of religion under the Virginia Company was its conscious utilization for disciplinary purposes. No less an authority on colonization than Richard Hakluyt had pointed to the advisability of taking along "one or two preachers that God may be honoured, the people instructed, mutinies better avoided, and obedience the better used." [29] The Company was quick to take the hint. Religion was used to screen prospective planters before their arrival in Virginia, and it was used to discipline them after their arrival. "We have thought it convenient to pronounce," stated the Company in a broadside of 1609, "that . . . we will receive no man that cannot bring or render some good testimony of his religion to God." [30] And during the time that Sir Thomas Dale's code of laws was sovereign in Virginia—from May, 1610, to April, 1619—the settlers were marched to church twice each day to pray for relief from dissension and for the showering of blessings upon the shareholders :

O Lord . . . defend us from the delusion of the devil, the malice of the heathen, the invasions of our enemies, & mutinies & dissentions of our own people. . . . Thou has moved . . . the hearts of so many of our nation to assist . . . with meanes and provision, and with their holy praiers . . . and for that portion of their substance which they willingly offer for thy honour

---

[28] *A True and Sincere Declaration* (London, 1609), in Brown, *Genesis*, I, 352.

[29] Quoted in Craven, *Southern Colonies*, p. 64.

[30] Appendix to *A True and Sincere Declaration*, in Brown, *Genesis*, I, 352.

& service in this action, recompence it to them and theirs, and reward it seven fold into their bosomes, with better blessinges.[31]

In a society of ranks and orders, deference is owed to certain persons by virtue of their social position, and the Company attempted to maximize the potentiality for discipline in such an arrangement by appointing to leading posts in Virginia those persons to whom obedience was due because of their high status. Insofar as it was possible, the Company selected only persons of high birth to be governor; when it was not possible, as in the case of Governor Yeardley, it quickly, and it seems surreptitiously, secured for him a knighthood.[32] And at all times the governors were urged to surround themselves with the pomp and circumstance of high office, the better to impress the governed. "You shall for the more regard and respect of yor place," read the Company's instructions to Sir Thomas Gates,

> to beget reverence to yor authority, and to refresh their mindes that obey the gravity of those lawes under wch they were borne at yor discrecon use such formes and Ensignes of government as by our letters Pattents wee are enabled to grant unto you, as also the attendance of a guarde uppon your pson.[33]

Ultimately, however, the Company relied upon a military regimen and upon the imposition of force to obtain labor discipline. Governor de la Warr had been instructed that his men were to be divided into groups and placed under the charge of officers "to be exercised and trayned up in Martiall manner and warlike Discipline." [34] Settlers were forbidden to return to England without permission, and their letters were sealed and sent first to the Company in London before being forwarded.[35] But the full code of military discipline was not worked out until the arrival in Jamestown of Captain Thomas Dale, marshal of the colony, who had been granted a leave of absence from his post in the Netherlands army at the behest of the Company. Dale supplemented the usual list of religious offenses and crimes against the state and the person with a series of enactments designed to protect the Company's interests. Slander against the Company, its officers, or any of its publications; unauthorized trading with the Indians; escaping to the Indians; theft; the killing of any domestic animal without consent; false accounting by any keeper of supplies—all were punishable by service in the galleys or death. Failure to keep regular hours of work subjected the offender to the pain of being forced to lie neck and heels together all night for the first

---

[31] *For the Colony in Virginea Britannia, Lawes Divine, Morall and Martiall, &c* (London, 1612), in Force (ed.), *op. cit.,* III, 68.

[32] Kingsbury (ed.), *Records,* III, 216–19.

[33] *Ibid.,* p. 15.

[34] *Ibid.,* p. 27.

[35] *Ibid.,* p. 22.

offense, whipping for the second, and one year's service in the galleys for the third.[36]

Moreover, Dale created a military rank for every person in Virginia and specified the duties of each in such a way as to provide us with important clues into the nature of labor discipline and what was expected to provide the motivation to work.

> Because we are not onely to exercise the duty of a Souldier, but that of the husbandman, and that in time of the vacancie of our watch and ward wee are not to live idly, therefore the Captaine . . . shall . . . demand . . . what service, worke, and businesse he hath in charge, from the Governor . . . in which worke the Captaine himselfe shall do exceeding worthily to take paines and labour, that his Souldiers seeing his industry and carefulnesse, may with more cheerfulnesse love him, and bee incouraged to the performance of the like.

Of the corporal:

> His duty is to provide that none of his Squadron, be absent, when the drumme shall call to any labour, or worke, or at what time soever they shall be commanded thereunto for the service of the Collonie, in the performance of which said workes he is to be an example of the rest of his Squadron by his owne labouring therein . . . that thereby giving incoraging to his superior officers he may be held by them worthy of a higher place.

Of the private soldier:

> He shall continue at his worke until the drumme beat, and . . . be conducted into the church to heare divine service, after which he may repayre to his house or lodging to prepare for his dinner, and to repose him until the drumme beate shall call him forth againe in the afternoone . . . the Generall having understanding of his promptitude and dilligence may conferre upon him, and call him into place of preferment and commaund.[37]

What is so striking about Dale's Code is the way in which it stripped from people all attributes save the one that really counted in the relationship which the Company sought to impose on them—their status in the organization. Behavior was expected to conform to a set of prescriptions the major characteristic of which was that the rights and obligations of persons depended on their position within the organization. In this respect, the contrast between Dale's Code and the first set of laws the settlers were able to enact for themselves at the General Assembly of 1619 is startling. For then, considerations other than status within an organization were fundamental:

---

[36] For the full text of the code see *For the Colony in Virginea Britannia, Lawes Divine, Morall and Martiall &c* (London, 1612), in Force (ed.), *op. cit.*, Vol. III.

[37] *For the Colony in Virginea Britannia*, in Force (ed.), *op. cit.*, III, 44, 55, 61–62.

All persons whatsoever upon the Sabaoth days shall frequente divine service and sermons both forenoon and afternoone. . . . And everyone that shall transgresse this lawe shall forfeicte three shillinges a time to the use of the churche. . . . But if a servant in this case shall wilfully neglecte his Mr's commande he shall suffer bodily punishment.

Or consider the following petition drafted by the Assembly:

. . . that the antient Planters . . . suche as before Sir T. Dales' depart were come hither . . . maye have their second, third and more divisions successively in as lardge and free manner as any other Planter. Also that they wilbe pleased to allowe to the male children, of them and of all others begotten in Virginia, being the onely hope of a posterity, a single share a piece.[38]

For the planters in Virginia, considerations of length of residence and of varying degrees of freedom now affected the rights and obligations of persons. No longer could relations be determined exclusively by the positions persons held within a single system—the organization of the Company. By 1619 Virginia was becoming a society, in which behavior was in some way determined by the totality of positions each person held in a network of sometimes complementary, sometimes contradictory, relationships. The key to this transformation from organization to society lies in the concessions the Company was forced to offer to induce persons to accept positions in the organizational relationship; for those concessions so multiplied the number of statuses and so altered the status of persons that a system of relationships was created where only one had existed before.

The fact is that the reforms the Company instituted in 1609 were not sufficient either to swell the supply of labor migrating to Virginia or to motivate the planters who were there to work with the will the Company expected. The Company had hoped that by its reforms it would be able to obtain not "idle and wicked persons; such as shame, or fear compels into this action [but] fit and industrious [persons], honest sufficient Artificers." [39] Yet so unproductive were they that as late as 1616 John Rolfe could indicate to Sir Robert Rich that what had been was still the Company's most serious problem. Our greatest want, he wrote, is "good and sufficient men as well of birth and quality to command, soldiers to marche, discover and defend the country from invasion, artificers, labourers, and husbandmen." [40] And so dissatisfied had the settlers become with their situation that, in a letter smuggled to the Spanish ambassador in London with the connivance of

---

[38] Kingsbury (ed.), *Records,* III, 173, 160.

[39] Appendix to *A True and Sincere Declaration* (1609), in Brown, *Genesis,* I, 352; Virginia Company broadside of 1610, in Brown, *Genesis,* I, 439.

[40] Quoted in Charles M. Andrews, *The Colonial Period of American History* (New Haven, 1934–38), I, 113–14.

English sailors, Don Diego de Molina, the prisoner in Jamestown, reported that "a good many have gone to the Indians . . . and others have gone out to sea . . . and those who remain do so by force and are anxious to see a fleet come from Spain to release them from this misery." [41] The hope that Don Diego attributed to the colonists was, no doubt, the wish of a patriotic Spaniard; but it is nevertheless true that some settlers did flee to the Indians, that the Company did succeed in obtaining authority to deport to Virginia those settlers who had escaped back to England, and that Coles and Kitchins, who had been Don Diego's guards, were executed in 1614 for organizing a plot to escape to Florida.[42]

Nor did the concessions granted to superior colonists in 1614, including a kind of modified right to private property and some relief from the obligation to work on the Company lands, suffice to solve the labor problem.[43] For the simple fact was, as Captain John Smith wrote, that "no man will go from hence to have less liberty there then here." [44] The Company, determined in 1619 to make a final effort to create of Virginia the profitable investment it had always hoped it would be, took his advice to heart. Though it was faced with declining financial resources, with internal bickering, and with increasing evidence that the king was losing patience with its meager achievement, the Company decided to pin its hopes on a quick return. The key to profits, it felt, lay in raising the value of the Company lands through increasing population and in diversifying products through the importation of labor skilled in many trades. The success of the effort, obviously, rested upon the strength of the additional inducements that could be offered to both investors and potential emigrants.[45]

As always, one of the principal devices used by the Company to attract labor and to increase productivity was that of easing the terms on which land could be acquired. The effect of the reform was to create within the Company a new group of statuses differentiated from one another in terms of the amount of property attached to each or the length of time required to obtain land on the part of those who were not yet entitled to it:

1. "Ancient planters" who had come to Virginia at their own cost before 1616 received 100 acres per share in perpetuity rent-free.
2. "Ancient planters" who had come to Virginia at Company expense

---

[41] Brown, *Genesis,* II, 648–49.

[42] Morris, *op. cit.,* pp. 169–71.

[43] Ballagh, *op. cit.,* pp. 22–23; Osgood, *op. cit.,* I, 75–77; Bruce, *Economic History,* I, 212–15; Craven, *Southern Colonies,* pp. 116–17; A. E. Smith, *op. cit.,* pp. 10–11.

[44] Quoted in Miller, "Religion and Society," *op. cit.,* p. 37.

[45] Craven, *Virginia Company, passim,* but esp. pp. 168–71; Craven, *Southern Colonies,* pp. 145–47; Scott, *op. cit.,* II, 266–88; Susan Myra Kingsbury, *An Introduction to the Records of the Virginia Company of London* (Washington, 1905), pp. 34–35, 40–41, 94–95.

received 100 acres at an annual rent of 2s. after the completion of their seven-year period of servitude on the Company's land.

3. All persons who came to Virginia after 1616 at their own expense received 50 acres at an annual rent of 1s.

4. All persons who came to Virginia after 1616 at Company expense were to receive 50 acres after having worked on the Company's land for seven years, during which time half their produce belonged to the Company and half to themselves.

5. All tradesmen received a house and 4 acres of land so long as they plied their trades.

6. All persons who paid for the transportation of emigrants received 50 acres per person.

7. Company officers not only were entitled to their regular land grants but were supported by the labor of tenants-at-halves on large tracts of land reserved by the Company for that purpose.

8. Indentured servants, whose transportation was paid by the Company or by private associations of investors and who were then sold to planters on their arrival in Virginia, were entitled to "freedom dues"—including a land grant—on the expiration of their servitude.[46]

Nor was this all. Determined to improve the morale of the colonists and, eventually, to relieve the Company of the burdensome cost of transporting labor from England, Sandys also began in 1620 to ship women to Virginia to become wives of the planters. There had been marriages in Virginia before, of course, but the supply of single women, restricted to the few female servants of married couples, was far smaller than the demand. Now, however, the Company organized the shipment of women on a business basis, forming a separate joint-stock company for the purpose. Though the women were, in any case, to be paid for by the planters at the rate of 120 pounds of the best leaf tobacco per person and though the Company conceded that it was dubious as to its authority to control marriages—"for the libertie of Mariadge we dare not infrindg"—it nevertheless discriminated between classes of planters in the bestowal of the women. "And though we are desireous that mariadge be free according to the law of nature," the Company wrote to the Governor and Council of Virginia, "yett would we not have these maids deceived and married to servants, but only to such freemen or tenants as have meanes to maintaine them." [47]

Finally, in a radical departure from previous policy, the Company limited

---

[46] "Instructions to Governor Yeardley, 1618," *Virginia Magazine of History and Biography*, II (1894–95), 161–62; Bruce, *Economic History*, I, 226–33, 511–14; Ballagh, *op. cit.*, pp. 25–28, 31; Craven, *Virginia Company*, pp. 50–57; Craven, *Southern Colonies*, pp. 127–29; A. E. Smith, *op. cit.*, pp. 11–17; Ballagh, *op. cit.*, pp. 28–30; Bruce, *Economic History*, II, 41–48; Morris, *op. cit.*, p. 395.

[47] Kingsbury (ed.), *Records*, III, 115, 493–94, 505.

the scope of martial law and ordered Governor Yeardley to convene an assembly of elected representatives from each district in Virginia. The Company did not intend to diminish its own authority, for the Governor was given the right to veto all enactments of the Assembly, and the General Court of the Company in London retained the right to disallow its decisions. Rather was it the Company's hope that the degree of acceptance of its program would be increased if it had the added sanction of approval by representatives of the planters themselves.[48]

In a sense, the Company's reforms suceeded too well. Lured by the new prospects in Virginia, about 4,800 emigrants departed from England between November, 1619, and February, 1625, nearly twice as many as had gone during the entire period from 1607 to 1619.[49] But, while the Company's propaganda could refer blandly to "each man having the shares of Land due to him" and to "the laudable forme of Justice and government,"[50] actual conditions in Virginia were quite different. Goodman Jackson "much marviled that you would send me a servant to the Companie," young Richard Freethorne wrote to his parents:

> He saith I had beene better knocked on the head, and Indeede so I fynde it now to my great greefe and miserie, and saith, that if you love me you will redeeme me suddenlie, for wch I doe Intreate and begg. . . . I thought no head had beene able to hold so much water as hath and doth daylie flow from mine eyes. . . . But this is Certaine I never felt the want of father and mother till now, but now deare freinds full well I knowe and rue it although it were too late before I knew it.

"To write of all crosses and miseries wᶜʰ have befallen us at this tyme we are not able," said Samuel Sharp. "So the truth is," Edward Hill wrote to his brother, "we lyve in the fearefullest age that ever Christians lived in."[51]

Though Company policy was not responsible for all the suffering endured by the settlers, it was responsible for intensifying their sense of deprivation by having promised too much. "My Master Atkins hath sould me," Henry Brigg wrote to his brother, Thomas:

> If you remember he tould me that for my Diett the worst day in the weeke should be better then the Sonday, & also he swore unto you that I should

---

[48] Thomas Jefferson Wertenbaker, *Virginia under the Stuarts* (Princeton, 1914), pp. 38–39; Craven, *Virginia Company*, pp. 70–80; Craven, *Southern Colonies*, pp. 127–29; "Proceedings of the First Assembly in Virginia, Held July 30, 1619," in *Colonial Records of Virginia* (Richmond, 1874).

[49] Samuel H. Yonge, "The Site of Old 'James Towne,' 1607–1698," *Virginia Magazine of History and Biography*, XI (1903–4), 399–400.

[50] *A Declaration of the State of the Colony* (1620), in Force (ed.), *op. cit.*, III, 5–6.

[51] Kingsbury (ed.), *Records*, IV, 59, 61–62, 239, 234; see also *ibid.*, pp. 41–42, 232, 235–36.

never serve any man but himselfe: And he also tould us that there they paled out their groundes from Deare & Hoggs. But in stead of them we pale out o^r Enemyes.

"If the Company would allow to each man a pound of butter and a pounde of Chese weekely," wrote a planter to Sir John Worsenholme,

> they would find more comfort therin then by all the Deere, Fish & Fowle is so talked of in England of wch I can assure yo^u yor poore servants have nott had since their cominge into the Contrey so much as the sent.

"I am pswaded," George Thorp wrote to John Smyth of Nibley,

> that more doe die of the disease of theire minde then of theire body by having this country victualls over-praised unto them in England & by not knowing, they shall drinke water here.[52]

No doubt the chasm between expectation and reality contributed to the planters' alienation from the organizational relationship into which they had been lured by the Company's promises. But that relationship was affected even more by the development of a network of relations that followed inevitably from the inducements to get men into the Company.

At one time in Virginia, the single relationship that existed between persons rested upon the positions they occupied in the Company's table of organization. As a result of the efforts made by the Company to get persons to accept that relationship, however, each person in Virginia had become the occupant of several statuses, for now there were rich and poor in Virginia, landowners and renters, masters and servants, old residents and newcomers, married and single, men and women; and the simultaneous possession of these statuses involved the holder in a network of relationships, some congruent and some incompatible, with his organizational relationship.

Once the men in Virginia had been bachelors who lived in Company-provided barracks. Now they lived in private houses with their families, and, though the Company attempted to make use of the new relationship by penalizing each "Master of a family" for certain crimes committed by those under his authority [53]—hoping thereby that the master would use his authority to suppress crime—it can hardly be doubted that its action involved the head of the family in a conflict of loyalties.

Once all persons had been equal before Company law, and penalties had been inflicted solely in accordance with the nature of the offense. Now, the General Assembly found that "persones of qualitie" were "not fitt to undergoe corporall punishment." [54]

---

[52] *Ibid.,* pp. 235–36, 312–32; III, 417; see also *ibid.,* III, 456.

[53] Proclamation of Governor Wyatt, June, 1622, in Kingsbury (ed.), *Records,* III, 659.

[54] Act of March, 1623/24 (*ibid.,* IV, 584).

Once length of residence was irrelevant in determining the obligations of persons to the Company. Now, however, it was enacted that all "yᵉ olde planters, yᵗ were heere before, or cam in at yᵉ laste cominge of Sr. Tho: Gates they and theire posteritie shalbe exempted from their psonall service to yᵉ warres, and any publique charge (Churche dewties excepted)." [55]

Once Virginians had been governed administratively through a chain of command originating in the Company's General Court. Now an authentic political system existed, and the members of the Assembly demanded the same right to disallow orders of the General Court that the Court had with respect to the Assembly.

Once all land had been owned by the Company. Now much of it was owned by private persons, and even more had been promised to them, and the opportunities for the creation of private fortunes involved the planters in a new relationship with the Company. No longer was the planter willing to have his tobacco exported through the Company at a fixed price, when, as a free landowner, he might strike his own bargain with the purchaser. No longer was the planter willing, at a time when labor meant profit, for the Company to commandeer his servants. Even officers of the Company, expected to administer its program in Virginia, saw the chance to subvert it to their own purposes; "The servants you allow them, or such as they hire," Captain John Smith told the Company, "they plant on their private Lands, not upon that belongeth to their office, which crop alwaies exceeds yours." Indeed, it became increasingly difficult to get planters to accept Company positions:

Sʳ George is taken up with his private. . . . Capt. Hamor is miserablie poore and necessities will inforce him to shift. . . . Capt: Mathews intends wholie his Cropp, and will rather hazard the payment of forfeictures, then performe our Injunctions. . . . Mʳ Blanie is now married in Virginia, and when he hath discharged your trust in the Magazine wilbee a Planter amongst us. . . . And I would you could persuade some of qualities and worth to come out.[56]

The increase in private wealth tended to subordinate status in the Company to status in a different relationship among the planters. The muster roll of early 1625 shows 48 families bearing various titles of distinction, most of which had been earned in Virginia. They alone held 266 of the approximately 487 white servants in Virginia, 20 of the 23 Negro servants, and 1 of the 2 Indian servants.[57] These were the families at the apex of Virginia so-

---

[55] Act of March, 1623/24 (*ibid.,* IV, 582).

[56] *Ibid.,* IV, 564, 581; Smith, *Generall Historie,* in Tyler (ed.), *op. cit.,* p. 356; George Sandys to John Ferrar, April 11, 1623, in Kingsbury (ed.), *Records,* IV, 110–11.

[57] The figures are derived from the muster rolls in John Camden Hotten, *The Original Lists of Persons of Quality; Emigrants, Religious Exiles . . . Who Went from Great Britain to the American Plantations, 1600–1700* (London, 1874).

ciety, determined to uphold their rights as over against other persons and sometimes going beyond their rights. Acting through the General Assembly, they insisted upon scrupulous enforcement of contracts of servitude, forbade servants to trade with the Indians, and, so as not to lose their labor, regulated the right of their servants to marry. Nor, as the chronic complaints bear witness, were they loath to keep their servants beyond the required time.[58] That aspect of the relationship between master and servant was eloquently revealed in a petition to the Governor by Jane Dickenson in 1624:

> [She] most humblie sheweth that whereas her late husband Ralph Dickenson Came ov^r into this Country fower Yeares since, obliged to Nicholas Hide deceased for ye tearme of seaven yeares, hee only to have for himselfe & yor petitioner ye one halfe of his labors, her said husband being slaine in the bloudy Masacre, & her selfe Caried away wth the Cruell salvages, amongst them Enduring much misery for teen monthes. At the Expiration it pleased God so to dispose the hartes of the Indians, y^t for a small ransome yor petitioner wth divers others should be realeased, In Consideration that Doctor Potts laid out two pounds of beades for her releasement, hee alleageth yor petitioner is linked to his servitude wth a towefold Chaine the one for her late husbandes obligation & thother for her ransome, of both wch shee hopeth that in Conscience shee ought to be discharged, of ye first by her widdowhood, of the second by the law of nations, Considering shee hath already served teen monthes, two much for two pound of beades.
>
> The pmises notwthstanding Dr Pott refuseth to sett yor peticioner at liberty, threatning to make her serve him the uttermost day, unless she pcure him 150^{li} waight of Tobacco, she therefore most humbly desireth, that you^{ll} wilbe pleased to take w^t Course shalbe thought iust for her releasement fro' his servitude, Considering that it much differeth not from her slavery wth the Indians.[59]

But that was only one aspect of the relationship. Conditions in Virginia were now more fluid than they had been, and persons of low estate might also rise. Secretary of State John Pory wrote Sir Dudley Carleton that "our cowekeeper here of James citty on Sundays goes accowtered all in freshe flaminge silke; and a wife of one that in England had professed the black arte, not of a scholler, but of a collier of Croydon, wears her rought bever hatt with a faire perle hat band." The Company was opposed to such unseemly displays of wealth on the part of persons of low estate,[60] but it could not prevent them.

The ultimate stage in the transition of Virginia from organization to society was reached when the settlers came to feel that the new relationships in

---

[58] A. E. Smith, *op. cit.,* pp. 226–29; Kingsbury (ed.), *Records,* IV, 128–30.

[59] Kingsbury (ed.), *Records,* IV, 473.

[60] Pory to Carleton, September 30, 1619, in Tyler (ed.), *op. cit.,* p. 285; Kingsbury (ed.), *Records,* III, 469.

which they were now involved were of greater importance than the Company relationship, when their statuses outside the organization came largely to dictate their behavior. For at that point they were no longer willing to accept the legitimacy of their organizational superiors. William Weldon warned Sir Edwin Sandys that the planters who now had land were grumbling at Company policy:

I acquainted them wth my restraint of plantinge Tobacco wch is a thinge so distastefull to them that they will wth no patience indure to heare of it bitterly Complayninge that they have noe other meanes to furnish themselves with aparell for the insuinge yere but are likely as they say (and for aught I Can see) to be starved if they be debarred of it.[61]

From general discontent it was but a short step to ridicule of Company officials and outright refusal to accept a Company assignment. Wrote planter William Capps to John Ferrar:

The old smoker our (I know not how to terme him but) Governor, so good so careful mild, Religious, just, honest that I protest I thinke God hath sent him in mercie for good to us, he undergoeth all your cares & ours and I feare not but god will bless him in all his pceedinges but who must be th'Instrument to make all this whole againe? Why Capps: all voyces can sett him forth about the business: But who must pay him his hyre? The Contrey is poore and the Companie is poore and Cappes is poore already, & poorer he will be if he follow this course.

Like other men, planter Capps believed that "Charity first beginnes at home," and he divorced his own interest from that of the Company:

I will forsweare ever bending my mind for publique good, and betake me to my own profit with some halfe a score men of my owne and lie rootinge in the earthe like a hog, and reckon Tobacco ad ungeum by hundrethes, and quarters.[62]

That the Company could no longer expect to command obedience was clear, for even its officers in Virginia perceived themselves as having a set of interests distinct from those of their London superiors and turned their backs to their authority. "Such is the disposicon of those who glorie in their wisdomes," wrote George Sandys, the treasurer in Virginia, to his brother, Sir Miles,

that they will rather Justifye and proceed in their Errors than to suffer a supposed disgrace by reforming them. . . . Who clere themselves by the wrong-

---

[61] Kingsbury (ed.), *Records*, III, 263.
[62] *Ibid.*, IV, 38–39.

ings of others; objecting unto us their Instructions, whereof manie are infeasible and the most inconvenient, for to say the truth they know nothing of Virginia.

"Such an Antipathy is there between theyr vast Comands and oᵣ grumbling Obedience," Sir Francis Wyatt wrote to his father:

Mingling matters of honor and profitt often overthrow both. They expect great retournes to pay the Companies debt. . . . For me I have not a third part of my men to inable me to either. . . . I often wish little Mᵣ Farrar here, that to his zeale he would add knowledge of this Contrey.[63]

In 1607 there had been no "Contrey," only the Virginia Company. It was the Company's fate to have created a country and to have destroyed itself in the process. More than a century later, James Otis wrote bitterly: "Those who judge of the reciprocal rights that subsist between a supreme and subordinate state of dominion, by no higher rules than are applied to a corporation of button-makers, will never have a very comprehensive view of them."[64] His comment was intended as an observation on contemporary political affairs, but we can detect in it a verdict on the past as well.

The Company had been faced with the problems of motivating its members to work for the ends which it was created to achieve and, at the same time, of maintaining the discipline that was essential for its organizational integrity. The solution it adopted for the first problem made it impossible to solve the second; and the burden of achieving order and discipline now became the responsibility not of an organization but of a society.

Among the papers in the Sackville collection is a document entitled "A Form of Policy for Virginia," written when it was already apparent that the Company had failed. The proposal was never adopted, but it is significant nonetheless, for, as Professor Fernand Braudel reminds us,

victorious events come about as a result of many possibilities, often contradictory, among which life finally has made its choice. For one possibility which actually is realized innumerable others have been drowned. These are the ones which have left little trace for the historians. And yet it is necessary to give them their place because the losing movements are forces which have at every moment affected the final outcome.[65]

The significance of the document, drafted as a royal proclamation, lies in its awareness of the problems of motivation and order, in its realization that

---

[63] *Ibid.,* pp. 71, 237; see also *ibid.,* pp. 455–57.

[64] *The Rights of the British Colonies asserted and proved* (Boston, 1764), in Samuel Eliot Morison (ed.), *Sources and Documents Illustrating the American Revolution* . . . (2d ed.; Oxford, 1929), p. 8.

[65] Quoted in Paul F. Lazarsfeld, "Public Opinion and the Classical Tradition," *Public Opinion Quarterly,* XXI, No. 1 (Spring, 1957), 53.

they could no longer be solved by instructions handed down through a chain of command, and in its conscious application of particular social inventions to solve them:

> Wee . . . knowinge that the perfection and happinesse of a commonwealth, lyeth . . . first and principally in the government, consisting in the mutuall duties of commandeing and obeyeing, next in the possessing thinges plentifully, necessarie for the life of man, doe professe that . . . we intend wholely the good of our subjects . . . endeavouringe to cause both England and Virginea, to endowe each other with their benefittes and profitts that thereby layeing aside force and our coactive power, we may by our justice and bountic marrye and combinde those our provinces to us and our soveraigntye in naturall love and obedience.

The problem of order was solved by the meticulous enumeration of every social status that was to exist in Virginia, with a specification of the rights and obligations that inhered in each. The problem of motivation was solved by the granting of both economic rewards and social privileges to each status and by the opportunity given to move from one to another:

> The meanest servant that goeth (God soe blessing him and his endeavours, that hee can purchase and [an] estate in England or compasse to carrie over or drawe over with him of his friends and adherences the number of 300 men) he may become a lord patriot which is the greatest place the commonwealth canne beare.

The problem of consensus was solved through devices to enhance the mutual affection of persons in these statuses:

> To the end that love may be mayntayned, and that theise degrees may not estrange the upper orders from the lower, we wish that the heires and eldest sonnes of the upper orders may marrie with the daughters of the lower orders. . . . And that the daughters of the upper orders being heires may marrye with the sonnes of the lower orders, makeing choice of the most vertuous . . . that all degrees may bee thereby bound togeather in the bonds of love that none may be scorned but the scorner. To this end alsoe, although we would not have you imitate the Irish in their wilde and barbarous manners, yet we will commend one custome of theires unto you, which is that the poorer sort sueing to gett the nurseing of the children of the lordes and gentrie, and breedeinge upp in their minorities as their own, this breedinge . . . doth begett anoether nature in them to love their foster children and brethren, as if they were naturally bread of the same parentes.

Written in the margin of the document, by whom we do not know, is a lengthy commentary. Concerning the importance of status and order, the following is written: "This maintenance of theire degrees will immoveably fixe the frame of the collonie." Concerning the importance of mobility and motivation, the following is written: "Soe framinge the government that it shall give all men both liberty and meanes of riseinge to the greatest places and honours therein, whereby they will receave such content that they will all strive to maintaine it in the same forme we shall now settle it." [66]

Shakespeare had written:

> Take but degree away, untune that string
> And hark, what discord follows.

The author of the document agreed. He rested his hopes for stability on the attachment of each person to a position in which recognized rights and responsibilities inhered. What he did not realize is what may be learned from the history of the Virginia Company—that each man is attached to many positions, that each position involves him in a separate relationship that imposes it own necessities, and that his behavior is the product of all the positions he holds and, because he has a memory, of all the positions he once held.

II

The generalizations that emerge from our study are of two kinds: those directly tied to the events of the time and place that we have analyzed and those of a more abstract kind that derive from the analysis of these historical particulars but can be stated in such a way as to be of more general applicability.

There seems little room for doubt about some of the conclusions we have drawn: that the character of seventeenth-century North American society was shaped decisively by the fact that, in contrast to the situation in Latin America, the creation of the society was accomplished through the recruitment of a voluntary labor force; that higher statuses in that society were created as a result of the need to induce persons to accept positions in lower statuses; and that the behavior of persons in that society was determined not only by opportunities for advancement, as Whiggish interpreters of our history would have us believe, but, as well, by the fact that these opportunities were less than people had been led to expect.

With respect to more general hypotheses, it may be suggested that the mechanism by which the change from organization to society was accomplished lay in the very effort to apply the blueprint that was intended to govern the relations between persons, for this so multiplied the number of statuses persons held, and therefore the relationships in which they were involved, as to alter their behavior in a decisive fashion.

The testing of these hypotheses, of course, would involve the examina-

---

[66] Kingsbury (ed.), *Records,* IV, 411, 417, 424–25, 416, 419.

tion of still other consciously selected historical situations for the purpose of comparison—the experience of the British in establishing other colonies in North America and in coping with a totally different problem in India, of the French in Canada and the Spanish in South America, of the reasons for the difference between the blueprint in accordance with which utopian communities were planned and the outcome of their establishment, and the like. Herein lies the design for a research in historical sociology.

EDMUND S. MORGAN

THE PURITANS AND SEX

Discussing sex in relation to Puritan culture, a subject long freighted with sensationalism and stereotypes, in a way that reflects upon a broad spectrum of ideas and social practices is an important achievement. In his brief article, Morgan not only succeeds in demolishing the tired contention that our Puritan forebears were prudes; he also shows how the Puritans' ways of mitigating the tension between their moral code and their sexual practices acknowledged the reality of human nature without compromising their principles. Morgan's article provides a model of how a fresh and original treatment of a subject can bring about a new understanding of a culture. The intellectual contours of this subject can be seen in Edmund S. Morgan, The Puritan Family, *rev. ed.* (1966).*

Henry Adams once observed that Americans have "ostentatiously ignored" sex. He could think of only two American writers who touched upon the subject with any degree of boldness—Walt Whitman and Bret Harte. Since the time when Adams made this penetrating observation, American writers have been making up for lost time in a way that would make Bret Harte, if not Whitman, blush. And yet there is still more truth than falsehood in Adams's statement. Americans, by comparison with Europeans or Asiatics, are squeamish when confronted with the facts of life. My purpose is not to account for this squeamishness, but simply to point out that the Puritans, those bogeymen of the modern intellectual, are not responsible for it.

At the outset, consider the Puritans' attitude toward marriage and the role of sex in marriage. The popular assumption might be that the Puritans frowned on marriage and tried to hush up the physical aspect of it as much as possible, but listen to what they themselves had to say. Samuel Willard, minister of the Old South Church in the latter part of the seventeenth century and author of the most complete textbook of Puritan divinity, more than once expressed his horror at "that Popish conceit of the Excellency of Virginity." [1] Another minister, John Cotton, wrote that

> Women are Creatures without which there is no comfortable Living for man: it is true of them what is wont to be said of Governments, *That bad ones are better than none:* They are a sort of Blasphemers then who dispise and decry them, and call them *a necessary Evil,* for they are *a necessary Good.*[2]

These sentiments did not arise from an interpretation of marriage as a spiritual partnership, in which sexual intercourse was a minor or incidental matter. Cotton gave his opinion of "Platonic love" when he recalled the case of

> one who immediately upon marriage, without ever approaching the *Nuptial Bed,* indented with the *Bride,* that by mutual consent they might both live such a life, and according did sequestring themselves according to the custom of those times, from the rest of mankind, and afterwards from one another too, in their retired Cells, giving themselves up to a Contemplative life; and this is recorded as an instance of no little or ordinary Vertue; but I must be pardoned in it, if I can account it no other than an effort of blind zeal, for they are the dictates of a blind mind they follow therein, and not of that Holy Spirit, which saith *It is not good that man should be alone.*[3]

---

[1] Samuel Willard, *A Compleat Body of Divinity* (Boston, 1726), 125 and 608–613.

[2] John Cotton, *A Meet Help* (Boston, 1699), 14–15.

[3] *A Meet Help,* 16.

FROM Edmund S. Morgan, "The Puritans and Sex," *The New England Quarterly,* Vol. XV, No. 4 (December 1942), pp. 591–607. Reprinted by permission.

Here is as healthy an attitude as one could hope to find anywhere. Cotton certainly cannot be accused of ignoring human nature. Nor was he an isolated example among the Puritans. Another minister stated plainly that "the Use of the Marriage Bed" is "founded in mans Nature," and that consequently any withdrawal from sexual intercourse upon the part of husband or wife "Denies all relief in Wedlock vnto Human necessity: and sends it for supply vnto Beastiality when God gives not the gift of Continency." [4] In other words, sexual intercourse was a human necessity and marriage the only proper supply for it. These were the views of the New England clergy, the acknowledged leaders of the community, the most Puritanical of the Puritans. As proof that their congregations concurred with them, one may cite the case in which the members of the First Church of Boston expelled James Mattock because, among other offenses, "he denied Coniugall fellowship vnto his wife for the space of 2 years together vpon pretense of taking Revenge upon himself for his abusing of her before marryage." [5] So strongly did the Puritans insist upon the sexual character of marriage that one New Englander considered himself slandered when it was reported, "that he Brock his deceased wife's hart with Greife, that he wold be absent from her 3 weeks together when he was at home, and wold never come nere her, and such Like." [6]

There was just one limitation which the Puritans placed upon sexual relations in marriage: sex must not interfere with religion. Man's chief end was to glorify God, and all earthly delights must promote that end, not hinder it. Love for a wife was carried too far when it led a man to neglect his God:

> . . . sometimes a man hath a good affection to Religion, but the love of his wife carries him away, a man may bee so transported to his wife, that hee dare not bee forward in Religion, lest hee displease his wife, and so the wife, lest shee displease her husband, and this is an inordinate love, when it exceeds measure. [7]

Sexual pleasures, in this respect, were treated like other kinds of pleasure. On a day of fast, when all comforts were supposed to be foregone in behalf of religious contemplation, not only were tasty food and drink to be abandoned but sexual intercourse, too. On other occasions, when food, drink, and recreation were allowable, sexual intercourse was allowable too, though of course only between persons who were married to each other. The Puritans

---

[4] Edward Taylor, Commonplace Book (manuscript in the library of the Massachusetts Historical Society).

[5] Records of the First Church in Boston (manuscript copy in the library of the Massachusetts Historical Society), 12.

[6] Middlesex County Court Files, folder 42.

[7] John Cotton, *A Practical Commentary . . . upon the First Epistle Generall of John* (London, 1656), 126.

were not ascetics; they never wished to prevent the enjoyment of earthly delights. They merely demanded that the pleasures of the flesh be subordinated to the greater glory of God: husband and wife must not become "so transported with affection, that they look at no higher end than marriage it self." "Let such as have wives," said the ministers, "look at them not for their own ends, but to be fitted for Gods service, and bring them nearer to God."[8]

Toward sexual intercourse outside marriage the Puritans were as frankly hostile as they were favorable to it in marriage. They passed laws to punish adultery with death, and fornication with whipping. Yet they had no misconceptions as to the capacity of human beings to obey such laws. Although the laws were commands of God, it was only natural—since the fall of Adam— for human beings to break them. Breaches must be punished lest the community suffer the wrath of God, but no offense, sexual or otherwise, could be occasion for surprise or for hushed tones of voice. How calmly the inhabitants of seventeenth-century New England could contemplate rape or attempted rape is evident in the following testimony offered before the Middlesex County Court of Massachusetts:

The examination of Edward Wire taken the 7th of october and alsoe Zachery Johnson, who sayeth that Edward Wires mayd being sent into the towne about busenes meeting with a man that dogd hir from about Joseph Kettles house to goody marches. She came into William Johnsones and desired Zachery Johnson to goe home with her for that the man dogd hir. accordingly he went with her and being then as far as Samuell Phips his house the man over tooke them. which man caled himselfe by the name of peter grant would have led the mayd but she oposed itt three times: and coming to Edward Wires house the said grant would have kist hir but she refused itt: wire being at prayer grant dragd the mayd between the said wiers and Nathanill frothinghams house. hee then flung the mayd downe in the streete and got atop hir; Johnson seeing it hee caled vppon the fellow to be sivill and not abuse the mayd then Edward wire came forth and ran to the said grant and took hold of him asking him what he did to his mayd, the said grant asked whether she was his wife for he did nothing to his wife: the said grant swearing he would be the death of the said wire. when he came of the mayd; he swore he would bring ten men to pul down his house and soe ran away and they followed him as far as good[y] phipses house where they mett with John Terry and George Chin with clubs in there hands and soe they went away together. Zachy Johnson going to Constable Heamans, and wire going home. there came John Terry to his house to ask for beer and grant was in the streete but afterward departed into the towne, both Johnson and Wire both aferme that when grant was vppon the mayd she cryed out severall times.

Deborah hadlocke being examined sayth that she mett with the man that cals himselfe peeter grant about good prichards that he dogd hir and followed hir to hir masters and there threw hir downe and lay vppon hir but had not

---

[8] *A Practical Commentary,* 126.

the use of hir body but swore several othes that he would ly with hir and gett hir with child before she got home.

Grant being present denys all saying he was drunk and did not know what he did.[9]

The Puritans became inured to sexual offenses, because there were so many. The impression which one gets from reading the records of seventeenth-century New England courts is that illicit sexual intercourse was fairly common. The testimony given in cases of fornication and adultery—by far the most numerous class of criminal cases in the records—suggests that many of the early New Englanders possessed a high degree of virility and very few inhibitions. Besides the case of Peter Grant, take the testimony of Elizabeth Knight about the manner of Richard Nevars's advances toward her:

> The last publique day of Thanksgiving (in the year 1674) in the evening as I was milking Richard Nevars came to me, and offered me abuse in putting his hand, under my coates, but I turning aside with much adoe, saved my self, and when I was settled to milking he agen took me by the shoulder and pulled me backward almost, but I clapped one hand on the Ground and held fast the Cows teatt with the other hand, and cryed out, and then came to mee Jonathan Abbot one of my Masters Servants, whome the said Never asked wherefore he came, the said Abbot said to look after you, what you doe unto the Maid, but the said Never bid Abbot goe about his businesse but I bade the lad to stay.[10]

One reason for the abundance of sexual offenses was the number of men in the colonies who were unable to gratify their sexual desires in marriage.[11] Many of the first settlers had wives in England. They had come to the new world to make a fortune, expecting either to bring their families after them or to return to England with some of the riches of America. Although these men left their wives behind, they brought their sexual appetites with them; and in spite of laws which required them to return to their families, they continued to stay, and more continued to arrive, as indictments against them throughout the seventeenth century clearly indicate.

Servants formed another group of men, and of women too, who could not ordinarily find supply for human necessity within the bounds of marriage. Most servants lived in the homes of their masters and could not marry without their consent, a consent which was not likely to be given unless the prospective husband or wife also belonged to the master's household. This

---

[9] Middlesex Files, folder 48.

[10] Middlesex Files, folder 71.

[11] Another reason was suggested by Charles Francis Adams in his scholarly article, "Some Phases of Sexual Morality and Church Discipline in Colonial New England," *Proceedings* of the Massachusetts Historical Society, xxvi, 477–516.

situation will be better understood if it is recalled that most servants at this time were engaged by contract for a stated period. They were, in the language of the time, "covenant servants," who had agreed to stay with their masters for a number of years in return for a specified recompense, such as transportation to New England or education in some trade (the latter, of course, were known more specifically as apprentices). Even hired servants who worked for wages were usually single, for as soon as a man had enough money to buy or build a house of his own and to get married, he would set up in farming or trade for himself. It must be emphasized, however, that anyone who was not in business for himself was necessarily a servant. The economic organization of seventeenth-century New England had no place for the independent proletarian workman with a family of his own. All production was carried on in the household by the master of the family and his servants, so that most men were either servants or masters of servants; and the former, of course, were more numerous than the latter. Probably most of the inhabitants of Puritan New England could remember a time when they had been servants.

Theoretically no servant had a right to a private life. His time, day or night, belonged to his master, and both religion and law required that he obey his master scrupulously.[12] But neither religion nor law could restrain the sexual impulses of youth, and if those impulses could not be expressed in marriage, they had to be given vent outside marriage. Servants had little difficulty in finding the occasions. Though they might be kept at work all day, it was easy enough to slip away at night. Once out of the house, there were several ways of meeting with a maid. The simplest way was to go to her bedchamber, if she was so fortunate as to have a private one of her own. Thus Jock, Mr. Solomon Phipps's Negro man, confessed in court

that on the sixteenth day of May 1682, in the morning, betweene 12 and one of the clock, he did force open the back doores of the House of Laurence Hammond in Charlestowne, and came in to the House, and went up into the garret to Marie the Negro.

He doth likewise acknowledge that one night the last week he forced into the House the same way, and went up to the Negro Woman Marie and that the like he hath done at severall other times before.[13]

Joshua Fletcher took a more romantic way of visiting his lady:

Joshua Fletcher . . . doth confesse and acknowledge that three severall nights, after bedtime, he went into Mr Fiskes Dwelling house at Chelmsford, at an open window by a ladder that he brought with him. the said windo

---

12 On the position of servants in early New England see *More Books,* XVII (September, 1942), 311–328.

13 Middlesex Files, folder 99.

opening into a chamber, whose was the lodging place of Gresill Juell servant to mr. Fiske. and there he kept company with the said mayd. she sometimes having her cloathes on, and one time he found her in her bed.[14]

Sometimes a maidservant might entertain callers in the parlor while the family were sleeping upstairs. John Knight described what was perhaps a common experience for masters. The crying of his child awakened him in the middle of the night, and he called to his maid, one Sarah Crouch, who was supposed to be sleeping with the child. Receiving no answer, he arose and

> went downe the stayres, and at the stair foot, the latch of doore was pulled in. I called severall times and at the last said if shee would not open the dore, I would breake it open, and when she opened the doore shee was all undressed and Sarah Largin with her undressed, also the said Sarah went out of doores and Dropped some of her clothes as shee went out. I enquired of Sarah Crouch what men they were, which was with them. Shee made mee no answer for some space of time, but at last shee told me Peeter Brigs was with them, I asked her whether Thomas Jones was not there, but shee would give mee no answer.[15]

In the temperate climate of New England it was not always necessary to seek out a maid at her home. Rachel Smith was seduced in an open field "about nine of the clock at night, being darke, neither moone nor starrs shineing." She was walking through the field when she met a man who

> asked her where shee lived, and what her name was and shee told him, and then shee asked his name, and he told her Saijing that he was old Good-man Shepards man. Also shee saith he gave her strong liquors, and told her that it was not the first time he had been with maydes after his master was in bed.[16]

Sometimes, of course, it was not necessary for a servant to go outside his master's house in order to satisfy his sexual urges. Many cases of fornication are on record between servants living in the same house. Even where servants had no private bedroom, even where the whole family slept in a single room, it was not impossible to make love. In fact many love affairs must have had their consummation upon a bed in which other people were sleeping. Take for example the case of Sarah Lepingwell. When Sarah was brought into court for having an illegitimate child, she related that one night when her master's brother, Thomas Hawes, was visiting the family, she went to bed early. Later, after Hawes had gone to bed, he called to her to get him a pipe of tobacco. After refusing for some time,

---

[14] Middlesex Files, folder 47.

[15] Middlesex Files, folder 52.

[16] Middlesex Files, folder 44.

at the last I arose and did lite his pipe and cam and lay doune one my one
bead and smoaked about half the pip and siting vp in my bead to giue him
his pip my bead being a trundell bead at the sid of his bead he reached beyond the pip and Cauth me by the wrist and pulled me on the side of his
bead but I biding him let me goe he bid me hold my peas the folks wold here
me and if it be replyed come why did you not call out I Ansar I was posesed
with fear of my mastar least my master shold think I did it only to bring a
scandall on his brothar and thinking thay wold all beare witnes agaynst me
but the thing is true that he did then begete me with child at that tim and
the Child is Thomas Hauses and noe mans but his.

In his defense Hawes offered the testimony of another man who was sleeping
"on the same side of the bed," but the jury nevertheless accepted Sarah's
story.[17]

The fact that Sarah was intimidated by her master's brother suggests that
maidservants may have been subject to sexual abuse by their masters. The
records show that sometimes masters did take advantage of their position to
force unwanted attentions upon their female servants. The case of Elizabeth
Dickerman is a good example. She complained to the Middlesex County
Court,

against her master John Harris senior for profiring abus to her by way of
forsing her to be naught with him: . . . he has tould her that if she tould
her dame: what cariag he did show to her shee had as good be hanged and
shee replyed then shee would run away and he sayd run the way is befor
you: . . . she says if she should liwe ther shee shall be in fear of her lif.[18]

The court accepted Elizabeth's complaint and ordered her master to be
whipped twenty stripes.

So numerous did cases of fornication and adultery become in seventeenth-
century New England that the problem of caring for the children of extra-
marital unions was a serious one. The Puritans solved it, but in such a way
as to increase rather than decrease the temptation to sin. In 1668 the General Court of Massachusetts ordered:

that where any man is legally convicted to be the Father of a Bastard childe,
he shall be at the care and charge to maintain and bring up the same, by
such assistance of the Mother as nature requireth, and as the Court from
time to time (according to circumstances) shall see meet to Order: and in
case the Father of a Bastard, by confession or other manifest proof, upon
trial of the case, do not appear to the Courts satisfaction, then the Man
charged by the Woman to be the Father, shee holding constant in it, (especially being put upon the real discovery of the truth of it in the time of her

---

[17] Middlesex Files, folder 47.
[18] Middlesex Files, folder 94.

Travail) shall be the reputed Father, and accordingly be liable to the charge of maintenance as aforesaid (though not to other punishment) notwithstanding his denial, unless the circumstances of the case and pleas be such, on the behalf of the man charged, as that the Court that have the cognizance thereon shall see reason to acquit him, and otherwise dispose of the Childe and education thereof.[19]

As a result of this law a girl could give way to temptation without the fear of having to care for an illegitimate child by herself. Furthermore, she could, by a little simple lying, spare her lover the expense of supporting the child. When Elizabeth Wells bore a child, less than a year after this statute was passed, she laid it to James Tufts, her master's son. Goodman Tufts affirmed that Andrew Robinson, servant to Goodman Dexter, was the real father, and he brought the following testimony as evidence:

Wee Elizabeth Jefts aged 15 ears and Mary tufts aged 14 ears doe testyfie that their being one at our hous sumtime the last winter who sayed that thear was a new law made concerning bastards that If aney man wear aqused with a bastard and the woman which had aqused him did stand vnto it in her labor that he should bee the reputed father of it and should mayntaine it Elizabeth Wells hearing of the sayd law she sayed vnto vs that If shee should bee with Child shee would bee sure to lay it vn to won who was rich enough abell to mayntayne it wheather it wear his or no and shee farder sayed Elizabeth Jefts would not you doe so likewise If it weare your case and I sayed no by no means for right must tacke place: and the sayd Elizabeth wells sayed If it wear my Caus I think I should doe so.[20]

A tragic unsigned letter that somehow found its way into the files of the Middlesex County Court gives more direct evidence of the practice which Elizabeth Wells professed:

der loue i remember my loue to you hoping your welfar and i hop to imbras the but now i rit to you to let you nowe that i am a child by you and i wil ether kil it or lay it to an other and you shal have no blame at al for I haue had many children and none have none of them. . . . [i.e., none of their fathers is supporting any of them.] [21]

In face of the wholesale violation of the sexual codes to which all these cases give testimony, the Puritans could not maintain the severe penalties which their laws provided. Although cases of adultery occurred every year, the death penalty is not known to have been applied more than three times.

---

[19] William H. Whitmore, editor, *The Colonial Laws of Massachusetts. Reprinted from the Edition of 1660* (Boston, 1889), 257.

[20] Middlesex Files, folder 52.

[21] Middlesex Files, folder 30.

The usual punishment was a whipping or a fine, or both, and perhaps a branding, combined with a symbolical execution in the form of standing on the gallows for an hour with a rope about the neck. Fornication met with a lighter whipping or a lighter fine, while rape was treated in the same way as adultery. Though the Puritans established a code of laws which demanded perfection—which demanded, in other words, strict obedience to the will of God, they nevertheless knew that frail human beings could never live up to the code. When fornication, adultery, rape, or even buggery and sodomy appeared, they were not surprised, nor were they so severe with the offenders as their codes of law would lead one to believe. Sodomy, to be sure, they usually punished with death; but rape, adultery, and fornication they regarded as pardonable human weaknesses, all the more likely to appear in a religious community, where the normal course of sin was stopped by wholesome laws. Governor Bradford in recounting the details of an epidemic of sexual misdemeanors in Plymouth, wrote resignedly:

> it may be in this case as it is with waters when their streames are stopped or damned up, when they gett passage they flow with more violence, and make more noys and disturbance, then when they are suffered to rune quietly in their owne chanels. So wickednes being here more stopped by strict laws, and the same more nerly looked unto, so as it cannot rune in a comone road of liberty as it would, and is inclined, it searches every wher, and at last breaks out wher it getts vente.[22]

The estimate of human capacities here expressed led the Puritans not only to deal leniently with sexual offenses but also to take every precaution to prevent such offenses, rather than wait for the necessity of punishment. One precaution was to see that children got married as soon as possible. The wrong way to promote virtue, the Puritans thought, was to "ensnare" children in vows of virginity, as the Catholics did. As a result of such vows, children, "not being able to contain," would be guilty of "unnatural pollutions, and other filthy practices in secret: and too oft of horrid Murthers of the fruit of their bodies," said Thomas Cobbett.[23] The way to avoid fornication and perversion was for parents to provide suitable husbands and wives for their children:

> Lot was to blame that looked not out seasonably for some fit matches for his two daughters, which had formerly minded marriage (witness the contract between them and two men in *Sodom,* called therfore for his Sons in Law, which had married his daughters, Gen. 19. 14.) for they seeing no man like

---

[22] William Bradford, *History of Plymouth Plantation* (Boston, 1912), II, 309.

[23] Thomas Cobbett, *A Fruitfull and Usefull Discourse touching the Honour due from Children to Parents and the Duty of Parents toward their Children* (London, 1656), 174.

to come into them in a conjugall way . . . then they plotted that incestuous course, whereby their Father was so highly dishonoured. . . .[24]

As marriage was the way to prevent fornication, successful marriage was the way to prevent adultery. The Puritans did not wait for adultery to appear; instead, they took every means possible to make husbands and wives live together and respect each other. If a husband deserted his wife and remained within the jurisdiction of a Puritan government, he was promptly sent back to her. Where the wife had been left in England, the offense did not always come to light until the wayward husband had committed fornication or bigamy, and of course there must have been many offenses which never came to light. But where both husband and wife lived in New England, neither had much chance of leaving the other without being returned by order of the county court at its next sitting. When John Smith of Medfield left his wife and went to live with Patience Rawlins, he was sent home poorer by ten pounds and richer by thirty stripes. Similarly Mary Drury, who deserted her husband on the pretense that he was impotent, failed to convince the court that he actually was so, and had to return to him as well as to pay a fine of five pounds. The wife of Phillip Pointing received lighter treatment: when the court thought that she had overstayed her leave in Boston, they simply ordered her "to depart the Towne and goe to Tanton to her husband." The courts, moreover, were not satisfied with mere cohabitation; they insisted that it be peaceful cohabitation. Husbands and wives were forbidden by law to strike one another, and the law was enforced on numerous occasions. But the courts did not stop there. Henry Flood was required to give bond for good behavior because he had abused his wife simply by "ill words calling her whore and cursing of her." The wife of Christopher Collins was presented for railing at her husband and calling him "Gurley gutted divill." Apparently in this case the court thought that Mistress Collins was right, for although the fact was proved by two witnesses, she was discharged. On another occasion the court favored the husband: Jacob Pudeator, fined for striking and kicking his wife, had the sentence moderated when the court was informed that she was a woman "of great provocation." [25]

Wherever there was strong suspicion that an illicit relation might arise between two persons, the authorities removed the temptation by forbidding the two to come together. As early as November, 1630, the Court of Assistants of Massachusetts prohibited a Mr. Clark from "cohabitacion and frequent keepeing company with Mrs. Freeman, vnder paine of such punish-

---

[24] Cobbett, 177.

[25] Samuel E. Morison and Zechariah Chafee, editors, *Records of the Suffolk County Court, 1671–1680, Publications* of the Colonial Society of Massachusetts, xxix and xxx, 121, 410, 524, 837–841, and 1158; George F. Dow, editor, *Records and Files of the Quarterly Courts of Essex County, Massachusetts* (Salem, 1911–1921), I, 274; and v, 377.

ment as the Court shall thinke meete to inflict." Mr. Clark and Mr. Freeman were both bound "in XX £ apeece that Mr. Clearke shall make his personall appearance att the nexte Court to be holden in March nexte, and in the meane tyme to carry himselfe in good behaviour towards all people and espetially towards Mrs. Freeman, concerneing whome there is stronge suspicion of incontinency." Forty-five years later the Suffolk County Court took the same kind of measure to protect the husbands of Dorchester from the temptations offered by the daughter of Robert Spurr. Spurr was presented by the grand jury

> for entertaining persons at his house at unseasonable times both by day and night to the greife of theire wives and Relations &c The Court having heard what was alleaged and testified against him do Sentence him to bee admonish't and to pay Fees of Court and charge him upon his perill not to entertain any married men to keepe company with his daughter especially James Minott and Joseph Belcher.

In like manner Walter Hickson was forbidden to keep company with Mary Bedwell, "And if at any time hereafter hee bee taken in company of the saide Mary Bedwell without other company to bee forthwith apprehended by the Constable and to be whip't with ten stripes." Elizabeth Wheeler and Joanna Peirce were admonished "for theire disorderly carriage in the house of Thomas Watts being married women and founde sitting in other mens Laps with theire Armes about theire Necks." How little confidence the Puritans had in human nature is even more clearly displayed by another case, in which Edmond Maddock and his wife were brought to court "to answere to all such matters as shalbe objected against them concerning Haarkwoody and Ezekiell Euerells being at their house at unseasonable tyme of the night and her being up with them after her husband was gone to bed." Haarkwoody and Everell had been found "by the Constable Henry Bridghame about tenn of the Clock at night sitting by the fyre at the house of Edmond Maddocks with his wyfe a suspicious weoman her husband being on sleepe [*sic*] on the bedd." A similar distrust of human ability to resist temptation is evident in the following order of the Connecticut Particular Court:

> James Hallett is to returne from the Correction house to his master Barclyt, who is to keepe him to hard labor, and course dyet during the pleasure of the Court provided that Barclet is first to remove his daughter from his family, before the sayd James enter therein.

These precautions, as we have already seen, did not eliminate fornication, adultery, or other sexual offenses, but they doubtless reduced the number from what it would otherwise have been.[26]

---

[26] *Records of the Suffolk County Court*, 442–443 and 676; John Noble, editor, *Records of the Court of Assistants of the Colony of Massachusetts Bay* (Boston, 1901–1928),

In sum, the Puritan attitude toward sex, though directed by a belief in absolute, God-given moral values, never neglected human nature. The rules of conduct which the Puritans regarded as divinely ordained had been formulated for men, not for angels and not for beasts. God had created mankind in two sexes; He had ordained marriage as desirable for all, and sexual intercourse as essential to marriage. On the other hand, He had forbidden sexual intercourse outside of marriage. These were the moral principles which the Puritans sought to enforce in New England. But in their enforcement they took cognizance of human nature. They knew well enough that human beings since the fall of Adam were incapable of obeying perfectly the laws of God. Consequently, in the endeavor to enforce those laws they treated offenders with patience and understanding, and concentrated their efforts on prevention more than on punishment. The result was not a society in which most of us would care to live, for the methods of prevention often caused serious interference with personal liberty. It must nevertheless be admitted that in maters of sex the Puritans showed none of the blind zeal or narrow-minded bigotry which is too often supposed to have been characteristic of them. The more one learns about these people, the less do they appear to have resembled the sad and sour portraits which their modern critics have drawn of them.

II, 8; *Records of the Particular Court of Connecticut, Collections* of the Connecticut Historical Society, XXII, 20; and a photostat in the library of the Massachusetts Historical Society, dated March 29, 1653.

SIDNEY MEAD

FROM COERCION TO PERSUASION
Another Look at the Rise
of Religious Liberty and the
Emergence of Denominationalism

Although the essays in this text insist upon the importance of ideas in history, they do not claim that the force of ideas can be understood apart from a particular set of social circumstances. The essay that follows, by a distinguished church historian, demonstrates the complex relationships that linked the ideology of religious toleration to the evolution of American colonial societies at a time when religious uniformity was still revered in Europe. While Mead does not deny that ideas of toleration and freedom affected colonial practice, he suggests that they gained acceptance in America out of a necessity composed of such disparate factors as the recruitment of settlers, the extent of physical space, the English policy of religious tolerance, and eighteenth-century revivalism. The Lively Experiment *(1963), also by Sidney Mead, offers still more on this subject.*

By the time English colonization got underway in the seventeenth century, the Reformation movement had shattered the once tangible unity of European Christendom. The spiritual reformation of the church was concurrent with the rising self-consciousness of the emerging nations. Quite naturally the reformation of the church found diverse expressions in the several countries—Lutheranism in the realms of the German princes and in the Scandinavian countries, Anglicanism in England, Reformed in Geneva and Scotland.

In general these right-wing Protestant groups agreed with Roman Catholics on the necessity for enforcing religious uniformity in doctrine and practice within a civil commonwealth. This view of many centuries' standing in Christendom the new churches accepted without question.

Meanwhile, in the social crevices created by universal upheaval, certain sects or left-wing groups were emerging as blades of grass spring up through the cracks once a cement sidewalk is broken. Throughout Europe, Catholics and Protestants alike tried to suppress these groups by force, branding them as heretics and schismatics who constituted a threat to the whole structure of Christian civilization.

All of the first settlements on that part of the continent that was to become the United States were made under the religious aegis of right-wing groups with the exception of Plymouth where a handful of separatists "made a small, bustling noise in an empty land." But Anglicans who were making a bigger noise on the James, as were Dutch Reformed on the Hudson, Swedes on the Delaware, and puritan Congregationalists on the Charles, all assumed that the pattern of religious uniformity would of necessity be transplanted and perpetuated in the colonies. And all took positive steps to insure this—even the Pilgrims. For as Plymouth colony prospered it made support of the church compulsory, demanded that voters be certified as "orthodox in the fundamentals of religion," and passed laws against Quakers and other heretics.[1]

The first Charter of Virginia of 1606 provided that "the true word and service of God and Christian faith be preached, planted, and used . . . according to the doctrine, rights, and religion now professed and established within our realm of England," and from the beginning laws provided for the maintenance of the church and clergy and for conformity.

---

[1] Evarts B. Greene, *Religion and the State: The Making and Testing of an American Tradition* (New York: New York University Press, 1941), p. 37. See also Joseph P. Thompson, *Church and State in the United States* (Boston: James R. Osgood & Co., 1873), p. 55.

FROM Sidney Mead, "From Coercion to Persuasion: Another Look at the Rise of Religious Liberty and the Emergence of Denominationalism," *The Lively Experiment: The Shaping of Christianity in America*, New York: Harper & Row, 1963. Reprinted by permission. This article first appeared in *Church History*, Vol. XXV (December 1956).

Orthodox ministers of the Dutch church came early to New Netherlands, and the new charter of freedoms and exemptions of 1640 stated that

> no other religion shall be publicly admitted in New Netherlands except the Reformed, as it is at present preached and practiced by public authority in the United Netherlands; and for this purpose the Company shall provide and maintain good and suitable preachers, schoolmasters, and Comforters of the sick.

When John Prinz was sent as Governor to the struggling Swedish colony in 1643 he was specifically instructed to

> labor and watch that he render in all things to Almighty God the true worship which is his due . . . and to take good measures that the divine service is performed according to the true confession of Augsburg, the Council of Upsala, and the ceremonies of the Swedish church . . .

After a brief stay he was happy to report that

> Divine service is performed here in the good old Swedish tongue, our priest clothed in the vestments of the Mass on high festivals, solemn prayer-days, Sundays, and Apostles' days, precisely as in old Sweden, and differing in every respect from that of the sects around us.[2]

That the New England Puritans' experiment in the Bible Commonwealth required uniformity hardly needs documentation. "There is no Rule given by God for any State to give an Affirmative Toleration to any false Religion, or Opinion whatsoever; they must connive in some cases, but may not concede in any," was the dictum of their self-appointed spokesman, Nathaniel Ward. Although the forthright clarity of this lawyer-minister disguised as a "Simple Cobler" was not typical of the more discreet apologists for the New England way, nevertheless Ward's sentiment was one of the stones in the foundation of their "due forme of Government both ciuell & ecclesiastical."

Yet in spite of such beginnings the intention to perpetuate uniformity in the several Protestant colonies that were gathered under the broad wings and "salutary neglect" of mother England during the seventeenth and eighteenth centuries was everywhere frustrated. The tradition of thirteen-centuries' standing was given up in the relatively brief time of one hundred and eighty years. By around the middle of the eighteenth century toleration was universally, however reluctantly, accepted in all the English colonies. Within fifty years complete religious freedom was declared to be the policy of the new nation formed from these colonies.

---

[2] As quoted in Frederick J. Zwierlein, *Religion in New Netherlands* (Rochester, N. Y.: John P. Smith Printing Co., 1910), pp. 140–41, 117, 118–19.

The importance of this change can hardly be overestimated. Professor W. E. Garrison has rightly called it one of "the two most profound revolutions which have occurred in the entire history of the church . . . on the administrative side"—and so it was.

I

There have been many studies of the rise of religious freedom in America. They range all the way from the sentimental to the cynical with a large number of very substantial works by careful scholars in between. There seems to be fairly wide agreement with Professor Philip Schaff's thesis that the Constitutional Convention "was shut up to this course" by the previous history of the colonies and the situation existing at the time. In this essay I do not intend a detailed historical explanation of this "profound revolution," but wish only to raise two questions: What was the situation in 1787? and How had it come to be?

In order to answer the second question two factors have to be weighed and balanced: that of the positive ideological thrust for such freedom made, for example, by the Baptists as a group, and by individual leaders in most of the other churches, and that of practical necessity. The latter position is ably represented by Perry Miller, who argues that Protestants by and large "did not [willingly] contribute to religious liberty, they stumbled into it, they were compelled into it, they accepted it at last because they had to, or because they saw its strategic value." [3]

It is my impression that Protestant writers have commonly stressed the first factor, usually suggesting that religious freedom was a natural concomitant of the Reformation. If in this essay I stress the second factor, it is primarily to bring into the discussion what I hope will be a corrective emphasis.

This emphasis necessarily reduces the historical importance Protestants have placed upon the positive, self-conscious, and articulated aspiration for religious freedom expressed in our popular folklore through such gems as Felicia Heman's poem on the landing of the Pilgrims. It does not deny the existence of important seminal ideas among left-wingers and other outcasts such as the Roman Catholics who established Maryland or even among the respectable Puritans and Presbyterians. Nor does it underestimate the long-term symbolic value of the steps taken along this road by the Baltimores, by Roger Williams and that motley collection of the banished in Rhode Island, and by William Penn and his Quakers in the Jerseys and Pennsylvania. Still it should be kept in mind that Protestants connived in the freedom extended to all by Roman Catholics in Maryland only so long as was necessary for them to do so. Rhode Island was the scandal of respectable Massachusetts

---

[3] Perry G. E. Miller, "The Contribution of the Protestant Churches to Religious Liberty in Colonial America," in *Church History,* IV (March, 1935), 57–66.

precisely because of its freedom and was commonly referred to by the Bay dignitaries as the sewer and loathsome receptacle of the land. They did not cleanse it because they could not. And by the time Penn launched his experiment with freedom in Pennsylvania, coerced uniformity had already broken down in the neighboring colonies, and England herself, having experimented extensively with toleration between 1648 and 1660 and unable to forget it during the Restoration, was trembling on the verge of toleration.

Accepting, then, the view that the original intention of the dominant and really powerful groups was to perpetuate the pattern of religious uniformity, I shall argue that this intention was frustrated by the unusual problems posed by the vast space with which the Planters had to deal, by a complex web of self-interest in which they were enmeshed, and by the practical necessity to connive at religious variety which both space and self-interest imposed. Finally, too, pressures from the motherland contributed to the process leading to religious freedom.

The web of self-interest was complex indeed, the strongest strands being Protestant, national, and personal. At a time when in England Protestant was synonymous with patriot, and the first feeble English settlements were encircled by the strong arms of French and Spanish Catholicism, whose fingers touched on the Mississippi, it is small wonder that all the early writings and charters stressed the planting of *Protestant* outposts of empire, and that a sentiment came to prevail that almost any kind of Protestantism was preferable to Catholicism. Perhaps this is why Dutch and English policy differed radically from French, in that the Protestant countries after a few random gestures such as the provision in the second Virginia Charter of 1609 that "none be permitted to pass in any Voyage . . . to be made into said Country but such as first shall have taken the Oath of Supremacy," let their dissenters go. Civil and ecclesiastical pressures ranging from slight disabilities to active persecution thus added an external push from the rear to the lure of land and of economic and social betterment operating in the colonists' minds. And this, coupled in many of them with a religious fervor that was always in danger of crossing the boundary into self-righteousness, pushed them out with the intention to become permanent settlers, to possess the land, and perchance to be an example for all mankind—as witness the Bay Puritans.

It is notable also that from the beginning the one outstanding Roman Catholic proprietor had to tolerate a majority of Protestants in his colony, and that eventually the heirs of the first Baltimore probably retained their lands and prerogatives only by becoming Protestants.

National self-interest mated easily with Protestant interests and spawned a desire for strong and profitable colonies that tended to overcome squeamishness about the religious complexion of the settlers. When Peter Stuyvesant came to New Netherlands in 1647 as Director General, he immediately took steps to put the religious house in order by limiting the sale of liquor on Sundays, instituting preaching twice rather than the former once a day, and compelling attendance thereon. When Lutherans, Jews, and Quakers arrived he tried to suppress them, finally shipping one notorious Quaker back to Holland. The Directors' reaction to this move is eloquent testimony to the mind that prevailed among them. They wrote in April 1663 that

> although it is our cordial desire that similar and other sectarians might not be found there, yet as the contrary seems to be the fact, we doubt very much if vigorous proceedings against them ought not to be discontinued, except you intend to check and destroy your population; which, however, in the youth of your existence ought rather to be encouraged by all possible means: Wherefore, it is our opinion, that some connivance would be useful; that the consciences of men, at least, ought ever to remain free and unshackled. Let everyone be unmolested, as long as he is modest; as long as his conduct in a political sense is irreproachable; as he does not disturb others, or oppose the government. This maxim of moderation has always been the guide of the magistrates of this city, and the consequence has been that, from every land, people have flocked to this asylum. Tread then in their steps, and, we doubt not, you will be blessed.[4]

So on another occasion Stuyvesant argues that "to give liberty to the Jews will be very detrimental . . . because the Christians there will not be able at the same time to do business." And besides, "giving them liberty, we cannot refuse the Lutherans and Papists." [5]

At the time he was backed by the doughty Reformed minister, Megapolensis, who thought the situation was already bad enough since there were "Papists, Mennonites and Lutherans amongst the Dutch, also many Puritans or Independents, and various other servants of Baal among the English under this government," all of whom "conceal themselves under the name of Christians." Nevertheless, the desire of the Directors not to "check and destroy" the population overruled the desire of both magistrate and clergy for a semblance of religious uniformity and Jews had to be granted permission to reside and traffic in New Netherlands only "provided they shall not become a charge upon the deaconry or the Company." [6]

II

Finally, from the beginning the ruling geniuses of the new age of expansion managed to mingle strong personal self-interest with the more abstract Protestant and national goals by making trading companies and proprietary-ships the instruments of planting. Dutch, Swedish, and English companies

---

[4] As quoted in W. W. Sweet, *Religion in Colonial America* (New York: Charles Scribner's Sons, 1942), pp. 151–52.

[5] Zwierlein, *op. cit.,* p. 261.

[6] *Ibid.,* pp. 257, 256.

organized the plantings in Virginia, Plymouth, New Netherlands, Massachusetts Bay, and Delaware, while proprietors were instrumental in the founding of Maryland, New Hampshire, New Jersey, the Carolinas, Pennsylvania, and Georgia. It might further be argued that William Coddington and his commercial-minded cohorts were the real backbone of Rhode Island, while obviously Theophilus Eaton, the merchant, was hand in hand with John Davenport, the minister, in the founding of the ultratheocratic New Haven.

By 1685, says Greene, more territory along the seaboard than New England and Virginia combined was under proprietary control, and there "governmental policies in relation to religion were radically different from those prevailing either in New England or Virginia." From the viewpoint of the proprietors, he continues, "it was obviously not good business to set up religious tests to exclude otherwise desirable immigrants." "The proprietors tried to attract settlers," Greene explained, "by promising, if not full religious equality, at least greater tolerance than was allowed elsewhere." [7]

But if self-interest dictated in more or less subtle and devious ways a kind of connivance with religious diversity that helped to spell out toleration in the colonies, the efforts even of the most authoritarian groups to enforce uniformity on principle was dissipated in the vast spaces of the new land.

The Anglicans tried it in Virginia, even resorting to the savage "Lavves Diuine, Morall and Martiall &c." published in 1612 which threatened the death penalty for speaking "impiously or maliciously against the . . . Trinitie," or "against the knowne Articles of the Christian faith," or for saying or doing anything which might "tend to the derision or despight of Gods Holy Word," and threatened loss of the "dayes allowance," whipping, "a bodkin thrust through his tongue," six months in the "gallies," or other punishments for failing, among other things, in respect for the clergy, for not attending divine services twice daily, for breaking the "Sabboth by any gaming, publique or private, or refusing religious instruction." [8]

No one supposes that such laws were enforced during the horrendous years between 1607 and 1624 when thirteen thousand of the fourteen thousand people sent over died from exposure, disease, starvation, and the weapons of the savages. Meanwhile the economic awards in the cultivation of tobacco had been discovered and this scattered the families to plantations along the rivers. Even honest clergymen began to despair of conducting the routine affairs of the English church in parishes that might be one hundred miles in length. In 1661 an acute observer argues in *Virginia's Cure* . . . that the chief difficulty was due to the "scattered Planting" for which there was "no other Remedy . . . but by reducing her Planters into towns." His proposal to build towns in every county, and then to make the Planters

---

[7] Greene, *op. cit.,* pp. 52–53.

[8] *For the Colony in Virginea Britannia. Lavves Diuine, Moral and Martiall, &c.* (Printed at London for Walter Burre, 1612); in Peter Force, *Tracts and Other Papers* (Washington: Wm. Q. Force, 1844), III, #ii, pp. 10–11.

bring their families and servants to these centers on weekends for catechetical instruction and church attendance was obviously the counsel of despairing, albeit ardent, churchmen who were beginning to realize that the snug parish life of settled England could not be duplicated in the wilderness.[9]

The Puritan theocrats on the Charles soon had one important aspect of the meaning of the great space available thrust upon them. They discovered that while they might protect their own religious uniformity by banishing all dissenters, they could neither keep the banished from settling in neighboring Rhode Island where "Justice did at greatest offenders wink," [10] nor prevent every wind from the south carrying their contagious ideas back to the Puritan stronghold. They did not foresee that the same inscrutable Providence that gave Puritans the opportunity to build their kind of Bible commonwealth on Massachusetts soil would offer dissenters the equal opportunity to build whatever kind of commonwealth they wished on Rhode Island soil.

Meanwhile the zeal of the dissenters, far from being dissipated by banishment, was truly enlarged by the knowledge thus forced upon them that even the long arms of civil and ecclesiastical authority could not encompass the vast spaces of the new land. In rather short order, belief in the effectiveness of suppression by force and the will to use it to maintain religious uniformity were undermined by the obvious futility of trying to land solid blows on the subversive men and women who were seldom there when the blows fell. Samuel Gorton, compelled to attend church in the Bay, wrote that the sermonic fare seemed adapted to the digestive capacities of the ostrich. But in spite of such capacities, the residents were unable to stomach the savage proceedings against the Quakers, and finally even the magistrates and ministers had to connive in their existence.[11]

There was of course another aspect of space—the distance from the motherland, which, relative to existing means of movement and communications, was immense. The Puritans began with the idea that

> God hath provided this place to be a refuge for many whome he meanes to
> save out of the generall callamity, and seeinge the Church hath noe place to

---

[9] *Virginia's Cure: Or an Advisive Narrative Concerning Virginia. Discovering the True Ground of That Unhappiness, and the Only True Remedy.* As it was presented to the Right Reverend Father in God *Gvilbert* Lord Bishop of London, September 2, 1661 (London: W. Godbid, 1662), reprinted in Force, *Tracts . . . , op. cit.,* III, #xv.

[10] Perry G. E. Miller and Thomas H. Johnson, eds., *The Puritans* (New York: American Book Co., 1938), p. 639.

[11] For the general factors at work, see Roland H. Bainton, "The Struggle for Religious Liberty," in *Church History,* X (June, 1941), 95–124. Professor Winthrop S. Hudson has argued that English Independents had developed a "denominational" conception of the church which, in spite of the rigors of the New England way, tended always to make its leaders inherently uncomfortable with persecution of dissenters; see his "Denominationalism as a Basis for Ecumenicity: A Seventeenth Century Conception," in *Church History,* XXIV (March, 1955), 32–50. This suggests a fruitful area for further exploration.

flie into but the wildernesse, what better worke can there be, then to goe and provide tabernacles and foode for her against she comes thether.[12]

They early sensed the protection inherent in the great distance. Their ingenious idea of taking the Charter and the Company with them to New England is evidence of this. Thereafter they perfected a system of sanctified maneuvering within the time granted by distance that succeeded for three generations in frustrating the attempts of English courts and Crown to control them.

Distance also militated against effective control of the Church of England in the Southern colonies. From the beginning, oversight fell somewhat accidentally to the Bishop of London. During the last quarter of the seventeenth century, the Bishops sought to instrument their supervision of church activities in the colonies through representatives called Commissaries. But without resident Bishops, effective supervision proved to be impossible. The church languished under too many second-rate and even fraudulent clergymen. Increasingly the control passed to parochial vestries composed of local laymen.

Turmoil in Britain at times reinforced distance in frustrating effective ecclesiastical control of the colonies. In 1638, after a series of reports and proclamations beginning in 1632, Archbishop Laud made arrangements to send a bishop to New England with sufficient troops to enforce conformity and obedience if necessary. The outbreak of troubles in Scotland sidetracked this interesting project, however, and "no records of any official connection between the Anglican episcopate and the colonies during the period 1638–1663" exist.[13]

Meanwhile through revolution, Protectorate, and Restoration, England was moving toward its rendezvous with the kind of toleration made manifest in the famous Act of 1689. Already in 1652 Dr. John Clarke had published in London his *Ill Newes from Newe England or a Narrative of New England's Persecution,* protesting the fining and whipping of three Baptists in Massachusetts under the aegis of a law passed in 1644. His telling thesis was that in matters of religious tolerance, "while Old England is becoming new, New England is become Old." [14]

From about that time the mother country took definite steps to curb persecution in the colonies. When the King was reminded by Edward Burroughs that the execution of Quakers in Boston meant that there was *"a Vein of innocent Blood opened in his Dominions, which, if it were not stopt would overrun all,"* he declared, *"But I will stop that Vein,"* and he did. A Mandamus was granted and carried to New England by Samuel Shattock, a resident

---

[12] As quoted in Charles M. Andrews, *The Colonial Period of American History* (New Haven: Yale University Press, 1934), I, 386.

[13] Arthur Lyon Cross, *The Anglican Episcopate and the American Colonies* (Cambridge: Harvard University Press, 1924), p. 22.

[14] In the *Massachusetts Historical Society Collections,* Ser. 4, II (1854), 1–113.

of Salem who had been banished on pain of death. Shattock and his fellow Quakers made the most of the occasion, which resulted in a suspension of the laws against the Quakers as such in November, 1661.[15]

Meanwhile, John Clarke's *Ill Newes from New England . . .* had resulted in a protest to the Governor of Massachusetts from ten Congregational ministers in London, who, seeking for more toleration in England, were embarrassed by this show of intolerance on the part of their New England brethren. Sir Richard Saltonstall added his protest in a letter to Cotton and Wilson of Boston's First Church. The Puritans' reply that it was better to have "hypocrites than profane persons" in their churches sounded outmoded.[16]

In 1663 the Crown, in giving its consent to Rhode Island's "lively experiment" with "full liberty in religious concernm[ts]" in the new Charter,[17] gave official sanction to the scandal of Massachusetts Bay and forestalled all future attempts on the part of the Bay Puritans to impose their kind of theocratic order on the neighboring chaos.

The most spectacular case of royal interference that worked for the broadening of colonial toleration was the revocation of the Massachusetts Bay Charter in 1684 and the coming of Sir Edmund Andros as the Royal Governor in 1686. Andros brought an Anglican chaplain with him. Seeking a place for Anglican Services, he tried to persuade the Puritan ministers to provide a church. When this proved unsuccessful, he took over one of their meetinghouses by force and had the English services conducted therein while King's Chapel was being built. The new charter of 1691, in which the New Englanders themselves had a part through the person and work of Increase Mather, wrote "the end" to the Puritan chapter on the preservation of uniformity in the new land.

III

Thus the new century found the original intention to perpetuate religious uniformity almost universally frustrated by the strange rope of circumstances woven from various kinds of self-interest and the problems posed by the great space. Effective interference from the motherland in the interests of broader toleration served only to hasten the process. When the two Mathers, father and son, took part in the ordination of a Baptist minister in Boston in

---

[15] Willem Sewel, *The History of the Rise, Increase, and Progress of the Christian People Called Quakers, Intermixed with Several Remarkable Occurrences,* written originally in Low-Dutch by Willem Sewel, and by himself translated into English, now rev. and published with some amendments (London: J. Sowle, 1722), p. 280.

[16] See Sanford H. Cobb, *The Rise of Religious Liberty in America* (New York: The Macmillan Co., 1902), p. 69.

[17] Andrews, *op. cit.,* II, 42.

1718, a new day was indeed dawning. But it is probably not to be wondered at that most of them adhered to the inherited standards and conceptions of the church with religious fervor sometimes bordering on desperation. It took the prolonged upheavals associated with the great revivals to break the dwindling hold of the old patterns and give the new an opportunity to grow, and, in the process, to scramble both inextricably with others emerging out of the immediate situation.

Once it was seen that uniformity was impracticable, two possible paths lay open before the churches: toleration, with a favored or established church and dissenting sects—the path actually taken in England—or freedom, with complete equality of all religious groups before the civil law. Favoring the first solution was the fact that transplanted offshoots of Europe's state churches were clearly dominant in all but two of the colonies, and indeed remained so until after the Revolution. Nine of the colonies actually maintained establishments—Congregationalism in New England, Anglicanism in the South and, nominally, in part of New York. Presbyterians in the South and Anglicans in New England were willing to acknowledge the prerogatives of establishments by assuming the role of dissenters. On the eve of the great revivals, then, these dominant churches had not as yet rejected the principle of religious uniformity but were compelled to recognize the fact of religious variety.

Meanwhile in Rhode Island and the stronger middle colonies religious freedom prevailed—in New York practically, ambiguously, and largely because of necessity, in Rhode Island and Pennsylvania actually and more clearly on principle and experience. As intimated above, the factors that had confounded the uniformitarian intentions of the churches originally established in the new land had also encouraged the numerical growth, geographical expansion, and bumptious self-confidence of the dissenting and free groups in all the colonies. However, they were as yet largely unconscious of their real strength which was to lie in their success with persuasion alone for recruiting members and maintaining their institutions in competition with other groups. An entry in Henry M. Muhlenberg's *Journal,* November 28, 1742, suggests how rapidly a minister, transplanted from a European state church, might size up the realities of the new situation in America and come to terms with them. Sent over to bring some order into the scrambled Lutheran affairs, he immediately ran into a squabble in one of the churches, and recorded:

> The deacons and elders are unable to do anything about it, for in religious and church matters, each has the right to do what he pleases. The government has nothing to do with it and will not concern itself with such matters. Everything depends on the vote of the majority. A preacher must fight his way through with the sword of the Spirit alone and depend upon faith in the

living God and His promises, if he wants to be a preacher and proclaim the truth in America.[18]

Such espousal of voluntaryism by these American offsprings of Europe's right-wing state churches meant that they accepted one aspect that had been common to the left-wing sectarian groups of Europe from their beginnings. But this was a triumph of a left-wing influence in America, as it is sometimes held, in a guilt-by-association sense only.

Much more important for the future than left-wing influence was the movement called Pietism. Originating in the European right-wing state churches during the last quarter of the seventeenth century, its leaders were seeking for more palatable spiritual food for the hungry souls of the common folk than current Protestant scholasticism and formalism afforded. Conceived and projected as a movement *within* churches aimed at the revitalization of the personal religious life of the members and a restoration of Christian unity, Pietism did tend to develop its own patterns of doctrine and polity. While assuming the validity and continuance of traditional standards and practices, Pietists tended to make personal religious experience more important than assent to correctly formulated belief and the observance of ecclesiastical forms. Here was an intimation that the essence of a church was the voluntary association of individuals who had had the experience.

Stress on the intuitive religion of the heart "strangely warmed" by "faith in Christ," as John Wesley was later to put it, became a possible seedbed for the dreaded religious "enthusiasm." However, in Europe the movement was always somewhat constrained by the sheer existence and accepted forms of the powerful state churches.

But, sprouting indigenously in America, or transplanted thereto by such leaders as Freylinghuysen, Muhlenberg, Zinzendorf, and the great Whitefield, where such constraining ecclesiastical forms were already weakened, Pietism, cross-fertilized by other movements, grew rankly and blossomed into the spectacular phenomena associated with the Great Awakenings. It swept the colonies from the 1720's to the Revolution, transforming the religious complexion of the land as it went.

Jonathan Edwards' experience in Northampton indicates how short was the step from preaching even the most traditional doctrines out of a heart "strangely warmed," to the outbreak of a surprising revival in the church that soon led to "strange enthusiastic delusions" which threatened to disrupt established parish customs.[19] To a modern student the emotional upheavals created by George Whitefield's preaching seem to be out of proportion to

---

[18] Henry Melchior Muhlenberg, *The Journals,* trans. by Theodore G. Tappert and John W. Doberstein (Philadelphia: Muhlenberg Press, 1942), I, 67.

[19] See Jonathan Edwards, "A Faithful Narrative of the Surprising Work of God in the Conversion of Many Hundred Souls, in Northampton . . . ," in his *The Works of President Edwards* (New York: Converse, 1830), IV, 70–71.

that noted evangelist's reputed powers that so impressed Benjamin Franklin.

Back of this was the peculiar religious situation that had been developing in the colonies for a century. Concurrent with the fracturing of uniformity had come the obvious decline of vital religion which concerned clergymen throughout the colonies during the twilight years of the seventeenth century and often turned their sermons into lamentations. The churches were not reaching the masses of the people, and they now confronted a greater proportion of unchurched adults than existed in any other Christian country. This grim statistic reflected the breakdown of the traditional pattern of church membership by birth into a commonwealth and baptism into a church that was coextensive with it, as well as the passing of support induced by coercion, at a time when no new, effective, and acceptable method for recruiting and holding members had emerged.

There was also the general cultural attrition associated with living on the frontier of western civilization where so much of the vital energy of the prosperous went into practical affairs—usually related to immediate profits—and of the poor in the even more engrossing problem of survival. The end of the seventeenth century has been called with reason the lowest ebb tide of the cultural amenities in America. Here was fertile soil for the growth of the kind of fearful and superstitious religiosity later so vividly pictured by Crèvecoeur in the twelfth of his *Letters from an American Farmer*. Hence, to change the figure, at the very time when the tried old dams of civil and ecclesiastical law and custom were crumbling, there was building up behind them a religious yearning waiting to be released in floods of religious enthusiasm. And the revivals came, doing just that.

Most of the early revivalists were pietistically inclined ministers who more or less unwittingly stumbled upon this technique. It so perfectly met the immediate needs of the churches that it seemed a direct answer to their prayers and a sign of the divine approbation of their doctrines.[20] The revivalists were obviously successful in carrying the gospel to the masses of indifferent people, in recruiting members from among the large body of the unchurched, and in filling the pews with convinced and committed Christians. The revivals demonstrated the spectacular effectiveness of persuasion alone to churches rapidly being shorn of coercive power.

---

[20] As, e.g., Jonathan Edwards' words: "The Beginning of the late work of God in this Place was so circumstanced, that I could not but look upon it as a remarkable Testimony of God's Approbation of the Doctrine of Justification by Faith alone, here asserted and vindicated: . . . And at that time, while I was greatly reproached for defending this Doctrine in the Pulpit, and just upon my suffering a very open Abuse for it, God's Work wonderfully brake forth amongst us, and souls began to flock to Christ, as the Saviour in whose Righteousness alone they hoped to be justified; So that this was the Doctrine on which this work in its Beginning was founded, as it evidently was in the whole progress of it." *Discourses on Various Important Subjects, Nearly Concerning the Great Affair of the Soul's Eternal Salvation* (Boston: S. Kneeland & T. Green, 1738), p. ii.

In the context of our general interpretation it is important to note two things. The first is that the revivals took place largely within the entrenched and dominant churches of right-wing tradition. The second is that everywhere, whether among Dutch Reformed and Presbyterians in the middle colonies, Congregationalists in New England or Anglicans in the South, head-on clashes developed between the pietistic revivalists and the powerful defenders of the traditional authoritarian Protestant patterns of doctrine and polity. For the latter correctly sensed that the revivalists stressed religious experience and results—namely conversion—more than correctness of belief, adherence to creedal statements, and proper observance of traditional forms. They knew that in the long run this emphasis might undermine all standards.

When the revivals broke out, traditionalists were largely in control in all these churches. Their attitude is fairly reflected in the Old Side Presbyterian condemnation of the revivalists for

> preaching the terrors of the law in such a manner, and dialect as has no precedent in the Word of God . . . and so industriously working on the passions and affections of weak minds, as to cause them to cry out in a hideous manner, and fall down in convulsion-like fits, to the marring of the profiting both of themselves and others, who are so taken up in seeing and hearing these odd symptoms, that they cannot attend to or hear what the preacher says; and then, after all, boasting of these things as the work of God, which we are persuaded do proceed from an inferior or worse cause.[21]

As for the greatest of the revivalists, George Whitefield, the Rev. John Thompson wrote that he was almost fully persuaded that Whitefield was either "a downright Deceiver, or else under a dreadful Delusion," and condemned his publications as "nothing but mere confused inconsistent religious jargon, contrived to amuse and delude the simple." [22]

Men like Thompson felt a strong sense of responsibility for order and decency in the churches. Still powerful in every colony, they used all available civil and ecclesiastical weapons against the revivalists.

The revivalists defended themselves primarily on the basic ground that personal religious experience was the important thing. They thought of course that the traditionalists neglected it. Gilbert Tennent struck their keynote in his sermon of March 8, 1740, which he called "The Danger of an Unconverted Ministry." Such ministers, he asserted, are "Pharisee-teachers, having no experience of a special work of the Holy Ghost, upon their own souls." They are merely "carnal," and have

---

[21] As quoted in Wesley M. Gewehr, *The Great Awakening in Virginia, 1740–1790* (Durham: Duke University Press, 1930), p. 16.

[22] In *ibid.*, p. 65.

discover'd themselves too plainly to be so in the Course of their lives; some by Ignorance of the Things of God, and Errors about them, bantering and ridiculing of them; some by vicious Practices, some both Ways, all by a furious Opposition to the Work of God in the Land; and what need have we of further Witnesses?

Of course, he added, "God, as an absolute Sovereign, may use what Means he pleases to accomplish his Work by," *but* "we only assert this, that Success by unconverted Ministers Preaching is very improbable, and very seldom happens, so far as we can gather." [23]

Here was the revivalists' most telling argument—they were obviously more successful than their traditionalist brethren. The experience of the Presbyterian churches divided into traditional and revivalist groups between 1745 and 1758 amounted to a demonstration. At the time of the separation the Old Side party numbered twenty-five ministers, at its close only twenty-two. Meanwhile the New Side revivalist party, which began with twenty-two ministers, had seventy-two in 1758 with churches and members proportionately in keeping with these figures. The success of the revivalists could be made very tangible and nicely measured merely by counting ministers, churches, and converts. Thereafter the emphasis upon success in numbers was to play havoc with all tradition-rooted standards of doctrine and polity in the American churches. One hundred and fifty years later Dwight L. Moody was to declare that it makes no difference how you got a man to God, just so you got him there. Moody's outlook was a natural culmination of the emphasis originating with his eighteenth-century forebears.

At this point it is worthwhile to note specifically that the battle was not one between tolerant left-wing sectarian revivalists riding the wave of the democratic future and anachronistic right-wing chairmen stubbornly defending the past and their own present prerogatives. It is important to stress this, because even Professor William Warren Sweet, dean of the historians of Christianity in America, gave the prestige of his name to the thesis that "it was the triumph of left-wing Protestantism in eighteenth century colonial America which underlay the final achievement of the separation of church and state." [24] This thesis has difficulties, chief of which is the plain fact that the left wing, whether defined institutionally or ideologically, never "triumphed" during the colonial period in America.[25] Colonial revivalism was largely a right-wing church affair.

---

[23] From Leonard J. Trinterud, *The Forming of an American Tradition, A Re-examination of Colonial Presbyterianism* (Philadelphia: The Westminster Press, 1944), pp. 89–91.

[24] W. W. Sweet, *The American Churches, an Interpretation* (New York: Abingdon-Cokesbury Press, 1948), pp. 30–31.

[25] See, e.g., Winthrop S. Hudson's review of Sweet's *The American Churches, an Interpretation* (*ibid.*), in *The Crozer Quarterly*, XXV (October, 1948), 358–60.

To be sure, the pietistic revivalists everywhere belabored what Tennent had called "The Danger of an Unconverted Ministry," and Jonathan Edwards was dismissed from his Northampton church in 1750 primarily for insisting, in that stronghold of right-wing sentiment locally known as "Stoddardeanism," that a conversion experience was the prime requisite for full communion in a Christian church—something he had perhaps learned in the revivals. The revivalists—harassed by traditionalists—naturally developed a kind of anticlericalism and antiecclesiasticism that helped to blur the lines between them and those of more authentic left-wing origin. Compounding this confusion between the revivalists and authentic left wingers was the fact that ever since the time of Munster, every departure from accepted order in the Protestant churches was apt to conjure up visions of an imminent upsurge of familism, antinomianism, anabaptism, and enthusiasm. These were terms that the traditionalists used freely but loosely during the heat of the controversies over revivalism.

Actually all the outstanding revivalists belonged to churches or right-wing tradition, and it might cogently be argued that what growth accrued to left-wing groups as a result of the revivals came largely through their ability to reap where others had sown. Thus, for example, the Baptists in New England apparently took little part in the Awakenings there, looking upon them as a movement within the churches of their Congregational oppressors.[26] But when conflict led to a separatist movement, and Separate Congregationalists were treated even more harshly than Baptists by their erstwhile Congregational brethren, many separatists became Baptists.

Once this point is clear, we see that during the clash between traditionalists and revivalists, the latter were thrown willy-nilly—but somewhat incidentally—on the side of greater toleration and freedom. It was not that they developed clearly formulated theories about religious freedom. In fact the striking thing about the whole pietistic movement, as A. N. Whitehead pointed out, was that it "was singularly devoid of new ideas." Rather it appears that the revivalists were prompted by a practical desire for freedom from the immediate restraints imposed by the dominant churchmen. They fought for the right to promote their own point of view in their own ways unmolested by traditional civil and ecclesiastical customs and laws.

Simultaneously the rationalist permeation of the intellectual world during the eighteenth century led to a situation where any man or group that appeared to be fighting for wider toleration of religious differences would attract the sympathetic attention of "enlightened" men in positions of social and political leadership. Furthermore, these men, unlike the Pietists, were in-

---

[26] Isaac Backus, *A History of New England, with Particular Reference to the Denomination of Christians Called Baptists*, 2d ed., with notes by David Weston (Newton, Mass.: The Backus Historical Society, 1871), II, 41. See also C. C. Goen, *Revivalism and Separatism in New England, 1740–1800* (New Haven: Yale University Press, 1962).

terested in giving religious freedom rational, theoretical justification. However much they might abhor "enthusiasm," they could take a sympathetic view of the practical moral application of the revivalist's gospel and the concomitant pietistic appeal to the teachings and simple religion of Jesus. As these rationalists observed the controversies in and between the religious "sects" occasioned by the revivals, along with the attempts of entrenched traditionalists to preserve order through the use of power, their sympathies were with the revivalists who appeared to be on the side of freedom.

Hence came that apparently strange coalition of rationalists with pietistic-revivalistic sectarians during the last quarter of the eighteenth century. Together, they provided much of the propelling energy behind the final thrust for the religious freedom that was written into the constitution of the new nation. This coalition seems less strange if we keep in mind that, at the time, religious freedom was for both more a practical and legal problem than a theoretical one. They agreed on the practical goal.

IV

Now to hark back to my guiding questions. Having suggested how it had come to be, we may briefly describe the situation in 1787 that necessitated the declaration for religious freedom in the new nation.

First, the churches of right-wing background were still dominant in every area. But no one of them, and no possible combination of them, was in a position to make a successful bid for a national establishment even if those of the Calvinistic tradition were numerous and powerful enough to give Jefferson reason to fear the possibility.[27] Meanwhile the sweep of pietistic sentiments through these right-wing churches during the revivals had undermined much of their desire for establishment. On the question of religious freedom for all, there were many shades of opinion in these churches, but all were practically unanimous on one point: each wanted freedom for itself. And by this time it had become clear that the only way to get it for themselves was to grant it to all others.

Second, the situation had actually made all previous distinctions between established churches and sects, between right- and left-wing groups, practically meaningless. In the South all but the Anglican Church were dissenting sects, as in New England were all but Congregational churches. In this respect, there was no difference between historically right-wing groups such as Presbyterians, Lutherans, and Anglicians and historically left-wing groups such as Quakers and Baptists. The latter, of course, had traditionally held for religious freedom on principle, while the former had recently come to accept it of necessity. But since the immediate problem of such freedom was

---

[27] Ralph Barton Perry, *Puritanism and Democracy* (New York: The Vanguard Press, 1944), p. 80.

practical and legal, all worked together for it—each for his own complete freedom to publish his own point of view in his own way.

Hence the true picture is not that of the "triumph" in America of right-wing or left-wing, of churches or sects, but rather a mingling through frustration, controversy, confusion, and compromise of all the diverse ecclesiastical patterns transplanted from Europe, with other patterns improvised on the spot. The result was a complex pattern of religious thought and institutional life that was peculiarly "American," and is probably best described as "denominationalism."

Most of the effectively powerful intellectual, social, and political leaders were rationalists, and these men made sense theoretically out of the actual, practical situation which demanded religious freedom. They gave it tangible form and legal structure. This the churches, each intent on its own freedom, accepted in practice but without reconciling themselves to it intellectually by developing theoretical defenses of religious freedom that were legitimately rooted in their professed theological positions. And they never have. Anson Phelps Stokes' massive three-volume work on *Church and State in the United States,* proceeding over the historical evidence like a vacuum cleaner over a rug, is notable for the paucity of positive Protestant pronouncements on religious freedom that it sweeps up.

The religious groups that were everywhere dominant in America throughout the colonial period seem to have placed their feet unwittingly on the road to religious freedom. Rather than following the cloud and pillar of articulated aspiration in that direction, they granted it (insofar as any can be said to have "granted" it) not as the kind of cheerful givers their Lord is said to love, but grudgingly and of necessity.

Meanwhile, by the time that the original intention to preserve religious uniformity was seen to be impossible of fulfillment in the new land, there had been incubated, largely within the dissenting groups (which were not necessarily left wing), ideas, theories, and practices that pointed the way toward a new kind of "church" consistent with the practice of religious freedom. During the colonial upheavals of the Great Awakenings, these dissenters' patterns of thought and practice infiltrated the dominant churches, and through the misty atmosphere of confusion and compromise, there began that historical merging of the traditional European patterns of "church" and "sect," "right" and "left" wings into a new kind of organization combining features of both plus features growing out of the immediate situation. The resulting organizational form was unlike anything that had preceded it in Christendom, and for purposes of distinctive clarity it is best known as the "denomination."

CARL BECKER

WHAT IS STILL LIVING
IN THE POLITICAL PHILOSOPHY
OF THOMAS JEFFERSON

Occasionally, a historian is able to speak to his own day about its values as eloquently as he is able to describe the values for it of another age. Carl Becker displayed this talent in several brilliant books and essays. In his essay on Jefferson, Becker considers the relationship of Jefferson's ideas to the American Revolution and their relevance for modern America. Readers of this essay have long found it worthwhile to ponder the distinction Becker makes between ends and means as they were originally understood by Jefferson. Carl Becker, Declaration of Independence * *(1922), discusses the ideological background of the revolutionary period with penetration.*

I believe. . . that there exists a right independent of force.

THOMAS JEFFERSON

Many nations have traced their history back to some fabled Golden Age, to the beginning of created things, when, as Hesiod said, men lived like gods, free from toil and grief. Our own history can likewise be traced, through its European origins, back to that mythical time. But we commonly think of it as beginning more recently, somewhat abruptly, in the clear light of day, with the settlement at Jamestown, the landing of the *Mayflower,* and the founding of Massachusetts Bay colony. Men did not then live like gods, or free from toil and grief; but there were among them men of heroic stature, round whom myths have gathered, and whom we delight, with good reason, to honor. The beginning of our history as an independent nation is still more recent, and still more open to critical inspection, in the still brighter light of the eighteenth century; and yet this is for us still more truly the time of our Golden Age and of our ancestors of heroic stature. Among the founders of the American federal republic (to name only the most distinguished) were Washington, Franklin and John Adams, Alexander Hamilton and John Jay, Robert Morris and James Wilson, Richard Henry Lee, James Madison, and Thomas Jefferson. No doubt we are apt to magnify these "Fathers" beyond their just merits. Their just merits are, nevertheless, sufficient, for it would be difficult to find in the history of any other country, or in the history of our own country at any other time, within a single generation, as many statesmen in proportion to the population of equal distinction for learning, probity, and political intelligence. And of these ten men none exhibited these qualities to better advantage or more lasting effect than Thomas Jefferson.

Jefferson, like Franklin, attained an international as well as a national eminence. Like Franklin, he was familiar with all of the ideas of his time, contributed something to its accumulated knowledge, and was identified with its most notable activities and events. There was indeed scarcely anything of human interest that was alien to his curious and far-ranging intelligence. Nevertheless, his name is for us inevitably associated with a certain general idea, a certain way of regarding man and the life of man, a certain political philosophy. The word that best denotes that philosophy is democracy. More than any other man we think of Jefferson as having formulated the funda-

---

FROM Carl Becker, "What Is Still Living in the Political Philosophy of Thomas Jefferson," *American Historical Review,* Vol. XLVIII, No. 4 (July 1943), pp. 691–706. Reprinted by permission. The Penrose Lecture, delivered before the American Philosophical Society in Philadelphia, April 22, 1943, in connection with the celebration of the two hundredth anniversary of the birth of Thomas Jefferson.

mental principles of American democracy, of what we now like to call the American way of life.

Any significant political philosophy is shaped by three different but closely related influences. The first of these is what Alfred North Whitehead has taught us to call the "climate of opinion"—those fundamental presuppositions which in any age so largely determine what men think about the nature of the universe and what can and cannot happen in it, and about the nature of man and what is essential to the good life. The second influence is more specific: it derives from the particular political and social conflicts of the time, which dispose groups and parties to accept a particular interpretation of current ideas as a theoretical support for their practical activities. The third influence is more specific still: it derives from the mind and temperament of the individual who gives to the political philosophy its ordered literary form. Whatever is original in the philosophy is usually contributed by the individual who gives it this form. Whatever value it has for its own time and place will depend largely on the extent to which it serves to illuminate or resolve the particular political issues of that time and place. But its value for other times and places will depend upon the extent to which the general presuppositions upon which it rests have a universal validity, the extent to which they express some enduring truth about nature and the life of man.

The political philosophy of Thomas Jefferson was not in essentials original with him. It was his only in the sense that he gave to ideas widely accepted at the time and genuinely entertained by him a Jeffersonian form and flavor. Nowhere is this peculiarity of form and flavor more evident than in the famous Declaration of Independence; but Jefferson did not claim that the ideas themselves were in any way novel. Some years later his old friend John Adams, a little irritated (as he was apt to be on slight provocation) by the laudation of Jefferson as the author of the Declaration, protested to Pickering that "there is not an idea in it that was not hackneyed in Congress two years before." [1] To this Jefferson replied that it was not his purpose "to say things which had never been said before, but to place before mankind the common sense of the subject," and to harmonize the "sentiments of the day, whether expressed in conversation, in letters, printed essays, or the elementary books of public right." [2] It was indeed Jefferson's merit, and the high value of the Declaration for his own time, that he expressed in lucid and persuasive form political ideas then widely accepted and thereby provided a reasoned justification for renouncing the authority of the British government. But the Declaration professes to do more than that. In providing the reasons for renouncing the authority of a particular government at a particular time, Jefferson took occasion to formulate the universal principles which, as he thought, could alone justify the authority of any government at any time.

---

[1] *The Works of John Adams* (Boston, 1850–56), II, 512.

[2] *The Writings of Thomas Jefferson* (Philadelphia, 1869–71), VII, 304, 407.

These principles are set forth in a single brief paragraph. We are all familiar with it, having read it or heard it read many times. But it will always, and at no time more than now, bear repeating; and so I will repeat it once more, not exactly as it appears in the Declaration but as Jefferson first wrote it in the original draft.

> We hold these truths to be sacred and undeniable; that all men are created equal and independent; that from that equal creation they derive rights inherent and inalienable, among which are the preservation of life, and liberty, and the pursuit of happiness; that to secure these ends, governments are instituted among men, deriving their just powers from the consent of the governed; that whenever any form of government shall become destructive of these ends, it is the right of the people to alter or to abolish it, and to institute new government, laying its foundation on such principles and organizing its powers in such form, as to them shall seem most likely to effect their safety and happiness.

This brief statement contains the substance of Jefferson's political philosophy, which may be reduced to four principles: (1) that the universe and man in it are governed by natural law; (2) that all men are endowed with certain natural and imprescriptible rights; (3) that governments exist to secure these rights; and (4) that all just governments derive their authority from the consent of the governed. These principles, made explicit in our Federal and state constitutions, are still the foundation of the political system which Thomas Jefferson did so much to establish. It is indeed appropriate, therefore, in this memorial year, for us to ask, What is still living in this political philosophy? In order to answer this question, I will break it down into two more specific questions. First, what did Jefferson understand by natural law and natural rights, and what form of government did he think best suited to secure those rights? And, second, to what extent is his conception of rights and of government still valid for our time?

The doctrine of natural law, as it was understood by Jefferson and his contemporaries, was revolutionary only in the sense that it was a reinterpretation, in secular and liberal terms, of the Christian theory of the origin, nature, and destiny of man. As commonly understood in the eighteenth century, it was perhaps never better defined than by the French writer Volney.

> Natural law is the regular and constant order of facts by which God rules the universe; the order which his wisdom presents to the sense and reason of men, to serve them as an equal and common rule of conduct, and to guide them, without distinction of race or sect, towards perfection and happiness.[3]

---

[3] *Oeuvres de Volney* (2d ed., Paris, 1826), I, 249.

For Jefferson, as for Volney, God still existed. But for them God the Father of Christian tradition had become attenuated into God the Creator, or First Cause. Having created the world for a beneficent purpose and on a rational plan, the Creator had withdrawn from the immediate and arbitrary control of human affairs into the dim recesses where absolute being dwells, leaving men to work out their own salvation as best they could. But this they could do very well, because the Creator had revealed his purposes, not in Holy Writ but in the open Book of Nature, which all men, in the light of reason, could read and interpret. "Is it simple," exclaimed Rousseau, "is it natural, that God should have gone in search of Moses to speak to Jean Jacques Rousseau?" To Jefferson, as to Volney, it seemed more natural to suppose that God had revealed his purpose in his works, from which it followed that the whole duty of man was progressively to discover the invariable laws of nature and of nature's God and to bring their ideas, their conduct, and their political and social institutions into harmony with them.

From this conception of natural law Jefferson derived the doctrine that all men are created equal and are endowed with certain natural rights. Many otherwise intelligent men have thought to refute Jefferson by pointing out that all men are in fact not equal. With the same ingenuity and poverty of imagination one could refute St. Augustine's doctrine of the brotherhood of man by pointing out that all men are in fact not brothers. St. Augustine would have said that all men are brothers in the sight of God, and Jefferson's doctrine of equality comes to the same thing. All men are equal in the possession of a common humanity, and if they are in fact not equal and have not in fact the same rights and privileges, the highest morality, both for the individual and for society, is to act on the assumption that all men should be accorded, so far as is humanly possible, the same consideration and opportunity. To act on this assumption would be, both for the individual and for society, to do the will of God and to live the good life.

In these respects—in respect to the primary values of life—the natural rights philosophy was essentially at one with the Christian faith; but in respect to the means by which these values might be realized, it differed sharply from current official Christian teaching. It denied that man is naturally prone to evil and error and for that reason incapable, apart from the compulsion of church and state, of arriving at the truth or living the good life. It affirmed, on the contrary, that men are endowed by their Creator with reason, in order that they may progressively discover that which is true, and with conscience, in order that they may be disposed, in the measure of their enlightenment, to follow that which is good. It was perhaps the dominant quality of Jefferson's mind and temperament, as it was of so many of his contemporaries, to have faith in the dignity and worth of the individual man, and it was for this reason that, in respect to the means for achieving the good life, they relied so confidently upon the negative principle of freedom of the individual from social constraint: freedom of opinion, in order that the truth might prevail; freedom of occupation and of enterprise, in order that careers might be open to talent; freedom from arbitrary political authority, in order that no man might be compelled against his will.

These freedoms were precisely what Jefferson meant by "liberty" as one of the natural rights of man, and it was through the fullest enjoyment of these freedoms that the "pursuit of happiness" would be most likely to result in the greatest happiness for the greatest number of men. And so we arrive at the central idea of the natural rights philosophy as to the proper function of government—the happy idea that the best way to secure the natural rights of men is just to leave them as free as possible to enjoy them, and that no form of government can secure these rights so well as the one that governs least. This idea was so engaging that anyone with an unbounded faith in the natural goodness of men and an equal faith in formal logic could push straight on to the conclusion arrived at by Proudhon—the conclusion that "property is theft," that all governments exist to condone it, and that men will never be free and happy until all governments are abolished.

Fortunately, Jefferson had not sufficient faith either in logic or in the native goodness of men to carry him that far. He had more faith in the goodness of men than some of his contemporaries—more, for example, than John Adams, but less than some others—less, for example, than Samuel Adams or Thomas Paine. He had a logical mind, but logic was not for him "a systematic way," as has been said, "of going wrong with confidence"—not, that is, a dialectical device for manipulating empty concepts in the void in vain—but a method of reaching sound conclusions on the basis of knowledge and common sense. History and political experience, rather than abstract political speculation, convinced Jefferson that men had been governed too much, and above all too arbitrarily, by kings claiming divine right, and that among the institutions that obscured the native goodness of men by depriving them of equal rights none was less defensible than a hereditary aristocracy enjoying privileges that were unearned and exacting a deference that was unmerited. It seemed to him self-evident, therefore, that men could govern themselves better than kings and aristocrats, whose powers rested upon the accident of birth, could do it for them. Not that the people could govern themselves in perfection or without difficulty. All forms of government had their evils, and the principal evil of popular government, Jefferson said, was "turbulence"; but "weigh this against the oppressions of monarchy, and it becomes nothing." [4]

Jefferson was thus profoundly convinced that republican government—government by representatives elected by the people—was the best form, because "it is the only form of government that is not eternally at open or se-

---

[4] *The Writings of Thomas Jefferson*, ed. Paul L. Ford (New York, 1892–99), IV, 362.

cret war with the rights of mankind." [5] But what, in concrete instances, did Jefferson mean by the people, and how was the consent of the governed to be obtained? The people in this sense might mean all the people in the world, or all the people in Virginia, or all the people composing a particular class or sect. Practical statesman that he was, Jefferson took the world, politically speaking, as he found it, divided into groups that by tradition and community of interest regarded themselves, and were commonly regarded, as nations. Such nations might at any time "assume, among the powers of the earth, that equal and independent station to which the laws of nature and of nature's God entitle them." Thus nations as well as individuals had their natural rights—the right of national self-determination. But nations are composed of individuals, and individuals necessarily differ in their interests and opinions; and it seemed to Jefferson self-evident that the only practical way of reconciling these differences was by majority vote. Even a monarchy with all of its trappings, or an aristocracy with all of its privileges, if supported by a majority vote, would be a "just government," because it would rest upon "the consent of the governed."

The right of national self-determination and majority vote—these were fundamental to all of Jefferson's ideas about the particular form of government best suited to any country at any time. Not that majority vote conferred upon the majority of the moment any fundamental right not shared by the minority. It was simply a necessary device imposed upon individuals bound by their nature to live together, and aiming to live together with the maximum degree of harmony and good will; and Jefferson justified it by saying that, this law disregarded, "no other remains but that of force, which ends necessarily in military despotism." [6] There is, of course, no more obdurate problem in political philosophy than the problem of the one and the many, the difficulty being to reconcile the desirable liberties of the individual with the necessary powers of society; and Jefferson was no more successful in solving it than other political philosophers have been. His solution, such as it is, is presented in a letter to Dupont de Nemours, some portions of which I venture to quote, because in it Jefferson states categorically, and perhaps better than anywhere else, the principal tenets of his political faith.

I believe with you that morality, compassion, generosity, are innate elements of the human constitution; that there exists a right independent of force; that the right to property is founded on our natural wants, in the measure with which we are endowed to satisfy these wants, and the right to what we acquire by those means without violating the similar rights of other sensible beings; that no one has a right to obstruct another exercising his faculty in-

---

[5] *Ibid.,* V, 147.
[6] *Ibid.,* X, 89.

nocently for the relief of sensibilities made a part of his nature; that justice is the fundamental law of society; that the majority, oppressing an individual, is guilty of a crime, abuses its strength, and by acting on the law of the strongest breaks up the foundations of society; that action by the citizens in person, in affairs within their reach and competence, and in all others by representatives, chosen immediately, and removable by themselves, constitutes the essence of a republic; that all governments are more or less republican in proportion as this principle enters more or less into their composition; and that government by a republic is capable of extension over a greater surface of country than any other form.[7]

In this passage, as in most of Jefferson's political writings, we can note the disposition to believe that man is naturally good but that men are prone to evil; or, translating it into political terms, that citizens in the mass are to be trusted but that citizens elected to office need to be carefully watched. I have quoted Jefferson as saying that the chief evil of republican government is "turbulence," but he did not really think so. On the contrary, he believed that a little turbulence now and then would do no harm, since it would serve to remind elected officials that their authority was merely a franchise from the people. What Jefferson really believed is that political power is inherently dangerous and that the chief evil of any form of government is to have too much of it. From this it followed that the chief aim in devising a republican government should be to disperse power among magistrates, separate it in respect to function, and otherwise to limit it by applying the grand negative principle of checks and balances. Jefferson agreed with Thomas Paine that whereas society is the result of our virtues government is the result of our vices and is therefore a necessary evil: necessary, in order to preserve order, protect property, and guarantee contracts; an evil, because inherently prone to magnify its authority and thereby impair the liberties of the individual.

Jefferson's ideal of a democratic society was best realized in a small agricultural community, such as he was familiar with at Monticello, composed of a few men of substance and learning, such as himself and his friend James Madison, and otherwise chiefly of industrious, upstanding yeoman farmers, making altogether a community of good neighbors in which everyone knows who is who and what is being done and who is doing it. The affairs of such a community, being easily within the "reach and competence" of the people, could be easily managed by them with the minimum of officials, exercising the minimum of authority, and attended with the minimum of palaver and ceremonial display. Unfortunately, this ideal community could not live to itself, and in managing the affairs of the larger area it was necessary for the people to act through representatives. This departure from the ideal was the beginning of danger, but there was no help for it except to prepare in good

---

[7] *Ibid.*, X, 24.

time by electing the representatives for very short terms and limiting their power to very specific matters.

The general principle would then be that the wider the area the less safe it would be to intrust representatives with power; and from this principle it followed that representatives from the counties to the state capital of Virginia could be safely intrusted with more power than could be safely intrusted to representatives from Virginia to Philadelphia. That the states must remain united Jefferson fully realized; but he was convinced that they should retain their sovereign powers, and at first the Articles of Confederation seemed to him very nearly the ideal form for such a union. When experience proved that a "more perfect union" was necessary, he approved of the Constitution of 1787 but insisted, as a safeguard against too much power in the hands of a government far removed from the people, that a bill of rights should be incorporated in the Constitution and that the powers therein granted to the Federal government should be strictly and narrowly interpreted.[8] As it happened, Jefferson's grasp of international political realities was destined to override this principle. He pushed through the purchase of Louisiana, in spite of the fact that in doing so he was exercising an authority which he believed he did not possess.[9] That perverse circumstances should have made Thomas Jefferson the man to usurp power from the people is ironical enough, and it troubled his political conscience not a little; but he could console himself with the reflection that he had tried, although in vain, to get an amendment to the Constitution to authorize the act and that in any case his conscience was clear, since he had acted solely for the public good.

Closely associated with Jefferson's fear of the open usurpation of political power was his fear of the secret and more insidious influences by which men become debased and corrupted. Republican government, he was well aware, could not be very successful unless the majority of the citizens were independent, honest, and reasonably intelligent. Intelligence could be sufficiently trained and directed by education—schools for the people and colleges for the leaders. But honesty and independence depended less upon precept than upon the conditions in which men lived. The best conditions were those of country life. "Cultivators of the earth," Jefferson said, "are the most virtuous citizens." Vice, he thought, flourished chiefly in cities and in industrial communities which produce cities. In cities, where most people are unacquainted with each other, unscrupulous men could push their selfish interests under cover of the general indifference; and industrial communities, making so much use of impalpable and evanescent forms of wealth, opened the door to speculation for unearned profit, encouraged greed, and rewarded

---

[8] *Ibid.,* V, 41–42, 45, 81.

[9] Jefferson's views are given in a letter to Robert R. Livingston, April 18, 1802 (*ibid.,* VIII, 143), in which he makes the much quoted statement about "marrying ourselves to the British fleet and nation." The reasons given by Jefferson for uniting with the British fleet and nation are as valid today as they were in 1802.

useless luxury: provided all the conditions, in short, for the rise of a corrupt and politically influential "money power." Jefferson regarded commerce and industry as necessary adjuncts to agriculture, but he had the farmer's settled antipathy to banks. "The exercise, by our own citizens, of so much commerce as may suffice to exchange our superfluities for our wants," he cautiously admitted, "may be advantageous to the whole"; but he was convinced that it would be fatal for us "to become a mere city of London, to carry on the commerce of half the world at the expense of waging eternal war with the other half." Capital invested in agriculture or useful industry was productively employed; but "all the capital employed in paper speculation is barren and useless, producing, like that on a gaming table, no accession to itself." And as for banks, they "are a blot left in all our constitutions, which, if not removed, will end in their destruction." [10] Jefferson was never weary of pointing to England as the most striking example of a country losing its freedom by the unchecked multiplication of such evils, and he was convinced that the United States would suffer the same loss if it did not profit in time by that example.

Such in brief was the political philosophy of Thomas Jefferson—his conception of human rights and of the form of government best suited to secure these rights. What then is still living in this political philosophy? To what extent is his conception of rights still valid for us? To what extent is the form of government recommended by him well adapted for securing the rights, whatever they are, that need to be secured in our time?

Any comprehensive study of Jefferson and his writings is apt, sooner or later, to leave one with the impression that he was more at home in the world of ideas than in the world of men and affairs. He had little of Franklin's zest for life in the rough, little of his genial, tolerant acceptance of men as they are, and none of his talent for being comfortable in crowds, or of hobnobbing on equal terms with persons of every station, from kings to scullions in the kitchen. Jefferson was a democrat by intellectual conviction but by training and temperament a Virginia aristocrat—a man of cultivated tastes and preferences, with an aversion from all that is crude and boisterous, vulgar and passionate, in human intercourse. It may be said that he felt with his mind, as some people think with the heart. John Adams said that Jefferson's writings were characterized by "a peculiar felicity of expression." [11] They were indeed—perhaps a little too much so. In reading Jefferson's writings one feels that it would be a relief to come now and then on a hard, uncompromising, passionate sentence, such as: "As for me, give me liberty or give me death!" What we expect to find is rather: "Manly sentiment bids us die freemen rather than live as slaves." Jefferson's ideas were also characterized by a peculiar felicity, and also perhaps a little too much

---

[10] *Ibid.,* III, 279; X, 28, 34.
[11] *Works of John Adams,* II, 514.

so. One feels that they come a little too easily to birth and rest a little precariously on the ideal aspirations of good men and not sufficiently on the harsh, brute facts of the world as it is. Jefferson was no visionary, and on occasions, such as the purchase of Louisiana, he exhibited a remarkable grasp of political realities. But it was entirely characteristic of him that, in respect to the Embargo, he should have taken the position that since our rights were in principle equally violated by England and France, they should be impartially defended against both countries, although England alone was in fact able to do us any material injury; equally characteristic that the high aim of his policy was to defend our rights by humane and peaceful methods, and the signal effect of it to inflict more material injury on the United States than on either of the countries by which its rights had been violated. One often feels that if there had been a little more humane sentiment and a good deal more passion in Jefferson's make-up, he would have been an out and out non-resistance pacifist. As it is, he presents us with the anomaly of a revolutionist who hated violence and a President of the United States who was disconcerted by the possession of political power.

If Jefferson was more at home in the world of ideas than in the world of men and affairs, it follows that, as a political philosopher, he was a better judge of ends than of means. In all that relates to the fundamental values of life, for the individual and for society, in all that relates to the ideal aims which the democratic form of government aims to realize, his understanding was profound. But in respect to the means, the particular institutions by which these values and ideal aims may be realized, he was often at fault, if not for his own time at least for ours; and when he was at fault he was so partly because he conceived of society as more static than it really is and partly because he conceived of American society as something that might remain predominantly agricultural and with relatively simple institutional devices be kept isolated in a relatively arcadian simplicity. But Jefferson's chief limitation as a political philosopher (and in fairness to him it should be remembered that it was the limitation of most political philosophers of his time) was that he was unduly influenced by the idea that the only thing to do with political power, since it is inherently dangerous, is to abate it. He failed to appreciate sufficiently the hard fact that political power always exists in the world and will be used by those who possess it; and as a consequence of this failure he was too much concerned with negative devices designed to obstruct the use of political power for bad ends and not sufficiently concerned with positive devices designed to make use of it for good ends.

This gives us then our general answer. In respect to fundamentals—the nature of human rights and the form of government best suited to secure them—Jefferson's philosophy is still valid for us; in respect to particular political forms and policies, much of it is now outmoded. In elaborating this general answer I can touch only on the main points.

None of Jefferson's ideas is so irrelevant to our needs as that concerning cities and industrial communities, not because there is not much truth in what he has to say about them but because his hope that the United States might remain a predominantly agricultural society was entirely misplaced. During Jefferson's time there was occurring a revolution of which he was unaware, or the significance of which he at all events entirely failed to grasp. I refer, of course, to the Industrial, or more properly the Technological, Revolution, brought about by the discovery of steam power, electricity, and radiation. It was one of the two or three major revolutions in the history of civilization, since by giving men an unprecedented control over material things it transformed, within a brief span of years, the relatively simple agricultural societies of the eighteenth century into societies far more complex and integrated and at the same time far more mobile and swiftly changing than any ever known before—formidable, blank-faced Leviathans that Thomas Jefferson would have regarded as unreal, fantastic, and altogether unsuited to liberty and equality as he understood those terms. That Jefferson did not foresee this momentous revolution is no discredit to him: no one in his time foresaw it more than dimly. But the point is that these are the societies in which we live and in connection with which we have to reconsider the nature of human rights and the institutions best suited to secure them; and it is now clear that Jefferson's favorite doctrine of laissez faire in respect to economic enterprise, and therefore in respect to political policy also, can no longer serve as a guiding principle for securing the rights of men to life, liberty, and the pursuit of happiness.

The doctrine of laissez faire, as it was understood by Jefferson and the social philosophers of the early nineteenth century, rested upon the assumption that if each individual within the nations, and each nation among the nations, was left as free as possible to pursue its own interest, something not themselves, God or Nature, would do whatever else was necessary for righteousness; or, better still, as Professor Carr puts it in his recent book, the assumption that from the unrestrained pursuit of individual self-interest a "harmony of interests" would more or less automatically emerge.[12] In the political realm this meant that the function of government should be confined in principle to the protection of life and property, the guaranteeing of contracts, the preservation of civil order, and the defense of the country against aggression. In the economic realm it meant that the free play of individual initiative, stimulated by the acquisitive instinct, would result in the maximum production of wealth, and that the competitive instinct, functioning through the price system, would result in as equitable a distribution of wealth as the qualities and defects of men permitted. In the international world it meant that the promotion of its own interest and power by each sovereign state would tend to create a balance of power and of interests which would serve,

---

[12] Edward H. Carr, *The Conditions of Peace* (Toronto, 1942), p. 105.

better than any other system, to promote commercial exchanges and cultural relations and to preserve the peace.

It is now sufficiently clear that the doctrine of laissez faire—of letting things go—however well adapted it may have been to the world in which Jefferson lived, is not well adapted to the world in which we live. In a world so highly integrated economically, a world in which the tempo of social change is so accelerated and the technological power at the disposal of corporations and governments is so enormous and can be so easily used for anti-social ends—in such a world the unrestrained pursuit of individual and national self-interest results neither in the maximum production or the equitable distribution of wealth, nor in the promotion of international comity and peace, but in social class conflicts and in total and global wars so ruthless as to threaten the destruction of all interests, individual and national, and even the foundations of civilized living. In such a world the inalienable right to life, liberty, and the pursuit of happiness can be secured, not by letting things go and trusting to God or Nature to see that they go right but in deciding beforehand where they ought to go and doing what is desirable and possible to make them go there. The harmony of interests, if there is to be any, must be deliberately and socially designed and deliberatively and co-operatively worked for. To bring this harmony of interests to pass is now the proper function of government; and it will assuredly not be brought to pass by any government that proceeds on the assumption that the best government is the one that governs least.

The history of the United States during a hundred years past confirms this conclusion and thereby refutes Jefferson's idea that the several states should retain their sovereign powers, and that the powers of the Federal government should be strictly and narrowly interpreted. Decade by decade the states have lost their sovereign powers, and the Federal government, by virtue of a liberal interpretation of the Constitution and of amendments to it, has assumed the authority to pass legislation limiting the activities of some individuals in order to secure the rights of others. This expansion of power and enlargement of function has been brought about, in spite of the inertia of traditional ideas and the pressure of interested groups, by the insistent need of regulating the activities of great corporations which, although in theory private enterprises, are in fact public utilities, and thereby possess irresponsible power which they are sometimes unwilling but more often unable to use for the public good. It is in respect to this situation that the engaging word "liberty" emerges in a guise unknown to Jefferson and his contemporaries. In his time the most obvious oppressions, for the majority of men, were the result of arbitrary governmental restrictions on the activities of individuals, so that liberty could be most easily conceived in terms of the emancipation of the individual from governmental constraint. But in our time the development of free economic enterprise has created a situation in which the most obvious oppressions, for the majority of men, arise not from an excess of governmental regulation but from the lack of it, so that in our time liberty can be understood only in terms of more and more intelligently designed supervision of free economic enterprise. Jefferson and his contemporaries, as James Bryce has well said, "mistook the pernicious channels in which selfish propensities had been flowing for those propensities themselves, which were sure to find new channels when the old had been destroyed." [13] The selfish propensities with which we have to deal are the same as those with which Jefferson and his contemporaries had to deal, but since the channels—the particular institutions and customs—through which they flow are different, the remedies have to be different also.

In this respect—in respect to the proper function of government—the political philosophy of Jefferson is now outmoded. But this is after all the more superficial aspect of Jefferson's philosophy, and if we turn to its more fundamental aspects—to the form of government as distinct from its function, and to the essential rights to be secured as distinct from the particular institutional forms for securing them—we find that Jefferson's political philosophy is as valid for our time as it was for his.

Jefferson was profoundly convinced that the best form of government was the republican—that is, government by elected representatives—because it was the only form, as he said, that "is not eternally at open or secret war with the rights of mankind." The form of government which Jefferson did so much to establish still exists, essentially unchanged; and today we accept it with even less qualification and divided loyalty than obtained in Jefferson's time. We accept it for many reasons, no doubt—because it has on the whole worked so well, because we have become habituated to it, and because there is in our political tradition no model for any other form. But we also accept it for the same reason that Jefferson accepted it—because we are profoundly convinced that it is the one form of government that is not at war with the rights of mankind, or at all events with those familiar rights and privileges which we regard as in some sense natural, because from long settled habit they seem to us so imprescriptibly American.

Recent events have greatly strengthened this conviction. Twenty years ago we were in a mood to ask whether the representative system of government might not be, if not at open, at least too often at secret, war with the rights of mankind. That was the result of comparing the democratic practice with the democratic ideal, with the inevitable if perhaps salutary effect of magnifying the defects and minimizing the virtues of democratic government as a going concern. But for ten years past now we have been permitted, have indeed been compelled, to reappraise democratic government in the light, not of the ideal, but of the practical alternative as presented for our admiration in Germany and elsewhere. And the result of this reappraisal has been to convince us that the defects of our system of government are, in comparison, trivial,

---

[13] *Modern Democracies* (New York, 1921), I, 49.

while its virtues are substantial. Indeed the incredible cynicism of Adolf Hitler's way of regarding man and the life of man, made real by the servile and remorseless activities of his bleak-faced, humorless Nazi supporters, has forced men everywhere to re-examine the validity of half-forgotten ideas and to entertain once more half-discarded convictions as to the substance of things not seen. One of these convictions is that "liberty, equality, fraternity," and the "inalienable rights" of man are phrases, glittering or not, that denote realities—the fundamental realities that men will always fight and die for rather than surrender.

In defense of these rights and of our democratic form of government, we are now fighting a desperate war; and in justification of our action we are advancing the same reasons that Jefferson proclaimed—that the democratic form of government is the one best adapted to secure the inalienable rights of man. We may be less sure than Jefferson was that a beneficent intelligence created the world for man's special convenience. We may think that the laws of nature, and especially the laws of human nature, are less easily discovered than he supposed. We may have found it more difficult to define the natural rights of man and to secure them by simple institutional forms than he anticipated. Above all, we may have learned that human reason is not quite so infallible an instrument for arriving at the truth as he supposed it to be and that men are less amenable to rational persuasion. Nevertheless, in essentials Jefferson's political philosophy is our political philosophy; in essentials democracy means for us what it meant for him.

Democracy is for us, as it was for him, primarily a set of values, a way of regarding man and the life of man. It is for us, as it was for him, also a set of concrete institutions through which these values may be realized. We now realize, as he did, but rather better than he did, that the institutional forms are bound to change: they have changed since Jefferson's time, they are changing now, and they will change still further in time to come. But we may believe, as Jefferson did, that the values themselves are enduring; one reason for believing so being the fact that the values we cherish are the same as those which Jefferson proclaimed and the same as those which for more than two thousand years the saints and sages of the world have regarded as the ideal aim and ultimate test of civilized living. If we were to write a Declaration of the modern democratic faith, it might run somewhat as follows:

We hold these truths to be self-evident: that the individual man has dignity and worth in his own right; that it is better to be governed by persuasion than by force; that fraternal good will is of greater worth than a selfish and contentious spirit; that in the long run all values, both for the individual and for society, are inseparable from the love of truth and the disinterested search for it; that the truth can be discovered only insofar as the mind of man is free; that knowledge and the power it gives should be used for promoting the welfare and happiness of all men rather than for the selfish interests of those individuals and classes whom intelligence and fortune have endowed with a temporary advantage; and that no form of government yet invented is so well adapted to realize these high ends as one that is designed to be a government of the people, by the people, for the people.

To this declaration of the modern democratic faith Thomas Jefferson would subscribe, I feel sure, without qualification. And it is in this sense, the most important sense of all, that his philosophy, and still more the humane and liberal spirit of the man himself, abides with us, as a living force, to clarify our purposes, to strengthen our faith, and to fortify our courage.

PART TWO

THE NINETEENTH CENTURY

RUTH MILLER ELSON

AMERICAN SCHOOLBOOKS AND "CULTURE" IN THE NINETEENTH CENTURY

The persistent moralism of nineteenth-century Americans, their devotion to utility in contrast to an indifference to esthetics, and their self-regarding nationalism continue to fascinate historians concerned with understanding and defining the national temper. Elson's discussion may not explain the origins of these cultural traits, but it goes a long way toward explaining how they were perpetuated and how they were modified over time. This article also deserves attention for still another reason: its meticulous examination of children's textbooks, a source of information about the American mentality that is usually ignored by cultural historians. Professor Elson's comments on these textbooks, studied in conjunction with the discussions of folk heroes and manifest destiny, will reveal much about the development of American values.

Students may wish to consult any of the great studies of American character from De Tocqueville on; they should also see Ruth Miller Elson, Guardians of Tradition: American Schoolbooks of the Nineteenth Century *(1964).*

113

$\mathbf{D}$oes America have a culture of its own? Has America contributed to that concept of culture which Noah Webster and the nineteenth century defined as "the enlightenment and refinement of taste acquired by intellectual and aesthetic training"? [1] This issue has been lightly and hotly debated across the Atlantic for a century and a half, and European criticisms of our contributions to scholarship and the fine arts made Americans painfully sensitive to any trans-Atlantic discussions in these areas. But the discussion in the United States was continuous; it reached points of egocentric frenzy at times when Americans were particularly proud of themselves in other respects vis-à-vis Europe, as in the periods after the American Revolution, the War of 1812, and World War II. The discussion has generally revolved around two questions: Has the United States produced art and scholarship of a quality comparable to that of Europe? Has the United States a literary and aesthetic culture of its own?

After the Revolution these issues were posed by American writers and intellectuals when they called for the development of a distinctively American culture. Immediately after the achievement of American political independence, Noah Webster hoped to separate America from Britain culturally by the creation of a distinctive American system of spelling. Charles Brockden Brown called on American literary men to use the resources of the American scene and, in his novel *Wieland,* illustrated his point by transposing the Gothic novel from the ruined castle of Europe to the American forest. In 1837 Ralph Waldo Emerson issued his famous declaration of independence for American scholars in an address at Harvard. The activities of James Fenimore Cooper, William Cullen Bryant, and others in calling for an American art as well as in creating one are well known.

That the American intellectual in the first part of our national existence wished to encourage American creativity in the fine arts and in scholarship cannot be questioned. But was the ordinary American aware of this? Was he encouraged to consider these fields worth cultivating in America? Was the intellectual climate in which the Americans lived favorable to the development of American scholars, or were potential scholars generally turned into the more useful field of schoolteaching? Was the American public encouraged to consider the fine arts an important element in national development?

What the a-verbal man of the past thought about anything is probably forever lost to historical research. But by examining the books that most Americans read one can at least discover those ideas to which they were exposed. In

---

[1] *Webster's New International Dictionary* (2nd ed., Springfield, Mass., 1946).

FROM Ruth Miller Elson, "American Schoolbooks and 'Culture' in the Nineteenth Century," *Mississippi Valley Historical Review,* Vol. XLVI (December 1959), pp. 411–34. Reprinted by permission.

the nineteenth century, apart from the Bible, the books most widely read were not those written by intellectuals, but schoolbooks written by printers, journalists, future lawyers earning their way through college, teachers, and ministers.[2] However ill-qualified to do so, the authors of schoolbooks both created and solidified American traditions. The selective process by which they decided what political, economic, social, cultural, and moral concepts should be presented to American youth undoubtedly helped to form the average American's view of the past, the present, and the possible future of man. The choice of what was to be admired in the past and present and preserved for the future was likely to be the first formal evaluation of man and his works to which the child was exposed, and it came to him from authority. The schoolbooks also delineated for the American child an idealized image of himself and of the history that had produced the much-admired American type. These books, then, were a kind of compendium of ideas popularly approved at the time, and they are an excellent index of concepts considered proper for the nineteenth-century American.[3] And while their nationalism demanded pride in American productions of any sort, they were far from encouraging to the potential artist or scholar. In these schoolbooks, scholarship and the fine arts were considered fields unfit for the American.

The primary intellectual value embodied in these books is that the only important knowledge is that which is "useful." The word "knowledge" is so often preceded by the word "useful" that it is clear only such knowledge is approved, and it is this kind of knowledge that is provided by a sound education. Useful knowledge is presumed to be uniquely characteristic of American education. The best definition of this "useful knowledge" as used in nineteenth-century schoolbooks comes from an 1807 reader, and was acceptable throughout the century:

> Our government and habits are republican; they cherish equal rights and tend to an equal distribution of property. Our mode of education has the same tendency to promote an equal distribution of knowledge, and to make us emphatically a "republic of letters." I would not be understood adept in the fine arts, but participants of useful knowledge. . . . We are all scholars in the useful; and employed in improving the works of nature, rather than in imitating them.[4]

---

[2] By the end of the century experts such as Arnold H. Guyot and Matthew F. Maury in geography and John Fiske and Edward Channing in history were used. But the books most read—the spellers and readers—continued to be turned out by those who were apparently learning by doing.

[3] This paper is part of a larger study of the social and cultural concepts in nineteenth-century schoolbooks. It is based on an analysis of 1,050 of the most popular readers, spellers, geographies, histories, and some arithmetics used in American schools from 1776 to 1900. Most of them are available in the Plimpton Collection in the Columbia University Library.

[4] Caleb Bingham, *The Columbian Orator* (Boston, 1807), 299.

And because of our special preparation in this kind of knowledge, the useful arts have become the peculiar province of the American. A reader of the 1850's notes: "In the arts which contribute to domestic culture and national aggrandizement, the American states will sustain no unfavorable comparison with Europe." [5] By the latter part of the century American achievements in this area have been recognized by all: "The ingenuity of the people of the United States has passed into a proverb. To them are due many of the inventions which have contributed most to the comfort and improvement of the race." [6] Thus useful knowledge is interpreted in a narrow sense; those arts that are functional to a more comfortable material life are equated to republicanism and to Americanism. Talents in these fields are inherent in the Americans and unique to them: "While many other nations are wasting the brilliant efforts of genius in monuments of ingenious folly, to perpetuate their pride, the Americans, according to the true spirit of republicanism, are employed almost entirely in works of public and private utility." [7]

In all of these books the fact that we have not produced scholars is noted with pride as a sign that knowledge is democratically diffused instead of being concentrated in the hands of an upper class:

> In the monarchical and aristocratic governments of Europe . . . . a few privileged orders monopolize not only the wealth and honors, but the knowledge of their country. They produce a few profound scholars, who make study the business of their lives; we acquire a portion of science as a necessary instrument of livelihood, and deem it absurd to devote our whole lives to the acquisition of implements, without having it in our power to make them useful to ourselves or others.[8]

Our institutions of higher learning are not designed to produce scholars; they are institutions

> Where homebred freemen seize the solid prize;
> Fixt in small spheres with safer beams to shine.
> They reach the useful and refuse the fine,
> Found on its proper base, the social plan,
> The broad plain truths, the common sense of man.[9]

---

[5] Epes Sargent, *The Standard Fourth Reader* (Boston, 1856), 167. See also William Swinton, *Swinton's Fifth Reader and Speaker* (New York, 1883), 411–13; Joel D. Steele and Esther B. Steele, *A Brief History of the United States* (New York, 1898), 307–308.

[6] George P. Quackenbos, *American History for Schools* (New York, 1879), 305.

[7] Jedidiah Morse, *Geography Made Easy* (Boston, 1791), 87. See also William H. McGuffey, *McGuffey's New Juvenile Speaker* (Cincinnati, 1860), 55–56.

[8] Bingham, *Columbian Orator*, 299.

[9] Rodolphus Dickinson, *The Columbian Reader* (Boston, 1815), 188, quoted from Joel Barlow.

Another book notes happily: "There are none of those splendid establishments such as Oxford and Cambridge in which immense salaries maintain the professors of literature in monastic idleness. . . . The People of this country have not yet been inclined to make much literary display—They have rather aimed at works of general utility." [10] Instead of such aristocratic institutions, public schools and small libraries have been set up in towns and villages all over the United States, "which serve a more valuable purpose, in the general diffusion of knowledge." [11] Instead of an isolated group of scholars toiling away in useless labor we produce educated men whose minds are bent to the improvement of society. "The greatest scholars of the country . . . have not deemed the latter [schoolbooks] an unworthy labor." [12] Most of our learned men "are so devoted to the instruction of youth, or the active employments of life, as to leave little opportunity for the prosecution of literary research, or scientific discovery." [13] And indeed the actual situation described here was sometimes elevated and abstracted into a principle of virtuous behavior for scholars: "It is not in literary production only, or chiefly, that the educated mind finds fit expression, and fulfills its mission in honor and beneficence. In the great theatre of the world's affairs there is a worthy and sufficient sphere." [14] Even on an elementary level scholarship was associated with Europe rather than with America. A delightful illustration of this occurs in an 1828 reader. Next to a picture entitled "German with Book" is the sentence: "The Germans read, write, and think a great deal." [15] Such activities were evidently not to be regarded by the child as part of the ordinary life of man, but were worthy of note as functions of a particular foreign culture.

Besides reserving education for the elite and sponsoring useless knowledge, the European universities have another serious disadvantage which is corrected in American institutions of higher learning. "The colleges and universities of Europe differ materially from those of the United States. They are rather places of study for such as wish to acquire knowledge. Scarcely any control or care is exercised over the character and conduct of the students, and their efforts are purely voluntary." [16] As a result, although the European university produced serious scholars it also produced men learned in the ways

---

10 John L. Blake, *A Geographical, Chronological, and Historical Atlas* (New York, 1826), 165.

11 William C. Woodbridge and Emma Willard, *Universal Geography, Ancient and Modern* (Hartford, 1824), 205.

12 William H. Venable, *A School History of the United States* (Cincinnati, 1872), 183.

13 William C. Woodbridge, *System of Modern Geography* (Hartford, 1866), 339.

14 Floyd B. Wilson, *Wilson's Book of Recitations and Dialogues* (New York, 1869), 159, quoted from George R. Putnam.

15 [Eliza Robbins], *American Popular Lessons* (New York, 1828), 22.

16 Woodbridge, *System of Modern Geography*, 345.

of drink, gambling, dissipation, and vice—activities that aroused transports of horror in the schoolbooks.[17]

The picture of the American college in these schoolbooks is one of an institution designed to inculcate moral values rather than intellectual ones; it should instill useful knowledge in the sense of principles useful to the maintenance of Christianity (Protestant, except in those books written for the parochial schools), the American form of government, and the American society. The colleges were firmly founded on the principle stated by Webster in a most popular 1805 reader: "How little of our peace and security depends on REASON and how much on *religion* and *government*." [18] The function of the American college was to produce men who were prepared to uphold the values already dominant in society rather than to examine them critically. It was the formation of character and sound principles rather than the pursuit of truth that was to engage the university student. This conception of the function of higher education in America has interesting implications for the principle of academic freedom. If the primary duty of the professor is to train the student in principles accepted as good by American society, then it is logical to contend that American society has the right to investigate the beliefs held by college teachers.

It was not the university, however, that was regarded in American schoolbooks as the most effective carrier of civilization; it was rather the common school that was to perpetuate what the authors considered most important in American civilization. Every author pointed with pride to the public school system as one of the most distinctive features of American civilization. A typical statement, emphasizing spread rather than depth, is the following: "Education is more widely diffused in this than in any other country in the world." [19] And America's devotion to universal education is old: "The idea of popular education was brought to the new world by our forefathers. Even in the wilderness, while the wolf prowled about the log-house, and the cry of the wild-cat was still heard, the school and even the college, were established." [20]

But it is clear from the books used in these schools that the purpose of the common school as well as of the university was to train the heart rather than the head. Emma Willard's preface to her 1868 history was quite explicit: "We have, indeed, been desirous to cultivate the memory, the intellect and the taste. But much more anxious have we been to sow the seeds of virtue by

---

[17] For an example of this see Lucius Osgood, *Osgood's American Fifth Reader* (New York, 1872), 170–73.

[18] Noah Webster, *An American Selection of Lessons in Reading and Speaking* (Salem, Mass., 1805), 147.

[19] Francis McNally, *An Improved System of Geography* (New York, 1875), 54.

[20] [Joel D. Steele], *A Brief History of the United States* (New York, 1889 [?]), 307.

showing the good in such amicable lights that the youthful heart shall kindle into desires of imitation." [21] That virtue is superior to knowledge or even to wisdom was stressed, as in this admonition by Alice Cary: "Little children, you must seek Rather to be good than wise"; [22] or, on a more advanced level, "Man's intellect is not man's sole nor best adorning." [23] It has often been stated in histories of American education that the American public school system was instituted to train citizens, native and immigrant, and to equalize classes, but the evidence of the schoolbooks would seem to indicate that this was to be accomplished by training character as well as by imparting knowledge. The "useful knowledge" offered in the school was useful to success in the material world, but it was also aimed to produce those qualities of character that we associate both with Puritanism and with the self-made man: thrift, hard work, and the rejection of frivolity.

In the early readers and spellers most of the literary excerpts are taken from *The Tatler* and *The Spectator,* from the writings of Franklin, Pope, Sterne, Dryden, Swift, and from various religious tracts. From the 1820's on the contemporary literature of Romanticism became dominant, and remained so throughout the century, disregarding newer trends in literature. Bryant, Longfellow, Whittier, Emerson, and watered down versions of these were fed to the child in a steady diet. Heroism, death, illness, decay, a mystical nationalism, a transcendental approach to nature, and the process of winning success against great odds were the popular subjects. But underlying all of these was the premise that the heart was more important than the head. The nearest approach to realism in the late nineteenth century was in the very large literature of the self-made man; here, although the head was important in achieving success, yet success came only to the pure in heart.

In the schoolbook characterizations of the great men of America some of the same attitudes are evident. All assumed that the function of American society was to produce men great in character as well as in achievements. And all were confident that America was peculiarly distinguished by these virtuous heroes; the United States "has already produced some of the greatest and best men who have ever lived." [24] And in the future:

---

[21] Emma Willard, *Abridged History of the United States or Republic of America* (New York, 1868), preface.

[22] H. I. Gourley and J. N. Hunt, *The Modern Third Reader* (New York, 1882), 196.

[23] Richard G. Parker and J. Madison Watson, *The National Fifth Reader* (New York, 1867), 338. See also William H. McGuffey, *McGuffey's New Fourth Eclectic Reader* (Cincinnati, 1866), 79–80; Epes Sargent, *Sargent's Standard Second Reader* ([1866?], title page missing), 101; Charles W. Sanders, *Sanders' Union Fourth Reader* (New York, 1870), 314–15; William H. McGuffey, *McGuffey's Fourth Eclectic Reader* (New York, [189?], 1879 copyright), 151–53.

[24] John L. Blake, *A Geography for Children* (Boston, 1831), 16–17.

But why may not Columbia's soil
Rear men as great as Britain's isle;
Exceed what Greece and Rome have done,
Or any land beneath the sun? [25]

The distinction between the great men of Europe and those of America was a sharp one in the schoolbooks. American heroes were distinguished for their virtue; European heroes were remembered for their vices as soldiers, or as "great scholars who were pensioned flatterers of power, and poets, who profaned the high gift of genius, to pamper the vices of a corrupted court." [26]

The two men who appeared most often and most emphatically as heroes were George Washington and Benjamin Franklin. In words attributed to John Quincy Adams: "What other two men, whose lives belong to the eighteenth century of Christendom, have left a deeper impression of themselves upon the age in which they lived, and upon all after time?" [27] The heroic stature of Washington was unique; he appeared rather as divinity than as man. As a Christlike liberator the contrast between Washington and European heroes was sharp indeed. That this greatest of all men appeared in the United States is sufficient justification for American civilization:

> At the grand and soothing idea that this greatest instance of human perfectibility, this conspicuous phenomenon of human elevation and grandeur should have been permitted to rise first on the horizon of America, every citizen of these states must feel his bosom beat with rapturous and honest pride, tempered with reverential gratitude to the great author and source of all perfection. . . . He will be penetrated with astonishment, and kindled into thanksgiving when he reflects that our globe had existed six thousand years before a Washington appeared on the theatre of the world; and that he was then destined to appear in America—to be the ornament, the deliverer, the protector, the delight! [28]

The same idea is contained in an excerpt from Daniel Webster's oration at Bunker Hill in 1843, which appears in many books: "America has furnished to the world the character of Washington! And if our American institutions

---

[25] Bingham, *Columbian Orator*, 58.

[26] John Goldsbury and William Russell, *The American Common-School Reader and Speaker* (Boston, 1844), 94–95. See also Sargent, *Standard Fourth Reader*, 313–16; Anon., *Fourth Progressive Reader* (New York, c. 1873), 239–41 (for Catholic schools); Noah Webster, *The Elementary Spelling Book* (New York, 1857), 50, 52.

[27] Goldsbury and Russell, *Common-School Reader*, 419–20; Swinton, *Fifth Reader and Speaker*, 318; [William H. McGuffey], *McGuffey's Alternate Fifth Reader* (Cincinnati, 1888), 299. See also Jesse Torrey, Jr., *Familiar Spelling Book* (Philadelphia, 1825), frontispiece; Epes Sargent, *The Standard Speller* (Boston, 1856), 157; John J. Anderson, *The United States Reader* (New York, 1873), 237–38.

[28] Ignatius Thomson, *The Patriot's Monitor, for New Hampshire* (Randolph, Vt., 1810), 70. See also George S. Hillard, *The Franklin Fifth Reader* (Boston, 1871), 342; Swinton, *Fifth Reader and Speaker*, 372.

had done nothing else, that alone would have entitled them to the respect of mankind." [29]

As they did with all hero-figures, the textbook authors attach to Washington's prestige-giving figure the virtues that they expect the child to emulate, whether these bear any resemblance to the hero's life or not. He is brave, charitable, industrious, religious, courteous, and a paragon of the domestic virtues. The best qualities of the self-made man are his, and from the 1840's on he is exalted as such in many books.[30] But in no instance are intelligence, learning, or disinterested inquiry associated with Washington. Indeed, in some of the later books he is specifically shown as a practical man who rejected the intellectual life. It is said that "He was more solid than brilliant, and had more judgment than genius. He had great dread of public life, cared little for books, and possessed no library." [31] As a child Washington "was fonder of playing out of doors than study in school, for he was a strong, manly boy, who could best all his school-mates in their sports." [32] This would seem to imply an unbridgeable abyss between the physically active boy and the student, between the successful man of affairs and the scholar. Manliness and scholarship would seem to be antithetical. And manliness was for the American, scholarship for the effete European.

Nor are intellectual qualities attached, as in this case they might logically be, to the second hero-figure of these books—Benjamin Franklin. It is not Franklin the scientist, cosmopolite, and democrat who appears here; it is rather Franklin the apotheosis of the self-made man. His temperance, industry, and thrift are praised to the highest degree as ends in themselves rather than as the conveniences that they seem to be to Franklin himself. His biography appears many times, and almost every schoolbook contains some of his adages with or without acknowledgment of their source. Washington is

---

[29] Goldsbury and Russell, *Common School Reader*, 386–88; Marcus Smith, *The Boston Speaker* (Boston, 1844), 19–23; Salem Town, *The Grammar School Reader* (Portland, Me., 1852), 351–53; Epes Sargent, *The Standard Third Reader* (Boston, 1859), 81–82; William H. McGuffey, *McGuffey's New Fifth Eclectic Reader* (Cincinnati, 1866), 273; Anderson, *United States Reader*, 307–308.

[30] Daniel Adams, *The Monitorial Reader* (Concord, N.H., 1845), 210; American Society for the Diffusion of Useful Knowledge, *The English Spelling Book* (New York, 1847), 120; Epes Sargent, *The First Class Standard Reader* (Boston, 1854), 249–51; Joseph B. Burleigh, *The Thinker: A Moral Reader, Part I* (Philadelphia, 1855), 41–43; Charles W. Sanders, *The School Reader, Third Book* (New York, 1864), 233–34; Epes Sargent and Amasa May, *The New American Fifth Reader* (Philadelphia, 1871), 65–66; Mrs. Lewis B. Monroe, *The Story of Our Country* (Boston, 1889), 179–80.

[31] Steele and Steele, *Brief History of the United States* (1898 edition), 150 (same in 1881 and 1889 editions); William T. Harris, Andrew J. Rickoff, and Mark Bailey, *The Fifth Reader* (New York, 1879), 367–69. See also *McGuffey's Alternate Fifth Reader*, 242–44; Monroe, *Story of Our Country*, 180; M. E. Thalheimer, *The Eclectic History of the United States* (Cincinnati, 1881 [actually probably 1888]), 187.

[32] Charles Morris, *Primary History of the United States* (Philadelphia, 1899 [actually includes material to 1904]), 131.

the hero of great actions and virtue; Franklin is the typical American writ large. But in both cases it is moral and patriotic rather than intellectual stature that elevates these Americans.

The only public figure to whom scholarship is ever a sign of distinction is Thomas Jefferson, but he is a quite minor figure in these books, only occasionally noted as a scholar. He is more than offset by Daniel Boone, a figure with obvious appeal to school-children, and one who was "ignorant of books, but versed in the forest and forest life." [33] The American hero-figure was stereotyped, then, as a practical, moral, hard-working man who needs "useful knowledge" to get ahead in the world, but finds scholarship unnecessary and even demeaning.

Was the child specifically encouraged to read on his own? He was exhorted to apply the Franklin virtues to his school work and to the acquisition of "useful knowledge" as a part of his struggle for success in the world. But doubts were frequently expressed as to both the quantity and the quality of books that he should read. He must be careful not to read too much: "She is a strange child. She will take a book and read it while the boys and girls run and play near her. I fear she reads and thinks too much. The brain must have rest." [34] Furthermore the frequent appearance of excerpts from the writings of Emerson and Wordsworth, shorn in this context of transcendental qualities, seems to recommend the achievement of the good life only by the rejection of the intellectual life in favor of direct experience. The following are typical examples:

> Up! up! my friend and quit your books
> Or surely you'll grow double;
> Books! 'Tis a dull and endless strife. . . .[35]
>
> I laugh at the lore and the pride of man,
> At the sophists' schools, and the learned clan;
> For what are they all in their high conceit,
> When man in the bush with God may meet.[36]

---

[33] James Baldwin, *School Reading by Grades: Fifth Year* (New York, 1897), 102. See also William T. Harris, Andrew J. Rickoff, and Mark Bailey, *The Fourth Reader* (New York, 1880), 165–68; Eliza H. Morton, *Potter's Advanced Geography* (Philadelphia, 1891), 78; George F. Holmes and Frank A. Hill, *Holmes' Fourth Reader* (New York, 1899), 221; Morris, *Primary History of the United States*, 172.

[34] Richard Soule and William Wheeler, *First Lessons in Reading* (Boston, 1866), 41. See also Marcius Willson, *The Fifth Reader* (New York, 1872), 163; George S. Hillard, *The Franklin Advanced Fourth or Intermediate Reader* (New York, 1874), 53; A. J. Demarest and William M. Van Sickle, *New Education Readers: Book Two* (New York, 1900), 132.

[35] From Wordsworth's "Vacation Song," quoted in Loomis J. Campbell, *The New Franklin Fourth Reader* (New York, 1884), 215–16.

[36] From Emerson's "Goodby," quoted in Campbell, *The New Franklin Fifth Reader* (New York, 1884), 109–10.

Taken out of context in this way, Wordsworth (more popular in the first half of the century) and Emerson (popular in the second half of the century) seem to stand for anti-intellectualism rather than awareness of the insufficiency of reason. There are countless tales of the value of direct experience over the value of book experience. A typical case is the tale of a boy forced by family difficulties to go to work rather than to go on with school. A merchant about to hire him gives him this advice: "Manhood is better than Greek. Self-reliance is worth more to a man than Latin." [37] Here, obviously, it is the self-reliance of self-support in a financial, not a spiritual, sense that is considered desirable. Emerson has been adapted to the market place.

Apart from the question of quantity, it was thought that reading must be carefully limited in quality to those books that impart "useful knowledge" and that strengthen character. William H. McGuffey, for example, believed that only "good" books are to be used—books that will inspire the reader with "love of what is right and useful." He continued: "Next to the fear of God, implanted in the heart nothing is a better safeguard to character, than the love of good books. They are the handmaids of virtue and religion." [38] Conversely: "Bad books are the public fountains of vice." [39] The reading of novels (and few distinctions are made among them) was almost always condemned in the first half of the century, and frequently in the latter half. An 1868 reader, in seeking the cause of the complete deterioration of a character under discussion, asks: "Is it the bottle or the betting book? Is it the billiard table or the theatre? Is it smoking? Is it laziness? Is it novel-reading?" [40] So the child was cautioned to read with great selectivity—a selectivity based not on training one's taste by wide reading but by canons laid down by authority. He was not only warned not to read too much, but his purpose in reading was to be censored. To read for pleasure was frowned upon: "A book which is torn and mutilated is abused, but one which is merely read for enjoyment is misused." [41]

---

[37] Mrs. Lewis B. Monroe, *The Fifth Reader* (Philadelphia, 1871), 58–59.

[38] *McGuffey's New Fifth Eclectic Reader,* 92.

[39] Henry N. Day, *The American Speller* (New York, 1869), 163. See also M. J. Kerney, *The First Class Book of History* (Baltimore, 1868), 216 (for Catholic schools); Sherman Williams, *Choice Literature: Book I for Grammar Grades* (New York, 1898), 330, 334; Sherman Williams, *Choice Literature: Book I for Primary Grades* (New York, 1898), pref., p. 3; George L. Aldrich and Alexander Forbes, *The Progressive Course in Reading, Fifth Book* (New York, 1900), Part I, 18–19.

[40] Richard G. Parker and J. Madison Watson, *The National Third Reader* (New York, 1868), 118. See also Sargent and May, *New American Fifth Reader,* 146–49; Sherman Williams, *Choice Literature: Book II for Grammar Grades* (New York, 1898), 136. Actually, certain "moral" novels were recommended, such as those by Scott and Cooper.

[41] Lillian Kupfer, *The Natural Speller and Word Book* (New York, 1890), 58. See also Epes Sargent, *The Standard Third Reader, Part II* (Boston, 1866), 129; Baldwin, *School Reading by Grades: Fifth Year,* 7–9; S. W. Black, *Fifth Reader* (Chicago, 1898), 7–12.

It is clear from this evidence that anti-intellectualism is not only not new in American civilization, but that it is thoroughly embedded in the school-books that have been read by generations of pupils since the beginning of the republic. The rejection of the intellectual required the rejection of an intellectual past—that of the Puritans and of the founders of the republic—as part of the American tradition. The frontier did not need scholarship, whereas "useful knowledge" was essential to survival. And the needs of the frontier were probably reinforced by the needs of expanding business. Thus an 1875 speller records current attitudes in saying: "We do not blame a man who is proud of his success, so much as one who is vain of his learning." [42]

To these schoolbook writers the concept of "usefulness" was perhaps even more important for the fine arts than for the intellectual elements of American culture. Historically, the arts occupied a quite different position from that of scholarship in American development. In undertaking to determine what was to be considered the American tradition it was possible to draw upon an actual scholarly heritage; but the arts had always been held in a distinctly subservient position in America. In the colonial period literary labors were made to serve theology and politics, but the visual and auditory arts were regarded with suspicion by New Englanders as being inconsistent with Puritan precautions against the seductiveness of the senses. It was also true that in a frontier environment relatively few had the leisure or the opportunity to participate, either as creator or as audience, in the fine arts and belles-lettres. Yet by the nineteenth century America had produced many creative artists whose art was not designed to serve some other cause; and the fact that their work was too important to be ignored raises questions as to how the schoolbooks evaluated their contributions. Was the American child in this period, for example, taught to regard the arts as worthy of serious attention? To what extent were they considered to be essential or, at the least, important to national development?

Music and the fine arts appeared in these schoolbooks primarily in discussions of three subjects: the self-made artist, national monuments, and evaluations of American art. Those paintings and sculptures that glorified American heroes and the American past were frequently noted. For example, the statues of Washington in Richmond, Baltimore, and Raleigh were almost always mentioned in the sections of the geographies devoted to those cities. But discussions of the aesthetic qualities of such works are absent; they are to be observed for nationalistic rather than for aesthetic reasons.

Discussions of the fine arts appear mainly in the examples of self-made men in the field of the arts, and it is evident that in these tales their self-achieved success is more important than their art. The career of the Italian sculptor, Antonio Canova, for example, is described in the same terms as those used to describe the career of a successful businessman of the nine-

---

[42] Lewis B. Monroe, *The Practical Speller* (Philadelphia, 1875), 144.

teenth century. The story of his boyhood act of carving a lion out of butter to provide a substitute for a centerpiece which had not been delivered was frequently told. He was praised, however, not as a man of artistic achievement but as one who "was diligent and regular in his habits," and who saw an opportunity for success and used it.[43] A similar tale that appeared more often in the schoolbooks was that the American painter, Benjamin West, too poor as a boy to buy paint brushes, made them of hairs plucked from his cat's tail and taught himself to paint. "Thus we see," runs the moral, "that, by industry, ingenuity, and perseverance, a little American boy became the most distinguished painter of his day in England." [44] Obviously, these are not discussions of talented artists but of self-made men who happened to be artists. Their success was accomplished by diligence combined with the ability to recognize opportunity.

The aesthetic theories held in these books necessarily settled the fine arts into a position inferior to that of literature. The statement that "statues and pictures are pleasing representations of nature" [45] expressed their attitude throughout the century, and Longfellow's aphorism, "Nature is a revelation of God, art is a revelation of man," [46] was quoted to show that as imitations of nature works of art could never approach nature itself. According to this theory a landscape is of necessity more beautiful than a pleasing representation of it, and God, who is manifest through nature itself, can be discerned but dimly, if at all, through an imperfect imitation. Consequently in the schoolbooks painting and sculpture acquire importance only for extra-artistic qualities. Sculpture was useful to commemorate the dead, and the schoolbooks were not alone in the nineteenth century in recommending tours of the cemeteries of Philadelphia and Boston. But more important than this, the fine arts were useful in engendering nationalism by portraying American heroes and historical events. This is made quite clear in what purports to be an aesthetic judgment of the field of painting: "Q. What are the most esteemed paintings? A. Those representing historical events." [47]

---

[43] Sargent, *Standard Second Reader,* 146–47. See also Richard G. Parker and J. Madison Watson, *The National Fourth Reader* ([1867?], title page missing), 73–77; Monroe, *Fifth Reader,* 156–57; Gourley and Hunt, *Modern Third Reader,* 225–27; *McGuffey's Alternate Fifth Reader,* 170–74; Black, *Fifth Reader,* 21–25.

[44] Josiah F. Bumstead, *Third Reading-Book in the Primary School* (Boston, 1844), 137–42. See also Bela B. Edwards, *The Eclectic Reader* (Boston, 1832), 297; Adams, *The Monitorial Reader,* 213; Sargent, *Standard Second Reader,* 76–78; Hillard, *Franklin Advanced Fourth or Intermediate Reader,* 156; Joseph E. Worcester, *Pronouncing Spelling-Book of the English Language* (Boston, 1874), 123.

[45] B. Brandreth, *A New System for the Instruction of Youth* (New York, 1836), 98. See also Charles Peirce, *The Arts and Sciences Abridged, with a Selection of Pieces from Celebrated Modern Authors* (Portsmouth, N.H., 1806), 48; Harris, Rickoff, and Bailey, *Fifth Reader,* 397–99; Kupfer, *Natural Speller and Word Book,* 63.

[46] Quoted in Samuel T. Dutton, *The Morse Speller* (New York, 1896), 114.

[47] Peirce, *The Arts and Sciences Abridged,* 48.

The most curious argument in favor of encouraging the fine arts in the United States, and indeed the only argument for encouraging them on any grounds, was presented in an 1826 reader under the heading "Usefulness of the Fine Arts." [48] In this article the fine arts are recommended partly because they would produce a new class of people to be fed and, in the case of sculpture, would stimulate the marble and granite industries. Furthermore, those artists who did not succeed in the fine arts would then turn their talents to the useful arts in the clay, glass, and cotton industries. This process of failure in the fine arts had given England her lead in manufacturing. So, concluded this ingenious author, America should encourage the fine arts not for their own sakes, but that they may be transmuted into the useful arts and so stimulate American industry.

When the arts serve no useful project, however, they are often looked on with suspicion. In statement and by implication the schoolbooks fear that too much concentration on the arts is unhealthy and indeed dangerous to civilization. An excerpt from the writings of Hannah More as quoted in an 1876 text specifically warns of the possibility of such subversion: "It will be prudent to reflect, that in all polished countries an entire devotedness to the fine arts has been one grand source of the corruption of women. . . . And while corruption brought on by an excessive cultivation of the arts has contributed its full share to the decline of states, it has always furnished an infallible symptom of their impending fall." [49] Art and the decadence of the individual and society are regarded as natural companions in many of these books. In a frequently quoted poem by Bayard Taylor, "Napoleon at Gotha," for example, the following lines describe a German duke:

> A handsome prince and courtly, of light and shallow heart,
> No better than he should be, but with a taste for art.

And when Napoleon invaded his country:

> But while the German people were silent in despair,
> Duke August painted pictures, and curled his yellow hair.[50]

In the geographies which survey the state of civilization in every country, Europe is always introduced as the seat of the arts and sciences. But the Europe that has produced great art is also the Europe of rigid class distinctions, vice, and degeneracy. In particular, "The Italians are celebrated for their mu-

---

[48] John Frost, *The Class Book of American Literature* (Boston, 1826), 43–44.

[49] Anon., *The Young Ladies' Progressive Reader* (New York, 1876), 203 (for Catholic schools).

[50] Lewis B. Monroe, *Monroe's New Fifth Reader* (New York, 1884), 380. See also Parker and Watson, *National Fifth Reader,* 247; Wilson, *Book of Recitations and Dialogues,* 118–20; Thalheimer, *Eclectic History of the United States,* 96.

sical skill and perfection in the fine arts"; [51] but the descriptions of Italian national character and Italian morals would hardly be a recommendation for accomplishments in the arts. Italy is generally described as a land of beggars, filth, and poverty, and the Italians as a degenerate, superstitious, revengeful, effeminate, and immoral people. This unfavorable view of the Italians was undoubtedly the result of a strong anti-Catholic bias in American schoolbooks, but the conjunction of such a national character with the greatest talents in the fine arts of any country in the world would hardly persuade the Americans that the cultivation of the fine arts was necessary for national development.

On the other hand, in the view of these schoolbooks art can and should have a moral purpose. It should show that virtue inevitably leads to beauty, and that the only true beauty is that which is equated to goodness:

> Would'st behold beauty
> Near thee, all round?
> Only hath duty
> Such a sight found.[52]

But it was to literature rather than to painting and sculpture that the schoolbooks turned for their discussion of the relationship between beauty and goodness. The literary man, according to one of them, "thinks beautiful thoughts, and tells them in beautiful words, and he helps to make people better by showing how beautiful goodness is." [53] Even here, however, it was content, not artistic form, that determined the merit of a literary production. The same piece (a comment on Henry Wadsworth Longfellow) goes on to say: "But it is not the way it is written that makes a poem, but rather the beautiful thought in it." Indeed it is clear from the literary excerpts in the spellers and readers (most of these, beyond the primer, are anthologies) that style was considered in the nature of a clever trick and was of very little importance to the authors and editors of these books. Wordsworth, Emerson, Irving, and Dickens are there, but they are outspaced by Alcott, Longfellow, Mrs. Hemans, Mrs. Sigourney, and Lydia Maria Child. Longfellow's poem "The Day Is Done" was taken to heart by these authors and editors, especially the passage in which the poet asks to have poetry read to him:

---

[51] McNally, *Improved System of Geography*, 75.

[52] Monroe, *Monroe's New Fifth Reader*, 366. See also Parker and Watson, *National Third Reader*, 46; Hillard, *Franklin Advanced Fourth or Intermediate Reader*, 155–56; William B. Watkins, *McGuffey's Alternate Spelling Book* (Cincinnati, 1888), 24; William H. McGuffey, *McGuffey's Third Eclectic Reader* (New York, 1896), 65; James Baldwin, *School Reading by Grades: Third Year* (New York, 1897), 208; Harry Pratt Judson and Ida C. Bender, *Graded Literary Readers: Third Book* (New York, 1900), 127.

[53] Sarah L. Arnold and Charles B. Gilbert, *Stepping Stones to Literature: A Reader for Seventh Grades* (New York, 1897), 29–30.

Not from the grand old masters,
Not from the bards sublime. . . .

Read from some humbler poet,
Whose songs gushed from his heart,
As showers from the clouds of summer
Or tears from the eyelids start.[54]

That good literature is thought to be moral, and to engender morality in its readers is evident in the following samples of the adjectives used in literary criticism in the schoolbooks: Bryant—"Lofty moral tone"; [55] Alcott—"Healthy tone"; [56] Whittier—"His verse is distinguished by vigor and a certain moral sweetness"; [57] Scott—"Healthfulness of tone." [58] And because moral qualities should be paramount in his writings, it was considered entirely proper to inquire into the author's moral behavior in life. Scott comes out very well in this respect. More attention is given in several books to his labors to pay back creditors than to his writings: "The sterling integrity of the man shown forth in this dark hour." [59] This portrayal of an honest and industrious man was used as an introduction to and an evaluation of his writings. Byron, on the other hand, is to be read with caution. His poems are of "startling power on new and original themes. The principles inculcated in some of these shocked his countrymen, and still offend the moral sense of readers." [60] Coleridge's use of opium [61] and the dissipation of Burns [62] interfered with and marred the work of these two writers. And ironically, Poe, the American writer of whom they could have been the most proud because of his European reputation, also falls into this category. Although his writings showed "marked ability, [they] are marred by their morbid subjects and their absence of moral feeling." [63] "He was intemperate, quarrelsome and without business ability. . . . Nothing that he has written can fairly be called of a high class. His chief fame rests on his cleverness in constructing plots, and his use of the

---

[54] Baldwin, *School Reading by Grades: Fourth Year,* 65–66.

[55] Hillard, *Franklin Fifth Reader,* 155.

[56] *Ibid.,* 294.

[57] Monroe, *Fifth Reader,* 314.

[58] George F. Holmes and Frank A. Hill, *Holmes' Fifth Reader* (New York, 1896), 161.

[59] Black, *Fifth Reader,* 162–65. See also *McGuffey's Alternate Fifth Reader,* 95; Williams, *Choice Literature: Book I for Grammar Grades,* 17–18.

[60] Campbell, *New Franklin Fifth Reader,* 238. See also Williams, *Choice Literature: Book II for Grammar Grades,* 289–94; Aldrich and Forbes, *Progressive Course in Reading, Fifth Book,* Part II, 76.

[61] *McGuffey's Alternate Fifth Reader,* 227.

[62] Williams, *Choice Literature: Book II for Grammar Grades,* 315.

[63] Aldrich and Forbes, *Progressive Course in Reading, Fifth Book,* Part II, 78.

grotesque and weird." [64] Only one book admits that although he led a dissipated life and died young in consequence, still "He left behind him some of the choicest treasures of American Literature." [65] Frequently the introduction to a literary excerpt, and its moral evaluation of the author, is more extensive than the piece of literature itself. Literature was to be interpreted according to its moral tone; should it lack moral qualities or embody the wrong ones it was not good literature.

It should be noted that the selectivity used in discarding improper pieces from the schoolbooks did not operate as effectively in some of the books published before 1820. Excerpts from Shakespeare and Molière used in that period did not always embody the "lofty moral tone" that later became standard in the schoolbooks. On the other hand, these pieces were often taken out of context in such peculiar ways that they made no sense, moral or otherwise. Pedagogical improvement changed the books in the latter respect, but also eliminated some subjects that had heretofore appeared.

From the 1820's on, all gambling, drinking, and laziness are condemned. All women are virtuous, or wish they had been as they sink into a miserable death; all widows are poor and honest; all married women are mothers with the virtues thereof; all self-respecting men try for financial success; there are no physical relations between the sexes even if hallowed by marriage. Yet this does not indicate a general denial of the material world, for the acquisition of goods by the individual and the nation is regarded as a national blessing. But just as Whitman is conspicuously absent from the anthologies, so the physical nature of man is a subject to be subdued if mentioned at all.

Throughout the century all of the schoolbooks were sensitive to such European criticisms as those of the Abbé Raynal, who had taken America to task for producing no important artists. Those published before 1830 responded by a simple rejection of Raynal's evaluation and by catalogues of the artists America had produced, such as Trumbull, Copley, West, Barlowe, and others. Many of the lists of American artists culminated with the name of George Washington! [66] This would seem to indicate that the textbook authors were not arguing that America had produced better artists than those of Europe, but that she had produced greater men; and one Washington would obviously outweigh any number of artists or scholars. A typical early evaluation of American arts asserted that "Printing, engraving and architecture among the fine arts, as well as the mechanic arts, exhibit as much native genius in the United States as in any part of the world. This genius has been

---

[64] Williams, *Choice Literature: Book I for Grammar Grades,* 223. See also Swinton, *Fifth Reader and Speaker,* 120.

[65] Arnold and Gilbert, *Stepping Stones to Literature,* 193.

[66] Alexander Thomas, *The Orator's Assistant* (Worcester, 1797), 211–13; William Biglow, *The Youth's Library* (2 vols., Salem, 1803), I, 164–65; Abner Alden, *The Speaker* (Boston, 1810), 127–30.

cultivated for the last few years to such a degree as, in some instances, to rival the most splendid and useful exhibitions of art in Europe." [67] A few of the authors at the beginning of the century complained, however, that the American artist found it hard to make a living by his art. They ascribed this situation to the snobbish attitude of some Americans who believed that the only good art was European and refused to give any attention to art produced by an American.

After 1830 the textbook writers changed the grounds for their defense of American art. Abandoning their simple refusal to accept the low evaluation of our arts by European critics, they admitted our inferiority in the arts with an explanation. This inferiority, they said proudly, came from the fact that we had deliberately neglected the fine arts in favor of the arts that produce a comfortable and happy life for everyone. If the founders of America produced no great music, painting, sculpture, architecture, or literature, "It was enough for them to lay the foundation of that noble fabric of civil liberty." [68] McGuffey in 1858 lists freedom, useful knowledge, and patriotism as American gifts to the world which more than make up for our lack of artistic contributions.[69] Our monuments are not Gothic cathedrals, said another commentary, but "an active, vigorous, intelligent, moral population." [70] Thus the American answer to European critics from 1830 through the Civil War held that although American artists might not be equal to those of Europe, America had been engaged in producing something of far greater significance to the world—a superior society.

After the Civil War, however, American schoolbooks aggressively placed American artists and writers on a level with those of Europe. Bolstered by a newly proved nationalism and backed by solid accomplishments in American literature they were ready to refute European criticisms. "It is not long," one of them said, "since it was asked 'Who reads an American book?' Now the question is, who does not cherish as household words the names of our charming fiction writers, Irving, Cooper and Hawthorne—our historians, Bancroft, Prescott and Motley—our poets, Bryant and Longfellow, Halleck and Whittier, Lowell and Holmes?" The same author, however, evidently had some slight doubt about the status of American belles-lettres, because he added: "In magazines and school-books especially, the United States has nothing to fear from a comparison with the most cultivated of the older nations." [71] By the 1870's there was general and confident agreement that

---

[67] William Darby, *Ewing's Geography* (New York, 1820), 91. See also Bingham, *Columbian Orator,* 296–99; Thomas, *Orator's Assistant,* 211–12.

[68] George B. Cheever, *The American Common-Place Book of Prose* (Boston, 1831), 417.

[69] William H. McGuffey, *McGuffey's New Eclectic Speaker* (Cincinnati, 1858), 259–60.

[70] Goldsbury and Russell, *Common-School Reader,* 119–20.

[71] Quackenbos, *American History for Schools,* 305–306. See also Charles Morris, *An Elementary History of the United States* (Philadelphia, 1890), 192.

America had her own literary culture. America has produced many authors, "some of whom have acquired a reputation even in the Old World, and whose works have now become sufficiently numerous and important to form an American literature." [72] Two late-nineteenth-century authors admit that in the past "The greatest triumphs achieved in the United States have been in the direction of mechanical ingenuity; and American literature, science, and art have not yet won the applause of the world quite so thoroughly as have American sewing machines and agricultural implements." [73] But both say that this is much less true in their day, and they are confident that it will be even less so in the future.

In rating American artists, the major criterion used in the schoolbooks is whether they compare favorably to European artists and whether they have been accepted abroad. Gilbert Stuart is proudly put into the first category: "Some critics think he is the best portrait painter of the age except for Joshua Reynolds." [74] And American historiography comes out well by comparison to that of Europe: "Bancroft, Hildreth, Prescott and Motley stand among the best writers of history the world has ever produced." [75] The great landmark in American literature came with its first recognition abroad. The distinction of being the first to achieve this is variously accorded to Irving and Cooper. The author who has brought greatest acclaim to American literature in the eyes of Europe is Emerson, and he is placed even above European writers. McGuffey records Matthew Arnold's opinion that Emerson's work was "the most important work done in prose" in the nineteenth century.[76] At the end of the century this was reaffirmed: "Abroad, Emerson was recognized as a master-mind." [77]

What made American literature American in the eyes of schoolbook writers? Was it part of American literature because it was produced by American citizens, or did it have characteristics of its own? Most of the schoolbooks echo the opinion of Noah Webster in 1783 that America must be culturally independent of Europe:

> While the Americans stand astonished at their former delusion and enjoy the pleasure of a final separation from their insolent sovereigns, it becomes their

---

[72] Mary L. Hall, *Our World: No. II, A Second Series of Lessons in Geography* (Boston, 1872), 49. See also John J. Anderson, *A Junior Class History of the United States* (New York, 1874), 236.

[73] Thomas Wentworth Higginson, *Young Folks' History of the United States* (Boston, 1875), 328; Morris, *Elementary History of the United States,* 223.

[74] John A. Doyle, *History of the United States* (New York, 1876), 224 (an English work adapted for American schools). See also Parker and Watson, *National Fourth Reader,* 82–84; Samuel Eliot, *History of the United States from 1492 to 1872* (Boston, 1881), 487.

[75] Anderson, *Junior Class History of the United States,* 237.

[76] *McGuffey's Alternate Fifth Reader,* 229.

[77] Arnold and Gilbert, *Stepping Stones to Literature,* 223.

duty to attend to the *arts of peace,* and particularly to the interests of literature to see if there be not some error to be corrected, some defects to be supplied, and some improvements to be introduced into our systems of education, as well as into those of civil policy. We find Englishmen practising upon very erroneous maxims in politics and religion: and possibly we shall find, upon careful examination, that their methods of education are equally erroneous and defective. . . . Europe is grown old in folly, corruption and tyranny—in that country laws are perverted, manners are licentious, literature is declining and human nature is debased. For America in her infancy to adopt the present maxims of the Old World, would be to stamp the wrinkles of decrepid [*sic*] age upon the bloom of youth and to plant the seeds of decay in a vigorous constitution.[78]

To implement his desire for cultural reform Webster himself engaged in a famous attempt to differentiate American from English spelling. Other authors of schoolbooks suggest that the American artist should find his inspiration in American landscape rather than in the Alps or Westminster Abbey. The American literary man should use American scenes and situations to illustrate American virtues.[79] In this way he will improve on European literature by teaching self-control, initiative, honesty, industry, and other characteristics that differentiate the American from the European. Just as European literature reflects the vices and crimes of Europe, so American literature should reflect the virtues of America, and should then be supported for moral as well as nationalistic reasons.[80] Bryant is frequently used as the ideal American man of letters: "We find in his pages all the most obvious and all the most retiring graces of our native landscapes, but nothing borrowed from books— nothing transplanted from a foreign soil." [81] A lofty moral tone is regarded as characteristic of American authors; it is this that makes American literature unique. Lacking this quality an American author is not considered to be a part of American literature. The most obvious case in point is Edgar Allan Poe. According to the major canon of literary eminence used in these books, European recognition, Poe should have replaced Emerson as our greatest writer by the end of the century. He was not only seriously read abroad, but he influenced the development of French literature. This accolade could not be transferred from the virtuous Emerson to the immoral Poe. Although Poe lived in America, it was said, he did not write American literature.

Whatever might be said of the past, American nationalism demanded that the future of American art be assured. With the establishment of our political and social foundations, our intellectual and artistic prospects were seen to be

---

[78] Noah Webster, *A Grammatical Institute of the English Language* (Hartford, 1783), Part I, Introduction.

[79] Goldsbury and Russell, *Common-School Reader,* 222–24.

[80] Ebenezer R. Porter, *The Rhetorical Reader* (New York, 1835), 218–19.

[81] George S. Hillard, *A First Class Reader* (Boston, 1856), 96.

boundless and unprecedented. To achieve this one need not sponsor or even encourage the arts; in fact, this is to be avoided. But it is our manifest destiny, when the time comes, to reach such eminence naturally. America is "ordained, we believe, to be the chosen seat of intelligence, of literature, of arts, and of science." [82] It shall be "The first in letters, as the first in arms." [83] Furthermore, American efforts, freed from class limitations, will provide a larger audience for the arts than Europe can afford: "The universal diffusion of knowledge, which distinguishes the United States from the rest of the world, by exciting a literary thirst among the people in general, must also render the patrons of ingenuity and taste infinitely more numerous than they can possibly be in those nations, where the means, the pleasures, and the advantages of information are confined within the limited circles of nobility and wealth." [84] This confidence in the future of America was apparently based on nationalistic optimism, but also on the assumption that a superior political and social system will inevitably breed great art. Since America has the former she will inevitably develop the latter in time:

> Be just, Columbians, and assert your name,
> Avow your genius, and protect your fame.
> The clime which gave a WASHINGTON to you,
> May give an OTWAY and a SHAKESPEARE too.[85]

Thus, although the future of American art was to be as glorious as were all things American, yet no preparation whatever was made in the schoolbooks to encourage the development either of future artists or of a public for art. The American was not expected to accept art, let alone sponsor it for its own sake. This was the attitude of an effete and declining Europe whose civilization the schoolbooks specifically and carefully reject. Only when art becomes propaganda for good morals, or nationalism, or when it is in the service of the useful arts is it worthy of serious attention. According to the schoolbooks it is this kind of art that Americans have produced and will continue to produce.

The child was of course influenced by things other than schoolbooks. But the latter came from authority, and laid a careful foundation particularly important in those areas of thought in which the child might have little personal experience. The nineteenth-century schoolbook, as compared to that of the

---

82 John Pierpont, *Introduction to the National Reader* (Boston, 1828), 167.

83 Noah Webster, *Instructive and Entertaining Lessons for Youth* (New Haven, 1835), 246. See also Bingham, *Columbian Orator,* 30–34; Herman Mann, *The Material Creation* . . . (Dedham, 1818), ix–xii; Sargent, *Standard Fourth Reader,* 238; Parker and Watson, *National Fifth Reader,* 164–65.

84 Thomas, *Orator's Assistant,* 211–13.

85 Joseph Chandler, *The Young Gentleman and Lady's Museum* (Hallowell, Me., 1811), 82.

twentieth century, had relatively little competition from outside sources of information, and poorly trained teachers were often entirely dependent on the text adopted for use in their schools. The method of the classroom in most schools consisted primarily in memorizing the schoolbook.

And the child who accepted the meaning of the words that he memorized would consider scholarship and the fine arts mere embellishments identified with Europe and therefore with a civilization that he was taught to reject as inferior to his own. He would expect men of talent in the arts to serve their nationality consciously in their art. He would think it a waste of time to engage himself in these fields; American creativity was and should be directed to the immediately practical. Only when the artist or the scholar used his talents for the extension of good morals, for the development of a comfortable material existence, or for the propagation of nationalism was his work to be respected as good art or scholarship. Guided by his schoolbooks the nineteenth-century American child would grow up to be honest, industrious, religious, and moral. He would be a useful citizen untouched by the effeminate and perhaps even dangerous influence of the arts or scholarship. The concept of American culture presented in these schoolbooks, therefore, had prepared him for a life devoted to the pursuit of material success and a perfected character, but a life in which intellectual and artistic achievements would seem important only when they could be made to subserve some useful purpose.

JULIUS W. PRATT

THE IDEOLOGY OF
AMERICAN EXPANSION

Ruth Miller Elson's discussion of nineteenth-century values helps prepare the reader for the ideas advanced in this essay by Julius Pratt. Nineteenth-century Americans, Pratt argues, invariably justified expansion westward with the claim that the Lord had preserved the New World for them. And though the contrast between the providence of the Puritans' errand into the wilderness and the providence of manifest destiny is great, both reflect the propensity of Americans to see their affairs as the working out of divine intentions. Pratt's article focuses on previously unknown elements in the American idea of manifest destiny and pays particular attention to the force of nineteenth-century attitudes toward nature, race, evolution, and territory.

Albert Weinberg, Manifest Destiny * *(1935), is a penetrating study of expansionist thought; Henry Nash Smith,* Virgin Land: The American West as Symbol and Myth * *(1950), discusses related problems.*

Lincoln Steffens has observed that Americans have never learned to do wrong knowingly; that whenever they compromise with principle or abandon it, they invariably find a pious justification for their action. One is reminded of this observation in reviewing the history of American territorial expansion. For every step in that process, ingenious minds have found the best of reasons. From the year 1620, when King James the First granted to the Council for New England certain "large and goodlye Territoryes" in order "to second and followe God's sacred Will," to the year 1898, when William McKinley alleged that he had divine sanction for taking the Philippine Islands, it has been found possible to fit each successive acquistion of territory into the pattern of things decreed by divine will or inescapable destiny. The avowal of need or greed, coupled with power to take, has never satisfied our national conscience. We needed Florida and the mouth of the Mississippi; we thought we needed Canada, Texas, Oregon, California. But when we took, or attempted to take, that which we needed, we persuaded ourselves that we were but fulfilling the designs of Providence or the laws of Nature. If some of the apologists for later ventures in expansion were more frank in avowing motives of "national interest," the pious or fatalistic justification was none the less present.

The idea of a destiny which presides over and guides American expansion has rarely, if ever, been absent from the national consciousness. The precise character of that destiny, however, as well as the ultimate goal to which it points, has varied with changing ideas and circumstances. One of its earliest forms was geographical determinism. Certain contiguous areas were thought of as surely destined for annexation because their location made them naturally part of the United States. This idea seems to have been the basis for Thomas Jefferson's sure conviction that Florida would inevitably become American territory. In this expectation his mind never wavered; he questiond only the time and the means. The settling of Americans in Florida, he wrote in 1791, "will be the means of delivering to us peaceably, what may otherwise cost us a war." [1] The failure of his own efforts to secure it did not shake his faith. In 1820, when it appeared likely that Spain would not ratify the Florida-purchase treaty, he wrote Monroe that this was not to be regretted. "Florida," he said, ". . . is ours. Every nation in Europe considers it such a right. We need not care for its occupation in time of peace, and, in war, the first cannon makes it ours without offence to anybody." [2] Jefferson's belief was widely shared. Florida, said *Niles' Register* in 1819, "will just as naturally come into

---

[1] P. L. Ford (ed.), *Writings of Thos. Jefferson* (10 vols.; New York, 1892–99), V, 316.
[2] *Ibid.*, X, 159.

our possession as the waters of the Mississippi seek the sea; . . . We believe this is the universal conclusion of the United States. . . ." [3] The young expansionists who led the country into war in 1812 in the hope of conquering Canada and Florida appealed to the God of Nature in behalf of their plans. "In point of territorial limit, the map will prove its importance," one of them proclaimed. "The waters of the St. Lawrence and the Mississippi interlock in a number of places, and the great Disposer of Human Events intended those two rivers should belong to the same people"; while to another it appeared that "the Author of Nature has marked our limits in the south, by the Gulf of Mexico; and on the north, by the regions of eternal frost." [4] If neither of these Congressmen was able to discern the westward limits set by the Author of Nature, this task was performed by a writer for a southwestern paper, who asked rhetorically: "Where is it written in the book of fate that the American republic shall not stretch her limits from the capes of the Chesapeake to Nootka sound, from the isthmus of Panama to Hudson bay?" [5] Even Cuba was thought of by some as drawn inevitably by geographic laws toward union with the United States. Upon this idea two men as dissimilar as Thomas H. Benton and John Quincy Adams could agree. The island, thought Benton, was "the geographical appurtenance of the valley of the Mississippi and eventually to become its political appurtenance." [6] Adams, as Secretary of State, likened Cuba to an apple which, when detached from the parent tree, would be drawn by a law of political gravitation to the United States. [7]

What were the "natural boundaries" of the young republic? One mode of determining them was defined by Jefferson. Writing to Madison in 1809 of the hope of acquiring Cuba, he said: "Cuba can be defended by us without a navy, and this develops the principle which ought to limit our views. Nothing should ever be accepted which would require a navy to defend it." [8] Northwardly, Jefferson visioned Canada as eventually to be drawn under the American flag; [9] southwardly, Florida, Cuba, and probably Texas. [10] On the west he apparently thought of the Rocky Mountains as forming the natural boundary. The West Coast would be peopled "with free and independent Americans, unconnected with us but by the ties of blood and interest, and employing like us the rights of self-government." [11] Sheer distance seemed an insuperable bar-

---

[3] *Niles' Weekly Register,* XVI, 225.

[4] *Annals of Congress,* 12th Congress, 1st Session, pp. 458, 657.

[5] *Democratic Clarion and Tennessee Gazette* (Nashville), April 28, 1812.

[6] W. M. Meigs, *Life of Thomas H. Benton* (Philadelphia and London, 1904), p. 101.

[7] *House Executive Document No. 121,* 32d Cong., 1st Sess., p. 7.

[8] H. A. Washington (ed.), *Writings of Thos. Jefferson* (9 vols.; Washington, 1853–54), V, 444–45.

[9] *Ibid.*

[10] Ford, *op. cit.,* X, 159.

[11] *Ibid.,* IX, 351 (to J. J. Astor, May 24, 1912).

rier to the incorporation of the Oregon country in the American Union. A representative from Oregon, it was asserted in 1825, if he visited his constituency once a year, would have but two weeks annually to spend in Washington; the remainder of the year would be spent in the journey to and fro.[12] Even Senator Benton, who predicted that the future route to Asia would follow the Missouri and Columbia rivers, and who in 1825 argued in favor of military occupation of Oregon by the United States, believed that in settling that territory Americans would be planting the seed of a new republic. The natural western limit of the United States was "the ridge of the Rocky Mountains. . . . Along the back of this ridge, the Western limit of this republic should be drawn, and the statue of the fabled god, Terminus, should be raised upon its highest peak, never to be thrown down." [13]

Such restricted ideas of the nation's natural boundaries were not to survive for many years. Indeed, some three years before Benton made this speech, the conservative weekly, *Niles' Register,* made an interesting prophecy. News had been received of the successful arrival at Santa Fe of one of the first parties of traders from Missouri. Commenting on this exploit, the *Register* predicted that crossing the Rockies would soon be as familiar to the western people as was the voyage to China to the easterners. "It was very possible that the citizens of St. Louis, on the *Mississippi,* may eat fresh salmon from the waters of the *Columbia!*—for distance seems as if annihilated by science and the spirit of adventure." [14] On July 4, 1828, the people of Baltimore, amid elaborate ceremony, watched Charles Carroll, of Carrollton, lay the cornerstone that marked the beginning of the Baltimore and Ohio Railroad. In his address from the president and directors of the company, Mr. John B. Morris assumed the rôle of prophet. "We are," he said, "about affording facilities of intercourse between the east and the west, which will bind the one more closely to the other, beyond the power of an increased population or sectional difficulties to disunite. We are in fact commencing a new era in our history.[15]

It was inevitable that the coming of the railroad and, later, of the telegraph should result in an expanding conception of the nation's natural boundaries. Daniel Webster could still maintain in 1845 that there would arise an independent "Pacific republic" on the west coast,[16] but for many others the "throne of Terminus" had moved on from the Rockies to the shores of the Pacific. The *Democratic Review,* leading organ of the expansionists of the Mexican War era, predicted in 1845 that a railroad to the Pacific would soon be a reality, and that "the day cannot be far distant which shall witness the conveyance of the representatives from Oregon and California to Washington

---

[12] *Congressional Debates,* 18th Cong., 2d Sess., I, 691–92.

[13] *Ibid.,* pp. 711–12. Cf. Meigs, *loc. cit.*

[14] *Niles' Weekly Register,* XXIII, 177 (Nov. 23, 1822).

[15] *Ibid.,* XXXIV, 316.

[16] *Ibid.,* LXIX, 167.

within less time than a few years ago was devoted to a similar journey by those from Ohio." The telegraph, furthermore, would soon enable Pacific coast newspapers "to set up in type the first half of the President's Inaugural, before the echoes of the latter half shall have died away beneath the lofty porch of the Capitol, as spoken from his lips." [17] In the debate on the Oregon question in the House of Representatives in January, 1846, the significance of the Pacific as a natural boundary was repeatedly stressed. From the Atlantic to the Pacific, said Bowlin of Missouri, "we were by nature, ay, we were stamped by the hand of God himself, as one nation of men." [18] Similarly, in the debate of 1844 and 1845 over the annexation of Texas, the Rio Grande with the neighboring strips of desert country had been portrayed as the divinely fixed natural boundary of the United States on the southwest.[19]

If a divine hand had shaped the outlines of the North American continent with a view to its attaining political unity, the divine mind was thought to be by no means indifferent to the type of political organism which should dominate it. The American god of the early nineteenth century was the God of Democracy, and his followers had no doubt that he had reserved the continent for a democratic nation. Jefferson may not have regarded this consummation as a divinely appointed destiny, but he certainly contemplated as probable and desirable the spread of democratic institutions throughout the continent.[20] The true flowering of this idea, however, belongs properly to the Jacksonian era, and its most enthusiastic exponent was the *Democratic Review,* a monthly magazine founded and for many years edited by Mr. John L. O'Sullivan.[21] This exuberant Irish-American, whose faith in the institutions of his adopted country was irrepressible, not only coined the phrase "manifest destiny" but for years expounded in the pages of the *Review* the idea which it embodied.

The *Democratic Review* was founded in 1837. In the issue for November, 1839, appeared an article, presumably by O'Sullivan, entitled "The Great Nation of Futurity." This rôle was to be America's, it was argued,

> because the principle upon which a nation is organized fixes its destiny, and that of equality is perfect, is universal. . . . Besides, the truthful annals of any nation furnish abundant evidence, that its happiness, its greatness, its duration, were always proportionate to the democratic equality in its system of government. . . . We point to the everlasting truth on the first page of

---

[17] *Democratic Review,* XVII, 9.

[18] *Congressional Globe,* 29th Cong., 1st Sess., *Appendix,* pp. 79–80. Cf. *ibid.,* p. 207, and *Appendix,* pp. 96, 321.

[19] *Niles' Weekly Register,* LXVI, 327; LXVII, 302, 408.

[20] Washington, *op. cit.,* V, 444–45; Ford, *op. cit.,* IX, 351.

[21] Julius W. Pratt, "John L. O'Sullivan and Manifest Destiny," *New York History,* XLV (July, 1933), 213–34.

our national declaration, and we proclaim to the millions of other lands, that "the gates of hell"—the powers of aristocracy and monarchy—"shall not prevail against it."

Thus happily founded upon the perfect principle of equality, the United States was destined to a unique success. Her shining example should "smite unto death the tyranny of kings, hierarchs, and oligarchs." What all this portended for the future boundaries of the United States the writer did not state except in poetic language. "Its floor shall be a hemisphere," he wrote, "its roof the firmament of the star-studded heavens, and its congregation an Union of many Republics, comprising hundreds of happy millions, . . . governed by God's natural and moral law of equality. . . ." [22] Within a few years, however, the *Democratic Review* became sufficiently concrete in its ideas of the extent of the democratizing mission of the United States. Texas, Oregon, California, Canada, and much or all of Mexico, were to receive the blessings of American principles. The American continent had been reserved by Providence for the dawn of a new era, when men should be ready to throw off the antique systems of Europe and live in the light of equality and reason. The time was now at hand, and no American should shrink from the task of spreading the principles of liberty over all the continent.[23] Cuba, too, had been left by Providence in the hands of a weak power until the United States was ready for it. Now it, like the rest, was "about to be annexed to the model republic." [24]

The ideas so fervently preached in the *Democratic Review* were echoed in Congress and elsewhere. With reference to the Oregon controversy, James Buchanan asserted in 1844 that Providence had given to the American people the mission of "extending the blessings of Christianity and of civil and religious liberty over the whole North American continent." [25] Breese of Illinois declared that "the impartial and the just" would see in the occupation of Oregon "a desire only to extend more widely the area of human freedom, . . . as an extension, sir, of that grand theatre, on which God, in his providence, and in his own appointed time, intends to work out that high destiny he has assigned for the whole human race." [26] California was not forgotten. A letter from an American in that Mexican state, published in the *Baltimore Patriot,* commented on the way in which "our people, like a sure heavy and sullen tide, are overflowing the country"; and the writer declared that, while not himself an advocate of territorial aggression, he thought he could "foresee in the inevitable destiny of this territory, one of the most efficient fortresses from

---

[22] *Democratic Review,* VI, 426–30.
[23] *Ibid.,* XVIII, 57–64 (Jan., 1846).
[24] *Ibid.,* XXV, 193–94 (Sept., 1849).
[25] *Cong. Globe,* 18th Cong., 1st Sess., *Appendix,* p. 350.
[26] *Ibid.,* 29th Cong., 1st Sess., *Appendix,* p. 383.

which new and liberal are to combat old and despotic institutions." [27] Kaufman of Texas was sure the day was near "when not one atom of kingly power will disgrace the North American continent." [28] Apologists for the war with Mexico were apt at urging its providential character and beneficent results. B. F. Porter, of Alabama, in an article on "The Mission of America," intimated that the war was a divine instrument for spreading American institutions and ideals to the Pacific; [29] and Robert J. Walker, Secretary of the Treasury, inserted in his report for December, 1847, a paragraph gratefully acknowledging the aid of a "higher than any earthly power" which had guided American expansion in the past and which "still guards and directs our destiny, impels us onward, and has selected our great and happy country as a model and ultimate centre of attraction for all the nations of the world." [30]

Neither natural boundaries nor divinely favored institutions were in themselves sufficient to insure the peopling of the continent by the favored race. The third essential factor was seen in what more than one Congressman termed "the American multiplication table." "Go to the West," said Kennedy of Indiana in 1846, "and see a young man with his mate of eighteen; after the lapse of thirty years, visit him again and instead of two, you will find twenty-two. This is what I call the American multiplication table." [31] Apparently Jefferson had in mind this same fecundity of the Anglo-Saxon race in America when he predicted in 1786 that "our confederacy must be viewed as the nest from which all America, North & South, is to be peopled," and when in 1803 he expressed full confidence in the growth of such an American population on the Mississippi "as will be able to do their own business" in securing control of New Orleans.[32] On the same principle, Barbour of Virginia foretold in 1825 the peopling of the Oregon country by Americans.[33]

It was partly, too, upon the basis of this unexampled growth in numbers that the editor of the *Democratic Review* founded his doctrine of "manifest destiny." It was in an unsigned article in the number for July–August, 1845, that the phrase first appeared. The writer charged foreign nations with attempting to impede the annexation of Texas, with the object of "checking the fulfilment of our manifest destiny to overspread the continent allotted by Providence for the free development of our yearly multiplying millions." Texas, he said, had been

---

[27] *Niles' Weekly Register,* LXIX, 244–45 (Dec. 20, 1845).

[28] *Cong. Globe,* 29th Cong., 1st Sess., *Appendix,* p. 805.

[29] *De Bow's Review,* IV, 108–22 (Sept., 1847).

[30] *Niles' Weekly Register,* LXXIII, 255.

[31] Quoted by E. I. McCormac in *James K. Polk, a Political Biography* (Berkeley, Calif., 1922), p. 588. Cf. Kaufman of Texas, *Cong. Globe,* 29th Cong., 1st Sess., *Appendix,* p. 805.

[32] Ford, *op. cit.,* IV, 188–89; VIII, 229.

[33] *Cong. Debates,* 18th Cong., 2d Sess., I, 689.

absorbed into the Union in the inevitable fulfilment of the general law which is rolling our population westward; the connexion of which with that ratio of growth in population which is destined within a hundred years to swell our numbers to the enormous population of *two hundred and fifty millions* (if not more), is too evident to leave us in doubt of the manifest design of Providence in regard to the occupation of this continent.[34]

When war with Mexico came, and the more rabid expansionists were seeking excuses for annexing large portions of Mexican territory, a different side of the idea of racial superiority was advanced. The Mexicans, it seemed, had a destiny too—how different from that of their northern neighbors! "The Mexican race," said the *Democratic Review,* "now see, in the fate of the aborigines of the north, their own inevitable destiny. They must amalgamate and be lost, in the superior vigor of the Anglo-Saxon race, or they must utterly perish." [35] The *New York Evening Post* indorsed the idea, sanctifying it in the name of Providence. "Providence has so ordained it; and it is folly not to recognize the fact. The Mexicans are *aboriginal Indians,* and they must share the destiny of their race." [36]

This pre-Darwinian version of the "survival of the fittest" was branded by the aged Albert Gallatin, an opponent of the war, as "a most extraordinary assertion." [37] That it persisted, that it constituted, in the 1850's, an integral part of the concept of manifest destiny is clear from the remarks of both friends and foes. John L. O'Sullivan was serving in 1855 as United States minister to Portugal. He reported to Secretary Marcy a conversation with some French imperialists in which he had said:

> I should be as glad to see our common race and blood overspread all Africa under the French flag and all India under the British, as they ought to be to see it overspread all the Western hemisphere under ours; and that probably enough that was the plan of Providence; to which we in America were accustomed to give the name of "manifest destiny." [38]

On the other hand, George Fitzhugh of Virginia, who believed in institutions (such as slavery) for the protection of weaker races, charged the members of the "Young American" party in Congress with boasting "that the Anglo-

---

[34] *Democratic Review,* XVII, 5–10. A British observer also took note of the "American multiplication table." Thomas Carlyle remarked that the sole achievement of American democracy had been to double its population every twenty years. "They have begotten, with a rapidity beyond recorded example, Eighteen Millions of the greatest *bores* ever seen in the world before" (*Collected Works* [Library ed., 1870], XIX, 26).

[35] *Democratic Review,* XX, 100.

[36] Quoted in *Niles' Weekly Register,* LXXIII, 334.

[37] *Ibid.,* p. 239.

[38] Pratt, *op. cit.,* p. 231.

Saxon race is manifestly destined to eat out all the other races, as the wire-grass destroys and takes the place of other grasses," and with inviting admiration for "this war of nature"—admiration which Fitzhugh, for one, refused to concede.[39]

Thus manifest destiny, which must be thought of as embracing all the ideas hitherto considered—geographical determinism, the superiority of democratic institutions, the superior fecundity, stamina, and ability of the white race—became a justification for almost any addition of territory which the United States had the will and the power to obtain.

Such ideas were not, as has been rather generally assumed, peculiarly southern. In their extreme form, at least, both the ideas and the imperialistic program which they were used to justify were repudiated by southern Whig leaders, and even by John C. Calhoun himself.[40] The southerner most closely associated with the program, Robert J. Walker, was of northern birth, was by no means an unwavering supporter of slavery, and was presently to sever entirely his connections with the South. The inventor of the phrase "manifest destiny" and one of the most persevering advocates of expansion was, as has been said, John L. O'Sullivan, who described himself in a letter to Calhoun as a "New York Free Soiler"; and he had the friendship and sympathy of prominent northern Democrats like Buchanan, Marcy, and Pierce. Indeed, if the manifest destiny of the 1840's and 1850's must be classified, it should be described as Democratic rather than sectional. Yet, even this generalization will not bear too close scrutiny, for William H. Seward, an antislavery Whig and Republican, was scarcely less intrigued by the idea than O'Sullivan himself. As early as 1846 he was predicting that the population of the United States was "destined to roll its resistless waves to the icy barriers of the North, and to encounter oriental civilization on the shores of the Pacific"; and in a speech at St. Paul, Minnesota, in 1860, he asserted with assurance that Russian, Canadian, and Latin on the American continents were but laying the foundations for future states of the American republic, whose ultimate capital would be the City of Mexico.[41]

Seward, in fact, supplies the chief link between the manifest destiny of the pre-Civil War years and the expansionist schemes of the decade following the war. As Secretary of State he had an opportunity to try his hand at a program of expansion; and though of all his plans the purchase of Alaska alone was carried through, the discussions of that and of other proposed acquisitions—the Danish West Indies, the Dominican Republic, the Hawaiian Islands, and Canada—demonstrated the continuity of ideas from 1850 to 1870. Professor

---

[39] George Fitzhugh, *Sociology for the South* (Richmond, 1854), pp. 31–32.

[40] Cf. A. C. Cole, *The Whig Party in the South* (Washington, 1913); C. S. Boucher, "*In re* That Aggressive Slavocracy," *Mississippi Valley Historical Review*, VIII (1921), 13–79.

[41] Frederick Bancroft, *Life of William H. Seward* (2 vols.; New York, 1900), II, 470–74.

T. C. Smith, who made an analysis of the expansionist arguments used in this period, found annexations urged on four principal grounds: economic value, strategic value to the navy, extension of republican institutions, and geographic determinism.[42] Only the second of these—the naval base argument —was at all new. It owed its vogue at the time to the navy's difficulties during the war. The first was always to be met with, and the third and fourth were carry-overs from the days of manifest destiny.

The collapse of the expansionist program of Seward and Grant was followed by a general loss of interest in such enterprises, which did not recover their one-time popularity until the era of the Spanish-American War. In the meantime, however, new arguments were taking shape which would eventually impinge on the popular consciousness and raise almost as keen an interest in expansion as that which had elected Polk in 1844. But while manifest destiny was a product indigenous to the United States, some of the new doctrines owed their origin to European trends of thought.

In 1859 Charles Darwin published his *Origin of Species,* setting forth the hypothesis that the evolution of the higher forms of life had come about through the preservation and perpetuation of chance variations by the "survival of the fittest" in the never ending struggle for existence. The authoritativeness of this work, and the stir which it made in the scientific world, gave a scientific sanction to the idea that perpetual struggle in the political and social world would lead upward along the evolutionary path. Many were the applications that might be made of such a principle—especially by nations and peoples considering themselves highly "fit." A nation with a faith in its political, moral, or racial superiority might take pleasure in the thought that in crushing its inferior neighbors it was at once obeying the law of destiny and contributing to the perfection of the species.

What did Darwinism signify for the future of the United States? One of the first to attempt an answer to that riddle was the historian, John Fiske, who spoke with double authority as a student of American institutions and a follower and popularizer of Darwin. Fiske's conclusion was sufficiently gratifying. Anglo-Saxons in the United States had evolved the "fittest" of all political principles—federalism—upon which all the world would at some future day be organized. Anglo-Saxons, moreover, excelled not only in institutions but in growth of numbers and economic power. So evident was the superior "fitness" of this race that its expansion was certain to go on "until every land on the earth's surface that is not already the seat of an old civilization shall become English in its language, in its religion, in its political habits and traditions, and to a predominant extent in the blood of its people." "The day is at hand," said Fiske, "when four-fifths of the human race will trace its pedigree to English forefathers, as four-fifths of the white people of the United States trace their

---

[42] T. C. Smith, "Expansion after the Civil War, 1865–1871" in *Political Science Quarterly,* XVI (1901), 412–36.

pedigree today." [43] This was surely encouraging doctrine to Americans or British who wanted an excuse to go a-conquering.

Conclusions very similar to Fiske's were reached by Josiah Strong, a Congregational clergyman, who in 1885 published what became a popular and widely read book entitled *Our Country: Its Possible Future and Its Present Crisis.* The Anglo-Saxon, thought Strong, as the chief representative of the two most valuable civilizing forces—civil liberty and "a pure *spiritual* Christianity"—was being divinely schooled for *"the final competition of races. . . ."* "If I read not amiss," he said, "this powerful race will move down upon Mexico, down upon Central and South America, out upon the islands of the sea, over upon Africa and beyond. And can any one doubt that the result of this competition of races will be the 'survival of the fittest'?" The extinction of inferior races before the conquering Anglo-Saxon might appear sad to some; but Strong knew of nothing likely to prevent it, and he accepted it as part of the divine plan. His doctrine was a curious blending of religious and scientific dogma. [44]

If Fiske and Strong could show that expansion was a matter of destiny, another scholar of the day preached it as a duty. In his *Political Science and Comparative Constitutional Law,* published in 1890, John W. Burgess, of Columbia University, surveyed the political careers of the principal civilized races and concluded that, of them all, only the Teutonic group had talent of the highest order. Greek and Roman, Slav and Celt, had exhibited their various abilities. Some had excelled in building city-states; others, in planning world-empires. Only Teutons had learned the secret of the national state, the form fittest to survive. The Teutonic nations—German and Anglo-Saxon— were "the political nations *par excellence,*" and this pre-eminence gave them the right "in the economy of the world to assume the leadership in the establishment and administration of states." Especially were they called "to carry the political civilization of the modern world into those parts of the world inhabited by unpolitical and barbaric races; i.e. they must have a colonial policy." There was "no human right to the status of barbarism." If barbaric peoples resisted the civilizing efforts of the political nations, the latter might rightly reduce them to subjection or clear their territory of their presence. If a population were not barbaric but merely incompetent politically, then too the Teutonic nations might "righteously assume sovereignty over, and undertake to create state order for, such a politically incompetent population." [45]

---

[43] John Fiske, "Manifest Destiny," *Harper's New Monthly Magazine,* LXX (Mar., 1885), 578–90. The quotation is from p. 588. The same essay is found in Fiske's *American Political Ideas Viewed from the Standpoint of Universal History* (New York, 1885).

[44] These ideas and quotations are found in chap. xiv, pp. 208–24, of the revised edition (New York, 1891). The first edition was published in New York in 1885.

[45] John W. Burgess, *Political Science and Comparative Constitutional Law* (2 vols.; Boston and London, 1890), I, 30–48.

There is in these pages of Burgess such a complete justification not only for British and German imperialism but also for the course of acquiring colonies and protectorates upon which the United States was to embark in 1898 that one learns with surprise from his rather naïve autobiography that Burgess was profoundly shocked by the war with Spain and felt that the adoption of an imperialistic career was a colossal blunder.[46] One would have supposed that he would have rejoiced that his country was assuming its share of world-responsibility as one of the Teutonic nations.

To Fiske and Strong, expansion was destiny; to Burgess, it was duty, though he apparently excused his own country from any share in its performance. To Alfred Thayer Mahan, the historian and prophet who frankly assumed the rôle of propagandist, it was both duty and opportunity. Mahan's *Influence of Sea Power upon History,* the result of a series of lectures at the Naval War College at Newport, Rhode Island, was published in 1890. Other books on naval history followed, but it is likely that Mahan reached a wider American public through the many magazine articles which he published at frequent intervals during the ensuing decade. History, as Mahan wrote it, was no mere academic exercise. Searching the past for lessons applicable to the here and now, he found them in full measure. Rather, he found *one,* which he never tired of driving home: Sea power was essential to national greatness. Sea power embraced commerce, merchant marine, navy, naval bases whence commerce might be protected, and colonies where it might find its farther terminals. One nation, Great Britain, had learned this lesson by heart and practiced it faithfully, with results that Mahan thought admirable. One other nation, he hoped, might walk in her footsteps.

Certain specific needs, beside the obvious one of a stronger navy and better coast defenses, Mahan urged upon his countrymen. If an Isthmian canal were to be built, the United States ought to build and control it, or, failing this, to control completely the approaches to it. This involved a willingness to accept islands in the Caribbean whenever they could be had by righteous means; sheer acts of conquest Mahan repudiated. It involved also a willingness to accept the Hawaiian Islands, partly as an outpost to the Pacific end of the canal, partly for another reason which weighed heavily with Mahan. The Pacific, he believed, was to be the theater of a vast conflict between Occident and Orient, with the United States holding the van of the Western forces. His deep religious sense assured him that the Deity was preparing the Christian powers for that coming cataclysm, but he was equally sure that mere human

---

[46] John W. Burgess, *Reminiscences of an American Scholar* (New York, 1934), chap. xi. "I have always regarded this war," he writes, "and the results of it as disastrous to American political civilization. It proved the entering wedge in separating all persons under the sovereignty of the United States into citizens and subjects" (p. 316). Equally naïve were his surprise and grief at learning that some suggestions in the same treatise on political science in regard to the importance of natural frontiers were thought to imply a justification of Germany's course in 1914 (*ibid.,* pp. 255–57).

agents must keep their powder dry. The United States must be ready, with a navy, a canal, and as many island outposts as she could righteously acquire, for her share in the great struggle between civilizations and religions.[47] Even the practical-minded naval officer must have a cosmic justification for the policy of national imperialism which he advocated.

It was such ideas as these of Fiske, Strong, Burgess, and Mahan which created a public opinion receptive to expansion overseas in 1898. Theodore Roosevelt and Henry Cabot Lodge, whose influence upon the events of that year was large indeed, were under the spell of Mahan's writings.[48] Roosevelt had been a pupil of Burgess while studying law at Columbia. In the debate over imperialism which ensued, the argument from Anglo-Saxon or Teutonic superiority and the divinely appointed mission of the race was probably as influential as the more practical strategic and economic arguments. Kipling's contribution, "The White Man's Burden," which appeared in 1898, fitted in well with the American temper. In the United States Senate, young Albert J. Beveridge, using language that might almost have been taken bodily from Burgess' treatise, declared that God "has made us [Anglo-Saxons and Teutons] the master organizers of the world to establish system where chaos reigns. . . . He has made us adepts in government that we may administer government among savage and senile peoples." [49] William Allen White, in the *Emporia Gazette,* proclaimed: "Only Anglo-Saxons can govern themselves. . . . It is the Anglo-Saxon's manifest destiny to go forth as a world conqueror. He will take possession of the islands of the sea. . . . This is what fate holds for the chosen people." [50] Senator O. H. Platt wrote President McKinley that in Connecticut "those who believe in Providence, see, or think they see, that God has placed upon this Government the solemn duty of providing for the people of these islands [the Philippines] a government based upon the principle of liberty no matter how many difficulties the problem may present." [51] A missionary from China was quoted as saying: "You will find that all American missionaries are in favor of expansion." [52]

Even those who stressed the economic value of new possessions could not refrain from claiming the special interest of Providence. That the war with Spain and the victory in the Philippines should have come just as the Euro-

---

[47] The pertinent passages are found in A. T. Mahan, *The Influence of Sea Power upon History, 1660–1783* (Boston, 1890), and *The Interest of America in Sea Power, Present and Future* (Boston, 1897). The latter is a collection of essays published in various American magazines from 1890 to 1897.

[48] Julius W. Pratt, "The 'Large Policy' of 1898," *Miss. Valley Hist. Rev.,* XIX (Sept., 1932), 219–42.

[49] Claude G. Bowers, *Beveridge and the Progressive Era* (New York, 1932), p. 121.

[50] Mark Sullivan, *Our Times* (New York, 1920–35), I, 50.

[51] L. A. Coolidge, *An Old-Fashioned Senator, Orville H. Platt of Connecticut* (New York and London, 1910), p. 287.

[52] Josiah Strong, *Expansion under New World Conditions* (New York, 1900), p. 249.

pean powers were attempting to partition China and monopolize its markets, seemed to the *American Banker* of New York "a coincidence which has a providential air." [53] Familiar to all students of the period is McKinley's story of how he prayed for divine guidance as to the disposition of the Philippines, and of how "one night it came to me this way—I don't know how it was but it came: . . . that we could not turn them over to France or Germany—our commercial rivals in the Orient—that would be bad business and discreditable." [54] Reasons of a more ideal character were vouchsafed to William McKinley on the same occasion, but McKinley's God did not hesitate to converse with him in terms that might better have befitted Mark Hanna. Perhaps McKinley did not misunderstand. Josiah Strong was a clergyman and hence in a better position than McKinley to interpret the wishes of the Deity; yet he found in Providence a concern for American business similar to that which McKinley detected. Strong, too, had in mind the Philippines and especially their relation to China and to the maintenance of the Open Door in the markets of that developing empire.

> And when we remember [he wrote] that our new necessities [markets for our manufactures] are precisely complementary to China's new needs, it is not difficult to see a providential meaning in the fact that, with no design of our own, we have become an Asiatic power, close to the Yellow Sea, and we find it easy to believe that
>
> > "There's a divinity that shapes our ends,
> > Rough-hew them how we will." [55]

Expansionists of different periods had invoked a God of Nature, a God of Democracy, a God of Evolution. It seems appropriate enough that those who inaugurated the last phase of territorial expansion, at the close of the nineteenth century, should have proclaimed their faith in a God of Business.

---

[53] *American Banker*, LXIII, 785 (May 11, 1898).

[54] J. F. Rhodes, *The McKinley and Roosevelt Administrations* (New York, 1922), p. 107.

[55] Strong, *op. cit.*, pp. 133–34.

DAVID BRION DAVIS

SOME THEMES OF COUNTER–SUBVERSION
An Analysis of Anti-Masonic, Anti-Catholic, and Anti-Mormon Literature

---

Historians have not usually contended that anti-Masonic, anti-Mormon, and anti-Catholic literature express similar values, though they have remarked the irrationality common to all these attitudes. Davis suggests that these movements of counter-subversion all found their impetus in a social situation marked by instability and change and within a psychological framework of repressed sexuality and sadism. His article is intriguing not only for its argument but also for the variety of techniques and assumptions he employs in supporting his thesis. In particular, the question of how historians may establish empirically the operations of the psychological mechanism usually called projection requires further study.

Of the excellent books cited by Davis in his footnotes, two merit especially careful reading: Ray A. Billington, The Protestant Crusade, 1800–1860 *(1938)* and Thomas F. O'Dea,* The Mormons ** (1958).*

149

During the second quarter of the nineteenth century, when danger of foreign invasion appeared increasingly remote, Americans were told by various respected leaders that Freemasons had infiltrated the government and had seized control of the courts, that Mormons were undermining political and economic freedom in the West, and that Roman Catholic priests, receiving instructions from Rome, had made frightening progress in a plot to subject the nation to popish despotism. This fear of internal subversion was channeled into a number of powerful counter-movements which attracted wide public support. The literature produced by these movements evoked images of a great American enemy that closely resembled traditional European stereotypes of conspiracy and subversion. In Europe, however, the idea of subversion implied a threat to the established order—to the king, the church, or the ruling aristocracy—rather than to ideals or a way of life. If free Americans borrowed their images of subversion from frightened kings and uneasy aristocrats, these images had to be shaped and blended to fit American conditions. The movements would have to come from the people, and the themes of counter-subversion would be likely to reflect their fears, prejudices, hopes, and perhaps even unconscious desires.

There are obvious dangers in treating such reactions against imagined subversion as part of a single tendency or spirit of an age.[1] Anti-Catholicism was nourished by ethnic conflict and uneasiness over immigration in the expanding cities of the Northeast; anti-Mormonism arose largely from a contest for economic and political power between western settlers and a group that voluntarily withdrew from society and claimed the undivided allegiance of its members.[2] Anti-Masonry, on the other hand, was directed against a group thoroughly integrated in American society and did not reflect a clear division of economic, religious, or political interests.[3] Moreover, anti-Masonry gained

---

[1] For an alternative to the method followed in this article, see John Higham's perceptive essay, "Another Look at Nativism," *Catholic Historical Review* (Washington), XLIV (July, 1958), 147–58. Higham rejects the ideological approach to nativism and stresses the importance of concrete ethnic tensions, "status rivalries," and face-to-face conflicts in explaining prejudice. Though much can be said for this sociological emphasis, as opposed to a search for irrational myths and stereotypes, the method suggested by Higham can easily lead to a simple "stimulus-response" view of prejudice. Awareness of actual conflicts in status and self-interest should not obscure the social and psychological functions of nativism, nor distract attention from themes that may reflect fundamental tensions within a culture.

[2] For a brilliant analysis of Mormon-Gentile conflict, see Thomas F. O'Dea, *The Mormons* (Chicago, 1958).

[3] Freemasons were blamed for various unrelated economic and political grievances, but anti-Masonry showed no uniform division according to class, occupation, or political affiliation. See Charles McCarthy, "The Anti-Masonic Party," American Historical

FROM David Brion Davis, "Some Themes of Counter-Subversion: An Analysis of Anti-Masonic, Anti-Catholic, and Anti-Mormon Literature," *Mississippi Valley Historical Review*, Vol. XLVII (September 1960), pp. 205–24. Reprinted by permission.

power in the late 1820's and soon spent its energies as it became absorbed in national politics; anti-Catholicism reached its maximum force in national politics a full generation later; [4] anti-Mormonism, though increasing in intensity in the 1850's, became an important national issue only after the Civil War.[5] These movements seem even more widely separated when we note that Freemasonry was traditionally associated with anti-Catholicism and that Mormonism itself absorbed considerable anti-Masonic and anti-Catholic sentiment.[6]

Despite such obvious differences, there were certain similarities in these campaigns against subversion. All three gained widespread support in the northeastern states within the space of a generation; anti-Masonry and anti-Catholicism resulted in the sudden emergence of separate political parties; and in 1856 the new Republican party explicitly condemned the Mormons' most controversial institution. The movements of counter-subversion differed markedly in historical origin, but as the image of an un-American conspiracy took form in the nativist press, in sensational exposés, in the countless fantasies of treason and mysterious criminality, the lines separating Mason, Catholic, and Mormon became almost indistinguishable.

The similar pattern of Masonic, Catholic, and Mormon subversion was frequently noticed by alarmist writers. The *Anti-Masonic Review* informed its readers in 1829 that whether one looked at Jesuitism or Freemasonry, "the organization, the power, and the secret operation, are the same; except that Freemasonry is much the more secret and complicated of the two." [7] William Hogan, an ex-priest and vitriolic anti-Catholic, compared the menace of Catholicism with that of Mormonism.[8] And many later anti-Mormon writers agreed with Josiah Strong that Brigham Young "out-popes the Roman" and

---

Association, *Annual Report for the Year 1902*, Vol. I (Washington, 1903), 370–73, 406–408. I am also indebted to Lorman A. Ratner, whose "Antimasonry in New York State: A Study in Pre-Civil War Reform" (M.A. thesis, Cornell University, 1958) substantiates this conclusion.

[4] For a detailed analysis of the issues and development of anti-Catholicism, see Ray A. Billington, *The Protestant Crusade, 1800–1860* (New York, 1938).

[5] It should be noted, however, that national attention was attracted by the Mountain Meadows Massacre and by Albert Sidney Johnston's punitive expedition to Utah.

[6] For anti-Catholic references in *The Book of Mormon*, see I Nephi 13:4–9; II Nephi 6:12, 28:18. Parallels between Masons and the "Gadianton robbers" have been frequently discussed.

[7] *Anti-Masonic Review and Magazine* (New York), II (October, 1829), 225–34. It was even claimed that Jesuits had been protected by Frederick the Great because they were mostly Freemasons and shared the same diabolical designs. See *Free Masonry: A Poem, In Three Cantos, Accompanied with Notes, Illustrative of the History, Policy, Principles, &c. of the Masonic Institution; Shewing the Coincidence of Its Spirit and Design with Ancient Jesuitism . . . By a Citizen of Massachusetts* (Leicester, Mass., 1830), 134.

[8] William Hogan, *Popery! As It Was and as It Is: Also, Auricular Confession: and Popish Nunneries,* two books in one edition (Hartford, 1855), 32–33.

described the Mormon hierarchy as being similar to the Catholic. It was probably not accidental that Samuel F. B. Morse analyzed the Catholic conspiracy in essentially the same terms his father had used in exposing the Society of the Illuminati, supposedly a radical branch of Freemasonry,[9] or that writers of sensational fiction in the 1840's and 1850's depicted an atheistic and unprincipled Catholic Church obviously modeled on Charles Brockden Brown's earlier fictional version of the Illuminati.[10]

If Masons, Catholics, and Mormons bore little resemblance to one another in actuality, as imagined enemies they merged into a nearly common stereotype. Behind specious professions of philanthropy or religious sentiment nativists [11] discerned a group of unscrupulous leaders plotting to subvert the American social order. Though rank-and-file members were not individually evil, they were blinded and corrupted by a persuasive ideology that justified treason and gross immorality in the interest of the subversive group. Trapped in the meshes of a machine-like organization, deluded by a false sense of loyalty and moral obligation, these dupes followed orders like professional soldiers and labored unknowingly to abolish free society, to enslave their fellow men, and to overthrow divine principles of law and justice. Should an occasional member free himself from bondage to superstition and fraudulent authority, he could still be disciplined by the threat of death or dreadful tortures. There were no limits to the ambitious designs of leaders equipped with such organizations. According to nativist prophets, they chose to subvert American society because control of America meant control of the world's destiny.

Some of these beliefs were common in earlier and later European interpretations of conspiracy. American images of Masonic, Catholic, and Mormon subversion were no doubt a compound of traditional myths concerning Jacobite agents, scheming Jesuits, and fanatical heretics, and of dark legends involving the Holy Vehm and Rosicrucians. What distinguished the stereotypes of Mason, Catholic, and Mormon was the way in which they were seen

---

[9] Jedidiah Morse, *A Sermon Preached at Charleston, November 29, 1798, on the Anniversary Thanksgiving in Massachusetts* (Boston, 1799); Vernon Stauffer, *The New England Clergy and the Bavarian Illuminati* (New York, 1918), 98–99, 233, 246–48.

[10] In Ned Buntline's *The G'hals of New York* (New York, 1850) the Jesuits seem to be connected with all secret conspiracies, and their American leader, Father Kerwin, is probably modeled on Brown's Carwin. George Lippard admired Brown, dedicated a novel to him, and was also fascinated by secret societies and diabolical plots to enslave America. In *New York: Its Upper Ten and Lower Million* (New York, 1853), the Catholic leaders are Illuminati-like atheists who plan revolutions, manipulate public opinion, and stop at no crime in their lust for wealth and power. These amoral supermen were clearly inspired by such characters as Brown's Ormond, as well as by the anti-Catholic writings of Eugène Sue and others.

[11] Though the term "nativist" is usually limited to opponents of immigration, it is used here to include anti-Masons and anti-Mormons. This seems justified in view of the fact that these alarmists saw themselves as defenders of native traditions and identified Masonry and Mormonism with forces alien to American life.

to embody those traits that were precise antitheses of American ideals. The subversive group was essentially an inverted image of Jacksonian democracy and the cult of the common man; as such it not only challenged the dominant values but stimulated those suppressed needs and yearnings that are unfulfilled in a mobile, rootless, and individualistic society. It was therefore both frightening and fascinating.

It is well known that expansion and material progress in the Jacksonian era evoked a fervid optimism and that nationalists became intoxicated with visions of America's millennial glory. The simultaneous growth of prosperity and social democracy seemed to prove that Providence would bless a nation that allowed her citizens maximum liberty. When each individual was left free to pursue happiness in his own way, unhampered by the tyranny of custom or special privilege, justice and well-being would inevitably emerge. But if a doctrine of laissez-faire individualism seemed to promise material expansion and prosperity, it also raised disturbing problems. As one early anti-Mormon writer expressed it: What was to prevent liberty and popular sovereignty from sweeping away "the old landmarks of Christendom, and the glorious old common law of our fathers"? How was the individual to preserve a sense of continuity with the past, or identify himself with a given cause or tradition? What, indeed, was to insure a common loyalty and a fundamental unity among the people?

Such questions acquired a special urgency as economic growth intensified mobility, destroyed old ways of life, and transformed traditional symbols of status and prestige. Though most Americans took pride in their material progress, they also expressed a yearning for reassurance and security, for unity in some cause transcending individual self-interest. This need for meaningful group activity was filled in part by religious revivals, reform movements, and a proliferation of fraternal orders and associations. In politics Americans tended to assume the posture of what Marvin Meyers has termed "venturesome conservatives," mitigating their acquisitive impulses by an appeal for unity against extraneous forces that allegedly threatened a noble heritage of republican ideals. Without abandoning a belief in progress through laissez-faire individualism, the Jacksonians achieved a sense of unity and righteousness by styling themselves as restorers of tradition.[12] Perhaps no theme is so evident in the Jacksonian era as the strained attempt to provide America with a glorious heritage and a noble destiny. With only a loose and often ephemeral attachment to places and institutions, many Americans felt a compelling need to articulate their loyalties, to prove their faith, and to demonstrate their allegiance to certain ideals and institutions. By so doing they acquired a sense of self-identity and personal direction in an otherwise rootless and shifting environment.

---

[12] For a lucid and provocative discussion of this "restoration theme," see Marvin Meyers, *The Jacksonian Persuasion* (Stanford, 1957), 162–64.

But was abstract nationalism sufficient to reassure a nation strained by sectional conflict, divided by an increasing number of sects and associations, and perplexed by the unexpected consequences of rapid growth? One might desire to protect the Republic against her enemies, to preserve the glorious traditions of the Founders, and to help insure continued expansion and prosperity, but first it was necessary to discover an enemy by distinguishing subversion from simple diversity. If Freemasons seemed to predominate in the economic and political life of a given area, was one's joining them shrewd business judgment or a betrayal of republican tradition? [13] Should Maryland citizens heed the warnings of anti-Masonic itinerants, or conclude that anti-Masonry was itself a conspiracy hatched by scheming Yankees? [14] Were Roman Catholics plotting to destroy public schools and a free press, the twin guardians of American democracy, or were they exercising democratic rights of self-expression and self-protection? [15] Did equality of opportunity and equality before the law mean that Americans should accept the land claims of Mormons or tolerate as jurors men who "swear that they have wrought miracles and supernatural cures"? Or should one agree with the Reverend Finis Ewing that "the 'Mormons' are the common enemies of mankind and ought to be destroyed"? [16]

Few men questioned traditional beliefs in freedom of conscience and the right of association. Yet what was to prevent "all the errors and worn out theories of the Old World, of schisms in the early Church, the monkish age and the rationalistic period," from flourishing in such salubrious air? [17] Nativists often praised the work of benevolent societies, but they were disturbed by the thought that monstrous conspiracies might also "show kindness and patriotism, when it is necessary for their better concealment; and oftentimes do much good for the sole purpose of getting a better opportunity to do evil." [18] When confronted by so many sects and associations, how was the patriot to distinguish the loyal from the disloyal? It was clear that mere dis-

---

[13] Hiram B. Hopkins, *Renunciation of Free Masonry* (Boston, 1830), 4–7.

[14] Jacob Lefever of Hagerstown appealed to regional loyalty and urged citizens of Maryland to forget their differences and unite against "foreign influence" from an area notorious for its "tricks and frauds." *Free-Masonry Unmasked: or Minutes of the Trial of a Suit in the Court of Common Pleas of Adams County, Wherein Thaddeus Stevens, Esq. Was Plaintiff, and Jacob Lefever, Defendant* (Gettysburg, 1835), pp. xiii–xiv.

[15] *The Cloven Foot: or Popery Aiming at Political Supremacy in the United States, By the Rector of Oldenwold* (New York, 1855), 170–79.

[16] William Mulder and A. Russell Mortensen (eds.), *Among the Mormons: Historic Accounts by Contemporary Observers* (New York, 1958), 76–79. The quotation is from the minutes of an anti-Mormon meeting in Jackson County, Missouri, July 20, 1833.

[17] John H. Beadle, *Life in Utah: or, the Mysteries and Crimes of Mormonism* (Philadelphia, [1872]), 5.

[18] *Anti-Masonic Review*, I (December, 1828), 3–4.

agreement over theology or economic policy was invalid as a test, since honest men disputed over the significance of baptism or the wisdom of protective tariffs. But neither could one rely on expressions of allegiance to common democratic principles, since subversives would cunningly profess to believe in freedom and toleration of dissent as long as they remained a powerless minority.

As nativists studied this troubling question, they discovered that most groups and denominations claimed only a partial loyalty from their members, freely subordinating themselves to the higher and more abstract demands of the Constitution, Christianity, and American public opinion. Moreover, they openly exposed their objects and activities to public scrutiny and exercised little discrimination in enlisting members. Some groups, however, dominated a larger portion of their members' lives, demanded unlimited allegiance as a condition of membership, and excluded certain activities from the gaze of a curious public.

Of all governments, said Richard Rush, ours was the one with most to fear from secret societies, since popular sovereignty by its very nature required perfect freedom of public inquiry and judgment.[19] In a virtuous republic why should anyone fear publicity or desire to conceal activities, unless those activities were somehow contrary to the public interest? When no one could be quite sure what the public interest was, and when no one could take for granted a secure and well-defined place in the social order, it was most difficult to acknowledge legitimate spheres of privacy. Most Americans of the Jacksonian era appeared willing to tolerate diversity and even eccentricity, but when they saw themselves excluded and even barred from witnessing certain proceedings, they imagined a "mystic power" conspiring to enslave them.

Readers might be amused by the first exposures of Masonic ritual, since they learned that pompous and dignified citizens, who had once impressed non-Masons with allusions to high degrees and elaborate ceremonies, had in actuality been forced to stand blindfolded and clad in ridiculous garb, with a long rope noosed around their necks. But genuine anti-Masons were not content with simple ridicule. Since intelligent and distinguished men had been members of the fraternity, "it must have in its interior something more than the usual revelations of its mysteries declare." [20] Surely leading citizens would not meet at night and undergo degrading and humiliating initiations just for the sake of novelty. The alleged murder of William Morgan raised an astonishing public furor because it supposedly revealed the inner secret of Freemasonry. Perverted by a false ideology, Masons had renounced all obligations to the general public, to the laws of the land, and even to the command

---

[19] Letter of May 4, 1831, printed in *The Anti-Masonic Almanac, for the Year 1832*, ed. by Edward Giddins (Utica, 1831), 29–30.

[20] *Anti-Masonic Review*, I (December, 1828), 6–7; Lebbeus Armstrong, *Masonry Proved to Be a Work of Darkness, Repugnant to the Christian Religion, and Inimical to a Republican Government* (New York, 1830), 16.

of God. Hence they threatened not a particular party's program or a denomination's creed, but stood opposed to all justice, democracy, and religion.[21]

The distinguishing mark of Masonic, Catholic, and Mormon conspiracies was a secrecy that cloaked the members' unconditional loyalty to an autonomous body. Since the organizations had corrupted the private moral judgment of their members, Americans could not rely on the ordinary forces of progress to spread truth and enlightenment among their ranks. Yet the affairs of such organizations were not outside the jurisdiction of democratic government, for no body politic could be asked to tolerate a power that was designed to destroy it.[22] Once the true nature of subversive groups was thoroughly understood, the alternatives were as clear as life and death. How could democracy and Catholicism coexist when, as Edward Beecher warned, "The systems are diametrically opposed: one must and will exterminate the other"?[23] Because Freemasons had so deeply penetrated state and national governments, only drastic remedies could restore the nation to its democratic purity.[24] And later, Americans faced an "irrepressible conflict" with Mormonism, for it was said that either free institutions or Mormon despotism must ultimately annihilate the other.[25]

We may well ask why nativists magnified the division between unpopular minorities and the American public, so that Masons, Catholics, and Mormons seemed so menacing that they could not be accorded the usual rights and privileges of a free society. Obviously the literature of counter-subversion reflected concrete rivalries and conflicts of interest between competing groups, but it is important to note that the subversive bore no racial or ethnic stigma and was not even accused of inherent depravity.[26] Since group membership was a matter of intellectual and emotional loyalty, no *physical* barrier pre-

---

[21] *The Anti-Masonic Almanack, for the Year 1828: Calculated for the Horizon of Rochester, N.Y. by Edward Giddins* (Rochester, 1827), entry for November and December, 1828; Armstrong, *Masonry*, 14.

[22] Hogan, *Popery*, 32–33.

[23] Edward Beecher, *The Papal Conspiracy Exposed, and Protestantism Defended, in the Light of Reason, History, and Scripture* (Boston, 1855), 29.

[24] *Anti-Masonic Review*, I (February, 1829), 71.

[25] Mulder and Mortensen (eds.), *Among the Mormons*, 407; Jennie Anderson Froiseth (ed.), *The Women of Mormonism: or, the Story of Polygamy as Told by the Victims Themselves* (Detroit, 1881–1882), 367–68.

[26] It is true that anti-Catholics sometimes stressed the inferiority of lower-class immigrants and that anti-Mormons occasionally claimed that Mormon converts were made among the most degraded and ignorant classes of Europe. This theme increased in importance toward the end of the century, but it seldom implied that Catholics and Mormons were physically incapable of being liberated and joined to the dominant group. Racism was not an original or an essential part of the counter-subversive's ideology. Even when Mormons were attacked for coarseness, credulity, and vulgarity, these traits were usually thought to be the product of their beliefs and institutions. See Mrs. B. G. Ferris, "Life among the Mormons," *Putnam's Monthly Magazine* (New York), VI (August, October, 1855), 144, 376–77.

vented a Mason, Catholic, or Mormon from apostatizing and joining the dominant in-group, providing always that he escaped assassination from his previous masters. This suggests that counter-subversion was more than a rationale for group rivalry and was related to the general problem of ideological unity and diversity in a free society. When a "system of delusion" insulated members of a group from the unifying and disciplining force of public opinion, there was no authority to command an allegiance to common principles. This was why oaths of loyalty assumed great importance for nativists. Though the ex-Catholic William Hogan stated repeatedly that Jesuit spies respected no oaths except those to the Church, he inconsistently told Masons and Odd Fellows that they could prevent infiltration by requiring new members to swear they were not Catholics. [27] It was precisely the absence of distinguishing outward traits that made the enemy so dangerous, and true loyalty so difficult to prove.

When the images of different enemies conform to a similar pattern, it is highly probable that this pattern reflects important tensions within a given culture. The themes of nativist literature suggest that its authors simplified problems of personal insecurity and adjustment to bewildering social change by trying to unite Americans of diverse political, religious, and economic interests against a common enemy. Just as revivalists sought to stimulate Christian fellowship by awakening men to the horrors of sin, so nativists used apocalyptic images to ignite human passions, destroy selfish indifference, and join patriots in a cohesive brotherhood. Such themes were only faintly secularized. When God saw his "lov'd Columbia" imperiled by the hideous monster of Freemasonry, He realized that only a martyr's blood could rouse the hearts of the people and save them from bondage to the Prince of Darkness. By having God will Morgan's death, this anti-Mason showed he was more concerned with national virtue and unity than with Freemasonry, which was only a providential instrument for testing republican strength.[28]

Similarly, for the anti-Catholic "this brilliant new world" was once "young and beautiful; it abounded in all the luxuries of nature; it promised all that was desirable to man." But the Roman Church, seeing "these irresistible temptations, thirsting with avarice and yearning for the reestablishment of her falling greatness, soon commenced pouring in among its unsuspecting people hordes of Jesuits and other friars." If Americans were to continue their narrow pursuit of self-interest, oblivious to the "Popish colleges, and nunneries, and monastic institutions," indifferent to manifold signs of corruption and decay, how could the nation expect "that the moral breezes of heaven should breathe upon her, and restore to her again that strong and healthy constitution, which her ancestors have left to her sons"? [29] The theme of an Adamic

[27] Hogan, *Popery*, 35.
[28] *Free Masonry: A Poem*, 55–58.
[29] Hogan, *Popery*, 7–8; *Auricular Confession*, 264–65.

fall from paradise was horrifying, but it was used to inspire determined action and thus unity. If Methodists were "criminally indifferent" to the Mormon question, and if "avaricious merchants, soulless corporations, and a subsidized press" ignored Mormon iniquities, there was all the more reason that the *"will of the people* must prevail." [30]

Without explicitly rejecting the philosophy of laissez-faire individualism, with its toleration of dissent and innovation, nativist literature conveyed a sense of common dedication to a noble cause and sacred tradition. Though the nation had begun with the blessings of God and with the noblest institutions known to man, the people had somehow become selfish and complacent, divided by petty disputes, and insensitive to signs of danger. In his sermons attacking such self-interest, such indifference to public concerns, and such a lack of devotion to common ideals and sentiments, the nativist revealed the true source of his anguish. Indeed, he seemed at times to recognize an almost beneficent side to subversive organizations, since they joined the nation in a glorious crusade and thus kept it from moral and social disintegration.

The exposure of subversion was a means of promoting unity, but it also served to clarify national values and provide the individual ego with a sense of high moral sanction and imputed righteousness. Nativists identified themselves repeatedly with a strangely incoherent tradition in which images of Pilgrims, Minute Men, Founding Fathers, and true Christians appeared in a confusing montage. Opposed to this heritage of stability and perfect integrity, to this society founded on the highest principles of divine and natural law, were organizations formed by the grossest frauds and impostures, and based on the wickedest impulses of human nature. Bitterly refuting Masonic claims to ancient tradition and Christian sanction, anti-Masons charged that the Order was of recent origin, that it was shaped by Jews, Jesuits, and French atheists as an engine for spreading infidelity, and that it was employed by kings and aristocrats to undermine republican institutions.[31] If the illustrious Franklin and Washington had been duped by Masonry, this only proved how treacherous was its appeal and how subtly persuasive were its pretensions.[32] Though the Catholic Church had an undeniable claim to tradition, nativists

---

[30] Froiseth (ed.), *Women of Mormonism*, 285–87, 291–92.

[31] *Free Masonry: A Poem*, 29–37; *Anti-Masonic Review*, I (June, 1829), 203–207. The charge was often repeated that higher degrees of Freemasonry were created by the "school of Voltaire" and introduced to America by Jewish immigrants. Masonry was also seen as an "auxiliary to British foreign policy."

[32] This question was most troubling to anti-Masons. Though some tried to side-step the issue by quoting Washington against "self-created societies," as if he had been referring to the Masons, others flatly declared that Washington had been hoodwinked, just as distinguished jurists had once been deluded by a belief in witchcraft. Of course Washington had been unaware of Masonic iniquities, but he had lent his name to the cause and had thus served as a decoy for the ensnarement of others. See *Free Masonry: A Poem*, 38; *Anti-Masonic Review*, I (January, 1829), 49, 54; *The Anti-Masonic Almanac, for the Year of the Christian Era 1830* (Rochester, 1829), 32.

argued that it had originated in stupendous frauds and forgeries "in comparison with which the forgeries of Mormonism are completely thrown into the shade." [33] Yet anti-Mormons saw an even more sinister conspiracy based on the "shrewd cunning" of Joseph Smith, who convinced gullible souls that he conversed with angels and received direct revelations from the Lord.[34]

By emphasizing the fraudulent character of their opponents' claims, nativists sought to establish the legitimacy and just authority of American institutions. Masonic rituals, Roman Catholic sacraments, and Mormon revelations were preposterous hoaxes used to delude naive or superstitious minds; but public schools, a free press, and jury trials were eternally valid prerequisites for a free and virtuous society.

Moreover, the finest values of an enlightened nation stood out in bold relief when contrasted with the corrupting tendencies of subversive groups. Perversion of the sexual instinct seemed inevitably to accompany religious error.[35] Deprived of the tender affections of normal married love, shut off from the elevating sentiments of fatherhood, Catholic priests looked on women only as insensitive objects for the gratification of their frustrated desires.[36] In similar fashion polygamy struck at the heart of a morality based on the inspiring influence of woman's affections: "it renders man coarse, tyrannical, brutal, and heartless. It deals death to all sentiments of true manhood. It enslaves and ruins woman. It crucifies every God-given feeling of her nature." [37] Some anti-Mormons concluded that plural marriage could only have been established among foreigners who have never learned to respect women. But the more common explanation was that the false ideology of Mormonism had deadened the moral sense and liberated man's wild sexual impulse from the normal restraints of civilization. Such degradation of women and corruption of man served to highlight the importance of democratic marriage, a respect for women, and careful cultivation of the finer sensibilities.[38]

But if nativist literature was a medium for articulating common values and exhorting individuals to transcend self-interest and join in a dedicated union against evil, it also performed a more subtle function. Why, we may ask, did nativist literature dwell so persistently on themes of brutal sadism and sexual immorality? Why did its authors describe sin in such minute de-

---

[33] Beecher, *Papal Conspiracy Exposed*, 391.

[34] Beadle, *Life in Utah*, 30–34.

[35] *Ibid.*, 332–33. According to Beadle, religious error and sexual perversion were related "because the same constitution of mind and temperament which gives rise to one, powerfully predisposes toward the other."

[36] *Cloven Foot*, 294–95.

[37] Froiseth (ed.), *Women of Mormonism*, 113.

[38] Though Horace Greeley was moderate in his judgment of Mormonism, he wrote: "I joyfully trust that the genius of the Nineteenth Century tends to a solution of the problem of Woman's sphere and destiny radically different from this." Quoted in Mulder and Mortensen (eds.), *Among the Mormons*, 328.

tails, endowing even the worst offenses of their enemies with a certain fascinating appeal?

Freemasons, it was said, could commit any crime and indulge any passion when "upon the square," and Catholics and Mormons were even less inhibited by internal moral restraints. Nativists expressed horror over this freedom from conscience and conventional morality, but they could not conceal a throbbing note of envy. What was it like to be a member of a cohesive brotherhood that casually abrogated the laws of God and man, enforcing unity and obedience with dark and mysterious powers? As nativists speculated on this question, they projected their own fears and desires into a fantasy of licentious orgies and fearful punishments.

Such a projection of forbidden desires can be seen in the exaggeration of the stereotyped enemy's powers, which made him appear at times as a virtual superman. Catholic and Mormon leaders, never hindered by conscience or respect for traditional morality, were curiously superior to ordinary Americans in cunning, in exercising power over others, and especially in captivating gullible women.[39] It was an ancient theme of anti-Catholic literature that friars and priests were somehow more potent and sexually attractive than married laymen, and were thus astonishingly successful at seducing supposedly virtuous wives.[40] Americans were cautioned repeatedly that no priest recognized Protestant marriages as valid, and might consider any wife legitimate prey.[41] Furthermore, priests had access to the pornographic teachings of Dens and Liguori, sinister names that aroused the curiosity of anti-Catholics, and hence learned subtle techniques of seduction perfected over the centuries. Speaking with the authority of an ex-priest, William Hogan described the shocking result: "I have seen husbands unsuspiciously and hospitably entertaining the very priest who seduced their wives in the confessional, and was the parent of some of the children who sat at the same table with them, each of the wives unconscious of the other's guilt, and the husbands of both, not even suspecting them." [42] Such blatant immorality was horrifying, but everyone was apparently happy in this domestic scene, and we may suspect that the image was

---

[39] It should be noted that Freemasons were rarely accused of sexual crimes, owing perhaps to their greater degree of integration within American society, and to their conformity to the dominant pattern of monogamy. They were sometimes attacked, however, for excluding women from their Order, and for swearing not to violate the chastity of wives, sisters, and daughters of fellow Masons. Why, anti-Masons asked, was such an oath not extended to include *all* women? David Bernard, *Light on Masonry: A Collection of all the Most Important Documents on the Subject* (Utica, 1829), 62 n.

[40] Anthony Gavin, *A Master-Key to Popery, Giving a Full Account of All the Customs of the Priests and Friars, and the Rites and Ceremonies of Popish Religion* (n.p., 1812), 70–72. Such traditional works of European anti-Catholicism were frequently reprinted and imitated in America.

[41] *Cloven Foot*, 224. The Mormons were also alleged to regard the wives of infidels "lawful prey to any believer who can win them," Beadle, *Life in Utah*, 233.

[42] Hogan, *Auricular Confession*, 289.

not entirely repugnant to husbands who, despite their respect for the Lord's Commandments, occasionally coveted their neighbors' wives.

The literature of counter-subversion could also embody the somewhat different projective fantasies of women. Ann Eliza Young dramatized her seduction by the Prophet Brigham, whose almost superhuman powers enchanted her and paralyzed her will. Though she submitted finally only because her parents were in danger of being ruined by the Church, she clearly indicated that it was an exciting privilege to be pursued by a Great Man.[43] When Anti-Mormons claimed that Joseph Smith and other prominent Saints knew the mysteries of Animal Magnetism, or were endowed with the highest degree of "amativeness" in their phrenological makeup, this did not detract from their covert appeal.[44] In a ridiculous fantasy written by Maria Ward, such alluring qualities were extended even to Mormon women. Many bold-hearted girls could doubtless identify themselves with Anna Bradish, a fearless Amazon of a creature, who rode like a man, killed without compunction, and had no pity for weak women who failed to look out for themselves. Tall, elegant, and "intellectual," Anna was attractive enough to arouse the insatiable desires of Brigham Young, though she ultimately rejected him and renounced Mormonism.[45]

While nativists affirmed their faith in Protestant monogamy, they obviously took pleasure in imagining the variety of sexual experience supposedly available to their enemies. By picturing themselves exposed to similar temptations, they assumed they could know how priests and Mormons actually sinned.[46] Imagine, said innumerable anti-Catholic writers, a beautiful young woman kneeling before an ardent young priest in a deserted room. As she confesses, he leans over, looking into her eyes, until their heads are nearly touching. Day after day she reveals to him her innermost secrets, secrets she would not think of unveiling to her parents, her dearest friends, or even her suitor. By skillful questioning the priest fills her mind with immodest and even sensual ideas, "until this wretch has worked up her passions to a tension almost snapping, and then becomes his easy prey." How could any man resist such provocative temptations, and how could any girl's virtue withstand such a test? [47]

---

[43] Ann Eliza Young, *Wife No. 19: or, the Story of a Life in Bondage, Being a Complete Exposé of Mormonism* (Hartford, 1875), 433, 440–41, 453.

[44] Maria Ward, *Female Life among the Mormons: A Narrative of Many Years' Personal Experience, By the Wife of a Mormon Elder, Recently Returned from Utah* (New York, 1857), 24; Beadle, *Life in Utah*, 339.

[45] Ward, *Female Life among the Mormons,* 68, 106, 374.

[46] The Mormons, for instance, were imagined to engage in the most licentious practices in the Endowment House ceremonies. See Nelson W. Green (ed.), *Fifteen Years among the Mormons: Being the Narrative of Mrs. Mary Ettie V. Smith* (New York, 1857), 44–51.

[47] Hogan, *Auricular Confession,* 254–55; *Cloven Foot,* 301–304.

We should recall that this literature was written in a period of increasing anxiety and uncertainty over sexual values and the proper role of woman. As ministers and journalists pointed with alarm at the spread of prostitution, the incidence of divorce, and the lax and hypocritical morality of the growing cities, a discussion of licentious subversives offered a convenient means for the projection of guilt as well as desire. The sins of individuals, or of the nation as a whole, could be pushed off upon the shoulders of the enemy and there punished in righteous anger.[48]

Specific instances of such projection are not difficult to find. John C. Bennett, whom the Mormons expelled from the Church as a result of his flagrant sexual immorality, invented the fantasy of "The Mormon Seraglio" which persisted in later anti-Mormon writings. According to Bennett, the Mormons maintained secret orders of beautiful prostitutes who were mostly reserved for various officials of the Church. He claimed, moreover, that any wife refusing to accept polygamy might be forced to join the lowest order and thus become available to any Mormon who desired her.[49]

Another example of projection can be seen in the letters of a young lieutenant who stopped in Utah in 1854 on his way to California. Convinced that Mormon women could be easily seduced, the lieutenant wrote frankly of his amorous adventures with a married woman. "Everybody has got one," he wrote with obvious pride, "except the Colonel and Major. The Doctor has got three—mother and two daughters. The mother cooks for him and the daughters sleep with him." But though he described Utah as "a great country," the lieutenant waxed indignant over polygamy, which he condemned as self-righteously as any anti-Mormon minister: "To see one man openly parading half a dozen or more women to church . . . is the devil according to my ideas of morality, virtue and decency." [50]

If the consciences of many Americans were troubled by the growth of red light districts in major cities, they could divert their attention to the "legalized brothels" called nunneries, for which no one was responsible but lecherous Catholic priests. If others were disturbed by the moral implications of divorce, they could point in horror at the Mormon elder who took his quota of wives all at once. The literature of counter-subversion could thus serve the double purpose of vicariously fulfilling repressed desires, and of releasing the tension and guilt arising from rapid social change and conflicting values.

Though the enemy's sexual freedom might at first seem enticing, it was always made repugnant in the end by associations with perversion or brutal cruelty. Both Catholics and Mormons were accused of practicing nearly every

---

[48] This point is ably discussed by Kimball Young, *Isn't One Wife Enough?* (New York, 1954), 26–27.

[49] *Ibid.*, 311.

[50] Quoted in Mulder and Mortensen (eds.), *Among the Mormons*, 274–78.

form of incest.[51] The persistent emphasis on this theme might indicate deep-rooted feelings of fear and guilt, but it also helped demonstrate, on a more objective level, the loathsome consequences of unrestrained lust. Sheer brutality and a delight in human suffering were supposed to be the even more horrible results of sexual depravity. Masons disemboweled or slit the throats of their victims; Catholics cut unborn infants from their mothers' wombs and threw them to the dogs before their parents' eyes; Mormons raped and lashed recalcitrant women, or seared their mouths with red-hot irons.[52] This obsession with details of sadism, which reached pathological proportions in much of the literature, showed a furious determination to purge the enemy of every admirable quality. The imagined enemy might serve at first as an outlet for forbidden desires, but nativist authors escaped from guilt by finally making him an agent of unmitigated aggression. In such a role the subversive seemed to deserve both righteous anger and the most terrible punishments.

The nativist escape from guilt was more clearly revealed in the themes of confession and conversion. For most American Protestants the crucial step in anyone's life was a profession of true faith resulting from a genuine religious experience. Only when a man became conscious of his inner guilt, when he struggled against the temptations of Satan, could he prepare his soul for the infusion of the regenerative spirit. Those most deeply involved in sin often made the most dramatic conversions. It is not surprising that conversion to nativism followed the same pattern, since nativists sought unity and moral certainty in the regenerative spirit of nationalism. Men who had been associated in some way with un-American conspiracies were not only capable of spectacular confessions of guilt, but were best equipped to expose the insidious work of supposedly harmless organizations. Even those who lacked such an exciting history of corruption usually made some confession of guilt, though it might involve only a previous indifference to subversive groups. Like ardent Christians, nativists searched in their own experiences for the meanings of sin, delusion, awakening to truth, and liberation from spiritual bondage. These personal confessions proved that one had recognized and conquered evil, and also served as ritual cleansings preparatory to full acceptance in a group of dedicated patriots.

Anti-Masons were perhaps the ones most given to confessions of guilt and most alert to subtle distinctions of loyalty and disloyalty. Many leaders of this movement, expressing guilt over their own "shameful experience and knowl-

---

[51] George Bourne, *Lorette: The History of Louise, Daughter of a Canadian Nun, Exhibiting the Interior of Female Convents* (New York, 1834), 176–77; Hogan, *Auricular Confession,* 271; Frances Stenhouse, *A Lady's Life among the Mormons: A Record of Personal Experience as One of the Wives of a Mormon Elder* (New York, 1872), 77.

[52] *Anti-Masonic Review,* I (December, 1828), 24 ff.; *Cloven Foot,* 325–42, 357–58; Froiseth (ed.), *Women of Mormonism,* 317–18; Ward, *Female Life among the Mormons,* 428–29.

edge" of Masonry, felt a compelling obligation to exhort their former associates to "come out, and be separate from masonic abominations." [53] Even when an anti-Mason could say with John Quincy Adams that "I am not, never was, and never shall be a Freemason," he would often admit that he had once admired the Order, or had even considered applying for admission.[54]

Since a willingness to sacrifice oneself was an unmistakable sign of loyalty and virtue, ex-Masons gloried in exaggerating the dangers they faced and the harm that their revelations supposedly inflicted on the enemy. In contrast to hardened Freemasons, who refused to answer questions in court concerning their fraternal associations, the seceders claimed to reveal the inmost secrets of the Order, and by so doing to risk property, reputation, and life.[55] Once the ex-Mason had dared to speak the truth, his character would surely be maligned, his motives impugned, and his life threatened. But, he declared, even if he shared the fate of the illustrious Morgan, he would die knowing that he had done his duty.

Such self-dramatization reached extravagant heights in the ranting confessions of many apostate Catholics and Mormons. Maria Monk and her various imitators told of shocking encounters with sin in its most sensational forms, of bondage to vice and superstition, and of melodramatic escapes from popish despotism. A host of "ex-Mormon wives" described their gradual recognition of Mormon frauds and iniquities, the anguish and misery of plural marriage, and their breath-taking flights over deserts or mountains. The female apostate was especially vulnerable to vengeful retaliation, since she could easily be kidnapped by crafty priests and nuns, or dreadfully punished by Brigham Young's Destroying Angels.[56] At the very least, her reputation could be smirched by foul lies and insinuations. But her willingness to risk honor and life for the sake of her country and for the dignity of all womankind was eloquent proof of her redemption. What man could be assured of so noble a role?

The apostate's pose sometimes assumed paranoid dimensions. William Hogan warned that only the former priest could properly gauge the Catholic threat to American liberties and saw himself as providentially appointed to save his Protestant countrymen. "For twenty years," he wrote, "I have warned them of approaching danger, but their politicians were deaf, and their Protestant theologians remained religiously coiled up in fancied security, overrating their own powers and undervaluing that of Papists." Pursued by vengeful Jesuits, denounced and calumniated for alleged crimes, Hogan pic-

---

[53] Armstrong, *Masonry,* 22.

[54] *Free Masonry: A Poem,* p. iv.

[55] *Ibid.,* pp. iii, 51; Hopkins, *Renunciation of Free Masonry,* 5, 9–11; *Anti-Masonic Almanac,* 1830, pp. 28–29; Bernard, *Light on Masonry,* p. iii.

[56] Stenhouse, *Lady's Life among the Mormons,* 142–43.

tured himself single-handedly defending American freedom: "No one, before me, dared to encounter their scurrilous abuse. I resolved to silence them; and I have done so. The very mention of my name is a terror to them now." After surviving the worst Catholic persecution, Hogan claimed to have at last aroused his countrymen and to have reduced the hierarchy to abject terror.[57]

As the nativist searched for participation in a noble cause, for unity in a group sanctioned by tradition and authority, he professed a belief in democracy and equal rights. Yet in his very zeal for freedom he curiously assumed many of the characteristics of the imagined enemy. By condemning the subversive's fanatical allegiance to an ideology, he affirmed a similarly uncritical acceptance of a different ideology; by attacking the subversive's intolerance of dissent, he worked to eliminate dissent and diversity of opinion by censuring the subversive for alleged licentiousness, he engaged in sensual fantasies; by criticizing the subversive's loyalty to an organization, he sought to prove his unconditional loyalty to the established order. The nativist moved even farther in the direction of his enemies when he formed tightly-knit societies and parties which were often secret and which subordinated the individual to the single purpose of the group. Though the nativists generally agreed that the worst evil of subversives was their subordination of means to ends, they themselves recommended the most radical means to purge the nation of troublesome groups and to enforce unquestioned loyalty to the state.

In his image of an evil group conspiring against the nation's welfare, and in his vision of a glorious millennium that was to dawn after the enemy's defeat, the nativist found satisfaction for many desires. His own interests became legitimate and dignified by fusion with the national interest, and various opponents became loosely associated with the un-American conspiracy. Thus Freemasonry in New York State was linked in the nativist mind with economic and political interests that were thought to discriminate against certain groups and regions; southerners imagined a union of abolitionists and Catholics to promote unrest and rebellion among slaves; gentile businessmen in Utah merged anti-Mormonism with plans for exploiting mines and lands.

Then too the nativist could style himself as a restorer of the past, as a defender of a stable order against disturbing changes, and at the same time proclaim his faith in future progress. By focusing his attention on the imaginary threat of a secret conspiracy, he found an outlet for many irrational impulses, yet professed his loyalty to the ideals of equal rights and government by law. He paid lip service to the doctrine of laissez-faire individualism, but preached selfless dedication to a transcendent cause. The imposing threat of subversion justified a group loyalty and subordination of the individual that would otherwise have been unacceptable. In a rootless environment shaken by bewildering social change the nativist found unity and meaning by conspiring against imaginary conspiracies.

---

[57] Hogan, *Auricular Confession,* 226–29, 233, 296–97.

JOHN L. THOMAS

ROMANTIC REFORM IN AMERICA
1815–1865

The following article deserves close reading for a number of reasons. It discusses the religious spirit that manifested itself in so many aspects of American reform in the nineteenth century, and it traces the complex ramifications of this basically conservative impulse in movements for far-reaching social reform. By focusing upon the romantic aspects of ante-bellum reform, Thomas provides a detailed analysis of such widespread nineteenth-century reformist assumptions and goals as perfectionism, immediatism, and anti-institutionalism as well as their strong belief in individualism. These forces are too frequently disregarded or ignored by the tendency to view Jacksonian democracy or the slavery controversy in exclusively political terms. Thomas briefly but perceptively explores the disruptive impact that the Civil War had upon these earlier reformist impulses and the role it had in shaping post-bellum reform. Finally, this essay establishes a historical framework within which the reform spirit so widespread among a growing segment of young Americans in the 1960's can be more readily understood.

Whitney R. Cross, The Burned-Over District * *(1950), is an excellent study of the genesis of reform movements in New York during the first half of the nineteenth century. And George M. Frederickson,* The Inner Civil War *(1965), contains an illuminating discussion of the effects of the Civil War upon the reform impulse in the North.*

$\mathbf{C}$onfronted by the bewildering variety of projects for regenerating American society, Emerson concluded his survey of humanitarian reform in 1844 with the observation that "the Church, or religious party, is falling away from the Church nominal, and . . . appearing in temperance and nonresistance societies; in movements of abolitionists and of socialists . . . of seekers, of all the soul of the soldiery of dissent." Common to all these planners and prophets, he noted, was the conviction of an "infinite worthiness" in man and the belief that reform simply meant removing "impediments" to natural perfection.[1]

Emerson was defining, both as participant and observer, a romantic revolution which T. E. Hulme once described as "spilt religion."[2] A romantic faith in perfectibility, originally confined by religious institutions, overflows these barriers and spreads across the surface of society, seeping into politics and culture. Perfectibility—the essentially religious notion of the individual as a "reservoir" of possibilities—fosters a revolutionary assurance "that if you can so rearrange society by the destruction of oppressive order then these possibilities will have a chance and you will get Progress." Hulme had in mind the destructive forces of the French Revolution, but his phrase is also a particularly accurate description of the surge of social reform which swept across Emerson's America in the three decades before the Civil War. Out of a seemingly conservative religious revival there flowed a spate of perfectionist ideas for the improvement and rearrangement of American society. Rising rapidly in the years after 1830, the flood of social reform reached its crest at midcentury only to be checked by political crisis and the counterforces of the Civil War. Reform after the Civil War, though still concerned with individual perfectibility, proceeded from new and different assumptions as to the nature of individualism and its preservation in an urban industrial society. Romantic reform ended with the Civil War and an intellectual counterrevolution which discredited the concept of the irreducible self and eventually redirected reform energies.

Romantic reform in America traced its origins to a religious impulse which was both politically and socially conservative. With the consolidation of independence and the arrival of democratic politics the new nineteenth-century generation of American churchmen faced a seeming crisis. Egalitari-

---

[1] Ralph Waldo Emerson, "The New England Reformers," *Works* (Centenary ed.), III, 251; "Man the Reformer," *Works,* I, 248–49.

[2] T. E. Hulme, "Romanticism and Classicism," *Speculations: Essays on Humanism and the Philosophy of Art,* ed. Herbert Read (London, 1924), reprinted in *Critiques and Essays in Criticism, 1920–1948,* ed. Robert Wooster Stallman (New York, 1949), pp. 3–16.

FROM John L. Thomas, "Romantic Reform in America, 1815–1865," *American Quarterly,* Philadelphia: University of Pennsylvania, 1965, Vol. XVII (Winter 1965), pp. 656–81. Copyright, 1965, Trustees of the University of Pennsylvania. Reprinted by permission.

anism and rising demands for church disestablishment suddenly appeared to threaten an inherited Christian order and along with it the preferred status of the clergy. Lyman Beecher spoke the fears of more than one of the clerical party when he warned that Americans were fast becoming "another people." When the attempted alliance between sound religion and correct politics failed to prevent disestablishment or improve waning Federalist fortunes at the polls, the evangelicals, assuming a defensive posture, organized voluntary benevolent associations to strengthen the Christian character of Americans and save the country from infidelity and ruin. Between 1815 and 1830 nearly a dozen moral reform societies were established to counter the threats to social equilibrium posed by irreligious democrats. Their intense religious concern could be read in the titles of the benevolent societies which the evangelicals founded: the American Bible Society, the American Sunday School Union, the American Home Missionary Society, the American Tract Society. By the time of the election of Andrew Jackson the benevolent associations formed a vast if loosely coordinated network of conservative reform enterprises staffed with clergy and wealthy laymen who served as self-appointed guardians of American morals.[3]

The clerical diagnosticians had little difficulty in identifying the symptoms of democratic disease. Infidelity flourished on the frontier and licentiousness bred openly in seaboard cities; intemperance sapped the strength of American workingmen and the saving word was denied their children. Soon atheism would destroy the vital organs of the republic unless drastic moral therapy prevented. The evangelicals' prescription followed logically from their diagnosis: large doses of morality injected into the body politic under the supervision of Christian stewards. No more Sunday mails or pleasure excursions, no more grog-shops or profane pleasures, no family without a Bible and no community without a minister of the gospel. Accepting for the moment their political liabilities, the moral reformers relied on the homeopathic strategy of fighting democratic excess with democratic remedies. The Tract Society set up three separate printing presses which cranked out hundreds of thousands of pamphlets for mass distribution. The Home Missionary Society subsidized seminarians in carrying religion into the backcountry. The Temperance Union staged popular conventions; the Peace Society sponsored public debates; the Bible Society hired hundreds of agents to spread its propaganda.

The initial thrust of religious reform, then, was moral rather than social, preventive rather than curative. Nominally rejecting politics and parties, the evangelicals looked to a general reformation of the American character achieved through a revival of piety and morals in the individual. By probing his conscience, by convincing him of his sinful ways and converting him to

---

[3] For discussions of evangelical reform see John R. Bodo, *The Protestant Clergy and Public Issues, 1812–1848* (Princeton, 1954), and Clifford S. Griffin, *Their Brothers' Keepers* (New Brunswick, N.J., 1960).

right conduct they hoped to engineer a Christian revolution which would leave the foundations of the social order undisturbed. The realization of their dream of a nonpolitical "Christian party" in America would ensure a one-party system open to moral talent and the natural superiority of Christian leadership. Until their work was completed, the evangelicals stood ready as servants of the Lord to manage their huge reformational apparatus in behalf of order and sobriety.

But the moral reformers inherited a theological revolution which in undermining their conservative defenses completely reversed their expectations for a Christian America. The transformation of American theology in the first quarter of the nineteenth century released the very forces of romantic perfectionism that conservatives most feared. This religious revolution advanced along three major fronts: first, the concentrated anti-theocratic assault of Robert Owen and his secular utopian followers, attacks purportedly atheistic and environmentalist but in reality Christian in spirit and perfectionist in method; second, the revolt of liberal theology beginning with Unitarianism and culminating in transcendentalism; third, the containment operation of the "new divinity" in adapting orthodoxy to the criticism of liberal dissent. The central fact in the romantic reorientation of American theology was the rejection of determinism. Salvation, however variously defined, lay open to everyone. Sin was voluntary: men were not helpless and depraved by nature but free agents and potential powers for good. Sin could be reduced to the selfish preferences of individuals, and social evils, in turn, to collective sins which, once acknowledged, could be rooted out. Perfectionism spread rapidly across the whole spectrum of American Protestantism as different denominations and sects elaborated their own versions of salvation. If man was a truly free agent, then his improvement became a matter of immediate consequence. The progress of the country suddenly seemed to depend upon the regeneration of the individual and the contagion of example.

As it spread, perfectionism swept across denominational barriers and penetrated even secular thought. Perfection was presented as Christian striving for holiness in the "new heart" sermons of Charles Grandison Finney and as an immediately attainable goal in the come-outer prophecies of John Humphrey Noyes. It was described as an escape from outworn dogma by Robert Owen and as the final union of the soul with nature by Emerson. The important fact for most Americans in the first half of the nineteenth century was that it was readily available. A romantic religious faith had changed an Enlightenment doctrine of progress into a dynamic principle of reform.

For the Founding Fathers' belief in perfectibility had been wholly compatible with a pessimistic appraisal of the present state of mankind. Progress, in the view of John Adams or James Madison, resulted from the planned operation of mechanical checks within the framework of government which balanced conflicting selfish interests and neutralized private passions. Thus a properly constructed governmental machine might achieve by artifact what men, left to their own devices, could not—gradual improvement of social institutions and a measure of progress. Perfectionism, on the contrary, as an optative mood demanded total commitment and immediate action. A latent revolutionary force lay in its demand for immediate reform and its promise to release the new American from the restraints of institutions and precedent. In appealing to the liberated individual, perfectionism reinforced the Jacksonian attack on institutions, whether a "Monster Bank" or a secret Masonic order, entrenched monopolies or the Catholic Church. But in emphasizing the unfettered will as the proper vehicle for reform it provided a millenarian alternative to Jacksonian politics. Since social evils were simply individual acts of selfishness compounded, and since Americans could attempt the perfect society any time they were so inclined, it followed that the duty of the true reformer consisted in educating them and making them models of good behavior. As the sum of individual sins social wrong would disappear when enough people had been converted and rededicated to right conduct. Deep and lasting reform, therefore, meant an educational crusade based on the assumption that when a sufficient number of individual Americans had seen the light, they would automatically solve the country's social problems. Thus formulated, perfectionist reform offered a program of mass conversion achieved through educational rather than political means. In the opinion of the romantic reformers the regeneration of American society began, not in legislative enactments or political manipulation, but in a calculated appeal to the American urge for individual self-improvement.

Perfectionism radically altered the moral reform movement by shattering the benevolent societies themselves. Typical of these organizations was the American Peace Society founded in 1828 as a forum for clerical discussions of the gospel of peace. Its founders, hoping to turn American attention from the pursuit of wealth to the prevention of war, debated the question of defensive war, constructed hypothetical leagues of amity, and in a general way sought to direct American foreign policy into pacific channels. Perfectionism, however, soon split the Peace Society into warring factions as radical nonresistants, led by the Christian perfectionist Henry C. Wright, denounced all use of force and demanded the instant creation of an American society modeled on the precepts of Jesus. Not only war but all governmental coercion fell under the ban of the nonresistants who refused military service and political office along with the right to vote. After a series of skirmishes the nonresistants seceded in 1838 to form their own New England Non-Resistant Society; and by 1840 the institutional strength of the peace movement had been completely broken.

The same power of perfectionism disrupted the temperance movement. The founders of the temperance crusade had considered their reform an integral part of the program of moral stewardship and had directed their campaign against "ardent spirits" which could be banished "by a correct and efficient public sentiment." Until 1833 there was no general agreement on a pledge of total abstinence: some local societies required it, others did not. At the first national convention held in that year, however, the radical advocates of temperance, following their perfectionist proclivities, demanded a pledge of total abstinence and hurried on to denounce the liquor traffic as "morally wrong." Soon both the national society and local and state auxiliaries were split betwen moderates content to preach to the consumer and radicals bent on extending moral suasion to public pressure on the seller. Afer 1836 the national movement disintegrated into scattered local societies which attempted with no uniform program and no permanent success to establish a cold-water America.

By far the most profound change wrought by perfectionism was the sudden emergence of abolition. The American Colonization Society, founded in 1817 as another key agency in the moral reform complex, aimed at strengthening republican institutions by deporting an inferior and therefore undesirable Negro population. The cooperation of Southerners hoping to strengthen the institution of slavery gave Northern colonizationists pause, but they succeeded in repressing their doubts until a perfectionist ethic totally discredited their program. The abolitionist pioneers were former colonizationists who took sin and redemption seriously and insisted that slavery constituted a flat denial of perfectibility to both Negroes and whites. They found in immediate emancipation a perfectionist formula for casting off the guilt of slavery and bringing the Negro to Christian freedom. Destroying slavery, the abolitionists argued, depended first of all on recognizing it as sin: and to this recognition they bent their efforts. Their method was direct and intensely personal. Slaveholding they considered a deliberate flouting of the divine will for which there was no remedy but repentance. Since slavery was sustained by a system of interlocking personal sins, their task was to teach Americans to stop sinning. "We shall send forth agents to lift up the voice of remonstrance, of warning, of entreaty, and of rebuke," the Declaration of Sentiments of the American Anti-Slavery Society announced. Agents, tracts, petitions and conventions— all the techniques of the moral reformers—were brought to bear on the consciences of Americans to convince them of their sin.

From the beginning, then, the abolitionists mounted a moral crusade rather than an engine of limited reform. For seven years, from 1833 to 1840, their society functioned as a loosely coordinated enterprise—a national directory of antislavery opinion. Perfectionist individualism made effective organization difficult and often impossible. Antislavery delegates from state and local societies gathered at annual conventions to frame denunciatory resolutions, listen to endless rounds of speeches and go through the motions of electing officers. Nominal leadership but very little power was vested in a self-perpetuating executive committee. Until its disruption in 1840 the national society was riddled with controversy as moderates, disillusioned by the failure of moral suasion, gradually turned to politics, and ultras, equally disenchanted by public hostility, abandoned American institutions altogether.

Faced with the resistance of Northern churches and state legislatures, the perfectionists, led by William Lloyd Garrison, deserted politics for the principle of secession. The come-outer abolitionists, who eventually took for their motto "No Union with Slaveholders," sought an alternative to politics in the command to cast off church and state for a holy fraternity which would convert the nation by the power of example. The American Anti-Slavery Society quickly succumbed to the strain of conflicting philosophies and warring personalities. In 1840 the Garrisonians seized control of the society and drove their moderate opponents out. Thereafter neither ultras nor moderates were able to maintain an effective national organization.

Thus romantic perfectionism altered the course of the reform enterprise by appealing directly to the individual conscience. Its power stemmed from a millennial expectation which proved too powerful a moral explosive for the reform agencies. In one way or another almost all of the benevolent societies felt the force of perfectionism. Moderates, attempting political solutions, scored temporary gains only to receive sharp setbacks. Local option laws passed one year were repealed the next. Despite repeated attempts the Sunday School Union failed to secure permanent adoption of its texts in the public schools. The Liberty Party succeeded only in electing a Democratic president in 1844. Generally, direct political action failed to furnish reformers with the moral leverage they believed necessary to perfect American society. The conviction spread accordingly that politicians and legislators, as Albert Brisbane put it, were engaged in "superficial controversies and quarrels, which lead to no practical results." [4] Political results, a growing number of social reformers were convinced, would be forthcoming only when the reformation of society at large had been accomplished through education and example.

The immediate effects of perfectionism, therefore, were felt outside politics in humanitarian reforms. With its confidence in the liberated individual perfectionism tended to be anti-institutional and exclusivist; but at the same time it posited an ideal society in which this same individual could discover his power for good and exploit it. Such a society would tolerate neither poverty nor suffering; it would contain no condemned classes or deprived citizens, no criminals or forgotten men. Impressed with the necessity for saving these neglected elements of American society, the humanitarian reformers in the years after 1830 undertook a huge rescue operation.

Almost to a man the humanitarians came from moral reform backgrounds. Samuel Gridley Howe was a product of Old Colony religious zeal and a Baptist education at Brown; Thomas Gallaudet a graduate of Andover and an ordained minister; Dorothea Dix a daughter of an itinerant Methodist minister, school mistress and Sunday school teacher-turned-reformer;

---

[4] Arthur Brisbane, *Social Destiny of Man: or, Association and Reorganization of Industry* (Philadelphia, 1840), introduction, p. vi.

E. M. P. Wells, founder of the reform school, a pastor of a Congregational church in Boston. Louis Dwight, the prison reformer, had been trained for the ministry at Yale and began his reform career as a traveling agent for the American Tract Society. Robert Hartley, for thirty years the secretary of the New York Association for Improving the Condition of the Poor, started as a tract distributor and temperance lecturer. Charles Loring Brace served as a missionary on Blackwell's Island before founding the Children's Aid Society.

In each of these cases of conversion to humanitarian reform there was a dramatic disclosure of deprivation and suffering which did not tally with pre-conceived notions of perfectibility—Dorothea Dix's discovery of the conditions in the Charlestown reformatory, Robert Hartley's inspection of contaminated milk in New York slums, Samuel Gridley Howe's chance conversation with Dr. Fisher in Boston. Something very much like a conversion experience seems to have forged the decisions of the humanitarians to take up their causes, a kind of revelation which furnished them with a ready-made role outside politics and opened a new career with which they could become completely identified. With the sudden transference of a vague perfectionist faith in self-improvement to urgent social problems there emerged a new type of professional reformer whose whole life became identified with the reform process.

Such, for example, was the conversion of Dorothea Dix from a lonely and afflicted schoolteacher who composed meditational studies of the life of Jesus into "D. L. Dix," the militant advocate of the helpless and forgotten. In a very real sense Miss Dix's crusade for better treatment of the insane and the criminal was one long self-imposed subjection to suffering. Her reports, which recorded cases of unbelievable mistreatment, completed a kind of purgative rite in which she assumed the burden of innocent suffering and passed it on as guilt to the American people. The source of her extraordinary energy lay in just this repeated submission of herself to human misery until she felt qualified to speak out against it. Both an exhausting schedule and the almost daily renewal of scenes of suffering seemed to give her new energies for playing her romantic reform role in an effective and intensely personal way. Intense but not flexible: there was little room for exchange and growth in the mood of atonement with which she approached her work. Nor was her peculiarly personal identification with the victims of American indifference easily matched in reform circles. Where other reformers like the abolitionists often made abstract pleas for "bleeding humanity" and "suffering millions," hers was the real thing—a perfectionist fervor which strengthened her will at the cost of psychological isolation. Throughout her career she preferred to work alone, deploring the tendency to multiply reform agencies and ignoring those that existed either because she disagreed with their principles, as in the case of Louis Dwight's Boston Prison Discipline Society, or because she chose the more direct method of personal appeal. In all her work, even the unhappy and frustrating last years as superintendent of nurses in the Union Army, she saw herself as a solitary spokesman for the deprived and personal healer of the suffering.

Another reform role supplied by perfectionism was Bronson Alcott's educator-prophet, the "true reformer" who "studied man as he is from the hand of the Creator, and not as he is made by the errors of the world." Convinced that the self sprang from divine origins in nature, Alcott naturally concluded that children were more susceptible to good than people imagined and set out to develop a method for uncovering that goodness. With the power to shape personality the teacher, Alcott was sure, held the key to illimitable progress and the eventual regeneration of the world. The teacher might literally make society over by teaching men as children to discover their own divine natures. Thus true education for Alcott consisted of the process of self-discovery guided by the educator-prophet. He sharply criticized his contemporaries for their fatal mistake of imposing partial and therefore false standards on their charges. Shades of the prison house obscured the child's search for perfection, and character was lost forever. "Instead of following it in the path pointed out by its Maker, instead of learning by observation, and guiding it in that path, we unthinkingly attempt to shape its course to our particular wishes. . . ." [5]

To help children avoid the traps set by their elders Alcott based his whole system on the cultivation of self-awareness through self-examination. His pupils kept journals in which they scrutinized their behavior and analyzed their motives. Ethical problems were the subject of frequent and earnest debate at the Temple School as the children were urged to discover the hidden springs of perfectibility in themselves. No mechanical methods of rote learning could bring on the moment of revelation; each child was unique and would find himself in his own way. The real meaning of education as reform, Alcott realized, came with an increased social sense that resulted from individual self-discovery. As the creator of social personality Alcott's teacher was bound by no external rules of pedagogy: as the primary social reformer he had to cast off "the shackles of form, of mode, and ceremony" in order to play the required roles in the educational process.

Alcott's modernity lay principally in his concept of the interchangeability of roles—both teacher and pupils acquired self-knowledge in an exciting give-and-take. Thus defined, education became a way of life, a continuing process through which individuals learned to obey the laws of their own natures and in so doing to discover the laws of the good society. This identification of individual development with true social unity was crucial for Alcott, as for the other perfectionist communitarians, because it provided the bridge over which they passed from self to society. The keystone in Alcott's construction was

---

[5] For a careful analysis of Alcott's educational theories see Dorothy McCuskey, *Bronson Alcott, Teacher* (New York, 1940), particularly pp. 25–40 from which these quotations are taken.

supplied by the individual conscience which connected with the "common conscience" of mankind. This fundamental identity, he was convinced, could be demonstrated by the learning process itself which he defined as "sympathy and imitation, the moral action of the teacher upon the children, of the children upon him, and each other." He saw in the school, therefore, a model of the good community where self-discovery led to a social exchange culminating in the recognition of universal dependency and brotherhood. The ideal society—the society he hoped to create—was one in which individuals could be totally free to follow their own natures because such pursuit would inevitably end in social harmony. For Alcott the community was the product rather than the creator of the good life.

Fruitlands, Alcott's attempt to apply the lessons of the Temple School on a larger scale, was designed to prove that perfectionist educational reform affected the "economies of life." In this realization lay the real import of Alcott's reform ideas; for education, seen as a way of life, meant the communitarian experiment as an educative model. Pushed to its limits, the perfectionist assault on institutions logically ended in the attempt to make new and better societies as examples for Americans to follow. Communitarianism, as Alcott envisioned it, was the social extension of his perfectionist belief in education as an alternative to politics.

In the case of other humanitarian reformers like Samuel Gridley Howe perfectionism determined even more precisely both the role and intellectual content of their proposals. Howe's ideal of the good society seems to have derived from his experiences in Greece where, during his last year, he promoted a communitarian plan for resettling exiles on the Gulf of Corinth. With government support he established his colony, "Washingtonia," on two thousand acres of arable land, selected the colonists himself, bought cattle and tools, managed its business affairs, and supervised a Lancastrian school. By his own admission these were the happiest days of his life: "I laboured here day & night in season & out; & was governor, legislator, clerk, constable, & everything but a patriarch." [6] When the government withdrew its support and brigands overran the colony, Howe was forced to abandon the project and return home. Still, the idea of an entire community under the care of a "patriarch" shouldering its collective burden and absorbing all its dependents in a cooperative life continued to dominate the "Doctor's" reform thinking and to determine his methods.

The ethical imperatives in Howe's philosophy of reform remained constant. "Humanity demands that every creature in human shape should command our respect; we should recognise as a brother every being upon whom God has stamped the human impress." Progress he likened to the American road. Christian individualism required that each man walk separately and at

---

[6] Letter from Howe to Horace Mann, 1857, quoted in Harold Schwartz, *Samuel Gridley Howe* (Cambridge, 1956) p. 37.

his own pace, but "the rear should not be left too far behind . . . none should be allowed to perish in their helplessness . . . the strong should help the weak, so that the whole should advance as a band of brethren." It was the duty of society itself to care for its disabled or mentally deficient members rather than to shut them up in asylums which were "offsprings of a low order of feeling." "The more I reflect upon the subject the more I see objections in principle and practice to asylums," he once wrote to a fellow-reformer. "What right have we to pack off the poor, the old, the blind into asylums? They are of us, our brothers, our sisters—they belong in families. . . . " [7]

In Howe's ideal society, then, the handicapped, criminals and defectives would not be walled off but accepted as part of the community and perfected by constant contact with it. Two years of experimenting with education for the feeble-minded convinced him that even "idiots" could be redeemed from what he called spiritual death. "How far they can be elevated, and to what extent they may be educated, can only be shown by the experience of the future," he admitted in his report to the Massachusetts legislature but predicted confidently that "each succeeding year will show even more progress than any preceding one." [8] He always acted on his conviction that "we shall avail ourselves of special institutions less and the common schools more" and never stopped hoping that eventually all blind children after proper training might be returned to families and public schools for their real education. He also opposed the establishment of reformatories with the argument that they only collected the refractory and vicious and made them worse. Nature mingled the defective in common families, he insisted, and any departure from her standards stunted moral growth. He took as his model for reform the Belgian town of Geel where mentally ill patients were boarded at public expense with private families and allowed maximum freedom. As soon as the building funds were available he introduced the cottage system at Perkins, a plan he also wanted to apply to reformatories. No artificial and unnatural institution could replace the family which Howe considered the primary agency in the perfection of the individual.

Howe shared his bias against institutions and a preference for the family unit with other humanitarian reformers like Robert Hartley and Charles Loring Brace. Hartley's "friendly visitors" were dispatched to New York's poor with instructions to bring the gospel of self-help home to every member of the family. Agents of the AICP dispensed advice and improving literature along with the coal and groceries. Only gradually did the organization incorporate "incidental labors"—legislative programs for housing reform, health regulations and child labor—into its system of reform. Hartley's real hope for the new urban poor lay in their removal to the country where a bootstrap opera-

---

[7] Letter from Howe to William Chapin, 1857, quoted in Laura E. Richards, *Letters and Journals of Samuel Gridley Howe* (2 vols.; New York, 1909), II, 48.

[8] Second Report of the Commissioners on Idiocy to the Massachusetts Legislature (1849), quoted in Richards, *Howe*, II, 214.

tion might lift them to sufficiency and selfhood. "Escape then from the city," he told them, "—for escape is your only recourse against the terrible ills of beggary; and the further you go, the better." [9] In Hartley's formula the perfectionist doctrine of the salvation of the individual combined with the conservative appeal of the safety-valve.

A pronounced hostility to cities also marked the program of Charles Loring Brace's Children's Aid Society, the central feature of which was the plan for relocating children of the "squalid poor" on upstate New York farms for "moral disinfection." The Society's placement service resettled thousands of slum children in the years before the Civil War in the belief that a proper family environment and a rural setting would release the naturally good tendencies in young people so that under the supervision of independent and hardworking farmers they would save themselves. [10]

There was thus a high nostalgic content in the plans of humanitarians who emphasized pastoral virtues and the perfectionist values inherent in country living. Their celebration of the restorative powers of nature followed logically from their assumption that the perfected individual—the truly free American—could be created only by the reunification of mental and physical labor. The rural life, it was assumed, could revive and sustain the unified sensibility threatened by the city. A second assumption concerned the importance of the family as the primary unit in the reconstruction of society. As the great debate among social reformers proceeded it centered on the question of the limits to which the natural family could be extended. Could an entire society, as the more radical communitarians argued, be reorganized as one huge family? Or were there natural boundaries necessary for preserving order and morality? On the whole, the more conservative humanitarians agreed with Howe in rejecting those communal plans which, like Fourier's, stemmed from too high an estimate of "the capacity of mankind for family affections." [11]

That intensive education held the key to illimitable progress, however, few humanitarian reformers denied. They were strengthened in their certainty by the absolutes inherited from moral reform. Thus Howe, for example, considered his work a "new field" of "practical religion." The mental defective, he was convinced, was the product of sin—both the sin of the parents and the sin of society in allowing the offspring to languish in mental and moral darkness. Yet the social evils incident to sin were not inevitable; they were not "inherent in the very constitution of man" but the "chastisements sent by a

---

[9] New York A.I.C.P., *The Mistake* (New York, 1850), p. 4, quoted in Robert H. Bremner, *From the Depths: the Discovery of Poverty in the United States* (New York, 1956), p. 38.

[10] Brace's views are set forth in his *The Dangerous Classes of New York and Twenty Years Among Them* (New York, 1872). For a brief treatment of his relation to the moral reform movement see Bremner, *From the Depths,* chap. iii.

[11] Letter from Howe to Charles Sumner, Apr. 8, 1847, quoted in Richards, *Howe,* II, 255–56.

loving Father to bring his children to obedience to his beneficent laws." [12]
These laws—infinite perfectibility and social responsibility—reinforced each
other in the truly progressive society. The present condition of the dependent
classes in America was proof of "the immense space through which society
has yet to advance before it even approaches the perfection of civilization
which is attainable." [13] Education, both the thorough training of the deprived
and the larger education of American society to its obligations, would meet
the moral challenge.

The perfectionist uses of education as an alternative to political reform
were most thoroughly explored by Horace Mann. Mann's initial investment in
public school education was dictated by his fear that American democracy,
lacking institutional checks and restraints, was fast degenerating into "the
spectacle of gladiatorial contests" conducted at the expense of the people.
Could laws save American society? Mann thought not.

> With us, the very idea of legislation is reversed. Once, the law prescribed the
> actions and shaped the wills of the multitude; here the wills of the multitude
> prescribe and shape the law . . . now when the law is weak, the passions of
> the multitude have gathered irresistible strength, it is fallacious and insane to
> look for security in the moral force of law. Government and law . . . will
> here be moulded into the similitude of the public mind. . . .[14]

In offering public school education as the only effective countervailing force in
a democracy Mann seemingly was giving vent to a conservative dread of unreg-
ulated change in a society where, as he admitted, the momentum of hereditary opinion was spent. Where there was no "surgical code of laws" reason,
conscience and benevolence would have to be provided by education. "The
whole mass of mind must be instructed in regard to its comprehensive and
enduring interests." In a republican government, however, compulsion was
theoretically undesirable and practically unavailable. People could not be
driven up a "dark avenue" even though it were the right one. Mann, like his
evangelical predecessors, found his solution in an educational crusade.

> Let the intelligent visit the ignorant, day by day, as the oculist visits the blind
> mind, and detaches the scales from his eyes, until the living sense leaps to
> light. . . . Let the love of beautiful reason, the admonitions of conscience,
> the sense of religious responsibility, be plied, in mingled tenderness and ear-
> nestness, until the obdurate and dark mass of avarice and ignorance and prej-
> udice shall be dissipated by their blended light and heat.[15]

---

[12] First Report of the Commissioners on Idiocy (1848), quoted in Richards, *Howe,*
II, 210–11.

[13] *Ibid.,* pp. 210–11.

[14] Horace Mann, "The Necessity of Education in a Republican Government," *Lectures
on Education* (Boston, 1845), pp. 152, 158.

[15] "An Historical View of Education; Showing Its Dignity and Its Degradation," *Lectures on Education,* pp. 260, 262.

Here in Mann's rhetorical recasting was what appeared to be the old evangelical prescription for tempering democratic excess. The chief problem admittedly was avoiding the "disturbing forces of party and sect and faction and clan." To make sure that education remained nonpartisan the common schools should teach on the *"exhibitory"* method, "by an actual exhibition of the principle we would inculcate."

Insofar as the exhibitory method operated to regulate or direct public opinion, it was conservative. But implicit in Mann's theory was a commitment to perfectionism which gradually altered his aims until in the twelfth and final report education emerges as a near-utopian device for making American politics simple, clean and, eventually, superfluous. In the Twelfth Report Mann noted that although a public school system might someday guarantee "sufficiency, comfort, competence" to every American, as yet "imperfect practice" had not matched "perfect theory." Then in an extended analysis of social trends which foreshadowed Henry George's classification he singled out "poverty" and "profusion" as the two most disturbing facts in American development. "With every generation, fortunes increase on the one hand, and some new privation is added to poverty on the other. We are verging toward those extremes of opulence and penury, each of which unhumanizes the mind." [16] A new feudalism threatened; and unless a drastic remedy was discovered, the "hideous evils" of unequal distribution of wealth would cause class war.

Mann's alternative to class conflict proved to be nothing less than universal education based on the exhibitory model of the common school. Diffusion of education, he pointed out, meant wiping out class lines and with them the possibility of conflict. As the great equalizer of condition it would supply the balance-wheel in the society of the future. Lest his readers confuse his suggestions with the fantasies of communitarians Mann hastened to point out that education would perfect society through the individual by creating new private resources. Given full play in a democracy, education gave each man the "independence and the means by which he can resist the selfishness of other men."

Once Mann had established education as an alternative to political action, it remained to uncover its utopian possibilities. By enlarging the "cultivated class" it would widen the area of social feelings—"if this education should be universal and complete, it would do more than all things else to obliterate factitious distinctions in society." Political reformers and revolutionaries based their schemes on the false assumption that the amount of wealth in

---

[16] This quotation and the ones from Mann that follow are taken from the central section of the *Twelfth Report* entitled "Intellectual Education as a Means of Removing Poverty, and Securing Abundance," Mary Peabody Mann, *Life of Horace Mann* (4 vols.; Boston, 1891), IV, 245–68. See also the perceptive comments on Mann in Rush Welter, *Popular Education and Democratic Thought in America* (New York, 1962), pp. 97–102, from which I have drawn.

America was fixed by fraud and force, and that the few were rich because the many were poor. By demanding a redistribution of wealth by legislative fiat they overlooked the power of education to obviate political action through the creation of new and immense sources of wealth.

Thus in Mann's theory as in the programs of the other humanitarians the perfection of the individual through education guaranteed illimitable progress. The constantly expanding powers of the free individual ensured the steady improvement of society until the educative process finally achieved a harmonious, self-regulating community. "And will not the community that gains its wealth in this way . . . be a model and a pattern for nations, a type of excellence to be admired and followed by the world?" The fate of free society, Mann concluded, depended upon the conversion of individuals from puppets and automatons to thinking men who were aware of the strength of the irreducible self and determined to foster it in others.

As romantic perfectionism spread across Jacksonian society it acquired an unofficial and only partly acceptable philosophy in the "systematic subjectivism" of transcendental theory.[17] Transcendentalism, as its official historian noted, claimed for all men what a more restrictive Christian perfectionism extended only to the redeemed. Seen in this light, self-culture—Emerson's "perfect unfolding of our individual nature"—appeared as a secular amplification of the doctrine of personal holiness. In the transcendentalist definition, true reform proceeded from the individual and worked outward through the family, the neighborhood and ultimately into the social and political life of the community. The transcendentalist, Frothingham noted in retrospect, "was less a reformer of human circumstances than a regenerator of the human spirit. . . . With movements that did not start from this primary assumption of individual dignity, and come back to that as their goal, he had nothing to do." [18] Emerson's followers, like the moral reformers and the humanitarians, looked to individuals rather than to institutions, to "high heroic example" rather than to political programs. The Brook-Farmer John Sullivan Dwight summed up their position when he protested that "men are anterior to systems. Great doctrines are not the origins, but the product of great lives." [19]

Accordingly the transcendentalists considered institutions—parties, churches, organizations—so many arbitrarily constructed barriers on the road to self-culture. They were lonely men, Emerson admitted, who repelled influences. "They are not good citizens; not good members of society. . . ." [20] A longing for solitude led them out of society, Emerson to the woods where he

---

[17] The phrase is Santayana's in "The Genteel Tradition in American Philosophy." For an analysis of the anti-institutional aspects of transcendentalism and reform see Stanley Elkins, *Slavery* (Chicago, 1959), chap. iii.

[18] Octavius Brooks Frothingham, *Transcendentalism in New England* (Harper Torchbooks ed.: New York, 1959), p. 155.

[19] John Sullivan Dwight as quoted in Frothingham, *Transcendentalism*, p. 147.

[20] "The Transcendentalist," *Works*, I, 347–48.

found no Jacksonian placards on the trees, Thoreau to his reclusive leadership of a majority of one. Accepting for the most part Emerson's dictum that one man was a counterpoise to a city, the transcendentalists turned inward to examine the divine self and find there the material with which to rebuild society. They wanted to avoid at all costs the mistake of their Jacksonian contemporaries who in order to be useful accommodated themselves to institutions without realizing the resultant loss of power and integrity.

The most immediate effect of perfectionism on the transcendentalists, as on the humanitarians, was the development of a set of concepts which, in stressing reform by example, opened up new roles for the alienated intellectual. In the first place, self-culture accounted for their ambivalence toward reform politics. It was not simply Emerson's reluctance to raise the siege on his hencoop that kept him apart, but a genuine confusion as to the proper role for the reformer. If government was simply a "job" and American society the senseless competition of the marketplace, how could the transcendentalist accept either as working premises? The transcendentalist difficulty in coming to terms with democratic politics could be read in Emerson's confused remark that of the two parties contending for the presidency in 1840 one had the better principles, the other the better men. Driven by their profound distaste for manipulation and chicanery, many of Emerson's followers took on the role of a prophet standing aloof from elections, campaigns and party caucuses and dispensing wisdom (often in oblique Emersonian terminology) out of the vast private resources of the self. In this sense transcendentalism, like Christian perfectionism, represented a distinct break with the prevailing Jacksonian views of democratic leadership and the politics of compromise and adjustment.

One of the more appealing versions of the transcendental role was the hero or genius to whom everything was permitted, as Emerson said, because "genius is the character of illimitable freedom." The heroes of the world, Margaret Fuller announced, were the true theocratic kings: "The hearts of men make music at their approach; the mind of the age is like the historian of their passing; and only men of destiny like themselves shall be permitted to write their eulogies, or fill their vacancies." [21] Margaret Fuller herself spent her transcendentalist years stalking the American hero, which she somehow confused with Emerson, before she joined the Roman Revolution in 1849 and discovered the authentic article in the mystic nationalist Mazzini.

Carlyle complained to Emerson of the "perilous altitudes" to which the transcendentalists' search for the hero led them. Despite his own penchant for hero-worship he came away from reading the *Dial* "with a kind of shudder." In their pursuit of the self-contained hero they seemed to separate themselves from "this same cotton-spinning, dollar-hunting, canting and shrieking, very

---

[21] Such was her description of Lamennais and Beranger as quoted in Mason Wade, *Margaret Fuller* (New York, 1940), p. 195.

wretched generation of ours." [22] The transcendentalists, however, were not trying to escape the Jacksonian world of fact, only to find a foothold for their perfectionist individualism in it. They sought a way of implementing their ideas of self-culture without corrupting them with the false values of materialism. They saw a day coming when parties and politicians would be obsolescent. By the 1850s Walt Whitman thought that day had already arrived and that America had outgrown parties.

> What right has any one political party, no matter which, to wield the American government? No right at all . . . and every American young man must have sense enough to comprehend this. I have said the old parties are defunct; but there remains of them empty flesh, putrid mouths, mumbling and speaking the tones of these conventions, the politicians standing back in shadow, telling lies, trying to delude and frighten the people. . . .[23]

Whitman's romantic alternative was a "love of comrades" cementing an American brotherhood and upholding a redeemer president.

A somewhat similar faith in the mystical fraternity informed Theodore Parker's plan for spiritual revolution. Like the other perfectionists, Parker began by reducing society to its basic components—individuals, the "monads" or "primitive atoms" of the social order—and judged it by its tendency to promote or inhibit individualism. "Destroy the individualtiy of those atoms, . . . all is gone. To mar the atoms is to mar the mass. To preserve itself, therefore, society is to preserve the individuality of the individual." [24] In Parker's theology perfectionist Christianity and transcendental method merged to form a loving brotherhood united by the capacity to apprehend primary truths directly. A shared sense of the divinity of individual man held society together; without it no true community was possible. Looking around him at ante-bellum America, Parker found only the wrong kind of individualism, the kind that said, "I am as good as you, so get out of my way." The right kind, the individualism whose motto was "You are as good as I, and let us help one another," [25] was to be the work of Parker's spiritual revolution. He explained the method of revolution as one of *"intellectual, moral* and *religious* education—everywhere and for all men." Until universal education had done its work Parker had little hope for political stability in the United States. He called instead for a new "party" to be formed in society at large, a party

---

[22] Quoted in Wade, *Margaret Fuller,* pp. 88–89.

[23] Walt Whitman, "The Eighteenth Presidency," an essay unpublished in Whitman's lifetime, in *Walt Whitman's Workshop,* ed. Clifton Joseph Furness (Cambridge, 1928), pp. 104–5.

[24] Quoted in Daniel Aaron, *Men of Good Hope* (Oxford paperback ed.: New York, 1961), p. 35.

[25] Theodore Parker, "The Political Destination of America and the Signs of the Times" (1848) excerpted in *The Transcendentalists,* ed. Perry Miller (Anchor ed.: Garden City, N.Y., 1957), p. 357.

built on the idea that "God still inspires men as much as ever; that he is immanent in spirit as in space." Such a party required no church, tradition or scripture. "It believes God is near the soul as matter to the sense. . . . It calls God father and mother, not king; Jesus, brother, not redeemer, heaven home, religion nature." [26]

Parker believed that this "philosophical party in politics," as he called it, was already at work in the 1850s on a code of universal laws from which to deduce specific legislation "so that each statute in the code shall represent a fact in the universe, a point of thought in God; so . . . that legislation shall be divine in the same sense that a true system of astronomy be divine." Parker's holy band represented the full fruition of the perfectionist idea of a "Christian party" in America, a party of no strict political or sectarian definition, but a true reform movement, apostolic in its beginnings but growing with the truths it preached until it encompassed all Americans in a huge brotherhood of divine average men. Party members, unlike time-serving Whigs and Democrats, followed ideas and intuitions rather than prejudice and precedent, and these ideas led them to question authority, oppose legal injustice and tear down rotten institutions. The philosophical party was not to be bound by accepted notions of political conduct or traditional attitudes toward law. When unjust laws interpose barriers to progress, reformers must demolish them.

So Parker himself reasoned when he organized the Vigilance Committee in Boston to defeat the Fugitive Slave Law. His reasoning epitomized perfectionist logic: every man may safely trust his conscience, properly informed, because it is the repository for divine truth. When men learn to trust their consciences and act on them, they naturally encourage others to do the same with the certainty that they will reach the same conclusions. Individual conscience thus creates a social conscience and a collective will to right action. Concerted right action means moral revolution. The fact that moral revolution, in its turn, might mean political revolt was a risk Parker and his perfectionist followers were willing to take.

Both transcendentalism and perfectionist moral reform, then, were marked by an individualist fervor that was disruptive of American institutions. Both made heavy moral demands on church and state; and when neither proved equal to the task of supporting their intensely personal demands, the transcendentalists and the moral reformers became increasingly alienated. The perfectionist temperament bred a come-outer spirit. An insistence on individual moral accountability and direct appeal to the irreducible self, the faith in self-reliance and distrust of compromise, and a substitution of universal education for partial reform measures, all meant that normal political and institutional reform channels were closed to the perfectionists. Alternate routes to the millennium had to be found. One of these was discovered by a new leadership which made reform a branch of prophecy. Another was

---

[26] Quoted in R. W. B. Lewis, *The American Adam* (Chicago, 1955), p. 182.

opened by the idea of a universal reawakening of the great god self. But there was a third possibility, also deeply involved with the educational process, an attempt to build the experimental community as a reform model. With an increasing number of reformers after 1840 perfectionist anti-institutionalism led to heavy investments in the communitarian movement.

The attraction that drew the perfectionists to communitarianism came from their conviction that the good society should be simple. Since American society was both complicated and corrupt, it was necessary to come out from it; but at the same [time] the challenge of the simple life had to be met. Once the true principles of social life had been discovered they had to be applied, some way found to harness individual perfectibility to a social engine. This urge to form the good community, as John Humphrey Noyes experienced it himself and perceived it in other reformers, provided the connection between perfectionism and communtarianism, or, as Noyes put it, between "Revivalism" and "Socialism." Perfectionist energies directed initially against institutions were diverted to the creation of small self-contained communities as educational models. In New England two come-outer abolitionists, Adin Ballou and George Benson, founded cooperative societies at Hopedale and Northampton, while a third Garrisonian lieutenant, John Collins, settled his followers on a farm in Skaneateles, New York. Brook Farm, Fruitlands and the North American Phalanx at Redbank acquired notoriety in their own day; but equally significant, both in terms of origins and personnel, were the experiments at Raritan Bay under the guidance of Marcus Spring, the Marlboro Association in Ohio, the Prairie Home Community of former Hicksite Quakers, and the Swedenborgian Brocton Community. In these and other experimental communities could be seen the various guises of perfectionism.

Communitarianism promised drastic social reform without violence. Artificiality and corruption could not be wiped out by partial improvements and piecemeal measures but demanded a total change which, as Robert Owen once explained, "could make an immediate, and almost instantaneous, revolution in the minds and manners of society in which it shall be introduced." Communitarians agreed in rejecting class struggle which set interest against interest instead of uniting them through association. "Whoever will examine the question of social ameliorations," Albert Brisbane argued in support of Fourier, "must be convinced that *the gradual perfecting of Civilization* is useless as a remedy for present social evils, and that the only effectual means of doing away with indigence, idleness and the dislike for labor is to do away with civilization itself, and organize Association . . . in its place." [27] Like the redemptive moment in conversion or the experience of self-discovery in transcendentalist thought, the communitarian ideal pointed to a sharp break

[27] Albert Brisbane, *Social Destiny of Man*, p. 286, quoted in Arthur Eugene Bestor, *Backwoods Utopias: The Sectarian and Owenite Phases of Communitarian Socialism in America: 1663–1829* (Philadelphia, 1950), p. 9.

with existing society and a commitment to root-and-branch reform. On the other hand, the community was seen as a controlled experiment in which profound but peaceful change might be effected without disturbing the larger social order. Massive change, according to communitarian theory, could also be gradual and harmonious if determined by the model.

Perfectionist religious and moral reform shaded into communitarianism, in the case of a number of social reformers, with the recognition that the conversion of the individual was a necessary preparation for and logically required communal experimentation. Such was John Humphrey Noyes' observation that in the years after 1815 "the line of socialistic excitement lies parallel with the line of religious Revivals. . . . The Revivalists had for their one great idea the regeneration of the soul. The great idea of the Socialists was the regeneration of society, which is the soul's environment. These ideas belong together and are the complements of each other." [28] So it seemed to Noyes' colleagues in the communitarian movement. The course from extreme individualism to communitarianism can be traced in George Ripley's decision to found Brook Farm. Trying to win Emerson to his new cause, he explained that his own personal tastes and habits would have led him away from plans and projects. "I have a passion for being independent of the world, and of every man in it. This I could do easily on the estate which is now offered. . . . I should have a city of God, on a small scale of my own. . . . But I feel bound to sacrifice this private feeling, in the hope of the great social good." That good Ripley had no difficulty in defining in perfectionist terms:

> . . . to insure a more natural union between intellectual and manual labor than now exists; to combine the thinker and the worker, as far as possible, in the same individual; to guarantee the highest mental freedom, by providing all with labor, adapted to their tastes and talents, and securing to them the fruits of their industry; to do away with the necessity of menial services, by opening the benefits of education and the profits of labor to all; and thus to prepare a society of liberal, intelligent, and cultivated persons, whose relations with each other would permit a more simple and wholesome life, than can be led amidst the pressure of our competitive institutions.[29]

However varied their actual experiences with social planning, all the communitarians echoed Ripley's call for translating perfectionism into concerted action and adapting the ethics of individualism to larger social units. Just as the moral reformers appealed to right conduct and conscience in individuals the communitarians sought to erect models of a collective conscience to educate Americans. Seen in this light, the communitarian faith in the model was simply an extension of the belief in individual perfectibility. Even the sense of

---

[28] John Humphrey Noyes, *History of American Socialism* (Philadelphia, 1870), p. 26.
[29] Letter from Ripley to Ralph Waldo Emerson, Nov. 9, 1840, in *Autobiography of Brook Farm*, ed. Henry W. Sams (Englewood Cliffs, N.J., 1958), pp. 5–8.

urgency characterizing moral reform was carried over into the communities where a millennial expectation flourished. The time to launch their projects, the social planners believed, was the immediate present when habits and attitudes were still fluid, before entrenched institutions had hardened the American heart and closed the American mind. To wait for a full quota of useful members or adequate supply of funds might be to miss the single chance to make the country perfect. The whole future of America seemed to them to hinge on the fate of their enterprises.

Some of the projects were joint-stock corporations betraying a middle-class origin; others were strictly communistic. Some, like the Shaker communities, were pietistic and rigid; others, like Oneida and Hopedale, open and frankly experimental. Communitarians took a lively interest in each others' projects and often joined one or another of them for a season before moving on to try utopia on their own. The division between religious and secular attempts was by no means absolute: both types of communities advertised an essentially religious brand of perfectionism. Nor was economic organization always an accurate means of distinguishing the various experiments, most of which were subjected to periodic constitutional overhauling and frequent readjustment, now in the direction of social controls and now toward relaxation of those controls in favor of individual initiative.

The most striking characteristic of the communitarian movement was not its apparent diversity but the fundamental similarity of educational purpose. The common denominator or "main idea" Noyes correctly identified as *"the enlargement of home—the extension of family union beyond the little man-and-wife circle to large corporations."* [30] Communities as different as Fruitlands and Hopedale, Brook Farm and Northampton, Owenite villages and Fourier phalansteries were all, in one way or another, attempting to expand and apply self-culture to groups. Thus the problem for radical communitarians was to solve the conflict between the family and society. In commenting on the failure of the Brook Farmers to achieve a real community, Charles Lane, Alcott's associate at Fruitlands, identified what he considered the basic social question of the day—"whether the existence of the marital family is compatible with that of the universal family, which the term 'Community' signifies." [31] A few of the communitarians, recognizing this conflict, attempted to solve it by changing or destroying the institution of marriage. For the most part, the perfectionist communitarians shied away from any such radical alteration of the family structure and instead sought a law of association by which the apparently antagonistic claims of private and universal love could be harmonized. Once this law was known and explained, they believed,

---

[30] Noyes, *American Socialisms,* p. 23.

[31] Charles Lane, "Brook Farm," *Dial,* IV (Jan. 1844), 351–57, reprinted in Sams, *Brook Farm,* pp. 87–92.

then the perfect society was possible—a self-adjusting mechanism constructed in accordance with their recently discovered law of human nature.

Inevitably communitarianism developed a "science of society," either the elaborate social mathematics of Fourier or the constitutional mechanics of native American perfectionists. The appeal of the blueprint grew overwhelming: in one way or another almost all the communitarians succumbed to the myth of the mathematically precise arrangement, searching for the perfect number or the exact size, plotting the precise disposition of working forces and living space, and combining these estimates in a formula which would ensure perfect concord. The appeal of Fourierism stemmed from its promise to reconcile productive industry with "passional attractions." "Could this be done," John Sullivan Dwight announced, "the word 'necessity' would acquire an altogether new and pleasanter meaning; the outward necessity and the inward prompting for every human being would be one and identical, and his life a living harmony." [32] Association fostered true individuality which, in turn, guaranteed collective accord. In an intricate calculation involving ascending and descending wings and a central point of social balance where attractions equalled destinies the converts to Fourierism contrived a utopian alternative to politics. The phalanx represented a self-perpetuating system for neutralizing conflict and ensuring perfection. The power factor—politics—had been dropped out; attraction alone provided the stimulants necessary to production and progress. Here in the mathematical model was the culmination of the "peaceful revolution" which was to transform America.

The communitarian experiments in effect were anti-institutional institutions. In abandoning political and religious institutions the communitarians were driven to create perfect societies of their own which conformed to their perfectionist definition of the free individual. Their communities veered erratically between the poles of anarchism and collectivism as they hunted feverishly for a way of eliminating friction without employing coercion, sure that once they had found it, they could apply it in a federation of model societies throughout the country. In a limited sense, perhaps, their plans constituted an escape from urban complexity and the loneliness of alienation. But beneath the nostalgia there lay a vital reform impulse and a driving determination to make American society over through the power of education.

The immediate causes of the collapse of the communities ranged from loss of funds and mismanagement to declining interest and disillusionment with imperfect human material. Behind these apparent reasons, however, stood the real cause in the person of the perfectionist self, Margaret Fuller's "mountainous me," that proved too powerful a disruptive force for even the

---

[32] John Sullivan Dwight, "Association in its Connection with Education," a lecture delivered before the New England Fourier Society, in Boston, Feb. 29, 1844. Excerpted in Sams, *Brook Farm*, pp. 104–5.

anti-institutional institutions it had created. It was the perfectionist ego which allowed the communitarian reformers to be almost wholly nonselective in recruiting their membership and to put their trust in the operation of an atomistic general will. Constitution-making and paper bonds, as it turned out, were not enough to unite divine egoists in a satisfactory system for the free expression of the personality. Perfectionist individualism did not make the consociate family. The result by the 1850s was a profound disillusionment with the principle of association which, significantly, coincided with the political crisis over slavery. Adin Ballou, his experiment at Hopedale in shambles, summarized the perfectionist mood of despair when he added that "few people are near enough right in heart, head and habits to live in close social intimacy." [33] Another way would have to be found to carry divine principles into social arrangements, one that took proper account of the individual.

The collapse of the communitarian movement in the 1850s left a vacuum in social reform which was filled by the slavery crisis. At first their failure to consolidate alternative social and educational institutions threw the reformers back on their old perfectionist individualism for support. It was hardly fortuitous that Garrison, Mann, Thoreau, Howe, Parker, Channing, Ripley and Emerson himself responded to John Brown's raid with a defense of the liberated conscience. But slavery, as a denial of freedom and individual responsibility, had to be destroyed by institutional forces which could be made to sustain these values. The antislavery cause during the secession crisis and throughout the Civil War offered reformers an escape from alienation by providing a new identity with the very political institutions which they had so vigorously assailed.

The effects of the Civil War as an intellectual counterrevolution were felt both in a revival of institutions and a renewal of an organic theory of society. The war brought with it a widespread reaction against the seeming sentimentality and illusions of perfectionism. It saw the establishment of new organizations like the Sanitary and the Christian Commissions run on principles of efficiency and professionalism totally alien to perfectionist methods. Accompanying the wartime revival of institutions was a theological reorientation directed by Horace Bushnell and other conservative churchmen whose longstanding opposition to perfectionism seemed justified by the war. The extreme individualism of the ante-bellum reformers was swallowed up in a Northern war effort that made private conscience less important than saving the Union. Some of the abolitionists actually substituted national unity for freedom for the slave as the primary war aim. Those reformers who contributed to the war effort through the Sanitary Commission or the Christian Commission found a new sense of order and efficiency indispensable. Older perfectionists, like Dorothea Dix, unable to adjust to new demands, found their usefulness dras-

---

[33] Letter from Ballou to Theodore Weld, Dec. 23, 1856, quoted in Benjamin P. Thomas, *Theodore Weld: Crusader for Freedom* (New Brunswick, N.J., 1950), p. 229.

tically confined. Young Emersonians returned from combat convinced that professionalism, discipline and subordination, dubious virtues by perfectionist standards, were essential in a healthy society. A new emphasis on leadership and performance was replacing the benevolent amateurism of the perfectionists.

Popular education and ethical agitation continued to hold the post-war stage, but the setting for them had changed. The three principal theorists of social reform in post-war industrial America—Henry George, Henry Demarest Lloyd and Edward Bellamy—denounced class conflict, minimized the importance of purely political reform, and, like their perfectionist precursors, called for moral revolution. The moral revolution which they demanded, however, was not the work of individuals in whom social responsibility developed as a by-product of self-discovery but the ethical revival of an entire society made possible by the natural development of social forces. Their organic view of society required new theories of personality and new concepts of role-playing, definitions which appeared variously in George's law of integration, Lloyd's religion of love, and Bellamy's economy of happiness. And whereas Nemesis in the perfectionist imagination had assumed the shape of personal guilt and estrangement from a pre-established divine order, for the post-war reformers it took on the social dimensions of a terrifying relapse into barbarism. Finally, the attitudes of the reformers toward individualism itself began to change as Darwinism with the aid of a false analogy twisted the prewar doctrine of self-reliance into a weapon against reform. It was to protest against a Darwinian psychology of individual isolation that Lloyd wrote his final chapter of *Wealth Against Commonwealth,* declaring that the regeneration of the individual was only a half-truth and that "the reorganization of the society which he makes and which makes him is the other half."

> We can become individual only by submitting to be bound to others. We extend our freedom only by finding new laws to obey. . . . The isolated man is a mere rudiment of an individual. But he who has become citizen, neighbor, friend, brother, son, husband, father, fellow-member, in one is just so many times individualized.[34]

Lloyd's plea for a new individualism could also be read as an obituary for perfectionist romantic reform.

---

[34] Henry Demarest Lloyd, *Wealth Against Commonwealth* (Spectrum paperback ed.: Englewood Cliffs, N.J., 1963), pp. 174, 178.

BERNARD WOLFE

UNCLE REMUS AND
THE MALEVOLENT RABBIT

Throughout American history, whites have viewed the Negro through the prism of their own expectations and desires; they have seen the Negro they wanted to see: the docile, infantile slave, the fawning, head-scratching, cackling "Uncle Tom," the disorganized, rhythmic, oversexed denizen of the Southern town and the urban ghetto. Whenever significant numbers of Negroes have visibly departed from these generalized behavior patterns, as in the years after both world wars, whites have exclaimed loudly and often fearfully about the rise of a "new negro." Rarely, however, have they been motivated to reexamine the stereotype itself by looking more carefully and more sensitively at Negro life and culture.

During and after the period of slavery, Negro Americans built up an impressive body of folk materials—tales, sermons, jokes, religious and secular music—that constitutes an indispensable source of information for those interested in the history and psychology of Negroes in America. Scholars have thus far been remiss in using such materials. In the following article Bernard Wolfe asserts the importance of the Brer Rabbit tales not only in providing new insights and perspectives on the attitudes and reactions of the slaves and freedmen to the society and institutions around them, but also in contributing to an enhanced understanding of the attitudes of whites toward Negroes and toward themselves.

190

The student who wishes to probe further into this neglected area may consult such studies as *Miles Mark Fisher,* Negro Slave Songs in the United States * (*1953*), *Charles Keil,* Urban Blues (*1966*), *and Roger D. Abrahams,* Deep Down in the Jungle: Negro Narrative Folklore from the Streets of Philadelphia (*1964*).

Aunt Jemima, Beulah, the Gold Dust Twins, "George" the Pullman-ad porter, Uncle Remus. . . . We like to picture the Negro as grinning at us. In Jack de Capitator, the bottle opener that looks like a gaping minstrel face, the grin is a kitchen utensil. At Mammy's Shack, the Seattle roadside inn built in the shape of a minstrel's head, you walk into the neon grin to get your hamburger. . . . And always the image of the Negro—as we create it—signifies some bounty—for us. Eternally the Negro gives—but (as they say in the theater) *really gives*—grinning from ear to ear.

Gifts without end, according to the billboards, movie screens, food labels, soap operas, magazine ads, singing commercials. Our daily bread: Cream O' Wheat, Uncle Ben's Rice, Wilson Ham ("The Ham What Am!"), those "happifyin' " Aunt Jemima pancakes for our "temptilatin' " breakfasts. Our daily drink, too: Carioca Puerto Rican Rum, Hiram Walker whiskey, Ballantine's Ale. Through McCallum and Propper, the Negro gives milady the new "dark Creole shades" in her sheer nylons; through the House of Vigny, her "grotesque," "fuzzy-wuzzy" bottles of Golliwogg colognes and perfumes. Shoeshines, snow-white laundry, comfortable lower berths, efficient handling of luggage; jazz, jive, jitterbugging, zoot, comedy, and the wonderful tales of Brer Rabbit to entrance the kiddies. Service with a smile. . . .

"The Negroes," writes Geoffrey Gorer, "are kept in their subservient position by the ultimate sanctions of fear and force, and this is well known to whites and Negroes alike. Nevertheless, the whites demand that the Negroes shall appear smiling, eager, and friendly in all their dealings with them."

But if the grin is extracted by force, may not the smiling face be a false-face—and just underneath is there not something else, often only half-hidden?

Uncle Remus—a kind of blackface Will Rogers, complete with standard minstrel dialect and plantation shuffle—has had remarkable staying power in our popular culture, much more than Daddy Long Legs, say, or even Uncle Tom. Within the past two years alone he has inspired a full-length Disney feature, three Hit Parade songs, a widely circulated album of recorded dialect stories, a best-selling juvenile picture book, a syndicated comic strip. And the wily hero of his animal fables, Brer Rabbit—to whom Bugs Bunny and perhaps even Harvey owe more than a little—is today a much bigger headliner than Bambi or Black Beauty, outclassing even Donald Duck.

For almost seventy years, Uncle Remus has been the prototype of the Negro grinner-giver. Nothing ever clouds the "beaming countenance" of the "venerable old darky"; nothing ever interrupts the flow of his "hearty," "mellow,"

FROM Bernard Wolfe, "Uncle Remus and the Malevolent Rabbit," Reprinted from *Commentary* (July 1949), pp. 31–41, by permission; copyright © 1949 by the American Jewish Committee.

"cheerful and good-humored" voice as, decade after decade, he presents his Brer Rabbit stories to the nation.

But Remus too is a white man's brainchild: he was created in the columns of the Atlanta *Constitution,* back in the early 1880's, by a neurotic young Southern journalist named Joel Chandler Harris (1848–1908).

When Remus grins, Harris is pulling the strings; when he "gives" his folk stories, he is the ventriloquist's dummy on Harris's knee.

The setting for these stories never varies: the little white boy, son of "Miss Sally" and "Mars John," the plantation owners, comes "hopping and skipping" into the old Negro's cabin down in back of the "big house" and the story telling session gets under way. Remus's face "breaks up into little eddies of smiles"; he takes his admirer on his knee, "strokes the child's hair thoughtfully and caressingly," calls him "honey." The little boy "nestles closer" to his "sable patron" and listens with "open-eyed wonder."

No "sanctions of fear and force" here, Harris insists—the relationship between narrator and auditor is one of unmitigated tenderness. Remus "gives," with a "kindly beam" and a "most infectious chuckle"; the little boy receives with mingled "awe," "admiration," and "delight." But, if one looks more closely, within the magnanimous caress is an incredibly malevolent blow.

Of the several Remus collections published by Harris, the first and most famous is *Uncle Remus: His Songs and His Sayings.* Brer Rabbit appears twenty-six times in this book, encounters the Fox twenty times, soundly trounces him nineteen times. The Fox, on the other hand, achieves only two very minor triumphs—one over the Rabbit, another over the Sparrow. On only two other occasions is the Rabbit victimized even slightly, both times by animals as puny as himself (the Tarrypin, the Buzzard); but when he is pitted against adversaries as strong as the Fox (the Wolf, the Bear, once the whole Animal Kingdom) he emerges the unruffled winner. The Rabbit finally kills off all three of his powerful enemies. The Fox is made a thorough fool of by all the weakest animals—the Buzzard, the Tarrypin, the Bull-Frog.

All told, there are twenty-eight victories of the Weak over the Strong; ultimately all the Strong die violent deaths at the hands of the Weak; and there are, at most, two very insignificant victories of the Strong over the Weak. . . . Admittedly, folk symbols are seldom systematic, clean-cut, or specific; they are cultural shadows thrown by the unconscious, and the unconscious is not governed by the sharp-edged neatness of the filing cabinet. But still, on the basis of the tally-sheet alone, is it too far-fetched to take Brer Rabbit as a symbol—about as sharp as Southern sanctions would allow—of the Negro slave's festering hatred of the white man?

It depends, of course, on whether these are animals who maul and murder each other, or human beings disguised as animals. Here Harris and Remus seem to differ. "In dem days," Remus often starts, "de creeturs wuz santer'n 'roun' same like fokes." But for Harris—so he insists—his anthropomorphism is only incidental. What the stories depict, he tells us, is only the "roaring comedy of animal life."

Is it? These are very un-Aesopian creatures who speak a vaudeville dialect, hold candy-pulls, run for the legislature, fight and scheme over gold mines, compete for women in elaborate rituals of courtship and self-aggrandizement, sing plantation ditties about "Jim Crow," read the newspapers after supper, and kill and maim each other—not in gusts of endocrine Pavlov passion but coldbloodedly, for prestige, plotting their crafty moves in advance and often using accomplices. . . . Harris sees no malice in all this, even when heads roll. Brer Rabbit, he explains, is moved not by "malice, but mischievousness." But Brer Rabbit "mischievously" scalds the Wolf to death, makes the innocent Possum die in a fire to cover his own crimes, tortures and probably murders the Bear by setting a swarm of bees on him—and, after causing the fatal beating of the Fox, carries his victim's head to Mrs. Fox and her children, hoping to trick them into eating it in their soup. . . .

One dramatic tension in these stories seems to be a gastronomic one: *Will the communal meal ever take place in the "Animal" Kingdom?*

The food-sharing issue is posed in the very first story. "I seed Brer B'ar yistiddy," the Fox tells the Rabbit as the story opens, "en he sorter rake me over de coals kaze you en me ain't make frens en live naborly." He then invites the Rabbit to supper—intending that his guest will be the main course in this "joint" feast. Brer Rabbit solemnly accepts the invitation, shows up, makes the Fox look ridiculous, and blithely scampers off: "En Brer Fox ain't kotch 'im yit, en w'at's mo', honey, he ain't gwine ter." The Rabbit can get along very well without the communal meal; but, it soon develops, Brer Fox and his associates can't live without it.

Without food-sharing, no community. Open warfare breaks out immediately after the Fox's hypocritical invitation; and the Rabbit is invariably the victor in the gory skirmishes. And after he kills and skins the Wolf, his other enemies are so cowed that now the communal meal finally seems about to take place: "de animals en de creeturs, dey kep' on gittin' mo' en mo' familious wid wunner nudder—bunchin' der perwishuns tergidder in de same shanty" and "takin' a snack" together too.

But Brer Rabbit isn't taken in. Knowing that the others are sharing their food with him out of fear, not genuine communality, he remains the complete cynic and continues to raid the Fox's goober patch and the Bear's persimmon orchard. Not until the closing episode does the Fox make a genuine food-sharing gesture—he crawls inside Bookay the Cow with Brer Rabbit and gratuitously shows him how to hack out all the beef he can carry. But the communal overture comes too late. In an act of the most supreme malevolence, the Rabbit betrays his benefactor to the farmer and stands by, "makin' like he mighty sorry," while the Fox is beaten to death. . . . And now the meal which aborted in the beginning, because the Fox's friendliness was only a ruse, almost does take place—with the Fox as the main course. Having brutally destroyed his arch enemy, Brer Rabbit tries to make Mrs. Fox cook a soup with her husband's head, and almost succeeds.

Remus is not an anthropomorphist by accident. His theme is a *human* one—neighborliness—and the communal meal is a symbol for it. His moral? There are no good neighbors in the world, neither equality nor fraternity. But the moral has an underside: the Rabbit can never be trapped.

Another tension runs through the stories: *Who gets the women?* In sex, Brer Rabbit is at his most aggressive—and his most invincible. Throughout he is engaged in murderous competition with the Fox and the other animals for the favors of "Miss Meadows en de gals."

In their sexual competition the Rabbit never fails to humiliate the Fox viciously. "I'll show Miss Meadows en de gals dat I'm de boss er Brer Fox," he decides. And he does: through the most elaborate trickery he persuades the Fox to put on a saddle, then rides him past Miss Meadows' house, digging his spurs in vigorously. . . . And in sex, it would seem, there are no false distinctions between creatures—all differences in status are irrelevant. At Miss Meadows' the feuds of the work-a-day world must be suspended, "kaze Miss Meadows, she done put her foot down, she did, en say dat w'en dey come ter her place dey hatter hang up a flag er truce at de front gate en 'bide by it."

The truce is all to the Rabbit's advantage, because if the competitors start from scratch in the sexual battle the best man must win—and the best man is invariably Brer Rabbit. The women themselves want the best man to win. Miss Meadows decides to get some peace by holding a contest and letting the winner have his pick of the girls. The Rabbit mulls the problem over. He sings ironically,

> Make a bow ter de Buzzard en den ter de Crow
> Takes a limber-toe gemmun fer ter jump Jim Crow.

Then, through a tricky scheme, he proceeds to outshine all the stronger contestants.

Food-sharing, sex-sharing—the Remus stories read like a catalogue of Southern racial taboos, all standing on their heads. The South, wearing the blinders of stereotype, has always tried to see the Negro as a "roaringly comic" domestic animal. Understandably; for animals of the tame or domestic variety are not menacing—they are capable only of mischief, never of malice. But the Negro slave, through his anthropomorphic Rabbit stories, seems to be hinting that even the frailest and most humble of "animals" can let fly with the most bloodthirsty aggressions. And these aggressions take place in the two most sacrosanct areas of Southern racial etiquette: the gastronomic and the erotic.

The South, with its "sanctions of fear and force," forbids Negroes to eat at the same table with whites. But Brer Rabbit, through an act of murder, *forces* Brer Fox and all his associates to share their food with him. The South enjoins the Negro, under penalty of death, from coming near the white man's women—although the white man has free access to the Negro's women. But Brer Rabbit flauntingly demonstrates his sexual superiority over all the other animals and, as the undisputed victor in the sexual competition, gets his choice of *all* the women.

And yet, despite these food and sex taboos, for two solid centuries—for the Rabbit stories existed long before Harris put them on paper—Southerners chuckled at the way the Rabbit terrorized all the other animals into the communal meal, roared at the Rabbit's guise in winning the girls away from the Fox *by jumping Jim Crow*. And they were endlessly intrigued by the O. Henry spasm of the miraculous in the very last story, right after the Fox's death: "Some say dat . . . Brer Rabbit married ole Miss Fox. . . ."

An interesting denouement, considering the sexual fears which saturate the South's racial attitudes. Still more interesting that Southern whites should even have countenanced it, let alone revelled in it. . . .

Significantly, the goal of eating and sex, as depicted in Uncle Remus, is not instinct-gratification. The overriding drive is for *prestige*—the South is a prestige-haunted land. And it is in that potent intangible that the Rabbit is always paid off most handsomely for his exploits. Throughout, as he terrorizes the Strong, the "sassy" Rabbit remains bland, unperturbed, sure of his invincibility. When he humiliates the Fox by turning him into a saddle-horse, he mounts him "same's ef he wuz king er de patter-rollers." ("Patter-rollers," Harris cheerfully points out, were the white patrols that terrorized Negro slaves so they wouldn't wander off the plantations.)

Brer Rabbit, in short, has all the jaunty topdog airs and attitudes which a slave can only dream of having. And, like the slave, he has a supremely cynical view of the social world, since he sees it from below. The South is the most etiquette-ridden region of the country; and the Rabbit sees all forms of etiquette as hypocritical and absurd. Creatures meet, address each other with unctuous politeness, inquire after each other's families, pass the time of day with oily clichés—and all the while they are plotting to humiliate, rob, and assassinate each other. The Rabbit sees through it all; if he is serene it is only because he can plot more rapidly and with more deadly efficiency than any of the others.

The world, in Brer Rabbit's wary eyes, is a jungle. Life is a battle-unto-the-death for food, sex, power, prestige, a battle without rules. There is only one reality in this life: who is on top? But Brer Rabbit wastes no time lamenting the mad unneighborly scramble for the top position. Because it is by no means ordained that the Weak can never take over. In his topsy-turvy world, to all practical purposes, the Weak *have* taken over. In one episode, the Rabbit falls down a well in a bucket. He can get back up only by enticing the Fox to climb into the other bucket. The Fox is duped: he drops down and the Rabbit rises, singing as he passes his enemy:

Good-by, Brer Fox, take keer yo' cloze
Fer dis is de way de worril goes
Some goes up en some goes down
You'll git ter de bottom all safe en soun'.

This is the theme song of the stories. The question remains, who sings it? The Rabbit is a creation of Uncle Remus's people; is it, then, Uncle Remus singing? But Uncle Remus is a creation of Joel Chandler Harris. . . .

There is a significant difference in age—some hundreds of years—between Uncle Remus and Brer Rabbit. The Rabbit had been the hero of animal stories popular among Negroes from the early days of slavery; these were genuine folk tales told by Negroes to Negroes and handed down in oral form. Uncle Remus was added only when Harris, in packaging the stories—using the Negro grin for gift-wrapping—invented the Negro narrator to sustain the dialect.

Harris, then, fitted the hate-imbued folk materials into a framework, a white man's framework, of "love." He took over the animal characters and situations of the original stories and gave them a human setting: the loving and lovable Negro narrator, the adoring white auditor. Within this framework of love, the blow was heavily padded with caresses and the genuine folk was almost emasculated into the cute folksy.

Almost, but not quite. Harris all his life was torn between his furtive penchant for fiction and his profession of journalism. It was the would-be novelist in him who created Remus, the "giver" of interracial caresses; but the trained journalist in him, having too good an eye and ear, reported the energetic folk blow in the caress. Thus the curious tension in his versions between "human" form and "animal" content.

Before Harris, few Southerners had ever faced squarely the aggressive symbolism of Brer Rabbit, or the paradox of their delight in it. Of course: it was part of the Southerner's undissected myth—often shared by the Negroes —that his cherished childhood sessions in the slave quarters were bathed in two-way benevolence. But Harris, by writing the white South and its Negro tale-spinners into the stories, also wrote in its unfaced paradoxes. Thus his versions helped to rip open the racial myth—and, with it, the interracial grin.

What was the slippery rabbit-hero doing in these stories to begin with? Where did he come from? As soon as Harris wrote down the oral stories for mass consumption, these questions began to agitate many whites. The result was a whole literature devoted to proving the "un-American" genealogy of Brer Rabbit.

Why, one Southern writer asks, did the Negro pick the Rabbit for a hero? Could it be because the Rabbit was "symbolic of his own humble and helpless condition in comparison with his master the owner of the plantation"? Perhaps the Rabbit represents the Negro "in revolt at . . . his own subordinate and insignificant place in society"?

But no: if the Negro is capable of rebelling against society—American society—even symbolically, he is a menace. The Negro must be in revolt against *Nature,* against the "subordinate and insignificant place" assigned to him by biological fate, not America. The writer reassures himself: the Negro makes animals act "like a low order of human intelligence, such as the Negro himself [can] comprehend." The Negro naturally feels "more closely in touch with [the lower animals] than with the white man who [is] so superior to him in every respect." No threat in Brer Rabbit; his genealogy, having no *American* roots, is a technical matter for "the psychologist or the student of folklore."

However, uneasy questions were raised; and as they were raised they were directed at Harris. Readers sensed the symbolic taunts and threats in the rabbit and insisted on knowing whether they were directed against white America—or against "Nature." Harris took refuge from this barrage of questions in two mutually contradictory formulas: (1) he was merely the "compiler" of these stories, a non-intellectual, a lowly humorist, ignorant of "folkloristic" matters; and (2) Brer Rabbit was most certainly, as Southerners intuited, an undiluted African.

"All that I know—all that we Southerners know—about it," Harris protested, "is that every old plantation mammy in the South is full of these stories." But, a sentence later, Harris decided there *was* one other thing he knew: "One thing is certain—the Negro did not get them from the whites; *probably they are of remote African origin.*" And if they come from the Congo, they offer no symbolic blows to Americans; they are simply funny. So Harris warns the folklorists: "First let us have the folktales told as they were intended to be told, for the sake of amusement. . . ."

But if the folklorists *should* find in them something "of value to their pretensions"? Then "let it be picked out and preserved with as little cackling as possible."

The South wavered; it could not shake off the feeling that Brer Rabbit's overtones were more than just funny. And Harris, too, wavered. To a British folklorist editor he wrote, suddenly reversing himself, that the stories were "more important than humorous." And in the introduction to his book he explains that "however humorous it may be in effect, its intention is perfectly serious. . . . It seems to me that a volume written wholly in dialect must have its solemn, not to say melancholy features."

What was it that Harris sporadically found "important," "solemn," even "melancholy" here? It turns out to be the *Americanism* of Brer Rabbit: "it needs no scientific investigation," Harris continues in his introduction, "to show why he [the Negro] selects as his hero the weakest and most harmless of all animals. . . . It is not virtue that triumphs, but helplessness. . . . Indeed, the parallel between the case of the 'weakest' of all animals, who must, perforce, triumph through his shrewdness, and the humble condition of the slave raconteur, is not without its pathos."

A suggestive idea. But such a "parallel" could not have been worked out in the African jungle, before slavery; it implies that Brer Rabbit, after all, was born much closer to the Mississippi than to the Congo. . . . This crucial sentence does not occur in later editions. Instead we read: "It would be presumptuous [sic] in me to offer an opinion as to the origins of these curious myth-stories; but, *if ethnologists should discover that they did not originate with the African, the proof to that effect should be accompanied with a good deal of persuasive eloquence."*

In this pressing sentence we can see Harris's whole fragmented psyche mirrored. Like all the South, he was caught in a subjective tug-of-war: his intelligence groped for the venomous American slave crouching behind the Rabbit, but his beleaguered racial emotions, in self-defense, had to insist on the "Africanism" of Brer Rabbit—and of the Negro. Then Miss Sally and Mars John could relish his "quaint antics" without recognizing themselves as his targets.

Against the African origin of Brer Rabbit one may argue that he is an eloquent white folk-symbol too, closely related to the lamb as the epitome of Christian meekness (the Easter bunny). May not the Negro, in his conversion to Christianity, have learned the standard Christian animal symbols from the whites? Could not his constant tale-spinning about the Rabbit's malevolent triumphs somehow, in some devious way, suggest the ascent of Christ, the meekness that shall inherit the earth; suggest, even, that the meek may stop being meek and set about inheriting the earth without waiting on the Biblical timetable?

But, there *is* more definite evidence as to Brer Rabbit's non-African origins—skimpy, not conclusive, but highly suggestive. Folklore study indicates that if the Negro did have stories about a rabbit back in Africa, they were not these stories, and the rabbit was most decidedly not this rabbit. Brer Rabbit's truer ancestor, research suggests, hails from elsewhere.

"Most of these Negro stories," reported a Johns Hopkins ethnologist— one of the "cackling" folklorists—". . . bear a striking resemblance to the large body of animal stories made on European soil, of which the most extensive is that known as the *Roman de Renard.* The episodes which form the substance of this French version circulated in the Middle Ages on the Flemish border. . . . The principal actors . . . are the fox, who plays the jokes, and the wolf, most frequently the victim of the fox."

In incident after incident, the Brer Rabbit situations parallel the Reynard the Fox situations: the same props appear, the same set-to's, the same ruses, the same supporting characters, often the same dialogue. But there is one big difference: "In *Uncle Remus* the parts are somewhat changed. Here the rabbit, who scarcely appears (under the name Couard) in the *Renard,* is the chief trickster. His usual butt is the fox. . . ."

In Christian symbolism, then, the rabbit is the essence of meekness and innocence. And in an important part of white folk culture he stands for the impotent, the cowardly, as against the cunning fox. Suddenly, with the beginning of slavery, the Negro begins to tell stories in which the rabbit, now the epitome of belligerence and guile, crops up as the *hero,* mercilessly badgering the fox.

Could the Negroes have got the Reynard fables from the whites? Not impossible. The stories originated among the Flemish peasants. During the 12th century they were written down in French, Latin, and German, in a variety of rhymed forms. The many written versions were then widely circulated throughout Western Europe. And more than a few of the first Negro slaves were brought to France, Spain, and Portugal; and some of their descendants were transplanted to America. Also, many early slaves were brought to plantations owned by Frenchmen—whether in the Louisiana Territory, the Acadian-French sections of North Carolina, or the West Indies.

And many white masters, of French and other backgrounds, told these delightful fox tales to their children. And, from the beginning of the slave trade, many Negroes—who may or may not have had pre-Christian rabbit fables of their own back in Africa—could have listened, smiling amiably, slowly absorbing the raw materials for the grinning folk "gift" that would one day be immortalized by Joel Chandler Harris, Walt Disney, Tin Pan Alley, and the comics. . . .

The Harris research technique, we learn, was first-hand and direct. Seeing a group of Negroes, he approaches and asks if they know any Brer Rabbit stories. The Negroes seem not to understand. Offhandedly, and in rich dialect, Harris tells one himself—as often as not, the famous "Tar-Baby" story. The Negroes are transfixed; then, suddenly, they break out in peals of laughter, kick their heels together, slap their thighs. Before long they are swapping Rabbit yarns with the white man as though he were their lifelong "hail-feller." "Curiously enough," Harris notes, "I have found few Negroes who will acknowledge to a stranger that they know anything of these legends; and yet to relate one of the stories is the surest road to their confidence and esteem."

Why the sudden hilarity? What magic folk-key causes these wary, taciturn Negroes to open up? Harris claims to have won their "esteem"; but perhaps he only guaranteed them immunity. He thinks he disarmed the Negroes—he may only have demonstrated that he, the white bossman, was disarmed.

And how much did the Negroes tell him when they "opened up"? Just how far did they really open up? Harris observes that "there are different versions of all the stories—the shrewd narrators of the mythology of the old plantations adapting themselves with ready tact to the years, tastes, and expectations of their juvenile audiences." But there seem to be gaps in Harris's own versions. At tantalizingly crucial points Uncle Remus will break off abruptly —"Some tells one tale en some tells nudder"—leaving the story dangling like a radio cliff-hanger. Did these gaps appear when the stories were told to Harris? When the slave is obliged to play the clown-entertainer and "give" his folk tales to his masters, young or old, his keen sense of the fitting might well delete the impermissible and blur the dubious—and more out of self-preservation than tact.

Of course, the original oral stories would not express the slave's aggressions straightforwardly either. A Negro slave who yielded his mind fully to his race hatreds in an absolutely white-dominated situation must go mad; and the function of such folk symbols as Brer Rabbit is precisely to prevent inner explosions by siphoning off these hatreds before they can completely possess consciousness. Folk tales, like so much of folk culture, are part of an elaborate psychic drainage system—they make it possible for Uncle Tom to retain his facade of grinning Tomism and even, to some degree, to believe in it himself. But the slave's venom, while subterranean, must nonetheless have been *thrillingly* close to the surface and its symbolic disguises flimsier, its attacks less roundabout. Accordingly his protective instincts, sensing the danger in too shallow symbolism, would have necessarily wielded a meticulous, if unconscious, blue pencil in the stories told to white audiences.

Harris tried hard to convince himself that Uncle Remus was a full-fledged, dyed-in-the-denim Uncle Tom—he describes the "venerable sable patron" as an ex-slave "who has nothing but pleasant memories of the discipline of slavery." But Harris could not completely exorcise the menace in the Meek. How often Remus steps out of his clown-role to deliver unmistakeable judgments on class, caste, and race! In those judgments the aggressions of this "white man's nigger" are astonishingly naked.

"Why the Negro Is Black" tells how the little boy makes the "curious" discovery that Remus's palms are white. The old man explains: "Dey wuz a time w'en all de w'ite folks 'us black—blacker dan me. . . . Niggers is niggers now, but de time wuz w'en we 'uz all niggers tergedder. . . ." How did some "niggers" get white? Simply by bathing in a pond which washed their pigmentation off and using up most of the waters, so that the latecomers could only dabble their hands and feet in it.

But the stragglers who were left with their dark skin tone are not trapped —they may be able to wriggle out of it. In "A Plantation Witch," Remus, explaining that there are witches everywhere in the world that "comes en conjus fokes," hints that these witches may be Negroes who have slipped out of their skins. And these witches conjure white folks from all sides, taking on the forms of owls, bats, dogs, cats—and rabbits.

And in "The Wonderful Tar-Baby Story"—advertised on the dust-jacket as the most famous of all the Remus stories—Remus reverts to the question of pigmentation. ("There are few negroes that will fail to respond" to this one, Harris advises one of his folklore "legmen.") The Fox fashions a "baby" out of tar and places it on the side of the road; the Rabbit comes along and addresses the figure. Not getting any answer, he threatens: "Ef you don't take off dat hat en tell me howdy, I'm gwineter bus' you wide open." (Here the Rabbit's bluster reads like a parody of the white man's demand for the proper bowing-and-scraping etiquette from the Negro; it is a reflection of the satiric mimicry of the whites which the slaves often indulged in among themselves.) He hits the Tar-Baby—his fist sticks in the gooey tar. He hits it with the other hand, then kicks it—all four extremities are stuck.

This is "giving" in a new sense; tar, blackness, by its very yielding, traps. Interesting symbol, in a land where the mere possession of a black skin requires you, under penalty of death, to yield, to *give,* everywhere. The mark of supreme impotence suddenly acquires the power to render impotent, merely by its flaccidity, its inertness; it is almost a Gandhi-like symbol. There is a puzzle here: it is the Rabbit who is trapped. But in a later story, "How Mr. Rabbit Was Too Sharp for Mr. Fox," it turns out that the Rabbit, through another cagey maneuver, gets the Fox to set him free from the tar-trap and thus avoids being eaten by his enemy. The Negro, in other words, is wily enough to escape from the engulfing pit of blackness, although his opponents, who set the trap, do their level best to keep him imprisoned in it. But it is not at all sure that anyone else who fell victim to this treacherous black yielding-ness—the Fox, say—would be able to wriggle out so easily.

The story about "A Plantation Witch" frightens his young admirer so much that Remus has to take him by the hand and lead him home to the "big house." And for a long time the boy lies awake "expecting an unseemly visitation from some mysterious source." Many of the other stories, too, must have given him uneasy nights. For within the "gift" that Uncle Remus gives to Miss Sally's little boy is a nightmare, a nightmare in which whites are Negroes, the Weak torture and drown the Strong, mere blackness becomes black magic— and Negroes cavort with cosmic forces and the supernatural, zipping their skins off at will to prowl around the countryside terrorizing the whites, often in the guise of rabbits. . . .

Harris's career is one of the fabulous success stories of American literary history. Thanks to Uncle Remus, the obscure newspaperman was catapulted into the company of Mark Twain, Bret Harte, James Whitcomb Riley, and Petroleum V. Nasby; Andrew Carnegie and Theodore Roosevelt traveled to Atlanta to seek him out; he was quoted in Congress. And all the while he maintained—as in a letter to Twain—that "my book has no basis in literary merit to stand upon; I know it is the matter and not the manner that has attracted public attention . . . my relations towards Uncle Remus are similar to those that exist between an almanac-maker and the calendar. . . ."

But how was it that Harris could apply his saccharine manner to such matter, dress this malevolent material, these nightmares, in such sweetness and light? For one thing, of course, he was only recording the tottering racial myth of the post-bellum South, doing a paste-job on its fissioning falseface. As it happened, he was peculiarly suited for the job; for he was crammed full of pathological racial obsessions, over and above those that wrack the South and, to a lesser degree, all of white America.

Even Harris's worshipful biographer, his daughter-in-law, can't prevent his story from reading like a psychiatric recital of symptoms. The blush and the stammer were his whole way of life. From early childhood on, we are told, he was "painfully conscious of his social deficiencies" and his "lack of size"; he felt "handicapped by his tendency to stutter" and to "blush furiously," believed himself "much uglier than he really was"; in his own words, he had "an absolute horror of strangers."

During his induction into the typographical union, Harris stutters so badly that he has to be excused from the initiation ceremony; trapped in a room full of congenial strangers, he escapes by jumping out of the window. "What a coarse ungainly boor I am," he laments, "how poor, small and insignificant. . . ." He wonders if he is mad: "I am morbidly sensitive . . . it is an affliction—a disease . . . the slightest rebuff tortures me beyond expression. . . . It is worse than death itself. It is *horrible*." Again, he speculates about his "abnormal quality of mind . . . that lacks only vehemence to become downright insanity. . . ." Harris's life, it appears, was one long ballet of embarrassment.

"I am nursing a novel in my brain," Harris announced archly more than once. All along he was consumed with the desire to turn out some "long work" of fiction, but, except for two inept and badly received efforts (published after his forty-eighth year), he never succeeded. Over and over he complained bitterly of his grinding life in the journalistic salt mines—but when the Century Company offered him a handsome income if he would devote all his time to creative work, he refused. This refusal, according to his daughter-in-law, "can be explained only by his abnormal lack of confidence in himself as a 'literary man.' "

The urge to create was strong in Harris, so strong that it gave him no peace; and he could not create. That is the central fact in his biography: his creative impulses were trapped behind a block of congealed guilts, granite-strong; the works he produced were not real gushings of the subjective but only those driblets that were able to seep around the edges of the block.

Harris's stammer—his literal choking on words—was like a charade of the novelist *manqué* in him; his blush was the fitful glow of his smothered self, a tic of the guilty blood. And that smothered self had a name: Uncle Remus.

Accused of plagiarizing folk materials, Harris replies indignantly: "I shall not hesitate to draw on the oral stories I know for incidents. . . . The greatest literary men, if you will remember, were very poor inventors." Harris all his life was a very poor inventor; his career was built on a merciless, systematic plagiarizing of the folk-Negro. Small wonder, then, that the "plantation darky" was such a provocative symbol for him. For, ironically, this lowly Negro was, when viewed through the blinders of stereotype, almost the walking image of Harris's ego-ideal—the un-selfconscious, "natural," free-flowing, richly giving creator that Harris could never become. Indeed, for Harris, as for many another white American, the Negro *seemed* in every respect to be a negative print of his own uneasy self: "happy-go-lucky," socializing, orally expressive, muscularly relaxed, never bored or passive, unashamedly exhibitionistic, free from self-pity even in his situation of concentrated pain, emotionally fluid. And every time a Remus opened his mouth, every time he flashed a grin, he wrote effortlessly another novel that was strangled a-borning in Harris.

"I despise and detest those false forms of society that compel people to suppress their thoughts," Harris wrote. But he was himself the most inhibited and abashed of men. What fascinates him in the Rabbit stories, he confesses, is "the humor that lies between *what is perfectly decorous in appearance* and *what is wildly extravagant in suggestion.*" But, a thorough slave to decorum, he was incapable of the "wildly extravagant," whether in his love-making ("My love for you," he informs his future wife, "is . . . far removed from that wild passion that develops itself in young men in their teens . . . it is not at all wild or unreasoning.") or in his writing.

Harris, then, was *awed* by Uncle Remus. It was the awe of the sophisticate before the spontaneous, the straitjacketed before the nimble. But was the Negro what Harris thought him to be? It is certainly open to question, for another irony of the South is that the white man, under his pretense of racial omniscience, actually knows the Negro not at all—he knows only the false-face which he has forced on the Negro. It is the white man who manufactures the Negro grin. The stereotype reflects the looker, his thwartings and yearnings, not the person looked at; it is born out of intense subjective need.

Harris's racial awe was only an offshoot of the problem that tormented him all his life: the problem of identifying himself. He was caught in the American who-am-I dilemma, one horn of which is white, the other often black. And there is abundant proof that, at least in one compartment of his being, Harris defined himself by identifying with the Negro.

As a child, Harris started the game of "Gully Minstrels" with his white playmates; and later in life, whenever he felt "blue" and wanted to relax, he would jump up and exclaim, "Let's have some fun—let's play minstrels!" Often, in letters and newspaper articles, and even in personal relations, he would *jokingly* refer to himself as "Uncle Remus," and when he started a one-man magazine, he decided to name it *Uncle Remus's Magazine* instead of *The Optimist!* Frequently he would lapse into a rich Negro dialect, to the delight of his admirers, from Andrew Carnegie down to the local trolley conductor. And, like Uncle Remus, he even toys with the idea that whites are only blanched Negroes: "Study a nigger right close," he has one of his characters say, "and you'll ketch a glimpse of how white folks would look and do without their trimmin's."

Harris seems to have been a man in permanent rebellion against his own skin. No wonder: for he was driven to "give," and it was impossible for him to give without first zipping out of his own decorous skin and slipping into Uncle Remus's. To him the artist and the Negro were synonymous.

And Harris virulently *hated* the Negro too. "The colored people of Macon," he writes in his paper, "celebrated the birthday of Lincoln again on Wednesday. This is the third time since last October. . . ." And: "A negro pursued by an agile Macon policeman fell in a well the other day. He says he knocked the bottom out of the concern." Again: "There will have to be another amendment to the civil rights bill. A negro boy in Covington was attacked by a sow lately and narrowly escaped with his life. We will hear next that the sheep have banded together to mangle the downtrodden race."

The malice here is understandable. Can the frustrate—the "almanac-maker"—ever love unequivocally the incarnation of his own taboo self—the "calendar"? What stillborn novelist can be undilutedly tender towards the objectivization of his squelched alter-ego, whose oral stories he feels impelled to "draw on" all his life?

Most likely, at least in Harris, the love went deeper than the hate—the hate was, in some measure, a *defense* against the love. *"Some goes up en some goes down."* Who sings this theme song? A trio: the Rabbit, Remus, *and* Harris. Literally, it is only a rabbit and a fox who change places. Racially, the song symbolizes the ascent of the Negro "Weak" and the descent of the white "Strong."

But to Harris, on the deepest personal level, it must have meant: collapse of the "perfectly decorous" (inhibition, etiquette, embarrassment, the love that is never wild, the uncreative journalist-compiler, the blush and the stammer) and the triumph of the "wildly extravagant" (spontaneity, "naturalness," the unleashed subjective, creativity, "Miss Meadows en de gals," exhibitionism, the folk-novelist). The song must have been *deliciously* funny to him. . . .

The Remus stories are a monument to the South's ambivalence. Harris, the archetypical Southerner, sought the Negro's love, and pretended he had received it (Remus's grin). But he sought the Negro's hate too (Brer Rabbit), and revelled in it in an unconscious orgy of masochism—punishing himself, possibly, for not being the Negro, the stereotypical Negro, the unstinting giver.

Harris's inner split—and the South's, and white America's—is mirrored in the fantastic disparity between Remus's beaming face and Brer Rabbit's acts. And such aggressive acts increasingly emanate from the grin, along with the hamburgers, the shoeshines, the "happifyin' " pancakes.

Today Negro attack and counter-attack becomes more straightforward. The NAACP submits a brief to the United Nations, demanding a redress of grievances suffered by the Negro people at the hands of white America. The election newsreels showed Henry Wallace addressing audiences that were heavily sprinkled with Negroes, protected by husky, alert, *deadpan* body-guards—Negroes. New York Negroes voted for Truman—but only after Truman went to Harlem. The Gandhi-like "Tar-Baby" begins to stir: Grant Reynolds and A. Phillips Randolph, announcing to a Senate committee that they will refuse to be drafted in the next war, revealed, at the time, that many Negroes were joining their civil-disobedience organization—the first movement of passive resistance this country had seen.

Increasingly Negroes themselves reject the mediating smile of Remus, the indirection of the Rabbit. The present-day animated cartoon hero, Bugs Bunny, is, like Brer Rabbit, the meek suddenly grown cunning—but without Brer Rabbit's facade of politeness. "To pull a Bugs Bunny," meaning to spectacularly outwit someone, is an expression not infrequently heard in Harlem.

There is today on every level a mass repudiation of "Uncle Tomism." Significantly the Negro comedian is disappearing. For bad or good, the *Dark Laughter* that Sherwood Anderson heard all around white New Orleans is going or gone.

The grin is faltering, especially since the war. That may be one of the reasons why, once more, the beaming Negro butler and Pullman porter are making their amiable way across our billboards, food labels, and magazine ads—and Uncle Remus, "fetchin' a grin from year to year," is in the big time again.

JOHN G. CAWELTI

FROM RAGS TO RESPECTABILITY
Horatio Alger

As Horatio Alger was transformed from the author of success novels into a symbol for the process of success itself, the precise content of the message that he successfully preached for so long became blurred and indistinguishable from all other literature exalting the self-made man. Anyone who raised himself by his own bootstraps, regardless of his methods or his goals, was awarded a place in the ever growing pantheon of "Alger" heroes. The "success myth" or "cult" has been too easily identified as a monolithic whole stretching from the nineteenth-century Alger to Norman Vincent Peale in the twentieth century.

In recent years scholars have been looking more closely at the various components of the success myth and have been concerned with showing changes over time. By emphasizing what Alger actually did and did not say, Cawelti illuminates the values central to Alger and, one would presume, to many of his ardent readers. His study helps us to recognize, and to better comprehend, the modifications in ideas of success that have occurred between Alger's time and ours.

The entire subject is discussed in greater detail in John G. Cawelti, Apostles of the Self-Made Man *(1965), as well as in Irvin G. Wyllie,* The Self-Made Man in America * *(1954), and Donald Meyer,* The Positive Thinkers * *(1965).*

Luke Walton is not puffed up by his unexpected and re-markable success. He never fails to recognize kindly, and help, if there is need, the old associates of his humbler days, and never tries to conceal the fact that he was once a Chicago Newsboy.

HORATIO ALGER, *Luke Walton*

Today his books are read more often by cultural historians than by children, and such erstwhile classics as *Struggling Upward* and *Mark, The Hatchboy* are no longer on the shelves of libraries, but the name of Horatio Alger has become synonymous with the self-made man. American businessmen who commission brief biographies often are described in the following manner:

> The Horatio Alger quality of William J. Stebler's rise to the presidency of General American Transportation Corporation makes one almost pause for breath.[1]

There is even a Horatio Alger award presented annually by the American Schools and Colleges Association to eight Americans who have reached positions of prominence from humble beginnings. In recent years, this award, a bronze desk plaque, has been presented to such leading industrialists and financiers as Benjamin F. Fairless, retired chairman of the United States Steel Corporation; James H. Carmichael, chairman of Capital Airlines; and Milton G. Hulme, president and chairman of a large investment banking firm in Pittsburgh. The creator of *Ragged Dick* has become a familiar idol to Americans concerned about the decline of what they refer to as "individualistic free enterprise." *Advertising Age* in December, 1947, tired of "government interference" in business, begged for a new Horatio Alger to inspire American youth with the independence and enterprise of their fathers.

Many of those who parade under Alger's mantle know little about their hero beyond the fact that he wrote books about success. They would probably be startled if they read one, for Alger was not a partisan of "rugged individualism," and only within limits an admirer of pecuniary success. For a patron saint of success, his life was rather obscure. Born in 1832 in Revere, Massachusetts, he was trained for the ministry at the insistence of his domineering father. He soon gave this up when he found he could support himself by writ-

---

[1] Quoted from "this 'n' that," a handout of the La Salle National Bank, Chicago, May, 1958, p. 3.

REPRINTED from "From Rags to Respectability: Horatio Alger," *Apostles of the Self-Made Man,* by John G. Cawelti, by permission of The University of Chicago. Copyright 1965 by The University of Chicago. All rights reserved.

ing children's books. He published a collection of sentimental tales in 1856, and his first widely popular juvenile, *Ragged Dick,* was published serially in Oliver Optic's (William T. Adams) *Student and Schoolmate* magazine, and as a book, in 1867. Alger moved to New York about 1866 and, aside from an occasional trip West and to Europe, spent most of his life in and around the Newsboys' Lodging House, an institution which figures in many of his stories. Its superintendent, Charles O'Connor, was one of his few close friends. Alger, whose books made fortunes for several publishers, died a relatively poor man. He sold most of his books outright for small sums, and spent what money he received in acts of spontaneous and unflagging charity to help almost anyone who applied to him. His amazingly rapid composition of books like *Grit, the Young Boatman of Pine Point* and *Jed, the Poorhouse Boy* was interspersed with occasional efforts at a serious novel, desultory participation in various reform movements—New York Mayor A. Oakey Hall, member of the Tweed ring, once named him chairman of an anti-vice commission—and brief forays into education (he sometimes tutored boys in Greek and Latin to supplement the income from his books).

Alger's death in 1899 did not put an end to the publication of Alger books. Publishers hired ghosts like Edward Stratemeyer, later the author of the Rover Boys series, to capitalize on Alger's popularity. Inevitably, there were signs of a reaction. Parents began to protest against what they considered the false values and unreality of the Alger stories, and a number of libraries removed his books from the shelves. They were republished less often in the second decade of the twentieth century, and, after World War I, sales declined rapidly. At the centennial of Alger's birth, in 1933, a survey of New York working children [2] showed that less than 20 per cent of the "juvenile proletariat" had ever heard of Alger; only 14 per cent had read an Alger book; and, even more threatening, a "large number" dismissed the theory of "work and win" as "a lot of bunk." A similar survey taken in the forties revealed that only 1 per cent of 20,000 children had read an Alger book.[3]

Alger and His Predecessors

There was a marked difference between Alger's work and that of his most important predecessor in the field of juvenile fiction. Jacob Abbott, author of the "Rollo" and "Caleb" books, began his extremely successful career as a writer of children's books in the early 1830's with a long, rather heavily theological, tome discussing the Christian duties of young boys and girls. A strong emphasis on evangelical Protestantism remained the central element in his

---

[2] "Cynical Youngest Generation," *Nation*, CXXXIV (February 17, 1932), p. 186.

[3] *The New York Times* for January 13, 1947, quoted in R. Richard Wohl, "The 'Rags to Riches' Story," Bendix and Lipset (eds.), *Class, Status and Power* (Glencoe, Illinois: Free Press, 1953), n. 4.

work. Alger, on the other hand, was not so concerned with the role of religion in the lives of his young heroes. There were other important differences between the Abbott boy and the Alger boy. A firm believer in the ethic of industry, frugality, integrity, and piety, Abbott rarely made ambition itself a significant element in his stories. Rollo and Caleb were not poor boys but the scions of well-to-do middle-class families. The typical Abbott book concerns everyday events from which Rollo or Caleb learns an important moral lesson. In *Rollo at Work,* for example, the hero learns how to work through a Lockean course of instruction which instils in him a progressively greater capacity for sustained effort.

Unlike Alger, Abbott chose to write about younger boys from well-established families for whom social mobility was not a significant problem, and his stories reflect the more conservative social views of the upper middle-class audience for which he wrote. As he presents American life, there are rightful and fundamental class distinctions, each class has its particular role, and there is relatively little movement between classes. At the same time, there is no conception of a leisure class in the Abbott books, and, in terms of worldly luxuries, the gulf between the higher and lower ranks is not great. According to Abbott, since every rank has its proper work, there should be no idlers.

In Alger's stories, on the other hand, rising and falling in society are characteristic phenomena. This is not the first appearance in American children's literature of the idea of mobility. Even in the period of Abbott's dominance, some juvenile authors began to write tales anticipating those of Alger. An interesting halfway house can be seen in the works of Mrs. Louisa M. Tuthill in the period 1830–50. Like Abbott, Mrs. Tuthill generally wrote about boys from well-established families, not the street boys who were Alger's favorite subjects. As an adherent of the Jeffersonian ideal of natural aristocracy, Mrs. Tuthill believed that American institutions properly encouraged the rise of talented and virtuous young men to whatever positions of eminence their merits entitled them. In her *I Will Be a Gentleman,* for example, she attacks the idea of hereditary distinction:

> Having no hereditary titles in the United States, there can be no higher distinction than that which belongs to moral worth, intellectual superiority, and refined politeness. A republican gentleman therefore need acknowledge no superior; he is a companion for nobles and kings, or, what is better, for the polite, the talented, the good. Since such are an American's only claims to distinction, it becomes the more important for him to cultivate all those graces which elevate and dignify humanity. No high ancestral claims can he urge for his position in society. Wealth he may possess, and there are those who will acknowledge that claim; but if the possessor have not intelligence and taste to teach him how to use his wealth, it will only make him a more conspicuous mark for ridicule. Those glorious institutions of New England, common schools, afford to every boy the opportunity to acquire that intelli-

gence and taste, and his associates there are from every class of society. There is no unsurmountable obstacle in any boy's way; his position in society must depend mainly upon himself.[4]

Mrs. Tuthill puts the same limits on rising in society as the didactic novelists of the same period. The candidate for distinction must be talented, virtuous, and refined, although he need not spring from an aristocratic family tradition. This emphasis on gentility and refinement, however acquired, also has an important role in the Alger books. Alger constantly emphasizes neatness, good manners, and the proper clothes, and yet his conception of gentility is far less elevated than Mrs. Tuthill's. In spite of her frequent protestations that the way was open to all, Mrs. Tuthill's heroes spring from respectable families who have the means to educate their children.

Most of the children's literature of the pre-Civil War period deals with the offspring of secure, middle-class families, but the orphaned boy of the city streets is not without his bards. As early as 1834, a putative autobiography of a bootblack who rose from poverty to be a member of Congress was published with the delightful title *A Spur to Youth; or, Davy Crockett Beaten.* In the following year, Charles F. Barnard published *The Life of Collin Reynolds, the Orphan Boy and Young Merchant.* In this tearful tale, dedicated to the pupils of the Hollis Street Sunday School in Boston, the hero is orphaned when his mother dies and his father goes to sea. Undaunted, he determines to support himself by peddling candy, peanuts, and sundries on the New York ferries. In good Alger fashion, he soon meets the wealthy Mr. J., who is impressed by the boy's history, his industry, and his enterprise and adopts him. Entering Mr. J.'s store, Collin is doing well when the opportunity to sigh forth a highly sentimental deathbed scene proves more attractive to his creator than the fulfilment of material promise. Poor Collin is disposed of in a fall from a horse.

Even closer to Alger formula is J. H. Ingraham's *Jemmy Daily: or, The Little News Vender,* published in 1843. Ingraham, a hack writer of astonishing fertility, made sentimental romance out of almost any subject. Ingraham's treatment of the newsboy foreshadowed both Alger's characteristic material and his method of treating it. Jemmy Daily and his noble mother, reduced to starvation by a drunken father, are saved when, in a chance encounter, the lovely daughter of a wealthy merchant gives Jemmy food and a sixpence. As a newsboy, Jemmy manages to support his mother. When father becomes intolerable, Jemmy and his mother leave him, a shock which happily reforms the drunkard. The rest of the story concerns Jemmy's fight with a bully and his foiling of the quack Dr. Wellington Smoot's lascivious designs on his mother. Once reformed, the father is granted a convenient death, and

---

[4] Mrs. Louisa C. Tuthill, *I Will be a Gentleman* (Boston: Crosby and Nichols, 1845), pp. 66–67.

Jemmy takes over the family, becoming a clerk under the benevolent tutelage of Mr. Weldon. Jemmy's reward is the promise of a junior partnership and the hand of Mr. Weldon's daughter, the girl who had originally befriended him.

The difference between Ingraham's tale and the typical Alger story is largely a matter of emphasis. The plot and characters are essentially the same, but Ingraham stresses religious conversion and "the great moral temperance reform, which is without question one of the agents of God in ameliorating the condition of fallen man." [5] Jemmy Daily's rise in society and his gradual acquisition of respectability are not as important to him as they were to Alger.

In the 1850's, as urban phenomena became of increasing interest and concern, newsboys and bootblacks were common figures in popular fiction. A. L. Stimson's *Easy Nat* includes an Alger-like street boy adopted by a benevolent farmer, and Seba Smith's wife, a sentimental novelist of considerable popularity, published a long novel, *The Newsboy,* in 1854.[6] This is a typical romantic adventure, containing as one of its many plots the narrative of a poor newsboy's rise to some prominence, through, as usual, the patronage of a benevolent merchant. One writer in the 1850's went so far as to proclaim the newsboy the symbol of a new age:

> Our clarion now, more potent than the Fontabrian horn, is the shrill voice of the news-boy, that modern Minerva, who leaped full blown from the o'er-fraught head of journalism; and, as the news-boy is in some respects the type of the time—an incarnation of the spirit of the day,—a few words devoted to his consideration may not be deemed amiss.[7]

Alger had considerable precedent for his dramatization of the street boy's rise to social respectability. Nor was he the only writer of his time to employ this subject. In fact, Alger neither created the Alger hero nor was he his only exponent. A flood of children's books by such authors as Oliver Optic, Mrs. Sarah Stuart Robbins, Mrs. Madeline Leslie, and the Rev. Elijah Kellog dealt with the rise to moderate security of a poor boy. Alger, however, outsold them all. Somehow he was able to seize upon just those combinations of characters and plot situations that most engrossed adolescent American boys of the nineteenth century.

---

[5] J. H. Ingraham, *Jemmy Daily; or, The Little News Vender* (New York: M. Y. Beach, Sun Office, 1843), p. 13.

[6] Elizabeth O. Smith, *The Newsboy* (New York: J. C. Derby, 1854). Mrs. Smith's treatment of the newsboy as a sentimental curiosity is indicated by her description of him in these terms (p. 9): "I learned to await the coming of the Newsboy with solemn expectancy, and the shuffling of his weary feet grew to have a majesty about them; his ragged habiliments were right royal robes over his great heart, and the brimless hat became him like a regal crown, for Bob had that innate dignity of soul which neither crown nor sceptre could augment."

[7] Joseph C. Neal, *Peter Ploddy* (Philadelphia: T. B. Peterson and Brothers, 1856), p. 64.

Alger's Message

Alger's contemporary position as a symbol of individualistic free enterprise has obscured the actual characteristics of his stories. A number of misconceptions must be cleared away before we can get to the heart of the Alger version of what constitutes success. Here, for example, is a typical interpretation of the Alger hero in a recent book:

> Alone, unaided, the ragged boy is plunged into the maelstrom of city life, but by his own pluck and luck he capitalizes on one of the myriad opportunities available to him and rises to the top of the economic heap. Here, in a nutshell, is the plot of every novel Alger ever wrote; here, too, is the quintessence of the myth. Like many simple formulations which nevertheless convey a heavy intellectual and emotional charge to vast numbers of people, the Alger hero represents a triumphant combination—and reduction to the lowest common denominator—of the most widely accepted concepts in nineteenth-century American society. The belief in the potential greatness of the common man, the glorification of individual effort and accomplishment, the equation of the pursuit of money with the pursuit of happiness and of business success with spiritual grace: simply to mention these concepts is to comprehend the brilliance of Alger's synthesis.[8]

This passage illustrates several important misconceptions concerning Alger's books. In the first place, Alger's heroes are rarely "alone and unaided," and do not win their success entirely through individual effort and accomplishment. From the very beginning of his career, the Alger boy demonstrates an astounding propensity for chance encounters with benevolent and useful friends, and his success is largely due to their patronage and assistance. In the course of his duties Fred Fenton, the hero of *The Erie Train Boy,* meets a wealthy young girl named Isabel Archer—presumably named in homage to Alger's literary idol, Henry James—who gives him money to pay his mother's rent. In addition, he encounters an eccentric miner, who later helps him sell some land belonging to his late father, and the uncle of a wealthy broker, who gives young Fred his chance in business. Alger's heroes are well aware of their indebtedness to these patrons, and modestly make no pretense of success through their own efforts, although Alger assures his readers that they deserve their advancement. Ragged Dick, congratulated on his achievement by one of the innumerable wealthy men who befriended him, replies: " 'I was lucky,' said Dick, modestly. 'I found some good friends who helped me along.' " [9]

Nor did the Alger hero rise "to the top of the economic heap." Some years ago a writer for *Time,* in a mathematical mood, calculated that the average Alger hero's fortune is only $10,000. Usually the hero is established in a se-

---

[8] Kenneth S. Lynn, *The Dream of Success* (Boston: Little, Brown, 1955), p. 7.
[9] Alger, *Mark, the Match Boy* (Philadelphia: Porter and Coates, n.d.), p. 38.

cure white-collar position, either as a clerk with the promise of a junior part-nership or as a junior member of a successful mercantile establishment. None achieve anything resembling economic or political prominence. Moderate eco-nomic security would best summarize the pecuniary achievements of the typi-cal Alger hero, in spite of such tantalizing titles as *Fame and Fortune, Striving for Fortune,* and *From Farm to Fortune.* For example, at the end of *Fame and Fortune,* the hero is in possession of a magnificent income of $1,400 a year, plus the interest on about $2,000 in savings. In Alger's mind, this was "fame and fortune."

We may admit that Alger's representation of economic reality was highly sentimentalized, but it is unfair to call him an uninhibited adulator of wealth who equated spiritual grace with business success. The true aim of the Alger hero is respectability, a happy state only partially defined by economic repute. Nor was Alger unaware that many men were successful as the result of ques-tionable practices. He may have lacked knowledge of these practices, but Al-ger frequently reminded his readers that many wealthy and successful men were undeserving of their fortunes. One of his favorite villains is the wealthy, unscrupulous banker who accumulates wealth by cheating widows and or-phans. On the whole, Alger's formula is more accurately stated as middle-class respectability equals spiritual grace.

Alger was no more an unrestrained advocate of the "potential greatness" of the common man than he was of the uninhibited pursuit of financial suc-cess. His heroes are ordinary boys only in the sense of their lowly origin. In ability and personal character they are far above average. Many boys in the Alger books are unable, in spite of their earnest efforts, to rise above a lowly position. Micky McGuire, a young slum boy who is a secondary character in the *Ragged Dick* series, is reformed at last through the efforts of Dick and his patron Mr. Rockwell. But the old maxim "No Irish Need Apply" still held for Alger.

> Micky has already turned out much better than was expected, but he is hardly likely to rise much higher than the subordinate position he now occu-pies. In capacity and education he is far inferior to his old associate, Richard Hunter, who is destined to rise much higher than at present.[10]

Who, then, is the Alger hero, and what is the nature of the adventures in which he is involved? Alger has two types of heroes. The first, and probably the more popular, is the poor, uneducated street boy—sometimes an orphan, more frequently the son of a widowed mother—who rises to moderate afflu-ence. The second is a well-born and well-educated middle-class youth whose

---

[10] *Mark, the Match Boy,* p. 141. Cf. also Ben Gibson in the same book and Peter Groot in *Strive and Succeed* (New York: New York Book Co., 1910).

father dies, leaving the son to fend for himself. In some cases a villainous squire or distant relative attempts to cheat the hero out of his rightful legacy, but, in the end, the hero is restored to his inheritance or succeeds in rising to his proper place.

Alger made desultory attempts to vary the character of his hero in each story, but such an achievement was beyond his skill, and the reader could be certain that, whatever the situation, and whether the hero smokes or uses slangy language, the same solid core of virtue is present. Alger's heroes, who range in age from around twelve to eighteen, are in the tradition of the didactic novels of self-improvement. One must give Alger some credit for making his young paragons a little less earnest and more lively than the placid prigs of T. S. Arthur. The Alger hero might begin as an intemperate spendthrift like Ragged Dick, but soon he becomes a master of the traditional virtues of industry, economy, integrity, and piety. He is manly and self-reliant—two of Alger's favorite words—and, in addition, kind and generous. Never a genius, he is usually a boy of above-average intelligence, particularly in the area of mathematics, and is also a strenuous devotee of self-culture. The Alger hero is never snobbish or condescending; indeed, he is the veritable apotheosis of modesty. Thoroughly democratic in his tastes, he befriends other poor boys and is uniformly courteous to people of all classes. The Alger hero demonstrates to a high degree those traits that might be called the employee virtues: fidelity, punctuality, and courteous deference. It is upon these latter traits that Alger places the greatest stress.

Against his hero, Alger sets three types of boys who serve as foils to the hero's sterling qualities. One of these may be called the lesser hero. He is usually a slightly younger and less vigorous edition of the major figure. The lesser hero often has greater advantages than his friend, but he lacks the enterprise, the courage, and the self-reliance of the hero, and frequently depends on him for protection against the harsh urban world, enabling the hero to demonstrate his courage and generosity. Another boy who appears in almost all the Alger books is the snob. Insisting that he is a gentleman's son, the snob looks down his nose at the hero's willingness to work at such lowly trades as that of bootblack or newsboy. Sometimes the snob is the son of a rich but grasping relative of the hero's, envious of his greater capabilities and endeavoring to get him into trouble. The young snob shows the obverse of all the hero's virtues: he is lazy, ignorant, arrogant, and unwilling to work because he considers it beneath his station. He is overtly contemptuous and secretly envious of the hero's successes. Alger delights in foiling this little monster, usually by arranging for his father to fail in business, thereby forcing the snob to go to work at a salary lower than the hero's.

Another type appearing somewhat less frequently in the Alger books is the poor boy who lacks the intelligence and ability of the hero and is more susceptible to the corruption of his environment. Often he becomes involved in plots against the hero, but is usually won over when he recognizes his true manliness and forgiving character. Although sometimes reformed through the hero's efforts, the Micky McGuire type is doomed to remain in a subordinate but respectable position by his lack of intelligence and enterprise. Curiously enough, these dim-minded characters are Alger's most interesting and vivid creations, and foreshadow the "bad boy" heroes of later juvenile books. In addition, they frequently represent immigrant groups—Irish, Italians, Germans—who, not all bad, play a distinctly inferior role in Alger's version of America.

The adult characters vary no more than the boys in the typical Alger book. The central adult figure is the benevolent businessman whose chance encounter with the hero gives him his big opportunity. Like all adults in Alger, this figure is thinly characterized, his major traits being the ability to recognize and reward the hero's potentialities. He is called upon to deliver long homilies on the virtues requisite to success. Generally, he is a merchant or a highly reputable stockbroker. In his business dealings he is honest and upright, scorning all but the most elevated commercial practices. In effect his role is to serve as an ideal adoptive father for the hero.

The second most important male adult in the Alger books is the villain, who usually has some important hold over the hero. Sometimes he is a mean stepfather, more often a grasping uncle or cousin who becomes the hero's guardian, and frequently a cruel, miserly squire who holds a mortgage on the family property. Whatever his mask, he invariably attempts to assert his tyrannical authority over the hero, and fails. One is tempted to describe him in Freudian terms as the overbearing father-figure whose authority the adolescent hero rejects and overthrows.

Few of the Alger heroes are orphans; the majority have a widowed mother dependent upon them for support. Here Alger differs appreciably from his predecessors. The Alger mother stands in a very different relationship to her doughty young offspring than do the mothers in the novels of T. S. Arthur. The "Arthurian" mother is pre-eminently a source of moral authority, an instructor and preceptor, whose gentle commands the young hero is expected to obey. In Alger, the mother rarely commands or instructs; although she presumably has some hand in her son's development, her authoritative function is mentioned only rarely. On the contrary, she is both a dependent and an admiring onlooker. Always gentle and supremely confident in her son's ability, she never criticizes or disciplines. Indeed, occasionally she is weak and indecisive, qualities which might lead the family into difficulty were it not for the manly self-reliance of her son. Characteristic of the Alger version of maternity is this interchange between Paul the peddler and his mother:

> "You see, mother, Phil would be sure of a beating if he went home without his fiddle. Now he doesn't like to be beaten, and the padrone gives harder beatings than you do, mother."

"I presume so," said Mrs. Hoffman, smiling. "I do not think I am very severe."

"No, you spoil the rod and spare the child." [11]

The benevolent merchant, the villainous father-figure, and the gentle and appreciative mother are at the center of most Alger books. They are joined by a variety of minor figures, all of whom can be traced to the traditional stereotypes of the sentimental novel: the warm-hearted Irish woman, poor and crude, kind and generous, who helps the hero escape from the villain; the snobbish female with aristocratic pretensions; the "stage Yankee" who appears in an occasional novel as a friend of the hero; and a variety of minor villains, such as the miserly moneylender, the petty swindler, and, in the Western stories, the stagecoach robber.

From such material, together with carefully accumulated local color—the books are filled with detailed descriptions of New York City—Alger constructed his tales. Almost invariably, they follow the same formula: by an amazing series of coincidences, and a few acts of personal heroism and generosity, the hero escapes from the plots laid by his enemies—usually an unholy alliance between the snobbish boy and the villainous father-figure—and attains the patronage of the benevolent merchant. In generating the action, chance and luck play a dominant role. Alger was apparently aware that the unbelievable tissue of coincidences which ran through his stories put some strain on the tolerance of his youthful readers. In *Struggling Upward,* for example, Linton Tomkins, the lesser hero, chances upon practically every other character in the book in the course of a twenty-minute promenade. Somewhat amazed at this feat, Alger can only remark that "Linton was destined to meet plenty of acquaintances." [12] At the book's conclusion he confesses:

So closes an eventful passage in the life of Luke Larkin. He has struggled upward from a boyhood of privation and self-denial into a youth and manhood of prosperity and honor. There has been some luck about it, I admit, but after all he is indebted for most of his good fortune to his own good qualities.[13]

However much the hero's good qualities may have been involved, and they often seem incidental, Alger is obsessed with luck. The chapter which contains the crucial turning point of the book is invariably entitled ———'s Luck, and every accession to the hero's fortunes stems from a coincidence: the land thought to be worthless suddenly becomes valuable because a town

---

[11] Alger, *Phil, the Fiddler* (Philadelphia, n.d.), pp. 145–46.

[12] Crouse (ed.) *Struggling Upward and Other Works* (New York: Crown Publishers, 1945), p. 135.

[13] *Ibid.,* p. 148.

has been built around it; the strongbox which the hero saves from thieves turns out to belong to an eccentric and wealthy old man who rewards the hero; the dead father's seemingly worthless speculation in mining stock is in fact a bonanza.

Alger's emphasis on luck resembles that found in the stories of T. S. Arthur and other apostles of the self-made man in the pre-Civil War era. Like them, he represents American society as an environment in which sudden and unaccountable prosperity frequently comes to the deserving like manna from heaven. To some extent, this reliance on luck or Providence is a literary shortcoming. Both Alger and Arthur turned out books at a tremendous rate; sloppiness and inadequacies in plotting and motivation could be concealed in part by defending coincidence. Furthermore, accident, luck, and chance have always played a large role in folk and popular literature, for they allow for exciting plot manipulation and the maintenance of suspense. It is equally true that the form which the accidental takes in a given work is some indication of the beliefs of an author and his intended audience.

In the case of Arthur and his contemporaries, the accidental assumes the form of the more or less direct intervention of Divine Providence. God acts to reward the deserving, punish the evil, and convert the doubting to a faith in his powers. Alger ignores the religious implications of the accidental. In his stories, luck is seemingly independent of the divine, inhering in the particular social environment of America, with its absence of hereditary class distinctions and the freedom it allows. Because most of the great merchants had been poor boys themselves, they were always on the lookout for deserving young men to assist. If the hero has the daring and self-assurance to seize one of his many opportunities to come to the attention of a benevolent patron, and is also blessed with the virtues of industry, fidelity, and good manners, he is certain to get ahead.

Religion itself does not play a major role in the life of the Alger hero. His heroes pray and go to Sunday School willingly enough, but Alger places greater stress on their obligations to others—loyalty to family and employer, and personal assistance to the less fortunate. His books encourage humanitarianism in their emphasis on practical good works and frequent insistence that Americans extend opportunities for worldly success to the juvenile proletariat of the cities. Although, like most writers in the tradition of self-improvement, Alger attributes success and failure to qualities within the individual, he occasionally points out to his young readers that a stifling and corrupting environment can be a major cause of vice and failure. An important factor in the rise of his streetboy heroes is their removal from the streets, where, if they remain, moral decay and poverty are certain. Alger can hardly be granted a profound understanding of the contemporary scene, but sympathy for the underprivileged is strong in his books. Judging from the prominence of his themes, there is as much evidence that Alger was an important influence on future reformers as a popular model for incipient robber barons.

Luck is not the only element in the success of the Alger hero. He has to deserve his luck by manifesting certain important traits which show him to be a fit candidate for a higher place in society. He carries the full complement of middle-class virtues, but these are not solely industry, frugality, and piety. Far more important are those qualities of character and intellect which make the hero a good employee and a reputable member of middle-class society. To his hero's cultivation of these qualities Alger devotes much of his attention. The hero has to learn how to dress neatly and modestly, to eliminate slang and colloquialisms from his speech, and to develop a facility with the stilted and pretentious language that Alger took to be the proper medium of verbal intercourse among respectable Americans. In addition, he has to educate himself. Alger's conception of the liberally educated man is also closely tied to social respectability. It is particularly desirable for the hero to have a neat hand and mathematical ability, but it is also important that he show a smattering of traditional culture. A foreign language is usually the prescribed curriculum. Ragged Dick studies French, for example. Since a foreign language plays no part in the hero's economic life, it is apparently intended by Alger as a certificate of a certain kind of respectability. The ability to learn French or Latin, although he might never have an opportunity to use such a skill, shows that the hero has a respect for learning as an end in itself and is no mere materialist. Thus, the Alger hero is a pale reflection of the ideal of self-culture as well as a devotee of rising in society.

Inner attainments are marked by characteristic external signs. The most crucial event in the hero's life is his acquisition of a good suit. The good suit, which is usually presented to the hero by his patron, marks the initial step in his advancement, his escape from the dirty and ragged classes and his entry upon respectability. It immediately differentiates the hero from the other bootblacks, and often leads to a quarrel with such dedicated proletarians as Micky McGuire. A second important event follows on the first: he is given a watch. The new watch marks the hero's attainment of a more elevated position, and is a symbol of punctuality and his respect for time as well as a sign of the attainment of young manhood. Alger makes much of the scene in which his hero receives from his patron a pocket watch suitably engraved.

Perhaps the most important group of qualities which operate in the hero's favor are those which make him the ideal employee: fidelity, dependability, and a burning desire to make himself useful. In a common Algerine situation, the hero, entrusted with some of his employer's money, is confronted by a villainous robber. At great risk to his own life, he defends his employer's property, preferring to lose his own money, or even his life, rather than betray his patron's trust. Under lesser stress, the hero demonstrates his superiority over the snobs by showing his willingness to perform any duties useful to his employer, and by going out of his way to give cheerful and uncomplaining service without haggling over wages. In *Fame and Fortune,* Roswell Crawford, a snob, is fired from his position as errand boy in a dry goods store when he not only complains of being required to carry packages—work too low for a "gentleman's son"—but has the additional temerity to ask for a raise. Ragged Dick, on the other hand, generously offers to carry Roswell's packages for him. Needless to say, Dick receives a raise without asking for it, because his patron recognizes his fidelity and insists on a suitable reward.

Emphasis on fidelity to the employer's interests is perhaps the worst advice Alger could have given his young readers if financial success was of major interest to them. Contrast the Alger hero's relations with his employers and Benjamin Franklin's as described in the *Memoirs*. Franklin keeps his eyes on his own interests when he works for his brother, and for the Philadelphia printers, Bradford and Keimer; indeed, he shows considerable satisfaction at his ability to turn Keimer's faults to his own benefit. By studying the inadequacies of his former employer he is able to make his own business a success. The Alger hero would never resort to such a self-serving device.

Placed against Emerson and his philosophy of self-reliance, Alger is simply another exponent of the idealized version of the self-made man found in the novels of T. S. Arthur, Sylvester Judd, and other sentimentalists of the 1840's and 1850's. His understanding of social mobility is on the same level of abstraction and idealization. Emerson, in comparison, has a much more profound understanding of the implications of social mobility and the actual characteristics likely to lead to economic and social advancement, as well as a broader ideal of self-culture. It is as true of Alger as of Arthur that he presents the mobile society through the rose-colored glasses of the middle-class ethical tradition of industry, frugality, and integrity, and the sentimental Christian version of a benevolent Providence.

The great attainment of Alger's hero is to leave the ranks of the "working class" and become an owner or partner in a business of his own. Yet few of Alger's heroes have any connection with such enterprises as mining, manufacturing, or construction, the industries in which most of the large fortunes of the late nineteenth century were made. Alger's favorite reward is a junior partnership in a respectable mercantile house. This emphasis is a throwback to the economic life of an earlier period, when American business was still dominated by merchants whose economic behavior in retrospect seemed refined and benevolent in comparison to the devastating strategies of transcontinental railroad builders, iron and steel manufacturers, and other corporate giants. Alger's version of success is, in effect, a reassertion of the values of a bygone era in an age of dramatic change and expansion.

Alger's Popularity

Today one would hardly expect adolescent boys to respond to Alger's vision of a dying past. His popularity with many older Americans—a phenomenon that continues into the present time—is certainly nostalgic. Alger is a teacher of traditional manners and morals rather than an exponent of free enterprise. His fictions embody the values that middle-class Americans have been taught to revere: honesty, hard work, familial loyalty; good manners, cleanliness, and neatness of appearance; kindness and generosity to the less fortunate; loyalty and deference on the part of employees, and consideration and personal interest on the part of employers. These "bourgeois virtues" are strenuously displayed by the Alger hero and his benevolent patron, along with that strong respect for education and self-culture which is a considerable part of the middle-class heritage. On the other hand, the Alger villains represent those vices particularly reprehensible to many nineteenth-century Americans: they have aristocratic pretensions and try to adopt the airs of the leisure-class; they frequent theaters and gaming houses and are intemperate; they are disloyal to their families and often try to cheat their relatives; they are avaricious, miserly, and usurious; and they lack integrity and are unscrupulous in business affairs. The conflict between middle-class virtues and vices is played out against a background of unlimited opportunities in which the virtues ultimately show themselves to be indispensable and the vices trip up their possessors.

At the time when Alger wrote, traditional commercial practices and ethics had been undermined by economic expansion. A lifetime of hard work often left a man worse off than when he began. The growing gulf between millionaire and employee and the increasing development of complex economic hierarchies were so circumscribing individual ownership and control that a clerk was better off working for others than attempting to found and operate his own business. Alger reasserts an older economic model, one that had begun to be out of date as early as 1830, but which still lingered in the minds of Americans as the ideal form of economic organization: a multiplicity of small individual businesses or partnerships. He certainly had little idea of the actuality of business enterprise in his day—nowhere in his novels do industrial corporations or the character types they produce appear—but he does have enough personal knowledge of New York City to give a certain plausibility and contemporaneity to his representation of American life. He is able to present the traditional pattern of middle-class economic ideals in late nineteenth-century dress and fill the bustling streets and thoroughfares of a nineteenth-century industrial metropolis with a nostalgic reincarnation of the ideal *eighteenth-century* merchant and his noble young apprentice. This moral and economic anachronism is an important source of Alger's popularity with adults. When, a generation or so later, the accumulation of social and economic change made it no longer tenable, even in fantasy, the books began to come down from the library shelves, classed as unrealistic and misleading, perhaps even dangerous, fairy tales.

Although parents encouraged their children to read Alger because he seemed to reassert the validity of hard work, economy, integrity, and family loyalty, this is probably not the source of his popularity with young boys. There were a great many reasons why children liked Alger. He writes of places that they were interested in. In these locales he places a set of characters whose activities have enough of the fantastic and unusual to be exciting, yet always retain enough connection with the ordinary activities of American boys to encourage an emotionally satisfying empathy. Alger's glorification of financial success has been overemphasized by commentators, but many of his young readers enjoyed dreaming of the day when they would be rich enough to buy gold watches, good clothes, and have others dependent on their beneficences. Furthermore, Alger has a simple and unsophisticated sense of justice, which punishes the enemies of boyhood. The snobs, the bullies, the uncles and spinster aunts who do not like boys get their comeuppances in ways that must have appealed to a juvenile audience. Alger is hardly a master stylist, but his narrative and dialogue are simple, clear, and relatively fast-moving; and his diction, if formal and stilted, is not arcane or difficult.

These elements were undoubtedly important factors in Alger's popularity with his juvenile audience; and there was a further dimension to the Alger formula. Legion are the dangers of Freudian interpretation of literary works, but Alger cries out for this kind of treatment. Consider the following brief summary, which can apply with variations to almost any of the Alger books: an adolescent boy, the support of a gentle, loving, and admiring mother, is threatened by a male figure of authority and discipline. Through personal heroism he succeeds in subverting the authority of this figure and in finding a new male supporter who makes no threats to his relationship with the mother and does not seek to circumscribe his independence. The pattern is too obvious to require extended comment. When we recall that the late nineteenth century was an era of relatively strict paternal discipline and control, it does not seem far-fetched to suggest that the Alger books may have been appreciated as phantasies of father-elimination. The rapid decline in the popularity of Alger books after World War I probably resulted in part from the changing character of familial relationships in the twenties and thirties. When new ideals of parent-child relationship became generally accepted, the Alger hero's victory over the villainous father-figure must have lost much of its bite.

RICHARD HOFSTADTER

THE MYTH OF THE HAPPY YEOMAN

It is both the historian's function and his most intricate problem to sepa-rate myth from reality—to be able to discern differences, often subtle, be-tween the ways in which a people conceived of themselves and what they ac-tually were—and to show the interaction between the two. In the following article from his more extensive study, The Age of Reform * (1955), *Richard Hofstadter has attempted to perform this task with reference to the American farmer living at the end of the nineteenth century. For a pioneering study of the impact that the image of the American West has had upon Amer-ican thought and action, see Henry Nash Smith,* Virgin Land: The American West as Symbol and Myth * (1950).

The United States was born in the country and has moved to the city. From the beginning its political values and ideas were of necessity shaped by country life. The early American politician, the country editor, who wished to address himself to the common man, had to draw upon a rhetoric that would touch the tillers of the soil; and even the spokesman of city people knew that his audience had been in very large part reared upon the farm.

But what the articulate people who talked and wrote about farmers and farming—the preachers, poets, philosophers, writers, and statesmen—liked about American farming was not, in every respect, what the typical working farmer liked. For the articulate people were drawn irresistibly to the noncommercial, non-pecuniary, self-sufficient aspect of American farm life. To them it was an ideal.

Writers like Thomas Jefferson and Hector St. John de Crèvecoeur admired the yeoman farmer not for his capacity to exploit opportunities and make money but for his honest industry, his independence, his frank spirit of equality, his ability to produce and enjoy a simple abundance. The farmer himself, in most cases, was in fact inspired to make money, and such self-sufficiency as he actually had was usually forced upon him by a lack of transportation or markets, or by the necessity to save cash to expand his operations.

For while early American society was an agrarian society, it was fast becoming more commercial, and commercial goals made their way among its agricultural classes almost as rapidly as elsewhere. The more commercial this society became, however, the more reason it found to cling in imagination to the noncommercial agrarian values. The more farming as a self-sufficient way of life was abandoned for farming as a business, the more merit men found in what was being left behind. And the more rapidly the farmers' sons moved into the towns, the more nostalgic the whole culture became about its rural past. Throughout the Nineteenth and even in the Twentieth Century, the American was taught that rural life and farming as a vocation were something sacred.

This sentimental attachment to the rural way of life is a kind of homage that Americans have paid to the fancied innocence of their origins. To call it a "myth" is not to imply that the idea is simply false. Rather the "myth" so effectively embodies men's values that it profoundly influences their way of perceiving reality and hence their behavior.

Like any complex of ideas, the agrarian myth cannot be defined in a phrase, but its component themes form a clear pattern. Its hero was the yeoman farmer, its central conception the notion that he is the ideal man and the ideal citizen. Unstinted praise of the special virtues of the farmer and the spe-

FROM Richard Hofstadter, *The Age of Reform*. Copyright 1955 by Richard Hofstadter. Reprinted by permission of Alfred A. Knopf, Inc.

cial values of rural life was coupled with the assertion that agriculture, as a calling uniquely productive and uniquely important to society, had a special right to the concern and protection of government. The yeoman, who owned a small farm and worked it with the aid of his family, was the incarnation of the simple, honest, independent, healthy, happy human being. Because he lived in close communion with beneficent nature, his life was believed to have a wholesomeness and integrity impossible for the depraved populations of cities.

His well-being was not merely physical, it was moral: it was not merely personal, it was the central source of civic virtue; it was not merely secular but religious, for God had made the land and called man to cultivate it. Since the yeoman was believed to be both happy and honest, and since he had a secure propertied stake in society in the form of his own land, he was held to be the best and most reliable sort of citizen. To this conviction Jefferson appealed when he wrote: "The small land holders are the most precious part of a state."

In origin the agrarian myth was not a popular but a literary idea, a preoccupation of the upper classes, of those who enjoyed a classical education, read pastoral poetry, experimented with breeding stock, and owned plantations or country estates. It was clearly formulated and almost universally accepted in America during the last half of the Eighteenth Century. As it took shape both in Europe and America, its promulgators drew heavily upon the authority and the rhetoric of classical writers—Hesiod, Xenophon, Cato, Cicero, Virgil, Horace, and others—whose works were the staples of a good education. A learned agricultural gentry, coming into conflict with the industrial classes, welcomed the moral strength that a rich classical ancestry brought to the praise of husbandry.

Chiefly through English experience, and from English and classical writers, the agrarian myth came to America, where, like so many other cultural importations, it eventually took on altogether new dimensions in its new setting. So appealing were the symbols of the myth that even an arch-opponent of the agrarian interest like Alexander Hamilton found it politic to concede in his *Report on Manufactures* that "the cultivation of the earth, as the primary and most certain source of national supply . . . has intrinsically a strong claim to pre-eminence over every other kind of industry." And Benjamin Franklin, urban cosmopolite though he was, once said that agriculture was "the only *honest way*" for a nation to acquire wealth, "wherein man receives a real increase of the seed thrown into the ground, a kind of continuous miracle, wrought by the hand of God in his favour, as a reward for his innocent life and virtuous industry."

Among the intellectual classes in the Eighteenth Century the agrarian myth had virtually universal appeal. Some writers used it to give simple, direct, and emotional expression to their feelings about life and nature; others linked agrarianism with a formal philosophy of natural rights. The application of the natural rights philosophy to land tenure became especially popular in America. Since the time of Locke it had been a standard argument that the land is the common stock of society to which every man has a right—what Jefferson called "the fundamental right to labour the earth"; that since the occupancy and use of land are the true criteria of valid ownership, labor expended in cultivating the earth confers title to it; that since government was created to protect property, the property of working landholders has a special claim to be fostered and protected by the state.

At first the agrarian myth was a notion of the educated classes, but by the early Nineteenth Century it had become a mass creed, a part of the country's political folklore and its nationalist ideology. The roots of this change may be found as far back as the American Revolution, which, appearing to many Americans as the victory of a band of embattled farmers over an empire, seemed to confirm the moral and civic superiority of the yeoman, made the farmer a symbol of the new nation, and wove the agrarian myth into his patriotic sentiments and idealism.

Still more important, the myth played a role in the first party battles under the Constitution. The Jeffersonians appealed again and again to the moral primacy of the yeoman farmer in their attacks on the Federalists. The family farm and American democracy became indissolubly connected in Jeffersonian thought, and by 1840 even the more conservative party, the Whigs, took over the rhetorical appeal to the common man, and elected a President in good part on the strength of the fiction that he lived in a log cabin.

The Jeffersonians, moreover, made the agrarian myth the basis of a strategy of continental development. Many of them expected that the great empty inland regions would guarantee the preponderance of the yeoman—and therefore the dominance of Jeffersonianism and the health of the state—for an unlimited future. The opening of the trans-Allegheny region, its protection from slavery, and the purchase of the Louisiana Territory were the first great steps in a continental strategy designed to establish an internal empire of small farms. Much later the Homestead Act was meant to carry to its completion the process of continental settlement by small homeowners. The failure of the Homestead Act "to enact by statute the fee-simple empire" was one of the original sources of Populist grievances, and one of the central points at which the agrarian myth was overrun by the commercial realities.

Above all, however, the myth was powerful because the United States in the first half of the Nineteenth Century consisted predominantly of literate and politically enfranchised farmers. Offering what seemed harmless flattery to this numerically dominant class, the myth suggested a standard vocabulary to rural editors and politicians. Although farmers may not have been much impressed by what was said about the merits of a noncommercial way of life, they could only enjoy learning about their special virtues and their unique services to the nation. Moreover, the editors and politicians who so flattered them need not in most cases have been insincere. More often than not they too were likely to have begun life in little villages or on farms, and what they had to say stirred in their own breasts, as it did in the breasts of a great many towns-people, nostalgia for their early years and perhaps relieved some residual feelings of guilt at having deserted parental homes and childhood attachments. They also had the satisfaction in the early days of knowing that in so far as it was based upon the life of the largely self-sufficient yeoman the agrarian myth was a depiction of reality as well as the assertion of an ideal.

Oddly enough, the agrarian myth came to be believed more widely and tenaciously as it became more fictional. At first it was propagated with a kind of genial candor, and only later did it acquire overtones of insincerity. There survives from the Jackson era a painting that shows Governor Joseph Ritner of Pennsylvania standing by a primitive plow at the end of a furrow. There is no pretense that the Governor has actually been plowing—he wears broad-cloth pants and a silk vest, and his tall black beaver hat has been carefully laid in the grass beside him—but the picture is meant as a reminder of both his rustic origin and his present high station in life. By contrast, Calvin Coolidge posed almost a century later for a series of photographs that represented him as haying in Vermont. In one of them the President sits on the edge of a hay rig in a white shirt, collar detached, wearing highly polished black shoes and a fresh pair of overalls; in the background stands his Pierce Arrow, a secret service man on the running board, plainly waiting to hurry the President away from his bogus rural labors. That the second picture is so much more pretentious and disingenuous than the first is a measure of the increasing hollowness of the myth as it became more and more remote from the realities of agriculture.

Throughout the Nineteenth Century hundreds upon hundreds of thousands of farm-born youths sought their careers in the towns and cities. Particularly after 1840, which marked the beginning of a long cycle of heavy country-to-city migration, farm children repudiated their parents' way of life and took off for the cities where, in agrarian theory if not in fact, they were sure to succumb to vice and poverty.

When a correspondent of the *Prairie Farmer* in 1849 made the mistake of praising the luxuries, the "polished society," and the economic opportunities of the city, he was rebuked for overlooking the fact that city life *"crushes, enslaves,* and *ruins so many thousands of our young men* who are insensibly made the victims of *dissipation,* of *reckless speculation,* and of *ultimate crime."* Such warnings, of course, were futile. "Thousands of young men," wrote the New York agriculturist Jesse Buel, "do annually forsake the plough, and the honest profession of their fathers, if not to win the fair, at least form an opinion, too often confirmed by mistaken parents, that agriculture is not the road to wealth, to honor, nor to happiness. And such will continue to be the case, until our agriculturists become qualified to assume that rank in society to which the importance of their calling, and their numbers, entitle them, and which intelligence and self-respect can alone give them."

Rank in society! That was close to the heart of the matter, for the farmer was beginning to realize acutely not merely that the best of the world's goods were to be had in the cities and that the urban middle and upper classes had much more of them than he did but also that he was losing in status and respect as compared with them. He became aware that the official respect paid to the farmer masked a certain disdain felt by many city people. "There has . . . a certain class of individuals grown up in our land," complained a farm writer in 1835, "who treat the cultivators of the soil as an inferior caste . . . whose utmost abilities are confined to the merit of being able to discuss a boiled potato and a rasher of bacon." The city was symbolized as the home of loan sharks, dandies, fops, and aristocrats with European ideas who despised farmers as hayseeds.

The growth of the urban market intensified this antagonism. In areas like colonial New England, where an intimate connection had existed between the small town and the adjacent countryside, where a community of interests and even of occupations cut across the town line, the rural-urban hostility had not developed so sharply as in the newer areas where the township plan was never instituted and where isolated farmsteads were more common. As settlement moved west, as urban markets grew, as self-sufficient farmers became rarer, as farmers pushed into commercial production for the cities they feared and distrusted, they quite correctly thought of themselves as a vocational and economic group rather than as members of a neighborhood. In the Populist era the city was totally alien territory to many farmers, and the primacy of agriculture as a source of wealth was reasserted with much bitterness. "The great cities rest upon our broad and fertile prairies," declared Bryan in his "Cross of Gold" speech. "Burn down your cities and leave our farms, and your cities will spring up again as if by magic; but destroy our farms, and the grass will grow in the streets of every city in the country." Out of the beliefs nourished by the agrarian myth there had arisen the notion that the city was a parasitical growth on the country. Bryan spoke for a people raised for generations on the idea that the farmer was a very special creature, blessed by God, and that in a country consisting largely of farmers the voice of the farmer was the voice of democracy and of virtue itself.

The agrarian myth encouraged farmers to believe that they were not themselves an organic part of the whole order of business enterprise and speculation that flourished in the city, partaking of its character and sharing in its risks, but rather the innocent pastoral victims of a conspiracy hatched in the distance. The notion of an innocent and victimized populace colors the whole history of agrarian controversy.

For the farmer it was bewildering, and irritating too, to think of the great contrast between the verbal deference paid him by almost everyone and the real economic position in which he found himself. Improving his economic position was always possible, though this was often done too little and too late; but it was not within anyone's power to stem the decline in the rural values and pieties, the gradual rejection of the moral commitments that had been expressed in the early exaltations of agrarianism.

It was the fate of the farmer himself to contribute to this decline. Like almost all good Americans he had innocently sought progress from the very beginning, and thus hastened the decline of many of his own values. Elsewhere the rural classes had usually looked to the past, had been bearers of tradition and upholders of stability. The American farmer looked to the future alone, and the story of the American land became a study in futures.

In the very hours of its birth as a nation Crèvecoeur had congratulated America for having, in effect, no feudal past and no industrial present, for having no royal, aristocratic, ecclesiastical, or monarchial power, and no manufacturing class, and had rapturously concluded: "We are the most perfect society now existing in the world." Here was the irony from which the farmer suffered above all others: the United States was the only country in the world that began with perfection and aspired to progress.

To what extent was the agrarian myth actually false? During the colonial period, and even well down into the Nineteenth Century, there were in fact large numbers of farmers who were very much like the yeomen idealized in the myth. They were independent and self-sufficient, and they bequeathed to their children a strong love of craftsmanlike improvisation and a firm tradition of household industry. These yeomen were all too often yeomen by force of circumstance. They could not become commercial farmers because they were too far from the rivers or the towns, because the roads were too poor for bulky traffic, because the domestic market for agricultural produce was too small and the overseas markets were out of reach. At the beginning of the Nineteenth Century, when the American population was still living largely in the forests and most of it was east of the Appalachians, the yeoman farmer did exist in large numbers, living much as the theorists of the agrarian myth portrayed him.

But when the yeoman practiced the self-sufficient economy that was expected of him, he usually did so not because he wanted to stay out of the market but because he wanted to get into it. "My farm," said a farmer of Jefferson's time, "gave me and my family a good living on the produce of it; and left me, one year with another, one hundred and fifty dollars, for I have never spent more than ten dollars a year, which was for salt, nails, and the like. Nothing to wear, eat, or drink was purchased, as my farm provided all. With this saving, I put money to interest, bought cattle, fatted and sold them, and made great profit." Great profit! Here was the significance of self-sufficiency for the characteristic family farmer. Commercialism had already begun to enter the American Arcadia.

For, whatever the spokesman of the agrarian myth might have told him, the farmer almost anywhere in early America knew that all around him there were examples of commercial success in agriculture—the tobacco, rice, and indigo, and later the cotton planters of the South, the grain, meat, and cattle exporters of the middle states.

The farmer knew that without cash he could never rise above the hardships and squalor of pioneering and log-cabin life. So the savings from his self-sufficiency went into improvements—into the purchase of more land, of herds and flocks, of better tools; they went into the building of barns and silos and better dwellings. Self-sufficiency, in short, was adopted for a time in order that it would eventually be unnecessary.

Between 1815 and 1860 the character of American agriculture was transformed. The rise of native industry created a home market for agriculture, while demands arose abroad for American cotton and foodstuffs, and a great network of turnpikes, canals, and railroads helped link the planter and the advancing western farmer to the new markets. As the farmer moved out of the forests onto the flat, rich prairies, he found possibilities for machinery that did not exist in the forest. Before long he was cultivating the prairies with horse-drawn mechanical reapers, steel plows, wheat and corn drills, and threshers.

The farmer was still a hard-working man, and he still owned his own land in the old tradition. But no longer did he grow or manufacture almost everything he needed. He concentrated on the cash crop, bought more and more of his supplies from the country store. To take full advantage of the possibilities of mechanization, he engrossed as much land as he could and borrowed money for his land and machinery. The shift from self-sufficient to commercial farming varied in time throughout the West and cannot be dated with precision, but it was complete in Ohio by about 1830 and twenty years later in Indiana, Illinois, and Michigan. All through the great Northwest, farmers whose fathers might have lived in isolation and self-sufficiency were surrounded by jobbers, banks, stores, middlemen, horses, and machinery.

This transformation affected not only what the farmer did but how he felt. The ideals of the agrarian myth were competing in his breast, and gradually losing ground, to another, even stronger ideal, the notion of opportunity, of career, of the self-made man. Agrarian sentiment sanctified labor in the soil and the simple life; but the prevailing Calvinist atmosphere of rural life implied that virtue was rewarded with success and material goods. Even farm boys were taught to strive for achievement in one form or another, and when this did not take them away from the farms altogether, it impelled them to follow farming not as a way of life but as a *career*—that is, as a way of achieving substantial success.

The sheer abundance of the land—that very internal empire that had been expected to insure the predominance of the yeoman in American life for centuries—gave the *coup de grâce* to the yeomanlike way of life. For it made of the farmer a speculator. Cheap land invited extensive and careless cultivation. Rising land values in areas of new settlement tempted early liquidation and frequent moves. Frequent and sensational rises in land values bred a boom psychology in the American farmer and caused him to rely for his margin of profit more on the appreciation in the value of his land than on the sale of crops. It took a strong man to resist the temptation to ride skyward on lands that might easily triple or quadruple their value in one decade and then double in the next.

What developed in America, then, was an agricultural society whose real attachment was not, like the yeoman's, to the land but to land values. The characteristic product of American rural society, as it developed on the prairies and the plains, was not a yeoman or a villager, but a harassed little country businessman who worked very hard, moved all too often, gambled with his land, and made his way alone.

While the farmer had long since ceased to act like a yeoman, he was somewhat slower in ceasing to think like one. He became a businessman in fact long before he began to regard himself in this light. As the Nineteenth Century drew to a close, however, various things were changing him. He was becoming increasingly an employer of labor, and though he still worked with his hands, he began to look with suspicion upon the working classes of the cities, especially those organized in trade unions, as he had once done upon the urban fops and aristocrats. Moreover, when good times returned after the Populist revolt of the 1890's, businessmen and bankers and the agricultural colleges began to woo the farmer, to make efforts to persuade him to take the businesslike view of himself that was warranted by the nature of his farm operations. "The object of farming," declared a writer in the *Cornell Countryman* in 1904, "is not primarily to make a living, but it is to make money. To this end it is to be conducted on the same business basis as any other producing industry."

The final change, which came only with a succession of changes in the Twentieth Century, wiped out the last traces of the yeoman of old, as the coming first of good roads and rural free delivery, and mail order catalogues, then the telephone, the automobile, and the tractor, and at length radio, movies, and television largely eliminated the difference between urban and rural experience in so many important areas of life. The city luxuries, once so derided by farmers, are now what they aspire to give to their wives and daughters.

In 1860 a farm journal satirized the imagined refinements and affectations of a city girl in the following picture:

> Slowly she rises from her couch. . . . Languidly she gains her feet, and oh! what vision of human perfection appears before us: Skinny, bony, sickly, hipless, thighless, formless, hairless, teethless. What a radiant belle! . . . The ceremony of enrobing commences. In goes the dentist's naturalization efforts; next the witching curls are fashioned to her "classically molded head." Then the womanly proportions are properly adjusted; hoops, bustles, and so forth,

follow in succession, then a profuse quantity of whitewash, together with a "permanent rose tint" is applied to a sallow complexion; and lastly the "killing" wrapper is arranged on her systematical and matchless form.

But compare this with these beauty hints for farmers' wives from the *Idaho Farmer,* April, 1935:

Hands should be soft enough to flatter the most delicate of the new fabrics. They must be carefully manicured, with none of the hot, brilliant shades of nail polish. The lighter and more delicate tones are in keeping with the spirit of freshness. Keep the tint of your fingertips friendly to the red of your lips, and check both your powder and your rouge to see that they best suit the tone of your skin in the bold light of summer.

Nothing can tell us with greater finality of the passing of the yeoman ideal than these light and delicate tones of nail polish.

HERBERT G. GUTMAN

PROTESTANTISM AND THE AMERICAN LABOR MOVEMENT : The Christian Spirit in the Gilded Age

---

Historians of late nineteenth-century America have reconstructed with sensitivity the relationships to Protestant Christianity of both the apologists for industrial capitalism and its middle-class critics. The defenders of the new industrial order espoused the Gospel of Wealth, a thinly disguised justification for rugged individualism; its attackers in turn proclaimed the Social Gospel, a call for the reform of society through the conversion of the individual to the Christian faith. In historical studies, the frame of mind of the worker, his values, and his commitment to attitudes of pre-industrial society have, according to Gutman, been neglected. Although he asserts that we need much more knowledge of working-class structure before we can reach firm conclusions about working-class attitudes, his own article substantially reduces our ignorance. Likening Gilded Age workers to first-generation immigrants, a group that usually looks backward to a familiar tradition, Gutman shows that workers of all varieties found in Protestant perfectionism a moral sanction for their challenge to business assumptions about the nature of life in America. And, Gutman explains, just as working-class Protestantism differed from business in its expectations of the new order, so also did it depart from the Social Gospel in defining the means to achieve its goals. Undoubtedly, this subject requires further study; but Gutman's focus of interest, his use of sociological technique, and his tapping of new sources of information all make this essay a valuable one.

Henry F. May, Protestant Churches and Industrial America * (*1949*), *considers the church's role in reform; Charles H. Hopkins,* The Rise of the Social Gospel in American Protestantism, 1865–1915 * (*1940*), *is a pioneering study of the Social Gospel movement.*

Labor historians and others have puzzled over precisely how and why American workers, especially those critical of the new industrial order, reacted to the profound changes in the nation's social and economic structure and in their own particular status between 1850 and 1900, but in seeking explanations they have studied almost exclusively working-class behavior and trade-union organization and have neatly catalogued the interminable wranglings between "business" unionists, "utopian" dreamers, and "socialist" radicals. Although their works have uncovered much of value, the "mind" of the worker—the modes of thought and perception through which he confronted the industrialization process and which helped shape his behavior—has received scant and inadequate attention. American workers, immigrant and native-born alike, brought more than their "labor" to the factory and did not view their changing circumstances in simple "economic" terms. So narrow an emphasis ignores the complexity of their lives and experiences and, in general, distorts human behavior. "Events, facts, data, happenings," J. L. Talmon reminds us, "assume their significance from the way in which they are experienced." [1] These pages examine one of several important but overlooked influences on the disaffected worker's thought: the way certain strands of pre-Gilded Age Protestantism affected him in a time of rapid industrialization and radical social change.

Before 1850 relatively few Americans had direct contact with an industrial *society,* but after that date rapid industrialization altered the social structure, and the process left few untouched. Depending upon circumstance, these social changes meant more or less opportunity for workers, but nearly all felt greater dependence and profoundly different patterns of work discipline. In addition, urbanization and immigration changed the structure and composition of the working class and affected its style of life. In ways that have not yet been adequately explored, class and status relationships took on new

---

[1] J. L. Talmon, "The Age of Revolution," *Encounter,* XXI (Sept. 1963), 14. See also Richard Hofstadter, *The Paranoid Style in American Politics and Other Essays* (New York, 1965), ix–x. Urging the study of popular ideology in order to understand more fully political thought and behavior, Hofstadter writes: "The political contest itself is deeply affected by the way in which it is perceived." "This does not mean," he hastens to warn, "that the material interests of politics can be psychologized away or reduced to episodes in intellectual history." A similar admonition is essential in studying labor thought.

FROM Herbert G. Gutman, "Protestantism and the American Labor Movement: The Christian Spirit in the Gilded Age," *American Historical Review,* Vol. LXXII (October 1966), pp. 74–101. Reprinted by permission. Mr. Gutman, professor at the University of Rochester and associate editor of *Labor History,* [was] at the Center for Advanced Study in the Behavioral Sciences for the year 1966–1967. He read a different version of this paper at the Organization of American Historians' joint session with the American Catholic Historical Association and the Labor Historians Group in Kansas City, Missouri, in April 1965.

meaning, too.[2] And a new ideology that sanctioned industrial laissez faire emerged because, as Ralph Gabriel has perceptively written, "the mores of a simpler agricultural and commercial era did not fit the conditions of an age characterized by the swift accumulation of industrial power."[3] The era found much "truth" in the frequent judgments of the Chicago *Times* that "the inexorable law of God" meant that "the man who lays up not for the morrow perishes on the morrow," that "political economy" was "in reality the autocrat of the age" and occupied "the position once held by the Caesars and the Popes," and that cheapened production counted for so much that men did not inquire "when looking at a piece of lace whether the woman who wove it is a saint or a courtesan."[4]

Legal and political theory, academic economics, amoral "social science," and institutional Protestantism emphasized that in industrial America interference with the entrepreneur's freedom violated "divine" or "scientific" laws, and historians have given much attention to the many ways Gilded Age social thought bolstered the virtues of "Acquisitive Man."[5] Two seemingly contradictory ideas especially sanctioned industrial laissez faire. Related to the decline of traditional religious sanctions and the growing importance of secular institutions and values, the first insisted that no connection existed between economic behavior and moral conduct. Gilded Age business practices, Edward C. Kirkland has argued, cannot be understood without realizing that for most entrepreneurs "economic activity stood apart from the sphere of moral and personal considerations."[6] Much contemporary evidence supports this view.[7] The second concept, identified with traditional Calvinist doctrine, re-

---

[2] Evidence on differing contemporary estimates of the status of industrialists and workers in large cities and small industrial towns is found in H. G. Gutman, "The Worker's Search for Power: Labor in the Guilded Age," in *The Gilded Age: A Reappraisal,* ed. H. Wayne Morgan (New York, 1963), 38–68.

[3] Ralph Gabriel, *The Course of American Democratic Thought* (New York, 1956), 154.

[4] Chicago *Times,* Aug. 24, 1874, Aug. 26, 1876.

[5] An able summary of the defense of laissez faire in the Gilded Age is found in Sidney Fine, *Laissez Faire and the General-Welfare State: A Study of Conflict in American Thought, 1865–1901* (Ann Arbor, Mich., 1956), 3–166. On the process of legitimizing newly achieved power, see Max Weber, *Essays in Sociology,* tr. and ed. H. W. Gerth and C. W. Mills (New York, 1946), 271.

[6] Edward C. Kirkland, "Divide and Rule," *Mississippi Valley Historical Review,* XLIII (June 1956), 3–17.

[7] Economist Arthur Perry explicitly said that "the grounds of economy and morals are independent and incommensurable," while the president of the American Exchange Bank found the "laws" of economics separate from but "as sacred and obligatory as . . . those of the Decalogue." Chicago, Burlington, and Quincy Railroad President C. E. Perkins advised an associate: "If I were able, I would found a school of political economy in order to harden men's hearts." Another time Perkins explained: "The question of political economy is not, What is noble? What is good? What is generous? What are the teachings of the Gospel?—But what, if anything, is it expedient to do about [the] production, distribution and consumption of property or wealth?" Like

inforced the business ethic by equating poverty and failure with sin.[8] Evidence gathered primarily from national denominational weekly and monthly periodicals, together with a Gilded Age premillennial evangelism (typified by the popular Dwight Moody) that insisted that "until Christ returned none of the basic problems of the world could be solved," convinces its historians that the Protestant denominations and their leaders mostly "lost their sense of estrangement from society" and "began . . . to bless and defend it in a jargon strangely compounded out of the language of traditional Christian theology, common-sense philosophy, and *laissez-faire* economics." [9] Henry May, Aaron Abell, and Charles Hopkins have shown that a small but quite influential group of Protestant clergymen and lay thinkers broke free from institutional Protestantism's social conservatism and traveled a difficult route in pioneering the social gospel,[10] but in the main Gilded Age Protestantism is viewed as a conformist, "culture-bound" Christianity that warmly embraced the rising industrialist, drained the aspiring rich of conscience, and confused or pacified the poor. The writings of an articulate minority suggest to historians that the wealthy busied themselves memorizing Herbert Spencer's aphorisms and purchasing expensive church pews, that the middle classes chased

---

many other men of new wealth and power, this railroad leader worried about those who denounced "the economic law of Adam Smith . . . as too cruel and heartless for a Christian People." (Quoted in Fine, *Laissez Faire,* 54, 56, 103; Kirkland, "Divide and Rule"; and Thomas Cochran, *Railroad Leaders, 1845–1890: The Business Mind in Action* [Cambridge, Mass., 1953], 436–37.)

[8] This view is identified most frequently with Henry Ward Beecher and Russell Conwell. "The general truth will stand," Beecher argued, "that no man in this land suffers from poverty unless it be more than his fault—unless it be his *sin.*" (Quoted in Henry F. May, *Protestant Churches and Industrial America* [New York, 1949], 69.) Conwell made the same point another way: "The number of poor to be sympathized with is very small. . . . To sympathize with a man whom God has punished for his sins, thus to help him when God will still continue a just punishment, is to do wrong, no doubt about it." (Quoted in Marquis Childs and Douglas Cater, *Ethics in a Business Society* [New York, 1954], 137.) A variant of this theme urged passivity upon complaining workers as when the Methodist *Christian Advocate* lectured readers: "John the Baptist set a good example . . . when he advised the Roman soldiers, 'Be content with your wages'. . . ." (Quoted in William G. McLoughlin, Jr., *Modern Revivalism: Charles Grandison Finney to Billy Graham* [New York, 1959], 267–68.)

[9] Sidney E. Mead, "American Protestantism Since the Civil War," *Journal of Religion,* XXXVI (Jan. 1956), 1–15. See also Winthrop Hudson, *American Protestantism* (Chicago, 1961), 136–40. Hudson also relates these developments to the new theology, "the doctrine of Incarnation, interpreted as divine immanence, which sanctified the 'natural' man and invested the culture itself with intrinsic redemptive tendencies." The new theology therefore surrendered "any independent basis of judgment." Excellent analysis of the post-Civil War evangelism typified by Dwight Moody is found in McLoughlin, *Modern Revivalism,* 166–281, and Bernard A. Weisberger, *They Gathered at the River: The Story of the Great Revivalists and Their Impact upon Religion in America* (Boston, 1958), 160–219.

[10] May, *Protestant Churches, passim,* but esp. 91–111, 163–203; A. I. Abell, *The Urban Impact on American Protestantism, 1865–1900* (Cambridge, Mass., 1943), *passim;* and C. H. Hopkins, *The Rise of the Social Gospel in American Protestantism, 1865–1915* (New Haven, Conn., 1940), *passim.*

wealth and cheered Horatio Alger, and that the wage earners, busy laboring, found little time to ponder existential questions and felt separated from institutional Protestantism. Workers wandered from the fold, and the churches lost touch with the laboring classes.

Accurate in describing certain themes characteristic of Gilded Age social and religious thought, this view nevertheless tells little about the relationship between Protestantism and the working class because the many functions of religion, particularly its effects on the lower classes, cannot be learned by analyzing what leading clergymen said and what social philosophy religious journals professed. Unless one first studies the varieties of working class community life, the social and economic structure that gave them shape, their voluntary associations (including churches, benevolent and fraternal societies, and trade-unions), their connections to the larger community, and their particular and shared values, one is likely to be confused about the relationship between the worker, institutional religion, and religious beliefs and sentiments.[11] It is suggested, for example, that a close tie between laissez faire and Gilded Age Protestantism developed partly because the post–Civil War "burst of technological and industrial expansion . . . created unbridled cheerfulness, confidence, and complacency among the American people" and because "the observational order coincided in a high degree with the conceptual order and . . . such coincidence defines social stability." [12] Such was probably the case for successful entrepreneurs and many lesser folk who benefited from rapid industrialization and the era's massive material gains, but the same cannot be inferred for those whose traditional skills became obsolete, who felt economic dependence for the first time, who knew recurrent seasonal and cyclical unemployment, and who suffered severe family and social disorganization in moving from farm and town to city and in adapting to industrial and urban priorities and work discipline patterns different from traditional norms. Day-to-day experiences for many such persons ("the observational order") did not entirely coincide with the religious and secular ideas and values ("the conceptual order") they carried with them from the immediate past. Some withdrew from the tensions stirred by such conflict, and others changed their beliefs. Many found in Gilded Age Protestantism reason to cheer material progress or comfort in premillennial evangelism. But some, especially trade-unionists and labor reformers and radicals, discovered that preindustrial ideology heightened rather than obliterated the moral dilemmas of a new social order and that the Protestantism of an earlier America offered a religious sanction for *their* discontent with industrial laissez faire and

---

[11] See the penetrating and original study of the role of voluntary associations and community institutions among Irish immigrant workers and their children in Newburyport, Massachusetts, between 1850 and 1880 in Stephan Thernstrom, *Poverty and Progress: Social Mobility in a Nineteenth Century City* (Cambridge, Mass., 1964), 166–91.

[12] Hudson, *American Protestantism;* Mead, "American Protestantism."

"Acquisitive Man." A preindustrial social order had nurtured particular religious beliefs that did not disappear with the coming of industrialism and did not easily or quickly conform to the Protestantism of a Henry Ward Beecher or a Dwight Moody and the secular optimism of an Andrew Carnegie or a Horatio Alger. The material conditions of life changed radically for these workers after 1850, but not the world of their mind and spirit. They saw the nation transformed, but were not themselves abruptly alienated from the past. Older traditions and modes of thought (religious and secular in origin) did not succumb easily to the imperatives of a disorganized industrial society, but, depending upon particular circumstances, often clung tenaciously and even deepened tensions generally characteristic of an early industrializing society.

The recent perspective emphasized by British historians of early industrial England helps clarify the particular relationship between Protestantism and Gilded Age labor reform. "In order to understand how people respond to industrial change," Asa Briggs has written, "it is necessary to examine fully what kind of people they were at the beginning of the process, to take account of continuities and traditions as well as new ways of thinking and feeling." [13] Edward P. Thompson has gathered and organized a mass of data in *The Making of the English Working Class* to argue persuasively that the English working class was not "the spontaneous generation of the factory-system" and that the early social history of industrial England was more than "an external force—the 'industrial revolution'—working upon some nondescript undifferentiated raw material of humanity." [14] Applied to the United States, this general point is quite simple although its particular American characteristics demand a level of conceptualization and a method of research not yet typical of "labor history." Protestantism in its many and even contradictory forms but particularly the Christian perfectionism of pre-Civil War evangelical and reform movements lingered on among many discontented *post-bellum* workers.[15] It was no different in the United States than in Great Britain where

---

[13] Asa Briggs, review of Edward P. Thompson, *The Making of the English Working Class, Labor History*, VI (Winter 1965), 84.

[14] Edward P. Thompson, *The Making of the English Working Class* (London, 1963), 194 *et passim*.

[15] See esp. Timothy L. Smith, *Revivalism and Social Reform in Mid-Nineteenth Century America* (New York, 1957), *passim*. Smith does not carry his important findings on the relationship between pre-Civil War evangelism, Christian perfectionism, and social reform beyond the Civil War. Clifton E. Olmstead argued that perfectionism "increased steadily in American evangelical Protestantism throughout and beyond the Civil War." It "flourished primarily in urban areas," Olmstead maintained, "where the social problems and the individual frustrations presented a peculiar challenge to those who believed that Christianity could 'work' to the betterment of mankind." (C. E. Olmstead, *History of Religion in the United States* [Englewood Cliffs, N.J., 1960], 352.) But Olmstead offered no concrete evidence to support this valuable insight. Although he makes little of the strain of labor Protestantism emphasized in these pages, W. G. McLoughlin offers a suggestive framework for understanding the effects of pietistic perfectionism on American social movements in his essay "Pietism and the American Character," *American Quarterly*, XVII (Summer 1965), 163–86.

labor and religious historians have documented the close relationship between Protestant Nonconformity, especially Methodism, and labor reform.[16] None of this should surprise students of social movements. "The bulk of industrial workers in all countries," Eric Hobsbawm notes, "began . . . as first-generation immigrants from preindustrial society . . . and like all first-generation immigrants, they looked backwards as much as forwards." The new industrial world "had no pattern of life suited to the new age," and so men and women often "drew on the only spiritual resources at their disposal, preindustrial custom and religion." [17]

An additional point stressed in Thompson's recent work offers insight into the Gilded Age labor reformer. "Behind every form of popular direct action," Thompson notes, "some legitimising notion of right is to be found." [18] Thus Boston labor leader and editor Frank K. Foster insisted in 1888: "The dry names and dates furnish but a small part of the history of the labor movement. To understand its real meaning one must comprehend the spirit animating it." [19] Leaders and followers of social movements that challenge an established order or question the direction of a rapidly changing society (such as the United States after the Civil War) are usually "animated" by a "spirit" that sanctions and legitimizes the particular alternative they espouse. It is not enough for them merely to criticize and to offer alternatives. This is the case whether they advocate trade-unions in a society hostile to collective activity or urge even more thorough and fundamental social reorganization. They must *feel* that what they propose is justified by values that transcend the particular social order they criticize. For this reason, they often crudely reinterpret the historical past. They either project "new" values or, as is more frequently the case, reinterpret vague and broadly shared national values to sanction their behavior. Then, they can argue that their critique of the dominant order and its ideology is "consistent with very basic values." [20] Such was the case with the generation of trade-unionists, labor reformers, and labor radicals who felt the transition from a preindustrial to an industrial society and who bore the social, economic, and psychological brunt of the American industrializing process after 1860.

Two broadly shared preindustrial national traditions especially offered the discontented nineteenth-century American worker a transcendent and sanctioning "notion of right." The first—the republican political tradition—is be-

---

[16] Thompson, *Making of the English Working Class*, 350–400; Eric Hobsbawm, *Labouring Men: Studies in the History of Labour* (London, 1964), 23–33; Robert F. Wearmouth, *Methodism and the Working-Class Movements of England, 1800–1850* (London, 1937), *passim*.

[17] E. J. Hobsbawm, *Social Bandits and Primitive Rebels: Studies in Archaic Forms of Social Movement in the 19th and 20th Centuries* (Glencoe, Ill., 1959), 108, 130.

[18] Thompson, *Making of the English Working Class*, 68.

[19] *Labor Leader* (Boston), Sept. 15, 1888.

[20] Alvin and Helen Gouldner, *Modern Sociology* (New York, 1963), 634–36.

yond the scope of these pages. The second was traditional American Protestantism. Frank Foster could explain in 1887: "John on Patmos, Jack Cade at the head of the populace, . . . Kropotkin indicting Russian imperialism, the rising wrath of American Democracy—these are all of kinship." Commenting on the American labor movement, Foster went on:

> The "cross of the new crusade" is the cross of an old crusade, old as the passions of the human heart. An idea may take different forms of expression and its ethical purport may be the same, and in whatever direction men may strive for this ambiguous thing we call social reform, if they mean anything at all, they but echo—be they Jew or Gentile, Greek or Christian, Deist or Atheist, Knight of Labor or Socialist—that carol of welcome which was sung to greet the coming of the Carpenter's Son in the centuries long gone by, "peace on earth, good will to men."

"Looking afar off, over the broad ocean of time and space," the Boston editor concluded, "we have faith, like St. Simon at death's door, [we] may exclaim, 'The furture is ours.' " [21] Similarly, the *Union Pacific Employees Magazine* comforted fearful trade-unionists by reminding them that after the Crucifixion "the rabble rejoiced." "Time," this journal insisted in explaining the difficulties encountered by trade-union advocates, "corrects errors. . . . The minority continue to urge their views until they become the majority or the fallacy of them be proven. Advance is made only thus. Time must be had to prepare the way for every step." [22] In another connection, the American Railway Union's *Railway Times* called "sublime idiocy . . . the idea that workingmen of the present, or of any other century, were the first to call attention to the rapacity of the rich." Instead, "The arraignment of the rich by God Himself and His Son, the Redeemer, set the pace for all coming generations of men who would be free from the crushing domination of wealth." Labor's complaints had "the unequivocal indorsement of the Holy Writ." [23] Here, then, was a religious faith that justified labor organization and agitation, encouraged workers to challenge industrial power, and compelled criticism of "natural" economic laws, the crude optimism of social Darwinism, and even the conformist Christianity of most respectable clergymen.

Protestantism affected the American working class in many ways, and a brief article cannot encompass its varied manifestations. But it is possible to indicate some of them.

A subordinate but distinct theme drew from pessimistic premillennialism

---

[21] *Labor Leader,* Aug. 27, 1888.

[22] *Union Pacific Employees Magazine,* n.d., reprinted in the *Journal of the Knights of Labor* (Philadelphia), July 16, 1891. The Crucifixion was but one example this journal cited. It also pointed to the mobbing of William Lloyd Garrison, the hanging of John Brown, and the jailing of Voltaire.

[23] *Railway Times* (Chicago), June 15, 1896.

the apocalyptic tradition that prophesied doom and imminent catastrophe before "redemption." In a period of rapid, unpredictable social and economic change, change itself meant decay and destruction to some. For them, the Christian prophetic tradition did not buoy up the spirit and command reform, but stimulated withdrawal. A Massachusetts ship joiner predicted destructive world-wide war as a result of "the sin of the people, 'covetousness.' " [24] A regular *Coast Seaman's Journal* columnist more than once made the same point.[25] Readers of the Denver *Labor Enquirer* learned from several sermons by Mrs. P. C. Munger of "The World's Final Crisis." She urged violence to speed the end of an evil social order and praised dynamite as a "blessing" from God:

> Socially, the ruling world is a dead leper. In the name of God and man bury it deep in the earth it has corrupted. . . . Dynamite in its line is the last scientific fruit of the Holy Ghost. . . . It is in every way worthy of the giver—God. . . . I thank, I praise, I bless God for dynamite. It is the blast of Gabriel's trumpet. . . . It does the deeds of God. . . . Its fruits are peace, love, joy, goodness, gentleness, meekness, and truth displayed in decent life and government. Is not this boon of heaven worth a blow; worth a blast on the trumpet of doom? . . . Dynamite is a weapon to win; a weapon to conquer, a weapon to kill. It is your only one. God Himself allows you no other; use it or tamely submit and sign your death warrant.[26]

Such violent and apparent psychotic anguish, however, was not typical of even the most extreme premillenarian visionaries. More characteristic was the complaint of an Indiana coal miner's wife who believed that "according to history" a "visitation" took place every two thousand years and quietly complained, "I have heard my mother talk about her girlhood days and how good and religious people were." The world had changed for the worse. "It is no wonder," she feared, "that God sends His voice in thunder through the air as wicked as this world stands to-day. . . . We are living in a land where shadows are continually falling in our pathway." [27] The extraordinary psychological strains of early industrialism thus found expression in the rejection of the secular order and the acceptance of a Protestantism of doom, despair, and destruction.[28]

More widespread than these premillennial prophecies was a postmillennial Christian justification of trade-unionism and even more radical social reform. Conservative trade-unionists and radical anarchists and socialists (except for the zealous followers of Daniel De Leon) often appealed to Christianity for

---

[24] *Labor Standard* (Boston), Feb. 22, 1879.

[25] *Coast Seaman's Journal* (San Francisco), Nov. 28, 1888, Jan. 30, 1889.

[26] *Labor Enquirer* (Denver), Apr.–May 1883.

[27] *United Mine Workers' Journal* (Columbus, Ohio), Mar. 8, 1900.

[28] Hobsbawm, *Labouring Men*, 376.

its sanction. A pre-Civil War utopian and afterward a Knight of Labor and builder of cooperatives, John Orvis claimed "the labor question" was "here in the Providence of Almighty God" and meant "the deliverance, exaltation, and ennobling of labor and the laboring classes to the first rank." [29] Conservative craft unionist and president of the Amalgamated Association of Iron, Steel, and Tin Workers, John Jarrett told a gathering of clergymen that "the climax of the mission of the Savior, beyond a question, . . . is that He came here so that the gospel would be preached to the poor." [30] After being sentenced to death in the aftermath of the Haymarket affair, German immigrant anarchist August Spies linked his beliefs to Thomas Münzer. "He," Spies said of Münzer, "interpreted the Gospel, saying that it did not merely promise blessings in heaven, but that it also commanded equality and brotherhood among men on earth." Spies insisted that "the spirit of the Reformation was the 'eternal spirit of the chainless mind,' and nothing could stay its progress." [31] This sentiment —radical criticism and labor discontent sanctioned by an appeal to Christian tradition—did not diminish by the end of the nineteenth century and remained as common in the 1890's as in the 1860's. No apparent connection existed between a particular brand of labor reform and Christianity; all shared in it.

Prophetic Protestantism offered labor leaders and their followers a transhistoric framework to challenge the new industrialism and a common set of moral imperatives to measure their rage against and to order their dissatisfactions. The intensity of religious commitment varied among individuals: it depended upon particular life experiences, and its sources drew from the many strands that made up the web of Protestant tradition. But the influence of the Christian perfectionism and postmillennialism identified with Charles G. Finney and other pre-Civil War and preindustrial evangelical revivalists seems predominant.[32] Even this tradition, which emphasized God's redemptive love and benevolence and insisted that "progress, in all its forms, was divinely directed toward the perfection of the world," took many forms.[33] A

---

[29] *American Workman* (Boston), June–July 1869.

[30] *Labor: Its Rights and Wrongs* (Washington, D.C., 1886), 252–61.

[31] *The Accused, the Accusers. The Famous Speeches of the Eight Chicago Anarchists in Court . . . On October 7th, 8th and 9th, 1886* (Chicago, 1886), 5–6.

[32] McLoughlin, *Modern Revivalism,* 65–165; Smith, *Revivalism, passim;* Olmstead, *History of Religion,* 347–62. See also the subtle but significant distinctions between the prophetic and the apocalyptic impulses stressed by Martin Buber in his essay "Prophecy, Apocalyptic, and Historical Hour" (1954), reprinted in *id., Pointing the Way: Collected Essays* (New York, 1957), 192–207. Although authoritative conclusions cannot yet be drawn, it appears that the prophetic rather than the apocalyptic tradition characterized the dominant religious sentiment of dissident Gilded Age workers.

[33] McLoughlin, *Modern Revivalism,* 167. There is little direct reference to Finney in post-Civil War labor thought. An exception is found in the *Iron Molder's Journal* (Cincinnati), Oct. 1876, which reported the following story about Finney: "He was passing an iron foundry when the works were in full blast and heard a workman swearing terribly. 'Young man,' said the revivalist, addressing the swearer, 'how hot do you suppose hell is?' The workman recognized the questioner, and placed his arms

few examples suffice. In the 1860's, William Sylvis, that decade's most prominent trade-unionist, pitted the God of Christian perfectionism against Malthusian doctrine and asked: "Is it not reasonable, is it not Christian, to suppose that the all-wise Being who placed us here, and whose attributes are benevolence and love, could find other means of controlling population than by war, famine, pestilence, and crime in all its forms?" [34] More than thirty years later, George E. Ward hailed the coming of the American Railway Union by arguing that "God is infinite and eternal justice" so that "he who strives to promote and establish justice upon earth is a co-worker with God." It followed that union men were "the rapidly-evolving God-men—the *genus homo* vivified by the eternal truths and energizing principles of the gospel of Christ." [35] Another perfectionist strain, more "emotional," told of man's "sin," but was nevertheless distinctly postmillennial. Celebrating Thanksgiving, a midwestern worker assured the Chicago Knights of Labor:

> God has given the earth to the children of men; that a few have stolen it all and disinherited the masses, is no fault of God's, but the wickedness of man. . . . We could not know the wickedness of man, could we not see the goodness of God. . . . It is perfectly safe to pray for His kingdom to come, and in that prayer you anathematize the present system as bitterly as words could do it. . . .[36]

"Pumpkin Smasher," a Newcomb, Tennessee, coal miner, typified extreme labor evangelism:

> Labor has made this country into a bed of roses so that a few may lie therein, and bask in the beautiful God-given sunshine, while the laborer or the creator of all this splendor is roaming in rags all tattered and torn. . . . Cheer up, my brothers, the longest night comes to an end. It may end by an honest use of the ballot box, but as that can never be until the great and glorious millennium with all its attendant beauties sets in, brothers we need not look for deliverance through the medium of the ballot box. But it will come just the same. It may come like it did to the Israelitish serfs from down yonder in Egypt, or it may come like it did in France in those long days of rebellion. Or, my brothers, it may come as it did to the colored slaves of the South by sword and fire. Let us be ready to eat the Paschal lamb at any moment the trumpet sounds.[37]

---

akimbo, and looking him squarely in the face, said, 'Well, Mr. Finney, I suppose it's so hot there that if somebody brought you a spoonful of melted iron, you'd swear 't was ice cream.' Mr. Finney had nothing more to say."

[34] James Sylvis, *Life, Speeches, Labors and Essays of William H. Sylvis* (Philadelphia, 1872), 152–65.

[35] *Railway Times,* Jan. 15, 1894.

[36] *Knights of Labor* (Chicago), Nov. 20, 1886.

[37] *United Mine Workers' Journal,* Mar. 29, 1894.

Even the more "conservative" *American Federationist* found room for labor evangelism. A contributor to the American Federation of Labor's official journal asked for nothing less than "A living Christ moving, living, breathing and dominant in the hearts of a people, not a dead Christianity, dreaming of a dead Christ, but live Christians as live Christs, scattering the table of the money changers in the temples, . . . going down in the poverty-stricken alleys of the robbed industrial slaves, and raising up its victims." This Christianity he called *"the real article!"* [38]

Not surprisingly, the labor evangels found the most essential characteristics of the rapidly developing new industrial social order un-Christian and violative of God's will. As early as the 1860's "Uncle Sam" told readers of *Fincher's Trades Review* that "the present system of labor . . . is a system begotten by the *evil one, hell-born*" and that it "warred against the heaven-born creation, the system instituted by *God* for the good of man." [39] And the Boston *Daily Evening Voice* justified a living wage and condemned the maldistribution of wealth by appealing to God: "It is because He has made of one blood all men—because all are brethren—that the differences instituted by men—the chief of which is the money difference—are so morally disastrous as they are. . . . The elevation of a false god dethrones the real one." [40]

Self-protection and trade-unionism especially enjoyed the blessings of God. A Louisville cigar maker argued: "The toilers are coming out of darkness into light and . . . have dared to organize, to come in closer touch with our Lord's will and the teachings of Jesus Christ." He prophesied: "The time is not far distant when the wage earners shall stand on the rock of independence and sing, 'Nearer, My God, to Thee.' We need not fire and sword, but [to] organize, unionize. . . ." [41] During the bitter bituminous coal strike of 1897 the *United Mine Workers' Journal* editorialized: "Blessed are the union men. They are the salt of the earth which keeps uncontaminated the pure principles of brotherhood in the breast of their fellow toilers, and which, if allowed to die, would make us doubt the fatherhood of God." [42] Biblical "history" served well J. A. Crawford, Illinois district president of the United Mine Workers, as he preached the divinity of unions:

The first labor organization mentioned in history, either profane or divine, was the one founded just outside of the historic Garden of Eden, by God Himself; the charter members being Adam and Eve. . . . Noah's campaign

---

[38] Louis Nash, "Is This A Christian Civilization?" *American Federationist,* I (Jan. 1895), 252.

[39] *Fincher's Trades Review* (Philadelphia), Feb. 2, 1864.

[40] Boston *Daily Evening Voice,* Sept. 2, 1865.

[41] *Cigar-Makers' Official Journal,* XIX (Jan. 1894), 3.

[42] *United Mine Workers' Journal,* Sept. 30, 1897.

among the Antediluvians favorably reminds us of the organizing campaigns of the United Mine Workers. . . . The third attempt at organizing labor was made by the authority of Jehovah, instituted and carried to a successful termination by "The Walking Delegates," Moses and Aaron, for the purpose of redeeming Israel from Egyptian task-masters. . . . The next labor movement of importance recorded in sacred history begins with the beginning of the ministry of the "Nazarene," opposed to all forms of oppression of the poor and antagonistic to the operation of "Wall street" in the house of His Father, the sanctuary of worship. . . . Choose you this day whom you shall serve. If plutocracy be God, serve it; if God be God, serve Him.[43]

A *Railway Times* writer summed it up by insisting that "so-called 'labor agitators,' who are such, *not* for the love of money, but for the love of humanity, are true followers of Christ and are striving to establish upon earth the kingdom of God, for which disciples are taught to pray." [44] Labor organizers had only to push ahead. "Brother Knights," a fellow unionist advised, "allow me to say that Moses, while fleeing from bondage and endeavoring to deliver his people from the hands of the Egyptian destroyer, received the imperative command from God, to 'go forward.' The same injunction still comes to us, 'go forward.' " [45]

The historic and divine person of Jesus Christ loomed large in the rhetoric and imagery of labor leaders. He served as a model to emulate, a symbol to inspire. An Illinois coal miner later elected to the state assembly admiringly described trade-unionist Richard Trevellick: "While not a preacher of Jesus and Him crucified, yet he was one of His most exemplary followers. . . . My wife thought Dick Trevellick the second Jesus Christ." [46] Much was made of the argument that "the Saviour Himself" had associated "with common fishermen and carpenters." [47] A West Coast seaman reminded his brothers that "Peter and James and John, . . . three sailors, were the chosen of our Saviour." [48] *Railway Times* called Jesus "an agitator such as the world has never seen before nor since, . . . despised and finally murdered to appease

---

[43] *Ibid.*, June 15, 1893.

[44] *Railway Times*, Jan. 15, 1894.

[45] *Journal of United Labor* (Philadelphia), Sept. 1882.

[46] O. T. Hicks, *Life of Richard Trevellick* (Joliet, Ill., 1898), 198–200.

[47] *Craftsman* (Washington, D.C.), May 30, 1885.

[48] *Coast Seaman's Journal*, Feb. 25, 1891. See also the editorials in the *National Labor Tribune* (Pittsburgh), Feb. 3, Mar. 7, 1877, in which trade-union organizers and labor reformers are called the "Apostles of Labor" and urged to go among the workers and talk with them as did the early Christians. The Apostles, the *Tribune* reminded readers, "were teachers who traveled without pay, and for no other reason than to spread the new gospel." "Looking back," it noted, "we may wonder how a few simple-minded men, without education, with nothing but plain, simple honesty, could make such mighty changes."

the wrath of the ruling class of His time." [49] William Mahon, the international president of the motorman's union, lectured the Businessman's Bible Class of the Detroit First Congregational Church that Christ was "crucified for disturbing the national order of things . . . [by] the conservative goody good people, whose plans Jesus spoilt." The businessmen learned that the speaker belonged to "the organizations . . . fighting for the very principles laid down by Jesus Christ." [50] The *Coast Seaman's Journal* explained Christ's death:

> Christ taught that all men had souls and were therefore equal in the finality of things. For that He was put to death. But it was not for preaching the doctrine of a common equality before God that the Saviour suffered. The Powers have never objected to changing the conditions and relations of the future: it is the conditions and relations of today they object to altering. Christ was crucified because the doctrine of common equality hereafter, which He preached, led inevitably to the doctrine of common equality now. This is the essence of Christ's teaching. [51]

Christ in an industrializing America would suffer as a labor leader or even a "tramp" suffered. "Had Christ lived in Connecticut, he would have been imprisoned for asking for a cup of water," believed the Washington *Craftsman*. [52]

If Gilded Age businessmen make sense only when it is realized that for them "economic activity stood apart from moral considerations," the opposite is true for most Gilded Age labor leaders. Protestantism helped many of them restore what Oscar Handlin calls "the sense of human solidarity infused with

---

[49] *Railway Times,* Feb. 1, 1897.

[50] *The Motorman and Conductor,* V (Jan. 1899), 1–3. See also *Labor Standard* (New York), Jan. 6, 1877. The socialist *Standard* condemned the New York *Herald* for praising Christ's life among the poor and for finding in it "a theory of the conduct of life and of society." The *Standard* believed that "if any man were to follow Christ's example by going amongst the brokers and doing as he did, he would soon find himself an inmate of a Lunatic asylum or a Jail." "Who in these days," asked the *Standard,* "does unto others as he wishes to be done by?"

[51] *Coast Seaman's Journal,* Feb. 22, 1897.

[52] *Craftsman,* Dec. 19, 1885; see also W. J. M., "Christmas Greeting," *Coast Seaman's Journal,* Dec. 21, 1887. The identification of Christ with "tramps" occurred earlier, too, especially during the antitramp hysteria of the middle and late 1870's. Defending "tramps," the *Weekly Worker* reminded readers: "About the only consolation left the truly unfortunate tramp is the thought that Christ was a tramping vagabond. . . ." (*Weekly Worker* [Syracuse, N.Y.], Aug. 15, 1875.) The *National Labor Tribune* and other labor journals echoed this point in the 1870's. "Christianity," the *Tribune* insisted, "was ushered into existence by tramps. . . . Great movements come from the bottom layer of society, who [sic] possess the truest instincts and noblest instincts. Our tramps are but the beginning of a worn-out system." (*National Labor Tribune,* Dec. 23, 1876.)

religious values." [53] Prominent Gilded Age trade-unionists, labor reformers, and even radicals—with the notable exception of Samuel Gompers and De Leon—shared a common faith in a just God, effused perfectionist doctrine, and warned of divine retribution against continuing injustice.[54] They often condemned the insensitivity of institutional Protestantism to the suffering brought about by rapid industrialization, but their speeches and writings also made frequent allusion to essential religious "truths" that gave meaning to their lives and that sanctioned organized opposition to the new industrialism.[55] Trade-unionists and reformers from Catholic backgrounds such as Joseph P. McDonnell, who had studied for the priesthood, and Terence V. Powderly frequently quoted the Sermon on the Mount.[56] Important trade-unionists and labor radicals reared as Protestants did the same. Sylvis found no contradiction between his sympathies for the First International and his belief that the worker's "task" was "to found the universal family—to build up the City of God" through trade-unions which Sylvis called an "association of souls" formed by "the sons of God." America's distinctiveness rested for Sylvis on "God's ordained equality of man . . . recognized in the laws and institutions of *our* country." [57] Early trained for the Baptist ministry, Knights of Labor founder Uriah Stephens called excessive hours of work "an artificial and man-made condition, not God's arrangement and order" and insisted the Knights build upon "the immutable basis of the Fatherhood of God and the logical principle of the Brotherhood of Man." Labor organizations had come "as messiahs have ever come, when the world was ready for them." The Knights brought workers together in local assemblies:

> The tabernacle—the dwelling-place of God—is among men. No longer shall men pine for justice, or perish for lack of judgment. "And He will dwell with

[53] Oscar Handlin, *The Americans* (Boston, 1963), 308.

[54] An unusual example of Gompers' making a direct appeal to religion occurred in an April 1891 Pittsburgh speech after the Morewood, Pennsylvania, murder of several East European coke workers. Gompers said: "I say to the capitalists, don't turn your backs on organized labor; don't widen the chasm. . . . Even the Bible lesson of our early childhood will change and we may be compelled to say, 'Whither thou goest I cannot go. . . . Thy people were not my people; thy God is not my God.' " (*United Mine Workers' Journal,* Apr. 23, 1891.) But see more typically Gompers' 1898 attack on "the church and the ministry as the apologists and defenders of the wrong committed against the interests of the people, simply because the perpetrators are possessors of wealth . . . whose real God is the almighty dollar . . ." (quoted in Hopkins, *Rise of the Social Gospel,* 85), and other examples of his critical attitude toward organized religion in Bernard Mandel, *Samuel Gompers: A Biography* (Yellow Springs, Ohio, 1963), 9–12.

[55] A good summary of the criticism by labor reformers and radicals of institutional Protestantism and "clerical *laissez-faire*" is found in May, *Protestant Churches,* 216–23.

[56] See, e.g., Powderly's speeches in the *Journal of United Labor,* July 17, 1890, Dec. 28, 1892, and McDonnell's editorials in the Paterson *Labor Standard,* Dec. 24, 1881, May 15, 1886, and in *Bakers' Journal,* Dec. 1, 1888.

[57] Sylvis, *Life . . . of William H. Sylvis,* 96–117, 443–46.

them, and they shall be His people." "God and Humanity." How inseparably connected! God, the Universal Father; Man, the Universal Brother! [58]

Trevellick found in God reason to ennoble human labor and asked: "Is He less because His mechanical hand formed the mountains? . . . No fellow toilers; He is not less because He worked; neither are you." [59] Eugene V. Debs bristled with Christian indignation at human suffering and cannot be understood outside that framework. From his prison cell after the Pullman debacle, Debs publicly celebrated Labor Day by declaring that it "would stand first in Labor's Millennium, that prophesied era when Christ shall begin in reign on the earth to continue a thousand years." [60] He compared his jailing with Daniel's treatment by the Persians.[61] Released from Woodstock jail, Debs told an admiring Chicago throng in an oration punctuated with religious images and analogies:

> Liberty is not a word of modern coinage. Liberty and slavery are primal words, like good and evil, right and wrong; they are opposites and coexistent. There has been no liberty in the world since the gift, like sunshine and rain, came down from heaven, for the maintenance of which man has not been required to fight. . . . Is it worth[while?] to reiterate that all men are created free and that slavery and bondage are in contravention of the Creator's decree and have their origin in man's depravity?

Courts, like the Supreme Court, had been "antagonizing the decrees of heaven since the day when Lucifer was cast into the bottomless pit." "God Himself had taught His lightning, thunderbolts, winds, waves, and earthquakes to strike," and men, too, would strike, "with bullets or ballots," until they walked "the earth free men." "Angels" had "transplanted" "sympathy," one of the "perennial flowers of the Celestial City" and the mainspring of human compassion for Debs, "in Eden for the happiness of Adam and Eve," and then "the winds had scattered the seed throughout the earth." Without sympathy, Debs concluded, there could be "no humanity, no elevating, refining, ennobling influences." [62]

The most eloquent Gilded Age labor reformer, George E. McNeill, was an abolitionist turned staunch American Federation of Labor trade-unionist and Christian socialist. He was also an essential link between preindustrial American reform and the Gilded Age labor movement. McNeill rarely spoke or

---

[58] Terence V. Powderly, *Thirty Years of Labor* (Columbus, Ohio, 1886), 160–72, 176–77.

[59] *National Labor Tribune,* Mar. 18, 1882.

[60] *Writings and Speeches of Eugene V. Debs,* ed. Arthur M. Schlesinger, Jr. (New York, 1948), 4–6.

[61] *Labor Leader,* Oct. 12, 1895.

[62] *Union* (Indianapolis), Jan. 17, 1896.

wrote without imparting a deep Christian fervor.[63] In 1876 he complained in the socialist *Labor Standard:* "It is the old, old story. . . . Have the Pharaoh's descendants nothing to learn from Pharaoh's fate?" [64] At a meeting eleven years later to condemn the hanging of Albert Parsons, McNeill announced: "I believe in the passive force of non-resistance as 'Him of old'. . . . I come here tonight as a Christian." [65] In 1890 he once again tied labor reform to Christian ethics:

> The Pilgrim leaven still works, true to the fundamental principles of the great Leader of men. . . . The influence of the teachings of the Carpenter's Son still tends to counteract the influence of Mammon. In this movement of the laborers toward equity, we will find a new revelation of the Old Gospel, when the Golden Rule of Christ shall measure the relations of men in all their duties toward their fellows. . . . Though the Mammon-worshippers may cry, "Crucify Him! Crucify Him!", the promise of the prophet and the poet shall be fulfilled . . . by the free acceptance of the Gospel that all men are of one blood. Then the new Pentecost will come, when every man shall have according to his needs.[66]

Three years later, McNeill found "the religious life" of the labor movement nothing less than "a protest against the mammonizing interpretation of religious truth." He wanted "the kingdom of Heaven (of equity and righteousness) to come on earth," but, more importantly, argued that "religious truth," adapted to the realities of industrial society, had meaning for his America. "A new interpretation of the old truth, 'That the chief end of man is to glorify God and to enjoy him forever,' reads that the glorification of God is the reinstatement of man in the likeness of God; that to enjoy God forever all things must be directed toward the securing for all the largest measure of happiness." [67] McNeill never changed. In 1902, sixty-five years old, he reaffirmed his continued faith in the supremacy of "moral power," but nevertheless warned: "Submission is good, but the order of God may light the torch of Revolution." [68]

Evangelical Protestantism that emphasized the possibility of perfect holiness in this world found expression among trade-unionists of less importance than McNeill and other national leaders. Negro activists in the early United

[63] Arthur Mann, *Yankee Reformers in the Urban Age* (Cambridge, Mass., 1954), 178-84, contains perceptive comments on the career and importance of McNeill, but most labor historians have minimized his importance.

[64] *Labor Standard,* Nov.–Dec. 1876.

[65] *Labor Enquirer,* Nov. 27, 1887.

[66] *Labor Leader,* Feb.–Mar. 1890.

[67] George E. McNeill, *The Philosophy of the Labor Movement* (Chicago, 1893), unpaged pamphlet.

[68] *American Federationist,* IX (Sept. 1902), 479–80.

Mine Workers of America (1890–1900) reveal such an influence.[69] A preacher and coal miner, William Riley won election in 1892 as secretary-treasurer of the Tennessee district and importuned fellow Negroes to join the union:

> Continue to battle on for the right, seek wisdom and be wise, act honest men and by so doing both white and colored men will love to respect you, and God Himself will bless you. . . . Yes, my people, wake up and ask yourselves these questions: How long am I to live in ignorance? How long am I to be a pullback to my race? How long am I to be a stumbling block for the cause of labor, justice, and humanity? Say as the prodigal did: I will arise and join the labor unions and rally for its [sic] rights, defend its [sic] cause and be known among my own craftsmen as a man among men.[70]

The tensions between an active, just God and the day-to-day realities of a Negro coal miner's life strained William E. Clark, a Rendville, Ohio, miner. He reported:

> My mind has wandered from world to world. My first wonder was, I wonder if the other worlds were inhabited? Did they have the same kind of law and government that we have? And my next wonder was, was this world of ours the hell we read about in the good book? If it is not, how can a man stand the punishment twice, and then live through eternity? They burn men alive, skin them, lynch them, shoot them, and torture them. . . .[71]

The most important early UMW Negro leader, Richard L. Davis, elected to the National Executive Board in 1896 and 1897, penned many letters that suggested the influence of evangelical imperatives. He found in the union a secular church that promised redemption from an evil social order. He gave to his work the zeal and devotion expected of a dedicated missionary. Miners who threatened to quit the UMW heard from him the words of Paul in the New Testament: "Except those abide in the ship, ye cannot be saved." Preachers designated the "ship as a church," but Davis called the UMW "the ship" and insisted: "I now exhort you that except ye abide in the ship ye cannot be saved." [72] A common religious rhetoric helped Davis ward against factionalism. He denied the charge of fellow Negroes who called the UMW "a white man's organization" and told them: "You yourselves are men and

---

[69] Further details on the role of Negroes in the early United Mine Workers of America are found in Herbert G. Gutman, "The Negro and the United Mine Workers. The Career and Letters of Richard L. Davis and Something of Their Meaning: 1890–1900," in "The Negro and the American Labor Movement," ed. Julius Jacobson (New York, in press).

[70] Riley to the editor, *United Mine Workers' Journal,* Sept. 8, 1892.

[71] Clark to the editor, *ibid.,* Aug. 9, 1894.

[72] Davis to the editor, *ibid.,* Aug. 15, 1895.

. . . have the same interest at stake as your white brother, because . . . I believe in the principle of the fatherhood of God and the brotherhood of all mankind no matter what the color of his [sic] skin may be." Davis' evangelical fervor was not otherworldly. "I know," he addressed these same Negroes, "that in former days you used to sing 'Give me Jesus, give me Jesus, you may have all the world, just give me Jesus.' But the day has now come that we want a little money along with our Jesus, so we want to change that old song and ask for a little of the world as well." [73] Urging compact labor organization, Davis argued that "we are taught by teachings of the Holy Writ that in unity there is strength." [74] The acquittal of a Pennsylvania sheriff involved in the shooting of several Polish anthracite miners in 1898 caused Davis to lament: "It is as we expected. . . . The miner has no rights that the coal barons are bound to respect. Surely, oh Heaven, this condition of things will not last forever." [75]

Just as Christianity motivated so many labor leaders who organized the reaction against the radical transition from preindustrial to industrial America, so, too, did it serve to condemn particular aspects of that new society and its ideology. A few examples illustrate. The *United Mine Workers' Journal* felt that legal convict leasing of coal miners proved "the laws of Tennessee . . . in conflict with Christianity, civilization and government." [76] Exploitative child factory labor caused the Chicago *Knights of Labor* to explode: "When Jesus said, 'Suffer little children to come unto me,' He did not have a shirt or cloak factory, nor a planing mill, that He wanted to put them into at 40 cents per day. He wanted to bless them and show them the light." [77] The San Francisco Manufacturer's and Employer's Association defense of "free contract" led Andrew Furuseth, secretary of the Sailors' Union of the Pacific, to exclaim indignantly: "If the present system be right, then Christianity is a lie; if the present system be right, then Robert Ingersoll is not a censer-boy in the Temple of Mammon, but the prophet of a new dispensation." [78] Critics of Labor Day learned that "Labor Day is one of the signs of the millennium." [79]

Those who saw in Christianity justification for industrial laissez faire especially felt the sting of labor critics. The *Locomotive Firemen's Magazine* declared the "theory" that "God assigns anyone a station in life . . . preposterous, repulsive, and degrading to God and man." [80] Men who argued

---

[73] Davis to the editor, *ibid.,* Apr. 18, 1892.

[74] Davis to the editor, *ibid.,* Feb. 11, 1897.

[75] Davis to the editor, *ibid.,* Mar. 3, 10, 1898.

[76] *Ibid.,* Dec. 8, 1892.

[77] *Knights of Labor,* Sept. 25, 1886.

[78] *Coast Seaman's Journal,* June 29, 1892.

[79] *Railway Times,* June 1, 1895.

[80] *Locomotive Firemen's Magazine,* XI (Apr. 1887), 207–208.

that "labor, like flour or cotton cloth, should always be bought in the cheapest market" did so because "an All-wise God, for some inscrutable purpose, has created them" so that workers could see "to what viciousness the antagonism to labor has arrived" and then "beat back to its native hell the theory that . . . laborers . . . are merchandise to be bought and sold as any other commodity—as cattle, mules, swine. . . ." [81] Clergymen who upheld the competitive system learned: "The church which allows the competitive system of each for himself, without a never-silent protest, is not a living Christian church; for 'each for himself' is a gospel of lies. That never was God's decree." [82] And the argument that poverty enjoyed God's blessings met the retort: "Do you think it is anything short of insulting to God to pretend to believe He makes of ninety-nine paving material for the one to walk into Heaven over?" [83] Paul's directive to Titus to "obey magistrates" was rejected. If followed "by the patriots of '76," explained the *Locomotive Firemen's Magazine*, "a new nation would not have been born." [84]

Christian example and religious exaltation proved especially important in times of severe discontent and defeat and in challenging dominant Gilded Age "myths." Two examples suffice. After the Pullman strike and boycott and Debs's imprisonment, a Portland, Oregon, railroad worker drew inferences and analogies only from sacred history:

Were Moses now living, and the Almighty should send him to a General Manager's office to protest against corporation robberies, he would be forthwith arrested and thrown into jail, and if Moses should appeal to the Supreme Court, the infamous proceedings would be sustained and declared constitutional; and therefore, the way I look at it, the corporation slaves of the United States are in a worse condition than were the slaves of Pharaoh. But in the case of Pharaoh, God put a curse upon him. The corporation Pharaohs are not to have their way always. There may be a Red Sea just ahead—but beyond it is the promised land.

Egypt had only one Pharaoh at a time on the throne. Here we have probably a hundred of the abnormal monsters, all engaged in enslaving working people. . . . The Egyptian Pharaoh did not send Moses to prison. . . . He could have done it. He had absolute power. He was a despot with a big D. . . . Here a labor leader is condemned and thrown into prison by a decree of one small contemptible Pharaoh at the suggestion of a General Manager Pharaoh . . . and there is no appeal except to the Buzzard's Bay Pharaoh [Gro-

[81] *Ibid.*, X (Sept. 1886), 519–20. See also Hermit of the Hills to the editor, *National Labor Tribune*, Jan. 1, 1876, who wrote: "No happiness can come to men or nations —no Kingdom of Heaven can descend upon earth—as long as this false system of antagonism—of working each against the other—continues."

[82] *Journal of United Labor*, Sept. 13, 1888.

[83] *Ibid.*, Sept. 20, 1888.

[84] *Locomotive Firemen's Magazine*, XVIII (Sept. 1894), 877–79.

ver Cleveland's Summer White House was in Buzzard's Bay], which would be like appealing from a pig stealing coyote to a grizzly bear.[85]

The second example concerns Andrew Carnegie and his belief in the "Gospel of Wealth," the notion of "stewardship." At the time of its enunciation, the *Locomotive Firemen's Magazine* scorned the "Gospel of Wealth" as "flapdoodle" and "slush." Of Carnegie, it said: "While asserting that the ' "Gospel of Wealth" but echoes Christ's words,' [he] endeavors to wriggle out of the tight place in which Christ's words place him." It required "patience" to read about "the 'right modes of using immense fortunes' known to be the product of cool, Christless robbery."[86] The Homestead conflict in 1892 caused the same journal to call Carnegie and Henry Clay Frick "brazen pirates [who] prate . . . of the 'spirit of Christ' [and] who plunder labor that they may build churches, endow universities and found libraries."[87] In 1894 the conservative *National Labor Tribune* joined in mocking Carnegie's professions:

> Oh, Almighty Andrew Philanthropist Library Carnegie, who are in America when not in Europe spending the money of your slaves and serfs, thou are a good father to the people of Pittsburgh, Homestead and Beaver Falls. . . . Oh, most adorable Carnegie, we love thee, because thou are the almighty iron and steel king of the world; thou who so much resembles the pharisee. . . . We thank thee and thy combines for the hungry men, women and children of the land. We thank thee and thy combines for the low price of iron and steel and the low price paid in iron and steel works. . . . Oh, master, we thank thee for all the free gifts you have given the public at the expense of your slaves. . . . Oh, master, we need no protection, we need no liberty so long as we are under thy care. So we commend ourselves to thy mercy and forevermore sing thy praise. Amen![88]

Such language could not be misunderstood.

Although the evidence emphasized in these pages indicates the existence

---

[85] *Railway Times,* Aug. 15, 1895.

[86] *Locomotive Firemen's Magazine,* XIV (Feb. 1890), 104–106.

[87] *Ibid.,* XVI (Aug. 1892), reprinted in *Writings and Speeches of Eugene V. Debs,* ed. Schlesinger, 378–82.

[88] *National Labor Tribune,* n.d., reprinted in *Coming Age,* Feb. 10, 1894. Such satiric use of traditional religious forms recurred in these years. See, for example, "A Miner's Prayer . . . ," *United Mine Workers' Journal,* May 16, 1895: "Oh! Almighty and allwise and powerful coal barons who art living in great and glorious palaces, when thou art not in secret meeting working for our interest and welfare, we hail thy blessed name as the great philanthropist of our commercial world to-day. We bow before thee in humble submission. . . . We are Americans of the modern type, not like Jefferson, Hancock and Washington. . . . We are your fools, liars, suckers; spit in our faces and rub it in. We have no business to want an education for our children or ourselves. We ain't got any sense. We don't want any; it don't take any sense to load coal for thee. . . . Did Dred Scott ever serve his master better? . . . Amen."

of a working-class social Christianity and suggests that Protestantism had a particular meaning for discontented Gilded Age labor leaders, social radicals, and even ordinary workers, it is hazardous to infer too much from it alone about the working class. Too little is yet known about nineteenth century American Protestant workers. Evidence on church affilation, for example, is contradictory. While many contemporaries like D. O. Kellogg, general secretary of the Charity Organization of Philadelphia, frequently worried over the "widespread skepticism and alienation from Christianity prevalent among the workingmen" and complained that institutional Protestantism often was "out of the poor man's reach," inadequate but significant statistics for church affiliation among the general population, not just workers, show an increase from 16 per cent in 1850 to 36 per cent in 1900.[89] Until more is known about particular groups of workers and their relations to institutional and noninstitutional religious sentiment and belief, however, it remains impossible to reconcile such seemingly contradictory evidence. Scattered but still inconclusive evidence hints at an apparent close connection between youthful religious conversion and subsequent labor militancy among certain workers.[90] The considerable but as yet largely neglected variations in the experience and outlook of factory workers and skilled craftsmen and of self-educated artisans and casual day laborers as well as the different social environments of small, semirural factory and mining villages, industrial cities, and large urban centers suggest other important analytic problems in explor-

---

[89] D. O. Kellogg, "Some Causes of Pauperism and Their Cure," *Penn Monthly,* XI (Apr. 1878), 275–76, 281–82; Olmstead, *History of Religion,* 447.

[90] Of the British experience, Hobsbawm writes: "The sect and the labour movement were—especially among the cadres and leaders of the movement—connected . . . by the process of conversion: that is to say, by the sudden, emotionally overpowering realizing of sin and the finding of grace. . . . Conversion indicated, reflected, or perhaps stimulated the kind of unselfish activity which labour militancy inevitably implied. . . . Conversion of some kind is, of course, a commonplace in labour movements." (Hobsbawm, *Social Bandits and Primitive Rebels,* 140.) Too little is known about this phenomenon among American trade-unionists and social reformers. But Gabriel perceptively points out that Henry George's beginning awareness of the "social problem" in New York in 1869 came to him as a "conversion after the pattern of evangelical Protestantism." George himself wrote: "Once, in daylight, and in a city street, there came to me a thought, a vision, a call—give it what name you please. But every nerve quivered. And there and then I made a vow." (Gabriel, *Course of American Democratic Thought,* 208–11.) There is also the case of Samuel Fielden, one of the anarchists convicted in the aftermath of the Haymarket bombing. As a Lancashire youth and factory worker, Fielden was converted to Primitive Methodism and became an active lay preacher. Years later, he wrote: "I felt that that religion . . . which I thought was calculated to better the world was something that was worth while for me to use my energies in propagating, and I did it. I could not help it. . . . So intense and earnest was I at that time that I was at one and the same time the Sunday school superintendent of a little Sunday school, a class teacher, a local preacher, and what was called an exhorter. . . ." Fielden came to the United States in 1868. Some years later he came into contact with secular radical ideology. His description of his "conversion" to socialism suggests a close parallel to evangelical conversion and the process Hobsbawm describes. Fielden explains

ing the relationship between Protestantism and the "working class." [91] And there are additional complexities. It is risky to assume too close a relationship between religious sentiment and rhetoric and everyday behavior, and it is equally perilous to view church attendance and affiliation as proof of religious belief or not attending church as presumptive evidence of the opposite. An example of the confusion that might result was the response of an unidentified worker when asked in 1898: "Why are so many intelligent workingmen non-church goers?" "Jesus Christ," he replied, "is with us outside the church, and we shall prevail with God." [92]

Despite these many difficulties, a perspective over more than one or two generations suggests tentative connections between the religious mode of expression of many Gilded Age trade-unionists and labor radicals and the behavior of larger numbers of disaffected Gilded Age Protestant workers. Except for those unions that drew support primarily from workers living in small towns and semirural or other isolated areas, the language of labor leaders and social radicals and the tone of their press after 1900 displayed a marked decline in religious emphasis when compared to the labor speeches, editorials, and letters penned between 1860 and 1900. In part this difference suggests the growing secularization of the national culture, but it also makes possible a particular view of Gilded Age workers, seeing them as a transitional generation that bridged two distinct social structures and was the first to encounter fully the profound strains accompanying the shift to an urban and industrial social order. Not separated emotionally or historically from a different past, they lived through an era of extreme social change and social disorder, but carried with them meaningful and deeply felt traditions and values rooted in the immediate and even more distant past. This process was not unique to the United States, but occurred at different times in other rapidly changing societies and greatly explains the behavior of the "first generation"

---

his growing discontent with industrial America and goes on: "My ideas did not become settled as to what was the remedy, but when they did, I carried the same energy and the same determination to bring about that remedy that I had applied to ideas which I had possessed years before. There is always a period in every individual's life when some sympathetic chord is touched by some other person. There is the open sesame that carries conviction. The ground may have all been prepared. The evidence may have all been accumulated but it has not formed in any shape; in fact, the child has not been born. The new idea has not impressed itself thoroughly when that sympathetic chord is touched, and the person is thoroughly convinced of the idea. It was so in my investigation of political economy. . . . A person said to me Socialism meant equal opportunities—and that was the touch. From that time on I became a Socialist. . . . I knew that I had found the right thing; and I had found the medicine that was calculated to cure the ills of society." (*The Accused, the Accusers*, 36–39.)

[91] Asa Briggs, *The Making of Modern England, 1784–1867* (New York, 1965), 287.

[92] H. Francis Perry, "The Workingman's Alienation from the Church," *American Journal of Sociology*, IV (Mar. 1899), 626.

to have contact with a radically different economic and social structure.[93] Although it is an exaggeration to argue that the violent and often disorganized protest characteristic of so much Gilded Age labor agitation resulted only from the tension between the outlook the worker brought to the Gilded Age and that era's rapidly changing economic and social structure, it is not too much to suggest that the thought and the behavior of Gilded Age workers were peculiar to that generation.

Vital in both pre-Civil War reform movements and evangelical crusades, perfectionist Christianity carried over into the Gilded Age and offered the uprooted but discontented Protestant worker ties with the certainties of his past and reasons for his disaffection with the present by denying for him the premises of Gilded Age America and the not yet "conventional wisdom" of that day. In 1874 the secretary of the Miners' Protective and Progressive Association of Western Pennsylvania, George Archbold, called the trade-union a "God-given right" and warned fellow unionists of employer opposition: "The Philistines are upon you, and the fair Delilah would rob you of your locks and shear you of your power." [94] Twenty-three years later and not in entirely dissimilar language, West Coast labor organizer and sailor Andrew Furuseth celebrated the twelfth anniversary of the Sailors' Union of the Pacific:

> Congress may rob us of our rights as men, and may make us bondsmen. The Judiciary may say "Well done" and uphold them. Yet we have our manhood from nature's God, and being true to our best interests we shall yet as free men turn our faces to the sun. . . . We must organize ourselves and align ourselves with the forces which in our country are making for that brotherhood for which Jesus died. So we must as individuals forget home, self and life if need be, to reconquer our liberty, to preserve the sacredness of our bodies, which by Paul were called "the temples of the living God." [95]

---

[93] Hobsbawm, *Social Bandits and Primitive Rebels*, 1–12, 126–49, but especially 3 when he writes of this generation: "They do not as yet grow with or into modern society: they are broken into it. . . . Their problem is how to adapt themselves to its life and struggles." See also Max Weber's compelling observation that "whenever modern capitalism has begun its work of increasing the productivity of human labor by increasing its intensity, it has encountered the immensely stubborn resistance of . . . pre-capitalistic labor" and the extensive comments on it in Thompson, *Making of the English Working Class*, 356 ff. Perceptive argument for a "generational" analysis by social historians is found in Marc Bloch, *The Historian's Craft* (New York, 1964), 185–87: "Men who are born into the same social environment about the same time necessarily come under analogous influences, particularly in their formative years. Experience proves that, by comparison with either considerably older or considerably younger groups, their behavior reveals certain distinctive characteristics which are ordinarily very clear. This is true even of their bitterest disagreements. To be excited by the same dispute even on opposing sides is still to be alike. This common stamp, deriving from a common age, is what makes a generation."

[94] *National Labor Tribune*, Jan. 31, 1874.

[95] *Coast Seaman's Journal*, Mar. 17, 1897.

Such an emphasis was common to men who disagreed on other matters such as trade-union strategy and the long-range purposes of labor organization and reform. That it is found among "business" unionists, Knights of Labor, and socialist and anarchist radicals and is as prevalent in the 1890's as in the 1860's suggests that it characterized no particular segment of organized labor, but was common to a generation of disaffected workers. Even the German Marxist immigrant Adolph Douai revealed its influence. Although he worried that "enthusiasm without reason engenders fanaticism and thus baffles the noblest purposes," Douai nevertheless pleaded in 1887: "Our age needs religious enthusiasm for the sake of common brotherhood, because infidelity is rampant and hypocrisy prevails in all churches—an infidelity of a peculiar kind, being a disbelief in the destiny of men to be brothers and sisters, in their common quality [sic] and rights." Douai depicted the Gilded Age labor movement as *"the* religion of common brotherhood." [96]

Preindustrial Christian perfectionism offered Gilded Age labor reformers absolute values in a time of rapid social change and allowed the labor reformer or radical to identify with "timeless truths" that legitimized his attack on the absolutes of Gilded Age social thought—the determinism of Spencerian dogma, the sanctity of property rights and freedom of contract, and the rigidity of political laissez faire.[97] "Conditions" had changed, but the "issues" remained as of old, wrote the *Printer's Labor Tribune,* immediate forerunner to the important Pittsburgh *National Labor Tribune,* in arguing that "the war between capital and labor" was being "fought all the time, and [was] . . . identical with civilization itself." Privilege and monopoly were not new. "When Adam commenced business as a farmer, he enjoyed a monopoly, and the same might be said of Noah, but this could not continue," wrote the *Tribune* in 1873. Industrialism merely altered the terms of a his-

---

[96] *Workmen's Advocate* (New Haven, Conn.), May 14, 1887.

[97] Vittorio Lanterari, *The Religion of the Oppressed: A Study of Modern Messianic Cults* (New York, 1965), x. "Although each history has its own theology," Lanterari writes, "the important fact is that the drive which motivates man's practical choices and causes him to struggle and suffer for a better future is common to all and rises out of a faith that is absolute. Thus, even while man is aware of the relativity of human values and goals, nonetheless he behaves 'as if' the goal were a final one (*eschaton*) and 'as if' the values he defends were absolute values." In this connection, an editorial in *Railway Times* (Nov. 1, 1895) is of great interest. The official journal of the American Railway Union worried why, although "truth" is "one of the attributes of deity, . . . the disciples of error, the devotees of lies, professing to be champions of truth, have betrayed it and placed it on a thousand scaffolds, from Calvary to Woodstock." The *Times* explained: "There is an intimate relation between truth and freedom. Christ said, 'Ye shall know the truth, and the truth shall make you free.' It is this declaration that solves the problem. If men are free, they will have found the truth, but they will be free only while they cling to it, maintain it, defend it, hold it aloft, swear by it, and fight for it on every battle field where its enemies appear; and if need be, die for it. . . ." But this labor newspaper worried that in the United States "error has erected its golden god and commands the nation to fall down and worship it."

toric conflict. "The age of steam, electricity and progress generally shows up a new phase of this old war. We have to fight against the old enemy of the masses, only under a new shape." [98] Coal miner and union organizer W. H. Haskins could declare: "Brothers, the principles of organized labor are as old as the old gray rocks and sand of Mt. Sinai." [99] And Knights of Labor leader Charles Litchman could promise:

> If you ask me to say how this system is to be changed, when the emancipation of the toiling millions on earth is to come, I can only say, "I know not *when* it will come, but I know it will come," because in the sight of God and God's angels the wrongs of the toiling millions on earth are a curse and a crime, and that as God is mercy and God is love, in His own good time the toiler will be free.[100]

Although the labor press frequently complained that institutional Protestantism had "come down to the level of merchandise, and our modern Levites worship the golden calf and offer their wares, like fakirs, to the highest bidder," [101] the *United Mine Workers' Journal* printed on its first page a sermon by Baptist minister J. Thalmus Morgan for good reason. Morgan warned from his Ohio mining village pulpit:

> God's laws of right and wrong are ever the same and cannot be changed until God and man's moral nature shall be changed. Opinions may change, but truth never. Truth is truth to the end of all reckoning. What was right in the time of Moses, Mordecai and Ehud will be right forever. . . . God shall judge the poor of the people; He shall save the children of the needy, and shall break into pieces the oppressor. Yes, He will do the poor justice, for He will delight in doing them good. . . . And [He] shall break into pieces oppression. He is strong to smite the foes of His people. Oppressors have been great breakers, but their time of retribution shall come, and they shall be broken themselves.[102]

---

[98] *Printer's Labor Tribune* (Pittsburgh), Nov. 27, 1873. See also the editorial in the Providence *Sun,* Apr. 14, 1875, a Rhode Island labor weekly, which insisted: "From the Old Testament times the Almighty has had a controversy with those who have robbed the laborer of his wages."

[99] *United Mine Workers' Journal,* Jan. 17, 1895.

[100] *Journal of United Labor* (Philadelphia), Aug. 27, 1888.

[101] *Coast Seaman's Journal,* Oct. 18, 1893. Earlier examples of this critical attitude toward the clergy's dominant social conservatism are found in reviews of Washington Gladden's *Working People and Their Employers* (Boston, 1876) in the *Workingman's Advocate* (Chicago), Aug. 26, 1876, and the *National Labor Tribune,* Sept. 16, 1876. The *Tribune* was especially hard on Gladden: "He is a shallow thinker and writer. Had his book never been written nothing would have been lost. Preachers, as a class, are not able to deal with the Labor problem, and Mr. Gladden is no exception."

[102] *United Mine Worker's Journal,* June 28, 1894. What Morgan's sermon typified cannot be known because the ideas and social outlook of local clergymen, particularly

The transcendent values that organized labor found in such postmillennial Christian exhortation helped steel it in a transitional era of deep crisis. "The mandate, 'Thou shalt glorify me in thy works,' is Labor's first article of faith," concluded the *Coast Seaman's Journal*.[103]

Although trade-unionists and labor radicals were not the only critics of Gilded Age industrial America, the social Christianity they espoused was different from the more widely known and well-studied social gospel put forth by middle- and upper-class religious critics of that society. Both groups reacted against the early disintegrating consequences of rapid industrialization and drew from the same broad religious tradition. But parallel developments are not necessarily synonymous even though they occur at the same time and share a common mode of expression. The available evidence sug-

---

those in industrial towns and cities and those with predominantly working-class congregations, have not yet been studied, and it is not helpful to infer their thoughts and behavior from national religious periodicals. Scattered but inconclusive evidence suggests that an unexplored dimension of the clerical social gospel may be uncovered by studying the clergy in such communities. A few examples suffice. After discontented and unpaid Erie Railroad shopworkers and repair mechanics stopped trains and took control of the repair shops in March 1874, eighteen hundred state militia went to Susquehanna Depot, Pennsylvania, to restore order. But a local minister preached a severe Sunday sermon against the railroad company. (H. G. Gutman, "Trouble on the Railroads in 1873–1874," *Labor History*, II [Spring 1961], 228.) In 1880 a socialist newspaper editor, Irish immigrant Joseph P. McDonnell, served time in a Passaic County, New Jersey, jail for libeling a brickyard owner by publishing a letter that exposed conditions in a Paterson brickyard. Two Paterson clergymen, one a Baptist and the other a Methodist, publicly supported McDonnell and sided with the workers. (*Id.*, "Industrial Invasion of the Village Green," *Transaction*, III [May–June 1966], 19–24.) After the fierce violence in 1892 between strikers and Pinkerton police that resulted in more than thirty deaths, a Homestead, Pennsylvania, Methodist preacher said of Henry Clay Frick at the funeral services for three dead strikers: "This town is bathed in tears today, and it is all brought about by one man, who is less respected by the laboring people than any other employer in the world. There is no more sensibility in that man than in a toad." (Leon Woolf, *Lockout. The Story of the Homestead Strike of 1892: A Study of Violence, Unionism, and the Carnegie Steel Empire* [New York, 1965], 133.) At the time of the 1894 Pullman strike and boycott, William Carwardine, pastor of the First Methodist Church of Pullman, bitterly attacked George Pullman and called his model town "a hollow mockery, a sham, an institution girdled with red tape, and as a solution to the labor problem most unsatisfactory." Carwardine supported the strikers and was joined by Morris L. Wickman, pastor of the Pullman Swedish Methodist Church, who sharply criticized the firm before the United States Strike Commission. (Almost Lindsay, *The Pullman Strike* [Chicago, 1942], 73, 103; May, *Protestant Churches*, 109–11.) Although he frequently criticized the social orthodoxy of most institutional Protestant churches and was himself without religious sentiment, Gompers nevertheless interestingly wrote in 1898 that not all clergymen deserved his condemnation: "The men who preach from their pulpits and breathe with every word their sympathy with the great struggling masses of humanity; . . . these ministers you will find always interesting, and not only interesting, but the churches filled with workers who go to hear them." (Perry, "Workingman's Alienation from the Church," 623.)

[103] *Coast Seaman's Journal*, Aug. 29, 1894.

gests few formal connections between the two "movements" and for several reasons. Before the 1890's, the two groups, so different in their social composition and in the way industrial and social change affected them, rarely addressed each other and usually spoke to different audiences. Despite many diversities (its "radical" and "conservative" fringes), the essential attributes of the early social gospel movement are characterized by Henry May in a way that makes it possible to distinguish it from its working-class counterpart:

> The Social Gospel of the American nineteenth century . . . did not grow out of actual suffering but rather out of moral and intellectual dissatisfaction with the suffering of others. It originated not with the "disinherited" but rather with the educated and pious middle class. It grew through argument, not through agitation; it pleaded for conversion, not revolt or withdrawal.[104]

Critical of business behavior and the individualist ethic of their time and anxious to infuse all social classes with a meaningful Christian ethic, few early advocates of the social gospel identified closely with organized labor and its particular forms of collective organization and protest. Few shared Henry George's belief that "the revolt everywhere" against the "hard conditions of modern society is really the religious spirit." [105] They sought first to mediate between the competing classes and frequently failed to understand the "immediacy" of labor discontent. Only a small number, May finds, arranged "a successful working relation between their ultimate confidence in the new social spirit and the drab realities of day-to-day struggle." [106] Even the young Richard T. Ely and Washington Gladden, both so typical of the

---

[104] May, *Protestant Churches*, 235.

[105] *Labor: Its Rights and Wrongs*, 261–68. George linked all contemporary protest movements, even the most radical, and compared them to early Christian history: "Who are these men, the Socialists, the Anarchists, the Nihilists, and what is it they seek? . . . Is it not for a state of greater equality, for a state of more perfect peace, for a condition where no one will want and no one will suffer for the material needs of existence? That is the ideal those men have before them, blind and wrong their methods though they be. And what is that ideal? Is it not the kingdom of God on earth? What was the reason that a doctrine preached by a humble Jewish carpenter, who was crucified between two thieves, propagated by slaves and fugitives meeting in caverns, overran the world and overthrew the might of legions and the tortures of the amphitheatre and dungeon? Was it for theological distinction that Rome, the tolerant Rome, that welcomed all Gods to her Pantheon, persecuted the adherents of this new Galilean superstition? No. . . . It was because they sought the kingdom of God on earth. It was because they hoped to bring it about there and then. . . . That doctrine of the fatherhood of a common Creator and the brotherhood of men struck at the roots of tyranny; struck at the privileges of those who were living in luxury on the toil and the blood and the sweat of the worker. . . ."

[106] May, *Protestant Churches*, 231–35.

mainstream social gospel movement and both profoundly at odds with the materialism of their times, found it difficult at the start to associate themselves with working-class organizations and their methods and objectives.[107] Of the early social gospel movement, Charles H. Hopkins concludes that its "inclusive panacea" was "Christianity itself." Quoting Gladden, he adds: " 'the power of Christian love' was declared to be strong enough 'to smooth and sweeten all relations of capitalists and labor.' " Society would change mainly "through the converted individual whose changed character would produce a social transformation." [108] Such thought and argument stimulated numerous middle- and upper-class reformers in late nineteenth-century America, but what May calls its "facile optimism" and its "fatal tendency to underestimate difficulties and to neglect mechanism" cut it off from working-class critics of industrial society.[109]

Protestantism in Gilded Age America permeated the social structure and the value system of the nation more deeply and in different ways than heretofore emphasized by that era's historians. The careers and writings of Henry Ward Beecher, Dwight Moody, Mary Baker Eddy, Washington Gladden, and the trade-unionists and labor radicals described in these pages illustrate the complexity of the relationship between religious belief and organization and the component parts of a particular social structure. Although what has been written here must not be interpreted as a single explanation for the little-studied subject of nineteenth-century working-class thought and behavior, it should be clear that the social gospel early found expression among those who professed to speak for the discontented lower classes and that the behavior of these critics of industrial capitalism cannot be understood without first exploring the religious (and secular) dimensions of their thought. For some workers and their leaders, including some of the most prominent Gilded Age trade-unionists and radicals, a particular strand of Protestantism offered what Hobsbawm calls "a passion and morality in which the most ignorant can compete on equal terms" and what Liston Pope describes as a religion "intimately related to the everyday struggles and vicissitudes of an in-

---

[107] In 1886 Ely, for example, defended trade-unions and attacked employer abuses in his significant *The Labor Movement in America,* but nevertheless urged discontented workers to "cast aside envy" and told them: "While the Bible is a good armory from which you may draw weapons of attack, it at the same time points out the right course for you to take. . . . It discourages no good effort; but even James followed his awful condemnation of the oppressor with these wise words, 'Be ye also patient.' " (R. T. Ely, *The Labor Movement in America* [New York, 1886], v–xiii.) Gladden early attacked the industrial abuses of his time, but still found labor unions "often unwise and unprofitable" and argued that "as a general thing' unions "result in more loss than gain to the laboring classes." (Quoted in John L. Shover, "Washington Gladden and the Labor Question," *Ohio Historical Quarterly,* LXVIII [Oct. 1959], 335–52.)

[108] Hopkins, *Rise of the Social Gospel,* 70, 89, 325.

[109] May, *Protestant Churches,* 233.

secure life" and "useful for interpretation and succor." [110] In 1893 one American pondered existential questions:

> While man is nothing more than a human, he has feeling. . . . While I am not a preacher nor one among the best of men, I am one who believes in Christ and His teachings and endeavor each day to live the life of a Christian. . . . My way is not everybody's way, and it would be wrong to even suppose it should be. . . . Now, what is my motive? . . . My reasoning is after this manner: Can man within himself accomplish as much while self exists as when he considers, Am I the only being that lives? and finds in answer, no. But I am one among millions, a pitiful drop in the bucket he thinks at once. . . . Am I right? Man wants everything but that which is best for him and his brother. [111]

These were not the words of Henry Ward Beecher, Russell Conwell, Mary Baker Eddy, Dwight Moody, William Lawrence, Lyman Atwater, John D. Rockefeller, Andrew Carnegie, or even Washington Gladden; they were penned by an unidentified but troubled Belleville, Ohio, coal miner.

---

[110] Hobsbawm, *Social Bandits and Primitive Rebels*, 132; Liston Pope, *Millhands and Preachers* (New Haven, Conn., 1942), 86.

[111] *United Mine Workers' Journal*, June 29, 1893.

MILTON M. GORDON

ASSIMILATION IN AMERICA
Theory and Reality

One of the salient and unique features of American history is its hetero-geneity. Racial, ethnic, and national groups bringing with them different cultures, different collective memories, different experiences, and different expectations peopled this continent and created this nation. There can be no thorough understanding of the development of the United States as a nation without an understanding of how these groups interacted with and reacted to one another.

Milton Gordon gets at the heart of this problem by examining the basic ideologies of assimilation in American history. His article points out that the idea of the melting pot, so familiar to generations of American school children, has been neither the only nor the predominant notion of assimilation. In fact, as it has often been propounded in American schools, the melting-pot theory resembles the classic notion of Crèvecoeur, Turner, and Zangwill less than it does the idea of Anglo-conformity that Gordon develops. That is, American society could more accurately be described as a crucible for the melting out *of differences, resulting in the emergence of the old Englishman, rather than as a crucible for the melting* down *of differences into a new man. Gordon expounds his ideas in greater detail in his book,* Assimilation in America * (1964).*

Three ideologies or conceptual models have competed for attention on the American scene as explanations of the way in which a nation, in the beginning largely white, Anglo-Saxon, and Protestant, has absorbed over 41 million immigrants and their descendants from variegated sources and welded them into the contemporary American people. These ideologies are Anglo-conformity, the melting pot, and cultural pluralism. They have served at various times, and often simultaneously, as explanations of what has happened—descriptive models—and of what should happen—goal models. Not infrequently they have been used in such a fashion that it is difficult to tell which of these two usages the writer has had in mind. In fact, one of the more remarkable omissions in the history of American intellectual thought is the relative lack of close analytical attention given to the theory of immigrant adjustment in the United States by its social scientists.

The result has been that this field of discussion—an overridingly important one since it has significant implications for the more familiar problems of prejudice, discrimination, and majority-minority group relations generally—has been largely preempted by laymen, representatives of belles lettres, philosophers, and apologists of various persuasions. Even from these sources the amount of attention devoted to ideologies of assimilation is hardly extensive. Consequently, the work of improving intergroup relations in America is carried out by dedicated professional agencies and individuals who deal as best they can with day-to-day problems of discriminatory behavior, but who for the most part are unable to relate their efforts to an adequate conceptual apparatus. Such an apparatus would, at one and the same time, accurately describe the present structure of American society with respect to its ethnic groups (I shall use the term "ethnic group" to refer to any racial, religious, or national origins collectivity), and allow for a considered formulation of its assimilation or integration goals for the foreseeable future. One is reminded of Alice's distraught question in her travels in Wonderland: "Would you tell me, please, which way I ought to go from here?" "That depends a good deal," replied the Cat with irrefutable logic, "on where you want to get to."

The story of America's immigration can be quickly told for our present purposes. The white American population at the time of the Revolution was largely English and Protestant in origin, but had already absorbed substantial groups of Germans and Scotch-Irish and smaller contingents of Frenchmen, Dutchmen, Swedes, Swiss, South Irish, Poles, and a handful of migrants from other European nations. Catholics were represented in modest numbers, par-

FROM Milton M. Gordon, "Assimilation in America: Theory and Reality," *Daedalus*, Vol. 90 (Spring 1961), pp. 263–85. Reprinted by permission of the American Academy of Arts and Sciences. The materials of this article are based on a larger study of the meaning and implications of minority group assimilation in the United States, which [was] carried out for the Russell Sage Foundation and which is scheduled to be published as a book by the Foundation.

ticularly in the middle colonies, and a small number of Jews were residents of the incipient nation. With the exception of the Quakers and a few missionaries, the colonists had generally treated the Indians and their cultures with contempt and hostility, driving them from the coastal plains and making the western frontier a bloody battleground where eternal vigilance was the price of survival.

Although the Negro at that time made up nearly one-fifth of the total population, his predominantly slave status, together with racial and cultural prejudice, barred him from serious consideration as an assimilable element of the society. And while many groups of European origin started out as determined ethnic enclaves, eventually, most historians believe, considerable ethnic intermixture within the white population took place. "People of different blood" [*sic*]—write two American historians about the colonial period, "English, Irish, German, Huguenot, Dutch, Swedish—mingled and intermarried with little thought of any difference." [1] In such a society, its people predominantly English, its white immigrants of other ethnic origins either English-speaking or derived largely from countries of northern and western Europe whose cultural divergences from the English were not great, and its dominant white population excluding by fiat the claims and considerations of welfare of the non-Caucasian minorities, the problem of assimilation understandably did not loom unduly large or complex.

The unfolding events of the next century and a half with increasing momentum dispelled the complacency which rested upon the relative simplicity of colonial and immediate post-Revolutionary conditions. The large-scale immigration to America of the famine-fleeing Irish, the Germans, and later the Scandinavians (along with additional Englishmen and other peoples of northern and western Europe) in the middle of the nineteenth century (the so-called "old immigration"), the emancipation of the Negro slaves and the problems created by post-Civil War reconstruction, the placing of the conquered Indian with his broken culture on government reservations, the arrival of the Oriental, first attracted by the discovery of gold and other opportunities in the West, and finally, beginning in the last quarter of the nineteenth century and continuing to the early 1920's, the swelling to proportions hitherto unimagined of the tide of immigration from the peasantries and "pales" of southern and eastern Europe—the Italians, Jews, and Slavs of the so-called "new immigration," fleeing the persecutions and industrial dislocations of the day—all these events constitute the background against which we may consider the rise of the theories of assimilation mentioned above. After a necessarily foreshortened description of each of these theories and their historical emergence, we shall suggest analytical distinctions designed to

---

[1] Allan Nevins and Henry Steele Commager, *America: The Story of a Free People* (Boston, Little, Brown, 1942), p. 58.

aid in clarifying the nature of the assimilation process, and then conclude by focusing on the American scene.

Anglo-Conformity

"Anglo-conformity" [2] is a broad term used to cover a variety of viewpoints about assimilation and immigration; they all assume the desirability of maintaining English institutions (as modified by the American Revolution), the English language, and English-oriented cultural patterns as dominant and standard in American life. However, bound up with this assumption are related attitudes. These may range from discredited notions about race and "Nordic" and "Aryan" racial superiority, together with the nativist political programs and exclusionist immigration policies which such notions entail, through an intermediate position of favoring immigration from northern and western Europe on amorphous, unreflective grounds ("They are more like us"), to a lack of opposition to any source of immigration, as long as these immigrants and their descendants duly adopt the standard Anglo-Saxon cultural patterns. There is by no means any necessary equation between Anglo-conformity and racist attitudes.

It is quite likely that "Anglo-conformity" in its more moderate aspects, however explicit its formulation, has been the most prevalent ideology of assimilation goals in America throughout the nation's history. As far back as colonial times, Benjamin Franklin recorded concern about the clannishness of the Germans in Pennsylvania, their slowness in learning English, and the establishment of their own native-language press.[3] Others of the founding fathers had similar reservations about large-scale immigration from Europe. In the context of their times they were unable to foresee the role such immigration was to play in creating the later greatness of the nation. They were not at all men of unthinking prejudices. The disestablishment of religion and the separation of church and state (so that no religious group—whether New England Congregationalists, Virginian Anglicans, or even all Protestants combined—could call upon the federal government for special favors or support, and so that man's religious conscience should be free) were cardinal points of the new national policy they fostered. "The Government of the United States," George Washington had written to the Jewish congregation of Newport during his first term as president, "gives to bigotry no sanction, to persecution no assistance."

---

[2] The phrase is the Coles's. See Stewart G. Cole and Mildred Wiese Cole, *Minorities and the American Promise* (New York, Harper & Brothers, 1954), ch. 6.

[3] Maurice R. Davie, *World Immigration* (New York, Macmillan, 1936), p. 36, and (cited therein) "Letter of Benjamin Franklin to Peter Collison, 9th May, 1753, on the condition and character of the Germans in Pennsylvania," in *The Works of Benjamin Franklin, with notes and a life of the author,* by Jared Sparks (Boston, 1828), vol. 7, pp. 71–73.

Political differences with ancestral England had just been written in blood; but there is no reason to suppose that these men looked upon their fledgling country as an impartial melting pot for the merging of the various cultures of Europe, or as a new "nation of nations," or as anything but a society in which, with important political modifications, Anglo-Saxon speech and institutional forms would be standard. Indeed, their newly won victory for democracy and republicanism made them especially anxious that these still precarious fruits of revolution should not be threatened by a large influx of European peoples whose life experiences had accustomed them to the bonds of despotic monarchy. Thus, although they explicitly conceived of the new United States of America as a haven for those unfortunates of Europe who were persecuted and oppressed, they had characteristic reservations about the effects of too free a policy. "My opinion, with respect to immigration," Washington wrote to John Adams in 1794, "is that except of useful mechanics and some particular descriptions of men or professions, there is no need of encouragement, while the policy or advantage of its taking place in a body (I mean the settling of them in a body) may be much questioned; for, by so doing, they retain the language, habits and principles (good or bad) which they bring with them." [4] Thomas Jefferson, whose views on race and attitudes towards slavery were notably liberal and advanced for his time, had similar doubts concerning the effects of mass immigration on American institutions, while conceding that immigrants, "if they come of themselves . . . are entitled to all the rights of citizenship." [5]

The attitudes of Americans toward foreign immigration in the first three-quarters of the nineteenth century may correctly be described as ambiguous. On the one hand, immigrants were much desired, so as to swell the population and importance of states and territories, to man the farms of expanding prairie settlement, to work the mines, build the railroads and canals, and take their place in expanding industry. This was a period in which no federal legislation of any consequence prevented the entry of aliens, and such state legislation as existed attempted to bar on an individual basis only those who were likely to become a burden on the community, such as convicts and paupers. On the other hand, the arrival in an overwhelmingly Protestant society of large numbers of poverty-stricken Irish Catholics, who settled in groups in the slums of Eastern cities, roused dormant fears of "Popery" and Rome. Another source of anxiety was the substantial influx of Germans, who made their way to the cities and farms of the mid-West and whose different language, separate communal life, and freer ideas on temperance and sab-

---

[4] *The Writings of George Washington,* collected and edited by W. C. Ford (New York, G. P. Putnam's Sons, 1889), vol. 12, p. 489.

[5] Thomas Jefferson, "Notes on Virginia, Query 8"; in *The Writings of Thomas Jefferson,* ed. A. E. Bergh (Washington, The Thomas Jefferson Memorial Association, 1907), vol. 2, p. 121.

bath observance brought them into conflict with the Anglo-Saxon bearers of the Puritan and Evangelical traditions. Fear of foreign "radicals" and suspicion of the economic demands of the occasionally aroused workingmen added fuel to the nativist fires. In their extreme form these fears resulted in the Native-American movement of the 1830's and 1840's and the "American" or "Know-Nothing" party of the 1850's, with their anti-Catholic campaigns and their demands for restrictive laws on naturalization procedures and for keeping the foreign-born out of political office. While these movements scored local political successes and their turbulences so rent the national social fabric that the patches are not yet entirely invisible, they failed to influence national legislative policy on immigration and immigrants; and their fulminations inevitably provoked the expected reactions from thoughtful observers.

The flood of newcomers to the westward expanding nation grew larger, reaching over one and two-thirds million between 1841 and 1850 and over two and one-half million in the decade before the Civil War. Throughout the entire period, quite apart from the excesses of the Know-Nothings, the predominant (though not exclusive) conception of what the ideal immigrant adjustment should be was probably summed up in a letter written in 1818 by John Quincy Adams, then Secretary of State, in answer to the inquiries of the Baron von Fürstenwaerther. If not the earliest, it is certainly the most elegant version of the sentiment, "If they don't like it here, they can go back where they came from." Adams declared: [6]

> They [immigrants to America] come to a life of independence, but to a life of labor—and, if they cannot accommodate themselves to the character; moral, political and physical, of this country with all its compensating balances of good and evil, the Atlantic is always open to them to return to the land of their nativity and their fathers. To one thing they must make up their minds, or they will be disappointed in every expectation of happiness as Americans. They must cast off the European skin, never to resume it. They must look forward to their posterity rather than backward to their ancestors; they must be sure that whatever their own feelings may be, those of their children will cling to the prejudices of this country.

The events that followed the Civil War created their own ambiguities in attitude toward the immigrant. A nation undergoing wholesale industrial expansion and not yet finished with the march of westward settlement could make good use of the never faltering waves of newcomers. But sporadic bursts of labor unrest, attributed to foreign radicals, the growth of Catholic institutions and the rise of Catholics to municipal political power, and the continuing association of immigrant settlement with urban slums revived fa-

---

[6] *Niles' Weekly Register*, vol. 18, 29 April 1820, pp. 157–158; also, Marcus L. Hansen, *The Atlantic Migration, 1607–1860*, pp. 96–97.

miliar fears. The first federal selective law restricting immigration was passed in 1882, and Chinese immigration was cut off in the same year. The most significant development of all, barely recognized at first, was the change in the source of European migrants. Beginning in the 1880's, the countries of southern and eastern Europe began to be represented in substantial numbers for the first time, and in the next decade immigrants from these sources became numerically dominant. Now the notes of a new, or at least hitherto unemphasized, chord from the nativist lyre began to sound—the ugly chord, or discord, of racism. Previously vague and romantic notions of Anglo-Saxon peoplehood, combined with general ethnocentrism, rudimentary wisps of genetics, selected tidbits of evolutionary theory, and naive assumptions from an early and crude imported anthropology produced the doctrine that the English, Germans, and others of the "old immigration" constituted a superior race of tall, blonde, blue-eyed "Nordics" or "Aryans," whereas the peoples of eastern and southern Europe made up the darker Alpines or Mediterraneans—both "inferior" breeds whose presence in America threatened, either by intermixture or supplementation, the traditional American stock and culture. The obvious corollary to this doctrine was to exclude the allegedly inferior breeds; but if the new type of immigrant could not be excluded, then everything must be done to instill Anglo-Saxon virtues in these benighted creatures. Thus, one educator writing in 1909 could state: [7]

> These southern and eastern Europeans are of a very different type from the north Europeans who preceded them. Illiterate, docile, lacking in self-reliance and initiative, and not possessing the Anglo-Teutonic conceptions of law, order, and government, their coming has served to dilute tremendously our national stock, and to corrupt our civic life. . . . Everywhere these people tend to settle in groups or settlements, and to set up here their national manners, customs, and observances. Our task is to break up these groups or settlements, to assimilate and amalgamate these people as a part of our American race, and to implant in their children, so far as can be done, the Anglo-Saxon conception of righteousness, law and order, and popular government, and to awaken in them a reverence for our democratic institutions and for those things in our national life which we as a people hold to be of abiding worth.

Anglo-conformity received its fullest expression in the so-called Americanization movement which gripped the nation during World War I. While "Americanization" in its various stages had more than one emphasis, it was essentially a consciously articulated movement to strip the immigrant of his native culture and attachments and make him over into an American along Anglo-Saxon lines—all this to be accomplished with great rapidity. To use an image of a later day, it was an attempt at "pressure-cooking assimila-

---

[7] Ellwood P. Cubberly, *Changing Conceptions of Education* (Boston, Houghton Mifflin, 1909), pp. 15–16.

tion." It had prewar antecedents, but it was during the height of the world conflict that federal agencies, state governments, municipalities, and a host of private organizations joined in the effort to persuade the immigrant to learn English, take out naturalization papers, buy war bonds, forget his former origins and culture, and give himself over to patriotic hysteria.

After the war and the "Red scare" which followed, the excesses of the Americanization movement subsided. In its place, however, came the restriction of immigration through federal law. Foiled at first by presidential vetoes, and later by the failure of the 1917 literacy test to halt the immigrant tide, the proponents of restriction finally put through in the early 1920's a series of acts culminating in the well-known national-origins formula for immigrant quotas which went into effect in 1929. Whatever the merits of a quantitative limit on the number of immigrants to be admitted to the United States, the provisions of the formula, which discriminated sharply against the countries of southern and eastern Europe, in effect institutionalized the assumptions of the rightful dominance of Anglo-Saxon patterns in the land. Reaffirmed with only slight modifications in the McCarran-Walter Act of 1952, these laws, then, stand as a legal monument to the creed of Anglo-conformity and a telling reminder that this ideological system still has numerous and powerful adherents on the American scene.

The Melting Pot

While Anglo-conformity in various guises has probably been the most prevalent ideology of assimilation in the American historical experience, a competing viewpoint with more generous and idealistic overtones has had its adherents and exponents from the eighteenth century onward. Conditions in the virgin continent, it was clear, were modifying the institutions which the English colonists brought with them from the mother country. Arrivals from non-English homelands such as Germany, Sweden, and France were similarly exposed to this fresh environment. Was it not possible, then, to think of the evolving American society not as a slightly modified England but rather as a totally new blend, culturally and biologically, in which the stocks and folkways of Europe, figuratively speaking, were indiscriminately mixed in the political pot of the emerging nation and fused by the fires of American influence and interaction into a distinctly new type?

Such, at any rate, was the conception of the new society which motivated that eighteenth-century French-born writer and agriculturalist, J. Hector St. John Crèvecoeur, who, after many years of American residence, published his reflections and observations in *Letters from an American Farmer*.[8] Who, he asks, is the American?

---

[8] J. Hector St. John Crèvecoeur, *Letters from an American Farmer* (New York, Albert and Charles Boni, 1925; reprinted from the 1st edn., London, 1782), pp. 54–55.

He is either an European, or the descendant of an European, hence that strange mixture of blood, which you will find in no other country. I could point out to you a family whose grandfather was an Englishman, whose wife was Dutch, whose son married a French woman, and whose present four sons have now four wives of different nations. *He* is an American, who leaving behind him all his ancient prejudices and manners, receives new ones from the new mode of life he has embraced, the new government he obeys, and the new rank he holds. He becomes an American by being received in the broad lap of our great *Alma Mater*. Here individuals of all nations are melted into a new race of men, whose labours and posterity will one day cause great changes in the world.

Some observers have interpreted the open-door policy on immigration of the first three-quarters of the nineteenth century as reflecting an underlying faith in the effectiveness of the American melting pot, in the belief "that all could be absorbed and that all could contribute to an emerging national character." [9] No doubt many who observed with dismay the nativist agitation of the times felt as did Ralph Waldo Emerson that such conformity-demanding and immigrant-hating forces represented a perversion of the best American ideals. In 1845, Emerson wrote in his Journal: [10]

I hate the narrowness of the Native American Party. It is the dog in the manger. It is precisely opposite to all the dictates of love and magnanimity; and therefore, of course, opposite to true wisdom. . . . Man is the most composite of all creatures. . . . Well, as in the old burning of the Temple at Corinth, by the melting and intermixture of silver and gold and other metals a new compound more precious than any, called Corinthian brass, was formed; so in this continent—asylum of all nations,—the energy of Irish, Germans, Swedes, Poles, and Cossacks, and all the European tribes,—of the Africans, and of the Polynesians,—will construct a new race, a new religion, a new state, a new literature, which will be as vigorous as the new Europe which came out of the smelting-pot of the Dark Ages, or that which earlier emerged from the Pelasgic and Etruscan barbarism. *La Nature aime les croisements.*

Eventually, the melting-pot hypothesis found its way into historical scholarship and interpretation. While many American historians of the late nineteenth century, some fresh from graduate study at German universities, tended to adopt the view that American institutions derived in essence from Anglo-Saxon (and ultimately Teutonic) sources, others were not so sure.[11] One of these was Frederick Jackson Turner, a young historian from Wiscon-

---

[9] Oscar Handlin, ed., *Immigration as a Factor in American History* (Englewood, Prentice-Hall, 1959), p. 146.

[10] Quoted by Stuart P. Sherman in his Introduction to *Essays and Poems of Emerson* (New York, Harcourt Brace, 1921), p. xxxiv.

[11] See Edward N. Saveth, *American Historians and European Immigrants, 1875–1925,* New York, Columbia University Press, 1948.

sin, not long emerged from his graduate training at Johns Hopkins. Turner presented a paper to the American Historical Association, meeting in Chicago in 1893. Called "The Significance of the Frontier in American History," this paper proved to be one of the most influential essays in the history of American scholarship, and its point of view, supported by Turner's subsequent writings and his teaching, pervaded the field of American historical interpretation for at least a generation. Turner's thesis was that the dominant influence in the shaping of American institutions and American democracy was not this nation's European heritage in any of its forms, nor the forces emanating from the eastern seaboard cities, but rather the experiences created by a moving and variegated western frontier. Among the many effects attributed to the frontier environment and the challenges it presented was that it acted as a solvent for the national heritages and the separatist tendencies of the many nationality groups which had joined the trek westward, including the Germans and Scotch-Irish of the eighteenth century and the Scandinavians and Germans of the nineteenth. "The frontier," asserted Turner, "promoted the formation of a composite nationality for the American people. . . . In the crucible of the frontier the immigrants were Americanized, liberated, and fused into a mixed race, English in neither nationality nor characteristics. The process has gone on from the early days to our own." And later, in an essay on the role of the Mississippi Valley, he refers to "the tide of foreign immigration which has risen so steadily that it has made a composite American people whose amalgamation is destined to produce a new national stock." [12]

Thus far, the proponents of the melting-pot idea had dealt largely with the diversity produced by the sizeable immigration from the countries of northern and western Europe alone—the "old immigration," consisting of peoples with cultures and physical appearance not greatly different from those of the Anglo-Saxon stock. Emerson, it is true, had impartially included Africans, Polynesians, and Cossacks in his conception of the mixture; but it was only in the last two decades of the nineteenth century that a large-scale influx of peoples from the countries of southern and eastern Europe imperatively posed the question of whether these uprooted newcomers who were crowding into the large cities of the nation and the industrial sector of the economy could also be successfully "melted." Would the "urban melting pot" work as well as the "frontier melting pot" of an essentially rural society was alleged to have done?

It remained for an English-Jewish writer with strong social convictions, moved by his observation of the role of the United States as a haven for the poor and oppressed of Europe, to give utterance to the broader view of the American melting pot in a way which attracted public attention. In 1908, Is-

---

[12] Frederick Jackson Turner, *The Frontier in American History* (New York, Henry Holt, 1920), pp. 22–23, 190.

rael Zangwill's drama, *The Melting Pot,* was produced in this country and became a popular success. It is a play dominated by the dream of its protagonist, a young Russian-Jewish immigrant to America, a composer, whose goal is the completion of a vast "American" symphony which will express his deeply felt conception of his adopted country as a divinely appointed crucible in which all the ethnic divisions of mankind will divest themselves of their ancient animosities and differences and become fused into one group, signifying the brotherhood of man. In the process he falls in love with a beautiful and cultured Gentile girl. The play ends with the performance of the symphony and, after numerous vicissitudes and traditional family opposition from both sides, with the approaching marriage of David Quixano and his beloved. During the course of these developments, David, in the rhetoric of the time, delivers himself of such sentiments as these: [13]

> America is God's crucible, the great Melting Pot where all the races of Europe are melting and re-forming! Here you stand, good folk, think I, when I see them at Ellis Island, here you stand in your fifty groups, with your fifty languages and histories, and your fifty blood hatreds and rivalries. But you won't be long like that, brothers, for these are the fires of God you've come to—these are the fires of God. A fig for your feuds and vendettas! Germans and Frenchmen, Irishmen and Englishmen, Jews and Russians—into the Crucible with you all! God is making the American.

Here we have a conception of a melting pot which admits of no exceptions or qualifications with regard to the ethnic stocks which will fuse in the great crucible. Englishmen, Germans, Frenchmen, Slavs, Greeks, Syrians, Jews, Gentiles, even the black and yellow races, were specifically mentioned in Zangwill's rhapsodic enumeration. And this pot patently was to boil in the great cities of America.

Thus around the turn of the century the melting-pot idea became embedded in the ideals of the age as one response to the immigrant receiving experience of the nation. Soon to be challenged by a new philosophy of group adjustment (to be discussed below) and always competing with the more pervasive adherence to Anglo-conformity, the melting-pot image, however, continued to draw a portion of the attention consciously directed toward this aspect of the American scene in the first half of the twentieth century. In the mid-1940's a sociologist who had carried out an investigation of intermarriage trends in New Haven, Connecticut, described a revised conception of the melting process in that city and suggested a basic modification of the theory of that process. In New Haven, Ruby Jo Reeves Kennedy [14] re-

---

13 Israel Zangwill, *The Melting Pot* (New York, Macmillan, 1909), p. 37.

14 Ruby Jo Reeves Kennedy, "Single or Triple Melting-Pot? Intermarriage Trends in New Haven, 1870–1940," *American Journal of Sociology,* 1944, *49:* 331–339. See also her "Single or Triple Melting-Pot? Intermarriage in New Haven, 1870–1950," *ibid.,* 1952, *58:* 56–59.

ported from a study of intermarriages from 1870 to 1940 that there was a distinct tendency for the British-Americans, Germans, and Scandinavians to marry among themselves—that is, within a Protestant "pool"; for the Irish, Italians, and Poles to marry among themselves—a Catholic "pool"; and for the Jews to marry other Jews. In other words, intermarriage was taking place across lines of nationality background, but there was a strong tendency for it to stay confined within one or the other of the three major religious groups, Protestants, Catholics, and Jews. Thus, declared Mrs. Kennedy, the picture in New Haven resembled a "triple melting pot" based on religious divisions, rather than a "single melting pot." Her study indicated, she stated, that "while strict endogamy is loosening, religious endogamy is persisting and the future cleavages will be along religious lines rather than along nationality lines as in the past. If this is the case, then the traditional 'single-melting-pot' idea must be abandoned, and a new conception, which we term the 'triple-melting-pot' theory of American assimilation, will take its place as the true expression of what is happening to the various nationality groups in the United States." [15] The triple-melting-pot thesis was later taken up by the theologian Will Herberg and formed an important sociological frame of reference for his analysis of religious trends in American society, *Protestant-Catholic-Jew*.[16] But the triple-melting-pot hypothesis patently takes us into the realm of a society pluralistically conceived. We turn now to the rise of an ideology which attempts to justify such a conception.

Cultural Pluralism

Probably all the non-English immigrants who came to American shores in any significant numbers from colonial times onward—settling either in the forbidding wilderness, the lonely prairie, or in some accessible urban slum —created ethnic enclaves and looked forward to the preservation of at least some of their native cultural patterns. Such a development, natural as breathing, was supported by the later accretion of friends, relatives, and countrymen seeking out oases of familiarity in a strange land, by the desire of the settlers to rebuild (necessarily in miniature) a society in which they could communicate in the familiar tongue and maintain familiar institutions, and, finally, by the necessity to band together for mutual aid and mutual protection against the uncertainties of a strange and frequently hostile environment. This was as true of the "old" immigrants as of the "new." In fact, some of the liberal intellectuals who fled to America from an inhospitable political climate in Germany in the 1830's, 1840's, and 1850's looked forward to the creation of an all-German state within the union, or, even more hopefully, to

---

[15] Ruby Jo Reeves Kennedy, "Single or Triple Melting-Pot? . . . 1870–1940," p. 332 (author's italics omitted).

[16] Will Herberg, *Protestant-Catholic-Jew*, Garden City, Doubleday, 1955.

the eventual formation of a separate German nation, as soon as the expected dissolution of the union under the impact of the slavery controversy should have taken place.[17] Oscar Handlin, writing of the sons of Erin in mid-nineteenth-century Boston, recent refugees from famine and economic degradation in their homeland, points out: "Unable to participate in the normal associational affairs of the community, the Irish felt obliged to erect a society within a society, to act together in their own way. In every contact therefore the group, acting apart from other sections of the community, became intensely aware of its peculiar and exclusive identity." [18] Thus cultural pluralism was a fact in American society before it became a theory—a theory with explicit relevance for the nation as a whole, and articulated and discussed in the English-speaking circles of American intellectual life.

Eventually, the cultural enclaves of the Germans (and the later arriving Scandinavians) were to decline in scope and significance as succeeding generations of their native-born attended public schools, left the farms and villages to strike out as individuals for the Americanizing city, and generally became subject to the influences of a standardizing industrial civilization. The German-American community, too, was struck a powerful blow by the accumulated passions generated by World War I—a blow from which it never fully recovered. The Irish were to be the dominant and pervasive element in the gradual emergence of a pan-Catholic group in America, but these developments would reveal themselves only in the twentieth century. In the meantime, in the last two decades of the nineteenth, the influx of immigrants from southern and eastern Europe had begun. These groups were all the more sociologically visible because the closing of the frontier, the occupational demands of an expanding industrial economy, and their own poverty made it inevitable that they would remain in the urban areas of the nation. In the swirling fires of controversy and the steadier flame of experience created by these new events, the ideology of cultural pluralism as a philosophy for the nation was forged.

The first manifestations of an ideological counterattack against draconic Americanization came not from the beleaguered newcomers (who were, after all, more concerned with survival than with theories of adjustment), but from those idealistic members of the middle class who, in the decade or so before the turn of the century, had followed the example of their English predecessors and "settled" in the slums to "learn to sup sorrow with the

---

[17] Nathan Glazer, "Ethnic Groups in America: From National Culture to Ideology," in Morroe Berger, Theodore Abel, and Charles H. Page, eds., *Freedom and Control in Modern Society* (New York, D. Van Nostrand, 1954), p. 161; Marcus Lee Hansen, *The Immigrant in American History* (Cambridge, Harvard University Press, 1940), pp. 129–140; John A. Hawgood, *The Tragedy of German-America* (New York, Putnam's, 1940), *passim*.

[18] Oscar Handlin, *Boston's Immigrants* (Cambridge, Harvard University Press, 1959, rev. edn.), p. 176.

poor." [19] Immediately, these workers in the "settlement houses" were forced to come to grips with the realities of immigrant life and adjustment. Not all reacted in the same way, but on the whole the settlements developed an approach to the immigrant which was sympathetic to his native cultural heritage and to his newly created ethnic institutions.[20] For one thing, their workers, necessarily in intimate contact with the lives of these often pathetic and bewildered newcomers and their daily problems, could see how unfortunate were the effects of those forces which impelled rapid Americanization in their impact on the immigrants' children, who not infrequently became alienated from their parents and the restraining influence of family authority. Were not their parents ignorant and uneducated "Hunkies," "Sheenies," or "Dagoes," as that limited portion of the American environment in which they moved defined the matter? Ethnic "self-hatred" with its debilitating psychological consequences, family disorganization, and juvenile delinquency, were not unusual results of this state of affairs. Furthermore, the immigrants themselves were adversely affected by the incessant attacks on their culture, their language, their institutions, their very conception of themselves. How were they to maintain their self-respect when all that they knew, felt, and dreamed, beyond their sheer capacity for manual labor—in other words, all that they *were*—was despised or scoffed at in America? And—unkindest cut of all—their own children had begun to adopt the contemptuous attitude of the "Americans." Jane Addams relates in a moving chapter of her *Twenty Years at Hull House* how, after coming to have some conception of the extent and depth of these problems, she created at the settlement a "Labor Museum," in which the immigrant women of the various nationalities crowded together in the slums of Chicago could illustrate their native methods of spinning and weaving, and in which the relation of these earlier techniques to contemporary factory methods could be graphically shown. For the first time these peasant women were made to feel by some part of their American environment that they possessed valuable and interesting skills— that they too had something to offer—and for the first time, the daughters of these women who, after a long day's work at their dank "needletrade" sweatshops, came to Hull House to observe, began to appreciate the fact that their mothers, too, had a "culture," that this culture possessed its own merit, and that it was related to their own contemporary lives. How aptly Jane Addams concludes her chapter with the hope that "our American citizenship might be built without disturbing these foundations which were laid of old time." [21]

---

[19] From a letter (1883) by Samuel A. Barnett; quoted in Arthur C. Holden, *The Settlement Idea* (New York, Macmillan, 1922), p. 12.

[20] Jane Addams, *Twenty Years at Hull House* (New York, Macmillan, 1914), pp. 231–258; Arthur C. Holden, *op. cit.*, pp. 109–131, 182–189; John Higham, *Strangers in the Land* (New Brunswick, Rutgers University Press, 1955), p. 236.

[21] Jane Addams, *op. cit.*, p. 258.

This appreciative view of the immigrant's cultural heritage and of its distinctive usefulness both to himself and his adopted country received additional sustenance from another source: those intellectual currents of the day which, however, overborne by their currently more powerful opposites, emphasized liberalism, internationalism, and tolerance. From time to time, an occasional educator or publicist protested the demands of the "Americanizers," arguing that the immigrant, too, had an ancient and honorable culture, and that this culture had much to offer an America whose character and destiny were still in the process of formation, an America which must serve as an example of the harmonious cooperation of various heritages to a world inflamed by nationalism and war. In 1916 John Dewey, Norman Hapgood, and the young literary critic, Randolph Bourne, published articles or addresses elaborating various aspects of this theme.

The classic statement of the cultural pluralist position, however, had been made over a year before. Early in 1915 there appeared in the pages of *The Nation* two articles under the title "Democracy *versus* the Melting-Pot." Their author was Horace Kallen, a Harvard-educated philosopher with a concern for the application of philosophy to societal affairs, and, as an American Jew, himself derivative of an ethnic background which was subject to the contemporary pressures for dissolution implicit in the "Americanization," or Anglo-conformity, and the melting-pot theories. In these articles Kallen vigorously rejected the usefulness of these theories as models of what was actually transpiring in American life or as ideals for the future. Rather he was impressed by the way in which the various ethnic groups in America were coincident with particular areas and regions, and with the tendency for each group to preserve its own language, religion, communal institutions, and ancestral culture. All the while, he pointed out, the immigrant has been learning to speak English as the language of general communication, and has participated in the over-all economic and political life of the nation. These developments in which "the United States are in the process of becoming a federal state not merely as a union of geographical and administrative unities, but also as a cooperation of cultural diversities, as a federation or commonwealth of national cultures," [22] the author argued, far from constituting a violation of historic American political principles, as the "Americanizers" claimed, actually represented the inevitable consequences of democratic ideals, since individuals are implicated in groups, and since democracy for the individual must by extension also mean democracy for his group.

The processes just described, however, as Kallen develops his argument, are far from having been thoroughly realized. They are menaced by "Americanization" programs, assumptions of Anglo-Saxon superiority, and mis-

---

[22] Horace M. Kallen, "Democracy *versus* the Melting-Pot," *The Nation,* 18 and 25 February 1915; reprinted in his *Culture and Democracy in the United States,* New York, Boni and Liveright, 1924; the quotation is on p. 116.

guided attempts to promote "racial" amalgamation. Thus America stands at a kind of cultural crossroads. It can attempt to impose by force an artificial, Anglo-Saxon oriented uniformity on its peoples, or it can consciously allow and encourage its ethnic groups to develop democratically, each emphasizing its particular cultural heritage. If the latter course is followed, as Kallen puts it at the close of his essay, then,[23]

> The outlines of a possible great and truly democratic commonwealth become discernible. Its form would be that of the federal republic; its substance a democracy of nationalities, cooperating voluntarily and autonomously through common institutions in the enterprise of self-realization through the perfection of men according to their kind. The common language of the commonwealth, the language of its great tradition, would be English, but each nationality would have for its emotional and involuntary life its own peculiar dialect or speech, its own individual and inevitable esthetic and intellectual forms. The political and economic life of the commonwealth is a single unit and serves as the foundation and background for the realization of the distinctive individuality of each *nation* that composes it and of the pooling of these in a harmony above them all. Thus "American civilization" may come to mean the perfection of the cooperative harmonies of "European civilization"—the waste, the squalor and the distress of Europe being eliminated—a multiplicity in a unity, an orchestration of mankind.

Within the next decade Kallen published more essays dealing with the theme of American multiple-group life, later collected in a volume.[24] In the introductory note to this book he used for the first time the term "cultural pluralism" to refer to his position. These essays reflect both his increasingly sharp rejection of the onslaughts on the immigrant and his culture which the coming of World War I and its attendant fears, the "Red scare," the projection of themes of racial superiority, the continued exploitation of the newcomers, and the rise of the Ku Klux Klan all served to increase in intensity, and also his emphasis on cultural pluralism as the democratic antidote to these ills. He has since published other essays elaborating or annotating the theme of cultural pluralism. Thus, for at least forty-five years, most of them spent teaching at the New School for Social Research, Kallen has been acknowledged as the originator and leading philosophical exponent of the idea of cultural pluralism.

In the late 1930's and early 1940's the late Louis Adamic, the Yugoslav immigrant who had become an American writer, took up the theme of America's multicultural heritage and the role of these groups in forging the country's national character. Borrowing Walt Whitman's phrase, he described America as "a nation of nations," and while his ultimate goal was closer to

---

[23] Kallen, *Culture and Democracy*, p. 124.
[24] *Op. cit.*

the melting-pot idea than to cultural pluralism, he saw the immediate task as that of making America conscious of what it owed to all its ethnic groups, not just to the Anglo-Saxons. The children and grandchildren of immigrants of non-English origins, he was convinced, must be taught to be proud of the cultural heritage of their ancestral ethnic group and of its role in building the American nation; otherwise, they would not lose their sense of ethnic inferiority and the feeling of rootlessness he claimed to find in them.

Thus in the twentieth century, particularly since World War II, "cultural pluralism" has become a concept which has worked its way into the vocabulary and imagery of specialists in intergroup relations and leaders of ethnic communal groups. In view of this new pluralistic emphasis, some writers now prefer to speak of the "integration" of immigrants rather than of their "assimilation." [25] However, with a few exceptions,[26] no close analytical attention has been given either by social scientists or practitioners of intergroup relations to the meaning of cultural pluralism, its nature and relevance for a modern industrialized society, and its implications for problems of prejudice and discrimination—a point to which we referred at the outset of this discussion.

Conclusions

In the remaining pages I can make only a few analytical comments which I shall apply in context to the American scene, historical and current. My view of the American situation will not be documented here, but may be considered as a series of hypotheses in which I shall attempt to outline the American assimilation process.

First of all, it must be realized that "assimilation" is a blanket term which in reality covers a multitude of subprocesses. The most crucial distinction is one often ignored—the distinction between what I have elsewhere called "behavioral assimilation" and "structural assimilation." [27] The first refers to the absorption of the cultural behavior patterns of the "host" society. (At the same time, there is frequently some modification of the cultural patterns of the immigrant-receiving country, as well.) There is a special term for this process of cultural modification or "behavioral assimilation"—

---

25 See W. D. Borrie *et al., The Cultural Integration of Immigrants* (a survey based on the papers and proceedings of the UNESCO Conference in Havana, April 1956), Paris, UNESCO, 1959; and William S. Bernard, "The Integration of Immigrants in the United States" (mimeographed), one of the papers for this conference.

26 See particularly Milton M. Gordon, "Social Structure and Goals in Group Relations"; and Nathan Glazer, "Ethnic Groups in America; From National Culture to Ideology," both articles in Berger, Abel, and Page, *op. cit.;* S. N. Eisenstadt, *The Absorption of Immigrants,* London, Routledge and Kegan Paul, 1954; and W. D. Borrie *et al., op. cit.*

27 Milton M. Gordon, "Social Structure and Goals in Group Relations," p. 151.

namely, "acculturation." "Structural assimilation," on the other hand, refers to the entrance of the immigrants and their descendants into the social cliques, organizations, institutional activities, and general civic life of the receiving society. If this process takes place on a large enough scale, then a high frequency of intermarriage must result. A further distinction must be made between, on the one hand, those activities of the general civic life which involve earning a living, carrying out political responsibilities, and engaging in the instrumental affairs of the larger comunity, and, on the other hand, activities which create personal friendship patterns, frequent home intervisiting, communal worship, and communal recreation. The first type usually develops so-called "secondary relationships," which tend to be relatively impersonal and segmental; the latter type leads to "primary relationships," which are warm, intimate, and personal.

With these various distinctions in mind, we may then proceed.

Built on the base of the original immigrant "colony" but frequently extending into the life of successive generations, the characteristic ethnic group experience is this: within the ethnic group there develops a network of organizations and informal social relationships which permits and encourages the members of the ethnic group to remain within the confines of the group for all of their primary relationships and some of their secondary relationships throughout all the stages of the life cycle. From the cradle in the sectarian hospital to the child's play group, the social clique in high school, the fraternity and religious center in college, the dating group within which he searches for a spouse, the marriage partner, the neighborhood of his residence, the church affiliation and the church clubs, the men's and the women's social and service organizations, the adult clique of "marrieds," the vacation resort, and then, as the age cycle nears completion, the rest home for the elderly and, finally, the sectarian cemetery—in all these activities and relationships which are close to the core of personality and selfhood—the member of the ethnic group may if he wishes follow a path which never takes him across the boundaries of his ethnic structural network.

The picture is made more complex by the existence of social class divisions which cut across ethnic group lines just as they do those of the white Protestant population in America. As each ethnic group which has been here for the requisite time has developed second, third, or in some cases, succeeding generations, it has produced a college-educated group which composes an upper middle class (and sometimes upper class, as well) segment of the larger groups. Such class divisions tend to restrict primary group relations even further, for although the ethnic-group member feels a general sense of identification with all the bearers of his ethnic heritage, he feels comfortable in intimate social relations only with those who also share his own class background or attainment.

In short, my point is that, while *behavioral assimilation* or acculturation has taken place in America to a considerable degree, *structural assimilation,* with some important exceptions, has not been extensive.[28] The exceptions are of two types. The first brings us back to the "triple-melting-pot" thesis of Ruby Jo Reeves Kennedy and Will Herberg. The "nationality" ethnic groups have tended to merge within each of the three major religious groups. This has been particularly true of the Protestant and Jewish communities. Those descendants of the "old" immigration of the nineteenth century, who were Protestant (many of the Germans and all the Scandinavians), have in considerable part gradually merged into the white Protestant "subsociety." Jews of Sephardic, German, and Eastern-European origins have similarly tended to come together in their communal life. The process of absorbing the various Catholic nationalities, such as the Italians, Poles, and French Canadians, into an American Catholic community hitherto dominated by the Irish has begun, although I do not believe that it is by any means close to completion. Racial and quasi-racial groups such as the Negroes, Indians, Mexican-Americans, and Puerto Ricans still retain their separate sociological structures. The outcome of all this in contemporary American life is thus pluralism—but it is more than "triple" and it is more accurately described as *structural pluralism* than as cultural pluralism, although some of the latter also remains.

My second exception refers to the social structures which implicate intellectuals. There is no space to develop the issue here, but I would argue that there is a social world or subsociety of the intellectuals in America in which true structural intermixture among persons of various ethnic backgrounds, including the religious, has markedly taken place.

My final point deals with the reasons for these developments. If structural assimilation has been retarded in America by religious and racial lines, we must ask why. The answer lies in the attitudes of both the majority and the minority groups and in the way these attitudes have interacted. A saying of the current day is, "It takes two to tango." To apply the analogy, there is no good reason to believe that white Protestant America has ever extended a firm and cordial invitation to its minorities to dance. Furthermore, the attitudes of the minority-group members themselves on the matter have been divided and ambiguous. Particularly for the minority religious groups, there is a certain logic in ethnic communality, since there is a commitment to the perpetuation of the religious ideology and since structural intermixture leads to intermarriage and the possible loss to the group of the intermarried family. Let us, then, examine the situation serially for various types of minorities.

With regard to the immigrant, in his characteristic numbers and socio-economic background, structural assimilation was out of the question. He

---

[28] See Erich Rosenthal, "Acculturation without Assimilation?" *American Journal of Sociology,* 1960, *66:* 275–288.

did not want it, and he had a positive need for the comfort of his own communal institutions. The native American, moreover, whatever the implications of his public pronouncements, had no intention of opening up his primary group life to entrance by these hordes of alien newcomers. The situation was a functionally complementary standoff.

The second generation found a much more complex situation. Many believed they heard the siren call of welcome to the social cliques, clubs, and institutions of white Protestant America. After all, it was simply a matter of learning American ways, was it not? Had they not grown up as Americans, and were they not culturally different from their parents, the "greenhorns"? Or perhaps an especially eager one reasoned (like the Jewish protagonist of Myron Kaufmann's novel, *Remember Me To God,* aspiring to membership in the prestigious club system of Harvard undergraduate social life) "If only I can go the last few steps in Ivy League manners and behavior, they will surely recognize that I am one of them and take me in." But, alas, Brooks Brothers suit notwithstanding, the doors of the fraternity house, the city men's club, and the country club were slammed in the face of the immigrant's offspring. That invitation was not really there in the first place; or, to the extent it was, in Joshua Fishman's phrase, it was a " 'look me over but don't touch me' invitation to the American minority group child." [29] And so the rebuffed one returned to the homelier but dependable comfort of the communal institutions of his ancestral group. There he found his fellows of the same generation who had never stirred from the home fires. Some of these had been too timid to stray; others were ethnic ideologists committed to the group's survival; still others had never really believed in the authenticity of the siren call or were simply too passive to do more than go along the familiar way. All could now join in the task that was well within the realm of the sociologically possible—the build-up of social institutions and organizations within the ethnic enclave, manned increasingly by members of the second generation and suitably separated by social class.

Those who had for a time ventured out gingerly or confidently, as the case might be, had been lured by the vision of an "American" social structure that was somehow larger than all subgroups and was ethnically neutral. Were they, too, not Americans? But they found to their dismay that at the primary group level a neutral American social structure was a mirage. What at a distance seemed to be a quasi-public edifice flying only the all-inclusive flag of American nationality turned out on closer inspection to be the clubhouse of a particular ethnic group—the white Anglo-Saxon Protestants, its operation shot through with the premises and expectations of its parental ethnicity. In these terms, the desirability of whatever invitation was grudg-

---

[29] Joshua A. Fishman, "Childhood Indoctrination for Minority-Group Membership and the Quest for Minority-Group Biculturism in America," in Oscar Handlin, ed., *Group Life in America* (Cambridge, Harvard University Press, forthcoming).

ingly extended to those of other ethnic backgrounds could only become a considerably attenuated one.

With the racial minorities, there was not even the pretense of an invitation. Negroes, to take the most salient example, have for the most part been determinedly barred from the cliques, social clubs, and churches of white America. Consequently, with due allowance for internal class differences, they have constructed their own network of organizations and institutions, their own "social world." There are now many vested interests served by the preservation of this separate communal life, and doubtless many Negroes are psychologically comfortable in it, even though at the same time they keenly desire that discrimination in such areas as employment, education, housing, and public accommodations be eliminated. However, the ideological attachment of Negroes to their communal separation is not conspicuous. Their sense of identification with ancestral African national cultures is virtually nonexistent, although Pan-Africanism engages the interest of some intellectuals and although "black nationalist" and "black racist" fringe groups have recently made an appearance at the other end of the communal spectrum. As for their religion, they are either Protestant or Catholic (overwhelmingly the former). Thus, there are no "logical" ideological reasons for their separate communality; dual social structures are created solely by the dynamics of prejudice and discrimination, rather than being reinforced by the ideological commitments of the minority itself.

Structural assimilation, then, has turned out to be the rock on which the ships of Anglo-conformity and the melting pot have foundered. To understand that behavioral assimilation (or acculturation) without massive structural intermingling in primary relationships has been the dominant motif in the American experience of creating and developing a nation out of diverse peoples is to comprehend the most essential sociological fact of that experience. It is against the background of "structural pluralism" that strategies of strengthening intergroup harmony, reducing ethnic discrimination and prejudice, and maintaining the rights of both those who stay within and those who venture beyond their ethnic boundaries must be thoughtfully devised.

PART THREE

THE TWENTIETH CENTURY

JOHN CHYNOWETH BURNHAM

PSYCHIATRY, PSYCHOLOGY, AND
THE PROGRESSIVE MOVEMENT

While the Progressive movement was primarily political in its emphasis, its ramifications touched every area of American life. Simply because progressivism was not confined to politics, historians cannot limit their study of the Progressive mentality to those people with a specifically political orientation. John Burnham's article, therefore, performs a dual service. It not only introduces the reader to aspects of the important and little-known history of psychiatry in America, but it relates that science's development to various aspects of the Progressive movement, thereby adding a new dimension to our understanding of that era and its thought. Morton White, Social Thought in America * (1949), provides important insights into other areas of intellectual development during the Progressive Era.*

R ecent interpretations have made the Progressive movement of the pre-1917 era one of the most interesting topics in American history. Much of this new scholarship represents the search of modern liberals for their own political identity. Currently a more thoroughgoing reinterpretation is being undertaken by a group of historians who are studying *social control* as the Progressives visualized it and put it into action.[1] This latest research on Progressivism ranges far beyond what is essentially political history.

A study of the two professions dealing with the human psyche, psychiatry and psychology, before World War I, contributes to a broader view of Progressivism by suggesting the hypothesis that the Progressive movement was not limited to politics, economics and social philosophy, but pervaded all of the endeavors of middle-class Americans. If the physicians and scientists of the mind were prototypical, an examination of the rest of national life—as it is ordinarily subdivided—will also show that early twentieth-century Americans in their occupations and other social capacities operated on "Progressive" assumptions or at least were aware of the relevance of their activities to "Progressive" ends.[2] The basis for the hypothesis is the striking fact that reformers in psychiatry and psychology shared with reformers in politics and economics a set of social assumptions that identified them all as Progressives.

From the more traditional research on the subject we already know the suppositions of Progressivism. The essence of the movement was the "firm belief that to a considerable degree man could make and remake his own world."[3] Although the Progressives did not all believe that man is inherently good, they agreed at least that the human being is malleable. The responsibility for the ills of the world rested, therefore, largely or entirely upon the social environment in which the individual lived.[4] Although modern environmentalism grew out of Darwinian thinking, the Progressives believed that

---

[1] For a partial treatment of social control, see Stow Persons, *American Minds, A History of Ideas* (New York: Henry Holt & Co., 1958), chap. xxv, and Henry F. May, *The End of American Innocence, A Study of the First Years of Our Own Time, 1912–1917* (New York: Alfred A. Knopf, 1959), pp. 154–58.

[2] Each area also had its conservatives analogous to Aldrich and Taft.

[3] George E. Mowry, *The Era of Theodore Roosevelt, 1900–1912* (New York: Harper & Bros., 1958), pp. 17–18, 37.

[4] *Ibid.*, pp. 49–51. David W. Noble, *The Paradox of Progressive Thought* (Minneapolis: University of Minnesota Press, 1958), summarizes the views of the high priest of Progressivism, Herbert Croly, on the subject, p. 62.

FROM John Chynoweth Burnham, "Psychiatry, Psychology, and the Progressive Movement," *American Quarterly*, Philadelphia: University of Pennsylvania, 1960, Vol. XII (Winter 1960), pp. 457–65. Copyright 1960, Trustees of the University of Pennsylvania. Reprinted by permission.

man could change his own environment and so reconstruct both societies and individuals.[5]

The most elusive element in the basic social thinking of the Progressives was—who should tamper with the environment and so foreordain the fates of his fellow men? It turned out, inevitably, that the Progressives themselves were to be the self-appointed arbiters of man's destiny. They were able, literate and largely professional groups, accustomed to the role of leadership and, like Theodore Roosevelt, unafraid of it.[6]

The Progressives were consciously motivated by altruism. Direction was to come from the Man of Good Will who had transcended his own interests; he governed by right of his moral superiority.[7] The Calvinistic background of many Progressives indicated a direct relationship as well as an analogy between Progressive leadership and the stewardship of the elect. Social responsibility inspired in many Progressives a feeling of guilt for all of the evil that a faulty society had caused, and the sophisticated with New England consciences equated righteousness with social reform.[8]

These, then, were the elements of Progressivism—optimism, environmentalism, moral fervor and leadership by an enlightened elite. None of them was new in American thought, but at the time they took on a special meaning because of the frequency with which they appeared and because of their application to social control. Although most obvious in political and social thinking, they also characterized, first, the psychotherapy movement in the psychiatry of that day and, second, the revolt of the behaviorists in contemporaneous psychology. In each case it turned out that an autonomous historical development within a science contained the same elements as a new political and social movement.

Psychiatry (which at that time included neurology) provides a nice ex-

---

[5] Eric F. Goldman, *Rendezvous with Destiny, A History of Modern American Reform* (New York: Alfred A. Knopf, 1952), p. 94; Mowry, *Era of Theodore Roosevelt,* p. 50. Such thinking was not far distant from other doctrines of the times, such as an economic interpretation of history.

[6] Richard Hofstadter, *The Age of Reform, From Bryan to F. D. R.* (New York: Alfred A. Knopf, 1955), has been pre-eminent in suggesting as a major factor in Progressivism the changing status of certain middle-class groups, chap. iv; and Mowry, *Era of Theodore Roosevelt,* has documented the middle-class nature of Progressive leadership, pp. 85 ff. (Psychiatrists and psychologists in general belonged to this dominant part of the middle class.) The Progressive reliance on the executive and the cult of the strong man were notable contemporaneous developments; *ibid.,* p. 88; Goldman, *Rendezvous with Destiny,* p. 80; Noble, *Paradox of Progressive Thought,* p. 74. Even the Progressives' faith in democracy was dependent upon their providing a proper environment for that democracy. See the sophisticated discussion of Progressivism in May, *End of American Innocence,* pp. 21–29.

[7] Hofstadter, *Age of Reform,* p. 258; compare the summary in Mowry, *Era of Theodore Roosevelt,* pp. 104–5.

[8] *Ibid.,* p. 87; Hofstadter, *Age of Reform,* pp. 204–6, 208–12.

ample. In the late nineteenth century, physicians who dealt with the mentally ill usually were "organicists" who adhered strictly to scientific materialism. They believed that behavior and thinking were but the expression of the functioning of the nervous system and that physical defects or diseases were at the bottom of all mental diseases. The organicists performed autopsies on the brains of deceased mental patients, searching for evidence of lesions or brain damage. The work of this group was vindicated by the discovery that a common type of insanity was caused by syphilis. Yet nothing is quite as depressing as the literature of psychiatry-neurology around the turn of the century—endless reports of post-mortem examinations of demented brains and discussions of the problems of keeping and managing the insane. The psychiatrist was expected to do little more than deliver a prognosis of the melancholy course of the disease and then supervise the housing, feeding and restraining of the patient.[9] Well into the twentieth century the three main causes of insanity were thought to be heredity, alcohol and syphilis.[10]

By the 1890's a great deal of discussion of hysteria (disease symptoms occurring in the absence of physical disease), hypnotism and faith healing, plus a rebellion against the dreary routine of prognosis and commitment, led to a revival of attention to so-called "moral treatment." Every experienced physician knew the importance of the patient's state of mind for the treatment of illness, and early in the first decade of the century, following developments in continental Europe, American medical practitioners took up the fad of psychotherapy. In large part the psychotherapy movement was a formal recognition of the medical value of a constructive intellectual and emotional environment, especially in the treatment of what we would now call neurotic diseases.[11]

Strict organicists who believed that insanity was caused by heredity, alcohol and syphilis were not necessarily outside of the Progressive movement. There were reform groups dedicated to the elimination of the baneful effects of all three. The eugenics movement, advocating the sterilization of insane, defective and criminal persons in order to improve the race, represented the Progressive attempt to deal with that part of man which was not malleable.[12] Many psychiatrists supported the efforts of the prohibitionists to remove

---

[9] The cure rate was about twenty per cent; A. I. Noble, "The Curability of Insanity," *American Journal of Insanity,* LXIX (1913), 715–17.

[10] E.g., H. M. Swift, "Insanity and Race," *American Journal of Insanity,* LXX (1913), 154.

[11] See Walter Bromberg, *Man Above Humanity, A History of Psychotherapy* (Philadelphia: J. B. Lippincott Co., 1954), chap. viii.

[12] Mark Hughlin Haller, "American Eugenics: Heredity and Social Thought, 1870–1930" (Ann Arbor: University Microfilms, 1960), especially pp. 4, 157–58, shows how Progressives' assumptions of environmentalism did not deter them from supporting the eugenics movement.

from commerce what they regarded as social poison. And one of the lasting reforms of Progressivism was effected by the crusaders (many of them physicians) who opposed both prostitution and promiscuity with the powerful argument that only prevention could control venereal diseases.[13] These were typical Progressive reform movements, but Progressive psychiatrists fought their finest—and most fundamental—battles in the name of psychotherapy.

Basically the physicians who employed or advocated psychotherapy in any of its many forms were unwilling to accept the pessimistic attitude of current psychiatry and neurology. Under the competitive pressure of Christian Science and other faith cures that were demonstrably effective, these physicians ignored materialism and undertook to cure patients by whatever method worked. Effective psychotherapy required hope—indeed, faith in the patient's ability to cure himself. C. P. Oberndorf, one of the first psychoanalytic psychotherapists in the United States, later attributed his early successes in treatment to his enthusiasm and to his confidence in the new tools with which he worked. Others using quite different methods of psychotherapy likewise showed an optimism that set them apart from conservatives in the psychiatric profession.[14]

The basis for the new hope was the conviction that an individual's behavior was determined—to a large extent—by his environment. A Boston physician in 1909 defined psychoneurotics "as people who, for one reason or another, are not well adapted to their environment." The conclusion was obvious; as one psychiatrist observed in 1911, "If the mental habits and the surroundings of an individual are largely responsible for the onset of a psychosis, we can look forward to accomplishments which may rival the success achieved in the crusade against tuberculosis." [15]

The psychotherapists' primary objective became, then, to re-educate the patient so that he adapted himself to his environment, adjusted himself to the reality that surrounded him. Thoughtful physicians quickly perceived that the largest part of the environment that required the patient to change his conduct was the society in which he lived, including his family. A New York asylum superintendent reported in 1913 that "The patient is no longer regarded simply as a separate individual, but also as a social unit, whose cure

---

[13] For somewhat different views, see Louis Filler, *Crusaders for American Liberalism* (2d ed., Yellow Springs, Ohio: Antioch Press, 1950), chap. xxii, and Harold Underwood Faulkner, *The Quest for Social Justice, 1898–1914* (New York: The Macmillan Co., 1931), pp. 159–62.

[14] C. P. Oberndorf, *A History of Psychoanalysis in America* (New York: Grune & Stratton, 1953), p. 152. E.g., see the revealing paper, Charles W. Burr, "The Prevention of Insanity and Degeneracy," *American Journal of Insanity*, LXXIV (1917), 409–24, and especially the discussion, 422–23.

[15] Richard C. Cabot, "The Analysis and Modification of Environment," *Psychotherapy*, III, No. 3 (1909), 5. James V. May, "The Modern Trend of Psychiatry," *Interstate Medical Journal*, XVIII (1911), 1098.

cannot be considered complete until he has been restored to social adaptability and efficiency." [16] At the same time physicians saw the possibility of altering not just the patient but also his environment. Since the important environment was social, the forward-looking psychiatrists found themselves committed to social meliorism, and therefore were Progressives indeed.[17]

The environment of children was especially a target for the social-reformer psychiatrists. Under the influence of early Freudian ideas, they asserted that childhood experiences were of overwhelming importance in later life. The most influential of these psychiatrists was William Healy, a conventionally trained specialist in nervous and mental diseases, who gave up his practice (at considerable sacrifice) in 1909 to work with juvenile delinquents in Chicago. Through his own experience with the motivations of youthful lawbreakers, Healy came to a strongly psychoanalytic point of view. His works (richly illustrated with interesting case histories) persuaded untold numbers of persons that favorable changes in the social environments of youngsters could prevent delinquency and promote not only mental health but social progress.[18]

The presumptuousness of psychiatrists in deciding how the world should be run was not different from that of other Progressives. Like Dr. George Van Ness Dearborn of Boston, physicians appealed to "the sound principle of *noblesse oblige.*" Moreover, as doctors they dealt with matters of life and death, and as psychotherapists in daily practice they undertook to interfere in and change the attitudes and ways of life of their patients. They were, therefore, accustomed to the responsibilities of leadership. As early as 1907 E. W. Taylor of Boston pointed out that the role of the physician was expanding and that he had to look after the social as well as the physical welfare of his

---

[16] E.g., see the systematic work of Morton Price, "The Subconscious Setting of Ideas in Relation to the Pathology of the Psychoneuroses," *The Journal of Abnormal Psychology,* XI (1916), 1–18. William L. Russell, "The Widening Field of Practical Psychiatry," *American Journal of Insanity,* LXX (1913), 460. E.g., William A. White, *The Principles of Mental Hygiene* (New York: The Macmillan Co., 1917), p. 316.

[17] E.g., C. C. Wholey, in *The Journal of the American Medical Association,* LXII (1914), 1036. Thomas W. Salmon, "Some New Fields in Neurology and Psychiatry," *The Journal of Nervous and Mental Disease,* XLVI (1917), 90–99.

[18] E.g., William Healy, *The Individual Delinquent: A Text-Book of Diagnosis and Prognosis for All Concerned in Understanding Offenders* (Boston: Little, Brown & Co., 1915); William Healy, *Mental Conflicts and Misconduct* (Boston: Little, Brown & Co., 1917), especially chap. xvii. Healy's case affords evidence of a situation in which political Progressives had a direct influence on the development of psychiatry. In an interview with the writer Dr. Healy remarked that the method of studying children (integrating medical, social, psychometric and psychiatric studies of a single individual) which yielded him such rich results was suggested in large part by a group of social reformers associated with Hull House and led by Jane Addams and Julia Lathrop, two of the best-known Progressives. The Hull House reformers found financial support for the work and invited Healy to undertake it.

patients. He was becoming, said Lewellys Barker of Johns Hopkins, the "moral director" of his patients.[19]

A number of theories were used by the psychotherapists in rationalizing their attempts to recast the world. A New York neurologist who advocated a type of psychotherapy called suggestion proposed in 1912 that physicians combat the psychic infections of civilization—noxious suggestion—with psychotherapy, that is, with suggestion that would foster what he believed to be the better cultural elements (surely an ambiguous goal for social control).[20] Most Americans were not strong on systematics, and hope sufficed to nourish many of their opinions; only those who used the most radical of the psychotherapies, psychoanalysis, invoked a fairly consistent theory to justify their reformism.[21]

The psychoanalysts, whose alleged commitment to a so-called "sexual" view of the world was notorious, illustrated most strikingly the intense moralism of the Progressive psychiatrists. By means of sublimation man's evil would be turned into good, they asserted; even the grossest sexual perversions would become artistic creations and love for fellow man. James Jackson Putnam, scion of the Puritans, married to a Cabot, and professor of neurology at Harvard, wrote: "It may well be urged that psychoanalysis does not take the cultivation of social ideals as an end for which it should directly strive. Technically, this is true. But psychoanalysts know well the evils that attend the over-assertion of personal desires, cultivated too exclusively in and for themselves, and the importance of the opposite course follows by inference." In their long, conventional textbook on nervous and mental diseases, two of the leading psychiatrists of the country, Smith Ely Jelliffe and William A. White, reminded their readers of the "socially useful ends" of psychotherapy. As sophisticated about right and wrong as the most advanced intellectual rebels of the time, Progressive psychiatrists found altruism medically justifiable.[22]

---

[19] George Van Ness Dearborn, *The Influence of Joy* (Boston: Little, Brown & Co., 1916), p. 35. E. W. Taylor, "The Attitude of the Medical Profession Toward the Psychotherapeutic Movement," *Boston Medical and Surgical Journal,* CLVII (1907), 845–46. Lewellys F. Barker, "On the Psychic Treatment of Some of the Functional Neuroses," *International Clinics,* I (17th ser., 1907), 13, 15, 17.

[20] George W. Jacoby, *Suggestion and Psychotherapy* (New York: Charles Scribner's Sons, 1912), chap. ii, especially pp. 207, 218–19.

[21] E.g., J. T. W. Rowe, "Is Dementia Praecox the 'New Peril' in Psychiatry?" *American Journal of Insanity,* LXIII (1907), 389, 393. Even most American psychoanalysists in this early period, it must be admitted, had less regard for theoretical consistency than their European counterparts.

[22] James J. Putnam, "The Psychoanalytic Movement," *Scientific American Supplement,* LXXVIII (1914), 391, 402. Freud commented regretfully on Putnam's inclination to make psychoanalysis "the servant of moral aims." Sigmund Freud, *An Autobiographical Study,* trans. by James Strachey (2d ed., London: Hogarth Press, 1946), p. 94. Smith Ely Jelliffe and William A. White, *Diseases of the Nervous System, A*

Some of the psychotherapists were psychologists who had abandoned strictly experimental psychology. Like the psychiatrists, these men tended to be lay preachers who sought to reform the world by means of re-education and retraining. The scholarly psychologist of Boston, L. E. Emerson, for example, repeatedly pointed out the ethical and reform possibilities of Freudianism. More orthodox psychologists were likewise led, when dealing with matters outside of experimental psychology, to dilate on the possibilities of fostering the "higher aspirations" of men through psychotherapy and psychoanalysis.[23] The best example of the foregoing is the famous book of E. B. Holt of Harvard on *The Freudian Wish and Its Place in Ethics*.[24] Holt asserted that Freudian psychology justified the ancient belief that knowledge is virtue, with the implication that evil need not be always with us. Holt saw man as an individual interacting with his environment and, significantly, utilized not only psychoanalytic psychology but also behaviorism. For within orthodox experimental psychology the Progressives were those who adhered to behaviorism.[25]

For years psychologists had been aware of ferment and discontent in their profession. Most of the criticism centered around the fact that dry, descriptive academic psychology was not useful. Then John B. Watson took leadership of the revolt of the behavioristic psychologists. They dispensed with consciousness and introspective methods and studied the human organism in its environment, using the methods of animal psychology. Watson began his behaviorist manifesto in 1913 by making the purpose of the revolt clear: "Psychology as the behaviorist views it is a purely objective experimental branch of natural science. Its theoretical goal is the *prediction and control of behavior*."[26] Here was usefulness with a vengeance.

The behaviorists had observed that animals' innate patterns of action could be modified by training, and the young Turks soon tended to embrace a radical environmentalism. Most psychologists more or less covertly subscribed to an instinct psychology such as that of William James or William

---

Text-Book of Neurology and Psychiatry (2d ed., Philadelphia: Lee & Febiger, 1917), p. 98. James J. Putnam, "On Some of the Broader Issues of the Psychoanalytic Movement," *The American Journal of the Medical Sciences*, CXLVII (1914), 397–402.

[23] E.g., Ernest K. Lindley, in *The Journal of the Indiana State Medical Association*, IX (1916), 7; Stephen S. Colvin, "What Dreams Mean," *The Independent*, LXXII (1912), 847.

[24] Edwin B. Holt, *The Freudian Wish and Its Place in Ethics* (New York: Henry Holt & Co., 1915).

[25] The social psychologies of men such as G. H. Mead and J. Mark Baldwin were too close to social philosophy to be properly included here. A case might be made, however, for including G. Stanley Hall and the genetic psychology of that time.

[26] John B. Watson, "Psychology as the Behaviorist Views It," *The Psychological Review*, XX (1913), 158; see also 168–69, 177. Italics added. For an interesting variation with Freudian elements, see John B. Watson and J. J. B. Morgan, "Emotional Reactions and Psychological Experimentation," *The American Journal of Psychology*, XXVIII (1917), 163–74.

McDougall. Now out of the laboratory itself came a challenge to essentially conservative nativism.[27] One would misunderstand behaviorism if he overlooked the explicit meliorism involved in the movement. Watson himself took pains to clarify the relation of behaviorism to social control, and the more alert members of the profession also realized what was involved.[28] The goal of behaviorism was, after all, merely a restatement of the classical purpose of any science including psychology: to predict. And prediction, to the Progressive behaviorists as to other scientists, involved control.[29]

The elements of Progressivism thus appeared as conspicuous features of reform movements within psychology and psychiatry. The mass of material in both sciences remained, as before, primarily descriptive. But the social attitudes of some of the practitioners of the two disciplines led to profound changes in the very nature of psychiatry and psychology, just as Progressivism left its mark on American political and social institutions.

Progressive psychiatry and Progressive psychology were uniquely American phenomena. The European professional literature was devoid of the optimistic social reformism of the New World versions of these disciplines. Psychologist Carl Rahn shrewdly epitomized the situation in his observation about psychoanalysis: "Where the European follower of Freud emphasizes the point that the formulation of the symbol is indicative of a 'renunciation of reality,'" wrote Rahn, "the American disciple sees it as a 'carrier of energy' exquisitely fitted for increasing man's control over his environment. . . ."[30]

One can easily account for the rise of psychotherapy and the rise of behaviorism in terms of the internal histories of psychiatry and psychology. But the fact that these movements coincided in time with the Progressive social reform movement, and the fact that social control was an aim of reformers in both politics and science, can be accounted for only by treating the developments in psychiatry and psychology and in all other middle-class endeavors as part and parcel of the Progressive movement itself.[31] The historian

---

27 E.g., see M. E. Haggerty, "The Laws of Learning," *The Psychological Review*, XX (1913), 411; Howard C. Warren, "The Mental and the Physical," *ibid.*, XXI (1914), 99.

28 E.g., see John B. Watson, "An Attempted Formulation of the Scope of Behavior Psychology," *ibid.*, XXIV (1917), 329–52; A. P. Weiss, "Relation Between Functional and Behavior Psychology," *ibid.*, pp. 353–68.

29 See John Dewey, "The Need for Social Psychology," *ibid.*, pp. 274–75.

30 See Edwin G. Boring, *A History of Experimental Psychology* (2d ed., New York: Appleton-Century-Crofts, Inc., 1950), pp. 642–43. Carl Rahn, in a review of W. A. White, *Mechanisms of Character Formation*, in *The Psychological Bulletin*, XIV (1917), 327. The absence of a British counterpart is especially striking in view of the nearly contemporaneous reform movement there.

31 The intellectual spokesmen for Progressivism were well aware of the possibilities of the new movements in psychiatry and psychology; e.g., see Walter Lippmann, *A Preface to Politics* (New York: M. Kennerley, 1913).

will discover the full dynamics of Progressivism only when he examines not just politics, economics and social philosophy, but all aspects of American life.[32]

---

[32] Even though not focusing on Progressivism, May, *End of American Innocence*, gives an idea of the light that can be shed on the movement by an approach such as the one suggested here.

JOHN WILLIAM WARD

THE MEANING OF LINDBERGH'S FLIGHT

The articles by Cawelti and Hofstadter in Part II reflect both the Americans' faith in progress and penchant for change and their tendency to look at the past as a golden age whose symbols and values must not be allowed to perish. Thus Horatio Alger attempted less to herald the birth of a new age than to keep alive the values of an old one, and the American farmer marched into the industrial era holding aloft the symbols of his yeoman past. As Ward points out, this duality, this mingling of progress and nostalgia for the past, has been an important theme throughout American history. Nor is this theme played out, as even a cursory study of our own age would show. Indeed, Ward's analysis of the reaction to Lindbergh's flight in the 1920's places these conflicting attitudes in sharp relief while helping to illuminate the adulation and rhetoric surrounding the American astronauts of the 1960's.

Other aspects of this theme, as exemplified in the nineteenth century, are examined in Leo Marx, The Machine in the Garden * (*1964*).*

On Friday, May 20, 1927, at 7:52 a.m., Charles A. Lindbergh took off in a silver-winged monoplane and flew from the United States to France. With this flight Lindbergh became the first man to fly alone across the Atlantic Ocean. The log of flight 33 of "The Spirit of St. Louis" reads: "Roosevelt Field, Long Island, New York, to Le Bourget Aerodrome, Paris, France. 33 hrs. 30 min." Thus was the fact of Lindbergh's achievement easily put down. But the meaning of Lindbergh's flight lay hidden in the next sentence of the log: "(Fuselage fabric badly torn by souvenir hunters.)"

When Lindbergh landed at Le Bourget he is supposed to have said, "Well, we've done it." A contemporary writer asked "Did what?" Lindbergh "had no idea of what he had done. He thought he had simply flown from New York to Paris. What he had really done was something far greater. He had fired the imagination of mankind." From the moment of Lindbergh's flight people recognized that something more was involved than the mere fact of the physical leap from New York to Paris. "Lindbergh," wrote John Erskine, "served as a metaphor." But what the metaphor stood for was not easy to say. The *New York Times* remarked then that "there has been no complete and satisfactory explanation of the enthusiasm and acclaim for Captain Lindbergh." Looking back on the celebration of Lindbergh, one can see now that the American people were trying to understand Lindbergh's flight, to grasp its meaning, and through it, perhaps, to grasp the meaning of their own experience. Was the flight the achievement of a heroic, solitary, unaided individual? Or did the flight represent the triumph of the machine, the success of an industrially organized society? These questions were central to the meaning of Lindbergh's flight. They were also central to the lives of the people who made Lindbergh their hero.

The flight demanded attention in its own right, of course, quite apart from whatever significance it might have. Lindbergh's story had all the makings of great drama. Since 1919 there had been a standing prize of $25,000 to be awarded to the first aviator who could cross the Atlantic in either direction between the United States and France in a heavier-than-air craft. In the spring of 1927 there promised to be what the *New York Times* called "the most spectacular race ever held—3,600 miles over the open sea to Paris." The scene was dominated by veteran pilots. On the European side were the French aces, Nungesser and Coli; on the American side, Commander Richard E. Byrd, in a big tri-motored Fokker monoplane, led a group of contestants. Besides Byrd, who had already flown over the North Pole, there were Commander Davis, flying a ship named in honor of the American Legion which had put up $100,000 to finance his attempt,

FROM John William Ward, "The Meaning of Lindbergh's Flight," *American Quarterly*, Philadelphia: University of Pennsylvania, 1958, Vol. X (Spring, 1958), pp. 3–16. Copyright 1958, Trustees of the University of Pennsylvania. Reprinted by permission.

Clarence Chamberlin, who had already set a world's endurance record of more than fifty-one hours in the air in a Bellanca tri-motored plane, and Captain René Fonck, the French war ace, who had come to America to fly a Sikorsky aircraft. The hero was unheard of and unknown. He was on the West Coast supervising the construction of a single-engined plane to cost only ten thousand dollars.

Then fate played its part. It seemed impossible that Lindbergh could get his plane built and east to New York in time to challenge his better equipped and more famous rivals. But in quick succession a series of disasters cleared his path. On April 16, Commander Byrd's "America" crashed on its test flight, crushing the leg of Floyd Bennett who was one of the crew and injuring Byrd's hand and wrist. On April 24, Clarence Chamberlin cracked up in his Bellanca, not seriously, but enough to delay his plans. Then on April 26, Commander Davis and his co-pilot lost their lives as the "American Legion" crashed on its final test flight. In ten days, accidents had stopped all of Lindbergh's American rivals. Nungesser and Coli, however, took off in their romantically named ship, "The White Bird," from Le Bourget on May 8. The world waited and Lindbergh, still on the West Coast, decided to try to fly the Pacific. But Nungesser and Coli were never seen again. As rumors filled the newspapers, as reports came in that "The White Bird" was seen over Newfoundland, over Boston, over the Atlantic, it soon became apparent that Nungesser and Coli had failed, dropping to their death in some unknown grave. Disaster had touched every ship entered in the trans-Atlantic race.

Now, with the stage cleared, Lindbergh entered. He swooped across the continent in two great strides, landing only at St. Louis. The first leg of his flight established a new distance record but all eyes were on the Atlantic and the feat received little notice. Curiously, the first time Lindbergh appeared in the headlines of the New York papers was Friday, the thirteenth. By this time Byrd and Chamberlin were ready once again but the weather had closed in and kept all planes on the ground. Then, after a week of fretful waiting, on the night of May 19, on the way into New York to see "Rio Rita," Lindbergh received a report that the weather was breaking over the ocean. He hurried back to Roosevelt Field to haul his plane out onto a wet, dripping runway. After mechanics painfully loaded the plane's gas by hand, the wind shifted, as fate played its last trick. A muddy runway and an adverse wind. Whatever the elements, whatever the fates, the decisive act is the hero's, and Lindbergh made his choice. Providing a chorus to the action, the *Herald Tribune* reported that Lindbergh lifted the overloaded plane into the sky "by his indomitable will alone."

The parabola of the action was as clean as the arc of Lindbergh's flight. The drama should have ended with the landing of "The Spirit of St. Louis" at Le Bourget. That is where Lindbergh wanted it to end. In *"WE,"* written immediately after the flight, and in *The Spirit of St. Louis,* written twenty-six years later, Lindbergh chose to end his accounts there. But the flight turned out to be only the first act in the part Lindbergh was to play.

Lindbergh was so innocent of his future that on his flight he carried letters of introduction. The hysterical response, first of the French and then of his own countrymen, had been no part of his careful plans. In *"WE,"* after Lindbergh's narrative of the flight, the publisher wrote: "When Lindbergh came to tell the story of his welcome at Paris, London, Brussels, Washington, New York, and St. Louis he found himself up against a tougher problem than flying the Atlantic." So another writer completed the account in the third person. He suggested that "the reason Lindbergh's story is different is that when his plane came to a halt on Le Bourget field that black night in Paris, Lindbergh the man kept on going. The phenomenon of Lindbergh took its start with his flight across the ocean; but in its entirety it was almost as distinct from that flight as though he had never flown at all."

Lindbergh's private life ended with his flight to Paris. The drama was no longer his, it was the public's. "The outburst of unanimous acclaim was at once personal and symbolic," said the *American Review of Reviews*. From the moment of success there were two Lindberghs, the private Lindbergh and the public Lindbergh. The latter was the construction of the imagination of Lindbergh's time, fastened on to an unwilling person. The tragedy of Lindbergh's career is that he could never accept the role assigned him. He always believed he might keep his two lives separate. But from the moment he landed at Le Bourget, Lindbergh became, as the *New Republic* noted, *"ours. . . .* He is no longer permitted to be himself. He is US personified. He is the United States." Ambassador Herrick introduced Lindbergh to the French, saying, "This young man from out of the West brings you better than anything else the spirit of America," and wired to President Coolidge, "Had we searched all America we could not have found a better type than young Lindbergh to represent the spirit and high purpose of our people." This was Lindbergh's fate, to be a type. A writer in the *North American Review* felt that Lindbergh represented "the dominant American character," he "images the best" about the United States. And an ecstatic female in the *American Magazine,* who began by saying that Lindbergh "is a sort of symbol. . . . He is the dream that is in our hearts," concluded that the American public responded so wildly to Lindbergh because of "the thrill of possessing, in him, our dream of what *we* really and truly want to be." The act of possession was so complete that articles since have attempted to discover the "real" Lindbergh, that enigmatic and taciturn figure behind the public mask. But it is no less difficult to discern the features of the public Lindbergh, that symbolic figure who presented to the imagination of his time all the yearnings and buried desires of its dream for itself.

Lindbergh's flight came at the end of a decade marked by social and political corruption and by a sense of moral loss. The heady idealism of the First World War had been succeeded by a deep cynicism as to the war's real purpose. The naive belief that virtue could be legislated was violated by the vast discrepancy between the law and the social habits of prohibition. A philosophy of relativism had become the uneasy rationale of a nation which had formerly believed in moral absolutes. The newspapers agreed that Lindbergh's chief worth was his spiritual and moral value. His story was held to be "in striking contrast with the sordid unhallowed themes that have for months steeped the imaginations and thinking of the people." Or, as another had it, "there is good reason why people should hail Lindbergh and give him honor. He stands out in a grubby world as an inspiration."

Lindbergh gave the American people a glimpse of what they liked to think themselves to be at a time when they feared they had deserted their own vision of themselves. The grubbiness of the twenties had a good deal to do with the shining quality of Lindbergh's success, especially when one remembers that Lindbergh's flight was not as unexampled as our national memory would have it. The Atlantic was not unconquered when Lindbergh flew. A British dirigible had twice crossed the Atlantic before 1919 and on May 8 of that year three naval seaplanes left Rockaway, New York, and one, the NC-4 manned by a crew of five, got through to Plymouth, England. A month later, Captain John Alcock, an Englishman, with Arthur W. Browne, an American, flew the first heavier-than-air land plane across the Atlantic nonstop, from Newfoundland to Ireland, to win twice the money Lindbergh did, a prize of $50,000 offered by the London *Daily Mail*. Alcock's and Browne's misfortune was to land in a soft and somnolent Irish peat bog instead of before the cheering thousands of London or Paris. Or perhaps they should have flown in 1927.

The wild medley of public acclaim and the Homeric strivings of editors make one realize that the response to Lindbergh involved a mass ritual in which America celebrated itself more than it celebrated Lindbergh. Lindbergh's flight was the occasion of a public act of regeneration in which the nation momentarily rededicated itself to something, the loss of which was keenly felt. It was said again and again that "Lindy" taught America "to lift its eyes up to Heaven." Heywood Broun, in his column in the *New York World,* wrote that this "tall young man raised up and let us see the potentialities of the human spirit." Broun felt that the flight proved that, though "we are small and fragile," it "isn't true that there is no health in us." Lindbergh's flight provided the moment, but the meaning of the flight is to be found in the deep and pervasive need for renewal which the flight brought to the surface of public feeling. When Lindbergh appeared at the nation's capital, the *Washington Post* observed, "He was given that frenzied acclaim which comes from the depths of the people." In New York, where 4,000,000 people saw him, a reporter wrote that the dense and vociferous crowds were swept, as Lindbergh passed, "with an emotion tense and inflammable." The *Literary Digest* suggested that the answer to the hero-worship of Lindbergh would "throw an interesting light on the psychology of our times and of the American people."

The *Nation* noted about Lindbergh that "there was something lyric as well as heroic about the apparition of this young Lochinvar who suddenly came out of the West and who flew all unarmed and all alone. It is the kind of stuff which the ancient Greeks would have worked into a myth and the medieval Scots into a border ballad. . . . But what we have in the case of Lindbergh is an actual, an heroic and an exhaustively exposed experience which exists by suggestion in the form of poetry." The *Nation* quickly qualified its statement by observing that reporters were as far as possible from being poets and concluded that the discrepancy between the fact and the celebration of it was not poetry, perhaps, but "magic on a vast scale." Yet the *Nation* might have clung to its insight that the public meaning of Lindbergh's flight was somehow poetic. The vast publicity about Lindbergh corresponds in one vital particular with the poetic vision. Poetry, said William Butler Yeats, contains opposites; so did Lindbergh. Lindbergh did not mean one thing, he meant many things. The image of itself which America contemplated in the public person of Lindbergh was full of conflict; it was, in a word, dramatic.

To heighten the drama, Lindbergh did it alone. He was the "lone eagle" and a full exploration of that fact takes one deep into the emotional meaning of his success. Not only the *Nation* found Sir Walter Scott's lines on Lochinvar appropriate: "he rode all unarmed and he rode all alone." Newspapers and magazines were deluged with amateur poems that vindicated one rhymester's wry comment, "Go conquer the perils / That lurk in the skies— / And you'll get bum poems / Right up to your eyes." The *New York Times,* that alone received more than two hundred poems, observed in trying to summarize the poetic deluge that "the fact that he flew alone made the strongest impression." Another favorite tribute was Kipling's "The Winners," with its refrain, "He travels the fastest who travels alone." The others who had conquered the Atlantic and those like Byrd and Chamberlin who were trying at the same time were not traveling alone and they hardly rode unarmed. Other than Lindbergh, all the contestants in the trans-Atlantic race had unlimited backing, access to the best planes, and all were working in teams, carrying at least one co-pilot to share the long burden of flying the plane. So a writer in the New York *Sun,* in a poem called "The Flying Fool," a nickname that Lindbergh despised, celebrated Lindbergh's flight: ". . . no kingly plane for him; / No endless data, comrades, moneyed chums; / No boards, no councils, no directors grim— / He plans ALONE . . . and takes luck as it comes."

Upon second thought, it must seem strange that the long distance flight of an airplane, the achievement of a highly advanced and organized technology, should be the occasion for hymns of praise to the solitary unaided man. Yet the National Geographic Society, when it presented a medal to Lindbergh, wrote on the presentation scroll, "Courage, when it goes alone, has ever caught men's imaginations," and compared Lindbergh to Robinson Crusoe and the trailmakers in our own West. But Lindbergh and Robinson Crusoe, the one in his helmet and fur-lined flying coat and the other in his wild goatskins, do not easily co-exist. Even if Robinson Crusoe did have a tidy capital investment in the form of a well-stocked shipwreck, he still did not have a ten thousand dollar machine under him.

Lindbergh, in nearly every remark about his flight and in his own writings about it, resisted the tendency to exploit the flight as the achievement of an individual. He never said "I," he always said "We." The plane was not to go unrecognized. Nevertheless, there persisted a tendency to seize upon the flight as a way of celebrating the self-sufficient individual, so that among many others an Ohio newspaper could describe Lindbergh as this "self-contained, self-reliant, courageous young man [who] ranks among the great pioneers of history." The strategy here was a common one, to make Lindbergh a "pioneer" and thus to link him with a long and vital tradition of individualism in the American experience. Colonel Theodore Roosevelt, himself the son of a famous exponent of self-reliance, said to reporters at his home in Oyster Bay that "Captain Lindbergh personifies the daring of youth. Daniel Boone, David Crocket [sic], and men of that type played a lone hand and made America. Lindbergh is their lineal descendant." In *Outlook* magazine, immediately below an enthusiastic endorsement of Lindbergh's own remarks on the importance of his machine and his scientific instruments, there was the statement, "Charles Lindbergh is the heir of all that we like to think is best in America. He is of the stuff out of which have been made the pioneers that opened up the wilderness, first on the Atlantic coast, and then in our great West. His are the qualities which we, as a people, must nourish." It is in this mood that one suspects it was important that Lindbergh came out of the West and rode all alone.

Another common metaphor in the attempt to place Lindbergh's exploit was to say that he had opened a new "frontier." To speak of the air as a "frontier" was to invoke an interpretation of the meaning of American history which had sources deep in American experience, but the frontier of the airplane is hardly the frontier of the trailmakers of the old West. Rather than an escape into the self-sufficient simplicity of the American past, the machine which made Lindbergh's flight possible represented an advance into a complex industrial present. The difficulty lay in using an instance of modern life to celebrate the virtues of the past, to use an extreme development of an urban industrial society to insist upon the significance of the frontier in American life.

A little more than a month after Lindbergh's flight, Joseph K. Hart in *Survey* magazine reached back to Walt Whitman's poem for the title of an article on Lindbergh: "O Pioneer." A school had made Lindbergh an honorary alumnus but Hart protested there was little available evidence "that he was educated in *schools.*" "We must look elsewhere for our explanation," Hart wrote and he looked to the experience of Lindbergh's youth when "everything that he ever did . . . he did by himself. He lived more to himself than most boys." And, of course, Lindbergh lived to himself in the only place conceivably possible, in the world of nature, on a Minnesota farm. "There he developed in the companionship of woods and fields, animals and machines, his audaciously natural and simple personality." The word, "machines," jars as it intrudes into Hart's idyllic pastoral landscape and betrays Hart's difficulty in relating the setting of nature upon which he wishes to insist with the fact that its product spent his whole life tinkering with machines, from motorcycles to airplanes. But except for that one word, Hart proceeds in uncritical nostalgia to show that "a lone trip across the Atlantic was not impossible for a boy who had grown up in the solitude of the woods and waters." If Lindbergh was "clear-headed, naif, untrained in the ways of cities," it was because he had "that 'natural simplicity' which Fenimore Cooper used to attribute to the pioneer hero of his Leatherstocking Tales." Hart rejected the notion that any student "bent to all the conformities" of formal training could have done what Lindbergh did. "Must we not admit," he asked, "that this pioneering urge remained to this audacious youth because he had never submitted completely to the repressions of the world and its jealous institutions?"

Only those who insist on reason will find it strange that Hart should use the industrial achievement of the airplane to reject the urban, institutionalized world of industrialism. Hart was dealing with something other than reason; he was dealing with the emotion evoked by Lindbergh's solitude. He recognized that people wished to call Lindbergh a "genius" because that "would release him from the ordinary rules of existence." That way, "we could rejoice with him in his triumph, and then go back to the contracted routines of our institutional ways [because] ninety-nine percent of us must be content to be shaped and moulded by the routine ways and forms of the world to the routine tasks of life." It is in the word, "must," that the pathos of this interpretation of the phenomenon of Lindbergh lies. The world had changed from the open society of the pioneer to the close-knit, interdependent world of a modern machine-oriented civilization. The institutions of a highly corporate industrial society existed as a constant reproach to a people who liked to believe that the meaning of its experience was embodied in the formless, independent life of the frontier. Like Thomas Jefferson who identified American virtue with nature and saw the city as a "great sore" on the public body, Hart concluded that "certainly, in the response that the world—especially the world of great cities —has made to the performance of this midwestern boy, we can read of the homesickness of the human soul, immured in city canyons and routine tasks, for the freer world of youth, for the open spaces of the pioneer, for the joy of battling with nature and clean storms once more on the frontiers of the earth."

The social actuality which made the adulation of Lindbergh possible had its own irony for the notion that America's strength lay in its simple uncomplicated beginnings. For the public response to Lindbergh to have reached the proportions it did, the world had by necessity to be the intricately developed world of modern mass communications. But more than irony was involved.

Ultimately, the emotion attached to Lindbergh's flight involved no less than a whole theory about American history. By singling out the fact that Lindbergh rode alone, and by naming him a pioneer of the frontier, the public projected its sense that the source of America's strength lay somewhere in the past and that Lindbergh somehow meant that America must look backward in time to rediscover some lost virtue. The mood was nostalgic and American history was read as a decline, a decline measured in terms of America's advance into an urban, institutionalized way of life which made solitary achievement increasingly beyond the reach of ninety-nine per cent of the people. Because Lindbergh's ancestors were Norse, it was easy to call him a "Viking" and extend the emotion far into the past when all frontiers were open. He became the "Columbus" of another new world to conquer as well as the "Lochinvar" who rode all alone. But there was always the brute, irreducible fact that Lindbergh's exploit was a victory of the machine over the barriers of nature. If the only response to Lindbergh had been a retreat to the past, we would be involved with a mass cultural neurosis, the inability of America to accept reality, the reality of the world in which it lived. But there was another aspect, one in which the public celebrated the machine and the highly organized society of which it was a product. The response to Lindbergh reveals that the American people were deeply torn between conflicting interpretations of their own experience. By calling Lindbergh a pioneer, the people could read into American history the necessity of turning back to the frontier past. Yet the people could also read American history in terms of progress into the industrial future. They could do this by emphasizing the machine which was involved in Lindbergh's flight.

Lindbergh came back from Europe in an American man-of-war, the cruiser *Memphis*. It seems he had contemplated flying on, around the whole world perhaps, but less adventurous heads prevailed and dictated a surer mode of travel for so valuable a piece of public property. The *New Republic* protested against bringing America's hero of romance home in a warship. If he had returned on a great liner, that would have been one thing. "One's first trip on an oceanliner is a great adventure—the novelty of it, the many people of all kinds and conditions, floating for a week in a tiny compact world of their own." But to return on the *Memphis*, "to be put on a gray battleship with a collection of people all of the same stripe, in a kind of ship that has as much relation to the life of the sea as a Ford factory has! We might as well have put him in a pneumatic tube and shot him across the Atlantic." The interesting thing about the *New Republic's* protest against the unromantic, regimented life of a battleship is that the image it found appropriate was the Ford assembly line. It was this reaction against the discipline of a mechanized society that probably led to the nostalgic image of Lindbergh as a remnant of a past when romance was possible for the individual, when life held novelty and society was variegated rather than uniform. But what the Ford Assembly Line represents, a society committed to the path of full mechanization, was what lay behind Lindbergh's romantic success. A long piece in the Sunday *New York Times,* "Lindbergh Symbolizes the Genius of America," reminded its readers of the too obvious fact that "without an airplane he could not have flown at all." Lindbergh "is, indeed, the Icarus of the twentieth century; not himself an inventor of his own wings, but a son of that omnipotent Daedalus whose ingenuity has created the modern world." The point was that modern America was the creation of modern industry. Lindbergh "reveres his 'ship' as a noble expression of mechanical wisdom. . . . Yet in this reverence . . . Lindbergh is not an exception. What he means by the Spirit of St. Louis is really the spirit of America. The mechanical genius, which is discerned in Henry Ford as well as in Charles A. Lindbergh, is in the very atmosphere of [the] country." In contrast to a sentiment that feared the enforced discipline of the machine there existed an attitude of reverence for its power.

Lindbergh led the way in the celebration of the machine, not only implicitly by including his plane when he said "we," but by direct statement. In Paris he told newspapermen, "You fellows have not said enough about that wonderful motor." Rarely have two more taciturn figures confronted one another than when Lindbergh returned to Washington and Calvin Coolidge pinned the Distinguished Flying Cross on him, but in his brief remarks Coolidge found room to express his particular delight that Lindbergh should have given equal credit to the airplane. "For we are proud," said the President, "that in every particular this silent partner represented American genius and industry. I am told that more than 100 separate companies furnished materials, parts or service in its construction."

The flight was not the heroic lone success of a single daring individual, but the climax of the co-operative effort of an elaborately interlocked technology. The day after Coolidge's speech, Lindbergh said at another ceremony in Washington that the honor should "not go to the pilot alone but to American science and genius which had given years of study to the advancement of aeronautics." "Some things," he said, "should be taken into due consideration in connection with our flight that have not heretofore been given due weight. That is just what made this flight possible. It was not the act of a single pilot. It was the culmination of twenty years of aeronautical research and the assembling together of all that was practicable and best in American aviation." The flight, concluded Lindbergh, "represented American industry."

The worship of the machine which was embodied in the public's response to Lindbergh exalted those very aspects which were denigrated in the celebration of the flight as the work of a heroic individual. Organization and careful method were what lay behind the flight, not individual self-sufficiency and daring romance. One magazine hailed the flight as a "triumph of mechanical engineering." "It is not to be forgotten that this era is the work not so much of brave aviators as of engineers, who have through patient and protracted effort been steadily improving the construction of airplanes." The lesson to be learned from Lindbergh's flight, thought a writer in the *Independent,* "is that the splendid human and material aspects of America need to be organized for the ordinary, matter of fact service of society." The machine meant organization, the careful rationalization of activity of a Ford assembly line, it meant planning, and, if it meant the loss of spontaneous individual action, it meant the material betterment of society. Lindbergh meant not a retreat to the free life of the frontier past but an emergence into the time when "the machine began to take first place in the public mind—the machine and the organization that made its operation possible on a large scale." A poet on this side of the matter wrote, "All day I felt the pull / Of the steel miracle." The machine was not a devilish engine which would enthrall mankind, it was the instrument which would lead to a new paradise. But the direction of history implicit in the machine was toward the future, not the past; the meaning of history was progress, not decline, and America should not lose faith in the future betterment of society. An address by a Harvard professor, picked up by the *Magazine of Business,* made all this explicit. "We commonly take Social Progress for granted," said Edwin F. Gay, "but the doctrine of Social Progress is one of the great revolutionary ideas which have powerfully affected our modern world." There was a danger, however, that the idea "may be in danger of becoming a commonplace or a butt of criticism." The speaker recognized why this might be. America was "worn and disillusioned after the Great War." Logically, contentment should have gone with so optimistic a creed, yet the American people were losing faith. So Lindbergh filled an emotional need even where a need should have been lacking. "He has come like a shining vision to revive the hope of mankind." The high ideals of faith in progress "had almost come to seem like hollow words to us—but now here he is, emblematic of heroes yet to inhabit this world. Our belief in Social Progress is justified symbolically in him."

It is a long flight from New York to Paris; it is a still longer flight from the fact of Lindbergh's achievement to the burden imposed upon it by the imagination of his time. But it is in that further flight that lies the full meaning of Lindbergh. His role was finally a double one. His flight provided an opportunity for the people to project their own emotions into his act and their emotions involved finally two attitudes toward the meaning of their own experience. One view had it that America represented a brief escape from the course of history, an emergence into a new and open world with the self-sufficient individual at its center. The other said that America represented a stage in historical evolution and that its fulfillment lay in the development of society. For one, the meaning of America lay in the past; for the other in the future. For one, the American ideal was an escape from institutions, from the forms of society, and from limitations put upon the free individual; for the other, the American ideal was the elaboration of the complex institutions which made modern society possible, an acceptance of the discipline of the machine, and the achievement of the individual within a context of which he was only a part. The two views were contradictory but both were possible and both were present in the public's reaction to Lindbergh's flight.

The Sunday newspapers announced that Lindbergh had reached Paris and in the very issue whose front pages were covered with Lindbergh's story the magazine section of the *New York Times* featured an article by the British philosopher, Bertrand Russell. The magazine had, of course, been made up too far in advance to take advantage of the news about Lindbergh. Yet, in a prophetic way, Russell's article was about Lindbergh. Russell hailed the rise to power of the United States because he felt that in the "new life that is America's" in the twentieth century "the new outlook appropriate to machinery [would] become more completely dominant than in the old world." Russell sensed that some might be unwilling to accept the machine, but "whether we like this new outlook or not," he wrote, "is of little importance." Why one might not was obvious. A society built on the machine, said Russell, meant "the diminution in the value and independence of the individual. Great enterprises tend more and more to be collective, and in an industrialized world the interference of the community with the individual must be more intense." Russell realized that while the co-operative effort involved in machine technology makes man collectively more lordly, it makes the individual more submissive. "I do not see how it is to be avoided," he concluded.

People are not philosophers. They did not see how the conflict between a machine society and the free individual was to be avoided either. But neither were they ready to accept the philosopher's statement of the problem. In Lindbergh, the people celebrated both the self-sufficient individual and the machine. Americans still celebrate both. We cherish the individualism of the American creed at the same time that we worship the machine which increasingly enforces collectivized behavior. Whether we can have both, the freedom of the individual and the power of an organized society, is a question that still haunts our minds. To resolve the conflict that is present in America's celebration of Lindbergh in 1927 is still the task of America.

DAVID BRION DAVIS

TEN-GALLON HERO

Americans looking at the cowboy see a face they yearn to wear, Davis tells us in his sketch of the cowboy as hero. It is a manly, honest, courageous face, which portrays a pure and simple soul. That it never existed in America (or anywhere else) makes it all the more precious and desirable, and the Americans hope to recover it. The legend of the cowboy has emerged, Davis contends, out of the tradition of the Western scout and the myth of the ante-bellum South. As a folk hero the cowboy symbolizes much in the American character that we do not especially admire but which we must acknowledge as our own. The cowboy has also provided a medium through which Americans have registered their yearning for a golden and romantic past uncluttered by the problems of industrial society, a past hospitable to the simple virtues of manliness, bravery, and action. Of course, the cowboy hero has assumed forms that have not been considered by Davis, particularly those rendered by naturalistic writers. It is also true that Europeans and Asians have found values in the cowboy hero resonant with their own. The universality of his appeal may suggest that the cowboy hero satisfies a romantic need common to modern industrial societies—or it may suggest something else, indeed. In any case, Davis' essay is an interesting probe of one segment of American folk culture.

Cowboys have been the subject of many studies. For an understanding of them as heroes the penetrating assessment in Henry Nash Smith's Virgin Land: The American West as Symbol and Myth * *is a good place to begin.*

In 1900 it seemed that the significance of the cowboy era would decline along with other brief but romantic episodes in American history. The Long Drive lingered only in the memories and imaginations of old cowhands. The "hoe-men" occupied former range land while Mennonites and professional dry farmers had sown their Turkey Red winter wheat on the Kansas prairies. To be sure, a cattle industry still flourished, but the cowboy was more like an employee of a corporation than the free-lance cowboy of old.[1] The myth of the cowboy lived on in the Beadle and Adams paper-back novels, with the followers of Ned Buntline and the prolific Colonel Prentiss Ingraham. But this seemed merely a substitution of the more up-to-date cowboy in a tradition which began with Leatherstocking and Daniel Boone.[2] If the mountain man had replaced Boone and the forest scouts, if the cowboy had succeeded the mountain man, and if the legends of Mike Fink and Crockett were slipping into the past, it would seem probable that the cowboy would follow, to become a quaint character of antiquity, overshadowed by newer heroes.

Yet more than a half-century after the passing of the actual wild and woolly cowboy, we find a unique phenomenon in American mythology. Gaudy-covered Western or cowboy magazines decorate stands, windows, and shelves in "drug" stores, bookstores, grocery stores and supermarkets from Miami to Seattle. Hundreds of cowboy movies and television shows are watched and lived through by millions of Americans. Nearly every little boy demands a cowboy suit and a Western six-shooter cap pistol. Cowboys gaze out at you with steely eye and cocked revolver from cereal packages and television screens. Jukeboxes in Bennington, Vermont, as well as Globe, Arizona, moan and warble the latest cowboy songs. Middle-age folk who had once thought of William S. Hart, Harry Carey, and Tom Mix as a passing phase, have lived to see several Hopalong Cassidy revivals, the Lone Ranger, Tim McCoy, Gene Autry, and Roy Rogers. Adolescents and even grown men in Maine and Florida can be seen affecting cowboy, or at least modified cowboy garb, while in the new airplane plants in Kansas, workers don their cowboy boots and wide-brimmed hats, go to work whistling a cowboy song, and are defiantly proud that they live in the land of lassos and sixguns.

When recognized at all, this remarkable cowboy complex is usually defined as the distortion of once-colorful legends by a commercial society.[3] The

---

[1] Edward Douglas Branch, *The Cowboy and His Interpreters* (New York: D. Appleton & Company, 1926), p. 69.

[2] Henry Nash Smith, *Virgin Land* (Cambridge: Harvard University Press, 1950), pp. v, vi.

[3] Smith, *Virgin Land,* p. 111.

FROM David Brion Davis, "Ten-Gallon Hero," *American Quarterly,* Philadelphia: University of Pennsylvania, 1954, Vol. VI (Summer 1954), pp. 111–25. Copyright 1954, Trustees of the University of Pennsylvania. Reprinted by permission.

obvious divergence between the real West and the idealized version, the standardization of plot and characters, and the ridiculous incongruities of cowboys with automobiles and airplanes, all go to substantiate this conclusion.

However, there is more than the cowboy costume and stage setting in even the wildest of these adventures. Despite the incongruities, the cowboy myth exists in fact, and as such is probably a more influential social force than the actual cowboy ever was. It provides the framework for an expression of common ideals of morality and behavior. And while a commercial success, the hero cowboy must satisfy some basic want in American culture, or there could never be such a tremendous market. It is true that the market has been exploited by magazine, song, and scenario writers, but it is important to ask why similar myths have not been equally profitable, such as the lumbermen of the early northwest, the whale fishermen of New Bedford, the early railroad builders, or the fur traders. There have been romances written and movies produced idealizing these phases of American history, but little boys do not dress up like Paul Bunyan and you do not see harpooners on cereal packages. Yet America has had many episodes fully as colorful and of longer duration than the actual cowboy era.

The cowboy hero and his setting are a unique synthesis of two American traditions, and echoes of this past can be discerned in even the wildest of the modern horse operas. On the one hand, the line of descent is a direct evolution from the Western scout of Cooper and the Dime Novel; on the other, there has been a recasting of the golden myth of the ante-bellum South.[4] The two were fused sometime in the 1880's. Perhaps there was actually some basis for such a union. While the West was economically tied to the North as soon as the early canals and railroads broke the river-centered traffic, social ties endured longer. Many Southerners emigrated West and went into the cattle business, and of course, the Long Drive originated in Texas.[5] The literary synthesis of two traditions only followed the two social movements. It was on the Great Plains that the descendants of Daniel Boone met the drawling Texas cowboy.

Henry Nash Smith has described two paradoxical aspects of the legendary Western scout, typified in Boone himself.[6] This woodsman, this buckskin-clad wilderness hunter is a pioneer, breaking trails for his countrymen to follow, reducing the savage wilderness for civilization. Nevertheless, he is also represented as escaping civilization, turning his back on the petty materialism of the world, on the hypocritical and self-conscious manners of community life, and seeking the unsullied, true values of nature.

---

[4] Emerson Hough, *The Story of the Cowboy* (New York: D. Appleton & Company, 1901), p. 200.

[5] Edward E. Dale, *Cow Country* (Norman, Okla.: University of Oklahoma Press, 1942), p. 15.

[6] Smith, *Virgin Land,* p. v.

These seemingly conflicting points of view have counterparts in the woodsman's descendant, the cowboy. The ideal cowboy fights for justice, risks his life to make the dismal little cowtown safe for law-abiding, respectable citizens, but in so doing he destroys the very environment which made him a heroic figure. This paradox is common with all ideals, and the cowboy legend is certainly the embodiment of a social ideal. Thus the minister or social reformer who rises to heroism in his fight against a sin-infested community would logically become a mere figurehead once the community is reformed. There can be no true ideal or hero in a utopia. And the civilization for which the cowboy or trailblazer struggles is utopian in character.

But there is a further consideration in the case of the cowboy. In our mythology, the cowboy era is timeless. The ranch may own a modern station wagon, but the distinguishing attributes of cowboy and environment remain. There is, it is true, a nostalgic sense that this is the last great drama, a sad knowledge that the cowboy is passing and that civilization is approaching. But it never comes. This strange, wistful sense of the coming end of an epoch is not something outside our experience. It is a faithful reflection of the sense of approaching adulthood. The appeal of the cowboy, in this sense, is similar to the appeal of Boone, Leatherstocking, and the later Mountain Man. We know that adulthood, civilization, is inevitable, but we are living toward the end of childhood, and at that point "childness" seems eternal; it is a whole lifetime. But suddenly we find it is not eternal, the forests disappear, the mountains are settled, and we have new responsibilities. When we shut our eyes and try to remember, the last image of a carefree life appears. For the nation, this last image is the cowboy.

The reborn myth of the ante-bellum South also involves nostalgia; not so much nostalgia for something that actually existed as for dreams and ideals. When the Southern myth reappeared on the rolling prairies, it was purified and regenerated by the casting off of apologies for slavery. It could focus all energies on its former rôle of opposing the peculiar social and economic philosophy of the Northeast. This took the form of something more fundamental than mere agrarianism or primitivism. Asserting the importance of values beyond the utilitarian and material, this transplanted Southern philosophy challenged the doctrine of enlightened self-interest and the belief that leisure time is sin.

Like the barons and knights of Southern feudalism, the large ranch owners and itinerant cowboys knew how to have a good time. If there was a time for work, there was a time for play, and the early rodeos, horse races, and wild nights at a cowtown were not occasions for reserve. In this respect, the cowboy West was more in the tradition of fun-loving New Orleans than of the Northeast. Furthermore, the ranch was a remarkable duplication of the plantation, minus slaves. It was a hospitable social unit, where travelers were welcome even when the owner was absent. As opposed to the hard-working, thrifty, and sober ideal of the East, the actual cowboy was overly cheerful at times, generous to the point of waste, and inclined to value friendly comradeship above prestige.[7]

The mythical New England Yankee developed a code of action which always triumphed over the more sophisticated city slicker, because the Yankee's down-to-earth shrewdness, common sense, and reserved humor embodied values which Americans considered as pragmatically effective. The ideal cowboy also had a code of action, but it involved neither material nor social success. The cowboy avoided actions which "just weren't done" because he placed a value on doing things "right," on managing difficult problems and situations with ease, skill, and modesty. The cowboy's code was a Western and democratic version of the Southern gentleman's "honor."

In the early years of the twentieth century, a Philadelphia lawyer, who affected a careless, loose-tied bow instead of the traditional black ribbon and who liked to appear in his shirt sleeves, wrote: "The nomadic bachelor west is over, the housed, married west is established." [8] In a book published in 1902 he had, more than any other man, established an idealized version of the former, unifying the Southern and Western hero myths in a formula which was not to be forgotten. Owen Wister had, in fact, liberated the cowboy hero from the Dime Novels and provided a synthetic tradition suitable for a new century. *The Virginian* became a key document in popular American culture, a romance which defined the cowboy character and thus the ideal American character in terms of courage, sex, religion, and humor. The novel served as a model for hundreds of Western books and movies for half a century. In the recent popular movie "High Noon" a Hollywood star, who won his fame dramatizing Wister's novel, reenacted the same basic plot of hero rejecting heroine's pleas and threats, to uphold his honor against the villain Trampas. While this theme is probably at least a thousand years old, it was Owen Wister who gave it a specifically American content and thus explicated and popularized the modern cowboy ideal, with its traditions, informality, and all-important code.

Of course, Wister's West is not the realistic, boisterous, sometimes monotonous West of Charlie Siringo and Andy Adams. The cowboy, after all, drove cattle. He worked. There was much loneliness and monotony on the range, which has faded like mist under a desert sun in the reminiscences of old cow hands and the fiction of idealizers. The Virginian runs some errands now and then, but there are no cattle-driving scenes, no monotony, no hard work. Fictional cowboys are never bored. Real cowboys were often so bored that they memorized the labels on tin cans and then played games to see how well they could recite them.[9] The cowboys in books and movies are far too

---

[7] Alfred Henry Lewis, *Wolfville Days* (New York: Stokes, 1902), p. 24.

[8] Branch, *The Cowboy and His Interpreters*, pp. 190 ff.

[9] Philip Ashton Rollins, *The Cowboy* (New York: Charles Scribner's Sons, 1922), p. 185.

busy making love and chasing bandits to work at such a dreary task as driving cattle. But then the Southern plantation owner did no work. The befringed hero of the forests did not work. And if any ideal is to be accepted by adolescent America, monotonous work must be subordinated to more exciting pastimes. The fact that the cowboy hero has more important things to do is only in keeping with his tradition and audience. He is only a natural reaction against a civilization which demands increasingly monotonous work, against the approaching adulthood when playtime ends.

And if the cowboy romance banishes work and monotony, their very opposites are found in the immensity of the Western environment. To be sure, the deserts and prairies can be bleak, but they are never dull when used as setting for the cowboy myth. There is always an element of the unexpected, of surprise, of variety. The tremendous distances either seclude or elevate the particular and significant. There are mirages, hidden springs, dust storms, hidden identities, and secret ranches. In one of his early Western novels William MacLeod Raine used both devices of a secret ranch and hidden identity, while Hoffman Birney combined a hidden ranch, a secret trail, and two hidden identities.[10] In such an environment of uncertainty and change men of true genius stand out from the rest. The evil or good in an individual is quickly revealed in cowboy land. A man familiar with the actual cowboy wrote that "brains, moral and physical courage, strength of character, native gentlemanliness, proficiency in riding or shooting—every quality of leadership tended to raise its owner from the common level." [11]

The hazing which cowboys gave the tenderfoot was only preliminary. It was a symbol of the true test which anyone must undergo in the West. After the final winnowing of men, there emerge the heroes, the villains, and the clowns. The latter live in a purgatory and usually attach themselves to the hero group. Often, after the stress of an extreme emergency, they burst out of their caste and are accepted in the élite.

While the Western environment, according to the myth, sorts men into their true places, it does not determine men. It brings out the best in heroes and the worst in villains, but it does not add qualities to the man who has none. The cowboy is a superman and is adorable for his own sake. It is here that he is the descendant of supernatural folk heroes. Harry Hawkeye, the creator of an early cowboy hero, Calvin Yancey, described him as:

> . . . straight as an arrow, fair and ruddy as a Viking, with long, flowing golden hair, which rippled over his massive shoulders, falling nearly to his waist; a high, broad forehead beneath which sparkled a pair of violet blue eyes, tender and soulful in repose, but firm and determined under excitement. His entire face was a study for a sculptor with its delicate aquiline nose,

---

[10] William MacLeod Raine, *Bucky O'Connor* (New York: Grosset & Dunlap, 1907); Hoffman Birney, *The Masked Rider* (New York: Penn, 1928).

[11] Rollins, *The Cowboy,* p. 352.

straight in outline as though chiselled from Parian marble, and its generous manly mouth, with full crimson and arched lips, surmounted by a long, silken blonde mustache, through which a beautiful set of even white teeth gleamed like rows of lustrous pearls.[12]

While the Virginian is not quite the blond, Nordic hero, he is just as beautiful to behold. His black, curly locks, his lean, athletic figure, his quiet, unassuming manner, all go to make him the most physically attractive man Owen Wister could describe. Later cowboy heroes have shaved their mustaches, but the great majority have beautiful curly hair, usually blond or red, square jaws, cleft chins, broad shoulders, deep chests, and wasp-like waists. Like the Virginian, they are perfect men, absolutely incapable of doing the wrong thing unless deceived.[13]

Many writers familiar with the real cowboy have criticized Wister for his concentration on the Virginian's love interest and, of course, they deplore the present degeneration of the cowboy plot, where love is supreme. There were few women in the West in the Chisholm Trail days and those few in Dodge City, Abilene, and Wichita were of dubious morality. The cowboy's sex life was intermittent, to say the least. He had to carry his thirst long distances, like a camel, and in the oases the orgies were hardly on a spiritual plane.[14] Since earlier heroes, like the woodsman, led celibate lives, it is important to ask why the cowboy depends on love interest.

At first glance, there would seem to be an inconsistency here. The cowboy is happiest with a group of buddies, playing poker, chasing horse thieves, riding in masculine company. He is contemptuous of farmers, has no interest in children, and considers men who have lived among women as effete. Usually he left his own family at a tender age and rebelled against the restrictions of mothers and older sisters. Neither the Virginian nor the actual cowboys were family men, nor did they have much interest in the homes they left behind. Thus it would seem that courting a young schoolteacher from Vermont would be self-destruction. At no place is the idealized cowboy further from reality than in his love for the tender woman from the East. Like the law and order he fights for, she will destroy his way of life.

But this paradox is solved when one considers the hero cowboy, not the plot, as the center of all attention. Molly Wood in *The Virginian,* like all her successors, is a literary device, a *dea ex machina* with a special purpose. Along with the Western environment, she serves to throw a stronger light on the hero, to make him stand out in relief, to complete the picture of an ideal. In the first place, she brings out qualities in him which we could not see other-

---

[12] Branch, *The Cowboy and His Interpreters,* p. 191.

[13] A Zane Grey hero is typical and is also seen through the eyes of a woman: "She saw a bronzed, strong-jawed, eagle-eyed man, stalwart, superb of height." Zane Grey, *The Light of Western Stars* (New York: Harper & Brothers, 1914), pp. 29–30.

[14] Charles A. Siringo, *A Lone Star Cowboy* (Santa Fe: C. A. Siringo, 1919), p. 64.

wise. Without her, he would be too much the brute for a real folk hero, at least in a modern age. If Molly Wood were not in *The Virginian,* the hero might seem too raucous, too wild. Of course, his affair with a blonde in town is handled genteelly; his boyish pranks such as mixing up the babies at a party are treated as good, clean fun. But still, there is nothing to bring out his qualities of masculine tenderness, there is nothing to show his conscience until Molly Wood arrives. A cowboy's tenderness is usually revealed through his kindness to horses, and in this sense, the Eastern belle's rôle is that of a glorified horse. A woman in the Western drama is somebody to rescue, somebody to protect. In her presence, the cowboy shows that, in his own way, he is a cultural ideal. The nomadic, bachelor cowboys described by Andy Adams and Charles Siringo are a little too masculine, a little too isolated from civilization to become the ideal for a settled community.

While the Western heroine brings out a new aspect of the cowboy's character, she also serves the external purpose of registering our attitudes toward him. The cowboy ideal is an adorable figure and the heroine is the vehicle of adoration. Female characters enable the author to make observations about cowboys which would be impossible with an all-male cast.[15] This rôle would lose its value if the heroine surrendered to the cowboy immediately. So the more she struggles with herself, the more she conquers her Eastern reservations and surmounts difficulties before capitulating, the more it enhances the hero.

Again, *The Virginian* is the perfect example. We do not meet Molly Wood in the first part of the book. Instead, the author, the I, who is an Easterner, goes to Wyoming and meets the Virginian. It is love at first sight, not in the sexual sense, of course (this was 1902), but there is no mistaking it for anything other than love. This young man's love for the Virginian is not important in itself; it heightens our worship of the hero. The sex of the worshiper is irrelevant. At first the young man is disconsolate, because he cannot win the Virginian's friendship. He must go through the ordeal of not knowing the Virginian's opinion of him. But as he learns the ways of the West, the Virginian's sublime goodness is unveiled. Though increasing knowledge of the hero's character only serves to widen the impossible gulf between the finite Easterner and the infinite, pure virtue of the cowboy, the latter, out of his own free grace and goodness recognizes the lowly visitor, who adores him all the more for it. But this little episode is only a preface, a symbol of the drama to come. As soon as the Virginian bestows his grace on the male adorer, Molly Wood arrives. The same passion is reenacted, though on a much larger frame. In this rôle, the sex of Molly *is* important, and the traditional romance plot is only superficial form. Molly's coyness, her reserve, her involved heritage of Ver-

---

[15] No male character could observe that, " 'Cowboys play like they work or fight,' she added. 'They give their whole souls to it. They are great big simple boys.' " Grey, *The Light of Western Stars,* p. 187.

mont tradition, all go to build an insurmountable barrier. Yet she loves the Virginian. And Owen Wister and his audience love the Virginian through Molly Wood's love. With the male adorer, they had gone about as far as they could go. But Molly offers a new height from which to love the Virginian. There are many exciting possibilities. Molly can save his life and nurse him back to health. She can threaten to break off their wedding if he goes out to fight his rival, and then forgive him when he disobeys her plea. The Virginian marries Molly in the end and most of his descendants either marry or are about to marry their lovely ladies. But this does not mean a physical marriage, children, and a home. That would be building up a hero only to destroy him. The love climax at the end of the cowboy drama raises the hero to a supreme height, the audience achieves an emotional union with its ideal. In the next book or movie the cowboy will be the carefree bachelor again.

The classic hero, Hopalong Cassidy, has saved hundreds of heroines, protected them, and has been adored by them. But in 1910 Hopalong, "remembering a former experience of his own, smiled in knowing cynicism when told that he again would fall under the feminine spell." [16] In 1950 he expressed the same resistance to actual marriage:

> "But you can't always move on, Hoppy!" Lenny protested. "Someday you must settle down! Don't you ever think of marriage?" "Uh-huh, and whenever I think of it I saddle Topper and ride. I'm not a marrying man, Lenny. Sometimes I get to thinkin' about that poem a feller wrote, about how a woman is only a woman but—" "The open road is my Fate!" she finished. "That's it. But can you imagine any woman raised outside a tepee livin' in the same house with a restless man?" [17]

The cowboy hero is the hero of the pre-adolescent, either chronologically or mentally. It is the stage of revolt against femininity and feminine standards. It is also the age of hero worship. If the cowboy romance were sexual, if it implied settling down with a real *girl,* there would be little interest. One recent cowboy hero summarized this attitude in terms which should appeal strongly to any ten-year-old: "I'd as soon fight a she-lion barehanded as have any truck with a gal." [18] The usual cowboy movie idol has about as much social presence in front of the leading lady as a very bashful boy. He is most certainly not the lover-type. That makes him lovable to both male and female Americans. There can be no doubt that Owen Wister identified himself, not with the Virginian, but with Molly Wood.

While some glorifiers of the actual cowboy have maintained that his close-

---

16 Clarence E. Mulford, *Hopalong Cassidy* (Chicago: A. C. McClurg & Company, 1910), p. 11.

17 Tex Burns, pseud. (Louis L'Amour), *Hopalong Cassidy and the Trail to Seven Pines* (New York: Doubleday, 1951), p. 187.

18 Davis Dresser, *The Hangmen of Sleepy Valley* (New York: Jefferson House, 1950), p. 77.

ness to nature made him a deeply religious being, thus echoing the devoutness of the earlier woodsman hero who found God in nature, this tradition has never carried over to the heroic cowboy. Undoubtedly some of the real cowboys were religious, though the consensus of most of the writers on the subject seems to indicate that indifference was more common.[19] Intellectualized religion obviously had no appeal and though the cowboy was often deeply sentimental, he did not seem prone to the emotional and frenzied religion of backwoods farmers and squatters. Perhaps his freedom from family conflicts, from smoldering hatreds and entangled jealousies and loves, had something to do with this. Despite the hard work, the violent physical conflicts, and the occasional debaucheries, the cowboy's life must have had a certain innocent, Homeric quality. Even when witnessing a lynching or murder, the cowboy must have felt further removed from total depravity or original sin than the farmer in a squalid frontier town, with his nagging wife and thirteen children.

At any rate, the cowboy hero of our mythology is too much of a god himself to feel humility. His very creation is a denial of any kind of sin. The cowboy is an enunciation of the goodness of man and the glory which he can achieve by himself. The Western environment strips off the artifice, the social veneer, and instead of a cringing sinner, we behold a dazzling superman. He is a figure of friendly justice, full of self-reliance, a very tower of strength. What need has he of a god?

Of course, the cowboy is not positively anti-religious. He is a respecter of traditions as long as they do not threaten his freedom. The Virginian is polite enough to the orthodox minister who visits his employer's ranch. He listens respectfully to the long sermon, but the ranting and raving about his evil nature are more than he can stand. He knows that his cowboy friends are good men. He loves the beauty of the natural world and feels that the Creator of such a world must be a good and just God. Beyond that, the most ignorant cowboy knows as much as this sinister-voiced preacher. So like a young Greek god leaving Mount Olympus for a practical joke in the interest of justice, the Virginian leaves his rôle of calm and straightforward dignity, and engages in some humorous guile and deceit. The minister is sleeping in the next room and the Virginian calls him and complains that the devil is clutching him. After numerous sessions of wrestling with his conscience, the sleepy minister acting as referee, morning comes before the divine finds he has been tricked. He leaves the ranch in a rage, much to the delight of all the cowboys. The moral, observes Wister, is that men who are obsessed with evil and morbid ideas of human nature, had better stay away from the cowboy West. As Alfred Henry Lewis put it, describing a Western town the year *The Virginian* was published, "Wolfville's a hard practical outfit, what you might call a heap obdurate, an' it's goin' to take more than them fitful an' o'casional sermons I

---

[19] Hough, *The Story of the Cowboy,* p. 199; Branch, *The Cowboy and His Interpreters,* p. 160; Rollins, *The Cowboy,* p. 84; Lewis, *Wolfville Days,* p. 216.

aloodes to,—to reach the roots of its soul." [20] The cowboy is too good and has too much horse sense to be deluded by such brooding theology. Tex Burns could have been describing the Virginian when he wrote that his characters "had the cow hand's rough sense of humor and a zest for practical jokes no cow hand ever outgrows." [21]

Coming as it did at the end of the nineteenth century, the cowboy ideal registered both a protest against orthodox creeds and a faith that man needs no formal religion, once he finds a pure and natural environment. It is the extreme end of a long evolution of individualism. Even the individualistic forest scout was dependent on his surroundings, and he exhibited a sort of pantheistic piety when he beheld the wilderness. The mighty captain of industry, while not accountable to anyone in this world, gave lip-service to the generous God who had made him a steward of wealth. But the cowboy hero stood out on the lonely prairie, dependent on neither man nor God. He was willing to take whatever risks lay along his road and would gladly make fun of any man who took life too seriously. Speaking of his mother's death, a real cowboy is supposed to have said:

> With almost her last breath, she begged me to make my peace with God, while the making was good. I have been too busy to heed her last advice. Being a just God, I feel that He will overlook my neglect. If not, I will have to take my medicine, with Satan holding the spoon.[22]

While the cowboy hero has a respect for property, he does not seek personal wealth and is generous to the point of carelessness. He gives money to his friends, to people in distress, and blows the rest when he hits town on Saturday night. He owns no land and, in fact, has only contempt for farmers, with their ploughed fields and weather-beaten buildings. He hates the slick professional gambler, the grasping Eastern speculator, and railroad man. How are these traits to be reconciled with his regard for property rights? The answer lies in a single possession—his horse. The cowboy's horse is what separates him from vagabondage and migratory labor. It is his link with the cavalier and plumed knight. More and more, in our increasingly property-conscious society, the cowboy's horse has gained in importance. A horse thief becomes a symbol of concentrated evil, a projection of all crime against property and, concomitantly, against social status. Zane Grey was adhering to this tradition when he wrote, "in those days, a horse meant all the world to a man. A lucky strike of grassy upland and good water . . . made him rich in all that he cared to own." On the other hand, "a horse thief was meaner than a poisoned coyote." [23]

---

[20] Lewis, *Wolfville Days,* p. 216.

[21] Burns, *Hopalong Cassidy,* p. 130.

[22] Siringo, *A Lone Star Cowboy,* p. 37.

[23] Zane Grey, *Wildfire* (New York: Harper & Brothers, 1917), pp. 10, 7.

When a cowboy is willing to sell his horse, as one actually does in *The Virginian,* he has sold his dignity and self-identity. It is the tragic mistake which will inevitably bring its nemesis. His love for and close relationship with his horse not only make a cowboy seem more human, they also show his respect for propriety and order. He may drift from ranch to ranch, but his horse ties him down to respectability. Yet the cowboy hero is not an ambitious man. He lacks the concern for hard work and practical results which typifies the Horatio Alger ideal. Despite his fine horse and expensive saddle and boots, he values his code of honor and his friends more than possessions. Because the cowboy era is timeless, the hero has little drive or push toward a new and better life. He fights for law and order and this implies civilization, but the cowboy has no visions of empires, industrial or agrarian.

One of the American traits which foreign visitors most frequently described was the inability to have a good time. Americans constantly appear in European journals as ill-at-ease socially, as feeling they must work every spare moment. Certainly it was part of the American Protestant capitalistic ethic, the Poor Richard, Horatio Alger ideal, that spare time, frivolous play, and relaxation were sins which would bring only poverty, disease, and other misfortunes. If a youth would study the wise sayings of great men, if he worked hard and made valuable friends but no really confidential ones, if he never let his hair down or became too intimate with any person, wife included, if he stolidly kept his emotions to himself and watched for his chance in the world, then he would be sure to succeed. But the cowboy hero is mainly concerned with doing things skillfully and conforming to his moral code for its own sake. When he plays poker, treats the town to a drink, or raises a thousand dollars to buy off the evil mortgage, he is not aiming at personal success. Most cowboy heroes have at least one friend who knows them intimately, and they are seldom reserved, except in the presence of a villain or nosey stranger.

Both the hero and real cowboy appear to be easy-going and informal. In dress, speech, and social manner, the cowboy sets a new ideal. Every cowboy knows how to relax. If the villains are sometimes tense and nervous, the hero sits placidly at a card game, never ruffled, never disturbed, even when his arch rival is behind him at the bar, hot with rage and whisky. The ideal cowboy is the kind of man who turns around slowly when a pistol goes off and drawls, "Ah'd put thet up, if Ah were yew." William MacLeod Raine's Sheriff Collins chats humorously with some train robbers and maintains a calm, unconcerned air which amuses the passengers, though he is actually pumping the bandits for useful information.[24] Previously, he had displayed typical cowboy individualism by flagging the train down and climbing aboard, despite the protests of the conductor. Instead of the eager, aspiring youth, the cowboy hero is like a young tomcat, calm and relaxed, but always ready to spring into action. An

---

[24] Raine, *Bucky O'Connor,* p. 22.

early description of one of the most persistent of the cowboy heroes summarizes the ideal characteristics which appeal to a wide audience:

> Hopalong Cassidy had the most striking personality of all the men in his outfit; humorous, courageous to the point of foolishness, eager for fight or frolic, nonchalant when one would expect him to be quite otherwise, curious, loyal to a fault, and the best man with a Colt in the Southwest, he was a paradox, and a puzzle even to his most intimate friends. With him life was a humorous recurrence of sensations, a huge pleasant joke instinctively tolerated, but not worth the price cowards pay to keep it. He had come onto the range when a boy and since that time he had laughingly carried his life in his open hand, and . . . still carried it there, and just as recklessly.[25]

Of course, most cowboy books and movies bristle with violence. Wild fist fights, brawls with chairs and bottles, gun play and mass battles with crashing windows, fires, and the final racing skirmish on horseback, are all as much a part of the cowboy drama as the boots and spurs. These bloody escapades are necessary and are simply explained. They provide the stage for the hero to show his heroism, and since the cowboy is the hero to the pre-adolescent, he must prove himself by their standards. Physical prowess is the most important thing for the ten- or twelve-year-old mind. They are constantly plagued by fear, doubt, and insecurity, in short, by evil, and they lack the power to crush it. The cowboy provides the instrument for their aggressive impulses, while the villain symbolizes all evil. The ethics of the cowboy band are the ethics of the boy's gang, where each member has a rôle determined by his physical skills and his past performance. As with any group of boys, an individual cowboy who had been "taken down a peg" was forever ridiculed and teased about his loss in status.[26]

The volume of cowboy magazines, radio programs and motion pictures would indicate a national hero for at least a certain age group, a national hero who could hardly help but reflect specific attitudes. The cowboy myth has been chosen by this audience because it combines a complex of traits, a way of life, which they consider the proper ideal for America. The actual drama and setting are subordinate to the grand figure of the cowboy hero, and the love affairs, the exciting plots, and the climactic physical struggles present opportunities for the definition of the cowboy code and character. Through the superficial action, the heroism of the cowboy is revealed, and each repetition of the drama, like the repetition of a sacrament, reaffirms the cowboy public's faith in their ideal.

Perhaps the outstanding cowboy trait, above even honor, courage, and generosity, is the relaxed, calm attitude toward life. Though he lives intensely,

---

[25] Mulford, *Hopalong Cassidy*, p. 65.
[26] Sam P. Ridings, *The Chisholm Trail* (Medford, Okla.: S. P. Ridings, 1936), p. 297.

he has a calm self-assurance, a knowledge that he can handle anything. He is good-humored and jovial.[27] He never takes women too seriously. He can take a joke or laugh at himself. Yet the cowboy is usually anti-intellectual and anti-school, another attitude which appeals to a younger audience.[28]

Above all, the cowboy is a "good joe." He personifies a code of personal dignity, personal liberty, and personal honesty. Most writers on the actual cowboy represented him as having these traits.[29] While many of these men obviously glorify him as much as any fiction writers, there must have been some basis for their judgment. As far as his light-hearted, calm attitude is concerned, it is amazing how similar cowboys appear, both in romances and non-fiction.[30] Millions of American youth subscribed to the new ideal and yearned for the clear, Western atmosphere of "unswerving loyalty, the true, deep affection, and good-natured banter that left no sting."[31] For a few thrilling hours they could roughly toss conventions aside and share the fellowship of ranch life and adore the kind of hero who was never bored and never afraid.

Whether these traits of self-confidence, a relaxed attitude toward life and good humor, have actually increased in the United States during the past fifty years is like asking whether men love their wives more now than in 1900. Certainly the effective influence of the cowboy myth can never be determined. It is significant, however, that the cowboy ideal has emerged above all others. And while the standardization of plot and character seems to follow other commercial conventions, the very popularity of this standard cowboy is important and is an overlooked aspect of the American character. It is true that this hero is infantile, that he is silly, overdone, and unreal. But when we think of many past ideals and heroes, myths and ethics; when we compare our placid cowboy with, say, the eager, cold, serious hero of Nazi Germany (the high-cheekboned, blond lad who appeared on the Reichsmarks); or if we compare the cowboy with the gangster heroes of the thirties, or with the serious, self-righteous and brutal series of Supermen, Batmen, and Human Torches; when, in an age of violence and questioned public and private morality, if we think of the many possible heroes we might have had—then we can be thankful for our silly cowboy. We could have chosen worse.

---

[27] The cowboy hero was judged to be "out of sorts when he could not vent his peculiar humor on somebody or something." Grey, *The Light of Western Stars*, pp. 118–19.

[28] This anti-intellectualism in the Western myth is at least as old as Cooper's parody of the scientist, Obed Bat, in *The Prairie*. More recently, Will James took pride in his son's poor attitude and performance in school. Will James, *The American Cowboy* (New York: Charles Scribner's Sons, 1942), p. 107.

[29] Ridings, *The Chisholm Trail*, pp. 278–94; Rollins, *The Cowboy*, p. 67; Dale, *Cow Country*, pp. 122, 153.

[30] According to Alfred Henry Lewis, surly and contentious people were just as unpopular in Wolfville as they appear to be in fiction. Lewis, *Wolfville Days*, p. 217.

[31] Mulford, *Hopalong Cassidy*, p. 155.

ROBERT WARSHOW

THE GANGSTER AS TRAGIC HERO

What happened to the Alger hero with the increasing urbanization, indus-trialization, and organization of the twentieth century is a problem historians have not yet explored sufficiently. When they finally do they will have to pay particular attention to the folk heroes of contemporary mass media. The widespread popularity of the classic gangster film, whose greatest popularity coincided with the Great Depression, constitutes an especially intriguing phe-nomenon for the student of American culture. As the depression obliterated the dream of unending economic progress and clogged the channels of eco-nomic mobility, millions of Americans flocked to theaters to watch such ac-tors as Edward G. Robinson and James Cagney portray individuals who were caricatures of the Alger hero in certain important respects. The gang-ster heroes also rose to success through diligence and self-reliance, but only by denying the values that Alger affirmed. They attained temporary eminence and power, but their ultimate reward was invariably violent destruction. Whether their eventual demise was punishment for their negation of tradi-tional virtues or, as Robert Warshow suggests, the consequence of their pre-sumption in setting themselves apart from, and above, the masses, the tragic outcome of their actions signified that the individual could no longer rise on his own and that he who chose to try was doomed. Certainly, there is much in these films to support the theory that the depression era helped give rise to the Organization Man of the post–World War II period.

Robert Warshow, whose early death cut short his career as one of the most perceptive critics of American popular culture, had many provocative *things to say about the gangster film, and his short essay merits several close readings. Warshow's interpretations of the cowboy film, funny papers, and many other aspects of popular culture can be found in his book* The Immediate Experience * (1962).

America, as a social and political organization, is committed to a cheerful view of life. It could not be otherwise. The sense of tragedy is a luxury of aristocratic societies, where the fate of the individual is not conceived of as having a direct and legitimate political importance, being determined by a fixed and supra-political—that is, non-controversial—moral order or fate. Modern equalitarian societies, however, whether democratic or authoritarian in their political forms, always base themselves on the claim that they are making life happier; the avowed function of the modern state, at least in its ultimate terms, is not only to regulate social relations, but also to determine the quality and the possibilities of human life in general. Happiness thus becomes the chief political issue—in a sense, the only political issue—and for that reason it can never be treated as an issue at all. If an American or a Russian is unhappy, it implies a certain reprobation of his society, and therefore, by a logic of which we can all recognize the necessity, it becomes an obligation of citizenship to be cheerful; if the authorities find it necessary, the citizen may even be compelled to make a public display of his cheerfulness on important occasions, just as he may be conscripted into the army in time of war.

Naturally, this civic responsibility rests most strongly upon the organs of mass culture. The individual citizen may still be permitted his private unhappiness so long as it does not take on political significance, the extent of this tolerance being determined by how large an area of private life the society can accommodate. But every production of mass culture is a public act and must conform with accepted notions of the public good. Nobody seriously questions the principle that it is the function of mass culture to maintain public morale, and certainly nobody in the mass audience objects to having his morale maintained.[1] At a time when the normal condition of the citizen is a state of anxiety, euphoria spreads over our culture like the broad smile of an idiot. In terms of attitudes towards life, there is very little difference between a "happy" movie like *Good News,* which ignores death and suffering, and a "sad" movie like *A Tree Grows in Brooklyn,* which uses death and suffering as incidents in the service of a higher optimism.

But, whatever its effectiveness as a source of consolation and a means of pressure for maintaining "positive" social attitudes, this optimism is fundamentally satisfying to no one, not even to those who would be most disoriented without its support. Even within the area of mass culture, there always

---

[1] In her testimony before the House Committee on Un-American Activities, Mrs. Leila Rogers said that the movie *None But the Lonely Heart* was un-American because it was gloomy. Like so much else that was said during the unhappy investigation of Hollywood, this statement was at once stupid and illuminating. One knew immediately what Mrs. Rogers was talking about; she had simply been insensitive enough to carry her philistinism to its conclusion.

FROM Robert Warshow, "The Gangster as Tragic Hero." "The Gangster as Tragic Hero" appeared first in *Partisan Review,* Vol. XV, No. 2 (February 1958), Reprinted by permission.

exists a current of opposition, seeking to express by whatever means are available to it that sense of desperation and inevitable failure which optimism itself helps to create. Most often, this opposition is confined to rudimentary or semi-literate forms: in mob politics and journalism, for example, or in certain kinds of religious enthusiasm. When it does enter the field of art, it is likely to be disguised or attenuated: in an unspecific form of expression like jazz, in the basically harmless nihilism of the Marx Brothers, in the continually reasserted strain of hopelessness that often seems to be the real meaning of the soap opera. The gangster film is remarkable in that it fills the need for disguise (though not sufficiently to avoid arousing uneasiness) without requiring any serious distortion. From its beginnings, it has been a consistent and astonishingly complete presentation of the modern sense of tragedy.[2]

In its initial character, the gangster film is simply one example of the movies' constant tendency to create fixed dramatic patterns that can be repeated indefinitely with a reasonable expectation of profit. One gangster film follows another as one musical or one Western follows another. But this rigidity is not necessarily opposed to the requirements of art. There have been very successful types of art in the past which developed such specific and detailed conventions as almost to make individual examples of the type interchangeable. This is true, for example, of Elizabethan revenge tragedy and Restoration comedy.

For such a type to be successful means that its conventions have imposed themselves upon the general consciousness and become the accepted vehicles of a particular set of attitudes and a particular aesthetic effect. One goes to any individual example of the type with very definite expectations, and originality is to be welcomed only in the degree that it intensifies the expected experience without fundamentally altering it. Moreover, the relationship between the conventions which go to make up such a type and the real experience of its audience or the real facts of whatever situation it pretends to describe is of only secondary importance and does not determine its aesthetic force. It is only in an ultimate sense that the type appeals to its audience's experience of reality; much more immediately, it appeals to previous experience of the type itself: it creates its own field of reference.

Thus the importance of the gangster film, and the nature and intensity of its emotional and aesthetic impact, cannot be measured in terms of the place of the gangster himself or the importance of the problem of crime in American life. Those European movie-goers who think there is a gangster on every corner in New York are certainly deceived, but defenders of the "positive" side of American culture are equally deceived if they think it relevant to point out that most Americans have never seen a gangster. What matters is that the

---

[2] Efforts have been made from time to time to bring the gangster film into line with the prevailing optimism and social constructiveness of our culture; *Kiss of Death* is a recent example. These efforts are usually unsuccessful; the reasons for their lack of success are interesting in themselves, but I shall not be able to discuss them here.

experience of the gangster *as an experience of art* is universal to Americans. There is almost nothing we understand better or react to more readily or with quicker intelligence. The Western film, though it seems never to diminish in popularity, is for most of us no more than the folklore of the past, familiar and understandable only because it has been repeated so often. The gangster film comes much closer. In ways that we do not easily or willingly define, the gangster speaks for us, expressing that part of the American psyche which rejects the qualities and the demands of modern life, which rejects "Americanism" itself.

The gangster is the man of the city, with the city's language and knowledge, with its queer and dishonest skills and its terrible daring, carrying his life in his hands like a placard, like a club. For everyone else, there is at least the theoretical possibility of another world—in that happier American culture which the gangster denies, the city does not really exist; it is only a more crowded and more brightly lit country—but for the gangster there is only the city; he must inhabit it in order to personify it: not the real city, but that dangerous and sad city of the imagination which is so much more important, which is the modern world. And the gangster—though there are real gangsters—is also, and primarily, a creature of the imagination. The real city, one might say, produces only criminals; the imaginary city produces the gangster: he is what we want to be and what we are afraid we may become.

Thrown into the crowd without background or advantages, with only those ambiguous skills which the rest of us—the real people of the real city —can only pretend to have, the gangster is required to make his way, to make his life and impose it on others. Usually, when we come upon him, he has already made his choice or the choice has already been made for him, it doesn't matter which: we are not permitted to ask whether at some point he could have chosen to be something else than what he is.

The gangster's activity is actually a form of rational enterprise, involving fairly definite goals and various techniques for achieving them. But this rationality is usually no more than a vague background; we know, perhaps, that the gangster sells liquor or that he operates a numbers racket; often we are not given even that much information. So his activity becomes a kind of pure criminality: he hurts people. Certainly our response to the gangster film is most consistently and most universally a response to sadism; we gain the double satisfaction of participating vicariously in the gangster's sadism and then seeing it turned against the gangster himself.

But on another level the quality of irrational brutality and the quality of rational enterprise become one. Since we do not see the rational and routine aspects of the gangster's behavior, the practice of brutality—the quality of unmixed criminality—becomes the totality of his career. At the same time, we are always conscious that the whole meaning of this career is a drive for success: the typical gangster film presents a steady upward progress followed by a very precipitate fall. Thus brutality itself becomes at once the means to success and the content of success—a success that is defined in its most general terms, not as accomplishment or specific gain, but simply as the unlimited possibility of aggression. (In the same way, film presentations of businessmen tend to make it appear that they achieve their success by talking on the telephone and holding conferences and that success *is* talking on the telephone and holding conferences.)

From this point of view, the initial contact between the film and its audience is an agreed conception of human life: that man is a being with the possibilities of success or failure. This principle, too, belongs to the city; one must emerge from the crowd or else one is nothing. On that basis the necessity of the action is established, and it progresses by inalterable paths to the point where the gangster lies dead and the principle has been modified: there is really only one possibility—failure. The final meaning of the city is anonymity and death.

In the opening scene of *Scarface,* we are shown a successful man; we know he is successful because he has just given a party of opulent proportions and because he is called Big Louie. Through some monstrous lack of caution, he permits himself to be alone for a few moments. We understand from this immediately that he is about to be killed. No convention of the gangster film is more strongly established than this: it is dangerous to be alone. And yet the very conditions of success make it impossible not to be alone, for success is always the establishment of an *individual* pre-eminence that must be imposed on others, in whom it automatically arouses hatred; the successful man is an outlaw. The gangster's whole life is an effort to assert himself as an individual, to draw himself out of the crowd, and he always dies *because* he is an individual; the final bullet thrusts him back, makes him, after all, a failure. "Mother of God," says the dying Little Caesar, "is this the end of Rico?"—speaking of himself thus in the third person because what has been brought low is not the undifferentiated *man,* but the individual with a name, the gangster, the success; even to himself he is a creature of the imagination. (T. S. Eliot has pointed out that a number of Shakespeare's tragic heroes have this trick of looking at themselves dramatically; their true identity, the thing that is destroyed when they die, is something outside themselves—not a man, but a style of life, a kind of meaning.)

At bottom, the gangster is doomed because he is under the obligation to succeed, not because the means he employs are unlawful. In the deeper layers of the modern consciousness, *all* means are unlawful, every attempt to succeed is an act of aggression, leaving one alone and guilty and defenseless among enemies: one is *punished* for success. This is our intolerable dilemma: that failure is a kind of death and success is evil and dangerous, is—ultimately—impossible. The effect of the gangster film is to embody this dilemma in the person of the gangster and resolve it by his death. The dilemma is resolved because it is *his* death, not ours. We are safe; for the moment, we can acquiesce in our failure, we can choose to fail.

MALCOLM COWLEY

WAR NOVELS: After Two Wars

Scholars have already discussed at some length the effects of World War II upon American foreign policy and America's role in the world community. To a lesser extent they have begun to investigate the changes that the war brought about in the economic and political spheres. But as yet they have had little to say about the impact of the war upon those who were engaged in fighting it—those who were torn from an environment familiar to them and thrown into a totally new milieu with its own rules and aims. War can often be cruel not only to those who die on its battlefields but also to those who survive it and have to adapt themselves for a period of years to different codes of morality and patterns of behavior than those that they had been brought up to respect and believe in. There is no truly conclusive way of documenting the effects of the war upon these men, but certainly the profusion of war novels published at the end of the hostilities constitutes a potentially fruitful source of information. The novels written after World War I described the attitudes and experiences of the generation of men that served in that war, and, as Malcolm Cowley's essay indicates, an analysis of these novels compared with those following World War II contributes to a deeper understanding of both war generations and their fundamental differences.

*Many of Cowley's conclusions are corroborated by the findings of an extensive sociological survey of the American soldier conducted during the war itself (see Samuel Stouffer et al., The American Soldier, vols. I and II * (1949)). If Cowley is correct in seeing in the novels written following World*

War II a pervasive distrust of all large institutions and of men acting in the mass, a turning away from idealism and from the concept of achieving progress through collective effort, and the material collected by Stouffer and his associates leads to similar conclusions, then we may well have an important explanation for the attitude of conservatism and apathy that developed in the decade after the war. For another account of the literature of this period, see John Aldridge, After the Lost Generation * (1951).*

There is one category of recent fiction that seems to be little affected by the standards of the newer critics: it consists of novels about World War II. Almost all of these are based on the wartime experience of their authors. The experience calls urgently to be retold and, much more than civilian life, it takes the shape of stories with a beginning, a middle, and an end. The hero enlists, has adventures, and at last comes home; or he goes into action, suffers, and is killed; or again there may be a collective hero, a platoon or a ship's company that is brought together, becomes a living unity, and then is dissolved at the end of a campaign.

In other words, the form of the novel is largely determined by the subject —which is always Americans at war, no matter where they fight—and the same formal structure may be used in stories about different types of combat service on different sides of the globe. The authors as a group haven't shown much interest in discovering new forms. That explains why American critics, with their specialized interest in structure and texture, have paid little attention to the novels of World War II. I can remember only three—*The Gallery, The Naked and the Dead,* and *From Here to Eternity*—that have been discussed at any length in the critical reviews. On the other hand, war novels as a class have been reaching an extremely wide public that doesn't listen to what the critics say.

It is time now for a long second look at the novels as a group. It is time to ask what they reveal about the behavior, the anxieties, and the aspirations of Americans in the Second World War. It is also time for one more attempt to answer the old question, how the novels compare with those written after 1920 by American veterans of another war.

I

I have read some fifty of the novels, most of them as printed books, but others as manuscripts in search of a publisher. Taken together, they cover a wide range of human experience and more than half of the terraqueous globe. They include stories laid in peacetime barracks, in training camps, at bomber fields in England, on Navy vessels patrolling all the oceans, and in combat units fighting in Africa, Europe, Asia, and Oceania—not to mention other stories dealing with prison camps, the liberated countries, and occupation forces in Germany and Japan. They also include first-hand accounts of every major battle from Pearl Harbor to Iwo Jima, with reports of the other battle that every veteran had to fight for himself when he returned to civilian life. And the novels as a group are comprehensive in other fashions as well. Here are characters—and authors too—from every economic level and almost

FROM "War Novels: After Two Wars," *The Literary Situation,* by Malcolm Cowley, New York: Viking Press, 1948, pp. 23–42. Copyright 1948 by Malcolm Cowley. Reprinted by permission of The Viking Press, Inc.

every racial strain in American society. Here are stories of their adventures in the three armed services and in special branches of each: infantry, artillery, engineers, paratroops, bombing and pursuit squadrons and their ground crews, ambulance sections, salvage outfits, Army Transport Service, Navy destroyers and cargo ships, War Crimes Commission, Military Government, and the psychiatric hospitals where some of the heroes were patients.

Had I looked farther I could have found other novels, published or in manuscript, about nurses, surgeons, Wacs, Waves, ski-troopers, tank crews, battle wagons, submarines, and the General Staff—in fact, about every arm and rank of all the services in every theater of operations. For having failed to read these other novels, I offer no apologies. Some of them, I am sure, are exciting or thoughtful stories, and most of them would broaden our picture of America's fighting men, but I doubt that any of them would change the general picture. And there *is* a general picture that, emerging from all these books, becomes their most impressive feature.

At this point I am thinking particularly of first novels about the war, to the exclusion of books that were written by somewhat older authors like Herman Wouk (*The Caine Mutiny*) and Irwin Shaw (*The Young Lions*) and James Gould Cozzens (*Guard of Honor,* which is a solider work than any of the novels by younger men). For these established writers the war was a subject that they chose like any other, but the first novelists were chosen by the subject and wrote about the war because it was their central experience. This immersion in the subject gives them a strong family resemblance. Different as they are in their social backgrounds and wartime adventures, they end by presenting the same American characters, the same conflicts of purpose, and the same message or group of messages. Some of the novels are so much alike that dialogues and episodes could be transposed from one to another without a change except in names. There are a few individualists among the new authors: notably there is James Jones, who is the only one to write about the Army as an institution and a permanent way of life; there is Norman Mailer, who has a political sense that is rare among writers of his generation; and there is John Horne Burns, with the strained but persuasive lyricism he achieved in *The Gallery* and never achieved again; but these and a few others are exceptions. Most of the young novelists might as well have been commissioned and trained in advance to write each his separate volume in a great collaborative history of World War II as seen by the fighting men. That is the great defect of the separate novels, but it is also a virtue of the undertaking as a whole. Together the novels form a production of lasting value, one that may well be richer and more complete than the account we possess of any nation's part in any other recent war.

To some extent the nature of this joint report is determined by the nature of its authors as observers and story-tellers. War novelists are not sociologists or historians, and neither are they average soldiers. The special training and talent of novelists lead them to express rather special moods. They are usually critical in temper and often they are self-critical to the point of being burdened with feelings of guilt. They are sensitive—about themselves in the beginning; but if they have imagination (and they need it) they learn to be sensitive for others, including the conquered peoples among whom American soldiers were forced to live. In military service many future writers were men of whom their comrades said that they were "always goofing off by themselves." They suffered more than others from the enforced promiscuity of Army and shipboard life. Most of them were rebels against discipline when they thought it was illogical—which they usually did—and rebels against the system that divides officers from enlisted men. Rather more than half of the novelists served in the ranks. The others were commissioned, but, being young, they seldom rose above the grade of Army captain or Navy lieutenant and they formed a lasting resentment toward senior officers. Politically most of them were indifferent or vaguely liberal without belonging to any party.

All these characteristics lend a special color to their joint report, which, before being accepted as historical fact, would have to be compared with reports by others having different temperaments and different types of specialized training. Yet the war novelists were trying hard to be accurate observers and to tell the true story of what they saw. When we find them in substantial agreement on a number of topics, we should listen attentively to what they say.

II

A first point on which almost all the novelists agree is that Americans in the mass remained a most unwarlike people, even when they were drilled, armed, and set to fighting all over the globe. *From Here to Eternity* is the only novel that presents a group of professional soldiers, thirty-year men, with sympathy and understanding. The other books are written from the standpoint of uniformed civilians, men for whom the war, although it lasted four years, was merely an interruption in their civilian lives. In the armed services they adopted an interim code of morality. Uncertain of the future, the soldiers depicted in the novels had ceased to judge any action by its distant effects. Most of their efforts were directed toward momentary gratifications—getting cash, getting drunk, getting laid—or simply toward keeping alive and out of trouble.

With a few exceptions they didn't know or couldn't say why they were fighting. "American soldiers rarely go in for ideological discussion and that kind of thing," says the hero of *The Gesture,* by John Cobb, a novel about bomber crews in England. Nevertheless the question was discussed in orientation lectures and sometimes by the men themselves, though it made them feel uncomfortably solemn. Almost all of them agreed that Hitler and the Japanese had to be stopped, but they couldn't understand why somebody else than they, individually, shouldn't have done the stopping. The exceptions among them were either radicals and bleeding hearts or else Polish and Jewish refugees, and both types are presented in the novels with a sort of distant incomprehension. In *The Gesture* a lieutenant colonel who understands and hates fascism nearly ruins the bombing squadron because he doesn't understand his fellow Americans. In *Point of Honor,* by M. L. Kadish—a thoughtful novel about the fighting in Italy—there is a Jewish soldier who had once served in the German army and now wants to destroy it. His fighting zeal makes him so unpopular with his American comrades that he ends by going insane.

This indifference about larger issues had some effect on morale, to judge by the novels, but less than might have been expected. Morale was good in some outfits, bad in others. The novels report that it was excellent in the Marines and the paratroops (see *Battle Cry,* by Leon M. Uris, and *Those Devils in Baggy Pants,* by Ross S. Carter), generally good in the Navy, except on small vessels commanded by incompetent officers (see *Mr. Roberts,* by Thomas Heggen), and mixed in the Army, where it was worst in battalions kept too long at the front (see *Day without End,* by Van Van Praag) and in segregated detachments of Negroes. Among aviators it was good in the air, bad on the ground (see *The Gesture*). Most men in all services accepted the war as they might have accepted an earthquake and tried to do their best in the circumstances.

To judge by their reported conversations, Americans in World War II were tougher and more sophisticated than their fathers in 1918. They were less ashamed of their vices, less religious (except for devout Catholics), and less affected by political propaganda. Often they proved refractory to discipline, and several novelists tell us that in the South Pacific they killed most of their prisoners. Although they were good fighting troops and highly skilled, if reckless and wasteful, in handling their superb mechanical equipment, they proved irresponsible and corrupt as garrison forces in conquered territory.

It is this last characteristic of Americans as soldiers that left the deepest impression on many of the novelists. Alfred Hayes and John Horne Burns writing about Italy, Lionel Shapiro about Germany, Robert Shaplen about ports on the China Sea, and Elliott Chaze about Japan all make it clear that the early occupation forces were leaving bitter memories behind them. In *The Stainless Steel Kimono,* a novel about seven tough paratroopers, Chaze tries to explain why the soldiers acted as they did. "The reaction of most occupation troops in Japan," he says, "is that of a person suddenly handed a brimming bedpan and told to guard its contents carefully. It comes as a shock to the average American to find himself custodian of such a smelly and strange country." In *A Corner of the World,* Robert Shaplen finds almost nothing but corruption in postwar Shanghai, Saigon, Manila, and Macao. The one truly honest man in his book, a German Jew, is murdered by the Macao police for his honesty. Alfred Hayes, in *All Thy Conquests,* quotes the Italians on their conquerors. "We have been liberated," they say. "We have been liberated from cigarettes, shoes, meat, gasoline, and our women." Lionel Shapiro's book, *The Sealed Verdict,* is a picture of demoralization in the American zone of Germany. Although the style is close to that of slick-paper magazines, some of the descriptions are hard to forget:

A Red Cross club for enlisted men occupied the most important building still standing in the street, the former Palast Kino. Just beyond the lights that brightened the entrance to the club, each dark doorway of the boarded, fire-gutted shops was populated by one or two girls. They were mostly children of thirteen or fourteen, and the rouge that was lumpily applied to their cheeks made them look like Halloween pranksters rather than apprentices on the dreary night watch of the camp follower. . . . A little man with sunken cheeks appeared at Lashley's elbow and walked with them briefly, whispering, "What got to sell? *Zigaretten? Amerikanische* dollars?" He fell away in the darkness and a boy, perhaps ten, took his place. "Want girl? Pretty girl. Young. No sick." He too slunk away. As they crossed in front of the Red Cross Club, two MP's saluted briskly.

The briskly saluted conquerors were themselves affected by the demoralization around them and helped to make it worse by profiteering at the expense of the conquered. "I don't know why," says Burns in *The Gallery,* "but most Americans had a blanket hatred of all Italians. They figured it this way: these Ginsoes have made war on us, so it doesn't matter what we do to them, boost their prices, shatter their economy, and shack up with their women. . . . I saw that we could mouth democratic catchwords and yet give the Neapolitans a huge black market. I saw that we could prate of the evils of fascism, yet be just as ruthless as Fascists with people who'd already been pushed around."

As a rule the soldiers made little distinction among the occupied, the liberated, and the Allied countries, since the people in all of them were foreigners—that is, frogs, limeys, heinies, ginsoes, yellow bastards, wogs, flips, or gooks. Yet the Americans themselves belonged to many racial strains, and this created a problem of discrimination that is a major or minor theme in many novels. A favorite device is to present a squad or platoon composed of different racial elements. There will be a Jew and an Italian (one of them from Brooklyn), a Texan, a farm boy (always from Iowa), a hillbilly, a Mexican, and an Anglo-Saxon from an Ivy League college—these are the required characters—and sometimes there will also be a Boston Irishman, an Indian from Arizona, a Pole from the Midwestern steel mills, and a Swedish lumberjack from Puget Sound. The Texan or the Irishman creates dissension by his racial prejudice, but the Jew and the Mexican turn out to be heroes, the Texan is killed or converted, and the squad becomes a family of blood brothers. Sometimes the squad stands for the whole nation, as we learn from one of the later novels, *Mask of Glory,* by Dan Levin. The book tells how Glenn Manson, born Kasimir Minkiewicz, enlists in the Marines and is accepted by his comrades. By dying on Iwo Jima he enables his Polish family in Cleveland to feel at home and proud in their adopted country.

Although the novelists are always opposed to racial discrimination, some of them are also opposed to the zealots who try to impose racial equality without sufficient preparation. In *The Gesture*—as also in *Guard of Honor,* by James Gould Cozzens—a liberal-minded officer tries to introduce Negro troops into an area reserved for whites, and the result comes close to being a military disaster. In *Last of the Conquerors,* by William Gardner Smith, we learn what the Negroes themselves were thinking. After a year in Germany, the author tells us, not one of them wanted to be sent home. "You know what the hell I learned?" one of them says on his last night in Berlin. "That a nigger ain't no different from nobody else. . . . I hadda come over here and let the Nazis teach me that. They don't teach that stuff back in the land of the free."

Almost all the novels have a great deal to say about the sexual behavior of the human male, and in many respects they support Dr. Kinsey's conclusions. On two points, however, they present so much opposing evidence that they make you wonder whether Kinsey's statistics are accurate. His first book says at some length that there were no significant changes in the male sexual pattern during the period of twenty-two years covered by his researches. "There is not even evidence," he says, "that patterns of sexual behavior are materially altered among men in the armed forces during a period of war." The novelists do not argue with these two statements, but they describe American soldiers as acting with vastly more freedom in sexual matters than any novelist, even Hemingway, described them in World War I. Moreover, the novelists show by many examples that Americans learned new patterns of behavior during their wartime service in Europe or Asia or the South Seas.

There is more sex than love in the novels, and the usual explanation is simply the stress of war. "Overseas," says John Cobb, "love, like everything else, is a form of direct action." Some of the authors hint that romantic love is difficult for self-centered and self-conscious Americans to achieve. Says John Horne Burns, who is given to making direct statements, "In America I remember a tension between the sexes. Human love is a disease for the isolation ward, not at all nice. Thus love in America is often divided into the classifications of Having Sex and Getting Married. Neither has much to do with love." He depicts several of his characters as learning naturalness and self-forgetfulness from the Neapolitan women. In *The Wolf That Fed Us,* Robert Lowry's soldiers are renewed and restored by Roman women, as if these were the she-wolf that suckled Romulus and Remus.

Few American women appear in the novels, and there are fewer still whom the authors seem to admire; many of the others are cold, selfish, even malignant. For some reason the prejudice against American women seems to be strongest in novels published shortly after the war.[1] I counted the romantic or tragic love stories in ten of these earlier books. Of the affairs that go beyond the category of merely Having Sex, there are four with Italians, two with Germans (including the love affair of the young Negro in *Last of the Conquerors*), two with Frenchwomen (of whom one is half Javanese), one with a Tonkinese, one with a New Zealander, and one with a Japanese "just like Madame Buttercup in the movies." Only two of the soldiers portrayed at length fall in love with American girls. One of these affairs ends in frustration and the other (in *All Thy Conquests*) is presented with cold disgust, like a dead mouse held out in a dustpan.

Rather more than half the novels, as I said, are written from the standpoint of enlisted men, and the others from that of commissioned officers— except for books like *The Naked and the Dead,* which try to include both standpoints by presenting all the ranks involved in a separate action or a minor campaign. Almost all the authors agree, however, that a gulf exists between the two military castes. Most of them show that there is sullen resentment on one side and uneasiness on the other. Often the men complain of special privileges granted to officers in respect to food, liquor, and liberty. Some of the more sensitive officers, but only a few, are depicted as being ashamed to enjoy the privileges, while the effect on others is to make them feel that they are living in an unreal world. "What am I doing with bars on me?" a captain asks his American mistress in *All Thy Conquests*. "I look in the mirror and I don't believe it. We're an army of phonies, baby, that's what we are. An army of jerks playing soldier."

The novels reveal a special conflict over the superior sexual opportunities enjoyed by officers. Apparently it was worst in the South Pacific; there the only white women in the advanced areas were nurses, who ranked as lieutenants and weren't allowed to associate with enlisted men. Michener, writing his *Tales of the South Pacific* from the naval officer's point of view, gives a pretty lurid picture of the situation. "There were," he says, "many other attacks or near attacks on nurses in the islands. They were grim, hushed-up affairs. Nobody ever knew exactly what had happened. Just rumor and surmises. But in time every nurse knew that she lived in danger. She could see in the baleful looks of enlisted men that they considered her little more than a plaything brought out to amuse the officers. With thousands of men for every white woman, with enlisted men forbidden to date the nurses, it was to be expected that vague and terrible things would occur."

Michener writes almost like a Southern planter in the Black Belt, living in fear that his womenfolk will be outraged by a sullen peasantry. Once when he paid a visit to the enlisted men in their quarters he was surprised to find that most of them were friendly. There was one man, however, who looked at him

---

[1] But later we find the case against American women stated at length, and classically, by James M. Michener in *Sayonara* (1954).

"with that grim stare which officers see so often and which always means: 'What the hell are you doing here?' " Norman Mailer describes the rivalry between Lieutenant Hearn and his platoon sergeant, who deliberately leads him into a Japanese ambush. After Hearn's death one of the men blurts out, "The Lootenant was a good guy." Another swears, "They ain't a———one of those officers is worth a goddam." "I wouldn't spit on the best one of them," a third man says furiously. "I ain't afraid of saying what I think. They're all bastards."

The war novels published after 1950 are less rancorous as a group, and some of them present a new hero who bridges the gulf between enlisted men and officers; he is a sergeant commanding a squad or a lieutenant commanding a platoon. In either case he is trusted by his superiors, while he serves as a father image to the soldiers, who follow him like children. Sometimes at the end of the book (see *Walk on the Water,* by Ralph Leveridge) he becomes a Christ who gives his life to save them. In *Victory Also Ends,* by Fred W. Booth, the father figure is a captain, but that is the highest rank he reaches in any war novel I have read. Majors continue to be represented as pompous fools, lieutenant colonels as butchers, generals as heartless villains—"And they're all bastards," most of the novelists might be saying.

Michener is almost the only author who accepts the caste system. The epauleted heroes of his *Tales of the South Pacific* come from wealthy homes, and more than once he celebrates "those graces of behavior which mark the true naval officer and distinguish him from men of the other services." One suspects him of ranking Army colonels with boatswains in the Navy. All the other novelists make it clear that they favor more democracy in the armed forces, and Norman Mailer offers an indirect but persuasive plea for democracy by allowing General Cummings, the villain of the novel, to state the arguments against it. Cummings' notion is that Americans, because of their high living standards, are naturally the worst soldiers in the world. "What you've got to do," he says, "is break them down. Every time an enlisted man sees an officer get an extra privilege, it breaks him down a little more. . . . The Army functions best when you're frightened of the man above you, and contemptuous of your subordinates."

A feeling present as an overtone in some novels is the fear that the military hierarchy will become the model and furnish the leaders for an American fascism. In *The Naked and the Dead* the feeling is discussed in a series of conversations between Hearn, the liberal-minded lieutenant, and the odious General Cummings. "The machine techniques of this century demand consolidation," Cummings says, "and with that you've got to have fear, because the majority of men must be subservient to the machine, and it's not a business they instinctively enjoy." Later he says, dotting the i's, "There are countries which have latent powers, latent resources, they are full of potential energy, so to speak. And there are great concepts which can unlock that, express it.

As kinetic energy a country is organization, coordinated effort, your epithet, fascism. . . . Historically the purpose of this war is to translate America's potential into kinetic energy." The general explains that we are about to take over the German dream. "You can consider the Army," he concludes, "as a preview of the future."

It would be wrong, however, to end on this political theme, since it appears in a minority of the novels and since Mailer has stronger political convictions than any of his colleagues. A note or at least an undertone to be heard more often is a sort of distrust for all human institutions larger than a squad or at most a platoon, and with it a feeling that goodness is to be found only in separate individuals. While describing horrors on the battlefield, bureaucracy at headquarters, and corruption in the occupied countries, the authors keep finding separate men who are not only heroes but martyrs and saints. Never have I read a group of novels that contained so many truly good persons—simple souls like Joey Goldstein, the Brooklyn mechanic, and his friend Ridges the sharecropper, in *The Naked and the Dead;* champions of the oppressed like Noah Ackerman in *The Young Lions;* Christs of a new dispensation like Sergeant Hervey in *Walk on the Water* (as Christ walked) and Lieutenant Shulman in *The Gallery;* and there are even saintly women, provided they are foreigners, like Carla in *All Thy Conquests,* Thémis Delisle in *The Sealed Verdict,* and the New Zealand widow in *Battle Cry.* The novelists are like the two angels who looked for virtue in Sodom that the city might be saved, and, luckier than the angels, each has come forward with a righteous few.

III

All this will serve as a partial answer to the first question, what the new writers have been saying about the war. There is still the second question, how the combat novels of this period compare with those written after 1920 by young veterans of the other war. The question must be simple to ask, since we have heard it on every side, but it isn't simple to answer. It calls for a series of explanations, some of which lead us into a curious borderland between literary history and military tactics. Besides a discussion of the novels themselves, in terms of method and purpose, it also involves a comparison between two wars fought in different fashions and leaving behind them different memories.

A few points, fortunately, are now beyond dispute. There is no longer any doubt that many more novels have been written about World War II than about World War I, that more of them reach a certain level of competence or merit, and that, as a group, they compose a sounder body of work. Writers of the second wartime generation have been quick to master the tools of their craft. On the average, their books are not only more smoothly and skillfully written than most war novels of the 1920s but are also better as reporting of "what really happened in action," to borrow a phrase from Ernest Hemingway.

Speaking of his early years, Hemingway said, "I was trying to write then and I found the greatest difficulty, aside from knowing truly what you really felt, rather than what you were supposed to feel, and had been taught to feel, was to put down what really happened in action." Most adventure-story writers had talked about the hero's emotion—that is, the fear or wonder or blind fury aroused in him by the events in which he was taking part. Hemingway wanted to arouse the same emotion in his readers instead of merely telling them how the hero had felt. He was trying to put down, so he said, "the actual things which produced the emotion that you experienced . . . the sequence of motion and fact which made the emotion and which would be as valid in a year or in ten years or, with luck and if you stated it purely enough, always."

Because his eyes were fixed on "actual things," Hemingway's battle scenes had a force and clarity that impressed the novelists who came after him. His method has become an accepted part of their technical equipment and it has led to a change in war fiction that I can illustrate by quoting some paragraphs written twenty-five years apart. The first is from Thomas Boyd's *Through the Wheat* (1923) and describes the taking of a village near Soissons:

> Bullets flew in every direction. Men toppled down from the windows of houses. Others raced up the steps of dwellings. Men ran through the streets, wild and tumultuous. They returned to the pavement, guarding their captives. Men poured the hate of their beings upon the town. They wept and cursed like lost souls in limbo. All of their fear, all of their anxiety, all of the restraint which had been forced upon them during the morning when they lay like animals in a slaughter-house and their brains numbed with apprehension, came out in an ugly fury.

Boyd is stressing the anxiety and rage of the Marines who took the village, rather than the events that produced those emotions. He is writing honestly, but awkwardly and in the fog of war, so that all his violence is dim and distant. He is also using elegant synonyms—if he writes "houses" in one sentence he has to write "dwellings" in the next—and fancy phrases like "hate of their beings" and "lost souls in limbo." A very few novelists of the Second World War still render combat scenes in this old-fashioned prose. Ralph Leveridge, in *Walk on the Water,* writes as if all his models for imitation had been selected from the ten-cent counter of a second-hand bookstore. Here is a typical paragraph:

> Men swore and raved. Men sweated with exquisite apprehension. They raised their fists, and their mouths slobbering, they wildly, incoherently jabbered obscenities, heaped every curse they knew upon the civilians back home, their

government, their mothers who had conceived them, and sometimes, upon the Japs.

Except for the one word "Japs," that might have been written by Thomas Boyd in 1923. It is, however, by no means typical of the second-war novelists, most of whom practice the new method of writing combat scenes, using the simplest language to set down "what really happened in action." Here, for example, is a paragraph by Norman Mailer describing a Japanese attack across a jungle river:

> "Shit." Croft's hand found the flare box, and he loaded the gun again. He was beginning to see in the darkness, and he hesitated. But something moved on the river and he fired the flare. As it burst, a few Japanese soldiers were caught motionless in the water. Croft pivoted his gun on them and fired. One of the soldiers remained standing for an incredible time. There was no expression on his face; he looked vacant and surprised even as the bullets struck him in the chest.

The paragraph begins with a formerly unprintable expletive. That sort of beginning is a habit of many novelists in this second postwar period, and Mailer is more addicted to it than most of his colleagues. But the chief feature of the paragraph, from the technical point of view, is the absence of terms like "fear," "hate," "fury," and "exquisite apprehension." Instead of stating the emotion of his characters, Mailer gives us "the sequence of motion and fact which made the emotion." He follows the method that Hemingway had discovered twenty-four years before him; and the fact is that Mailer's paragraph is reminiscent of one that Hemingway included in his second booklet, *in our time,* which was privately printed in Paris in 1924, a year before his book of stories with the same title was published in New York. The earlier paragraph reads:

> We were in a garden in Mons. Young Buckley came in with his patrol from across the river. The first German I saw climbed up over the garden wall. We waited till he got one leg over and then potted him. He had so much equipment on and looked awfully surprised and fell down into the garden. Then three more came over further down the wall. We shot them. They all came just like that.

It happens that among the second-war novelists Mailer reveals less kinship with Hemingway than most of the others. The spirit is different, the style is different, the characters are seen with different eyes. If Mailer has clearly contracted a literary debt it is rather to James T. Farrell, so that his first novel has been described as the Studs Lonigan boys in the South Pacific. Yet even Mailer depends on the Hemingway method when he describes men in battle, and his dying Japanese "looked vacant and surprised," almost exactly like the

German climbing over the garden wall in Mons. The truth is that Hemingway discovered what has so far proved to be the most effective method of rendering a battle scene. It can be learned from his books or studied in college courses, and most of the younger war novelists have followed it instinctively.

They are good technicians, good reporters, and I should judge that they are also good historians. Perhaps the most serious criticism of their work is that the group of books is more impressive than the separate works of fiction. These are on a higher level of competence than almost all the first-war novels, but what they form is a tableland, not a chain of mountains. I may be speaking as a prejudiced witness, proud of his long memory, but it seems to me that none of the authors, not even Norman Mailer and James Jones, has had the separate impact for these times that Dos Passos and Cummings and Hemingway had in the early 1920s.

IV

Partly the lack of impact may be the fault of their readers more than that of the writers. The American public has become so familiar with horrors recounted from life that it is no longer much impressed with those described in novels, even if the novels are also based on life. Although the slaughter of Japanese prisoners in *The Naked and the Dead* is more shocking than any battle scene in the first-war novels, it produced no such public outcry. In *Three Soldiers* (1922) Dos Passos described an Army stockade for American prisoners, the one commanded in life by Captain "Hardboiled" Smith. Congressmen debated his charges of cruelty, and I seem to remember that the Army promised reforms. There is a still worse stockade in *From Here to Eternity,* described from more intimate experience, but it has produced no public protests. In the matter of horror the novelists are always a step behind reality, and the public is too stunned by reality to demand action. Even the novelists have developed an attitude of acquiescence in horror, and some of them—not James Jones—have lost the capacity for indignation; their books contribute to the general picture of a situation which they do not attempt to change.

The earlier group of postwar writers, those of the 1920s, were often described as being "disillusioned," but I have always felt that the adjective was badly chosen. They were something quite different: rebels in life and art. To be a rebel implies faith in one's ability to do things better than those in power. Young writers of the 1920s had that faith, which was sometimes close to being an illusion; they believed that a world in which their standards prevailed would be gayer, more tolerant, and more natural than the world of their elders. It would have no armies. Never again—and this is what they kept saying in novel after novel—must there be such a pointless sacrifice of lives as in the battles on the Western Front.

Even a professional soldier would now admit that their rebellion was based on a valid complaint, since the Western battles of World War I were most of them useless and stupid from the military point of view. Until 1918 the commanding generals on both sides had no real military objectives. Their imaginations were deadened by the sheer quantity of manpower and material at their disposal. They planned their massive offensives merely to gain terrain, when yielding it might have been the wiser strategy, or merely to inflict losses on the enemy. Verdun is the archetypical example. The battle was started by the Germans in the hope—as General von Falkenhayn confessed in his memoirs—that the French would "bleed to death." It lasted five months without interruption and was several times renewed; it killed a million men, including as many Germans as Frenchmen, and ended with both sides almost exactly where they began.

In that same year the British attacked on the Somme and lost sixty thousand men on the first day without gaining any ground whatever. The war continued on the same premises, behind the same barbed-wire entanglements that were like climbproof factory fences; it was death on the production line. Death, not victory, was in the air and the two most famous poems of the war were "In Flanders Fields"—about poppies in the mass graveyards—and "I Have a Rendezvous with Death." Even Blackjack Pershing caught the contagion. When he offered his men to Foch after the German break-through of March 1918, he said, not "We are here to win," but "We are here to be killed." This background has to be kept in mind when we are judging the books that grew out of World War I. The military leaders of the time, and most of the politicians too, had shown their inability to think except in quantities of material and numbers of corpses. The young men who wrote the books were in revolt because their elders had betrayed them and slaughtered their friends and because they believed that the world would be better if all the principles of the elders were set aside. They said, and deeply felt, "The war was wrong," then rushed on to a broader conclusion: "All wars are evil, like the munitions makers who foment them for dividends and like the governments that order young men to be killed."

Today their broad conclusion seems wrong-headed or simple-minded, but it gave emotional force and a broad perspective to the novels that some of them wrote. There is no such conclusion to be found in the novels of World War II. Emotionally it would be less justified, because the new war wasn't fought in the same blindly stupid and life-destructive fashion. Civilians died pointlessly by the hundreds of thousands, but this time the leaders were not so eager to have our soldiers die. The war included battles where the losses were on the same scale as in 1914–18, not to mention separate actions like Tarawa and Iwo Jima where they were proportionately higher, but these were not useless sacrifices like Verdun for the Germans or Passchendaele for the British, and they usually ended in clear-cut victories or defeats. If the soldiers didn't know why they, individually, were fighting, they still accepted the war as a fact of nature and could usually see the military logic of the campaigns in which they were engaged.

All this helps to explain why novels about the Second World War have no such message of simple pacifism as we find in many books of the 1920s. There are still rebellions, but they are on a smaller scale and have limited objects of attack: racial prejudice among soldiers, the military caste system, and the self-centeredness of American women. Many of the novels—especially those written after 1950, under the shadow of another world conflict—are not rebellious at all; instead they are celebrations of squad-room comradeship, Navy traditions, or the fighting Marines.

The novelists write as if they were wholly immersed in the war and as if, instead of being an exterior event to describe, it had become an inner condition of their lives. Sergeant Holloway, one of the two principal characters in *Point of Honor,* goes into action with a battery of howitzers. As the guns fire, "Holloway eases into a kind of peace. Now he lives compact within the space of action. He can eye the present the way he saw a small snake eye a bird's nest once before the war." Many of the novels give us just such a narrow-focused, intent, and snake's-eye picture of the fighting. Even when they soar over the battlefront, the picture remains narrow. Lieutenant Evans, the other hero of the same novel, is an artillery observer in a Piper Cub who muses as the battle unrolls beneath him. "Had he thought once that the war had an issue? Anti-fascism, perhaps? Under aerial observation, war shed issues. War was Fact, Thing-in-Itself. Existence sheer beyond argument; it spoke from the Rapido and beyond. 'I AM THAT I AM,' it declared to you. 'I AM MY OWN JUSTIFICATION.'"

In general the new novelists do not presume to judge the war. They do not suggest that it was foolish in its aims or that, given the temper of the people, it might have been avoided by wiser statesmanship. They are not in revolt against the war itself so much as they are disappointed by the fruits of victory, and more than disappointed: some of them are heartbroken at the contrast between our aims and efforts on one hand and our achievements on the other; between soldiers dying in the jungle and soldiers drunk in Japanese houses of prostitution; between the delirious joy with which our men were greeted as they marched into a liberated city and the despair of the inhabitants when they learned that we could be—to quote from John Horne Burns—"just as ruthless as Fascists with people who'd been pushed around already. That," he says, "was why my heart broke in Naples in August 1944."

Many of the novelists have begun to question the whole idea of progress through collective effort. It was the idea that dominated the 1930s, both in the democracies and in the totalitarian countries, but now the novelists are asking what can come of such an effort, except more cruelty and more corruption. They have even begun to question themselves and are not at all sure that they could have done better in the circumstances than our actual leaders. In a word, many of the novelists are really disillusioned this time, instead of being rebellious, and the disillusion lends a more conservative tone to their writing.

Their conservatism, or conservative liberalism, is also expressed in their literary technique. Here they offer a contrast with many novelists of the First War, who were always trying experiments and hoping to make discoveries on the order of Hemingway's method for describing battle scenes. Novelists of this later group are apparently more concerned with using and perfecting discoveries already made by their predecessors.

Many war novelists of the 1920s were deeply influenced by French literature and especially by the French Symbolist tradition. Speaking in the broadest terms, one can say that Flaubert was their model, either directly or else as his ideals were refracted through the work of James Joyce and others in the same line. Like Flaubert they wanted to achieve the qualities of precision, economy, and formal balance in hard, new books that shocked the middle classes—books in which, as Edmund Wilson said, "every word, every cadence, every detail, should perform a definite function in producing an intense effect." That was a European ideal, or so it seemed at the time, but the young writers also wanted to use American subject matter and a new literary idiom developed from American speech. They were determined to write truly what they really felt, as Hemingway said, "rather than what you were supposed to feel, and had been taught to feel." The result was that their novels, when they finally appeared, were so different from anything in the past that no French critic could recognize the source of their inspiration. They illustrated an old rule of comparative literature, that the same methods translated from one culture into another are likely to produce radically different results. They may even produce a literary renaissance, and that, in a modest way, was what happened during the 1920s.

In the novels of the Second War I can find very few signs that their authors have been reading French, German, or even English books. There is a touch of Joseph Conrad in *The Gesture* and a few other novels; a touch of Graham Greene in some of the stories about occupied Germany; a suggestion of Kipling's atmosphere in Michener's *Tales of the South Pacific*. Although Kafka, Gide, and Sartre were the Continental authors in fashion during the 1940s, and although they influenced many novels about civilian life, they had no effect on the war novels I have been reading—unless there is a hint of Gide in *The Gallery,* and of that one can't be sure. American influences, on the other hand, are easy to recognize. They even form a sort of pattern that was evident as early as John Hersey's *A Bell for Adano,* published in 1944. One might say that a great many novels of the Second War are based on Dos Passos for structure, since they have collective heroes, in the Dos Passos fashion, and since he invented a series of structural devices for dealing with such heroes in unified works of fiction. At the same time they are based on Scott Fitzgerald for mood, on Steinbeck for humor, and on Hemingway for action and dialogue.

From Here to Eternity was more directly influenced by Thomas Wolfe, and I have already remarked that *The Naked and the Dead* is written in the mood of James T. Farrell. Sometimes—though not in these two cases—the relation of a new writer with an older one is close enough to make the reader uncomfortable; for example, *Mr. Roberts*—the novel, not the play—is Steinbeck's *Cannery Row* towed out to sea. *All Thy Conquests,* by Alfred Hayes, and his later war novel, *The Girl on the Via Flaminia,* are convincing stories that would have been better still if the author hadn't adopted Hemingway's point of view along with his style, so that he seems to be looking at Rome through borrowed spectacles. In most of the books, however, the influence of older American novelists is a little less evident on the surface, though just as pervasive, and it suggests a conclusion about the two periods in fiction. During the 1920s writers were trying to create a new tradition in American literature because the older one had broken down or couldn't be accepted. Now, in the middle of the century, most American writers are trying to develop a tradition that already exists. Some of them, as we shall see, are entirely too faithful to the tradition as expounded by the newer critics.

HORTENSE POWDERMAKER

THE CHANNELING
OF NEGRO AGGRESSION
BY THE CULTURAL PROCESS

It has long been a truism among Negro Americans that they understand whites far better than whites understand them. While this interpretation can be unduly stressed, there is a good deal of substance in it, not only because of white indifference but because Negroes have taken pains not to let whites know them too well. W. E. B. DuBois spoke of a veil that prevents whites from perceiving Negroes accurately. The Negro poet Paul Laurence Dunbar refers to a mask: "Why should the world be overwise/In counting all our tears and sighs?/Nay, let them only see us while/We wear the mask." A popular Negro song repeats the theme: "Got one mind for white folks to see, 'nother for what I know is me; he don't know, he don't know my mind." One of the greatest problems confronting the Negro writer, Ralph Ellison observed in the 1960's, "was the difficulty, based upon our long habit of deception and evasion, of depicting what really happened within our areas of American life. . . ."

Unfortunately, the devices of deception and evasion have too long eluded students of the Negro in America. By drawing too clear a line between behavior patterns of protest and of accommodation, they have frequently failed to discern the fact that protest is often built into accommodative behavior. In the following article anthropologist Hortense Powdermaker discusses the different forms of behavior that Negroes have adopted as a means of chan-

neling their aggressive feelings. Her article focuses on various aspects of ac-
commodative behavior, which often conceal the Negroes' feelings towards
whites. Powdermaker has written at greater length of this and related matters
in After Freedom (*1939*), *her excellent study of the Negro community in a*
Southern town.

$\mathbf{W}$e shall attempt in this article to look at one small segment of our cultural process—namely, a changing pattern of aggressive behavior—caused by the interracial situation. We limit ourselves to considering, at this time, only the Negro side of this complex of interpersonal relations; and we shall do no more than offer a few rather broad hypotheses on the relation between the forms aggression has taken during different historical periods and changes in the cultural processes at these times. For our hypotheses we are indebted to history, anthropology, sociology, and psychoanalysis; to the first three for understanding how social patterns come into being at a given point in time and how they are related to each other; and to the fourth, psychoanalysis, for a clue to the mechanisms by which individuals adopt particular social patterns. We shall concentrate on an analysis of two forms of adaptation where the aggression seems to have been concealed and, therefore, less understood. The two forms are that of the faithful slave and that of the meek, humble, unaggressive Negro who followed him after the Civil War. Since there is much more data on the latter role, this is the one we shall discuss in detail.

Education includes learning to play certain roles, roles which are advantageous to the individual in adapting himself to his particular culture. As the culture changes, so does the role. Adaptation to society begins at birth and ends at death. Culture is not a neatly tied package given to the child in school. It is an ever changing process, gropingly and gradually discovered.[1] The family, church, movies, newspapers, radio programs, books, trade-unions, chambers of commerce, and all other organized and unorganized interpersonal relations are part of education. All these are part of the cultural process, which determines how behavior and attitudes are channeled.

The cultural milieu of the Negro in the United States has run the gamut from slavery to that of a free but underprivileged group, who are slowly but continuously raising their status. From the time slaves were first brought to this country until today there have been barriers and restrictions which have prevented the Negro from satisfying social needs and attaining those values prized most highly by our society. How the resentment against these deprivations is channeled depends largely on cultural factors. Each historical period has produced certain types of adaptation.

Much has been written as to whether slaves emotionally accepted their status or whether they rebelled against it, with the consequent aggressive impulses turned against their masters. There is no categorical answer. Aggres-

---

[1] For further elaboration of this point see Edward Sapir, "The Emergence of the Concept of Personality in a Study of Cultures," *Journal of Social Psychology,* V, 408–15.

REPRINTED from Hortense Powdermaker, "The Channeling of Negro Aggression," *American Journal of Sociology,* Vol. 48 (May 1943), pp. 750–58 by permission of the University of Chicago Press. Copyright 1942, 1943 by the University of Chicago.

sion can be channeled in many ways, and some of these are not discernible except to the trained psychiatrist. But others are quite obvious. The fact that thousands of slaves ran away clearly indicates dissatisfaction with their status.[2] Crimes committed by the slaves are another evidence of lack of acceptance of status and of aggressive feelings toward the whites.

> Many people have assumed that there was little or no crime by Negroes during the slave regime. The impression will be quickly dispelled if one consults the elaborate studies contained in *Judicial Cases concerning American Slavery and the Negro.* . . . In these lists can be found cases of murder, rape, attempted rape, arson, theft, burglary, and practically every conceivable crime.[3]

The fact that these crimes were committed in the face of the most severe deterrents—cutting-off of ears, whipping, castration, death by mutilation—bears witness to the strength of the underlying aggression. Equally cruel was the punishment of those slaves who broke the laws against carrying firearms, assembling, and conspiring to rebel. The Gabriel conspiracy in Richmond, the Vesey conspiracy in Charleston, the Nat Turner rebellion, and others resulted in the massacre of whites and in the burning, shooting, and hanging of the Negroes. These attempts were undertaken despite the fact that the superior power of the whites made it virtually impossible for a slave revolt to be successful.

But the overt aggression was very probably only a small part of the total hostility. The punishments imposed by the culture for failure were too severe and the chances for success too slight to encourage the majority of slaves to rebel to any considerable extent. There were large numbers of loyal and faithful slaves, loyal to the system and to the masters. It is this loyalty that we try to understand.

Psychologically, slavery is a dependency situation. The slave was completely dependent upon the white master for food, clothing, shelter, protection—in other words, for security. If he could gain the good will or affection of the master, his security was increased. In return for this security the Negro gave obedience, loyalty, and sometimes love or affection. With certain limitations the situation of slave and master corresponds to that of child and parent. The young child is completely dependent on his parents for food, shelter, love, and everything affecting his well-being and security. The child learns to be obedient because he is taught that disobedience brings punishment and the withdrawal of something he needs for security. Basic infantile and childhood

---

[2] From 1830 to 1860 about fifty thousand escaped, chiefly through Ohio and Philadelphia. In an earlier period many escaped to near-by Indian tribes, others to Canada and the free states (see E. B. Reuter, *The American Race Problem* [New York, 1938], pp. 117–18).

[3] Quoted in W. D. Weatherford and C. S. Johnson, *Race Relations* (New York, 1934), p. 265.

disciplines relating to sex are imposed on this level. In our culture, parents forbid and punish deviations by a child, who in turn renounces his gratification to gain the parent's approval. "The parent is needed and feared, and must therefore be obeyed; but the hatred to the frustrating parent, though suppressed, must be present somewhere." [4]

We mentioned above that there are certain limitations to our analogy. Obviously, the bondage is greater for the slave than for the child. Equally obviously, while there was love in some master-slave relationships, it was certainly not so prevalent as between parents and children. Again, the child always has a weak and undeveloped ego while the adult slave may have a strong, developed one. But most important is the difference in the reasons for the dependency attitude. The limited strength and resources of the child and his resulting helplessness and anxiety are due to biological causes. But the slave's dependency is imposed on him by culture and has nothing to do with biological factors. The structure of the two dependency situations is, therefore, very different. Nevertheless, functionally they have something in common. To attain the only security available to them, both the slave and the child repress, consciously or unconsciously, their hatred for the object which restricts their desires and freedom. At this late date it is impossible to determine to what degree aggression occurred in slaves' fantasies or in minor overt acts.[5] It probably varied from one slave to another, as it does for children. Neither all children nor all slaves repress their aggression all the time. Running away is a pattern for both groups. Disobedience is followed by punishment for both. Another alternative for both is open rebellion. Finally, children and slaves may accept their dependency and repress their aggression when compensations are adequate. They may even identify with the frustrating object. The picture of the faithful slave who helped the white mistress run the plantation while the master was away fighting, fighting the men who would liberate the slave, is only superficially paradoxical.

Data from psychoanalysis indicate that those children who do not permit their aggressive impulses to break through even in fantasy, not to mention overt behavior, have great difficulty as adults in entering into any personal relationship which does not duplicate the dependency pattern of parent and child. A legal edict of freedom did not immediately change the security system for the slave, conditioned over years to depend on the white man for all security. Time was needed for the compensations of freedom to become part of the ex-slave's security system. The process of growing up, or becoming less dependent, is a long and difficult one.

With emancipation the slave, from being a piece of property with no rights

---

[4] A. Kardiner and R. Linton, *The Individual and Society* (New York, 1939), p. 24.

[5] I know of no accurate way of getting data on this point. The memories of old ex-slaves would be colored by what has happened to them since slavery was abolished. Aggressive impulses which may have been completely repressed during slavery could be released and brought into consciousness after slavery ceased.

at all, attained the status of a human being—but an underprivileged one. Psychological dependency did not vanish with the proclamation of freedom. In the period following the Civil War the slave's illiteracy, his complete lack of capital and property, the habituation to the past, and the continuous forces wielded by the whites in power created new conditions for the continuance of the old dependency. The recently freed Negro was dependent on the whites for jobs, for favors, for grants of money to set up schools, and for much of his security. In the South, following the Reconstruction Period, it was by obtaining favors from whites rather than by insisting on his rights that the Negro was able to make any progress or attain any security. The set of mores which insured the colored man's status being lower than that of the whites was and is still firmly intrenched. The denial of the courtesy titles (Mr., Mrs., Miss); the Jim Crowism in schools, buses, and trains, in places of residence; the denial of legal rights; the threat of lynching—these are among the more obvious ways of "keeping the Negro in his place." He is deprived of what are considered legal, social, and human rights, without any of the compensations for his deprivation which he had under slavery.

The same questions we asked about the slave occur again. Did the Negro really accept his position? Or was aggression aroused, and, if so, how did the culture channel it? This is an easier situation to study than the slavery of the past; for varied ways of reacting or adapting to this situation became stereotyped and still persist today. They are therefore susceptible of direct study.

First, there is direct aggression against its true object. Since the whites had, and still have, superior power and since Negroes are highly realistic, they rarely use this method on any large scale except in times of crisis, and then as a climax to a long series of more indirect aggressive behavior patterns. The knocking-down of a white overseer, the direct attack on other whites, has occurred, but only occasionally. One of the reasons advanced by many southern white planters for their preference for colored share-croppers to white ones is that the former do not fight back like the latter.

A second method consists in substituting a colored object for the white object of aggression. This was, and still is, done very frequently. The high degree of intra-Negro quarreling, crime, and homicide, revealed by statistics and observation, can be directly correlated with the Negro's frustration in being unable to vent his hostility on the whites. The mechanism of the substitution of one object of aggression for another is well known to the scientist and to the layman.[6] The substitution of Negro for white is encouraged by the culture pattern of white official and unofficial leniency toward intra-Negro crime. Courts, more particularly southern ones, are mild in their view of intra-Negro

---

[6] This is reflected in the jokes and stories about the man who has a bad day at the office and then "takes it out" on his wife or children when he comes home in the evening.

offenses, and the prevailing white attitude is one of indulgence toward those intra-Negro crimes which do not infringe on white privileges.[7]

A third possibility is for the Negro to retreat to an "ivory tower" and attempt to remain unaffected by the interracial situation. But this type of adjustment is very difficult and consequently a rare one.

Another form of adaptation consists in the Negro's identification with his white employer, particularly if the latter has great prestige. Some of the slaves also identified themselves with the great families whom they served. This pattern may likewise be observed in white servants. Still another adaptation is the diversion of aggression into wit, which has been and still is a much-used mechanism. We have not sufficient data on these two mechanisms to discuss them in detail.

But we do want to analyze in some detail a very frequent type of adjustment which occurred after the Civil War and which has persisted. We mean the behavior of the meek, humble, and unaggressive Negro, who is always deferential to whites no matter what the provocation may be. The psychological mechanism for this form of adaptation is less obvious than some of the other types, and a more detailed analysis is therefore needed. We have called this Negro "unaggressive," and that is the way his overt behavior could be correctly described. All our data, however, indicate that he does have aggressive impulses against whites, springing from the interracial situation. He would be abnormal if he did not have them. Over and over again field studies reveal that this type of Negro is conscious of these resentments. But he conceals his true attitude from the whites who have power. How has he been able to conceal his aggression so successfully? His success here is patent. What is the psychological mechanism which enables the Negro to play this meek, deferential role?

A clue appears in certain similarities of this kind of behavior to that of the masochist, particularly through the detailed analysis of masochism by Dr. Theodor Reik in his recent book on that subject.[8] The seeming paradox of the masochist enjoying his suffering has been well known to psychoanalysts. He derives pleasure, because, first, it satisfies unconscious guilt feeling. Second (and here is where Dr. Reik has gone beyond the other psychoanalysts in his interpretation), the masochist derives another kind of pleasure, because his suffering is a prelude to his reward and eventual triumph over his adversary. In other words, he gets power through his suffering. We must not be misunderstood at this point. The meek Negro is neither neurotic nor masochistic any more than the slave was biologically a child. But the unaggressive behavior has some elements in common with (and some different from) the

---

[7] For further elaboration see H. Powdermaker, *After Freedom* (Viking Press, 1939), pp. 172–74.

[8] *Masochism in Modern Man* (New York: Farrar & Rinehart, 1941).

behavior of the masochist; and a comparison of the two gives a clue to an understanding of the strength behind the meek, humble role played by so many Negroes.

First, there are essential differences between the Negroes we are describing and the masochists analyzed by Dr. Reik and others. The Negro's sufferings and sacrifices are not unconsciously self-inflicted (as are those of the masochist) but are inflicted on him by the culture. The Negro plays his social masochistic role consciously, while the psychologically compulsive masochist does it unconsciously. These two important differences should be kept in mind while the similarities are discussed.

Our hypothesis is that the meek, unaggressive Negro, who persists today as a type and whom we have opportunity to study, feels guilty about his conscious and unconscious feelings of hostility and aggression toward the white people. These Negroes are believing Christians who have taken very literally the Christian doctrine that it is sinful to hate. Yet on every hand they are faced with situations which must inevitably produce hatred in any normal human being. These situations run the scale from seeing an innocent person lynched to having to accept the inferior accommodations on a Jim Crow train. The feeling of sin and guilt is frequently and openly expressed. In a Sunday-school class in a southern rural colored church a teacher tells the tale of a sharecropper who had worked all season for a white planter, only to be cheated out of half his earnings. The teacher's lesson is that it is wrong to hate this planter, because Christ told us to love our enemies. The members of the class say how hard it is not to hate but that since it is a sin they will change their hate to love. They regard this as possible, although difficult.[9]

One woman in the same community, who plays the deferential role to perfection and who, whites say, never steps out of "her place," tells me she feels guilty because she hates the whites, who do not seem to distinguish between her, a very moral, respectable, and law-abiding person, and the immoral, disreputable colored prostitutes of the community. She says that God and Jesus have told her not to hate but to love—and so she must drive the hatred and bitterness away. Almost every human being in our culture carries a load of guilt (heavy or light as the case may be) over his conscious and unconscious aggressive impulses. It is easy then to imagine how heavy is the load of guilt for the believing Christian Negro who lives in an interracial situation which is a constant stimulus to aggressive thoughts and fantasies. By acting in exactly the opposite manner—that is, meekly and unaggressively—he can appease his guilt feelings consciously and unconsciously. It is this appeasement which accounts, in part, for his pleasure in the unaggressive role he plays with the whites.

But only in part. The unaggressive Negro enjoys his role also because through it he feels superior to the whites. Like the masochist, he thinks of his

---

[9] Cf. Powdermaker, *op. cit.*, pp. 247–48.

present sufferings as a contrasting background for his future glory. His is the final victory, and so he can afford to feel superior to his white opponent who is enjoying a temporary victory over him. My own field work and the work of others give many examples. Dr. Charles S. Johnson, in his recent book on rural colored youth in the South, discusses the dissimulation of many of the young people studied. He says:

> Outward submissiveness and respect may thus be, as often as not, a mask behind which these youth conceal their attitude. George Cator is an example of this behavior. He has learned to flatter as a means of preserving his own estimate of himself. . . . "When I'm around them, I act like they are more than I am. I don't think they are, but they do. I hear people say that's the best way to act." [10]

Any expression of antagonism would be dangerous, but this is not the whole story. It is not just that this boy and others avoid danger by meek negative behavior. There is a positive element in that he and others are insuring eventual victory. This was expressed by a colored servant who is a model of deferential behavior when with the whites. However, to me she says, partly scornfully and partly jokingly, that she considers it ridiculous that having cleaned the front porch and entrance she has to use the back entrance. She hates having to walk in the back door, which in this case is not only the symbol of status for a servant but the symbol that a whole race has a servant status. She adds that she expects to go to Heaven and there she will find rest—and no back doors.[11]

The Christian doctrines, "The last shall be first, and the first shall be last" and "The meek shall inherit the earth," and all the promises of future reward for suffering give strong homiletic sanction to the feeling that the Negroes' present status and suffering is a prelude to their future triumph. Colored ministers give very concise expression to this attitude. A sermon heard in a colored church in rural Mississippi related

> the story of a rich woman who lived in a big house and had no time for God. When she went to Heaven she was given an old shanty in which to live and she exclaimed: "Why that's the shanty my cook used to live in!" The cook, who on earth had given all her time to God, was now living in a big house in Heaven, very much like the one in which her former mistress used to live.[12]

The Christian missionaries of the pre-Civil War period emphasized the reward for the meek and their contrasting glories in the future partly because it

---

[10] Charles S. Johnson, *Growing Up in the Black Belt* (American Council on Education, 1941), pp. 296–97.

[11] From the author's field notes in rural Mississippi.

[12] Powdermaker, *op. cit.,* p. 243.

was an important part of Christian doctrine and partly because it was only by negating the present and emphasizing the future that the evangelists could get permission from the planters to preach to the slaves. The general theme of many of these sermons was that the greater the suffering here, the greater would be the reward in the world to come. One minister, referring to the case of a slave who was unjustly punished by his masters, says, "He [God] will reward you for it in heaven, and the punishment you suffer unjustly here shall turn to your exceeding great glory thereafter." [13] Sermons, past and current, quite frequently picture Heaven as a place where whites and Negroes are not just equal but where their respective status is the opposite of what it is here.

This fantasy of turning the tables on the oppressor is not always confined to the other world; sometimes the setting is our own world. An example of this is the fantasy of a young colored girl in a northern town who had publicly taken quite meekly a decision that the colored people could not use the "Y" swimming pool at the same time white people were using it. Privately she shows her anger and says that she wishes the colored people would build a great big, magnificent "Y," a hundred times better than the white one, and make that one look like nothing. Her fantasy of triumph over the whites obviously gives her real pleasure and allows her to carry the present situation less onerously. Another example of the same type of fantasying occurs in the joking between two colored teachers who obey a disliked white official with deferential meekness. The joking consists of one of them boasting in some detail about how he has fired the white official; and the other one, in the same tone, describing how he "cussed out" the white official over the telephone.

Another aspect of the unaggressive Negro's pleasure is his feeling of superiority because he thinks he is so much finer a Christian than his white opponent. He, the Negro, is following Christ's precepts, while the white man does the opposite. The white man oppresses the poor and is unjust; in other words, he sins. He, the Negro, is virtuous and will be rewarded. One Negro, referring to a white man's un-Christian behavior, says, "It reflects back on him."

This feeling of superiority is a third characteristic of the unaggressive Negro's pleasure and is not limited to the feeling of Christian virtue. He feels superior to the whites because he is fooling them. His triumph is not completely limited to the distant future, but he enjoys at least a small part of it now. One of my informants in Mississippi, who plays this role to perfection, told me how he has the laugh on the whites because they never know his real thoughts. He quite consciously feels that he and the other Negroes like him have the upper hand through their dissimulation. He says very clearly that it makes him feel superior. One woman who presents an appearance of perfect meekness laughs with a kind of gleeful irony when she tells me how she really feels, and her meekness drops away from her as if she were discarding a cloak. Another chuckles when she relates how much she has been able to ex-

---

[13] Revor Bowen, *Divine White Right* (1934), p. 111.

tract from white people, who would never give her a thing if they knew how she really felt about them. A Negro official who holds a fairly important position in his community knows that he is constantly being watched to see that he does not overstep his place, that his position and contact with whites has not made him "uppity." As he goes around humbly saying, "Yes, ma'am" and "Yes, sir," waiting his turn long after it is due, appearing not to heed insulting remarks, he is buoyed up with a feeling of superiority because he is really fooling all these whites. He is quite aware of his mask and knows it is such and not his real self. This mask characteristic comes out particularly when one of these individuals is seen with the whites and then later with his own group. One woman who has been particularly successful in the deferential, humble role with the whites gives a clear impression of meekness and humility. Her eyes downcast, her voice low, she patiently waits to be spoken to before she speaks, and then her tone is completely deferential. An hour later she is in the midst of her own group. No longer are her eyes downcast. They sparkle! Her laugh flashes out readily. Instead of patiently waiting, she is energetically leading. Her personality emerges, vibrant and strong, a complete contrast to the picture she gives the whites. These people enjoy wearing their mask because they do it so successfully and because its success makes them feel superior to the whites whom they deceive.

The deferential, unaggressive role just described and well known to students of Negro life has a very real function besides the obvious one of avoiding trouble. As Dr. Reik says in his book on masochism, "The supremacy of the will is not only expressed in open fights." It is, as he says, likewise expressed "in the determination to yield only exteriorly and yet to cling to life, nourishing such phantasies anticipating final victory." [14] Our unaggressive Negro, like the masochist, imagines a future where his fine qualities are acknowledged by the people who had formerly disdained him. This, in good Christian manner, will be brought about through suffering. This philosophy and its resulting behavior obviously make the Negroes (or any minority group) who have them very adaptable to any circumstance in which they find themselves, no matter how painful. They continue to cling to life, in the assurance of ultimate victory. They cannot be hurt in the way that people without this faith are hurt. The adaptability of the Negro has often been noted. This hypothesis may give some further clue to understanding it.

A special combination of cultural factors—namely, oppression of a minority group and a religion which promises that through suffering power will be gained over the oppressors—has channeled one type of adaptive behavior similar to that of the masochist. This behavior pattern has given the Negro a way of appeasing his guilt over his aggressive impulses and a method of adapting to a very difficult cultural situation. Because of the understanding given us by psychoanalysis of the pleasure derived through suffering, of the

---

[14] *Op. cit.*, p. 322.

near and distant aims of the masochist, we are given a clue to the psychological mechanism underlying the so-called "unaggressive" Negro's behavior. This Negro is not a masochist, in that his sufferings are not self-inflicted and he plays his role consciously. He knows he is acting, while the masochist behavior springs from inner compulsion. Again, there is a real difference in structure, as there was in the dependency situations of the child and the slave; and again there is a real similarity in function. The masochist and the meek, unaggressive Negro derive a similar kind of pleasure from their suffering. For the Negro as well as for the masochist there is pleasure in appeasing the guilt feeling; for each there is the pleasure derived from the belief that through his suffering he becomes superior to his oppressors; and, finally, for each the suffering is a prelude to final victory.

Neither the slave nor the obsequious, unaggressive Negro, whom we have described, learned to play his role in any school. They learned by observation and imitation; they were taught by their parents; they observed what role brought rewards. Since the Civil War the Negro has likewise seen the meek, humble type presented over and over again with approval in sermons, in literature, in movies, and, more recently, through radio sketches. By participating in the cultural processes, the Negro has learned his role. This was his education, far more powerful than anything restricted to schools; for the kind of education we are discussing is continuous during the entire life of the individual. It is subtle as well as direct. One part of the cultural process strengthens another part, and reinforcement for the role we described comes from every side.

But the cultural process continues to change with resulting changes in behavior. Just as the completely loyal and faithful slave disappeared, so the meek, unaggressive, and humble Negro, the "good nigger" type, is declining in numbers. In the rural South, and elsewhere too, the tendency of Negro young people (in their teens and twenties) is to refuse to assume the unaggressive role. The passing of the "good nigger" from the scene does not entail a civil war as did the passing of the faithful slave. But it does indicate a psychological revolution. For the slave the Civil War altered the scope of the dependency situation. Today, without a Civil War, equally significant cultural changes are taking place. The Negro is participating now in a very different kind of cultural process from that which he underwent fifty years ago.

Some of the differences occurring today are here briefly indicated. There is a decline in religious faith. The vivid "getting-religion" experience prevalent in the past has become increasingly rare for young people. Today they use the church as a social center. Gone is the intensity of religious belief that their parents knew. The young people are not atheists, but they do not have the fervor and sincerity of belief in a future world. They are much more hurt by slights and minor insults than are their parents, because they do not put their faith in the promise of a heavenly victory.

Along with changes in the form of religious participation have come many other changes. The illiteracy of the past has disappeared. A lengthening of schooling and a steady improvement in educational standards tend to give the Negro the same knowledge and the same tools enjoyed by the white man and to minimize cultural differences between the two. A more independent and rebellious Negro type is making its appearance in literature, as, for instance, the character of Bigger in the best seller, *Native Son*.

The steady trek of the rural Negroes to cities, North and South, has changed the milieu of masses of Negroes from the rural peasant life to the industrial urban one.[15] Here they come under the influence of the trade-union movement, which slowly but gradually is shifting its attitude from one of jealous exclusion to one of inclusion, sometimes cordial and sometimes resigned. The shift is not anywhere near completion yet, but the trend is there. In the city the Negro is influenced by the same advertisements, the same radio sketches, the same political bosses, the same parties (left or right), and all the other urban forces which influence the white man.

The Negro's goals for success are thus becoming increasingly the same as those of the white person; and these goals are primarily in the economic field, although those in other fields, such as art and athletics, are not to be minimized either. The securing of these goals is in this world rather than in a future one. They are attained through the competition and aggressive struggle so characteristic of our culture rather than through meekness and subservience. The compensations available to the loyal slave and the humble, unaggressive, free Negro no longer exist or, at least, are steadily diminishing. The white man can no longer offer security in return for devotion, because he himself no longer has security. The whites of all classes have known a mounting social insecurity over the past decade, and they obviously cannot give away something which they do not possess. Thus the material rewards for obsequiousness and unaggressiveness are fading away. Gone, too, is the religious emphasis on rewards in Heaven. When the cultural process takes away rewards for a certain type of behavior, dissatisfaction with that behavior appears and there is a gradual change to another form which is more likely to bring new compensations. Obviously, one can expect, and one finds, a growing restlessness and uncertainty which occur in any transition period, when old goals have been lost. The new goals are the standard American ones. But the means for attaining these goals are not yet as available to the Negro as they are to the white. Economic and social discriminations still exist. Unless some other form of adaptation takes place and unless discriminations are lessened, we may expect a trend toward greater overt aggression.

However, there are no sudden revolutions in behavior patterns, and this holds for the patterns of aggression. They change slowly; the old ones persist while new ones are being formed, and opposing patterns exist side by side.

---

15 Between 1920 and 1930 over a million Negroes migrated from the country to the cities. The figures for the past decade are not yet available.

But change occurs. The cultural process in which the Negro has participated from the time when he was first brought to this country until today has involved a constant denial of privileges. The denial has taken various forms, from the overt one involved in slavery to the more subtle ones of today. The compensations for the denial have varied from different degrees of material security to promises of future blessings in Heaven, and from the feeling of being more virtuous than the white to the feeling of fooling him. Today these compensations are fading away. Equally important, ideological fetters of the past have been broken by the Negro's increasing participation in the current urban industrial processes.

The Negro's education, formal and informal, has consisted of his participation in this ever changing cultural process, one small part of which we have briefly examined. Slavery, religion, economic and other social factors, have channeled his activities, offering him alternatives within a certain cultural range. We have examined only two of the alternatives in any detail—namely, the roles of the faithful slave and of the humble, meek Negro who was a fairly common stereotype following the Civil War; we have concentrated on the latter because he still exists and we therefore have more data on him. Both appear unaggressive. A functional comparison with the psychoanalytical analysis of the dependency situation of the child and of the problem of masochism has indicated how the aggression may have been present, although concealed, in these two roles.

RICHARD HOFSTADTER

FUNDAMENTALISM AND
STATUS POLITICS ON THE RIGHT

In seeking an explanation for the emergence in the past two decades of movements like McCarthyism and the proliferation of extreme right-wing groups such as the John Birch Society, a number of historians and commentators have focused upon the fact that since World War II Americans have experienced a series of extreme and unprecedented shocks. They had defeated Germany and Japan only to be confronted almost immediately by the hostility of another and even greater power, the Soviet Union, and they saw that power increase its influence over large parts of the world; they fought a war in Korea and emerged not with a victory but with a fragile stalemate; they have witnessed the rise of a vast anti-colonialist movement around the world, in which the United States, traditionally anti-colonial, was cast not as a hero but as a villain; they have watched the Soviet Union forge ahead of us in certain phases of the scientific contest being waged and have listened uneasily to its leaders boast that they would surge ahead economically as well in the near future—that they would "bury" us. It has been argued that these threats to the nation's power and security have led Americans to question their own destiny and to doubt their omnipotence, giving rise to an anxiety which provides fertile ground for the unreasoning fear and the wild charges of the extreme right wing to take root.

Certainly, the force of this explanation cannot be gainsaid, but, in itself, it leaves too many important questions unanswered: Why do only certain groups in America respond to these common shocks by embracing the radical

361

right? Why do they tend to react to external threats by focusing not upon the external enemy but upon a supposed internal enemy, by attacking not only real and fancied Communists and left-wingers but also entrenched elements of the American establishment—the clergy, the major parties, the judiciary, and at times even the military and big business? In his attempt to get at these more complex problems, Richard Hofstadter relates the right-wing movements of our own day to the larger context of American culture and history as a whole, and he discusses the various economic, religious, and psychological factors that have contributed to the reemergence of fundamentalism in politics. In exploring this issue and that of status politics, he draws upon some of the same material that is found in earlier articles in this collection. Hofstadter has still more to say about these and related problems in a number of the other essays in his collection, The Paranoid Style in American Politics * *(1965). Additional commentary on aspects of this general problem by a variety of contemporary social scientists can be found in Daniel Bell, ed.,* The Radical Right * *(1963).*

Over the past three decades, right-wing movements have appealed to segments of the public which, though overlapping, have been significantly different. In the 1930s the chief vehicle of right-wing discontent was Father Coughlin's Social Justice movement, a depression phenomenon drawing the bulk of its support from those who suffered most from bad times—the working class and the unemployed, farmers and some of the lower middle class. Its tone was more pseudo-radical than pseudo-conservative. It played on old Populist themes, attacked international bankers, demanded free silver and other changes in the money and credit system, and resorted to an anti-Semitic rhetoric far more virulent than anything the Populists would have dreamed of. It was stronger in rural areas and small towns than in cities, and much stronger among Catholics, particularly Irish Catholics, than among Protestants. Its isolationist and Anglophobic note drew support from Germans, both Catholic and Lutheran. It was strongest in two areas: the West Central states, where its appeal was both ethnic and agrarian, and in New England, where it attracted Irish Catholics. That Coughlin had little strength in the South is perhaps an interesting token of surviving religious prejudice; also, up to the time of Huey Long's assassination, the South had its own native and more appealing messiah.

Coughlinism died with the war and the subsequent prosperity. The new right wing of the McCarthy era showed both continuity and discontinuity with Coughlinism. McCarthy, as an Irish Catholic, picked up much of the ethnic and religious following that had once been Coughlin's, as well as some support from ethnic groups drawn from the "captive" nations of Eastern Europe. But as a phenomenon of prosperity McCarthyism was almost entirely devoid of economic content and had no economic program. Since McCarthy appealed both to Republicans who resented their party's continuing domination by its eastern wing and to those in both parties who were swept up by the anti-Communist passions of the cold war, his following was much greater than Coughlin's. On the whole, he received a measure of support disproportionate to their numbers in the general population from Catholics and from the ill-educated, but also from Republicans, Irish Americans, the lower classes, and the aged. Along with economic issues, McCarthy abruptly dropped the old right-wing appeal to anti-Semitism.

Part of McCarthy's strength lay in his ability to combine a mass appeal with a special appeal to a limited stratum of the upper classes. As compared with Coughlin, whose following had been almost entirely a low-status public, McCarthy was able to win considerable support from the middle and upper ranks of society, mobilizing Republicans who had never accepted the changes

REPRINTED by permission of Alfred A. Knopf, Inc., from "Pseudo-Conservatism Revisited—1965," *The Paranoid Style in American Politics,* pp. 68–92, by Richard Hofstadter. Copyright © 1965 by Richard Hofstadter.

Fundamentalism and Status Politics on the Right   363

brought by the New Deal and whose rage at the long exclusion of the party from presidential power was reaching a peak. There is evidence also that McCarthy had a special appeal to the postwar newly rich. Most prophetic too of the future of the right wing was his strong appeal for fundamentalist-oriented Protestants, who now took a significant place along with their Catholic counterparts.[1]

This is strikingly illustrated by the changing views of Baptists. Probably because of Coughlin's priestly vocation, Baptists had ranked low among the evangelical denominations that supported him, but McCarthy, though a lay Catholic, commanded more support from them than from any other Protestant denomination. It was in the McCarthyist era that the anti-Communist issue became so salient for members of this evangelical denomination (and presumably others) that they abandoned their traditional anti-Catholic animus in order to take part in right-wing ecumenical anti-Communism.

The right wing of the 1960s, whose leadership has fallen to the John Birch Society, continues to move up the socio-economic ladder. With its strong commitment to ultraconservative economic ideas, the Birch Society makes little appeal to the economically deprived. It is primarily an organization of well-educated middle- and upper-status Republicans who are deviants among the educated strata in several ways—including a greater disposition to ethnic prejudice than the population as a whole.[2] As an elite corps, the Birch Society is, of course, much better educated than the members of other right-wing groups. It has also brought out an interesting polarity within the educated upper classes of American society, which is related to party affiliation. Among Democrats, increasing education is correlated with increas-

---

[1] McCarthyism, it must also be remembered, was a phenomenon of much broader significance than the far right itself. During 1953 and 1954, when McCarthy was at the peak of his influence, there was no poll in which less than 34 per cent of the public was found approving him, and at one point, January 1954, the figure rose to 50 per cent. No sensible observer has ever imagined that extreme right-wing ideas command the loyalty of one third, much less one half, of the American public. In July 1964, for example, at a time of great right-wing ferment, a major national poll found that only 4 per cent of the public would be influenced to vote for a presidential candidate because he was endorsed by the John Birch Society, as against 47 per cent who would be more disposed to vote against him; the remainder would have been unaffected or expressed no opinion. *The New York Times*, July 31, 1964. Characteristically, from about 5 to 10 per cent of the public will express approval of the Birch Society (see Daniel Bell (ed.): *The Radical Right* (New York: 1963), pp. 201–2, 349–63), though right-wing positions often receive the endorsement of as much as 15 per cent of the public.

[2] Birchite prejudice, it should be said, is directed more significantly against Negroes, Mexicans, and Orientals than it is against Jews. Birchites are a shade *less* prejudiced against Catholics than anti-Birchites. (Seymour M. Lipset: "Three Decades of the Radical Right," in Bell (ed.): *op. cit.*, p. 361.) Though all polls agree on the relatively high level of formal education among Birchites, they do not provide information about the kind of colleges they attended, and it would be interesting to know to what extent these were the great cosmopolitan universities and colleges or denominational institutions.

ing disapproval of the Birch Society; but among Republicans, increasing education is correlated with increasing support for the society.

Although the Birch Society as a whole draws its most vital public support from affluent Republican Protestants, it has some special appeal, when party affiliation is held constant, to Catholics. Its sociological profile is that of a group enjoying a strong social position, mainly well-to-do and educated beyond the average, but manifesting a degree of prejudice and social tension not customarily found among the affluent and the educated.

Although it is doubtful that extreme rightists in the 1960s are any more numerous than they were in the McCarthyist period, the right wing has learned the secret of organization, which largely accounts for its greater successes. Coughlinism and McCarthyism were largely the creation of astute and voluminous publicity on the radio and in the press, which was not matched by their organizational efforts. Coughlin's organized groups were of relatively little consequence, and McCarthy could barely organize his own files, much less a national movement. The John Birch Society, with only a fraction of McCarthy's support among the public, has won its successes through tightly organized and militant cadres of workers, operating in a manner resembling that of Communist cells, and linked to the Republican party not through publicity but by active work in district, precinct, and community organizations where ideological affinities can be translated into power.

At the grass roots the extreme right now draws its primary support from two basic (and at points overlapping) social types: first, the affluent (perhaps newly affluent) suburban educated middle class, largely outside the Northeast, which responds to ultraconservative economic issues as well as to militant nationalism and anti-Communism, and which seeks to win a place in the political structure proportionate to the secure place it has won in society; and second, a large lower middle class, somewhat less educated and less charmed than the first group by old-fashioned economic liberalism but even more fearful of Communism, which it perceives rather abstractly in the light of a strong evangelical-fundamentalist cast of thought.

II

The re-emergence of fundamentalism in politics, invigorated by the conditions of the cold war and the stimulus of the affluent society, is a notable development of the past fifteen years. Of necessity I use the term "fundamentalism" in a rather extended way to describe a religious style rather than firm doctrinal commitments, since no one knows how many evangelical right-wingers adhere to a literal view of Scripture and other fundamentalist tenets. Two other qualifications should be made: first, there are large numbers of fundamentalists who interpret their religious commitment as a reason to withdraw from worldly politics, in which they see no more hope than they do in the other things of this world; and second, many fundamentalists have inherited generous views on domestic economic reforms which they do not easily give up. But on certain issues of cultural politics fundamentalists have always been rigid, and when such issues become more salient the fundamentalists become more responsive to the blandishments of pseudo-conservative prophets. Moreover, the Manichean and apocalyptic style of thought prevalent in the fundamentalist tradition can easily be carried over into secular affairs and transmuted into a curiously crude and almost superstitious form of anti-Communism.

Not only is the entire right-wing movement infused at the mass level with the fundamentalist style of mind, but the place in its ranks of fundamentalist preachers, ex-preachers, and sons of preachers is so prominent as to underline the mutual congeniality of thought. Leading right-wing spokesmen have brought into politics the methods and the style of the evangelical revivalists, just as many preachers have discovered that they can arouse more fervor and raise more cash by politicizing their message than they can by appealing solely to the religious sensibilities of their audiences.[3]

Under the aegis of right-wing politics, rigid Protestants of a type once intensely anti-Catholic can now unite with Catholics of similar militancy in a grand ecumenical zeal against Communism and in what they take to be a joint defense of Christian civilization. The malevolent energy formerly used in the harassment of Catholics can now be more profitably spent in the search for Communists, or even in attacks on the alleged subversiveness of liberal Protestant denominations. The Manichean conception of life as a struggle between absolute good and absolute evil and the idea of an irresistible Armageddon have been thinly secularized and transferred to the cold war. The conflict between Christianity and Communism is conceived as a war to the death, and Christianity is set forth as the only adequate counterpoise to the Communist credo.

Fundamentalist leaders play a part in right-wing organizations far out of proportion to the strength of fundamentalism in the population at large.

---

[3] This is not the first period in our history in which fundamentalist leaders, anguished over the general repudiation of their beliefs and values, lent their energies to political reaction. During the 1920s they gave heavy support to the Ku Klux Klan, particularly in the South. During the years 1922 to 1928, 26 of 39 anti-Catholic lecturers employed by the Klan were Protestant ministers of the fundamentalist type, and 16 of such ministers were Klan officials. Klansmen were regularly entertained in the homes of such ministers, and churches were used for Klan meetings. The two chief leaders of the new Klan had fundamentalist backgrounds—its initiator, Colonel William J. Simmons, had been a religious camp-meeting exhorter, and its most successful promoter, Edward Y. Clarke, went into the fundamentalist movement after giving up his efforts in the Klan. In return, the Klan often fought for passage of the anti-evolution laws. On the relation between the preachers of certain denominations and Klan activities, see Michael Williams: *The Shadow of the Pope* (New York, 1932), pp. 317 ff. On the limitations of this connection and Protestant opposition to the Klan, see Robert Moats Miller: "A Note on the Relation Between the Protestant Churches and the Revival of the Klan," *Journal of Southern History*, XXII (August 1956), pp. 355–68.

Among them are Robert H. Welch, Jr., the founder of the John Birch Society; Dr. Fred C. Schwartz, the head of the Christian Anti-Communism Crusade; and Reverend Billy Hargis, of the Christian Crusade, which flourishes in the Southwest.[4]

A large part of the rise of fundamentalist ultraconservatism may be linked with the astonishing growth of the Southern Baptist Church, which increased from 2,300,000 members in 1936 to 10,000,000 in 1962. A comparable growth has also been enjoyed by the right-wing Churches of Christ. The increase in these groups has far outstripped that of more moderate Protestant denominations in the same period.[5] Such church groups have created a vast religious public, once poor and depression-ridden but now to a large degree moderately prosperous, whose members sometimes combine the economic prejudices of the newly well-to-do with the moral prejudices of the revolt against modernity.

We know more, of course, about the role of fundamentalist leaders in right-wing groups than we do about fundamentalism among the mass following. The presence of two kinds of subcultures in the Christian Anti-Communism Crusade is suggested in a study by Raymond F. Wolfinger and his associates of a sample of its members in Oakland, California. Their findings point to a

---

[4] Welch, who was raised as a pious fundamentalist Baptist in North Carolina, chose to name his organization after a young fundamentalist Baptist preacher from Macon, Georgia, who was killed by the Chinese Communists. As a prosperous candy manufacturer, once very active in the National Association of Manufacturers, Welch embodies the union of fundamentalist inspiration and small-business parochial conservatism that animates the extreme right. Schwarz is the son of an Australian pentecostal preacher; he had considerable experiences in his native country as a lay preacher before coming to the United States on the invitation of some anti-modernist preachers. He began his American career with an evangelical-style tour. Preachers and ex-preachers figure prominently in the "faculty" he has recruited for his anti-Communist "schools." Hargis moved on from evangelism to right-wing politics in much the same way as such predecessors as Gerald L. K. Smith, Gerald Winrod, and J. Frank Norris. He is the product of Ozark Bible College in Arkansas and of the Disciples of Christ, though his ministry is now independent. Another successful southwestern leader is Dr. George Benson, a former Church of Christ missionary in China, now president of the church-affiliated Harding College in Searcy, Arkansas. This organization still holds forth against Darwin, but its main claim to fame is its role as the source of right-wing political radio broadcasts and films, on the strength of which it has attracted munificent contributions from businessmen. In the East, the Reverend Carl McIntire of the Bible Presbyterian Church in Collingswood, New Jersey, reaches large audiences with his radio broadcasts. A former disciple of the highbrow fundamentalist H. Gresham Machen, McIntire set up his own after being expelled from the General Assembly of the Presbyterian Church, and he has been vociferous in fighting modernist Christianity and the ecumenical movement. Finally, there is the Church League of America, founded in 1937 to fight liberal Protestantism but now a right-wing organization managed by Edgar Bundy, a minister ordained in the Southern Baptist Convention.

[5] Kenneth H. Bailey: *Southern White Protestantism in the Twentieth Century* (New York, 1964), p. 152. See Chs. 3 and 4 of this work on the fundamentalist background in the South. On internal tensions that have come with this fantastic growth, see Samuel S. Hill, Jr.: "The Southern Baptists," *Christian Century,* LXXX (January 1963), pp. 39–42.

bifurcation between a relatively affluent, educated, and "sophisticated" wing, concerned most intensely with the economic content of ultra-conservatism, and a more deeply religious wing, leaning toward fundamentalism, primarily concerned with religious and moral issues. Among 308 people who consented to be interviewed, persons belonging to fundamentalist churches constituted 20 per cent (they would be a larger proportion in southern California). Those who reported that they came to the "schools" of this right-wing movement because of church influence differed from the whole sample in important respects: they were more fundamentalist, more active in politics. They were more favorably disposed than other respondents to such reforms as medicare and federal aid to education, and were more willing to accept the legitimacy of trade unions. Their more intense Christian convictions were perhaps also reflected in their taking a less sympathetic view than other members of the South's position on racial integration. But they were more anti-evolution, more disturbed about the threat of Communism to theistic belief, and more anxious about the alleged internal threat of Communism to the nation.[6] An impressionistic study by participant observers of the membership of the same movement in a small midwestern industrial city found the members predominantly Baptist-fundamentalist, educated, with few exceptions, only to the high-school level, aggressively anti-intellectual, anxious about the preservation of the old-fashioned moral virtues, and rather disposed to see the world in the paranoid style.[7]

III

One way of adding to our understanding of the politics of the 1950s and 1960s is to compare it with that of the 1920s. During the 1920s our political life was profoundly affected, and at times dominated, by certain cultural struggles, which were interrupted and deflected by the depression, the New Deal, and the war, but which have in a measure reasserted themselves in the different setting of the postwar decades. Both the 1920s and the postwar

---

[6] Wolfinger et al.: "America's Radical Right: Politics and Ideology," in David E. Apter (ed.): Ideology and Discontent (Glencoe, Ill., 1964), pp. 281–3. This study does not purport to be a representative sample. Among other difficulties was the hostility of a large proportion of members to student interviewers. Their refusal to be interviewed or to answer mailed questionnaires suggests that the Wolfinger group's respondents represent the less extreme members of the movement. The Crusaders were drawn, out of proportion to their numbers in the population, from professional and technical workers and business managers, from income brackets over $10,000, and from those who had graduated from or attended college. Their average age was also somewhat higher than that of the general population of the Bay area. Their profile bears a fairly close resemblance to those approving the Birch Society in a national sample. See Lipset: op. cit., p. 350.

[7] Mark Chesler and Richard Schmuck: "Participant Observation in a Super-Patriot Discussion Group," Journal of Social Issues, XIX (April 1963), pp. 18–30.

years, as periods of relative prosperity, saw some diminution in the force of economic issues and an upsurge in the issues of status politics—issues of religion, morals, personal style, and culture. It is significant that the election campaign which, of all the campaigns in our history, was most completely dominated by status politics was the Smith-Hoover campaign of 1928, conducted when the ill-fated boom of the twenties was nearing its peak. In 1964, again under prosperous conditions, the issues of status politics once more played an unusually significant part.

During the 1920s small-town and rural Protestants were waging a vigorous defense of their cultural values against their rapidly gaining foes—the advancing Catholics and minority ethnic groups on one side and the modernists in religion and secularists in intellectual culture on the other. The Ku Klux Klan, Prohibitionism, the campaign against evolution in the schools, anti-Catholicism and the whispering campaign against Al Smith were all aspects of this struggle. On one count, immigration restriction, the old guard scored an important and permanent victory and on another, Prohibition, they scored a gratifying if temporary success. But on the others they continued to lose ground. They substantially lost the fight against teaching evolution in the public schools, which exposed them to humiliating ridicule throughout the world. Lost, too, was the fight against modern relaxation in manners, morals, and censorship. Again the effort to contain the influence of immigrants in politics was lost within the Democratic party. The rural Protestant Democrats fought in 1924 to keep their party free of urban ethnic domination, and the two factions nearly tore the Democratic party apart at its 1924 convention. By 1928 the enemy was in control and Smith was nominated. He paid a heavy price for his religion and his defiance of establishment manners and morals, but he did succeed, partly by mobilizing the ethnic Catholic vote, in rehabilitating his party and raising it from the desperate condition it had reached in the two previous elections. The Democratic party became the coalition party of the new urban polyglot America. What Smith had begun, Roosevelt completed; F.D.R.'s consolidation of the ethnic and working-class elements in the country into an effective political force was almost as important as his economic reforms.

The problems of the depression and the Second World War somewhat eclipsed these cultural antagonisms, though they were often visible beneath the surface. Fundamentalist-evangelical America was, in fact, so long divided or quiescent as a political force that many intellectuals have forgotten that it still exists. Nor has it surrendered its commitment to Prohibitionism or its dislike of evolution in popular education.[8] Even as recently as 1959, according to a Gallup poll, 34 per cent of all Protestants favored national Prohibition. Three fifths of all Protestant farmers and two fifths of all Protestants living in

---

[8] I have tried to account for the background of the revolt against modernity in *Anti-intellectualism in American Life* (New York, 1963), esp. Ch. 5.

towns of less than 10,000 population took this view.[9] Again, only a few years earlier, another survey showed the effects of a resolute if quiet effort being made to protect the young against Darwinism and secularism. In a poll of adolescents based on an unusually large sample, only 35 per cent responded by checking "Yes" alongside the statement: "Man was evolved from lower forms of animals." As many as 40 per cent marked "No," and 24 per cent "Don't know." [10]

Now the point of all this is not to say that the old cultural issues of the 1920s are important manifest issues under present conditions, but rather that ascetic Protestantism remains a significant undercurrent in contemporary America, and that its followers have found new-fangled ways of reaffirming some of their convictions. They cannot bring back Prohibition or keep evolution entirely out of the schools. They have been unable even to defend school prayer or prevent *Life* magazine from featuring the topless bathing suit. But they can recriminate against and punish the new America that outrages them, and they have found powerful leaders to echo their views.[11] As the old fight against immigration has waned in significance, the Negro "revolution" has frightened many of them, and has given a new focus to ethnic conflict. The participants in this revolt against modernity are no longer rubes and hicks, and they have gained something both in sophistication and in cohesiveness through modern urbanization. They too live in the cities and the suburbs, at closer and more irritating range to the things that disturb them, but also closer to each other, and more susceptible to organization.

Above all, they have found a fighting issue that helps them to surmount their previous isolation, an issue on which at last they have common ground with all America: they are implacably and consumingly anti-Communist, and in the grand ecumenicism of their anti-Communist passion they welcome all allies. They are particularly happy to have made terms with the Catholics and to accept members of minority ethnic groups as comrades-in-arms. That the Whore of Babylon now sits in Moscow, not Rome, is to their incalculable advantage, for they have been able to turn a powerful domestic foe, the Church, into an ally, and in its former place they have installed the impotent American Communist. Nor does it trouble them that genuine Communists are all but impossible to find. Liberals, pacifists, beatniks, agitators for racial justice, radicals of other persuasions—what Robert Welch calls "comsymps"—will do as well.

People who share this outlook have a disposition to interpret issues of secular politics as though they were solely moral and spiritual struggles. They

---

[9] Seymour M. Lipset: "Religion and Politics in the American Past and Present," in Robert Lee and Martin Marty (eds.): *Religion and Social Conflict* (New York, 1964), pp. 114–15.

[10] H. H. Remmers and D. H. Radler: *The American Teenager* (Indianapolis, 1957).

[11] For example, see Richard Hofstadter: *The Paranoid Style in American Politics* (New York: 1965), pp. 116–24.

are less concerned with the battle against Communism in the world theater than they are with the alleged damage it does to politics and morals at home. The cold war serves as a constant source of recriminations about our moral and material failure, but as an objective struggle in the arena of world politics it is less challenging to them than it is as a kind of spiritual wrestling match with the minions of absolute evil, who, as is so often the case with Satanic powers, exercise an irresistible attractiveness. Those who look at the world in this way see their fundamental battle as one to be conducted against other Americans at home, and they respond eagerly to the notion, so pervasive in the right wing, that the worst enemy of American liberties is to be found in Washington. Moreover, whereas in the past only an occasional wealthy crank was interested in subsidizing attacks on Catholicism, the anti-Communist crusade brings lavish outpourings from right-wing foundations and from some of the nation's large business firms.

Though many Americans with fundamentalist leanings have traditionally been sympathetic to economic and social reforms, there is one aspect of right-wing thought that invariably attracts them—the moralistic quality of its economic ideas. Christian economic moralism, to be sure, has often buttressed benevolence and inspired social reform. But it has another side: insofar as economic life is regarded as a sphere for the fulfillment of the ascetic Protestant virtues, Christian moralism has worked for right-wing discontent. One strain in Protestant thinking has always looked to economic life not just for its efficacy in producing goods and services but as a vast apparatus of moral discipline, of rewards for virtue and industry and punishments for vice and indolence. In the past, vocational life was supposed to inculcate prudence, economy, and diligence—and many writers seem to have felt that economic discipline would be more effective in this task than sermons and exhortations. The vocational life was a moral testing ground. Today these assumptions have been flouted. The modern economy, based on advertising, lavish consumption, installment buying, safeguards to social security, relief to the indigent, government fiscal manipulation, and unbalanced budgets, seems reckless and immoral, even when it happens to work. In the intellectual synthesis of contemporary ultraconservatism, the impulses of Protestant asceticism can thus be drawn upon to support business self-interest and the beautiful mathematical models of neoclassical economists.

IV

We can now return to our original interest: to what extent are the newly affluent, the fundamentalist, and the other constituent elements of the modern American right animated by status resentments and anxieties? This question does not seem to have the same urgency it had ten years ago, because the point which the various authors of *The Radical Right* then sought to make has been widely accepted. At that time we were all struck by a salient fact: the literature of the American right was a literature not of those who felt themselves to be in possession but of those who felt dispossessed—a literature of resentment, profoundly anti-establishment in its impulses.[12] We were all struck by the flimsiness of its pretensions to conservatism, and by its profound hostility to the culture and institutions by which it was surrounded.

If the essays in *The Radical Right* dwelled on status resentments, it was not because the authors thought they had found a final, single explanation of the right-wing line of thought, but because we had come upon a hitherto neglected and unexplained side of the movement. Our ideas were offered as an addition to the store of what was already known about the right wing, not as an attempt to displace the undeniable structural and historical setting in which the right wing arose. We were, in short, not trying to deny the obvious, but to go beyond it.

Our emphasis, then, on certain social and psychological forces at work in American society was not intended to deny the plurality of circumstances that gave birth to the right-wing resurgence—the shock of the Korean War, the failures of our foreign policy, the frustrations of Republicans too long defeated in presidential politics, the traditional irritations of big money, the continued high taxes, the impact of inflation, revelations of Communist espionage and of political corruption, the long-standing pent-up resentment against the New Deal and the social reforms it had established, the dislike of the type of national leadership that it had installed. We were trying to bring to the surface the additional sociological and psychological forces that helped all these circumstances come to a center and find a rhetorical form, and that gave to their anti-establishment animus its particular edge. We were impressed by the way in which the processes of prosperity yield their own kind of discontent, which, if not so widely shared as that of hard times, is nonetheless as bitter.

The emphasis given to status resentments and anxieties in the essays in *The Radical Right* was based partly on inferences from poll data about the socio-economic status and the education of McCarthyists, partly from impressionistic observation of contemporary social changes, and partly from the rhetoric of McCarthyism and the social objects against which its grievances were directed. What seemed important was not only the wrongs the McCarthyist right-wingers thought had been committed but who they thought had committed them; and repeated denunciations of "striped-pants diplomats," Ivy League graduates, high-ranking generals, college presidents, intellectuals, the Eastern upper classes, Harvard professors, and members of Phi Beta Kappa seemed to be serving psychological purposes which had little to do

---

[12] One is struck also by the disparity between the actual social position of these segments of the population and the intensity of their discontent. As Daniel Bell observes, they come from disparate groups many of which are doing very well. "In identifying 'the dispossessed,' it is somewhat misleading to seek their economic location, since it is not economic interest alone that accounts for their anxieties." Bell (ed.): *op. cit.*, p. 19.

with arriving at a realistic historical account of the nation's difficulties and failures.[13] As McCarthy put it in his famous speech at Wheeling, the nation had been sold out by "those who have had all the benefits that the wealthiest nation on earth has to offer—the finest homes, the finest college education, and the finest jobs in Government. . . . The bright young men who are born with silver spoons in their mouths are the ones who have been worst." [14]

This seemed to voice certain status resentments, but it was hard to gauge them quantitatively or to measure their place among the many forces that were at work. To my knowledge only one study has been made to try to define felt status grievances in such a way as to put the notion to the test, and it reports a modest confirmation of the hypothesis of *The Radical Right*.[15] Other empirical studies have stressed quite correctly the large number of variables that have gone into the making of the right wing, but have not effectively argued that status resentments should be excluded from them.[16]

The essays in *The Radical Right* were prompted by a curiosity about certain facts hitherto taken for granted. We wanted to know why Americans who were affected in a similar way by many events reacted to them so differently. Of course, party affiliation, socio-economic status, and geographical region always affect political opinions, but in this case the aggregate of these readily perceptible factors did not yield a satisfactory or exhaustive answer. There was a wide range of reaction to the events of the 1950s, for example, among people in the same social class and in the same political party. People responded to political events, as they always do, not merely with profoundly different opinions about the policies that should be pursued but in strikingly

---

[13] See Immanuel Wallerstein: "McCarthyism and the Conservative," unpublished M.A. essay, Columbia University (1954), pp. 46 ff.

[14] *Congressional Record,* 81st Cong., 2nd. sess. (February 20, 1950), p. 1954.

[15] Robert Sokol: "Status Inconsistency," unpublished doctoral dissertation, Columbia University (1961), esp. pp. 87–95, 120–5, 175, 198–200.

[16] The best evaluation, I believe, of available information from various sources remains that of Seymour Lipset in "Three Decades of the Radical Right," esp. pp. 326–48.
   The study most frequently cited as having effectively contradicted the status hypothesis is Martin Trow's survey of McCarthyist opinion in Bennington, Vermont, in 1954, "Small Businessmen, Political Tolerance, and Support for McCarthy," *American Journal of Sociology,* LXIV (November 1958), pp. 270–81. Why it is so construed I do not understand. Though it differs clearly enough on a rather marginal point, it puts strong emphasis on the anti-conservative, anti-establishment element in McCarthyism, finds it directed "precisely against the conservative authorities and institutions—the 'big shots,' the 'stuffed shirts,' the 'bureaucrats,' " sees support for McCarthy as "the channeling of certain dissatisfactions with aspects of the social, economic, and political order," finds McCarthyists "angrily confused and deeply resentful of a world that continually offends their deepest values," and reports them animated by resentment and indignation that has "no effective and institutionalized channels of expression" and by a "generalized fear of the dominant currents and institutions of modern society"—and in this respect offers an analysis not remarkably dissimilar to that of the authors it is held to refute. See esp. pp. 273, 276, 277. In any case, there was no reason to believe that Bennington was a good or representative place to study Mc-

different mental and rhetorical styles. It was understood that the Korean War and the overlong exclusion of Republicans from the White House had much to do with the temper of the times, but why did some Republicans welcome the peace in Korea while others branded the Republican President who made it as a traitor? Again, millionaires cannot be expected to like progressive taxation, but how could we account for the political differences between a first- or second-generation oil millionaire in Texas and a third-generation oil millionaire in New York? Why did taxpayers enjoying the same income and belonging to the same political party have such profoundly different views of the social reforms inherited from the New Deal?

I confess to mixed feelings about the term "status politics" as a means of explaining the discontents animated by the right wing. On one hand, I have no desire to overstate the role of status, narrowly defined, in the right wing of the 1950's or of today. There are a large number of factors, social and economic, that enter into the composition of the right wing, and, like any other single explanation, this one is bound to have its limitations. Yet I should be sorry if, because of its limited utility in this context, the fundamental importance of the distinction between status politics and interest politics should be lost. I chose the term "status politics" because I was looking for a way to designate an impulse held in common by a variety of discontented elements. If there is something misleading in the word "status," it is because its meaning is somewhat too specific to account for what it attempts to describe, and takes the part for the whole. Few critics have denied the presence or significance of what is intended, but it has been suggested that such terms as "cultural politics" and "symbolic politics" will serve better.

In [another] essay I used the term "status politics" to refer to three things that are related but not identical: first is the problem of American identity, as it

Carthyism, and, as Lipset has pointed out, some of its key findings were not replicated by national data. "Three Decades of the Radical Right," pp. 340–1.

Two of the most valuable studies of the extreme right that have raised serious questions about the status hypothesis are those of Nelson W. Polsby: "Towards an Explanation of McCarthyism," *Political Studies,* VIII (1960), pp. 250–71, and Wolfinger: *op. cit.* But some of the difficulties of the subject are exemplified in their positive conclusions. Polsby dwells (p. 258) on "the rather heavy evidence supporting the hypothesis that McCarthy succeeded at the grass roots primarily among Republicans," and he is echoed by Wolfinger in his study of right-wing Christian Crusaders of the 1960's, which finds as "the most salient fact about the Crusaders: whatever else they may be, they are not Democrats." The scarcity of Democrats, he says, was "the most striking single characteristic of our sample" (pp. 285, 288). These conclusions—that McCarthy appealed more to Republicans than to Democrats and that the right-wingers of the 1960's are overwhelmingly Republican in partisan affiliation— have the great advantage that they are likely to go ringing down the corridors of time unchallenged and unimpaired. They have an attractive solidity, but they do not offer an arresting new idea to our store of understanding. What would be most pertinent would be to find out just what characteristics divide those Republicans who have joined the extreme right from those who believe that it is a menace to the body politic, and what were the social characteristics of the rather substantial number of Democrats who were pro-McCarthy.

is complicated by our immigrant origins and the problem of ethnic minorities; second, the problem of social status, defined as the capacity of various groups and occupations to command personal deference in society; and, finally, the effort of Americans of diverse cultural and moral persuasions to win reassurance that their values are respected by the community at large. The purpose of the term was to heighten our awareness of a constant political struggle arising not out of the real or imagined contest for gain that is familiar in our interest-group politics—that is, the historical struggles for cheap land, cheap credit, higher farm prices, larger profits, market protection of various kinds, more jobs, more bargaining power, economic security—but out of commitments to certain other values, which are taken by the persons who share them to be ultimate moral goals, disinterestedly pursued. Such persons believe that their prestige in the community, even indeed their self-esteem, depends on having these values honored in public. Besides their economic expectations, people have deep emotional commitments in other spheres—religion, morals, culture, race relations—which they also hope to see realized in political action. Status politics seeks not to advance perceived material interests but to express grievances and resentments about such matters, to press claims upon society to give deference to noneconomic values. As a rule, status politics does more to express emotions than to formulate policies. It is in fact hard to translate the claims of status politics into programs or concrete objectives (national Prohibition was an exception, though ultimately an unsuccessful one); and for the most part the proponents of such politics, being less concerned with the uses of power than with its alleged misuse, do not offer positive programs to solve social problems. The operative content of their demands is more likely to be negative: they call on us mainly to prohibit, to prevent, to censor and censure, to discredit, and to punish.

The most useful attempt to apply the concept of status politics to an aspect of our history is Joseph R. Gusfield's recent book on the temperance movement, *Symbolic Crusade: Status Politics and the Temperance Movement*. Defining status politics rather sharply as "political conflict over the allocation of prestige," he argues that its importance "lies precisely in identifying noneconomic segments as crucial in certain social and political conflicts." [17]

---

[17] *Symbolic Crusade* (Urbana, Ill., 1963), p. 18. "A political issue becomes one of status when its tangible, instrumental consequences are subordinated to its significance for the conferral of prestige . . . The argument is less over the effect of the proposed measures on concrete actions than it is over the question of whose culture is to be granted legitimacy by the public action of government" (p. 148).

Gusfield is gratifyingly careful to avoid the reductionist fallacy: he recognizes the profoundly genuine concern of temperance advocates with the moral issues, and does not try to reduce it to a preoccupation with their status. He shows how their moral commitment comes to affect their status, and offers much evidence that in the end they become quite aware of this process. (See esp. Ch. 5.) In his book the concern with status is treated not as something that displaces the substantive purpose of the movement but as an important additional aspect of it. (See pp. 57–60.)

Gusfield distinguishes between the political aims of those he calls "cultural fundamentalists" and "cultural modernists"—the fundamentalists having a character more rigidly and exclusively oriented toward production, work, and saving, while the modernists are more concerned with consumption and enjoyment. The fundamentalists are "locals" in Robert Merton's terminology: that is, they take their values from the traditions of local society; the modernists are "cosmopolitans" in that they are more *au courant* with what is going on in the nation-wide mass society, whether or not they approve of it. Both are engaged with politics, but the fundamentalists have a special edge because they want to restore the simple virtues of a bygone age and feel themselves to be fighting in a losing cause.

This is exemplified by the temperance movement, whose political commitments Gusfield traces from the early days of the Republic to recent times. The temperance movement of the late nineteenth and the early twentieth century, he points out, was often associated with progressive causes—feminism, Christian pacifism, the Progressive movement of the Roosevelt-Wilson era —but as its members have felt an increasing sense of alienation from modernity, and as its more moderate adherents have been drawn away into the orbit of cosmopolitan society, temperance advocates have become more and more embittered. They know that they are regarded as oddities and that the most respectable and honored people no longer support their cause. Since the New Deal—a heavily urban and cosmopolitan administration—gave the *coup de grâce* to national Prohibition, the members of the movement have moved to the political right. The Prohibition party no longer attempts, as it did a generation ago, to appeal to reformers and liberals, but, as Gusfield concludes, "has moved toward an open appeal to the right-wing elements of both major parties."

In many areas of life, the style of status politics has been shaped in large measure by rigid moral and religious attitudes, and those who are moved by the issues of status politics transfer these attitudes to social and economic questions. On many occasions they approach economic issues as matters of faith and morals rather than matters of fact. For example, people often oppose certain economic policies not because they have been or would be economically hurt by such policies, or even because they have any carefully calculated views about their economic efficacy, but because they disapprove *on moral grounds* of the assumptions on which they think the policies rest.

A prominent case in point is the argument over fiscal policy. Deficit spending is vehemently opposed by great numbers of people in our society who have given no serious thought—indeed, are hardly equipped to do so—to the complex questions bearing on its efficacy as an economic device. They oppose it because their personal experience or training in spending, debts, and prudential management leads them to see in deficit spending a shocking repudiation of the moral precepts upon which their lives have been based. As a matter of status politics, deficit spending is an affront to millions who have been raised to live (and in some cases have been forced by circumstances to live) abstemious, thrifty, prudential lives. As a matter of interest politics, deficit spending might work to their advantage; but the moral and psychological effect, which is what they can really understand and feel, is quite otherwise: when society adopts a policy of deficit spending, thrifty small-businessmen, professionals, farmers, and white-collar workers who have been managing their affairs by the old rules feel that their way of life has been officially and insultingly repudiated.

Historians and social critics of the present generation have a particularly urgent need for such an analytical instrument as status politics: it serves to keep their conception of political conflict from being imbued with the excessive rationalism that infused the work of the two preceding generations of historians and political scientists. Under the guidance of such writers as Charles A. Beard, Frederick Jackson Turner, V. L. Parrington, Arthur F. Bentley, and others, we used to think of political man basically as a rational being who reckons as well as he can what his economic interests are, forms pressure groups and parties to advance these interests, and as a citizen casts his vote in order to see them realized.

Of course, the writers of this school understood that men can make miscalculations as to the nature of their interests and the best ways of pursuing them, and they also knew that at times noneconomic factors entered significantly into political behavior. But they persisted in seeking fundamental economic motives in almost all political conflict. When they dealt with noneconomic factors, as their sense of reality compelled them to do, they tended to discount the significance of these factors and to look upon them as momentary aberrations, and felt no need to develop a theory that would take adequate account of them. They were strongest when writing about those political conflicts that did in fact rest squarely on economic issues, and weakest when other issues came to the foreground. Their conceptions of historical change were least suited to deal with the kind of discontents that have developed during prosperity and which to a significant degree cut across class lines.

This rationalistic bias has very largely broken down in our time, partly under the impact of political events, partly because of what has been learned through public-opinion polling and depth psychology.[18] A conception of poli-

---

[18] Even the pollsters, however, were slow to break away from the older pattern of thought. The realization that socio-economic status was a fundamental category was at the very foundation of commercial polling, but the importance of religious affiliation was not realized. George Gallup found it hard to believe when Paul Lazarsfeld first told him that religious affiliation has a powerful and independent relation to voting habits; and even as recently as 1959 Elmo Roper asserted that there is no relation between religious affiliation and voting. Lipset: "Religion and Politics in the American Past and Present," already cited, p. 70. On religion as an independent force in American politics, and on the conservative drive of ascetic Protestantism, see Benton Johnson: "Ascetic Protestantism and Political Preference," *Public Opinion Quarterly*, XXVI (Spring 1962), pp. 35–46.

tics which dealt with the public largely as a set of economic blocs had no adequate way of coping with the variety of other factors that have entered into our political history—among them the sheer weight of habit and party loyalty, ethnic origins and traditions, religious affiliations and religious styles, racial and ethnic prejudices, attitudes toward liberty and censorship, feelings about foreign policy quite unrelated to commercial goals and of dubious relationship to the national interest. In American history the combined effect of such forces has been singularly large. The wealth of the country and the absence of sharp class-consciousness have released much political energy for expression on issues not directly connected with economic conflict; and our unusually complex ethnic and religious mixture has introduced a number of complicating factors of great emotional urgency.

Significantly, the periods in which status politics has been most strikingly apparent have been the relatively prosperous 1920s and the 1960s. In periods of prosperity, when economic conflicts are blunted or subordinated, the other issues become particularly acute. We have noticed that whereas in depressions or during great bursts of economic reform people vote for what they think are their economic interests, in times of prosperity they feel free to vote their prejudices. In good times, with their most severe economic difficulties behind them, many people feel that they can afford the luxury of addressing themselves to larger moral questions, and they are easily convinced that the kind of politics that results is much superior to the crass materialism of interest politics. They have fewer inhibitions about pressing hard for their moral concerns, no matter how demanding and ill-formulated, as an object of public policy, than they have in pressing for their interests, no matter how reasonable and realistically conceived.

DWIGHT MACDONALD

OUR INVISIBLE POOR

During the past half-century, as formal education—especially higher edu-cation—increasingly became a prerequisite for the exercise of leadership in American business and society, the self-made man of nineteenth-century America was gradually transformed into a mythic figure. In his penetrating study of American economic problems, Challenge to Affluence *(1963), the Swedish economist Gunnar Myrdal noted that in our own period the demand for skilled and educated workers has begun to affect jobs in the middle- and even lower-income brackets. As the need for formal training and education grew, those without it were, in Myrdal's terms, relegated to the status of a redundant "underclass" with little or no hope of rising and without any means of changing their own fate. Finding it impossible to become part of the mainstream of a nation enjoying the greatest period of prosperity and op-portunity in its history, they constituted "a useless and miserable substra-tum." "There is," Myrdal concluded, "an ugly smell rising from the base-ment of the stately American mansion."*

Not until a number of studies publicized these facts in the early 1960's did an awareness of the situation begin to intrude itself upon the conscious-ness of the nation at large. In the following article Dwight Macdonald dis-cusses the earliest of these studies, using them as a springboard for his own comments on the American scene. There has been some improvement since Macdonald wrote in 1963. Congress has passed a Medicare bill, a segment of the farm workers in California have begun to organize successfully, and the federal government has taken official notice of the poverty existing in the

379

United States and has inaugurated a few programs to deal with aspects of it. But the fundamental conditions afflicting the poor, of which Macdonald wrote, remain unchanged, and without taking them into account there can be no understanding of the needs of contemporary American society. For still another excellent study of existing American poverty, published after Macdonald's article, read Herman P. Miller, Rich Man, Poor Man * (1964).

In his significantly titled *The Affluent Society* (1958) Professor J. K. Galbraith states that poverty in this country is no longer "a massive affliction [but] more nearly an afterthought." Dr. Galbraith is a humane critic of the American capitalist system, and he is generously indignant about the continued existence of even this nonmassive and afterthoughtish poverty. But the interesting thing about his pronouncement, aside from the fact that it is inaccurate, is that it was generally accepted as obvious. For a long time now, almost everybody has assumed that, because of the New Deal's social legislation and—more important—the prosperity we have enjoyed since 1940, mass poverty no longer exists in this country.

Dr. Galbraith states that our poor have dwindled to two hard-core categories. One is the "insular poverty" of those who live in the rural South or in depressed areas like West Virginia. The other category is "case poverty," which he says is "commonly and properly related to [such] characteristics of the individuals so afflicted [as] mental deficiency, bad health, inability to adapt to the discipline of modern economic life, excessive procreation, alcohol, insufficient education." He reasons that such poverty must be due to individual defects, since "nearly everyone else has mastered his environment; this proves that it is not intractable." Without pressing the similarity of this concept to the "Social Darwinism" whose fallacies Dr. Galbraith easily disposes of elsewhere in his book, one may observe that most of these characteristics are as much the result of poverty as its cause.

Dr. Galbraith's error is understandable, and common. Last April the newspapers reported some exhilarating statistics in a Department of Commerce study: the average family income increased from $2,340 in 1929 to $7,020 in 1961. (These figures are calculated in current dollars, as are all the others I shall cite.) But the papers did not report the fine type, so to speak, which showed that almost all the recent gain was made by families with incomes of over $7,500, and that the rate at which poverty is being eliminated has slowed down alarmingly since 1953. Only the specialists and the statisticians read the fine type, which is why illusions continue to exist about American poverty.

Now Michael Harrington, an alumnus of the *Catholic Worker* and the Fund for the Republic who is at present a contributing editor of *Dissent* and the chief editor of the Socialist Party biweekly, *New America,* has written *The Other America: Poverty in the United States* (Macmillan). In the admirably short space of under two hundred pages, he outlines the problem, describes in imaginative detail what it means to be poor in this country today, summarizes the findings of recent studies by economists and sociologists, and

---

FROM Dwight Macdonald, "Our Invisible Poor," *The New Yorker* (January 19, 1963). Reprinted by permission. © 1963 The New Yorker Magazine, Inc.

analyzes the reasons for the persistence of mass poverty in the midst of general prosperity. It is an excellent book—and a most important one.

My only serious criticism is that Mr. Harrington has popularized the treatment a bit too much. Not in the writing, which is on a decent level, but in a certain vagueness. There are no index, no bibliography, no reference footnotes. In our overspecialized culture, books like this tend to fall into two categories: Popular (no scholarly "apparatus") and Academic (too much). I favor something intermediate—why should the academics have *all* the footnotes? The lack of references means that the book is of limited use to future researchers and writers. A pity, since the author has brought together a great range of material.

I must also object that Mr. Harrington's treatment of statistics is more than a little impressionistic. His appendix, which he calls a coming to grips with the professional material, doesn't live up to its billing. "If my interpretation is bleak and grim," he writes, "and even if it overstates the case slightly, that is intentional. My moral point of departure is a sense of outrage. . . . In such a discussion it is inevitable that one gets mixed up with dry, graceless, technical matters. That should not conceal the crucial fact that these numbers represent people and that any tendency toward understatement is an intellectual way of acquiescing in suffering." But a fact is a fact, and Mr. Harrington confuses the issue when he writes that "these numbers represent people." They do—and one virtue of his book is that he never forgets it—but in dealing with statistics, this truism must be firmly repressed lest one begin to think from the heart rather than from the head, as he seems to do when he charges those statisticians who "understate" the numbers of the poor with having found "an intellectual way of acquiescing in suffering." This is moral bullying, and it reminds me, *toutes proportions gardées,* of the habitual confusion in Communist thinking between facts and political inferences from them. "A sense of outrage" is proper for a "moral point of departure," but statistics are the appropriate *factual* point of departure, as in the writings of Marx and Engels on the agony of the nineteenth-century English working class—writings that are by no means lacking in a sense of moral outrage, either.

These objections, however, do not affect Mr. Harrington's two main contentions: that mass poverty still exists in the United States, and that it is disappearing more slowly than is commonly thought. Two recent dry, graceless, and technical reports bear him out. One is that Commerce Department study, already mentioned. More important is *Poverty and Deprivation in the U.S.,* a bulky pamphlet issued by the Conference on Economic Progress, in Washington, whose national committee includes Thurman Arnold, Leon H. Keyserling (said to be the principal author of the pamphlet), and Walter P. Reuther.

In the last year we seem to have suddenly awakened, rubbing our eyes like Rip van Winkle, to the fact that mass poverty persists, and that it is one of our two gravest social problems. (The other is related: While only eleven per cent of our population is non-white, twenty-five per cent of our poor are.) Two other current books confirm Mr. Harrington's thesis: *Wealth and Power in America* (Praeger), by Dr. Gabriel Kolko, a social historian who has recently been at Harvard and the University of Melbourne, Australia, and *Income and Welfare in the United States* (McGraw-Hill), compiled by an imposing battery of four socio-economists headed by Dr. James N. Morgan, who rejoices in the title of Program Director of the Survey Research Center of the Institute for Social Research at the University of Michigan.

Dr. Kolko's book resembles Mr. Harrington's in several ways: It is short, it is based on earlier studies, and it is liberally inclined. It is less readable, because it is written in an academic jargon that is merely a vehicle for the clinching Statistic. Although it is impossible to write seriously about poverty without a copious use of statistics—as this review will demonstrate—it *is* possible to bring thought and feeling to bear on such raw material. Mr. Harrington does this more successfully than Dr. Kolko, whose prose is afflicted not only with academic blight but also with creeping ideology. Dr. Kolko leans so far to the socialist side that he sometimes falls on his nose, as when he clinches the inequality of wealth in the United States with a statistic: "In 1959, 23% of those earning less than $1,000 [a year] owned a car, compared to 95% of those earning more than $10,000." The real point is just the opposite, as any citizen of Iran, Ghana, Yemen, or the U.S.S.R. would appreciate—not that the rich have cars but that almost a quarter of the extremely poor do. Similarly, although Dr. Kolko has two chapters on poverty that confirm Mr. Harrington's argument, his main point is a different and more vulnerable one: "The basic distribution of income and wealth in the United States is essentially the same now as it was in 1939, or even 1910." This is a half fact. The rich are almost as rich as ever and the poor are even poorer, in the percentage of the national income they receive. Yet, as will become apparent later, there have been major changes in the distribution of wealth, and there has been a general improvement in living standards, so that the poor are much fewer today than they were in 1939. "Most low-income groups live substantially better today," Dr. Kolko admits. "But even though their real wages have mounted, their percentage of the national income has not changed." That in the last half century the rich have kept their riches and the poor their poverty is indeed a scandal. But it is theoretically possible, assuming enough general increase in wealth, that the relatively poor might by now have achieved a decent standard of living, no matter how inferior to that of the rich. As the books under consideration show, however, this theoretical possibility has not been realized.

Inequality of wealth is not necessarily a major social problem per se. Poverty is. The late French philosopher Charles Péguy remarks, in his classic essay on poverty, "The duty of tearing the destitute from their destitution and the duty of distributing goods equitably are not of the same order. The first is an urgent duty, the second is a duty of convenience. . . . When all men are provided with the necessities . . . what do we care about the distribution of luxury?" What indeed? Envy and emulation are the motives—and not very good ones—for the equalization of wealth. The problem of poverty goes much deeper.

Income and Welfare in the United States differs from the other works reviewed here in length (531 big pages) and in being the result of original research; 2,800 families were interviewed "in depth." I must confess that, aside from a few interesting bits of data, I got almost nothing out of it. I assume the authors think poverty is still an important social problem, else why would they have gone to all this labor, but I'm not at all sure what their general conclusions are; maybe there aren't supposed to be any, in the best tradition of American scholarship. Their book is one of those behemoths of collective research financed by a foundation (in this case, largely by Ford) that daunt the stoutest-hearted lay reader (in this case, me). Based on "a multi-stage area probability sample that gives equal chance of selection to all non-institutional dwelling units in the conterminous United States [and that] was clustered geographically at each stage and stratified with interlaced controls," it is a specimen of what Charles Lamb called *biblia abiblia*—things that have the outward appearance of books but are not books, since they cannot be read. Methodologically, it employs something called the "multivariate analysis," which is explained in Appendix E. Typographically, Appendix E looks like language, but it turns out to be strewn with booby traps, all doubtless well known in the trade, like "dummy variables," "F ratios," "regression coefficients," "beta coefficients" (and "partial beta coefficients"), and two kinds of "standard deviations"—"of explanatory variable A" and "of the dependent variable."

My experience with such works may be summarized as follows: (alpha) the coefficient of comprehensibility decreases in direct ratio to the increase in length, or the longer the incomprehensibler, a notion that is illustrated here by the fact that Dr. Kolko's short work is more understandable than Dr. Morgan *et al.*'s long one; (beta) the standard deviation from truism is inversely related to the magnitude of the generalization, or the bigger the statement the more obvious. (Beta) is illustrated by the authors' five general proposals for action ("Implications for Public Policy"). The second of these is: "Fuller employment and the elimination of discrimination based on prejudice would contribute greatly to the independence of non-white persons, women, teenagers, and some of the aged." That is, if Negroes and the rest had jobs and were not discriminated against, they would be better off—a point that doesn't need to be argued or, for that matter, stated. The authors have achieved such a mastery of truism that they sometimes achieve the same monumental effect even in non-magnitudinous statements, as: "Table 28–1 shows that the proportion of parents who indicated that their children will attend private colleges is approximately twice as large for those with incomes over $10,000 as for those with incomes under $3,000." Could be.

What is "poverty"? It is a historically relative concept, first of all. "There are new definitions [in America] of what man can achieve, of what a human standard of life should be," Mr. Harrington writes. "Those who suffer levels of life well below those that are possible, even though they live better than medieval knights or Asian peasants, are poor. . . . Poverty should be defined in terms of those who are denied the minimal levels of health, housing, food, and education that our present stage of scientific knowledge specifies as necessary for life as it is now lived in the United States." His dividing line follows that proposed in recent studies by the United States Bureau of Labor Statistics: $4,000 a year for a family of four and $2,000 for an individual living alone. (All kinds of income are included, such as food grown and consumed on farms.) This is the cutoff line generally drawn today.

Mr. Harrington estimates that between forty and fifty million Americans, or about a fourth of the population, are now living in poverty. Not just below the level of comfortable living, but real poverty, in the old-fashioned sense of the word—that they are hard put to it to get the mere necessities, beginning with enough to eat. This is difficult to believe in the United States of 1963, but one has to make the effort, and it is now being made. The extent of our poverty has suddenly become visible. The same thing has happened in England, where working-class gains as a result of the Labour Party's post-1945 welfare state blinded almost everybody to the continued existence of mass poverty. It was not until Professor Richard M. Titmuss, of the London School of Economics, published a series of articles in the *New Statesman* last fall, based on his new book, *Income Distribution and Social Change* (Allen & Unwin), that even the liberal public in England became aware that the problem still persists on a scale that is "statistically significant," as the economists put it.

Statistics on poverty are even trickier than most. For example, age and geography make a difference. There is a distinction, which cannot be rendered arithmetically, between poverty and low income. A childless young couple with $3,000 a year is not poor in the way an elderly couple might be with the same income. The young couple's statistical poverty may be a temporary inconvenience; if the husband is a graduate student or a skilled worker, there are prospects of later affluence or at least comfort. But the old couple can look forward only to diminishing earnings and increasing medical expenses. So also geographically: A family of four in a small town with $4,000 a year may be better off than a like family in a city—lower rent, no bus fares to get to work, fewer occasions (or temptations) to spend money. Even more so with a rural family. Although allowance is made for the value of the vegetables they may raise to feed themselves, it is impossible to calculate how much money they *don't* spend on clothes, say, or furniture, because they don't have to keep up with the Joneses. Lurking in the crevices of a city, like piranha fish in a Brazilian stream, are numerous tempting opportunities for expenditure, small but voracious, which can strip a budget to its bones in a surprisingly short time. The subtlety and complexity of poverty statistics may be discovered by a look at Dr. Kolko's statement that in 1959 "23% of those earning less than $1,000 owned a car." Does this include college students, or are they included in their families' statistics? If the first is true, then Dr. Kolko's figure loses much of its meaning. If the second is, then it is almost *too* meaningful, since it says that one-fourth of those earning less than twenty dollars a week are able to afford a car. Which it is, deponent sayeth not.

It is not, therefore, surprising to find that there is some disagreement about just how many millions of Americans are poor. The point is that all these recent studies agree that American poverty is still a mass phenomenon. One of the lowest estimates appears in the University of Michigan's *Income and Welfare,* which states, "Poor families comprise one-fifth of the nation's families." The authors do not develop this large and crucial statement, or even give sources for it, despite their meticulous pedantry in all unimportant matters. So one can only murmur that the other experts put the number of poor much higher. (Though even a fifth is still over 35,000,000 people.) The lowness of the Michigan estimate is especially puzzling since its cutoff figure for poverty is $4,330, which is slightly higher than the commonly accepted one. The tendentious Dr. Kolko is also unconvincing, in the opposite direction. "Since 1947," he writes, "one-half of the nation's families and unattached individuals have had an income too small to provide them with a maintenance standard of living," which he sets at $4,500 a year for a family. He does give a table, with a long supporting footnote that failed to make clear to me how he could have possibly decided that 90,000,000 Americans are now living on less than $4,500 a year; I suspect some confusion between a "maintenance" and a "minimum-comfort" budget.

More persuasive estimates appear in the Conference on Economic Progress pamphlet, *Poverty and Deprivation.* Using the $4,000 cutoff, the authors conclude that 38,000,000 persons are now living in poverty, which is slightly less than Mr. Harrington's lowest estimate. One reason may be that the pamphlet discriminates, as most studies don't, between "multiple-person families" and "unattached individuals," rating the latter as poor only if they have less than $2,000 a year. But there is more to it than that, including a few things I don't feel competent to judge. Income statistics are never compiled on exactly the same bases and there are all kinds of refinements, which vary from one study to another. Thus the Commerce Department's April report estimates there are 17,500,000 families *and* "unattached individuals" with incomes of less than $4,000. How many of the latter are there? *Poverty and Deprivation* puts the number of single persons with under $2,000 at 4,000,000. Let us say that in the 17,500,000 under $4,000 there are 6,500,000 single persons—the proportion of unattached individuals tends to go down as income rises. This homemade estimate gives us 11,000,000 families with incomes of under $4,000. Figuring the average American family at three and a half persons—which it is—this makes 38,500,000 individuals in families, or a grand total, if we add in the 4,000,000 "unattached individuals" with under $2,000 a year, of 42,500,000 Americans now living in poverty, which is close to a fourth of the total population.

The reason Dr. Galbraith was able to see poverty as no longer "a massive affliction" is that he used a cutoff of $1,000, which even in 1949, when it was adopted in a Congressional study, was probably too low (the C.I.O. argued for $2,000) and in 1958, when *The Affluent Society* appeared, was simply fantastic.

The model postwar budgets drawn up in 1951 by the Bureau of Labor Statistics to "maintain a level of adequate living" give a concrete idea of what poverty means in this country—or would mean if poor families lived within their income and spent it wisely, which they don't. Dr. Kolko summarizes the kind of living these budgets provide:

> Three members of the family see a movie once every three weeks, and one member sees a movie once every two weeks. There is no telephone in the house, but the family makes three pay calls a week. They buy one book a year and write one letter a week.
>
> The father buys one heavy wool suit every two years and a light wool suit every three years; the wife, one suit every ten years or one skirt every five years. Every three or four years, depending on the distance and time involved, the family takes a vacation outside their own city. In 1950, the family spent a total of $80 to $90 on all types of home furnishings, electrical appliances, and laundry equipment. . . . The family eats cheaper cuts of meat several times a week, but has more expensive cuts on holidays. The entire family consumes a total of two five-cent ice cream cones, one five-cent candy bar, two bottles of soda, and one bottle of beer a week. The family owes no money, but has no savings except for a small insurance policy.

One other item is included in the B.L.S. "maintenance" budget: a new car every twelve to eighteen years.

This is an ideal picture, drawn up by social workers, of how a poor family *should* spend its money. But the poor are much less provident—installment debts take up a lot of their cash, and only a statistician could expect an actual live woman, however poor, to buy new clothes at intervals of five or ten years. Also, one suspects that a lot more movies are seen and ice-cream cones and bottles of beer are consumed than in the Spartan ideal. But these necessary luxuries are had only at the cost of displacing other items—necessary necessities, so to speak—in the B.L.S. budget.

The Conference on Economic Progress's *Poverty and Deprivation* deals not only with the poor but also with another large section of the "underprivileged," which is an American euphemism almost as good as "senior citizen";

namely, the 37,000,000 persons whose family income is between $4,000 and $5,999 and the 2,000,000 singles who have from $2,000 to $2,999. The authors define "deprivation" as "above poverty but short of minimum requirements for a modestly comfortable level of living." They claim that 77,000,000 Americans, or *almost half the population,* live in poverty or deprivation. One recalls the furor Roosevelt aroused with his "one-third of a nation—ill-housed, ill-clad, ill-nourished." But the political climate was different then.

The distinction between a family income of $3,500 ("poverty") and $4,500 ("deprivation") is not vivid to those who run things—the 31 per cent whose incomes are between $7,500 and $14,999 and the 7 per cent of the topmost top dogs, who get $15,000 or more. These two minorities, sizable enough to feel they *are* the nation, have been as unaware of the continued existence of mass poverty as this reviewer was until he read Mr. Harrington's book. They are businessmen, congressmen, judges, government officials, politicians, lawyers, doctors, engineers, scientists, editors, journalists, and administrators in colleges, churches, and foundations. Since their education, income, and social status are superior, they, if anybody, might be expected to accept responsibility for what the Constitution calls "the general welfare." They have not done so in the case of the poor. And they have a good excuse. It is becoming harder and harder simply to *see* the one-fourth of our fellow-citizens who live below the poverty line.

> The poor are increasingly slipping out of the very experience and consciousness of the nation [Mr. Harrington writes]. If the middle class never did like ugliness and poverty, it was at least aware of them. "Across the tracks" was not a very long way to go. . . . Now the American city has been transformed. The poor still inhabit the miserable housing in the central area, but they are increasingly isolated from contact with, or sight of, anybody else. . . . Living out in the suburbs, it is easy to assume that ours is, indeed, an affluent society. . . .
>
> Clothes make the poor invisible too: America has the best-dressed poverty the world has ever known. . . . It is much easier in the United States to be decently dressed than it is to be decently housed, fed, or doctored. . . .
>
> Many of the poor are the wrong age to be seen. A good number of them are sixty-five years of age or better; an even larger number are under eighteen. . . .
>
> And finally, the poor are politically invisible. . . . They are without lobbies of their own; they put forward no legislative program. As a group, they are atomized. They have no face; they have no voice. . . . Only the social agencies have a really direct involvement with the other America, and they are without any great political power. . . .
>
> Forty to fifty million people are becoming increasingly invisible.

These invisible people fall mostly into the following categories, some of them overlapping: poor farmers, who operate 40 per cent of the farms and get

7 per cent of the farm cash income; migratory farm workers; unskilled, unorganized workers in offices, hotels, restaurants, hospitals, laundries, and other service jobs; inhabitants of areas where poverty is either endemic ("peculiar to a people or district"), as in the rural South, or epidemic ("prevalent among a community at a special time and produced by some special causes"), as in West Virginia, where the special cause was the closing of coal mines and steel plants; Negroes and Puerto Ricans, who are a fourth of the total poor; the alcoholic derelicts in the big-city skid rows; the hillbillies from Kentucky, Tennessee, and Oklahoma who have migrated to Midwestern cities in search of better jobs. And, finally, almost half our "senior citizens."

The only pages in *Poverty and Deprivation* that can be read are the statistical tables. The rest is a jungle of inchoate data that seems deliberately to eschew, like other collective research projects, such human qualities as reason (the reader has to do most of the work of ordering the material) and feeling (if Mr. Harrington sometimes has too much, it is a venial sin compared to the bleakness of this prose). My hypothesis is that *Poverty and Deprivation* was composed on that TX–0 "electronic brain" at M.I.T. This would account both for the vitality of the tables and for the deadness of the text.

And what shall one say about the University of Michigan's *Income and Welfare in the United States?* Even its *tables* are not readable. And its text makes *Poverty and Deprivation* look like the Federalist Papers. On the first page, the authors unloose a generalization of stupefying generality: "The United States has arrived at the point where poverty could be abolished easily and simply by a stroke of the pen. [Where have we heard *that* before?] To raise every individual and family in the nation now below a subsistence income to the subsistence level would cost about $10 billion a year. This is less than 2 per cent of the gross national product. It is less than 10 per cent of tax revenues. [They mean, but forgot to say so, *federal* taxes, since if state and local taxes were added, the total would be much higher than $100 billion.] It is about one-fifth of the cost of national defense." (They might have added that it is slightly more than three times the $3 billion Americans spend on their dogs and cats and canaries every year.) This got big headlines in the press, as must have been expected: "'STROKE OF PEN' COULD ELIMINATE POVERTY IN U.S., 4 SCIENTISTS SAY." But the authors, having dropped the $10 billion figure on the first page, never explain its meaning—is it a seedbed operation or a permanent dole? They are not clear even on how they arrived at it. At their own estimate of 35,000,000 poor, $10 billion would work out to slightly less than $300 per person. This seems too little to abolish poverty "easily and simply by a stroke of the pen."

There are other vaguenesses: "A careful analysis of the characteristics of families whose incomes are inadequate reveals that they should earn considerably more than they do on the basis of their education and other characteristics. The multivariate analysis . . . indicates that heads of poor families should average $2,204 in earnings. In fact heads of poor families earned an average of only $932 in 1959." I have already confessed my inability to understand the multivariate analysis, but the compilers seem to be saying that according to the variables in their study (race, age, sex, education, physical disabilities, and locale), heads of poor families should now be making twice as much as they are. And why don't they? "The discrepancy may arise from psychological dependency, lack of motivation, lack of intelligence, and a variety of other factors that were not studied." One wonders why they were not studied—and what those "other factors" were, exactly. Also, whether such a discrepancy—the earnings the researchers expected to find were actually less than half those they *did* find—may not indicate some ghastly flaw in that "multivariate analysis." There is, of course, no suggestion in the book that Dr. Morgan and his team are in any way worried.

The most obvious citizens of the Other America are those whose skins are the wrong color. The folk slogans are realistic: "Last to be hired, first to be fired" and "If you're black, stay back." There has been some progress. In 1939, the non-white worker's wage averaged 41.4 per cent of the white worker's; by 1958 it had climbed to 58 per cent. A famous victory, but the non-whites still average only slightly more than half as much as the whites. Even this modest gain was due not to any Rooseveltian or Trumanian social reform but merely to the fact that for some years there was a war on and workers were in demand, whether black, white, or violet. By 1947, the non-whites had achieved most of their advance—to 54 per cent of white earnings, which means they have gained, in the last fifteen years, just 4 per cent.

The least obvious poverty affects our "senior citizens"—those over sixty-five. Mr. Harrington estimates that half of them—8,000,000—live in poverty, and he thinks they are even more atomized and politically helpless than the rest of the Other America. He estimates that one-fourth of the "unrelated individuals" among them, or a million persons, have less than $580 a year, which is about what is allotted *for food alone* in the Department of Agriculture's minimum-subsistence budget. (The average American family now spends only 20 per cent of its income for food—an indication of the remarkable prosperity we are all enjoying, except for one-quarter of us.) One can imagine, or perhaps one can't, what it would be like to live on $580 a year, or $11 a week. It is only fair to note that most of our senior citizens do better: The average per-capita income of those over sixty-five is now estimated to be slightly over $20 a week. That is, about $1,000 a year.

The aged poor have two sources of income besides their earnings or savings. One is contributions by relatives. A 1961 White House Conference Report put this at 10 per cent of income, which works out to $8 a week for an income of $4,000—and the 8,000,000 aged poor all have less than that. The other is Social Security, whose benefits in 1959 averaged $18 a week. Even this modest sum is more than any of the under–$4,000 got, since payments are proportionate to earnings and the poor, of course, earned less than the rest. A quarter of them, and those in general the neediest, are not covered by

Social Security. The last resort is relief, and Mr. Harrington describes most vividly the humiliations the poor often have to put up with to get that.

The problem of the aged poor is aggravated by the fact that, unlike the Italians or the English, we seem to have little respect for or interest in our "senior citizens," beyond giving them that honorific title, and we don't include them in family life. If we can afford it, we are likely to send them to nursing homes—"a storage-bin philosophy," a Senate report calls it—and if we can't, which is the case with the poor, they must make do with the resources noted above. The Michigan study has a depressing chapter on "The Economics of Living with Relatives." Nearly two-thirds of the heads of families queried were opposed to having their aged parents live with their children. "The old do not understand the young, and the young do not understand the old or the young," observed one respondent, who must have had a sense of humor. Other replies were "Old people are pretty hard to get along with" and "The parents and the children try to boss each other and when they live with you there's always fighting." The minority in favor gave practical reasons, like "It's a good thing to have them with you so you can see after them" and "The old folks might get a pension or something, so they could help you out." Hardly anyone expressed any particular respect for the old, or a feeling that their experience might enrich family life. The most depressing finding was "People most able to provide support for relatives are most opposed to it. Older people with some college education are eleven to one against it." The most favorable toward including older people in the home were Negroes, and even they were mostly against it.

The whole problem of poverty and the aged is especially serious today because Americans are living longer. In the first half of this century, life expectancy increased 17.6 years for men and 20.3 years for women. And between 1950 and 1960 the over-sixty-five group increased twice as fast as the population as a whole.

The worst part of being old and poor in this country is the loneliness. Mr. Harrington notes that we have not only racial ghettos but geriatric ones, in the cheap rooming-house districts of large cities. He gives one peculiarly disturbing statistic: "One-third of the aged in the United States, some 5,000,000 or more human beings, have no phone in their place of residence. They are literally cut off from the rest of America."

Ernest Hemingway's celebrated deflation of Scott Fitzgerald's romantic notion that the rich are "different" somehow—"Yes, they have money" —doesn't apply to the poor. They are different in more important ways than their lack of money, as Mr. Harrington demonstrates:

> Emotional upset is one of the main forms of the vicious circle of impoverishment. The structure of the society is hostile to these people. The poor tend to become pessimistic and depressed; they seek immediate gratification instead of saving; they act out.
>
> Once this mood, this unarticulated philosophy becomes a fact, society can

change, the recession can end, and yet there is no motive for movement. The depression has become internalized. The middle class looks upon this process and sees "lazy" people who "just don't want to get ahead." People who are much too sensitive to demand of cripples that they run races ask of the poor that they get up and act just like everyone else in the society.

The poor are not like everyone else. . . . They think and feel differently; they look upon a different America than the middle class looks upon.

The poor are also different in a physical sense: they are much less healthy. According to *Poverty and Deprivation,* the proportion of those "disabled or limited in their major activity by chronic ill health" rises sharply as income sinks. In reasonably well-off families ($7,000 and up), 4.3 per cent are so disabled; in reasonably poor families ($2,000 to $3,999), the proportion doubles, to 8 per cent; and in unreasonably poor families (under $2,000), it doubles again, to 16.5 per cent. An obvious cause, among others, for the very poor being four times as much disabled by "chronic ill health" as the well-to-do is that they have much less money to spend for medical care— in fact, almost nothing. This weighs with special heaviness on the aged poor. During the fifties, Mr. Harrington notes, "all costs on the Consumer Price Index went up by 12 per cent. But medical costs, that terrible staple of the aged, went up by 36 per cent, hospitalization rose by 65 per cent, and group hospitalization costs (Blue Cross premiums) were up by 83 per cent."

This last figure is particularly interesting, since Blue Cross and such plans are the A.M.A.'s alternative to socialized medicine, or, rather, to the timid fumblings toward it that even our most liberal politicians have dared to propose. Such figures throw an unpleasant light on the Senate's rejection of Medicare. The defeat was all the more bitter because, in the usual effort to appease the conservatives (with the usual lack of success—only five Republicans and only four Southern Democrats voted pro), the bill was watered down in advance. Not until he had spent $90 of his own money—which is 10 per cent of the annual income of some 3,000,000 aged poor—would a patient have been eligible. And the original program included only people already covered by Social Security or Railroad Retirement pensions and excluded the neediest of all—the 2,500,000 aged poor who are left out of both these systems. These untouchables were finally included in order to placate five liberal Republican senators, led by Javits of New York. They did vote for Medicare, but they were the only Republicans who did.

Mental as well as physical illness is much greater among the poor, even though our complacent cliché is that nervous breakdowns are a prerogative of the rich because the poor "can't afford" them. (They can't, but they have them anyway.) This bit of middle-class folklore should be laid to rest by a study made in New Haven: *Social Class and Mental Illness,* by August B. Hollingshead and Frederick C. Redlich (Wiley). They found that the rate of "treated psychiatric illness" is about the same from the rich down through decently paid workers—an average of 573 per 100,000. But in the bottom fifth it shoots up to 1,659 per 100,000. There is an even more striking difference in the *kind* of mental illness. Of those in the four top income groups who had undergone psychiatric treatment, 65 per cent had been treated for neurotic problems and 35 per cent for psychotic disturbances. In the bottom fifth, the treated illnesses were almost all psychotic (90 per cent). This shows there is something to the notion that the poor "can't afford" nervous breakdowns— the milder kind, that is—since the reason the proportion of *treated* neuroses among the poor is only 10 per cent is that a neurotic can keep going, after a fashion. But the argument cuts deeper the other way. The poor go to a psychiatrist (or, more commonly, are committed to a mental institution) only when they are completely unable to function because of psychotic symptoms. Therefore, even that nearly threefold increase in mental disorders among the poor is probably an underestimate.

The poor are different, then, both physically and psychologically. During the fifties, a team of psychiatrists from Cornell studied "Midtown," a residential area in this city that contained 170,000 people, of all social classes. The area was 99 per cent white, so the findings may be presumed to understate the problem of poverty. The description of the poor—the "low social economic status individual"—is blunt: "[They are] rigid, suspicious, and have a fatalistic outlook on life. They do not plan ahead. . . . They are prone to depression, have feelings of futility, lack of belongingness, friendliness, and a lack of trust in others." Only a Dr. Pangloss would expect anything else. As Mr. Harrington points out, such characteristics are "a realistic adaptation to a socially perverse situation."

As for the isolation that is the lot of the American poor, that is a point on which Mr. Harrington is very good:

America has a self-image of itself as a nation of joiners and doers. There are social clubs, charities, community drives, and the like. [One might add organizations like the Elks and Masons, Rotary and Kiwanis, cultural groups like our women's clubs, also alumni associations and professional organizations.] And yet this entire structure is a phenomenon of the middle class. Some time ago, a study in Franklin, Indiana [this vagueness of reference is all too typical of "The Other America"], reported that the percentage of people in the bottom class who were without affiliations of any kind was eight times as great as the percentage in the high-income class.

Paradoxically, one of the factors that intensifies the social isolation of the poor is that America thinks of itself as a nation without social classes. As a result, there are few social or civic organizations that are separated on the basis of income and class. The "working-class culture" that sociologists have described in a country like England does not exist here. . . . The poor person who might want to join an organization is afraid. Because he or she will have less education, less money, less competence to articulate ideas than anyone else in the group, they stay away.

One reason our society is a comparatively violent one is that the French and Italian and British poor have a communal life and culture that the American poor lack. As one reads *The Other America,* one wonders why there is not even more violence than there is.

The richest city of all, New York, has been steadily growing poorer, if one looks beyond Park Avenue and Wall Street. Of its 2,080,000 families, just under half (49 per cent) had incomes in 1959 of less than $6,000; for the city's non-white families, the percentage was 71. And a fourth of all New York families in 1959 were below the poverty line of $4,000. These percentages are at present slightly higher than the national average—an ominous reversal of the city's earlier position. In 1932, the average national weekly wage was only 67 per cent of the New York City average. In 1960, it was 108 per cent. The city's manufacturing workers in 1946 earned $11 more a week than the national average; in 1960 they earned $6.55 a week less. The two chief reasons are probably the postwar influx of Puerto Ricans and the exodus to the suburbs of the well-to-do. But whatever the reasons, the city seems to be turning into an economically backward area, like Arkansas or New Hampshire. Even the bankers—the "non-supervisory" ones, that is—are modestly paid: 54 per cent of the males and 78 per cent of the females make less than $80 a week. All these statistics come from John O'Rourke, president of Joint Council 16, International Brotherhood of Teamsters, which has 168,000 members in the area. Mr. O'Rourke has been campaigning to persuade Mayor Wagner to raise the city's minimum hourly wage to $1.50. (The Mayor has gone as far as $1.25.) The New York teamsters are motivated by enlightened self-interest: the more other wages stagnate, the harder it will be to maintain their own comparatively high level of pay. They complain especially about the low wages in the highly organized garment trade, to which Mr. Dubinsky's International Ladies' Garment Workers' Union replies that if it presses for higher wages the manufacturers will simply move to low-wage, non-union areas, mostly in the South, as the New England textile manufacturers did many years ago—a riposte that is as realistic as it is uncheering. However, Mr. O'Rourke has an enterprising research staff, plenty of persistence, and a sharp tongue. "New Yorkers," he says, "are accustomed to thinking of themselves as pacesetters in an allegedly affluent society [but] at the rate we are going, we will soon qualify for the title 'Sweatshop Capital of the Nation.' "

The main reason the American poor have become invisible is that since 1936 their numbers have been reduced by two-thirds. Astounding as it may seem, the fact is that President Roosevelt's "one-third of a nation" was a considerable understatement; over two-thirds of us then lived below the poverty line, as is shown by the tables that follow. But today the poor are a minority, and minorities can be ignored if they are so heterogeneous that they cannot be organized. When the poor were a majority, they simply could not be overlooked. Poverty is also hard to see today because the middle class ($6,000 to $14,999) has vastly increased—from 13 per cent of all families in 1936 to a near-majority (47 per cent) today. That mass poverty can persist despite this rise to affluence is hard to believe, or see, especially if one is among those who have risen.

Two tables in *Poverty and Deprivation* summarize what has been happening in the last thirty years. They cover only multiple-person families; all figures are converted to 1960 dollars; and the income is before taxes. I have omitted, for clarity, all fractions.

The first table is the percentage of families with a given income:

	1935–36	1947	1953	1960
Under $ 4,000	68%	37%	28%	23%
$4,000 to $ 5,999	17	29	28	23
$6,000 to $ 7,499	6	12	17	16
$7,500 to $14,999	7	17	23	31
Over $15,000	2	4	5	7

The second table is the share each group had in the family income of the nation:

	1935–36	1947	1953	1960
Under $ 4,000	35%	16%	11%	7%
$4,000 to $ 5,999	21	24	21	15
$6,000 to $ 7,499	10	14	17	14
$7,500 to $14,999	16	28	33	40
Over $15,000	18	18	19	24

Several interesting conclusions can be drawn from these tables:

(1) The New Deal didn't do anything about poverty: The under–$4,000 families in 1936 were 68 per cent of the total population, which was slightly *more* than the 1929 figure of 65 per cent.

(2) The war economy (hot and cold) did do something about poverty: Between 1936 and 1960 the proportion of all families who were poor was reduced from 68 per cent to 23 per cent.

(3) If the percentage of under–$4,000 families decreased by two-thirds between 1936 and 1960, their share of the national income dropped a great deal more—from 35 per cent to 7 per cent.

(4) The well-to-do ($7,500 to $14,999) have enormously increased, from 7 per cent of all families in 1936 to 31 per cent today. The rich ($15,000 and over) have also multiplied—from 2 to 7 per cent. But it should be noted that the very rich, according to another new study, *The Share of Top Wealth-Holders in National Wealth, 1922–1956,* by Robert J. Lampman (Princeton), have experienced a decline. He finds that the top 1 per cent

of wealth-holders owned 38 per cent of the national wealth in 1929 and own only 28 per cent today. (Though let's not get sentimental over that "only.") Thus, *pace* Dr. Kolko, there has in fact been a redistribution of wealth—in favor of the well-to-do and the rich at the expense of the poor and the very rich.

(5) The reduction of poverty has slowed down. In the six years 1947–53, the number of poor families declined 9 per cent, but in the following seven years only 5 per cent. The economic stasis that set in with Eisenhower and that still persists under Kennedy was responsible. (This stagnation, however, did not affect the over–$7,500 families, who increased from 28 per cent to 38 per cent between 1953 and 1960.) In the *New York Times Magazine* for last November 11th, Herman P. Miller, of the Bureau of the Census, wrote, "During the forties, the lower-paid occupations made the greatest relative gains in average income. Laborers and service workers . . . had increases of about 180% . . . and professional and managerial workers, the highest paid workers of all, had the lowest relative gains—96%." But in the last decade the trend has been reversed; laborers and service workers have gained 39% while professional-managerial workers have gained 68%. This is because in the wartime forties the unskilled were in great demand, while now they are being replaced by machines. Automation is today the same kind of menace to the unskilled—that is, the poor—that the enclosure movement was to the British agricultural population centuries ago. "The facts show that our 'social revolution' ended nearly twenty years ago," Mr. Miller concludes, "yet important segments of the American public, many of them highly placed Government officials and prominent educators, think and act as though it were a continuing process."

"A reduction of about 19% [in the under–$6,000 families] in more than thirty years, or at a rate of about 0.7% per year, is no ground for complacency," the authors of *Poverty and Deprivation* justly observe. There is even less ground for complacency in the recent figures on *extreme* poverty. The authors estimate the number of families in 1929 with incomes of under $2,000 (in current dollars) at 7,500,000. By 1947 there were less than 4,000,000, not because of any philanthropic effort by their more prosperous fellow-citizens but entirely because of those first glorious years of a war economy. Six years later, in 1953, when the economy had begun to slow down, there were still 3,300,000 of these families with incomes of less than $2,000, and seven years later, in 1960, "there had been no further reduction." Thus in the last fifteen years the bottom dogs have remained on the bottom, sharing hardly at all in the advances that the income groups above them have made in an ascending scale that is exquisitely adjusted, by the automatic workings of capitalism, so that it is inversely proportionate to need.

There are, finally, the bottomest bottom dogs; i.e., *families* with incomes of *under* $1,000. I apologize for the italics, but some facts insist on them. According to *Poverty and Deprivation,* the numbers of these families "appear to have risen slightly" of late (1953–60), from 800,000 to about 1,000,000. It is only fair, and patriotic, to add that according to the Commerce Department study, about 10,000,000 of our families and unattached individuals now enjoy incomes of $10,000 a year and up. So while some 3,500,000 Americans are in under–$1,000 families, ten times as many are in over–$10,000 families. Not bad at all—in a way.

The post-1940 decrease in poverty was not due to the policies or actions of those who are not poor, those in positions of power and responsibility. The war economy needed workers, wages went up, and the poor became less poor. When economic stasis set in, the rate of decrease in poverty slowed down proportionately, and it is still slow. Kennedy's efforts to "get the country moving again" have been unsuccessful, possibly because he has, despite the suggestions of many of his economic advisers, not yet advocated the one big step that might push the economy off dead center: a massive increase in government spending. This would be politically courageous, perhaps even dangerous, because of the superstitious fear of "deficit spending" and an "unbalanced" federal budget. American folklore insists that a government's budget must be arranged like a private family's. Walter Lippmann wrote, after the collapse of the stock market last spring:

> There is mounting evidence that those economists were right who told the Administration last winter that it was making the mistake of trying to balance the budget too soon. It will be said that the budget is not balanced: it shows a deficit in fiscal 1962 of $7 billion. . . . But . . . the budget that matters is the Department of Commerce's income and product accounts budget. Nobody looks at it except the economists [but] while the Administrative budget is necessary for administration and is like a man's checkbook, the income budget tells the real story. . . .
>
> [It] shows that at the end of 1962 the outgo and ingo accounts will be virtually in balance, with a deficit of only about half a billion dollars. Thus, in reality, the Kennedy administration is no longer stimulating the economy, and the economy is stagnating for lack of stimulation. We have one of the lowest rates of growth among the advanced industrial nations of the world.

One shouldn't be hard on the President. Franklin Roosevelt, a more daring and experimental politician, at least in his domestic policy, listened to the American disciples of J. M. Keynes in the early New Deal years and unbalanced his budgets, with splendid results. But by 1936 he had lost his nerve. He cut back government spending and there ensued the 1937 recession, from which the economy recovered only when war orders began to make up for the deficiency in domestic buying power. *Poverty and Deprivation* estimates that between 1953 and 1961 the annual growth rate of our economy was "only 2.5 per cent per annum contrasted with an estimated 4.2 per cent required to maintain utilization of manpower and other productive resources." The poor, who always experience the worst the first, understand quite personally the meaning of that dry statistic, as they understand Kipling's "The toad beneath the harrow knows / Exactly where each tooth-point goes." They are also most intimately acquainted with another set of statistics: the steady postwar rise in the unemployment rate, from 3.1 per cent in 1949 to 4.3 per cent in 1954 to 5.1 per cent in 1958 to over 7 per cent in 1961. (The Tory Government is worried because British unemployment is now at its highest point for the last three years. This point is 2.1 per cent, which is less than our lowest rate in the last fifteen years.)

Some of the post-1940 gains of the poor have been their own doing. "Moonlighting"—or holding two or more jobs at once—was practiced by about 3 per cent of the employed in 1950; today this percentage has almost doubled. Far more important is what might be called "wife-flitting": Between 1940 and 1957, the percentage of wives with jobs outside the home doubled, from 15 per cent to 30 per cent. The head of the United States Children's Bureau, Mrs. Katherine B. Oettinger, announced last summer, not at all triumphantly, that there are now two-thirds more working mothers than there were ten years ago and that these mothers have about 15,000,000 children under eighteen—of whom 4,000,000 are under six. This kind of economic enterprise ought to impress Senator Goldwater and the ideologues of the *National Review,* whose reaction to the poor, when they think about such an uninspiring subject, is "Why don't they *do* something about it?" The poor have done something about it and the family pay check is bigger and the statistics on poverty look better. But the effects on family life and on those 4,000,000 pre-school children is something else. Mrs. Oettinger quoted a roadside sign, "IRONING, DAY CARE AND WORMS FOR FISHING BAIT," and mentioned a baby-sitter who pacified her charge with sleeping pills and another who met the problem of a cold apartment by putting the baby in the oven. "The situation has become a 'national disgrace,' with many unfortunate conditions that do not come to public attention until a crisis arises," the *Times* summed up her conclusion. This crisis has finally penetrated to public attention. The President recently signed a law that might be called Day-care. It provides $5,000,000 for such facilities this fiscal year, which works out to $1.25 for each of the 4,000,000 under-six children with working mothers. Next year, the program will provide all of $2.50 per child. This is a free, democratic society's notion of an adequate response. Almost a century ago, Bismarck instituted in Germany state-financed social benefits far beyond anything we have yet ventured. Granted that he did it merely to take the play away from the Social Democratic Party founded by Marx and Engels. Still, one imagines that Count Bismarck must be amused—in the circle of Hell reserved for reactionaries—by that $2.50 a child.

It's not that Public Opinion doesn't become Aroused every now and then. But the arousement never leads to much. It was aroused twenty-four years ago when John Steinbeck published *The Grapes of Wrath,* but Mr. Harrington reports that things in the Imperial Valley are still much the same: low wages, bad housing, no effective union. Public Opinion is too public—that is, too general; of its very nature, it can have no sustained interest in California agriculture. The only groups with such a continuing interest are the workers and the farmers who hire them. Once Public Opinion ceased to be Aroused, the battle was again between the two antagonists with a real, personal stake in the outcome, and there was no question about which was stronger. So with the rural poor in general. In the late fifties, the average annual wage for white male American farm workers was slightly over $1,000; women, children, Negroes, and Mexicans got less. One recalls Edward R. Murrow's celebrated television program about these people, "Harvest of Shame." Once more everybody was shocked, but the harvest is still shameful. One also recalls that Mr. Murrow, after President Kennedy had appointed him head of the United States Information Agency, tried to persuade the B.B.C. not to show "Harvest of Shame." His argument was that it would give an undesirable "image" of America to foreign audiences.

There is a monotony about the injustices suffered by the poor that perhaps accounts for the lack of interest the rest of society shows in them. Everything seems to go wrong with them. They never win. It's just boring.

Public housing turns out not to be for them. The 1949 Housing Act authorized 810,000 new units of low-cost housing in the following four years. Twelve years later, in 1961, the A.F.L.-C.I.O. proposed 400,000 units to complete the lagging 1949 program. The Kennedy administration ventured to recommend 100,000 to Congress. Thus, instead of 810,000 low-cost units by 1953, the poor will get, if they are lucky, 500,000 by 1963. And they are more likely to be injured than helped by slum clearance, since the new projects usually have higher rents than the displaced slum-dwellers can afford. (There has been no dearth of government-financed *middle*-income housing since 1949.) These refugees from the bulldozers for the most part simply emigrate to other slums. They also become invisible; Mr. Harrington notes that half of them are recorded as "address unknown." Several years ago, Charles Abrams, who was New York State Rent Administrator under Harriman and who is now president of the National Committee Against Discrimination in Housing, summed up what he had learned in two decades in public housing: "Once social reforms have won tonal appeal in the public mind, their slogans and goal-symbols may degenerate into tools of the dominant class for beleaguering the minority and often for defeating the very aims which the original sponsors had intended for their reforms." Mr. Abrams was probably thinking, in part, of the Title I adventures of Robert Moses in dealing with New York housing. There is a Moses or two in every American city, determined to lead us away from the promised land.

And this is not the end of tribulation. The poor, who can least afford to lose pay because of ill health, lose the most. A National Health Survey, made a few years ago, found that workers earning under $2,000 a year had twice as many "restricted-activity days" as those earning over $4,000.

The poor are even fatter than the rich. (The cartoonists will have to revise their clichés.) "Obesity is seven times more frequent among women of the lowest socio-economic level than it is among those of the highest level," state Drs. Moore, Stunkard, and Srole in a recent issue of the *Journal of the American Medical Association.* (The proportion is almost the same for men.) They also found that overweight associated with poverty is related to mental disease. Fatness used to be a sign of wealth, as it still is in some parts of Africa, but in more advanced societies it is now a stigma of poverty, since it means too many cheap carbohydrates and too little exercise—which has changed from a necessity for the poor into a luxury for the rich, as may be confirmed by a glance at the models in any fashion magazine.

Although they are the most in need of hospital insurance, the poor have the least, since they can't afford the premiums; only 40 per cent of poor families have it, as against 63 per cent of all families. (It should be noted, however, that the poor who are war veterans can get free treatment, at government expense, in Veterans Administration Hospitals.)

The poor actually pay more taxes, in proportion to their income, than the rich. A recent study by the Tax Foundation estimates that 28 per cent of incomes under $2,000 goes for taxes, as against 24 per cent of the incomes of families earning five to seven times as much. Sales and other excise taxes are largely responsible for this curious statistic. It is true that such taxes fall impartially on all, like the blessed rain from heaven, but it is a form of egalitarianism that perhaps only Senator Goldwater can fully appreciate.

The final irony is that the Welfare State, which Roosevelt erected and which Eisenhower, no matter how strongly he felt about it, didn't attempt to pull down, is not for the poor, either. Agricultural workers are not covered by Social Security, nor are many of the desperately poor among the aged, such as "unrelated individuals" with incomes of less than $1,000, of whom only 37 per cent are covered, which is just half the percentage of coverage among the aged in general. Of the Welfare State, Mr. Harrington says, "Its creation had been stimulated by mass impoverishment and misery, yet it helped the poor least of all. Laws like unemployment compensation, the Wagner Act, the various farm programs, all these were designed for the middle third in the cities, for the organized workers, and for the . . . big market farmers. . . . [It] benefits those least who need help most." The industrial workers, led by John L. Lewis, mobilized enough political force to put through Section 7(a) of the National Industrial Recovery Act, which, with the Wagner Act, made the C.I.O. possible. The big farmers put enough pressure on Henry Wallace, Roosevelt's first Secretary of Agriculture—who talked a good fight for liberal principles but was a Hamlet when it came to action—to establish the two basic propositions of Welfare State agriculture: subsidies that now cost $3 billion a year and that chiefly benefit the big farmers; and the exclusion of share-

croppers, tenant farmers, and migratory workers from the protection of mini-
mum-wage and Social Security laws.

No doubt the Kennedy administration would like to do more for the poor
than it has, but it is hampered by the cabal of Republicans and Southern
Democrats in Congress. The 1961 revision of the Fair Labor Standards Act,
which raised the national minimum wage to the not exorbitant figure of $1.15
an hour, was a slight improvement over the previous act. For instance, it increased coverage of retail-trade workers from 3 per cent to 33 per cent. (But
one-fourth of the retail workers still excluded earn less than $1 an hour.)
There was also a considerable amount of shadowboxing involved: Of the
3,600,000 workers newly covered, only 663,000 were making less than $1 an
hour. And there was the exclusion of a particularly ill-paid group of workers.
Nobody had anything against the laundry workers *personally*. It was just that
they were weak, unorganized, and politically expendable. To appease the conservatives in Congress, whose votes were needed to get the revision through,
they were therefore expended. The result is that of the 500,000 workers in the
laundry, dry-cleaning, and dyeing industries, just 17,000 are now protected by
the Fair Labor Standards Act.

In short, one reaches the unstartling conclusion that rewards in class societies, including Communist ones, are according to power rather than need. A
recent illustration is the campaign of an obscure organization called Veterans
of World War I of the U.S.A. to get a bill through Congress for pensions of
about $25 a week. It was formed by older men who think other veterans' or-
ganizations (such as the American Legion, which claims 2,500,000 members
to their 200,000) are dominated by the relatively young. It asks for pensions
for veterans of the First World War with incomes of under $2,400 (if single)
or $3,600 (if married)—that is, only for *poor* veterans. The editorials have
been violent: "STOP THIS VETERANS' GRAB," implored the *Herald Tribune;*
"WORLD WAR I PENSION GRAB," echoed the *Saturday Evening Post.* Their
objection was, in part, that many of the beneficiaries would not be bona fide
poor, since pensions, annuities, and Social Security benefits were excluded
from the maximum income needed to qualify. Considering that the average
Social Security payment is about $1,000 a year, this would not put any poten-
tial beneficiary into the rich or even the comfortably-off class, even if one assumes another $1,000, which is surely too high, from annuities and pensions.
It's all very confusing. The one clear aspect is that the minuscule Veterans of
World War I of the U.S.A. came very near to bringing it off. Although their
bill was opposed by both the White House and by the chairman of the House
Committee on Veterans' Affairs, two hundred and one members of the House
signed a petition to bring the measure to a vote, only eighteen less than
needed "to accomplish this unusual parliamentary strategy," as the *Times* put
it. These congressmen were motivated by politics rather than charity, one may
assume. Many were up for reelection last November, and the two hundred
thousand Veterans of World War I had two advantages over the fifty million

poor: They were organized, and they had a patriotic appeal only a wink away from the demagogic. Their "unusual parliamentary strategy" failed by eighteen votes in the Congress. But there will be another Congress.

It seems likely that mass poverty will continue in this country for a long time. The more it is reduced, the harder it is to keep on reducing it. The poor, having dwindled from two-thirds of the population in 1936 to one-quarter today, no longer are a significant political force, as is shown by the Senate's rejection of Medicare and by the Democrats' dropping it as an issue in the elections last year. Also, as poverty decreases, those left behind tend more and more to be the ones who have for so long accepted poverty as their destiny that they need outside help to climb out of it. This new minority mass poverty, so much more isolated and hopeless than the old majority poverty, shows signs of becoming chronic. "The permanence of low incomes is inferred from a variety of findings," write the authors of the Michigan survey. "In many poor families the head has never earned enough to cover the family's present needs." They give a vignette of what the statistics mean in human terms:

> For most families, however, the problem of chronic poverty is serious. One such family is headed by a thirty-two-year-old man who is employed as a dishwasher. Though he works steadily and more than full time, he earned slightly over $2,000 in 1959. His wife earned $300 more, but their combined incomes are not enough to support themselves and their three children. Although the head of the family is only thirty-two, he feels that he has no chance of advancement partly because he finished only seven grades of school. . . . The possibility of such families leaving the ranks of the poor is not high.

Children born into poor families today have less chance of "improving themselves" than the children of the pre-1940 poor. Rags to riches is now more likely to be rags to rags. "Indeed," the Michigan surveyors conclude, "it appears that a number of the heads of poor families have moved into less skilled jobs than their fathers had." Over a third of the children of the poor, according to the survey, don't go beyond the eighth grade and "will probably perpetuate the poverty of their parents." There are a great many of these children. In an important study of poverty, made for a Congressional committee in 1959, Dr. Robert J. Lampman estimated that eleven million of the poor were under eighteen. "A considerable number of younger persons are starting life in a condition of 'inherited poverty,' " he observed. To which Mr. Harrington adds, "The character of poverty has changed, and it has become more deadly for the young. It is no longer associated with immigrant groups with high aspirations; it is now identified with those whose social existence makes it more and more difficult to break out into the larger society." Even when children from poor families show intellectual promise, there is nothing in the values of their friends or families to encourage them to make use of it. Dr.

Kolko, citing impressive sources, states that of the top 16 per cent of high-school students—those scoring 120 and over in I.Q. tests—only half go on to college. The explanation for this amazing—and alarming—situation is as much cultural as economic. The children of the poor now tend to lack what the sociologists call "motivation." At least one foundation is working on the problem of why so many bright children from poor families don't ever try to go beyond high school.

Mr. Raymond M. Hilliard, at present director of the Cook County (i.e., Chicago) Department of Public Aid and formerly Commissioner of Welfare for New York City, recently directed a "representative-sample" investigation, which showed that more than half of the 225,000 able-bodied Cook County residents who were on relief were "functionally illiterate." One reason Cook County has to spend $16,500,000 a month on relief is "the lack of basic educational skills of relief recipients which are essential to compete in our modern society." An interesting footnote, apropos of recent happenings at "Ole Miss," is that the illiteracy rate of the relief recipients who were educated in Chicago is 33 per cent, while among those who were educated in Mississippi and later moved to Chicago it is 77 per cent.

The problem of educating the poor has changed since 1900. Then it was the language and cultural difficulties of immigrants from foreign countries; now it is the subtler but more intractable problems of internal migration from backward regions, mostly in the South. The old immigrants wanted to Better Themselves and to Get Ahead. The new migrants are less ambitious, and they come into a less ambitious atmosphere. "When they arrive in the city," wrote Christopher Jencks in an excellent two-part survey, "Slums and Schools," in the *New Republic* last fall, "they join others equally unprepared for urban life in the slums—a milieu which is in many ways utterly dissociated from the rest of America. Often this milieu is self-perpetuating. I have been unable to find any statistics on how many of these migrants' children and grandchildren have become middle-class, but it is probably not too inaccurate to estimate that about 30,000,000 people live in urban slums, and that about half are second-generation residents." The immigrants of 1890–1910 also arrived in a milieu that was "in many ways utterly dissociated from the rest of America," yet they had a vision—a rather materialistic one, but still a vision—of what life in America could be if they worked hard enough; and they did work, and they did aspire to something more than they had; and they did get out of the slums. The disturbing thing about the poor today is that so many of them seem to lack any such vision. Mr. Jencks remarks:

> While the economy is changing in a way which makes the eventual liquidation of the slums at least conceivable, young people are not seizing the opportunities this change presents. Too many are dropping out of school before graduation (more than half in many slums); too few are going to college. . . . As a result there are serious shortages of teachers, nurses, doctors, technicians, and scientifically trained executives, but 4,500,000 unemployables.

"Poverty is the parent of revolution and crime," Aristotle wrote. This is now a half truth—the last half. Our poor are alienated; they don't consider themselves part of society. But precisely because they don't they are not politically dangerous. It is people with "a stake in the country" who make revolutions. The best—though by no means the only—reason for worrying about the Other America is that its existence should make us feel uncomfortable.

The federal government is the only purposeful force—I assume wars are not purposeful—that can reduce the numbers of the poor and make their lives more bearable. The authors of *Poverty and Deprivation* take a dim view of the Kennedy administration's efforts to date:

> The Federal Budget is the most important single instrument available to us as a free people to induce satisfactory economic performance, and to reduce poverty and deprivation. . . .
> Projected Federal outlays in the fiscal 1963 Budget are too small. The items in this Budget covering programs directly related to human improvement and the reduction of mass poverty and deprivation allocate far too small a portion of our total national production to these great purposes.

The effect of government policy on poverty has two quite distinct aspects. One is the indirect effect of the stimulation of the economy by federal spending. Such stimulation—though by war-time demands rather than government policy—has in the past produced a prosperity that did cut down American poverty by almost two-thirds. But I am inclined to agree with Dr. Galbraith that it would not have a comparable effect on present-day poverty:

> It is assumed that with increasing output poverty must disappear [he writes]. Increased output eliminated the general poverty of all who worked. Accordingly it must, sooner or later, eliminate the special poverty that still remains. . . . Yet just as the arithmetic of modern politics makes it tempting to overlook the very poor, so the supposition that increasing output will remedy their case has made it easy to do so too.

He underestimates the massiveness of American poverty, but he is right when he says there is now a hard core of the specially disadvantaged—because of age, race, environment, physical or mental defects, etc.—that would not be significantly reduced by general prosperity. (Although I think the majority of our present poor *would* benefit, if only by a reduction in the present high rate of unemployment.)

To do something about this hard core, a second line of government policy would be required; namely, direct intervention to help the poor. We have had this since the New Deal, but it has always been grudging and miserly, and we have never accepted the principle that every citizen should be provided, at state expense, with a reasonable minimum standard of living regardless of any other considerations. It should not depend on earnings, as does Social Security, which continues the inequalities and inequities and so tends to keep the poor forever poor. Nor should it exclude millions of our poorest citizens because they lack the political pressure to force their way into the Welfare State. The governmental obligation to provide, out of taxes, such a minimum living standard for all who need it should be taken as much for granted as free public schools have always been in our history.

It may be objected that the economy cannot bear the cost, and certainly costs must be calculated. But the point is not the calculation but the principle. Statistics—and especially statistical forecasts—can be pushed one way or the other. Who can determine in advance to what extent the extra expense of giving our 40,000,000 poor enough income to rise above the poverty line would be offset by the lift to the economy from their increased purchasing power? We really don't know. Nor did we know what the budgetary effects would be when we established the principle of free public education. The rationale then was that all citizens should have an equal chance of competing for a better status. The rationale now is different: that every citizen has a right to become or remain part of our society because if this right is denied, as it is in the case of at least one-fourth of our citizens, it impoverishes us all. Since 1932, "the government"—local, state, and federal—has recognized a responsibility to provide its citizens with a subsistence living. Apples will never again be sold on the street by jobless accountants, it seems safe to predict, nor will any serious political leader ever again suggest that share-the-work and local charity can solve the problem of unemployment. "Nobody starves" in this country any more, but, like every social statistic, this is a tricky business. Nobody starves, but who can measure the starvation, not to be calculated by daily intake of proteins and calories, that reduces life for many of our poor to a long vestibule to death? Nobody starves, but every fourth citizen rubs along on a standard of living that is below what Mr. Harrington defines as "the minimal levels of health, housing, food, and education that our present stage of scientific knowledge specifies as necessary for life as it is now lived in the United States." Nobody starves, but a fourth of us are excluded from the common social existence. Not to be able to afford a movie or a glass of beer is a kind of starvation—if everybody else can.

The problem is obvious: the persistence of mass poverty in a prosperous country. The solution is also obvious: to provide, out of taxes, the kind of subsidies that have always been given to the public schools (not to mention the police and fire departments and the post office)—subsidies that would raise incomes above the poverty level, so that every citizen could feel he is indeed such. *"Civis Romanus sum!"* cried St. Paul when he was threatened with flogging—and he was not flogged. Until our poor can be proud to say *"Civis Americanus sum!,"* until the act of justice that would make this possible has been performed by the three-quarters of Americans who are not poor—until then the shame of the Other America will continue.

ROBERT N. BELLAH

CIVIL RELIGION IN AMERICA

What Robert Bellah designates as the civil religion is derived from Chris-
tian and Hebraic traditions without being either Christian or Jewish. Bellah
points to the existence of a religious dimension in American political life that
manifests itself in various ceremonies and rituals as opposed to a particular
dogma. In its origins at the time of the Revolution, the civil religion drew out
of both traditions a set of beliefs and symbols that expressed the obligation
of Americans to "carry out God's will on earth." In the following article,
Bellah examines the development of the civil religion from the Revolutionary
period in America through its times of trial, discussing with great insight the
accretions made to it, and the new meaning it assumed, in the crisis of the
Civil War. One of the strengths of his analysis is its insistence that this form
of American religious understanding has significantly affected public policy.
Today, he suggests, in a revolutionary world Americans can draw strength
from the civil religion. It should, by reminding us of our standards, chasten
and guide us in the exercise of our power, and aid us in the reevaluation of our
role in the world.

In thinking further about the problems raised by this essay, two books
deserve special consideration: Sidney Mead, The Lively Experiment *(1963),*
and H. Richard Niebuhr, The Kingdom of God in America * *(1937).*

406

$\mathbf{W}$hile some have argued that Christianity is the national faith, and others that church and synagogue celebrate only the generalized religion of "the American Way of Life," few have realized that there actually exists alongside of and rather clearly differentiated from the churches an elaborate and well-institutionalized civil religion in America. This article argues not only that there is such a thing, but also that this religion—or perhaps better, this religious dimension—has its own seriousness and integrity and requires the same care in understanding that any other religion does.[1]

The Kennedy Inaugural

Kennedy's inaugural address of 20 January 1961 serves as an example and a clue with which to introduce this complex subject. That address began:

> We observe today not a victory of party but a celebration of freedom— symbolizing an end as well as a beginning—signifying renewal as well as change. For I have sworn before you and Almighty God the same solemn oath our forebears prescribed nearly a century and three quarters ago.
>
> The world is very different now. For man holds in his mortal hands the power to abolish all forms of human poverty and to abolish all forms of human life. And yet the same revolutionary beliefs for which our forebears fought are still at issue around the globe—the belief that the rights of man come not from the generosity of the state but from the hand of God.

And it concluded:

> Finally, whether you are citizens of America or of the world, ask of us the same high standards of strength and sacrifice that we shall ask of you. With a

---

[1] Why something so obvious should have escaped serious analytical attention is in itself an interesting problem. Part of the reason is probably the controversial nature of the subject. From the earliest years of the nineteenth century, conservative religious and political groups have argued that Christianity is, in fact, the national religion. Some of them have from time to time and as recently as the 1950's proposed constitutional amendments that would explicitly recognize the sovereignty of Christ. In defending the doctrine of separation of church and state, opponents of such groups have denied that the national polity has, intrinsically, anything to do with religion at all. The moderates on this issue have insisted that the American state has taken a permissive and indeed supportive attitude toward religious groups (tax exemption, et cetera), thus favoring religion but still missing the positive institutionalization with which I am concerned. But part of the reason this issue has been left in obscurity is certainly due to the peculiarly Western concept of "religion" as denoting a single type of collectivity of which an individual can be a member of one and only one at a time. The Durkheimian notion that every group has a religious dimension, which would be seen as obvious in southern or eastern Asia, is foreign to us. This obscures the recognition of such dimensions in our society.

FROM Robert N. Bellah, "Civil Religion in America," *Daedalus*, Vol. 96 (Winter 1967), pp. 1–21. Reprinted by permission of the American Academy of Arts and Sciences.

good conscience our only sure reward, with history the final judge of our deeds, let us go forth to lead the land we love, asking His blessing and His help, but knowing that here on earth God's work must truly be our own.

These are the three places in this brief address in which Kennedy mentioned the name of God. If we could understand why he mentioned God, the way in which he did it, and what he meant to say in those three references, we would understand much about American civil religion. But this is not a simple or obvious task, and American students of religion would probably differ widely in their interpretation of these passages.

Let us consider first the placing of the three references. They occur in the two opening paragraphs and in the closing paragraph, thus providing a sort of frame for the more concrete remarks that form the middle part of the speech. Looking beyond this particular speech, we would find that similar references to God are almost invariably to be found in the pronouncements of American presidents on solemn occasions, though usually not in the working messages that the president sends to Congress on various concrete issues. How, then, are we to interpret this placing of references to God?

It might be argued that the passages quoted reveal the essentially irrelevant role of religion in the very secular society that is America. The placing of the references in this speech as well as in public life generally indicates that religion has "only a ceremonial significance"; it gets only a sentimental nod which serves largely to placate the more unenlightened members of the community, before a discussion of the really serious business with which religion has nothing whatever to do. A cynical observer might even say that an American president has to mention God or risk losing votes. A semblance of piety is merely one of the unwritten qualifications for the office, a bit more traditional than but not essentially different from the present-day requirement of a pleasing television personality.

But we know enough about the function of ceremonial and ritual in various societies to make us suspicious of dismissing something as unimportant because it is "only a ritual." What people say on solemn occasions need not be taken at face value, but it is often indicative of deep-seated values and commitments that are not made explicit in the course of everyday life. Following this line of argument, it is worth considering whether the very special placing of the references to God in Kennedy's address may not reveal something rather important and serious about religion in American life.

It might be countered that the very way in which Kennedy made his references reveals the essentially vestigial place of religion today. He did not refer to any religion in particular. He did not refer to Jesus Christ, or to Moses, or to the Christian church; certainly he did not refer to the Catholic Church. In fact, his only reference was to the concept of God, a word which almost all Americans can accept but which means so many different things to so many different people that it is almost an empty sign. Is this not just another indication that in America religion is considered vaguely to be a good thing, but that people care so little about it that it has lost any content whatever? Isn't Eisenhower reported to have said, "Our government makes no sense unless it is founded in a deeply felt religious faith—and I don't care what it is," [2] and isn't that a complete negation of any real religion?

These questions are worth pursuing because they raise the issue of how civil religion relates to the political society, on the one hand, and to private religious organization, on the other. President Kennedy was a Christian, more specifically a Catholic Christian. Thus, his general references to God do not mean that he lacked a specific religious commitment. But why, then, did he not include some remark to the effect that Christ is the Lord of the world or some indication of respect for the Catholic Church? He did not because these are matters of his own private religious belief and of his relation to his own particular church; they are not matters relevant in any direct way to the conduct of his public office. Others with different religious views and commitments to different churches or denominations are equally qualified participants in the political process. The principle of separation of church and state guarantees the freedom of religious belief and association, but at the same time clearly segregates the religious sphere, which is considered to be essentially private, from the political one.

Considering the separation of church and state, how is a president justified in using the word *God* at all? The answer is that the separation of church and state has not denied the political realm a religious dimension. Although matters of personal religious belief, worship, and association are considered to be strictly private affairs, there are, at the same time, certain common elements of religious orientation that the great majority of Americans share. These have played a crucial role in the development of American institutions and still provide a religious dimension for the whole fabric of American life, including the political sphere. This public religious dimension is expressed in a set of beliefs, symbols, and rituals that I am calling the American civil religion. The inauguration of a president is an important ceremonial event in this religion. It reaffirms, among other things, the religious legitimation of the highest political authority.

Let us look more closely at what Kennedy actually said. First he said, "I have sworn before you and Almighty God the same solemn oath our forebears prescribed nearly a century and three quarters ago." The oath is the oath of office, including the acceptance of the obligation to uphold the Constitution. He swears it before the people (you) and God. Beyond the Constitution, then, the president's obligation extends not only to the people but to God. In American political theory, sovereignty rests, of course, with the people, but implicitly, and often explicitly, the ultimate sovereignty has been attributed to God. This is the meaning of the motto, "In God we trust," as well as the in-

---

[2] Quoted in Will Herberg, *Protestant-Catholic-Jew* (New York, 1955), p. 97.

clusion of the phrase "under God" in the pledge to the flag. What difference does it make that sovereignty belongs to God? Though the will of the people as expressed in majority vote is carefully institutionalized as the operative source of political authority, it is deprived of an ultimate significance. The will of the people is not itself the criterion of right and wrong. There is a higher criterion in terms of which this will can be judged; it is possible that the people may be wrong. The president's obligation extends to the higher criterion.

When Kennedy says that "the rights of man come not from the generosity of the state but from the hand of God," he is stressing this point again. It does not matter whether the state is the expression of the will of an autocratic monarch or of the "people"; the rights of man are more basic than any political structure and provide a point of revolutionary leverage from which any state structure may be radically altered. That is the basis for his reassertion of the revolutionary significance of America.

But the religious dimension in political life as recognized by Kennedy not only provides a grounding for the rights of man which makes any form of political absolutism illegitimate, it also provides a transcendent goal for the political process. This is implied in his final words that "here on earth God's work must truly be our own." What he means here is, I think, more clearly spelled out in a previous paragraph, the wording of which, incidentally, has a distinctly Biblical ring:

> Now the trumpet summons us again—not as a call to bear arms, though arms we need—not as a call to battle, though embattled we are—but a call to bear the burden of a long twilight struggle, year in and year out, "rejoicing in hope, patient in tribulation"—a struggle against the common enemies of man: tyranny, poverty, disease and war itself.

The whole address can be understood as only the most recent statement of a theme that lies very deep in the American tradition, namely the obligation, both collective and individual, to carry out God's will on earth. This was the motivating spirit of those who founded America, and it has been present in every generation since. Just below the surface throughout Kennedy's inaugural address, it becomes explicit in the closing statement that God's work must be our own. That this very activist and non-contemplative conception of the fundamental religious obligation, which has been historically associated with the Protestant position, should be enunciated so clearly in the first major statement of the first Catholic president seems to underline how deeply established it is in the American outlook. Let us now consider the form and history of the civil religious tradition in which Kennedy was speaking.

The Idea of a Civil Religion

The phrase *civil religion* is, of course, Rousseau's. In Chapter 8, Book 4, of *The Social Contract*, he outlines the simple dogmas of the civil religion:

the existence of God, the life to come, the reward of virtue and the punishment of vice, and the exclusion of religious intolerance. All other religious opinions are outside the cognizance of the state and may be freely held by citizens. While the phrase *civil religion* was not used, to the best of my knowledge, by the founding fathers, and I am certainly not arguing for the particular influence of Rousseau, it is clear that similar ideas, as part of the cultural climate of the late-eighteenth century, were to be found among the Americans. For example, Franklin writes in his autobiography,

> I never was without some religious principles. I never doubted, for instance, the existence of the Deity; that he made the world and govern'd it by his Providence; that the most acceptable service of God was the doing of good to men; that our souls are immortal; and that all crime will be punished, and virtue rewarded either here or hereafter. These I esteemed the essentials of every religion; and, being to be found in all the religions we had in our country, I respected them all, tho' with different degrees of respect, as I found them more or less mix'd with other articles, which, without any tendency to inspire, promote or confirm morality, serv'd principally to divide us, and make us unfriendly to one another.

It is easy to dispose of this sort of position as essentially utilitarian in relation to religion. In Washington's Farewell Address (though the words may be Hamilton's) the utilitarian aspect is quite explicit:

> Of all the dispositions and habits which lead to political prosperity, Religion and Morality are indispensable supports. In vain would that man claim the tribute of Patriotism, who should labour to subvert these great Pillars of human happiness, these firmest props of the duties of men and citizens. The mere politician, equally with the pious man, ought to respect and cherish them. A volume could not trace all their connections with private and public felicity. Let it simply be asked where is the security for property, for reputation, for life, if the sense of religious obligation *desert* the oaths, which are the instruments of investigation in Courts of Justice? And let us with caution indulge the supposition, that morality can be maintained without religion. Whatever may be conceded to the influence of refined education on minds of peculiar structure, reason and experience both forbid us to expect that National morality can prevail in exclusion of religious principle.

But there is every reason to believe that religion, particularly the idea of God, played a constitutive role in the thought of the early American statesmen.

Kennedy's inaugural pointed to the religious aspect of the Declaration of Independence, and it might be well to look at that document a bit more closely. There are four references to God. The first speaks of the "Laws of Nature and of Nature's God" which entitle any people to be independent. The second is the famous statement that all men "are endowed by their Creator with certain inalienable Rights." Here Jefferson is locating the fundamental legitimacy of the new nation in a conception of "higher law" that is itself based on both classical natural law and Biblical religion. The third is an appeal to "the Supreme Judge of the world for the rectitude of our intentions," and the last indicates "a firm reliance on the protection of divine Providence." In these last two references, a Biblical God of history who stands in judgment over the world is indicated.

The intimate relation of these religious notions with the self-conception of the new republic is indicated by the frequency of their appearance in early official documents. For example, we find in Washington's first inaugural address of 30 April 1789:

> It would be peculiarly improper to omit in this first official act my fervent supplications to that Almighty Being who rules over the universe, who presides in the councils of nations, and whose providential aids can supply every defect, that His benediction may consecrate to the liberties and happiness of the people of the United States a Government instituted by themselves for these essential purposes, and may enable every instrument employed in its administration to execute with success the functions allotted to his charge.
>
> No people can be bound to acknowledge and adore the Invisible Hand which conducts the affairs of man more than those of the United States. Every step by which we have advanced to the character of an independent nation seems to have been distinguished by some token of providential agency. . . .
>
> The propitious smiles of Heaven can never be expected on a nation that disregards the eternal rules of order and right which Heaven itself has ordained. . . . The preservation of the sacred fire of liberty and the destiny of the republican model of government are justly considered, perhaps, as *deeply*, as *finally*, staked on the experiment intrusted to the hands of the American people.

Nor did these religious sentiments remain merely the personal expression of the president. At the request of both Houses of Congress, Washington proclaimed on October 3 of that same first year as president that November 26 should be "a day of public thanksgiving and prayer," the first Thanksgiving Day under the Constitution.

The words and acts of the founding fathers, especially the first few presidents, shaped the form and tone of the civil religion as it has been maintained ever since. Though much is selectively derived from Christianity, this religion is clearly not itself Christianity. For one thing, neither Washington nor Adams nor Jefferson mentions Christ in his inaugural address; nor do any of the subsequent presidents, although not one of them fails to mention God.[3] The God

---

[3] God is mentioned or referred to in all inaugural addresses but Washington's second, which is a very brief (two paragraphs) and perfunctory acknowledgment. It is not without interest that the actual word *God* does not appear until Monroe's second inaugural, 5 March 1821. In his first inaugural, Washington refers to God as "that Almighty Being who rules the universe," "Great Author of every public and private

of the civil religion is not only rather "unitarian," he is also on the austere side, much more related to order, law, and right than to salvation and love. Even though he is somewhat deist in cast, he is by no means simply a watchmaker God. He is actively interested and involved in history, with a special concern for America. Here the analogy has much less to do with natural law than with ancient Israel; the equation of America with Israel in the idea of the "American Israel" is not infrequent.[4] What was implicit in the words of Washington already quoted becomes explicit in Jefferson's second inaugural when he said: "I shall need, too, the favor of that Being in whose hands we are, who led our fathers, as Israel of old, from their native land and planted them in a country flowing with all the necessaries and comforts of life." Europe is Egypt; America, the promised land. God has led his people to establish a new sort of social order that shall be a light unto all the nations.[5]

This theme, too, has been a continuous one in the civil religion. We have already alluded to it in the case of the Kennedy inaugural. We find it again in President Johnson's inaugural address:

> They came here—the exile and the stranger, brave but frightened—to find a place where a man could be his own man. They made a covenant with this land. Conceived in justice, written in liberty, bound in union, it was meant one day to inspire the hopes of all mankind; and it binds us still. If we keep its terms, we shall flourish.

---

good," "Invisible Hand," and "benign Parent of the Human Race." John Adams refers to God as "Providence," "Being who is supreme over all," "Patron of Order," "Fountain of Justice," and "Protector in all ages of the world of virtuous liberty." Jefferson speaks of "that Infinite Power which rules the destinies of the universe," and "that Being in whose hands we are." Madison speaks of "that Almighty Being whose power regulates the destiny of nations," and "Heaven." Monroe uses "Providence" and "the Almighty" in his first inaugural and finally "Almighty God" in his second. See *Inaugural Addresses of the Presidents of the United States from George Washington 1789 to Harry S. Truman 1949,* 82d Congress, 2d Session, House Document No. 540, 1952.

[4] For example, Abiel Abbot, pastor of the First Church in Haverhill, Massachusetts, delivered a Thanksgiving sermon in 1799, *Traits of Resemblance in the People of the United States of America to Ancient Israel,* in which he said, "It has been often remarked that the people of the United States come nearer to a parallel with Ancient Israel, than any other nation upon the globe. Hence OUR AMERICAN ISRAEL is a term frequently used; and common consent allows it apt and proper." Cited in Hans Kohn, *The Idea of Nationalism* (New York, 1961), p. 665.

[5] That the Mosaic analogy was present in the minds of leaders at the very moment of the birth of the republic is indicated in the designs proposed by Franklin and Jefferson for a seal of the United States of America. Together with Adams, they formed a committee of three delegated by the Continental Congress on 4 July 1776, to draw up the new device. "Franklin proposed as the device Moses lifting up his wand and dividing the Red Sea while Pharaoh was overwhelmed by its waters, with the motto 'Rebellion to tyrants is obedience to God.' Jefferson proposed the children of Israel in the wilderness 'led by a cloud by day and a pillar of fire at night.'" Anson Phelps Stokes, *Church and State in the United States,* Vol. 1 (New York, 1950), pp. 467–68.

What we have, then, from the earliest years of the republic is a collection of beliefs, symbols, and rituals with respect to sacred things and institutionalized in a collectivity. This religion—there seems no other word for it—while not antithetical to and indeed sharing much in common with Christianity, was neither sectarian nor in any specific sense Christian. At a time when the society was overwhelmingly Christian, it seems unlikely that this lack of Christian reference was meant to spare the feelings of the tiny non-Christian minority. Rather, the civil religion expressed what those who set the precedents felt was appropriate under the circumstances. It reflected their private as well as public views. Nor was the civil religion simply "religion in general." While generality was undoubtedly seen as a virtue by some, as in the quotation from Franklin above, the civil religion was specific enough when it came to the topic of America. Precisely because of this specificity, the civil religion was saved from empty formalism and served as a genuine vehicle of national religious self-understanding.

But the civil religion was not, in the minds of Franklin, Washington, Jefferson, or other leaders, with the exception of a few radicals like Tom Paine, ever felt to be a substitute for Christianity. There was an implicit but quite clear division of function between the civil religion and Christianity. Under the doctrine of religious liberty, an exceptionally wide sphere of personal piety and voluntary social action was left to the churches. But the churches were neither to control the state nor to be controlled by it. The national magistrate, whatever his private religious views, operates under the rubrics of the civil religion as long as he is in his official capacity, as we have already seen in the case of Kennedy. This accommodation was undoubtedly the product of a particular historical moment and of a cultural background dominated by Protestantism of several varieties and by the Enlightenment, but it has survived despite subsequent changes in the cultural and religious climate.

Civil War and Civil Religion

Until the Civil War, the American civil religion focused above all on the event of the Revolution, which was seen as the final act of the Exodus from the old lands across the waters. The Declaration of Independence and the Constitution were the sacred scriptures and Washington the divinely appointed Moses who led his people out of the hands of tyranny. The Civil War, which Sidney Mead calls "the center of American history," [6] was the second great event that involved the national self-understanding so deeply as to require expression in the civil religion. In 1835, De Tocqueville wrote that the American republic had never really been tried, that victory in the Revolutionary War was more the result of British preoccupation elsewhere and the

[6] Sidney Mead, *The Lively Experiment* (New York, 1963), p. 12.

presence of a powerful ally than of any great military success of the Americans. But in 1861 the time of testing had indeed come. Not only did the Civil War have the tragic intensity of fratricidal strife, but it was one of the bloodiest wars of the nineteenth century; the loss of life was far greater than any previously suffered by Americans.

The Civil War raised the deepest questions of national meaning. The man who not only formulated but in his own person embodied its meaning for Americans was Abraham Lincoln. For him the issue was not in the first instance slavery but "whether that nation, or any nation so conceived, and so dedicated, can long endure." He had said in Independence Hall in Philadelphia on 22 February 1861:

> All the political sentiments I entertain have been drawn, so far as I have been able to draw them, from the sentiments which originated in and were given to the world from this Hall. I have never had a feeling, politically, that did not spring from the sentiments embodied in the Declaration of Independence.[7]

The phrases of Jefferson constantly echo in Lincoln's speeches. His task was, first of all, to save the Union—not for America alone but for the meaning of America to the whole world so unforgettably etched in the last phrase of the Gettysburg Address.

But inevitably the issue of slavery as the deeper cause of the conflict had to be faced. In the second inaugural, Lincoln related slavery and the war in an ultimate perspective:

> If we shall suppose that American slavery is one of those offenses which, in the providence of God, must needs come, but which, having continued through His appointed time, He now wills to remove, and that He gives to both North and South this terrible war as the woe due to those by whom the offense came, shall we discern therein any departure from those divine attributes which the believers in a living God always ascribe to Him? Fondly do we hope, fervently do we pray, that this mighty scourge of war may speedily pass away. Yet, if God wills that it continue until all the wealth piled by the bondsman's two hundred and fifty years of unrequited toil shall be sunk, and until every drop of blood drawn with the lash shall be paid by another drawn with the sword, as was said three thousand years ago, so still it must be said "the judgements of the Lord are true and righteous altogether."

But he closes on a note if not of redemption then of reconciliation—"With malice toward none, with charity for all."

With the Civil War, a new theme of death, sacrifice, and rebirth enters the civil religion. It is symbolized in the life and death of Lincoln. Nowhere is it stated more vividly than in the Gettysburg Address, itself part of the Lin-

---

[7] Quoted by Arthur Lehman Goodhart in Allan Nevins (ed.), *Lincoln and the Gettysburg Address* (Urbana, Ill., 1964), p. 39.

colnian "New Testament" among the civil scriptures. Robert Lowell has recently pointed out the "insistent use of birth images" in this speech explicitly devoted to "these honored dead": "brought forth," "conceived," "created," "a new birth of freedom." He goes on to say:

> The Gettysburg Address is a symbolic and sacramental act. Its verbal quality is resonance combined with a logical, matter of fact, prosaic brevity. . . . In his words, Lincoln symbolically died, just as the Union soldiers really died— and as he himself was soon really to die. By his words, he gave the field of battle a symbolic significance that it had lacked. For us and our country, he left Jefferson's ideals of freedom and equality joined to the Christian sacrificial act of death and rebirth. I believe this is a meaning that goes beyond sect or religion and beyond peace and war, and is now part of our lives as a challenge, obstacle and hope.[8]

Lowell is certainly right in pointing out the Christian quality of the symbolism here, but he is also right in quickly disavowing any sectarian implication. The earlier symbolism of the civil religion had been Hebraic without being in any specific sense Jewish. The Gettysburg symbolism (". . . those who here gave their lives, that that nation might live") is Christian without having anything to do with the Christian church.

The symbolic equation of Lincoln with Jesus was made relatively early. Herndon, who had been Lincoln's law partner, wrote:

> For fifty years God rolled Abraham Lincoln through his fiery furnace. He did it to try Abraham and to purify him for his purposes. This made Mr. Lincoln humble, tender, forbearing, sympathetic to suffering, kind, sensitive, tolerant; broadening, deepening and widening his whole nature; making him the noblest and loveliest character since Jesus Christ. . . . I believe that Lincoln was God's chosen one.[9]

With the Christian archetype in the background, Lincoln, "our martyred president," was linked to the war dead, those who "gave the last full measure of devotion." The theme of sacrifice was indelibly written into the civil religion.

The new symbolism soon found both physical and ritualistic expression. The great number of the war dead required the establishment of a number of national cemeteries. Of these, the Gettysburg National Cemetery, which Lincoln's famous address served to dedicate, has been overshadowed only by the Arlington National Cemetery. Begun somewhat vindictively on the Lee estate across the river from Washington, partly with the end that the Lee family

---

[8] *Ibid.*, "On the Gettysburg Address," pp. 88–89.

[9] Quoted in Sherwood Eddy, *The Kingdom of God and the American Dream* (New York, 1941), p. 162.

could never reclaim it,[10] it has subsequently become the most hallowed monument of the civil religion. Not only was a section set aside for the Confederate dead, but it has received the dead of each succeeding American war. It is the site of the one important new symbol to come out of World War I, the Tomb of the Unknown Soldier; more recently it has become the site of the tomb of another martyred president and its symbolic eternal flame.

Memorial Day, which grew out of the Civil War, gave ritual expression to the themes we have been discussing. As Lloyd Warner has so brilliantly analyzed it, the Memorial Day observance, especially in the towns and smaller cities of America, is a major event for the whole community involving a rededication to the martyred dead, to the spirit of sacrifice, and to the American vision.[11] Just as Thanksgiving Day, which incidentally was securely institutionalized as an annual national holiday only under the presidency of Lincoln, serves to integrate the family into the civil religion, so Memorial Day has acted to integrate the local community into the national cult. Together with the less overtly religious Fourth of July and the more minor celebrations of Veterans Day and the birthdays of Washington and Lincoln, these two holidays provide an annual ritual calendar for the civil religion. The public-school system serves as a particularly important context for the cultic celebration of the civil rituals.

The Civil Religion Today

In reifying and giving a name to something that, though pervasive enough when you look at it, has gone on only semiconsciously, there is risk of severely distorting the data. But the reification and the naming have already begun. The religious critics of "religion in general," or of the "religion of the

---

[10] Karl Decker and Angus McSween, *Historic Arlington* (Washington, D.C., 1892), pp. 60–67.

[11] How extensive the activity associated with Memorial Day can be is indicated by Warner: "The sacred symbolic behavior of Memorial Day, in which scores of the town's organizations are involved, is ordinarily divided into four periods. During the year separate rituals are held by many of the associations for their dead, and many of these activities are connected with later Memorial Day events. In the second phase, preparations are made during the last three or four weeks for the ceremony itself, and some of the associations perform public rituals. The third phase consists of scores of rituals held in all the cemeteries, churches, and halls of the associations. These rituals consist of speeches and highly ritualized behavior. They last for two days and are climaxed by the fourth and last phase, in which all the separate celebrants gather in the center of the business district on the afternoon of Memorial Day. The separate organizations, with their members in uniform or with fitting insignia, march through the town, visit the shrines and monuments of the hero dead, and, finally, enter the cemetery. Here dozens of ceremonies are held, most of them highly symbolic and formalized." During these various ceremonies Lincoln is continually referred to and the Gettysburg Address recited many times. W. Lloyd Warner, *American Life* (Chicago, 1962), pp. 8–9.

'American Way of Life,'" or of "American Shinto" have really been talking about the civil religion. As usual in religious polemic, they take as criteria the best in their own religious traditions and as typical the worst in the tradition of the civil religion. Against these critics, I would argue that the civil religion at its best is a genuine apprehension of universal and transcendent religious reality as seen in or, one could almost say, as revealed through the experience of the American people. Like all religions, it has suffered various deformations and demonic distortions. At its best, it has neither been so general that it has lacked incisive relevance to the American scene nor so particular that it has placed American society above universal human values. I am not at all convinced that the leaders of the churches have consistently represented a higher level of religious insight than the spokesmen of the civil religion. Reinhold Niebuhr has this to say of Lincoln, who never joined a church and who certainly represents civil religion at its best:

> An analysis of the religion of Abraham Lincoln in the context of the traditional religion of his time and place and of its polemical use on the slavery issue, which corrupted religious life in the days before and during the Civil War, must lead to the conclusion that Lincoln's religious convictions were superior in depth and purity to those, not only of the political leaders of his day, but of the religious leaders of the era.[12]

Perhaps the real animus of the religious critics has been not so much against the civil religion in itself but against its pervasive and dominating influence within the sphere of church religion. As S. M. Lipset has recently shown, American religion at least since the early nineteenth century has been predominantly activist, moralistic, and social rather than contemplative, theological, or innerly spiritual.[13] De Tocqueville spoke of American church religion as "a political institution which powerfully contributes to the maintenance of a democratic republic among the Americans"[14] by supplying a strong moral consensus amidst continuous political change. Henry Bargy in 1902 spoke of American church religion as *"la poésie du civisme."* [15]

It is certainly true that the relation between religion and politics in Amer-

---

[12] Reinhold Niebuhr, "The Religion of Abraham Lincoln," in Nevins (ed.), *op. cit.*, p. 72. William J. Wolfe of the Episcopal Theological School in Cambridge, Massachusetts, has written: "Lincoln is one of the greatest theologians of America—not in the technical meaning of producing a system of doctrine, certainly not as the defender of some one denomination, but in the sense of seeing the hand of God intimately in the affairs of nations. Just so the prophets of Israel criticized the events of their day from the perspective of the God who is concerned for history and who reveals His will within it. Lincoln now stands among God's latter-day prophets." *The Religion of Abraham Lincoln* (New York, 1963), p. 24.

[13] Seymour Martin Lipset, "Religion and American Values," Chapter 4, *The First New Nation* (New York, 1964).

[14] Alexis de Tocqueville, *Democracy in America,* Vol. 1 (New York, 1954), p. 310.

[15] Henry Bargy, *La Religion dans la Société aux États-Unis* (Paris, 1902), p. 31.

ica has been singularly smooth. This is in large part due to the dominant tradition. As De Tocqueville wrote:

> The greatest part of British America was peopled by men who, after having shaken off the authority of the Pope, acknowledged no other religious supremacy: they brought with them into the New World a form of Christianity which I cannot better describe than by styling it a democratic and republican religion.[16]

The churches opposed neither the Revolution nor the establishment of democratic institutions. Even when some of them opposed the full institutionalization of religious liberty, they accepted the final outcome with good grace and without nostalgia for an *ancien régime*. The American civil religion was never anticlerical or militantly secular. On the contrary, it borrowed selectively from the religious tradition in such a way that the average American saw no conflict between the two. In this way, the civil religion was able to build up without any bitter struggle with the church powerful symbols of national solidarity and to mobilize deep levels of personal motivation for the attainment of national goals.

Such an achievement is by no means to be taken for granted. It would seem that the problem of a civil religion is quite general in modern societies and that the way it is solved or not solved will have repercussions in many spheres. One needs only to think of France to see how differently things can go. The French Revolution was anticlerical to the core and attempted to set up an anti-Christian civil religion. Throughout modern French history, the chasm between traditional Catholic symbols and the symbolism of 1789 has been immense.

American civil religion is still very much alive. Just three years ago we participated in a vivid re-enactment of the sacrifice theme in connection with the funeral of our assassinated president. The American Israel theme is clearly behind both Kennedy's New Frontier and Johnson's Great Society. Let me give just one recent illustration of how the civil religion serves to mobilize support for the attainment of national goals. On 15 March 1965 President Johnson went before Congress to ask for a strong voting-rights bill. Early in the speech he said:

> Rarely are we met with the challenge, not to our growth or abundance, or our welfare or our security—but rather to the values and the purposes and the meaning of our beloved nation.

---

[16] De Tocqueville, *op. cit.*, p. 311. Later he says, "In the United States even the religion of most of the citizens is republican, since it submits the truths of the other world to private judgment, as in politics the care of their temporal interests is abandoned to the good sense of the people. Thus every man is allowed freely to take that road which he thinks will lead him to heaven, just as the law permits every citizen to have the right of choosing his own government" (p. 436).

The issue of equal rights for American Negroes is such an issue. And should we defeat every enemy, and should we double our wealth and conquer the stars and still be unequal to this issue, then we will have failed as a people and as a nation.

For with a country as with a person, "What is a man profited, if he shall gain the whole world, and lose his own soul?"

And in conclusion he said:

Above the pyramid on the great seal of the United States it says in Latin, "God has favored our undertaking."

God will not favor everything that we do. It is rather our duty to divine His will. I cannot help but believe that He truly understands and that He really favors the undertaking that we begin here tonight.[17]

The civil religion has not always been invoked in favor of worthy causes. On the domestic scene, an American-Legion type of ideology that fuses God, country, and flag has been used to attack nonconformist and liberal ideas and groups of all kinds. Still, it has been difficult to use the words of Jefferson and Lincoln to support special interests and undermine personal freedom. The defenders of slavery before the Civil War came to reject the thinking of the Declaration of Independence. Some of the most consistent of them turned against not only Jeffersonian democracy but Reformation religion; they dreamed of a South dominated by medieval chivalry and divine-right monarchy.[18] For all the overt religiosity of the radical right today, their relation to the civil religious consensus is tenuous, as when the John Birch Society attacks the central American symbol of Democracy itself.

With respect to America's role in the world, the dangers of distortion are greater and the built-in safeguards of the tradition weaker. The theme of the American Israel was used, almost from the beginning, as a justification for the shameful treatment of the Indians so characteristic of our history. It can be overtly or implicitly linked to the idea of manifest destiny which has been used to legitimate several adventures in imperialism since the early nineteenth century. Never has the danger been greater than today. The issue is not so much one of imperial expansion, of which we are accused, as of the tendency to assimilate all governments or parties in the world which support our immediate policies or call upon our help by invoking the notion of free institutions and democratic values. Those nations that are for the moment "on our side" become "the free world." A repressive and unstable military dictatorship in South Viet-Nam becomes "the free people of South Viet-Nam and their government." It is then part of the role of America as the New Jerusalem and

---

[17] U. S., *Congressional Record,* House, 15 March 1965, pp. 4924, 4926.

[18] See Louis Hartz, "The Feudal Dream of the South," Part 4, *The Liberal Tradition in America* (New York, 1955).

"the last hope of earth" to defend such governments with treasure and eventually with blood. When our soldiers are actually dying, it becomes possible to consecrate the struggle further by invoking the great theme of sacrifice. For the majority of the American people who are unable to judge whether the people in South Viet-Nam (or wherever) are "free like us," such arguments are convincing. Fortunately President Johnson has been less ready to assert that "God has favored our undertaking" in the case of Viet-Nam than with respect to civil rights. But others are not so hesitant. The civil religion has exercised long-term pressure for the humane solution of our greatest domestic problem, the treatment of the Negro American. It remains to be seen how relevant it can become for our role in the world at large, and whether we can effectively stand for "the revolutionary beliefs for which our forebears fought," in John F. Kennedy's words.

The civil religion is obviously involved in the most pressing moral and political issues of the day. But it is also caught in another kind of crisis, theoretical and theological, of which it is at the moment largely unaware. "God" has clearly been a central symbol in the civil religion from the beginning and remains so today. This symbol is just as central to the civil religion as it is to Judaism or Christianity. In the late eighteenth century this posed no problem; even Tom Paine, contrary to his detractors, was not an atheist. From left to right and regardless of church or sect, all could accept the idea of God. But today, as even *Time* has recognized, the meaning of the word *God* is by no means so clear or so obvious. There is no formal creed in the civil religion. We have had a Catholic president; it is conceivable that we could have a Jewish one. But could we have an agnostic president? Could a man with conscientious scruples about using the word *God* the way Kennedy and Johnson have used it be elected chief magistrate of our country? If the whole God symbolism requires reformulation, there will be obvious consequences for the civil religion, consequences perhaps of liberal alienation and of fundamentalist ossification that have not so far been prominent in this realm. The civil religion has been a point of articulation between the profoundest commitments of the Western religious and philosophical tradition and the common beliefs of ordinary Americans. It is not too soon to consider how the deepening theological crisis may affect the future of this articulation.

The Third Time of Trial

In conclusion it may be worthwhile to relate the civil religion to the most serious situation that we as Americans now face, what I call the third time of trial. The first time of trial had to do with the question of independence, whether we should or could run our own affairs in our own way. The second time of trial was over the issue of slavery, which in turn was only the most salient aspect of the more general problem of the full institutionalization of democracy within our country. This second problem we are still far from solving though we have some notable successes to our credit. But we have been overtaken by a third great problem which has led to a third great crisis, in the midst of which we stand. This is the problem of responsible action in a revolutionary world, a world seeking to attain many of the things, material and spiritual, that we have already attained. Americans have, from the beginning, been aware of the responsibility and the significance our republican experiment has for the whole world. The first internal political polarization in the new nation had to do with our attitude toward the French Revolution. But we were small and weak then, and "foreign entanglements" seemed to threaten our very survival. During the last century, our relevance for the world was not forgotten, but our role was seen as purely exemplary. Our democratic republic rebuked tyranny by merely existing. Just after World War I we were on the brink of taking a different role in the world, but once again we turned our back.

Since World War II the old pattern has become impossible. Every president since Roosevelt has been groping toward a new pattern of action in the world, one that would be consonant with our power and our responsibilities. For Truman and for the period dominated by John Foster Dulles that pattern was seen to be the great Manichaean confrontation of East and West, the confrontation of democracy and "the false philosophy of Communism" that provided the structure of Truman's inaugural address. But with the last years of Eisenhower and with the successive two presidents, the pattern began to shift. The great problems came to be seen as caused not solely by the evil intent of any one group of men, but as stemming from much more complex and multiple sources. For Kennedy, it was not so much a struggle against particular men as against "the common enemies of man: tyranny, poverty, disease and war itself."

But in the midst of this trend toward a less primitive conception of ourselves and our world, we have somehow, without anyone really intending it, stumbled into a military confrontation where we have come to feel that our honor is at stake. We have in a moment of uncertainty been tempted to rely on our overwhelming physical power rather than on our intelligence, and we have, in part, succumbed to this temptation. Bewildered and unnerved when our terrible power fails to bring immediate success, we are at the edge of a chasm the depth of which no man knows.

I cannot help but think of Robinson Jeffers, whose poetry seems more apt now than when it was written, when he said:

> Unhappy country, what wings you have! . . .
> Weep (it is frequent in human affairs), weep for
> the terrible magnificence of the means,
> The ridiculous incompetence of the reasons, the
> bloody and shabby
> Pathos of the result.

But as so often before in similar times, we have a man of prophetic stature, without the bitterness or misanthropy of Jeffers, who, as Lincoln before him, calls this nation to its judgment:

> When a nation is very powerful but lacking in self-confidence, it is likely to behave in a manner that is dangerous both to itself and to others.
>
> Gradually but unmistakably, America is succumbing to that arrogance of power which has afflicted, weakened and in some cases destroyed great nations in the past.
>
> If the war goes on and expands, if that fatal process continues to accelerate until America becomes what it is not now and never has been, a seeker after unlimited power and empire, then Vietnam will have had a mighty and tragic fallout indeed.
>
> I do not believe that will happen. I am very apprehensive but I still remain hopeful, and even confident, that America, with its humane and democratic traditions, will find the wisdom to match its power.[19]

Without an awareness that our nation stands under higher judgment, the tradition of the civil religion would be dangerous indeed. Fortunately, the prophetic voices have never been lacking. Our present situation brings to mind the Mexican-American war that Lincoln, among so many others, opposed. The spirit of civil disobedience that is alive today in the civil rights movement and the opposition to the Viet-Nam war was already clearly outlined by Henry David Thoreau when he wrote, "If the law is of such a nature that it requires you to be an agent of injustice to another, then I say, break the law." Thoreau's words, "I would remind my countrymen that they are men first, and Americans at a late and convenient hour," [20] provide an essential standard for any adequate thought and action in our third time of trial. As Americans, we have been well favored in the world, but it is as men that we will be judged.

Out of the first and second times of trial have come, as we have seen, the major symbols of the American civil religion. There seems little doubt that a successful negotiation of this third time of trial—the attainment of some kind of viable and coherent world order—would precipitate a major new set of symbolic forms. So far the flickering flame of the United Nations burns too low to be the focus of a cult, but the emergence of a genuine trans-national sovereignty would certainly change this. It would necessitate the incorporation of vital international symbolism into our civil religion, or, perhaps a better way of putting it, it would result in American civil religion becoming simply one part of a new civil religion of the world. It is useless to speculate on

---

[19] Speech of Senator J. William Fulbright of 28 April 1966, as reported in *The New York Times,* 29 April 1966.

[20] Quoted in Yehoshua Arieli, *Individualism and Nationalism in American Ideology* (Cambridge, Mass., 1964), p. 274.

the form such a civil religion might take, though it obviously would draw on religious traditions beyond the sphere of Biblical religion alone. Fortunately, since the American civil religion is not the worship of the American nation but an understanding of the American experience in the light of ultimate and universal reality, the reorganization entailed by such a new situation need not disrupt the American civil religion's continuity. A world civil religion could be accepted as a fulfillment and not a denial of American civil religion. Indeed, such an outcome has been the eschatological hope of American civil religion from the beginning. To deny such an outcome would be to deny the meaning of America itself.

Behind the civil religion at every point lie Biblical archetypes: Exodus, Chosen People, Promised Land, New Jerusalem, Sacrificial Death and Rebirth. But it is also genuinely American and genuinely new. It has its own prophets and its own martyrs, its own sacred events and sacred places, its own solemn rituals and symbols. It is concerned that America be a society as perfectly in accord with the will of God as men can make it, and a light to all the nations.

It has often been used and is being used today as a cloak for petty interests and ugly passions. It is in need—as is any living faith—of continual reformation, of being measured by universal standards. But it is not evident that it is incapable of growth and new insight.

It does not make any decision for us. It does not remove us from moral ambiguity, from being, in Lincoln's fine phrase, an "almost chosen people." But it is a heritage of moral and religious experience from which we still have much to learn as we formulate the decisions that lie ahead.